ALFA ROMEO GIULIA

WORKSHOP MANUAL
1962-1975 ALL MODELS
1300, 1600, 1750 & 2000cc

© 2019 Veloce Enterprises Inc., San Antonio, Texas USA
All rights reserved. This work may not be reproduced or
transmitted in any form without the express consent of the publisher

Introduction

Welcome to the world of digital publishing ~ the book you now hold in your hand, was printed using the latest state of the art digital technology. The advent of print-on-demand has forever changed the publishing process, never has information been so accessible and it is our hope that this book serves your informational needs for years to come. If this is your first exposure to digital publishing, we hope that you are pleased with the results. Many more titles of interest to the classic automobile and motorcycle enthusiast, collector and restorer are available via our website at www.VelocePress.com. We hope that you find this title as interesting as we do.

Note from the Publisher

The information presented is true and complete to the best of our knowledge. All recommendations are made without any guarantees on the part of the author or the publisher, who also disclaim all liability incurred with the use of this information.

Trademarks

We recognize that some words, model names and designations, for example, mentioned herein are the property of the trademark holder. We use them for identification purposes only. This is not an official publication.

Information on the use of this Publication

This manual is an invaluable resource for those interested in performing their own maintenance. However, in today's information age we are constantly subject to changes in common practice, new technology, availability of improved materials and increased awareness of chemical toxicity. As such, it is advised that the user consult with an experienced professional prior to undertaking any procedure described herein. While every care has been taken to ensure correctness of information, it is obviously not possible to guarantee complete freedom from errors or omissions or to accept liability arising from such errors or omissions. Therefore, any individual that uses the information contained within, or elects to perform or participate in do-it-yourself repairs or modifications acknowledges that there is a risk factor involved and that the publisher or its associates cannot be held responsible for personal injury or property damage resulting from the use of the information or the outcome of such procedures.

Warning!

One final word of advice, this publication is intended to be used as a reference guide, and when in doubt the reader should consult with a qualified technician.

PAGE NUMBERING & MAIN INDEX

As each of the individual factory publications in this manual have their own index, the page numbers corresponding to that index are printed to the top corner of each page. The number printed to the center bottom of the page is the page number within the manual which is the page number referenced in this main index.

SHOP MANUAL No.1		1
ENGINE	Technical features	5
	Identification	6
	Specifications & Cutaway views	8
	Tune up	12
	Overhaul without removing engine	21
	Engine overhaul on bench	35
	Fuel pump (mechanical)	55
	Solex C. 32 PAIA 7 carburettor	57
	Lubrication system	62
	Cooling system	64
	Exhaust	66
	Dimensions & Tolerances	67
CLUTCH	Overhaul & Adjustments	75
GEARBOX	Overhaul & Adjustments	81
SPECIAL INSTRUCTIONS FOR Ti SUPER		97
	Technical features	98
	Ignition	99
	Fuel pump (electric)	100
	Weber 45 DCOE 14 carburettor	101
	Valve clearances	113
	Dimensions & Tolerances	113
SPECIAL INSTRUCTIONS FOR SPRINT G.T.		114
	Technical features	114
	Ignition	115
	Weber 40 DCOE 4 carburettor	115
	Valve clearances	116
SHOP MANUAL No. 2 - PROPELLER SHAFT & REAR AXLE		117
	Propeller shaft	121
	Rear axle	128
	Rear suspension	146
SHOP MANUAL No. 3 - BRAKES		153
	Drum brakes	154
	Hydraulic system	156
	Dunlop disc brakes	158
	ATE disc brakes	162

SHOP MANUAL No. 4 - FRONT SUSPENSION — 173

Suspension behaviour	177
Checking & adjusting the car trim	186
Checking front end geometry	193
Dismantling & servicing the suspension	194
Trouble shooting	195
Suspension specifications	196
Wheel hubs	212
Shock absorbers & stabilizer rod	213
ZF steering box	214
Burman steering box	215
Steering linkage	216
Steering adjustments	217

SHOP MANUAL No. 5 - ELECTRICAL SYSTEM — 219

Bosch alternator	221
Control box & regulator	249
Generator	250
Starter motor	252
Windscreen wiper motor (Marelli)	254
Windscreen wiper motor (Bosch)	255
Lamps & lighting	256
Wiring diagrams (see list on page 220)	257

SHOP MANUAL No. 6 - AIR CONDITIONING — 273

SHOP MANUAL No. 7 - BODY — 291

REMOVAL & INSTALLATION

Windscreen & rear window glass	293
Doors, trim, glass, locks, windows & weatherstriping	298
Front seats	311
Instrument panel - facia	312
Console	316
Headliner	319
Body insulation & sound deadening	327

CHECKING & ADJUSTING

Door locks	328
Hood - bonnet	331
Trunk lid - boot lid	334
Door weather strip	335
Sealing the trunk - boot area	336

Alfa Romeo Giulia Workshop Manual 1962-1975 All Models 1300cc, 1600cc, 1750cc & 2000cc

A Guide to Understanding the Alfa Romeo Giulia Factory 'Manuals'

Alfa Romeo never published an 'all inclusive' workshop manual for the Giulia series of automobiles. Instead, they produced a number of individual 'Mechanical Repair' publications that were focused on the overhaul and service of various mechanical and electrical components plus individual 'Technical Characteristics' publications that provided model specific information. The intention was that these two separate publications were to be used in conjunction with each other in order to provide both technical and mechanical data for a particular model.

This manual is compiled using data from seven of those individual factory 'Mechanical Repair' publications plus a number of additional pages of maintenance, repair, overhaul and wiring diagrams that were not included in the factory publications. Consequently, it provides a generic 'Workshop Manual' for the repair and overhaul of the 1965-1971 Giulia series of automobiles. However, as the 1962-1975 series of Alfa models shared many of the same mechanical components, these 'Mechanical Repair' publications are also of use to owners of both the earlier and later models. For example, even though the engines were of four different capacities they are sufficiently alike for a single set of instructions to suffice for their maintenance and overhaul.

The additional pages in this manual include maintenance and repair information on:

Drum brakes, hydraulic braking system, Dunlop disc brakes and additional information on ATE disc brakes. Front hubs, shock absorbers and stabilizer rod, ZF steering box, Burman steering box, steering linkage and steering adjustments. Electrical components including control box, regulator, generator, starter motor, windscreen wiper motor (both Bosch & Marelli), lamps and lighting and wiring diagrams for 14 different models.

The factory 'Mechanical Repair' publications included in this compilation are:

(1) Engine, Clutch & Gearbox Manual for the 1600 Giulia TI, Sprint GT & TI Super. (1968 Publication)

(2) Propeller Shaft, Rear Axle & Suspension for the Giulia 1300, 1300TI the Giulia 1600 TI Super, Sprint GT, GTC, TI, Super, Sprint GT Veloce & Spider 1600. (1971 Publication)

(3) ATE Disc Brakes all models, as appropriate. (1969 Publication)

(4) Wheel, Suspension & Front End Geometry, for all Giulia and 1750 Models. (1970 Publication - Only sections that are 'owner appropriate' are included).

(5) Electrical for the 1600 Giulia Super, 1750 Berlina, 1750 GT Veloce & 1750 Spider Veloce. (1969 Publication - Only sections that are 'owner appropriate' are included).

(6) Air Conditioning all models, as appropriate. (1972 Publication)

(7) Body, for all Giulia and 1750 Models. (1970 Publication - Only sections that are 'owner appropriate' are included).

Finally, it should be noted that Alfa Romeo never issued a publication that was exclusive to the repair and maintenance of the SPICA fuel injection system. However, that information is included in the appropriate technical publications for the fuel injected cars.

Giulia Model Designations

To aid in better understanding the Alfa Romeo Giulia model designations GT, GTV and Sprint refer to 2 door coupes, Spider to 2 door convertibles and Berlina, Super and Ti to the 4 door sedans. The individual model types within each of these designations may (or may not!) include the engine capacity (1300, 1600, 1750 & 2000) before, after or somewhere within the particular model designation. The identification of a particular body style by the model designation plus the random positioning of the engine size within the model description often creates confusion among those unfamiliar with the Alfa Giula model line.

Measurements and Values

The metric system is the primary measurement method used in both the manufacture of these vehicles and in the production of the factory 'Mechanical Repair' and 'Technical' publications. As such, the reader is urged to verify that the conversion of those metric measurements to other forms of measurement is correct. All measurements and values contained within this compilation of the factory publications are made without any guarantees on behalf of the publisher, who also disclaims any and all liability incurred with the use of this manual.

The importance of using the Alfa Romeo Factory 'Technical Characteristics' publications in conjunction with this Manual

As noted previously, Alfa Romeo also issued a specific 'Technical Characteristics' publication for each individual model (or series of models). While these publications were issued under a variety of different titles, they would be considered to be predominately 'Technical Maintenance & Specifications Manuals'. As these publications were meant to be used in conjunction with the 'Mechanical Repair' publications, we feel it is important that the reader is made aware of the associated technical manuals that compliment this workshop manual.

Alfa Romeo Giulia Technical Manual for 1962 and onwards 1300cc, 1600cc and 1750cc Carbureted Models ISBN 9781588502261

This manual is a compilation of the factory 'Technical' publications listed below and, while the list is not inclusive, the publications were selected as being representative for the 1300cc, 1600cc and 1750cc series of carbureted Alfa Romeo Giulia models.

Factory 'Technical Characteristics' Publications for the Carbureted Giulia Series include:

(1) 1300cc GT 1300 Junior (1967 Publication)

(2) 1300cc Spider 1300 Junior (1968 Publication - plus 1969 Supplement)

(3) 1300cc Giulia TI (1969 Publication)

(4) 1600cc Giulia Ti, Spider & Sprint (1963 Publication)

(5) 1600cc Spider (1966 Publication)

(6) 1600cc Sprint GT Veloce (1966 Publication)

(7) 1600cc Giulia Super (1970 Publication)

(8) 1750cc Berlina, GT Veloce & Spider Veloce (1968 publication)

Alfa Romeo Giulia Technical Manual for 1969 and onwards 1750cc and 2000cc SPICA Fuel Injected Models ISBN 9781588502278

This manual is a compilation of the factory 'Technical' publications listed below and, while the list is not inclusive, the publications were selected as being representative for the 1750cc and 2000cc series of SPICA fuel injected Alfa Romeo Giulia models. It should be noted that the technical publications included in this manual are the only documents that were ever issued by the factory that contain the appropriate maintenance, repair, service, adjustment and trouble shooting information for the SPICA Fuel Injection system.

Technical Characteristics and Principal Inspection Specifications Manual for:

(1) 1750 Berlina, 1750 GT Veloce & 1750 Spider Veloce (1969 publication)

Instruction and Maintenance Manuals for Fuel Injection Models USA:

(2) 1750 All Models USA (1969 publication)

(3) 1750 All Models USA (1971 publication)

(4) 2000 All Models USA (1972 publication)

Technical Characteristics and Principal Inspection Specifications Manual for:

(5) 2000 Berlina, 2000 GT Veloce & 2000 Spider Veloce (1973 publication)

Instruction and Maintenance Manual for Fuel Injection Models USA:

(6) 2000 All models USA including Alfetta (1975 publication)

NOTES

SHOP MANUAL No. 1

ENGINE
CLUTCH
GEARBOX

(FACTORY MANUAL)

GIULIA Ti
GIULIA SPRINT GT
GIULIA Ti SUPER

CONTENTS

- 5 Technical features
- 6 Identification

ENGINE

- 8 Cutaway views and engine specifications

Engine tune up

- 10 Ignition
- 12 Fuel feed
- 13 Fan belt, cylinder head nuts
- 14 Cylinder compression, timing chain tension
- 15 Valve clearance
- 16 Valve timing
- 17 Cooling system, oil and water leakage
- 18 Battery

Overhaul without removing engine

- 19 Preparatory steps for cylinder head removal
- 20 Cylinder head
- 25 Lubricating system units
- 28 Cooling system
- 29 Water pump, engine mountings
- 30 Crankcase front cover
- 32 Flywheel

Engine overhaul on bench

- 33 Removal of engine
- 35 Disassembly
- 37 Inspection and checking
- 44 Reassembly
- 48 Checking the valve timing
- 51 Engine running in

Auxiliary equipment

- 53 Fuel pump
- 55 Solex C. 32 PAIA 7 carburettor
- 60 Lubrication
- 62 Cooling system
- 64 Exhaust system

Engine dimensions and tolerances

- 66 Valves
- 68 Camshafts
- 69 Cylinder barrels, pistons
- 70 Connecting rods
- 71 Crankshaft

CLUTCH

- 74 Adjustment data and ispection specifications
- 75 Removal and disassembly
- 76 Inspection and checking
- 78 Reassembly, checking and reinstallation

GEARBOX

- 82 Removal from car
- 83 Disassembly
- 85 Direct drive & mainshaft
- 87 Countershaft
- 88 Synchromesh: operating principle
- 90 Changing silentblock mounting pads
- 90 Inspection and checking
- 92 Reassembly
- 94 Adjustment of control linkage

SPECIAL INSTRUCTIONS

Giulia T.I. Super

- 96 Technical features
- 97 Ignition
- 98 Electric fuel pump
- 99 Weber 45 DCOE 14 carburettor
- 109 Valve clearances - Timing check
- 109 Dimensions and tolerances

Giulia Sprint G.T.

- 110 Technical features
- 111 Ignition
- 111 Weber 40 DCOE 4 carburettor
- 112 Valve clearances - Timing check

GENERAL SERVICING INSTRUCTIONS

To avoid damage to parts when disassembling and reassembling, always work with the correct wrenches, extractors and tools (special and general).

If a few taps are needed to loosen tight-fitting, use a copper or aluminium mallet for steel parts; for light alloy parts (covers, housings, etc.) use a wooden or plastic mallet.

When disassembling, check that parts which should be marked are stamped with the correct number or reference mark; any original parts (previously replaced) found unmarked should be so stamped.

Components of different assemblies should be kept separate, and nuts should be loosely screwed onto their original studs or bolts.

Before washing parts, brush or wipe off the thickest dirt (to avoid soiling the solvent in the washing tank); then wash with paraffin or hot water and soda and remove any remaining dirt with compressed air; dry all parts immediately after washing so that they do not rust.

A hydraulic press or some other suitable means of applying pressure should be used if parts have to be trued; hammering reduces mechanical strength and should be strictly avoided.

After parts have been ground or honed, wash them thoroughly and blast with compressed air to remove all traces of abrasive powder. When reassembling, clean components (particularly after regrinding) with compressed air blast or a clean, dry brush.

When reassembling, lubricate all mechanical parts properly (except graphite bushings) to prevent seizing and scoring when the engine is first run.

Use a brush and absolutely clean oil to apply a film of oil to all parts which have to be lubricated on reassembly; the brush, the oil and its container should be kept completely free from dust and should be used for the above purpose only.

Use adhesive paper or clean rags to protect those parts of the engine into which dust or foreign particles could penetrate as a result of their being uncovered during disassembling.

When reassembling, renew all gaskets, oil seals, spring washers, tabwashers and lockplates, palnuts and any component not in perfect condition.

Always use genuine ALFA ROMEO spares.

GIULIA 1600 TI

TECHNICAL FEATURES

Engine
- Number and layout of cylinders . . . . 4 in line
- Bore and stroke . . . . 78 x 82 mm
- Total displacement . . . . 1570 cc
- Maximum power at 6000 rpm . . . . HP { DIN 92 / SAE 106

Chassis
- Front wheel track . . . . 1310 mm
- Rear wheel track . . . . 1270 mm
- Wheel base . . . . 2510 mm
- Minimum turning circle . . . . 10,900 mm
- Overall length . . . . 4140 mm
- Overall width . . . . 1560 mm
- Overall height . . . . 1430 mm
- Dry weight . . . . 1060 kgs
- Number of seats 6
- Tyres (Michelin X - Pirelli Cinturato S) 155-15

Inflation pressures with cold tyres
- FRONT 1.6 kg/cm² (22.7 psi) } with low load and short bursts of speed
- REAR 1.7 kg/cm² (24.1 psi)
- FRONT 1.8 kg/cm² (25.6 psi) } with full load and max. continuous speed on highways
- REAR 2.1 kg/cm² (29.8 psi)

Performance after running in period

Maximum speeds for each gear with **41 : 8** final drive
- 1st .... **40 km/h** — 25 mph
- 2nd .... **66 km/h** — 41 mph
- 3rd .... **97 km/h** — 60 mph
- 4th .... **131 km/h** — 82 mph
- 5th .... **165 km/h** — 103 mph
- Reverse .. **44 km/h** — 27 mph

To avoid damaging engine, do not exceed these maximum speeds.
The performances shown are intended for use in ambient conditions as found in center Europe.

Fuel consumption Per **100 km** (62 mi.) to italian CUNA standard approx. **10.4 lts** (27.1 mpg GB-22.6 mpg US)

FUEL, OIL AND WATER

- **Water** (engine and radiator) . . . . approx. 7.5 lts (1.65 gals GB) (1.98 gals US)
- **Fuel:** for best engine performance, we recommend premium grade fuel with an octane number of not less than 92 (RM) . . . . . approx. 46 lts (10.1 gals GB) (12.1 gals US)
- Fuel reserve approx. 6-7 lts (1.3-1.5 gals GB) (1.6-1.8 gals US)

RECOMMENDED LUBRICANTS

Part		kg ▼	GB units	US units	Classification	Commercial equivalents AGIP	Commercial equivalents SHELL	REMARKS
Engine sump — when full		5.80	5.75 qts	6.90 qts	SAE 20 W 40 API MS	F.1 Supermotoroil Multigrade 20 W/40	X-100 Multigrade 20 W/40 Super Motor-Oil « 100 »	
Quantity needed for regular changing — danger level		4.00	3.95 qts	4.7 qts				
Total amount of oil in circuit (sump, filter and passages)		6.55	6.5 qts	7.8 qts				
Gearbox		1.65	3.2 pts	3.8 pts	SAE 90	F.1 Rotra SAE 90	Dentax 90	
Gearbox *					SAE 90 EP	F.1 Rotra Hypoid SAE 90	Spirax 90 EP	* as specified by the red transfer, if any, on gearbox.
Rear axle		1.25	2.5 pts	3.0 pts	SAE 90 API EP	F.1 Rotra Hypoid SAE 90	Spirax 90 EP	
Steering box		.25	.5 pt	.6 pt				
Propeller shaft universal joints & sliding sleeve					NLGI 1	F.1 Grease 15	Retinax G	
Front wheel bearings					NLGI 2/3	F.1 Grease 33FD	Retinax AX	
Fluid reservoir	drum brake				SAE 70 R 3	F.1 Brake Fluid	Donax B 70 R 3	It is advisable not to mix fluids of different makes.
	disc brake				—		ATE « Blau H »	

In countries where the recommended lubricants are not available, it is possible to replace them with products of other leading makes provided that in accordance with the prescribed specifications and grades.

SAE - Society of Automotive Engineers
API - American Petroleum Institute
NLGI - National Lubricating Grease Institute

IDENTIFICATION

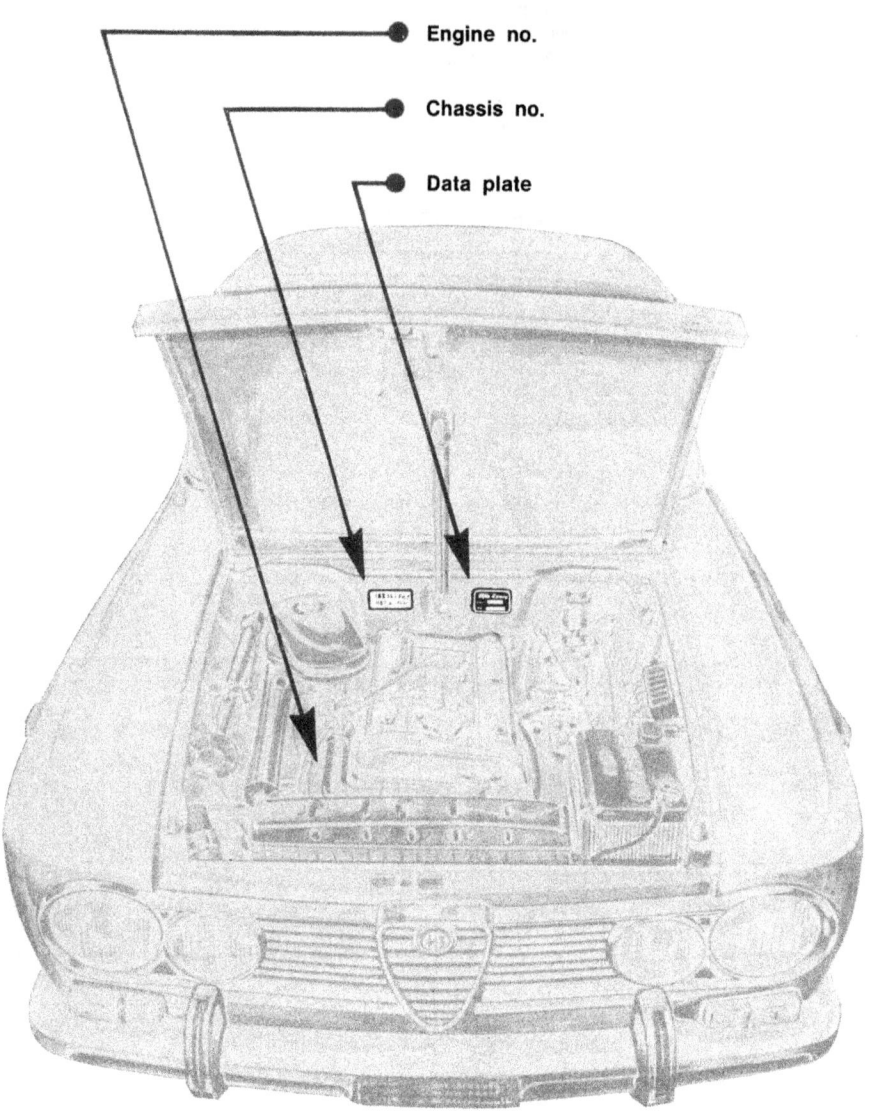

Engine No.

Model and serial no. of engine are stamped on right-hand side of crankcase.

Chassis No.

Chassis serial no. is stamped on bulkhead right-hand top (in the engine compartment).

Data plate

Data plate is attached to bulkhead top (in the engine compartment) and stamped with car model and type approval no.

Paint specifications

Paint specification plate is attached to bulkhead top (in the engine compartment) and stamped with paint type, color and manufacturer's name.

ENGINE

ENGINE SPECIFICATIONS

Engine type	00.514
Cylinder block	light alloy.
Cylinder liners	special cast iron, removable.
Cylinder head	light alloy, water cooled, valve seat inserts.
Crankshaft	treated alloy steel, with counterweights, on five main bearings.
Connecting rods	forged treated steel, with bronze small end bushing.
Pistons	light alloy, with chromium-plated, compression ring, oil scraper ring and oil control ring.
Main and connecting rod bearings	thin steel shell, lined with antifriction metal.
Valve timing gear	two chain-driven overhead camshafts.
Valves	overhead, two per cylinder, directly operated by camshafts.
Oil sump	light alloy.
Fuel feed system	mechanically-operated diaphragm pump and twin **Solex C32 PAIA 7** downdraft carburettor with choke, accelerating pump and vacuum control of second barrel throttle.
Ignition	battery and distributor with vacuum advance regulator.
Lubricating system	forced lubrication by gear pump; the system includes a relief valve.
Cooling system	water coolant, with radiator and fan; forced circulation by centrifugal pump; coolant temperature controlled by a thermostat.
Filters	oil: full-flow filter in series with the delivery circuit, with clogged-element bypass. air: silencer-type cleaner with dry element.
Starting	with 12-volt cranking motor.

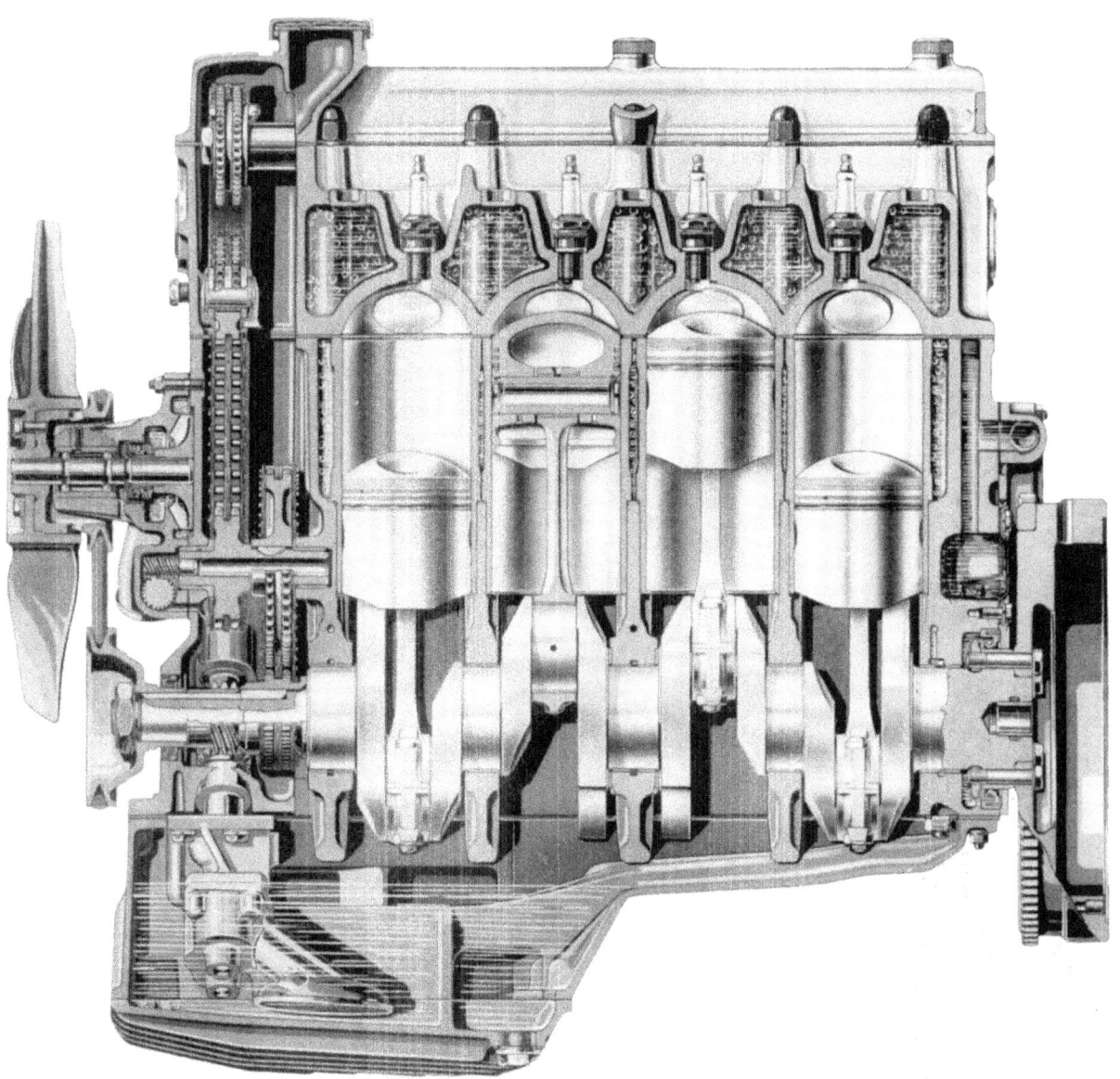

9A

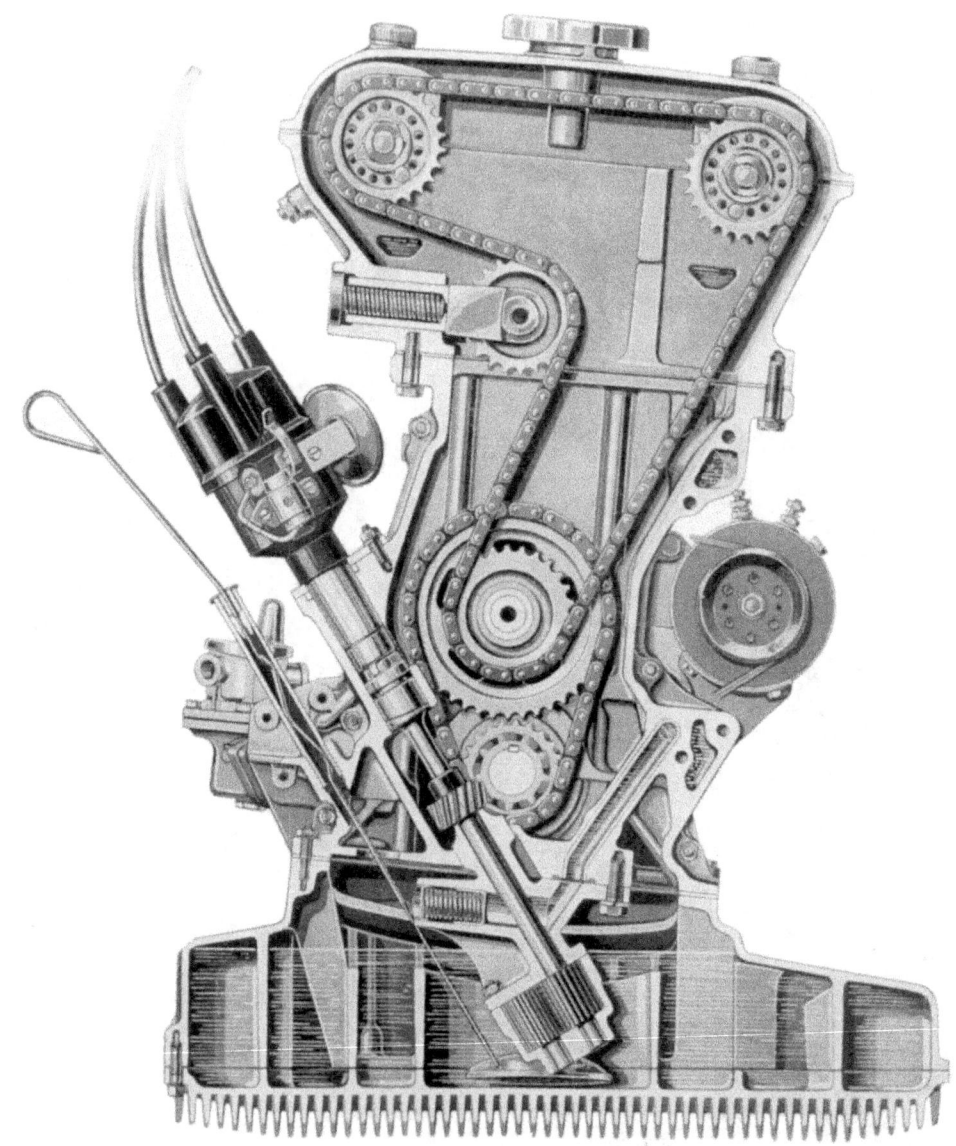

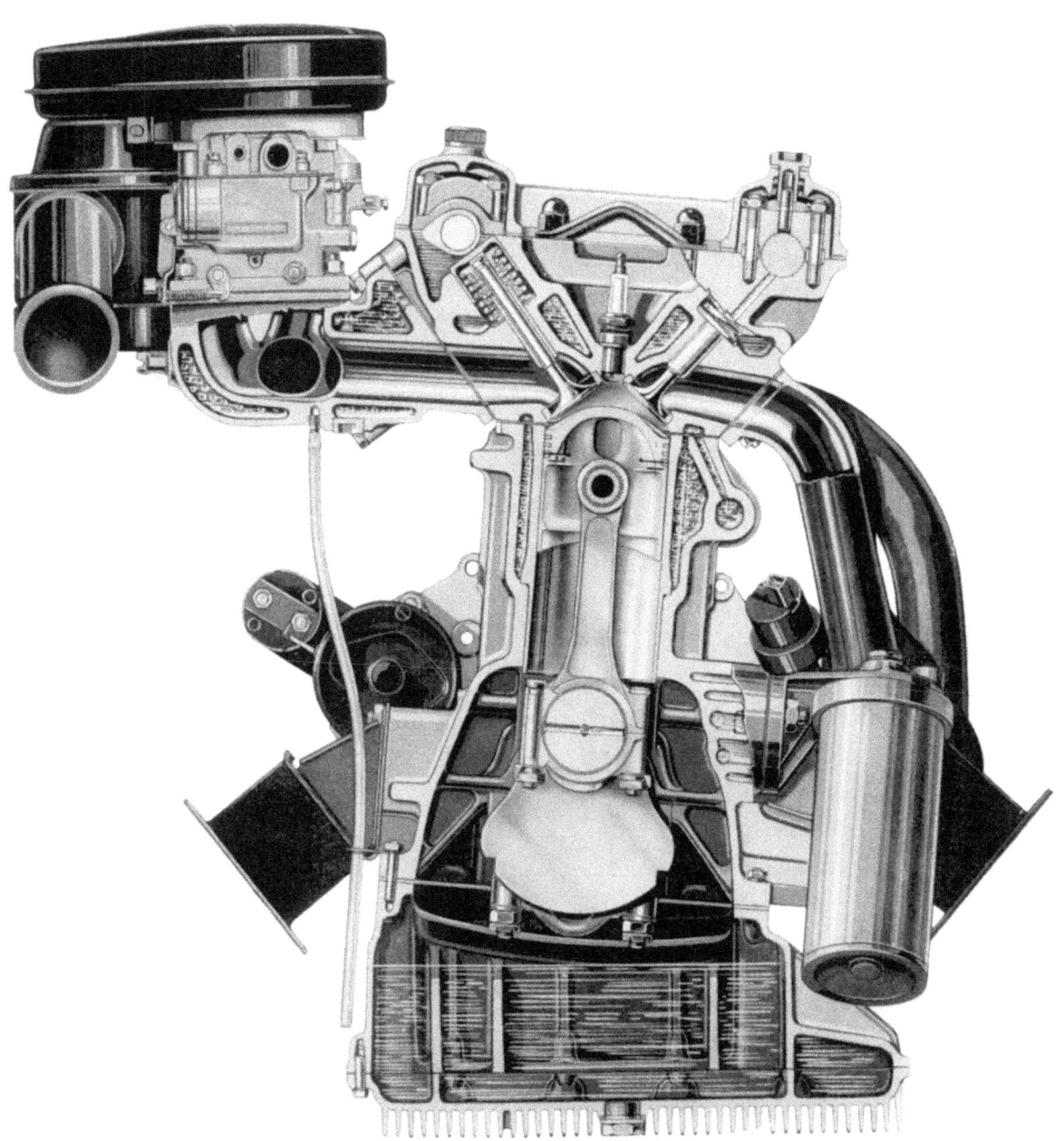

ENGINE TUNE UP

IGNITION

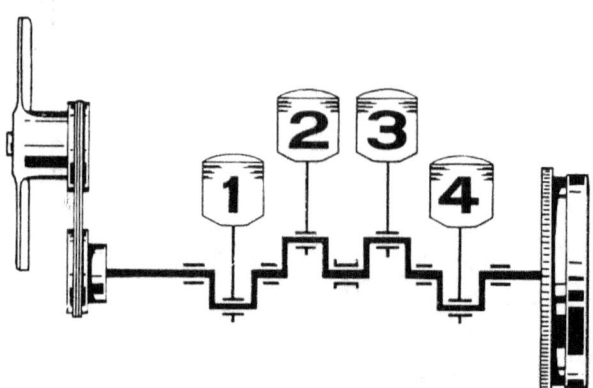

Firing order **1-3-4-2**

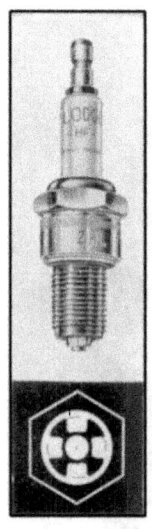

LODGE 2 HL

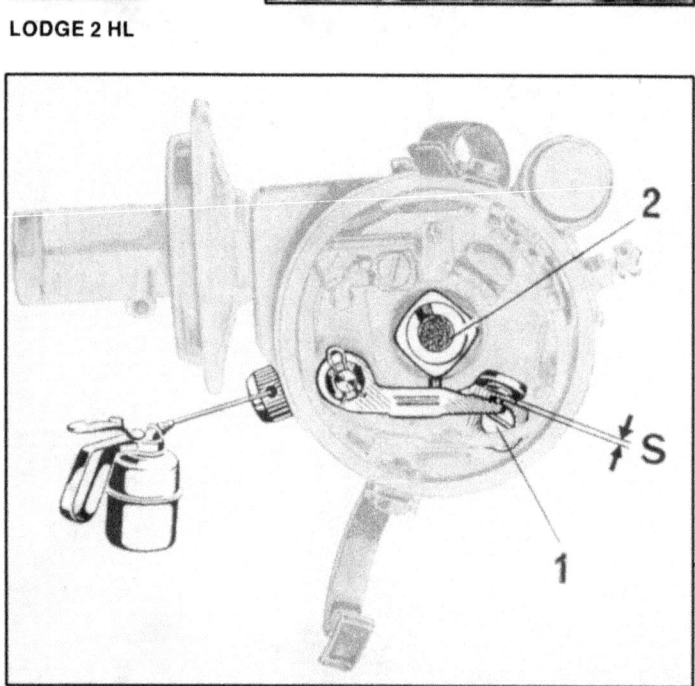

Spark plug inspection

- The plugs are of the type with a power electrode centred among four «earthed» points. **No adjustment of the distance between electrodes is necessary.**

- Using a screwdriver, earth the central electrode of a plug. If the plug sparked properly, the speed of the engine will decrease.

- WARNING: do not disconnect the plug cables when the engine is running, of the distributor capacitor may be damaged.

- If necessary, remove the plugs and clean them with a wire brush.

- Test the plugs on the bench, making sure that the spark jumps properly at a pressure of about **8 kg/cm²** (114 psi).

- Tighten the plugs when cold to **2.5-3.5 kgm** (18 - 25.3 ft. lbs.) with a torque wrench and tool **A.5.0115**; before installing on engine, lubricate plug threaded shank with graphite grease.

Distributor: BOSCH JFU 4

Inspection of cap and contact points:

- Check:
  - that the interior of the cap shows no signs of moisture, carbon deposits or cracking;
  - that the centre carbon brush works freely in its holder and that the spring is functioning properly;
  - the insulation of the rotor arm;
  - the condition of the terminals, both on the rotor arm and on the cap;
  - that contact breaker points are clean and smooth.

- Check by means of a feeler gauge that the gap between the points is as specified:
  S = .35 to .40 mm (.014-.016 in.).

- If the points are corroded, smooth them with a very fine file and then wash them with petrol.

- Adjust the contact gap to the specified value by means of the adjusting screw **1** (use a screwdriver and feeler gauge).

- Apply some drops of oil through the suitable oiler and soak the felt **2**.

- Clean the cam with a lint-free cloth and smear it with petrolatum.

- Sparingly lubricate the contact-breaker arm pin with grease.

ENGINE TUNE UP

IGNITION

Check the static advance

- Bring the static advance mark **F** cut in the drive pulley into line with the reference plate by slightly rotating the crankshaft.

- Check that, in this position, the contact breaker points are about to separate; when a 12-volt lamp is connected between the distributor input terminal **1** and the ground, it should light up immediately the points open.

- Slacken bolt **2** and turn the body of the distributor to make the required adjustment. (Clockwise to retard and counter-clockwise to advance).

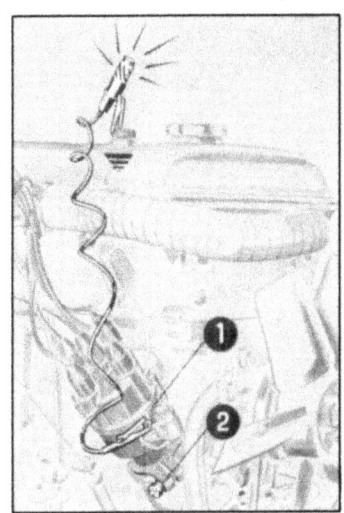

Check the automatic advance with a stroboscopic gun

- Disconnect the rubber pipe from the vacuum advance regulator.

- Make the connections (see diagram).

- Run the engine at about 5,000 rpm and direct the light from the stroboscopic gun onto the pulley; if the timing is correct, the **M** (max. advance) stamped on the pulley will be seen in line with the reference plate.

- If it is found that the max. advance is greater or less than the prescribed value, adjust the static advance accordingly, as it is better to have correct timing at high speeds.

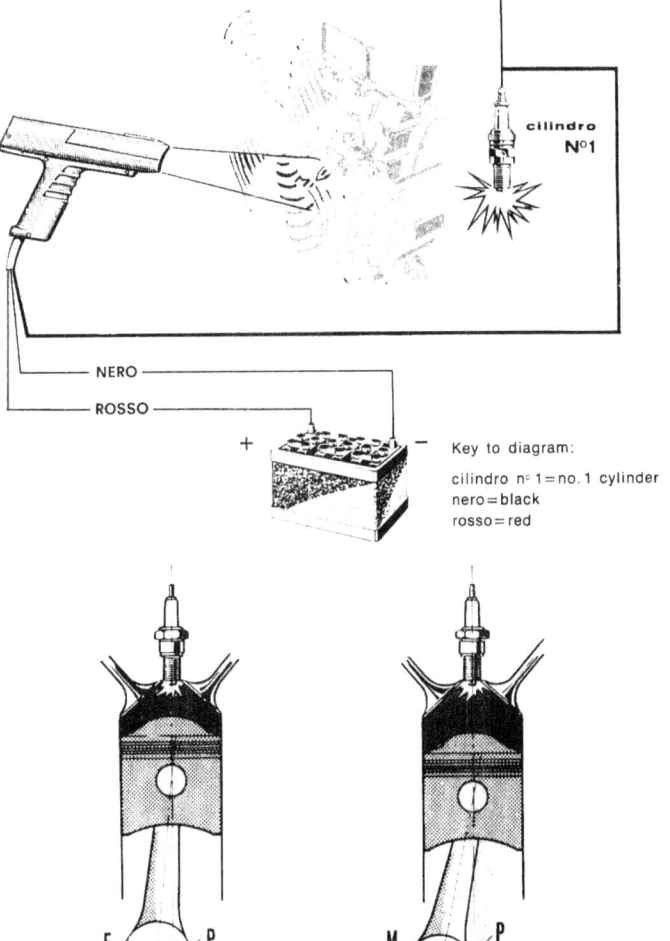

Key to diagram:
cilindro n° 1 = no. 1 cylinder
nero = black
rosso = red

Advance values (before **T.D.C.**)

- Static **F = 3° ± 2°**

- Maximum **M = 43° ± 3°** at 5,000 rpm.

ENGINE TUNE UP

FUEL FEED

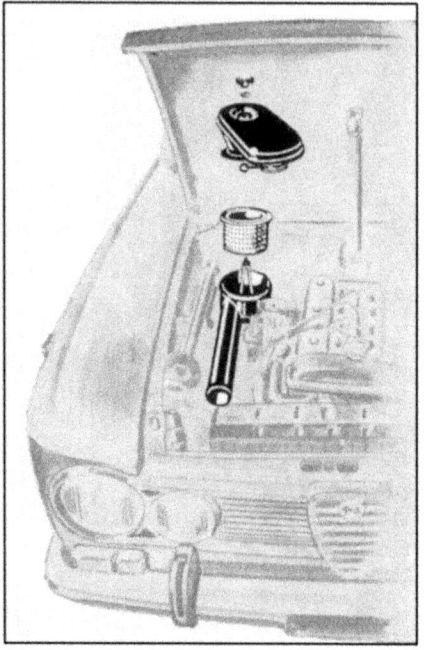

AIR CLEANER

Cleaning or replacement of the element

- Loosen the clamp which fastens the air inlet duct to the carburettor.
- Unscrew the wing nut fastening the duct to cleaner body.
- Remove the duct and withdraw the element.
- Thoroughly wash the element with petrol.
- Replace the element if damaged or if impossible to clean properly.

SOLEX C 32 PAIA-7 CARBURETTOR

Cleaning and inspection of jets:

- Remove jets **1**, **2**, **8** and **9** and blow through with compressed air. Do not use a metal probe as this could alter the jet diameter.
- Check that the numbers stamped on the jets are the same as those given in the table.

Idling adjustment (with engine hot)

- Tighten the screw **11** for a quarter turn (to prevent binding of the 2nd throttle) and lock in the jam nut.
- Screw slowly in the screw **4** to make the engine run faster.
- Loosen the screw **5** until the engine begins to « hunt », then gradually screw it in until the engine runs smoothly.
- Unscrew the screw **4** very slowly until the engine speed is approximately 500-600 rpm.
- If the engine again begins to « hunt », slightly tighten screw **5**; **in no case must this screw be tightened to its maximum extent.**

1 Idling jet, no. 1 barrel
2 Main jet, no. 1 barrel
3 Accelerating pump
4 Adjusting screw for minimum opening of 1st throttle
5 Idling mixture adjusting screw
6 Choke control lever
7 Vacuum capsule
8 Main jet, no. 2 barrel
9 Idling jet, no. 2 barrel
10 Filter
11 Adjusting screw for minimum opening of 2nd throttle

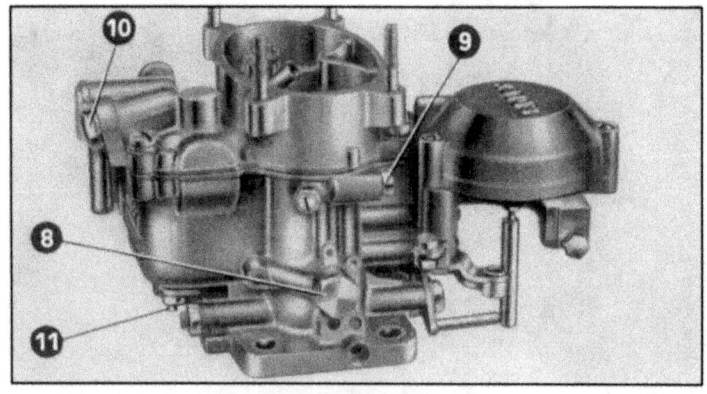

Jet specifications	1st barrel	2nd barrel
Venturi	23	23
Main	125	130
Idling	45	70
Main air metering	190	190
Idling air metering	100	60
Accelerating pump	45	—
Choke	120	—

14

ENGINE TUNE UP

FAN BELT
CYLINDER HEAD NUTS

FAN AND GENERATOR DRIVING BELT
PIRELLI: model n. 60675

Tension check

- Belt tension should be enough to drive generator and fan pulley without slipping nor straining the bearings.
  When the tension is correct the sag of the belt tested as shown should be: **10 to 15 mm** (about 1/2").

Tension adjustment

- Loosen the nut on adjusting arm pivot pin and the nut on the generator securing bolt.
- Move the generator outwards by rotating it on its hinge; if necessary use a screwdriver or similar as a lever; then relock the nuts.
- Check that sag is as stated above.
- Check that warning light on dashboard goes off when engine speed exceeds 1100 rpm.

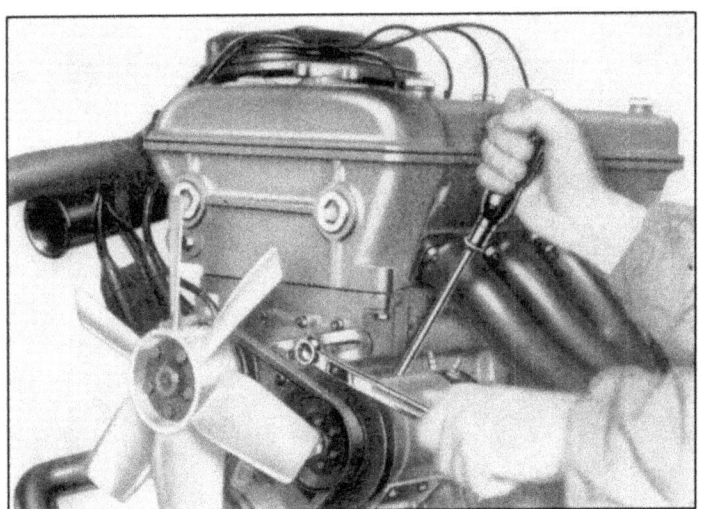

CYLINDER HEAD NUTS

Tightening torque specifications

- **After reconditioning:**

  lubetorque when cold to:
  6.2 to 6.4 kgm (44.7 to 46.2 ft-lbs).
  Then, warm up the engine (better if actually driving the car) and relock without slackening to **6.6 to 6.7 kgm** (47.7 to 48.5 ft-lbs).
  After tested the car, when cold and in correct sequence, slacken the nuts by one and one half turn and lubetorque to **6.2 to 6.4 kgm** (44.7 to 46.2 ft-lbs).

  Warning - Whenever performing any repair involving the removal of cylinder head the gasket must be replaced with a new one.

Tightening sequence

- Tighten the cylinder head nuts in the sequence shown to avoid harmful straining and to allow the gasket to bed in perfectly between the two joining surfaces.

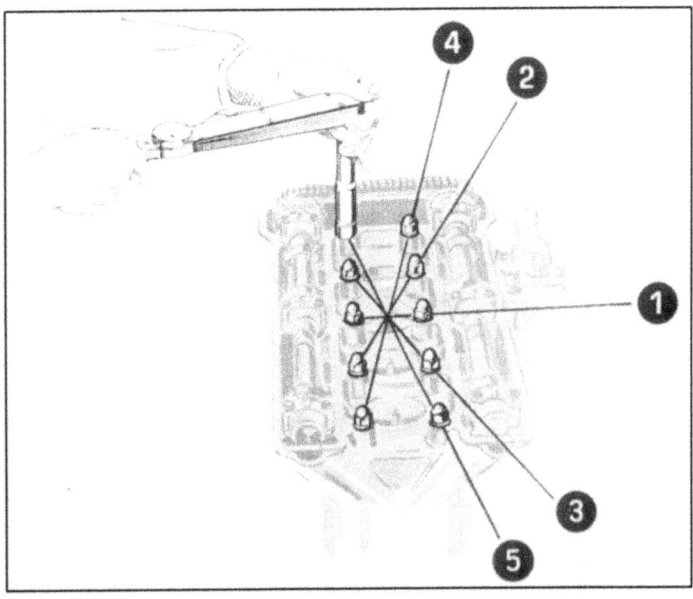

ENGINE TUNE UP

CYLINDER COMPRESSION TIMING CHAIN TENSION

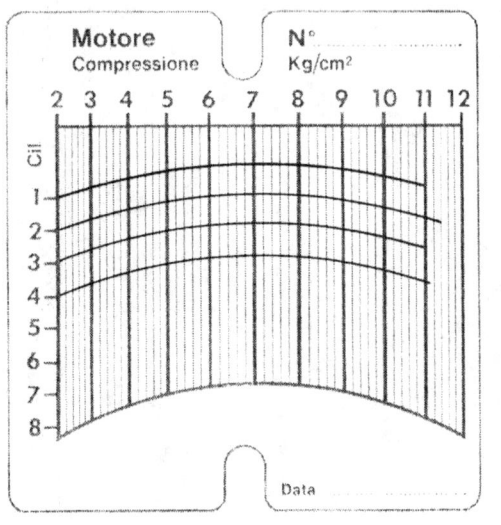 

Cylinder compression check

To check the cylinder compression use a suitable recording gauge and proceed as follows:

- warm up the engine to normal operating temperature;
- remove all spark plugs and obtain recordings by cranking the engine with the starting motor.
Pressure variation between cylinders shoud not exceed 10% of the highest reading.

Motore = Engine
Compressione = Compression
Data = Date

Adjust chain tension

- Unscrew the camshaft cover retaining nuts and remove the cover.

N.B. - On reassembly, check that the gasket is in good condition; if not, replace it with a new one. Then relock the cover retaining nuts gradually and in diagonal order so as to avoid straining the camshaft journal bearings which house the cover retaining studs.

- Unlock without removing the setscrew of chain tensioner.
- Check the tensioner spring for proper working conditions.
- Crank the engine for a few seconds to allow the tensioner to tight the chain.
- Lock chain tensioner setscrew firmly.

ENGINE TUNE UP

VALVE CLEARANCE

Check valve clearance

- Check that clearance **G**, measured when the engine is cold at the unlobed profile of the cam, falls within the following limits:

  Intake .475 - .500 mm
  (.0187 - .0197 in.)

  Exhaust .525 - .550 mm
  (.0206 - .0216 in.)

Valve clearance adjustment

- Measure and record the clearance found along with the excess to be taken up to reset the correct clearance.

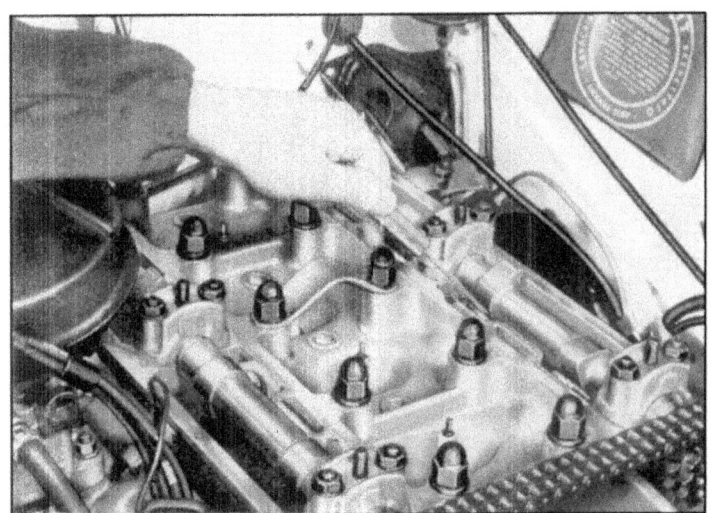

Example

Clearance		CYLINDER			
		1	2	3	4
INTAKE .0197" (.500 mm)	Clearance recorded	.450 mm .0177"	.475 mm .0187"	.425 mm .0167"	.500 mm .0197"
	Correction required	—.050 mm —.0020"	—.025 mm —.0010"	—.075 mm —.0030"	—
EXHAUST .0216" (.550 mm)	Clearance recorded	.400 mm .0156"	.450 mm .0176"	.400 mm .0156"	.600 mm .0236"
	Correction required	—.150 mm —.0060"	—.100 mm —.0040"	—.150 mm —.0060"	+.050 mm +.0020"

- Rotate the crankshaft until the timing marks cut in the camshaft journals are in line with those on the journal bearings.

- Move the chain tensioner backwards, slacken the chain and secure the tensioner in retracted position.

- Remove the journal bearings from the camshaft at the intake side and, taking care that the chain does not move with respect to the sprocket, take out the camshaft together with the chain; then rest the unit on the center of the head.
  The same applies to the camshaft at the exhaust side.

- Using suitable pliers, remove the valve cups.

- Withdraw the valve adjusting pad and measure its thickness.

- Fit a new pad of correct thickness **S**. For the selection of the proper adjusting pad use the dial gauge **7600.31.002** complete with the bracket **C.5.0111/1** (Ref. Tool Bulletin no. 51/2).

  Note: the adjusting pads are made available in a series of thicknesses ranging from **1.3 to 3.5 mm** (.051 to .138 in.) in increments of **.025 mm** (.001 in.).

- Refit valve cups, camshafts and chain.

- **Recheck valve clearance.**

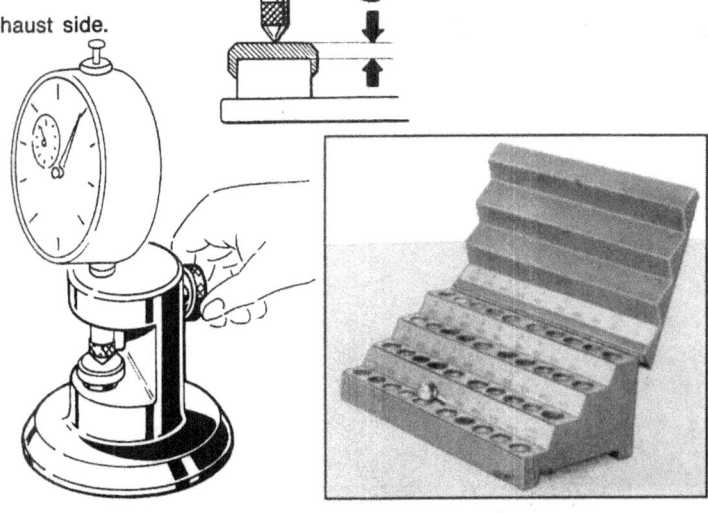

ENGINE TUNE UP

VALVE TIMING

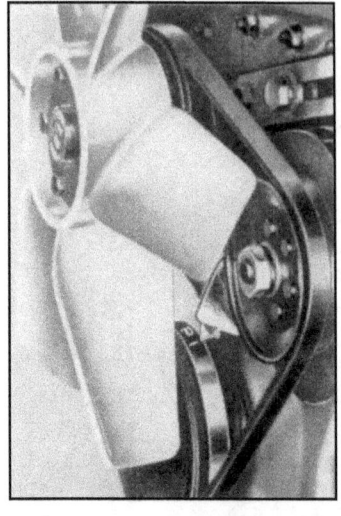 

Valve timing adjustment

(to be performed when valve clearance and chain tension are correct).

- Rotate the crankshaft until the timing mark **P** (TDC) cut in the pulley is in line with the reference plate on front cover.

- Check that timing marks, cut in the camshaft front journals, are aligned with those on the journal bearings when no. 1 cylinder cams are pointing outwards as shown.

 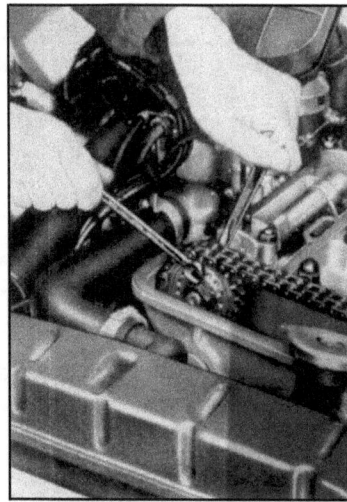

- If the marks are misaligned, loosen the screw locking the sprocket to the camshaft.

- Remove the locating bolt which keys the sprocket to the camshaft flange.

- Using tool **A.5.0103** (Ref. Tool Bulletin no. 61/2) turn the camshafts without moving the chain so as to bring the reference marks into alignment.

- In the holes which are now aligned, refit the locating bolt and lock the screw again.

ENGINE TUNE UP

COOLING SYSTEM
OIL AND WATER LEAKAGE

COOLING SYSTEM

- Disconnect the hose from intake manifold.
- Withdraw the thermostat from its housing.
- Check that thermostat starts to open at about **82° - 87° C** (180° to 190 °F) and replace it if not within these limits.
- Check the radiator cap, making sure that the spring is not broken, that the seal is in good condition and that the pressure-reducing valve is working properly.

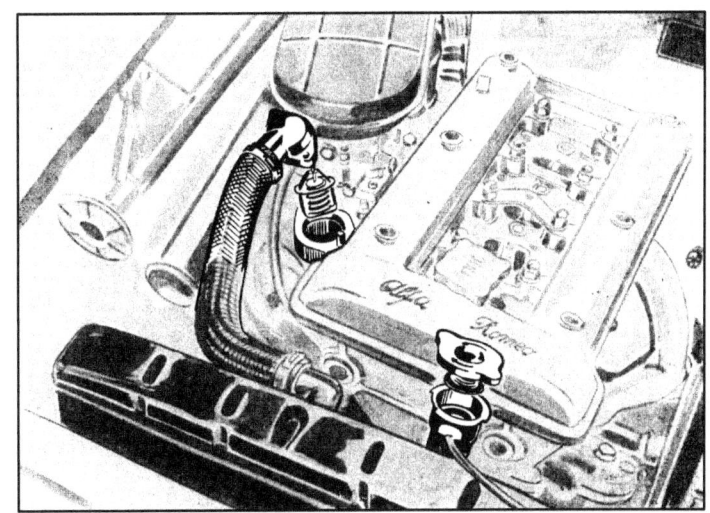

OIL AND WATER LEAKAGE

Check for any sign of oil leaks from:

1. camshaft cover
2. joining surface between cylinder block and head
3. joining surface between fuel pump mounting flange and crankcase
4. sump gaskets
5. crankcase front cover
6. crankshaft front and rear packings.

Check for any sign of water leaks from:

2. joining surface between cylinder block and head
7. radiator
8. joining surface between water pump and front cover.

Check the following units for good conditions:

9. hose from intake manifold to radiator
10. hose from radiator to water pump
11. rubber hoses and connections of heating system.

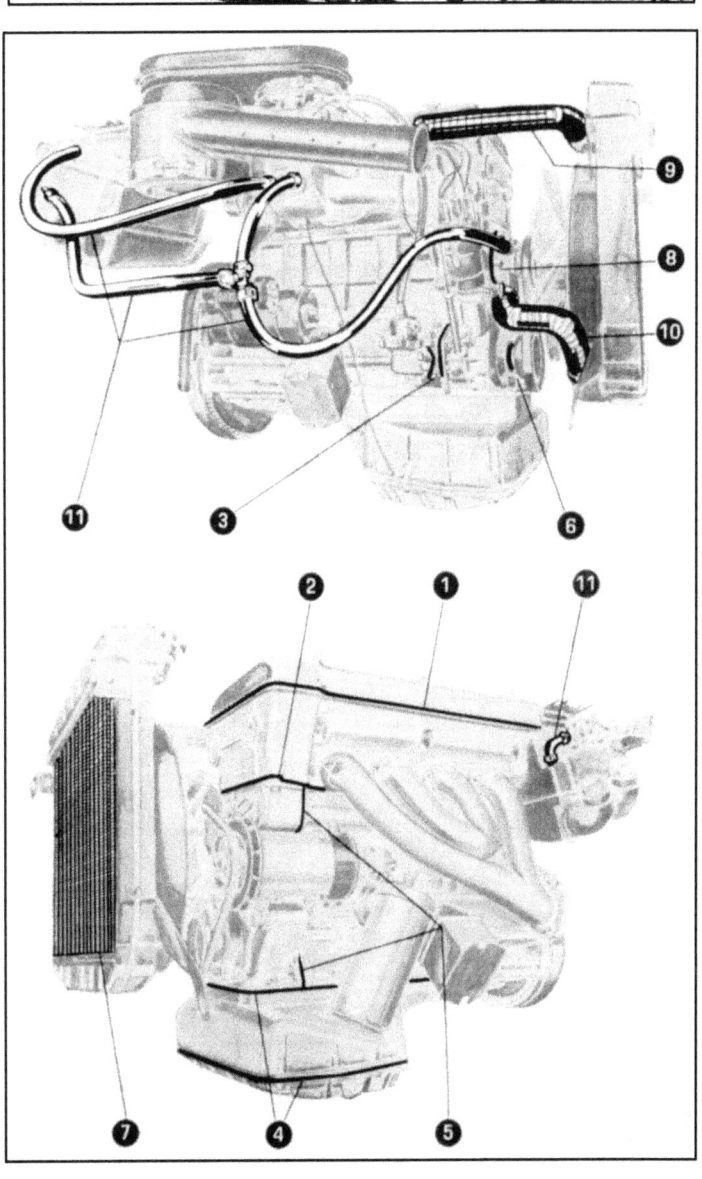

ENGINE TUNE UP

BATTERY

- Using a wooden rule as a dipstick check that water level is not more than **4-5 mm** (3/16") above the plates.
- Top up with distilled water only.

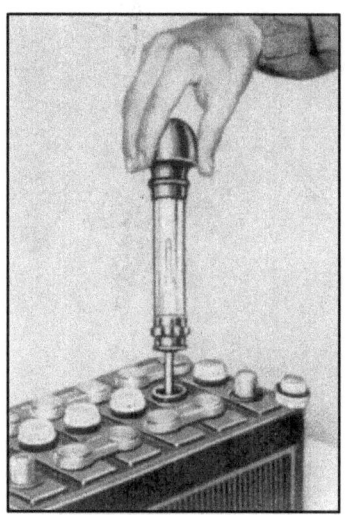 

- Check the charge of battery cells using a hydrometer as shown; the specific gravity should be **1.23 to 1.28** (equivalent to 27 to 31.5 Baumè).
  If distilled water has been added to a battery, the specific gravity shall not be measured until mixing is complete; to facilitate mixing, charge the battery for about half an hour.
- If no hydrometer is available, test the charge of the battery cells with a fork voltmeter: each cell should give an output of **1.9 - 2** volts.
  When a voltmeter is used it partially discharges the cell; it should therefore be kept in contact with the terminals for **a few seconds** only.

OVERHAUL WITHOUT REMOVING ENGINE

PREPARATORY STEPS FOR CYLINDER HEAD REMOVAL

- Drain coolant from:
  1 radiator
  2 cylinder block
- Remove:
  3 exhaust manifold from cylinder head
  4 air cleaner assembly (loose clamp 5 on carburettor and 6 on cylinder head)
  6 clamp from cylinder head
  7 spark plug leads
  8 cooling water hose from cylinder head
  9 choke flexible cable from carburettor
  10 water thermometer sender lead
  11 fuel delivery hose
  12 vacuum advance regulator hose from ignition distributor
  13 fuel drain pipe
  14 throttle control
  15 two water pipes from intake manifold.

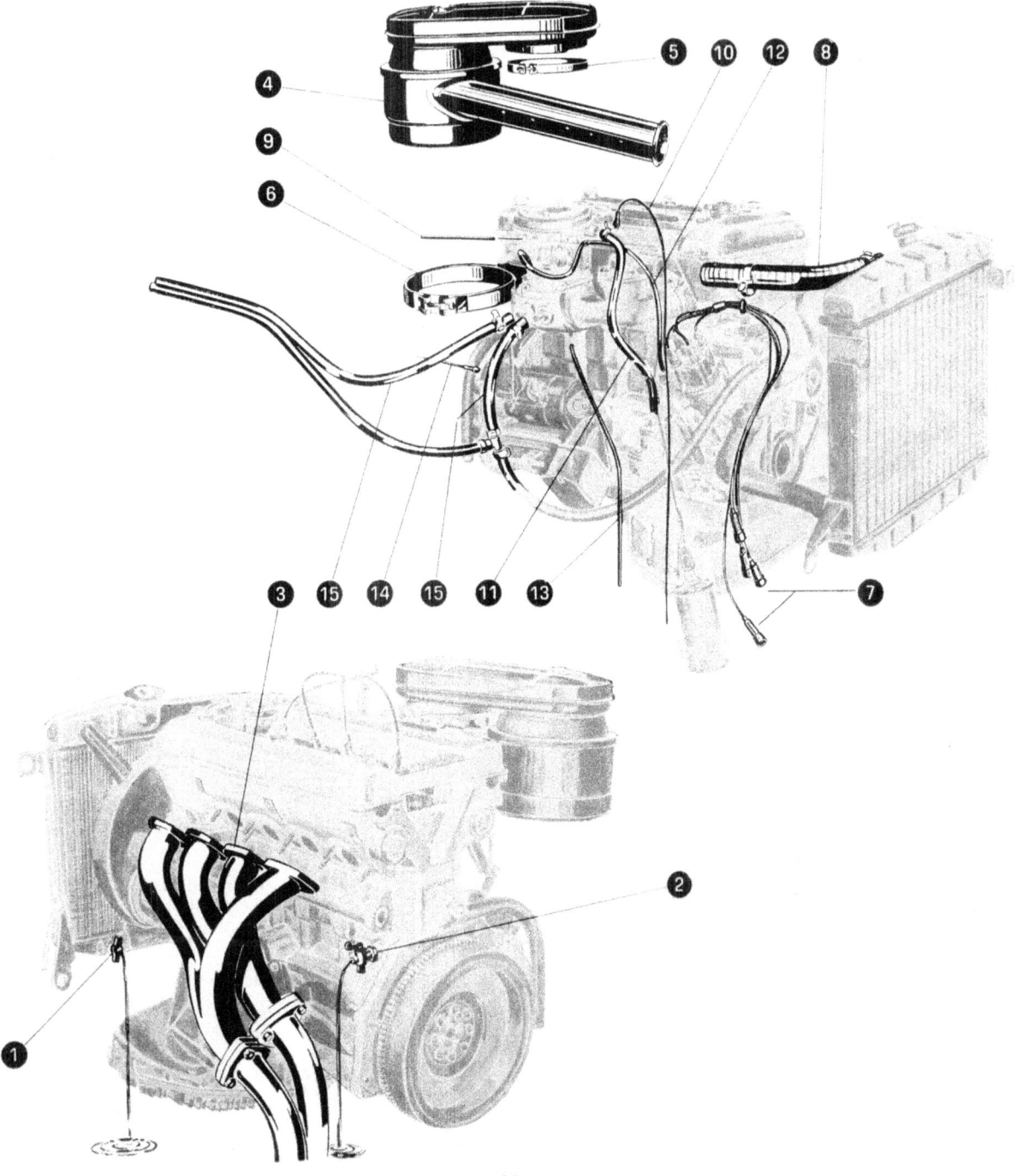

OVERHAUL WITHOUT REMOVING ENGINE

CYLINDER HEAD

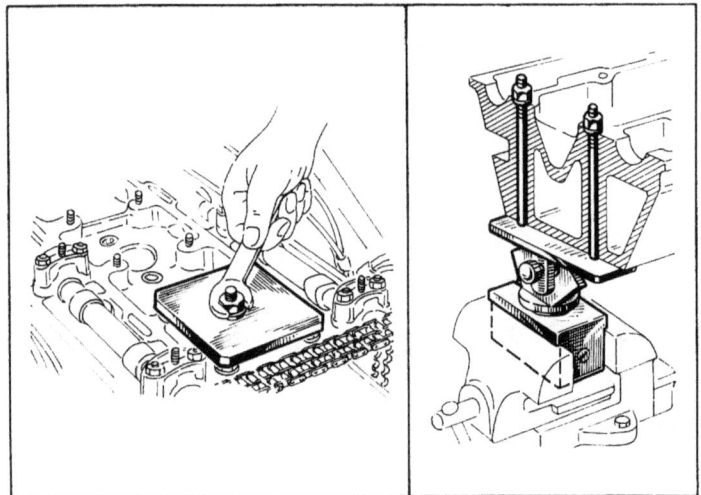

Removal from cylinder block

- Remove camshaft cover from cylinder head.
- Disconnect the timing chain and secure its ends to prevent them from dropping into cylinder block.
- Unscrew the nuts fixing head to block and the two screws securing front cover to head.
- Take the head away with tool **A.2.0146** (Ref. Tool Bulletin no. 130).

Caution: do not remove the cylinder head assembly when still hot to prevent possible warping.

Disassembly and overhaul

- Drain oil from camshaft housing and clean the head thoroughly.
- Remove the intake manifold and carburettor as a unit with the wrench **A.5.0133**.

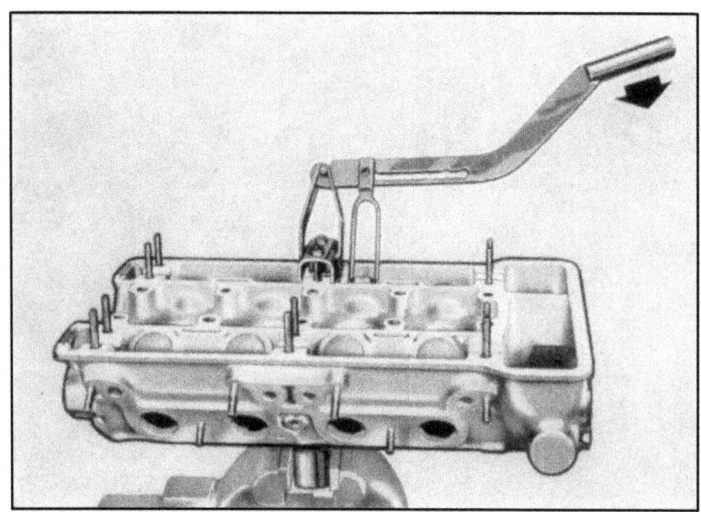

- Unscrew the spark plugs.
- Grip the jig B (**A.2.0128/1** - Ref. Tool Bulletin no. 76/1) in a vice, install the head on the jig and lock in place with the two nuts.
- Remove the journal bearing caps and take camshafts, valve cups and adjusting pads away (see page 15).
- Hold the valves in position with tool A (**A.2.0121** - Ref. Tool Bulletin no. 88).
- Remove the valve cotters by depressing the springs with the tool **A.3.0103/1-2-6** (Ref. Tool Bulletin no. 11/2).
- Withdraw from the top:
  - the upper spring seats
  - the springs
  - the shims
  - the lower spring seats.
- Remove tool A from the cylinder head and withdraw the pair of valves from below.
- Repeat the same procedure for the other pairs of valves.

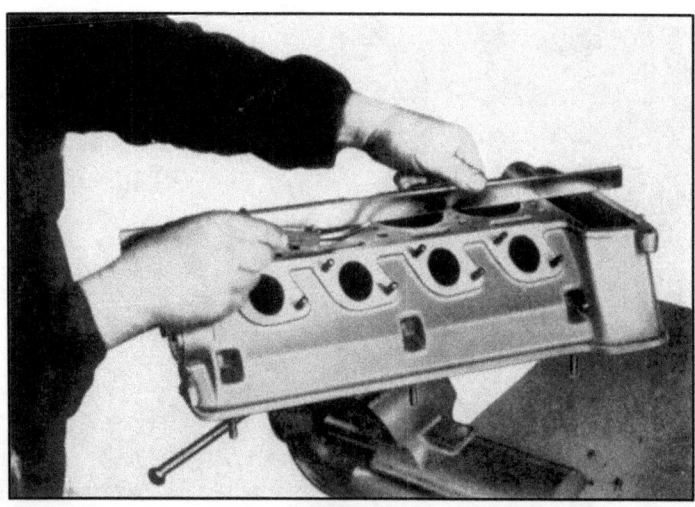

- Loosen the setscrew and withdraw the chain tensioner from its housing along with the spring and tapered retaining plate.
- Check that cylinder head is not warped out of flat.
- Using a straight rule and a feeler gauge as shown, check that out of flat is not more than **.1 mm** (.0039 in.).
- If this limit is exceeded, rework the surface true with a scraper; grinding is not advisable unless strictly necessary.

OVERHAUL WITHOUT REMOVING ENGINE

CYLINDER HEAD

Valve guides

- Check that the bore of valve guides shows no sign of seizing; if there are gummy or carbon deposits, clean the guides with a suitable swab.
- Check with the gauge **C.5.0115** (Ref. Tool Bulletin no. 103) that the inside diameter of guides is **9.000-9.015 mm** (.3544-.3549").

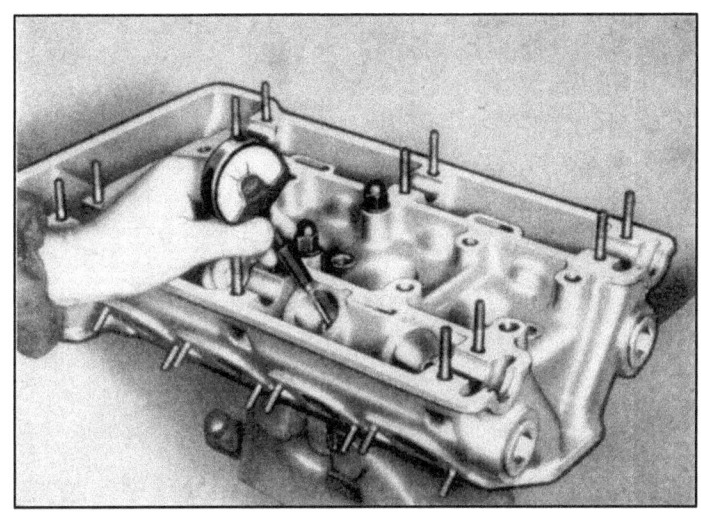

A If valve guides are badly scored, remove them with tool **A.3.0134** (Ref. Tool Bulletin no. 80/2).
To withdraw the valve guide seals, use tool no. **A.3.0247** (Ref. Tool Bulletin no. 141).

B Insert new valve guides with the tool **A.3.0133** - exhaust side and **A.3.0246** - intake side (Ref. Tool Bulletin no. 80/2) and check for correct inside diameter. Before inserting the guides heat the cylinder head to **100 °C**.
To drive the valve guide seals, use tool no. **A.3.0244** (Ref. Tool Bulletin no. 141).

- If enlarging is needed, bore the guide as required (Ref. Tool Bulletin no. 96/1).

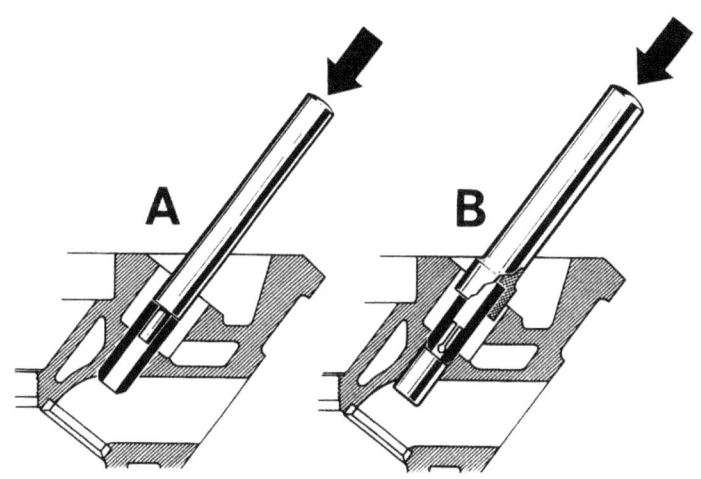

Valve seat inserts

- Check that valve seat inserts are not cracked and flush with the countersink in the cylinder head. If cracked or flush, reney the inserts as follows:

  • insert the spindle of the tool **A.3.0053** complete of tap and spacer (Ref. Tool Bulletin no. 118):

  intake: tap **U.4.0004** with **42.5 mm** (1.675") dia. spacer

  exhaust: tap **U.4.0002** with **38.5 mm** (1.516") dia. spacer

  • screw all the way in the tap into the valve insert;

  • with a lead or copper mallet, eject tool and seat insert from cylinder head as shown;

  • heat the cylinder head to **100° - 120 °C** (212° - 248° F) and fit a new insert.

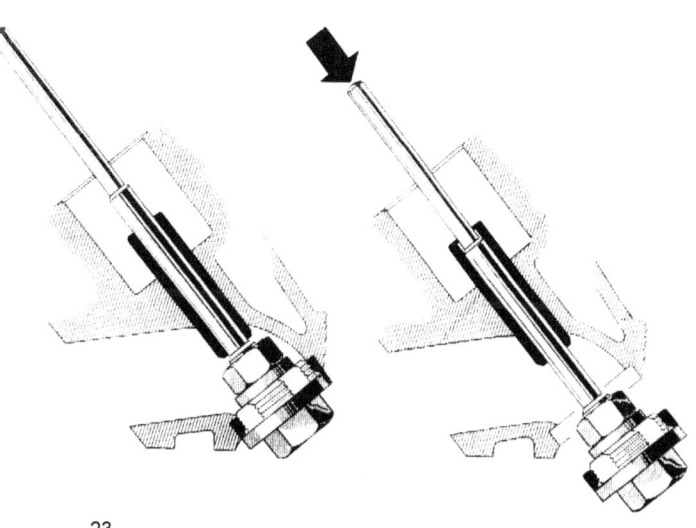

OVERHAUL WITHOUT REMOVING ENGINE

CYLINDER HEAD

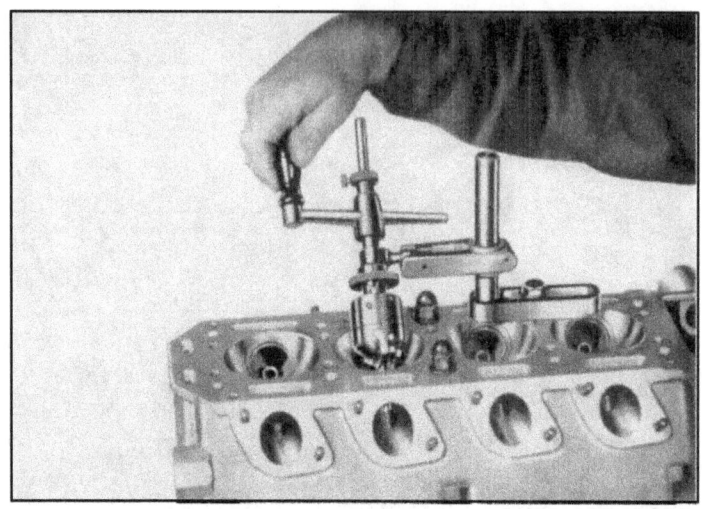

- After the installation, countersink the new insert to an angle of **30°** with the tool **A.1.0002** (Ref. Tool Bulletin no. 14).

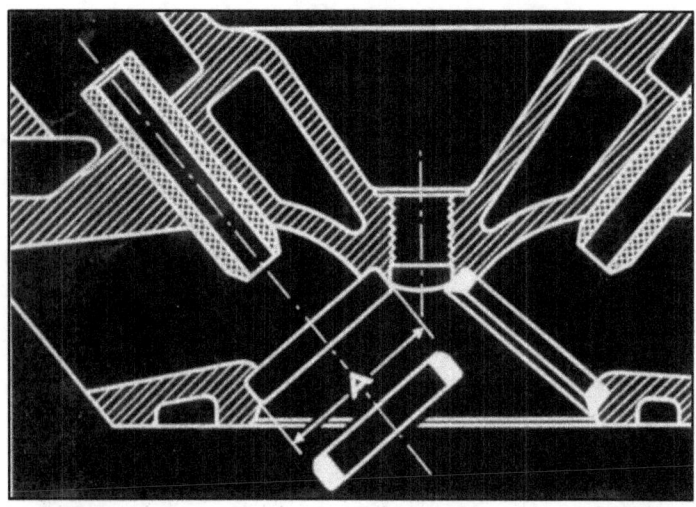

Note

- If the housing of valve seat insert is worn or scored it shall be counterbored with the tool **A.1.0002** (Ref. Tool. Bulletin no. 14) up to the following oversize:

    intake   A = **42.772 - 42.797 mm**
    (1.6840 - 1.6849 in.)

    exhaust A = **38.772 - 38.797 mm**
    (1.5265 - 1.6274 in.).

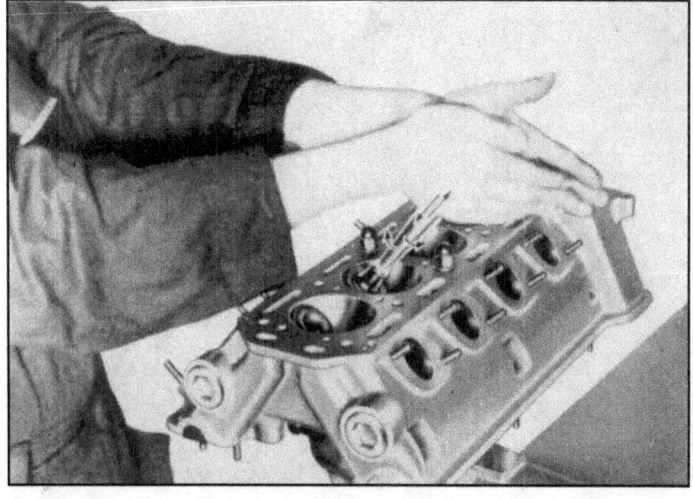

Valves

- Check that valves are not warped and that valve poppet is not burnt; if damaged, renew the valves.

- Check valve stem for correct diameter:

    intake valve: **8.960 - 8.987 mm**
    (.3527 - .3538 in.)

    exhaust valve: **8.935 - 8.960 mm**
    (.3518 - .3527 in.).

- Lap each valve in its seat with the aid of a suitable tool and using a fine grain lapping powder suspended in oil.
  Take care not to interchange the valves; refer to figures stamped on them.
  After lapping, wash carefully with fuel oil and dry with compressed air.

OVERHAUL WITHOUT REMOVING ENGINE

CYLINDER HEAD

- Check springs for proper calibration with a suitable test rig:

		Free length	Loaded condition	
			Length	Test load
SPRING	large	51.3 mm (2.02 in.)	27.5 mm (1.08 in.)	35.6 to 37.1 kg (78.5 to 81.8 lbs)
	small	46.5 mm (1.83 in.)	26.0 mm (1.02 in.)	21.2 to 23.16 kg (46.7 to 51.1 lbs)

- Check that valve cotters, spring seats and shims are not worn or damaged.

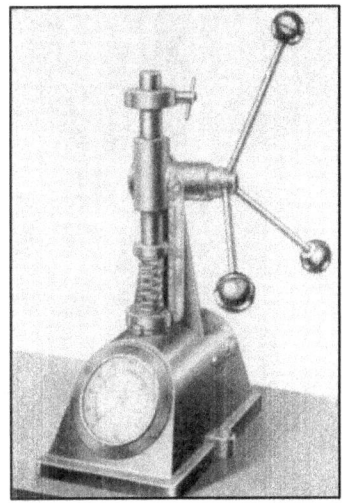
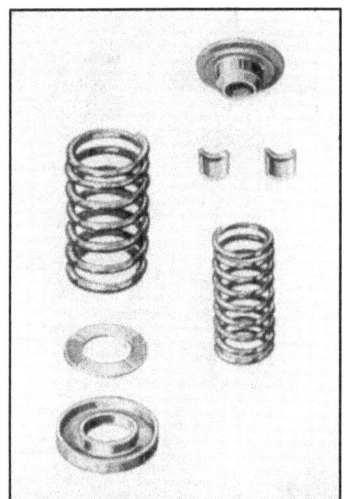

- After installation of valve springs, spring seats, shims and cotters, check the valves for leakage as follows.
- Fill the combustion chamber with petrol and blow compressed air into intake and exhaust ports.
- Air bubbles will be seen if the valves and seats do not seal properly: in this case lap valves and seats together again.

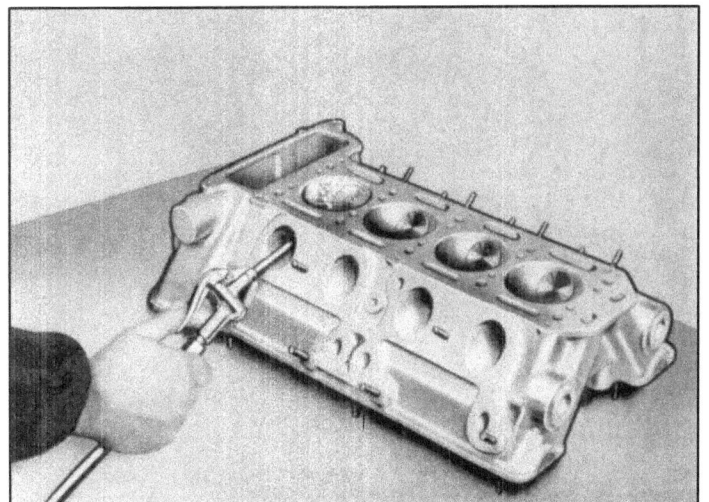

- Inspect the valve cups to make sure that the top surface is flat and shows no sign of scoring or seizing.
- Check that top surface of the adjusting pads is not damaged.
- Check that outside diameter of valve cups and inside diameter of their housings in cylinder head fall within the following limits:

Diameter	Standard	Oversized
d	34.973 to 34.989 mm (1.3773 to 1.3775 in.)	35.173 to 35.189 mm (1.3848 to 1.3853 in.)
D	35.000 to 35.025 mm (1.3779 to 1.3789 in.)	35.200 to 35.225 mm (1.3859 to 1.3868 in.)

Clearance **G = .011 to .052 mm** (.0005 to .0020 in.).

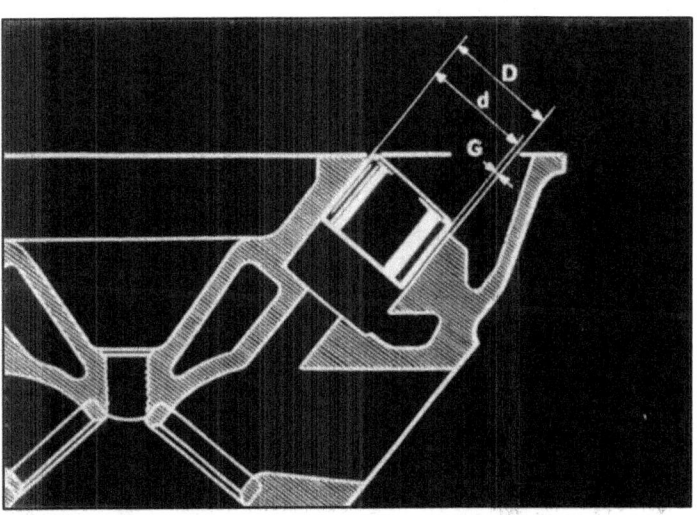

OVERHAUL WITHOUT REMOVING ENGINE

CYLINDER HEAD

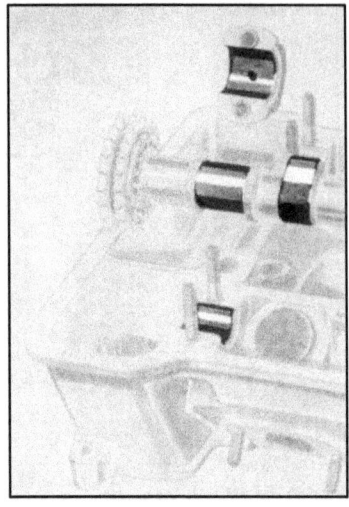

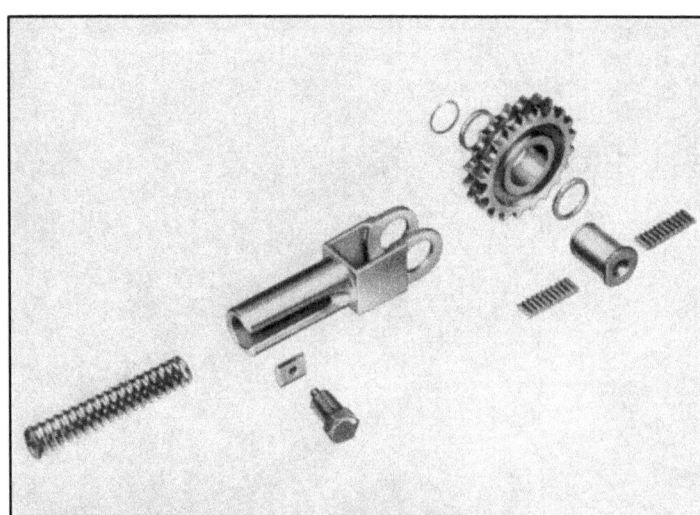

Camshafts

- Check cam working surface for excessive wear and working surface of journals and journal bearings for scoring and any sign of seizing. If only minor or skin defects are found, they must be smoothed out with an oil stone. However, if the affected parts are severely damaged or worn, renew them.
- Assemble the camshafts on cylinder head and lock (in oil) the bearing retaining nuts with a torque wrench to **2.00 to 2.25 kgm** (14.5 to 16.3 ft-lbs).

Chain tensioner

- Check the spring for proper calibration with a suitable test rig:
  free length: **98 mm** (3.9 in.);
  length under test load: **58 mm** (2.3 in.);
  test load: **20.8 to 22.8 kg** (46 to 50 lbs).
- Inspect the locking plate and its thrust faces for damage and excessive wear.
- Check pin and rollers for wear.
- For removal and inspection of camshaft drive chain follow this procedure:
  - tie a length of wire — about 1.5 meters (5 feet) — to an end of the chain;
  - slide out the chain from the end opposite the wire leading the wire to follow the chain;
  - in this way, when chain is withdrawn the wire will stay in place of the chain ready for an easier installation.
- Chain inspection:
  - check that rollers are not broken or seized on pins;
  - check links for free movement;
  - check the chain as a whole for binding.
- Whenever the chain is disconnected it is a good rule to replace the detachable end link and the clip with new parts.

Note: after the chain has been reassembled, check the valve timing as outlined on page 16.

Reassemble the cylinder head

- Fit the intake manifold and carburettor assembly on cylinder head.
- Install the head on cylinder block taking care to renew the gasket and to lock the retaining nuts according to tightening specifications given on page 13.
- To complete the assembly of engine components, reverse the order of removal given on page 19.

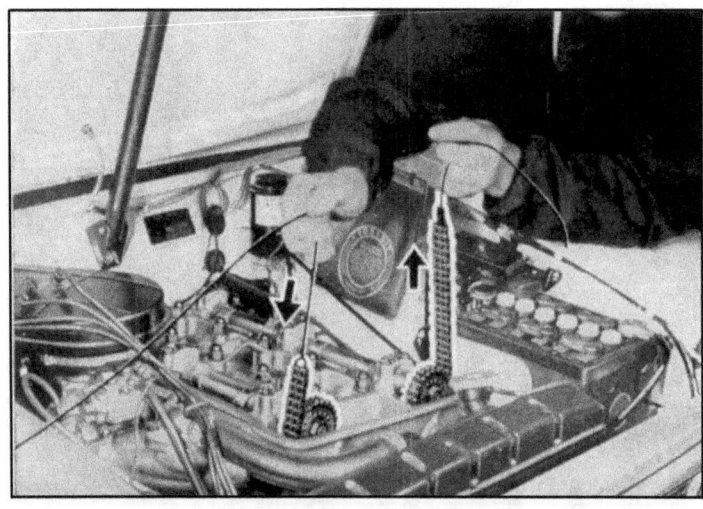

OVERHAUL WITHOUT REMOVING ENGINE

LUBRICATING SYSTEM UNITS

OIL SUMP

- Unscrew the drain plug with the wrench **A.5.0106** (Ref. Tool Bulletin no. 66/2) and drain oil from sump.

- Loosen and remove the nuts securing sump to crankcase and, by tilting it conveniently, take the sump off from the front end of car.

- Remove the screws joining sump bottom to sump.

  On reassembly renew the gaskets between sump bottom and sump as well as those between sump and crankcase.

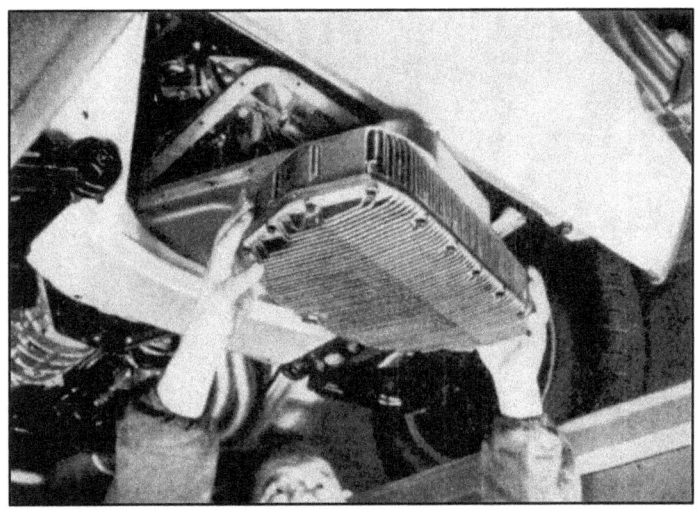

OIL PUMP

To remove the oil pump from crankcase proceed as follows:

- take the oil sump off;

- bring no. 1 piston at **TDC** on compression stroke: reference **P** on crankshaft pulley in line with the reference plate on front cover and distributor rotor arm pointing toward the engine front end.

- Remove the screws fixing the oil pump to crankcase.

OVERHAUL WITHOUT REMOVING ENGINE

LUBRICATING SYSTEM UNITS

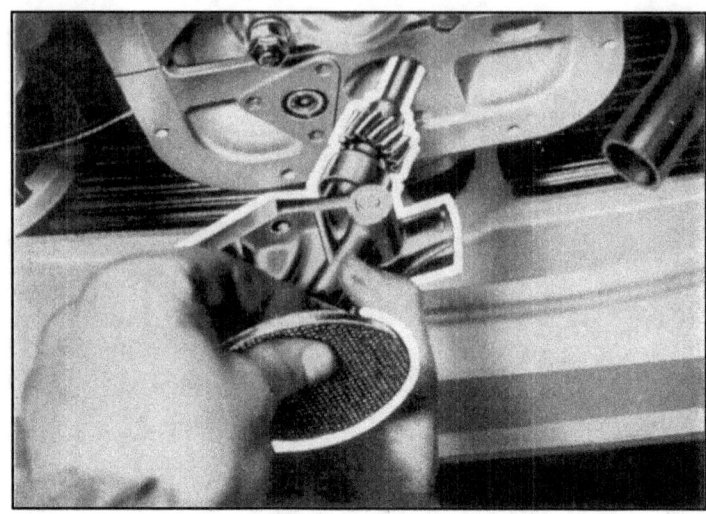

- Take out the pump by withdrawing it from the bottom.
- For pump overhaul refer to page 60.

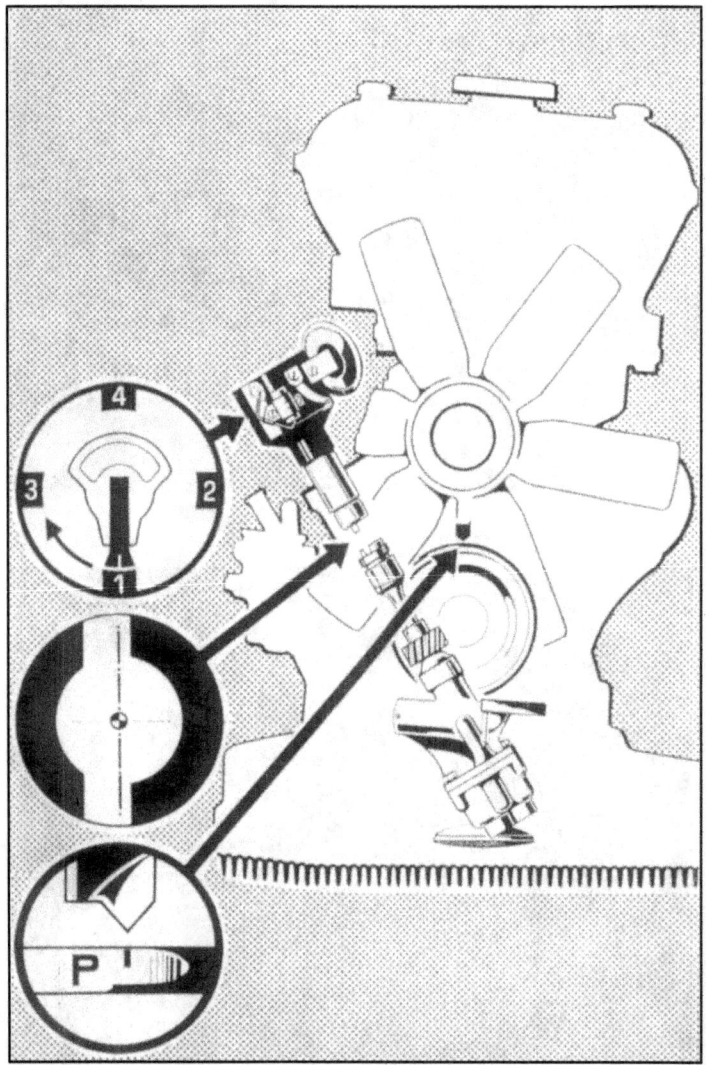

To reassemble the pump to crankcase follow the instructions below:

- align the coupling on pump drive shaft as shown, that is the tooth on distributor shaft shall engage the off-set slot in the pump shaft (no. **1** piston at **TDC** on compression stroke: reference **P** on crankshaft pulley in line with the reference plate on front cover and rotor arm pointing toward the engine front end).

- Install the pump into crankcase.
  If the rotor-to-pump coupling should not fit properly for the tooth is misaligned with respect to slot, take the pump out again and rotate the drive shaft so as to engage the drive pinion in the next tooth in either direction until the coupling engages.

- Secure the pump to crankcase by locking the retaining screws.
- Refit the sump and replenish with oil.
- Check ignition timing as outlined on page 11.

OVERHAUL WITHOUT REMOVING ENGINE

LUBRICATING SYSTEM UNITS

OIL FILTER

To change the filter element unscrew the threaded plug which joins together filter bracket and housing and take the housing off from the bottom by tilting it conveniently as shown.

Change the filter element and wash the housing with gasoline; then dry it with compressed air.

Check that the following gaskets are in good conditions:

- between filter housing and bracket;
- on threaded plug;
- between filter element and housing bottom.

Check gasket retaining cups for good conditions.
Replenish the housing with the oil specified for the engine.
On reassembling do not overtighten the plug securing filter housing to bracket or warping will result.
While the engine is running make certain there is no oil leakage from filter.

- To remove the filter bracket for inspection purposes, unscrew from the underside of car the fastening nuts.
- For inspection of pressure relief valve, refer to page 61.

OVERHAUL WITHOUT REMOVING ENGINE

COOLING SYSTEM

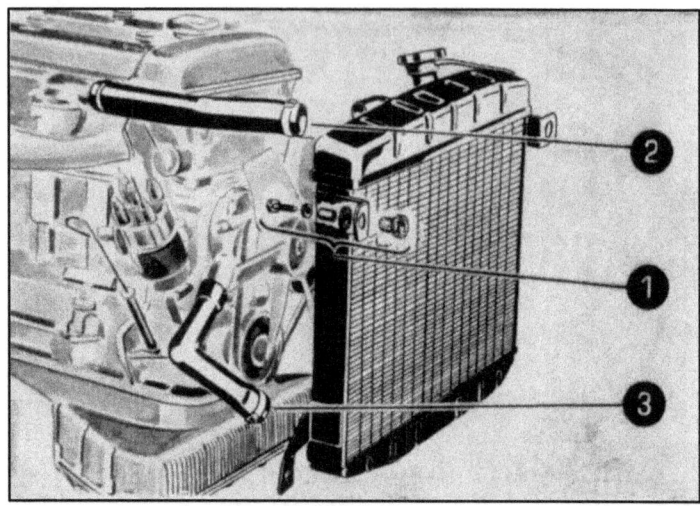

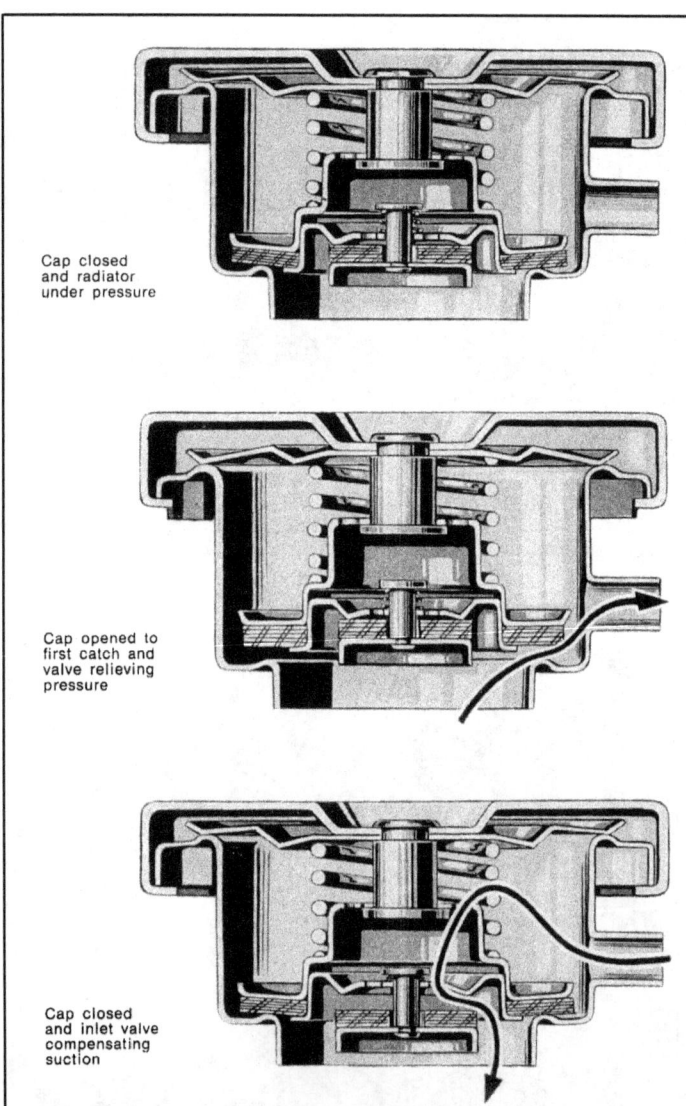

Cap closed and radiator under pressure

Cap opened to first catch and valve relieving pressure

Cap closed and inlet valve compensating suction

RADIATOR

Drain coolant from radiator and engine as instructed on page 19.

Remove the radiator attaching parts **1**. Disconnect:

- hose **2**, from radiator to cylinder head
- hose **3**, from radiator to water pump.

Take the radiator off paying attention not to damage the fan blades.

Inspect the radiating elements for good appearance.

Examine the weldings of brackets, side straps and connections.

Make sure that inside surfaces of radiator are not excessively scaled. If scale deposits have formed refit the radiator and flush the system as follows:

- fill the cooling system with a solution of 300 grs (10.6 ozs) of sodium bicarbonate in 8 lts (1.8 Imp. gals) (2.1 U.S. gals) of water;
- run the engine slowly for 10 to 15 minutes;
- drain the solution off thoroughly;
- allow the engine to cool down and then circulate running water while leaving the drain cocks open;
- refill cooling system with clean water and run the engine slowly for a few minutes;
- drain system once more and replenish with coolant again.

Radiator cap

Examine the cap to make sure the spring is not broken, the gasket is in good condition and the relief and inlet valves operate properly.

After reassembly of radiator and with the engine running check the hoses for possible leakage.

OVERHAUL WITHOUT REMOVING ENGINE

WATER PUMP - ENGINE MOUNTINGS

Water pump

Remove the radiator as previously described.

- Disconnect:
  - tachometer flexible shaft;
  - hose for water return from intake manifold to pump.

Loosen the nut fixing generator to adjusting arm.

Rotate the generator inwards.

Free the belt from pulleys.

Remove the belt tension adjusting arm.

Rotate the generator outwards.

Take off the pump body and fan assembly.

For water pump overhaul refer to page 62.

Note: to reassemble the pump on cylinder block reverse the disassembly procedure; after installation of the pump, adjust the belt tension as described on page 13.

 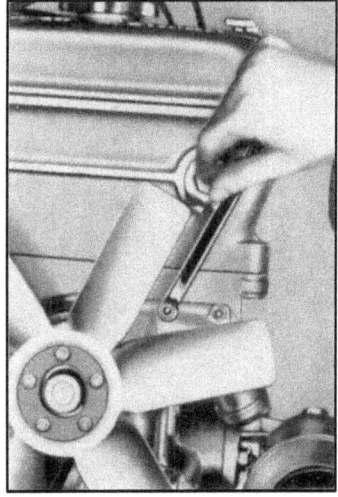

Motore = Engine
Batteria = Battery

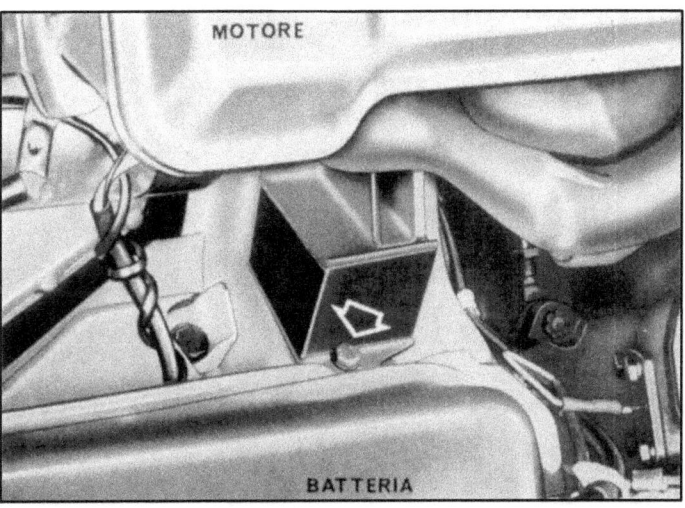

Replacement of engine mountings

- Remove the bonnet support from chassis.
- Hook the engine to a hoist and slightly release the load on mounting pads.
- Unscrew the nuts fastening the mounting pads to engine and body.
- To remove the mounting from the exhaust side, take off oil filter housing and bracket as outlined on page 27.

31

OVERHAUL WITHOUT REMOVING ENGINE

CRANKCASE FRONT COVER

Preparatory steps

Remove:

- radiator (refer to page 28);
- water pump (page 29);
- generator and its mounting flange;
- cylinder head (page 19);
- oil sump (page 25);
- fuel pump and bracket;
- crankshaft pulley.

Removal - Inspection and repairs

Remove the front cover - oil pump - ignition distributor group from the crankcase (on reassembly, replace the two gaskets between cover and crankcase).

- Slide out sprockets, chain, oil pump drive pinion and idle sprocket as a unit.
- Check:
  - gear teeth for good appearance;
  - chain rollers for any sign of damage or seizing on their pins;
  - links for free movement and the chain as a whole for binding.

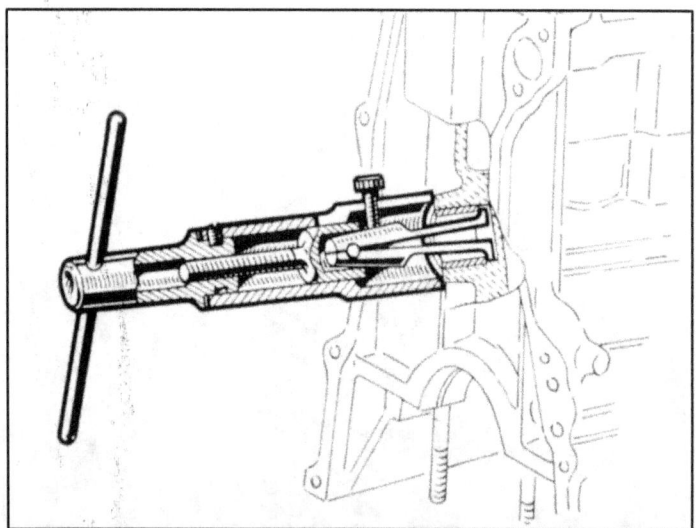

- If the spacer between idle sprocket shoulder and the abutment on crankcase is worn down, replace it with a new one.
- Measure the diameters and calculate the clearance between bushing in crankcase and idle shaft, and the clearance between idle shaft and bushing in front cover:

  permissible clearance: **.040 to .074 mm** (.0016 to .0029 in.);

  wear limit: **.1 mm** (.0039 in).

- If necessary pull out the bushings from cover and crankcase with the puller **A.3.210.** (Ref. Tool Bulletin no. 126) and replace them with new ones by following this procedure:

OVERHAUL WITHOUT REMOVING ENGINE

CRANKCASE FRONT COVER

- install the new bushings into their seats in cover and crankcase;
- fit and secure the cover onto crankcase;
- assemble the guide **A.4.0112** and ream the bushings to an inside diameter from **20.677 to 20.698 mm** (.8141 to .8148 in.) by means of the reamers **U.2.0040** for roughing and **U.2.0041** for finishing. Check diameter and alignment of bores with the tool **C.8.0103** (Ref. Tool Bulletin no. 94).

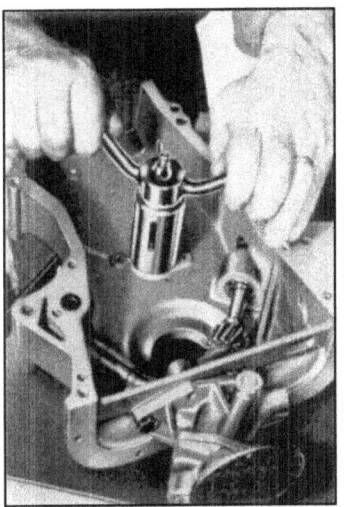
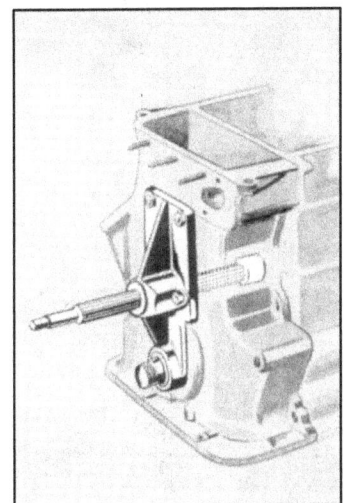

Reassemble the front cover

- Install chain, sprockets and spacer as a unit **taking care to align the timing reference marks on sprockets.**
- Rotate the ignition distributor shaft so that the rotor arm is pointing toward the front en as shown.
- Fit the cover on cranckcase and make sure the rotor arm is positioned as described above; if necessary, take the cover out again and rotate the oil pump drive shaft so as to position the rotor arm properly.

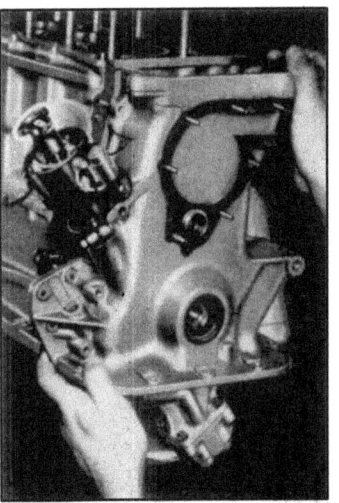

- Secure the cover to the crankcase.
- Insert the packing into front cover with the driver **A.3.0146**.
  Before inserting the packing into its housing make sure the cover fits the crankcase in such a way that the tools is centered on crankshaft.
- Assemble the drive pulley onto the shaft and secure it with the locknut.
- Complete the assembly by reversing the disassembly procedure.
- On completion of assembly check the valve timing as described on page 16.

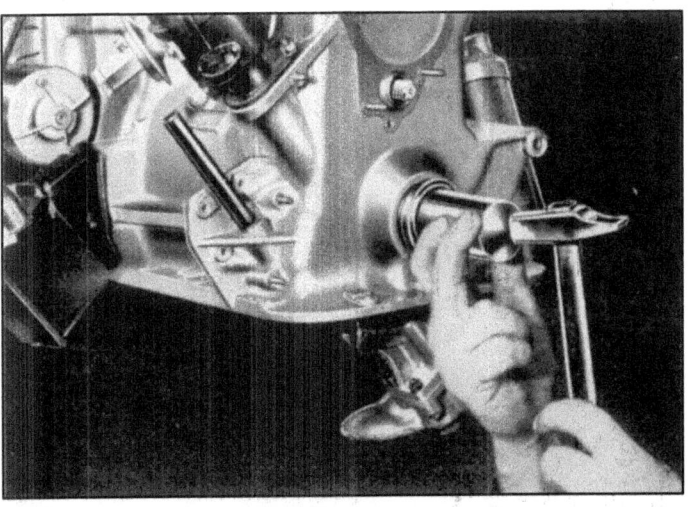

OVERHAUL WITHOUT REMOVING ENGINE

FLYWHEEL

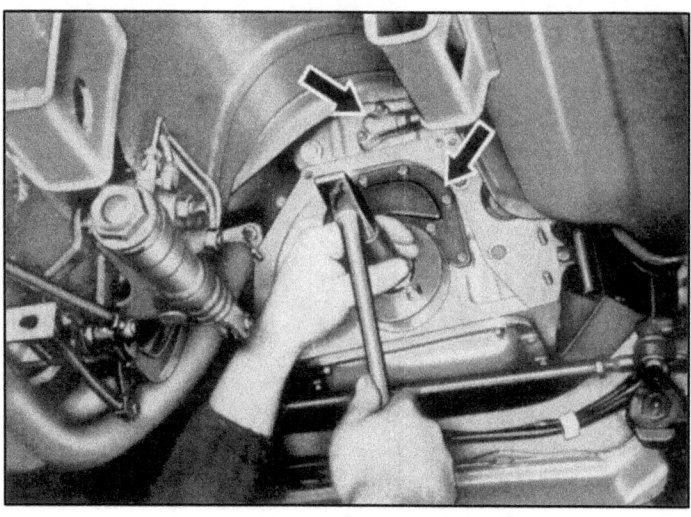

Replace the flywheel ring gear

- Remove:
  - the gearbox (see page 82);
  - the clutch (see page 75).

- Loosen and remove in alternate sequence 4 of the 8 bolts which fasten the flywheel to the crankshaft and screw in 4 studs in their place in order to avoid the half-rings from getting out of the seat; then remove the remaining 4 bolts and take the flywheel off.

- If oil leakage is found, check the following:
  - the gasket on cover of oil vent chamber and on vent pipe connection;
  - the crankshaft rear packing; if necessary, replace it with a new one by using the driver **A.3.0178**.

- When cold separate the ring gear from flywheel with a hydraulic press.

- Heat the new ring gear to 100° C (212° F) in an oil bath and fit it onto the flywheel.

- Rotate the crankshaft to bring no. 1 piston at TDC; then install the flywheel on crankshaft and align the mark cut in the flywheel with the centerline of crankpins 1 and 4.

- Fit new safety plates.

- Smear the bolts with oil and tighten to **4.2 - 4.5 kgm** (30.4 - 32.5 ft-lbs) with a torque wrench.

- Carefully bend the tabs of safety plates.

ENGINE OVERHAUL ON BENCH

REMOVAL OF ENGINE

Preparatory steps

- Drain off water from engine and radiator through the drain cocks.
- Drain off oil from sump (see page 25).
- Disconnect battery cables.

From the underside of car:

Detach:

1 the front section of propeller shaft from the rear section at the intermediate joint flange;
2 the support of propeller shaft central bearing;
3 the cross plate;
4 the odometer flexible shaft;
5 the exhaust pipe bracket from gearbox;

6 the clutch protection cover;
7 the gear selection lever;
8 the cables of back up lamp switch;
9 the clutch disengaging lever;
10 the manifold from exhaust pipe;
11 the gear engaging lever;

12 the tachometer flexible shaft.

ENGINE OVERHAUL ON BENCH

REMOVAL OF ENGINE

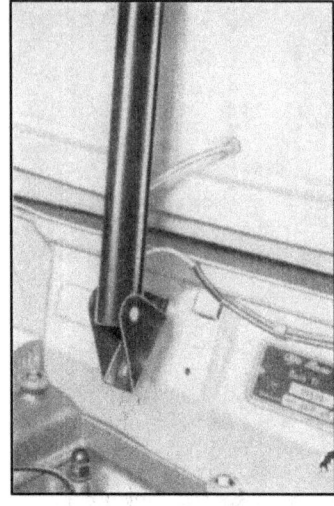 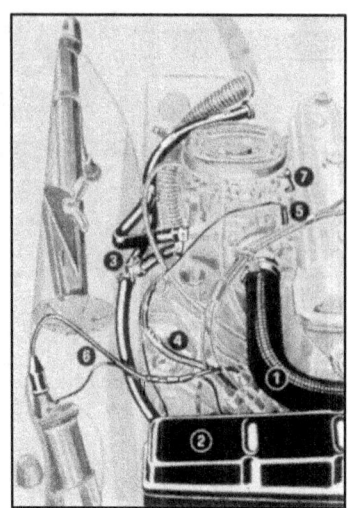

From the engine compartment

- Remove:
    - the strut for supporting bonnet from body;
    - the air cleaner;
    - 1 the hose from cylinder head to radiator;
    - the hose from radiator to water pump;
    - 2 the radiator from body (as shown on page 28);
    - 3 the hose from water pump to intake manifold and the hoses to heater;
    - 4 the petrol delivery pipe from tank to pump;
    - 5 the lead from water thermometer bulb;
    - 6 the leads from coil;
    - 7 the choke control cable;
    - the throttle control tie rod;

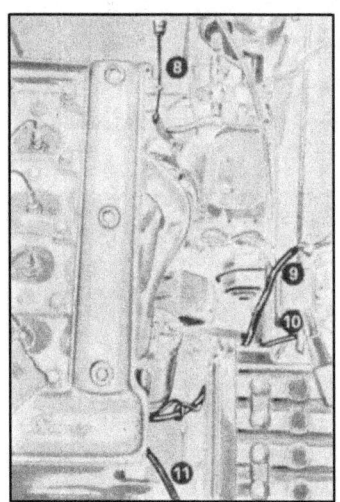 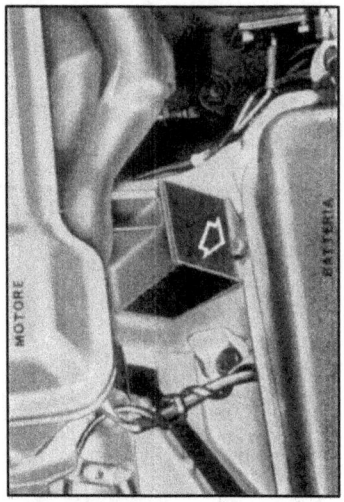

- 8 the accelerator hand control cable;
- 9 the generator leads;
- 10 the cable from oil pressure gauge union;
- 11 the engine bonding wire;
- the starting motor leads.

Batteria = Battery

Motore = Engine

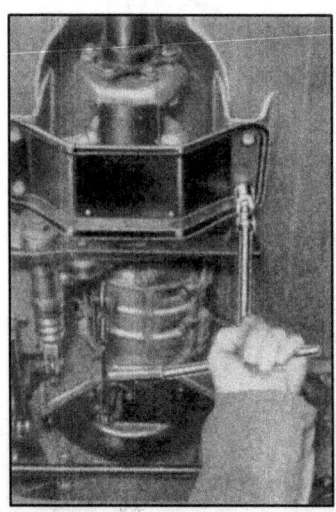 

Removal of engine-gearbox unit

- Hook up the engine with a hoist and give a light pull.
- Unscrew the bolts fastening the gearbox supporting cross member to car floor.
- Unscrew the bolt festening the gearbox to cross member and remove the latter.
- Detach the engine mountings from chassis.
- Take the engine-gearbox unit out by tilting it conveniently.

ENGINE OVERHAUL ON BENCH

DISASSEMBLY

- Remove the gearbox and the front section of propeller shaft.
- Put the engine on a stand.
- Remove from cylinder block:
  - the cylinder head (page 20);
  - the oil sump (page 25);
  - the oil filter and its bracket (page 27);
  - the starting motor.
- Fit the parts of tool **A.2.0117**, (Ref. Tool Bulletin no. 77/1) for retaining the cylinder barrels, on cylinder head studs.
- Mount the tool **A.2.0122**, for turning the crankshaft, on flywheel.

Con. rods and pistons

- Unscrew the nuts on con. rod bearing caps and remove the caps and the half shells.
- Withdraw the pistons along with con. rods from the top of cylinder block; to do this push the con. rods upward taking care not to hit or scratch the barrels with the con. rod big end.
- Mark the pistons for reassembly in the original order.

Crankshaft

- Unscrew the nut securing the crankshaft pulley and remove nut and pulley.
- Remove the front cover, the water pump, the ignition distributor and the oil pump as a unit (see page 30).
- Slide out sprockets and chain, oil pump drive pinion and idle sprocket as a unit (see page 30).

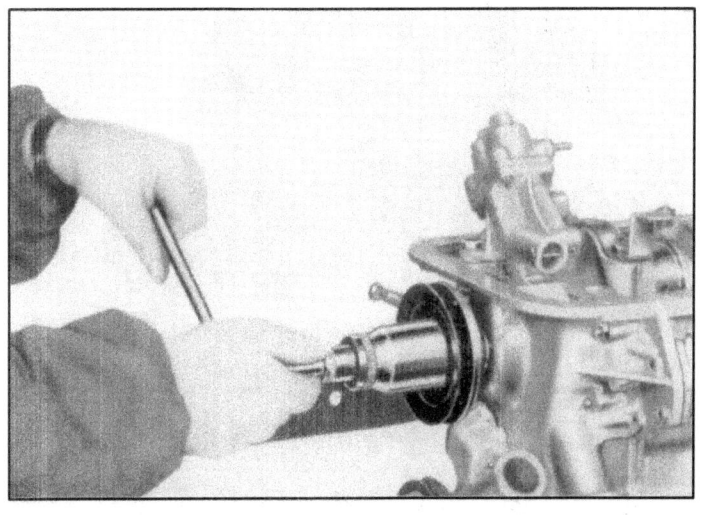

ENGINE OVERHAUL ON BENCH

DISASSEMBLY

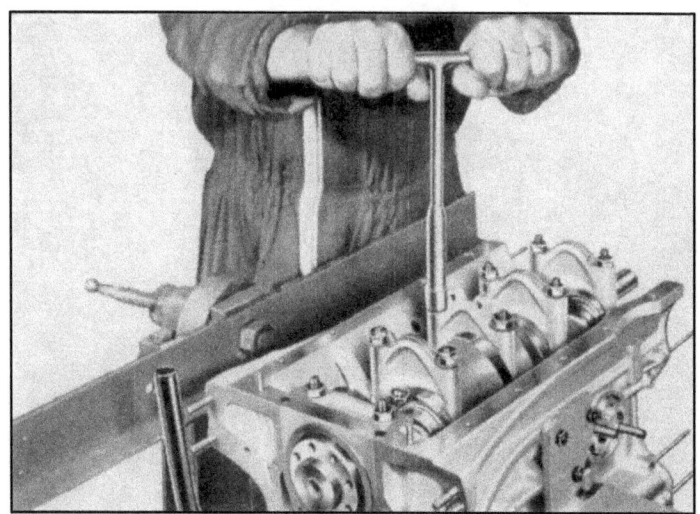

- Remove the tool **A.2.0122** from the flywheel.
- Unscrew the nuts securing the flywheel and remove the flywheel.
- Unscrew the nuts securing the main bearing caps starting from the central bearing.

- Remove the rear main bearing cap with the aid of the lever **A.3.0139/1** and the puller **A.3.0139/2** (Ref. Tool Bulletin no. 87).

- Remove the other main bearing caps with the tool **A.3.0182**.
- Take a careful note of the assembly order of main bearing shells so as to reassemble them in the original positions.
- Remove the crankshaft from crankcase.

ENGINE OVERHAUL ON BENCH

INSPECTION AND CHECKING

Con. rods

- Inspect the surface of con. rod bearings for no sign of scratching or seizing and that antifriction layer is not worn down to the pink metal underneath, even in small spots.

- Check the clearance between crankshaft journals and big end bearings as follows:
  - measure the inside diameter of big end bearing seat with a suitable dial gauge;
  - measure the outside diameter of relative journal with a micrometer gauge in two positions at right angle;
  - to measure the actual thickness of the antifriction bearing without errors or damage, insert a 10 mm (3/8 in.) dia. ball between bearing and gauge as shown;
  - the clearance is the difference between diameters of big end bearing seat and its journal plus twice the bearing thickness.

  If the clearance exceeds **.15 mm** (.0059 in.) the journal must be reground without exceeding the minimum allowable diameter; then replace the bearings with the oversized ones (see page 70).
  Never scrape the bearings; renew them when the pink layer under the friction metal appears even in small spots.

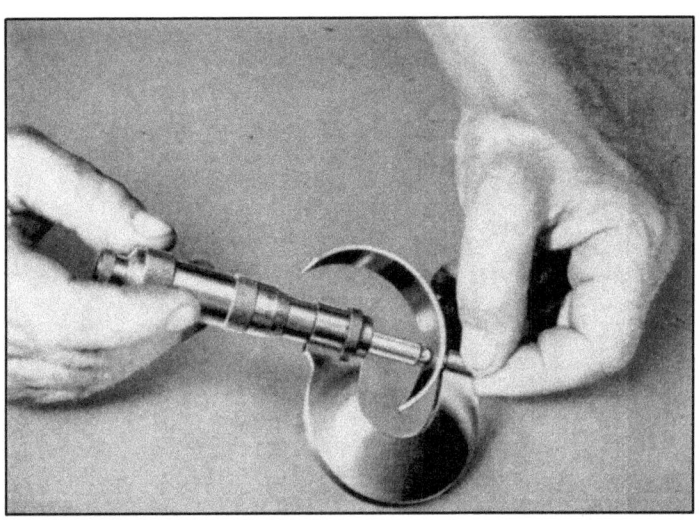

- Remove the piston pin retainer ring with a suitable tool.
  Withdraw the piston pin and check for no sign of scratching or binding.
  Measure the pin diameter and the inside diameter of hole in piston and check that clearance falls within the specified limits (see page 70).

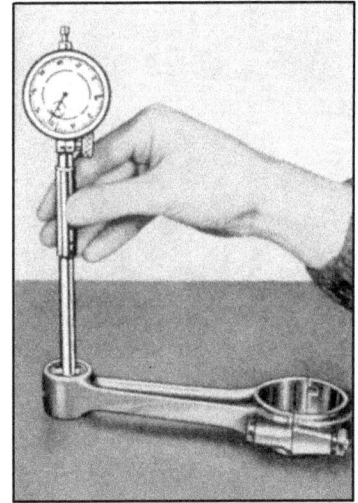 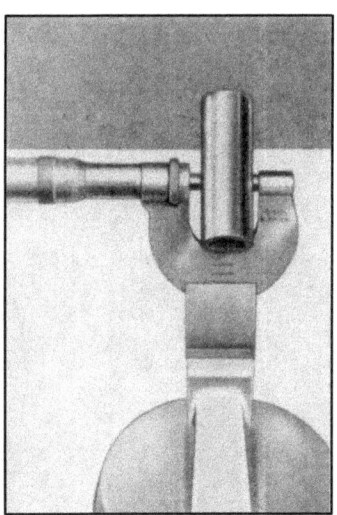

- Check the inner surface of small end bearing for any sign of binding.
  Check with a suitable dial gauge the inside diameter of small end bearing and that the bearing-to-pin clearance falls within the specified limits (see page 70). If not, take the small end bearing off and replace it with a new one using a suitable tool and a press. After the installation bore the bearing to

  22.005 - 22.015 mm (.8664 - .8667 in.)

  in diameter.

- Check that centerline of big end hole is parallel with centerline of small end hole as shown.
  The maximum out of parallelism is **.05 mm** (.002 in.) measured over a base of **100 mm** (3.94 in.).
  If required, straighten the con. rod with a press.
  Examine the con. rods with a magnaflux detector for no sign of cracking.

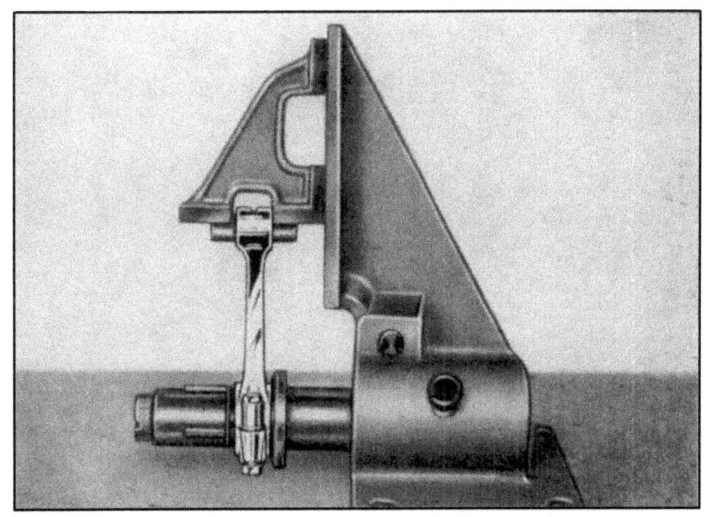

ENGINE OVERHAUL ON BENCH

INSPECTION AND CHECKING

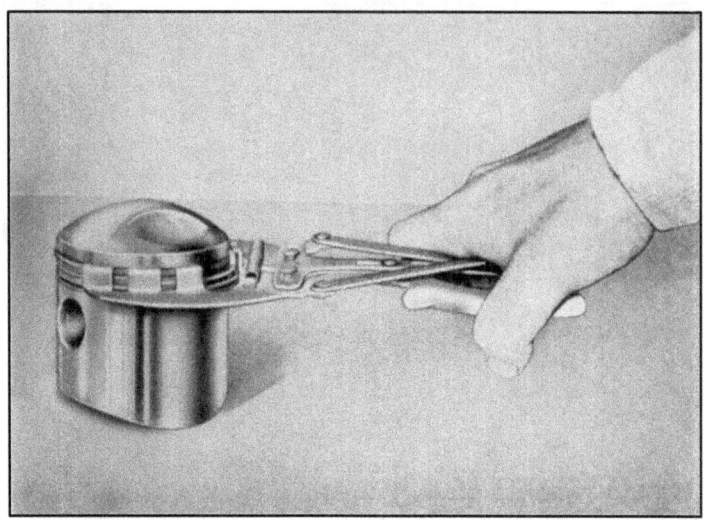

Pistons

- Remove the piston rings from their grooves by using suitable pliers. In order to avoid breakage, stretch the piston ring ends only as strictly required for withdrawal.
- Get rid of carbon deposits and wash the piston rings in petrol; after cleaning check that rings show no deep scratches or any sign of binding.

- Insert the piston rings one at a time into their cylinder barrel taking care they lie flat at right angle to cylinder bore.
- Measure the ring gap with a feeler gauge:

specified gap: .3 to .45 mm
                (.012 to .017 in.)

wear limit: 1.0 mm (.039 in.)

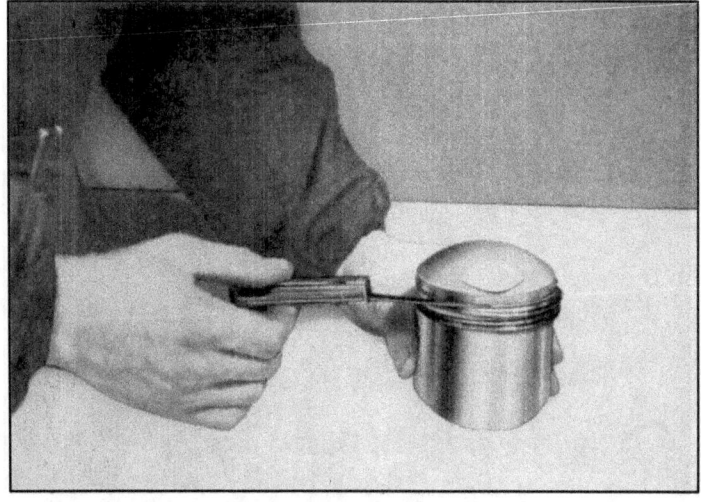

- Scrape down the carbon deposits built up on piston head; clean the ring grooves and wash the pistons with a solvent.
- Check that piston skirt shows no sign of binding or deep scratches.
- Refit piston rings in their grooves with the same pliers as outlined in the disassembly procedure.
- With a feeler gauge check that the end play of rings in their grooves is:

chromium-plated compression ring:	.045 - .072 mm (.0018 - .0028 in.)
oil scraper ring:	.035 - .062 mm (.0014 - .0024 in.)
oil control ring:	.025 - .052 mm (.0010 - .0020 in.)

ENGINE OVERHAUL ON BENCH

INSPECTION AND CHECKING

- On a central zero scale, check that the difference in weight between con. rods of the same engine complete with caps, bearings and bolts does not exceed **2 grammes** (.07 ozs.).

- Repeat the weighing with the pistons completely assembled to the con. rods. The difference in weight should not exceed **5 grammes** (.17 ozs.).

- If necessary, grind off the flash from con. rod forging seam.

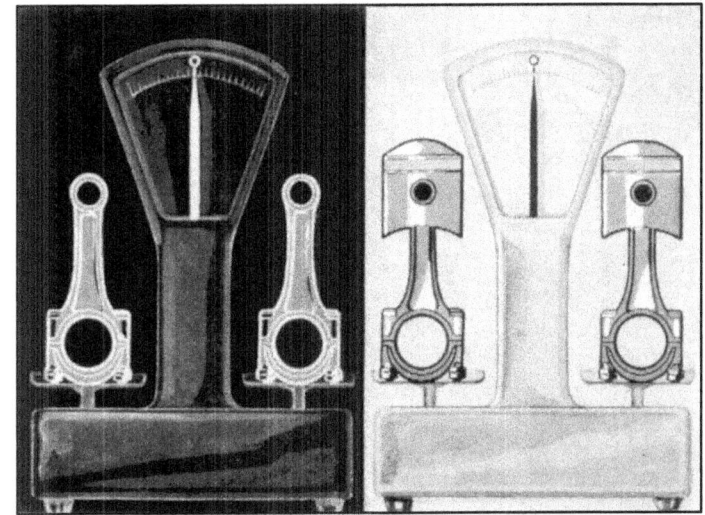

Cylinder barrels

- Remove barrels and inspect the inner surface for good condition.

- Zero set a bore dial gauge on the reference ring **C.8.0100** and check the inside diameter, the elongation and taper of barrels at the positions shown in the illustration and in two directions at right angle (see table on page 69).

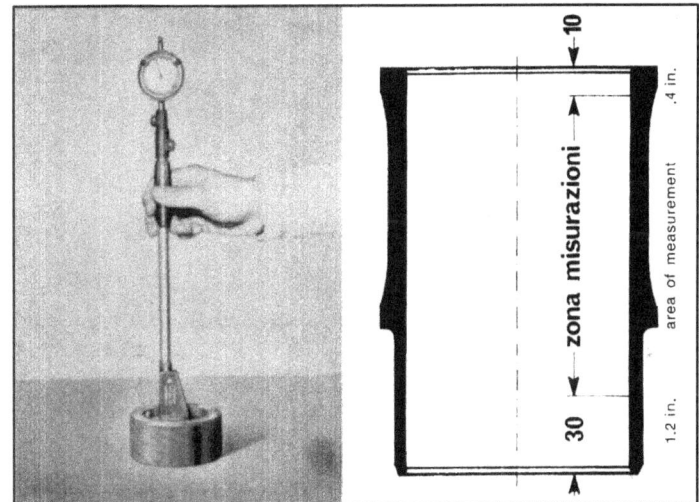

- Measure the outside diameter of pistons at right angle to the wrist pin hole and at a position of:
  11 mm (.43 in.) (Mahle make)
  12 mm (.47 in.) (Borgo make)
  from lower edge of skirt.

- The clearance between piston and barrel should be:

  specified clearance = $\begin{cases} .055 - .074 \text{ mm } (.0022 - .0029 \text{ in.}) \text{ (Borgo)} \\ .030 - .049 \text{ mm } (.0012 - .0019 \text{ in.}) \text{ (Mahle)} \end{cases}$

  wear limit = **.150 mm** (.0059 in.)

- If clearance does not fall within the above limits replace the unit (barrel, piston, rings and pin).
  Replace the gasket between barrel and cylinder block at every reassembly.

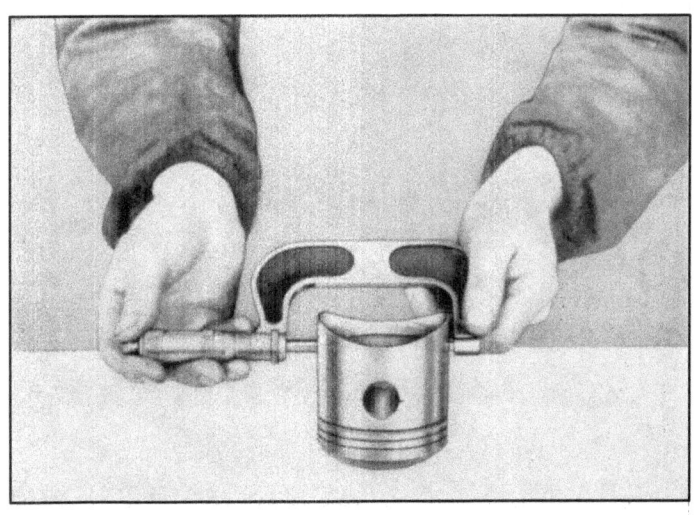

ENGINE OVERHAUL ON BENCH

INSPECTION AND CHECKING

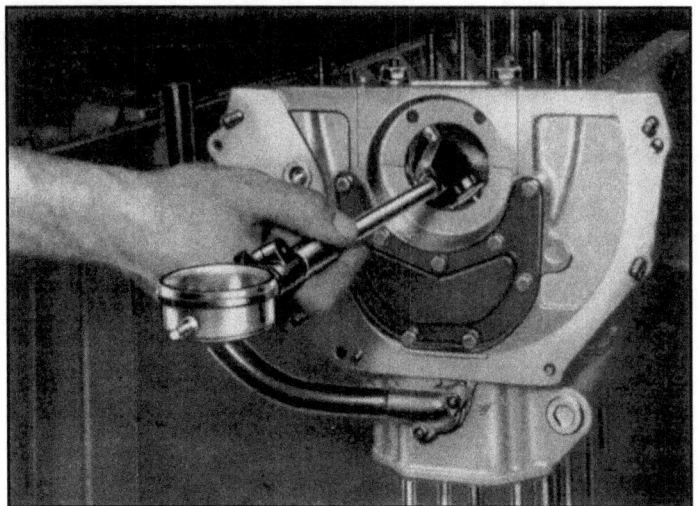

Crankshaft

- Examine the crankshaft with a magnaflux detector; if it shows any sign of crackings discard it.

- Inspect the surfaces of crankshaft journals and remove possible minor scratches with an oil stone.

- If these surfaces are deeply scored, scratched or show sign of binding, regrind the journals without exceeding the minimum dimensions given in the table on page 71.

- Check the main bearing-to-journal clearance as follows:

  · measure the inside diameter of main bearing seat with a dial gauge;

  · measure the outside diameter of the respective journal with a micrometer gauge on two positions at right angle;

  · to measure the actual thickness of the antifriction bearing without errors or damage, insert a 10 mm (3/8 in.) dia. ball between bearing and gauge;

  · the clearance is the difference between diameters of main bearing seat and its crankshaft journal plus twice the bearing thickness:

  specified clearance: .014 to .058 mm
  (.0006 to .0022 in.)
  wear limit: .150 mm
  (.0059 in.)

- Check that elongation and taper of journals fall within the specified limits given in the table on page 71. To this end take at least two readings in positions at right angles at both ends of each journal.

- Place the crankshaft between centers of a test rig.
  Check the alignment of main journals with a dial gauge:

  maximum permissible misalignment: .01 mm (.0004 in.).

ENGINE OVERHAUL ON BENCH

INSPECTION AND CHECKING

- Check:
  - the alignment of the pairs of crankpins:

    maximum permissible misalignment: .07 mm (.0027 in.)

    as measured on full length of each crankpin;

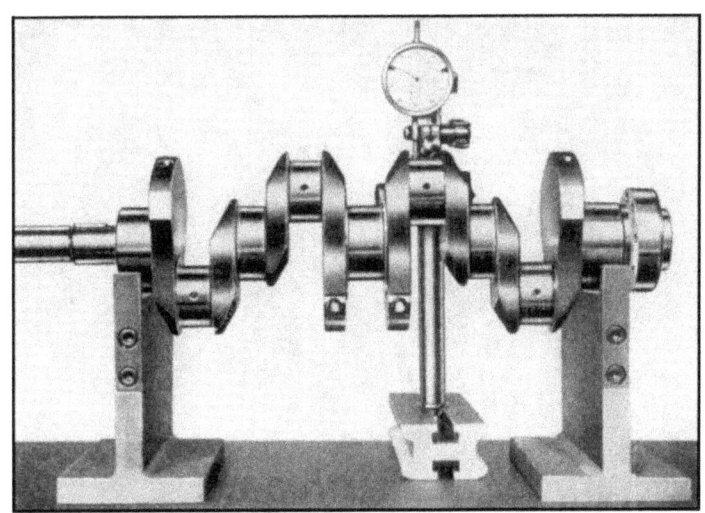

  - the parallelism between crankpins and main journals:

    maximum permissible error: A = .015 mm (.00059 in.)

    as measured on full length of each crankpin and main journal with respect to crankshaft centerline;

  - that centerlines of crankpins lie in the same plane as the main journal centerline:

    maximum deviation: S = .07 mm (.0027 in.).

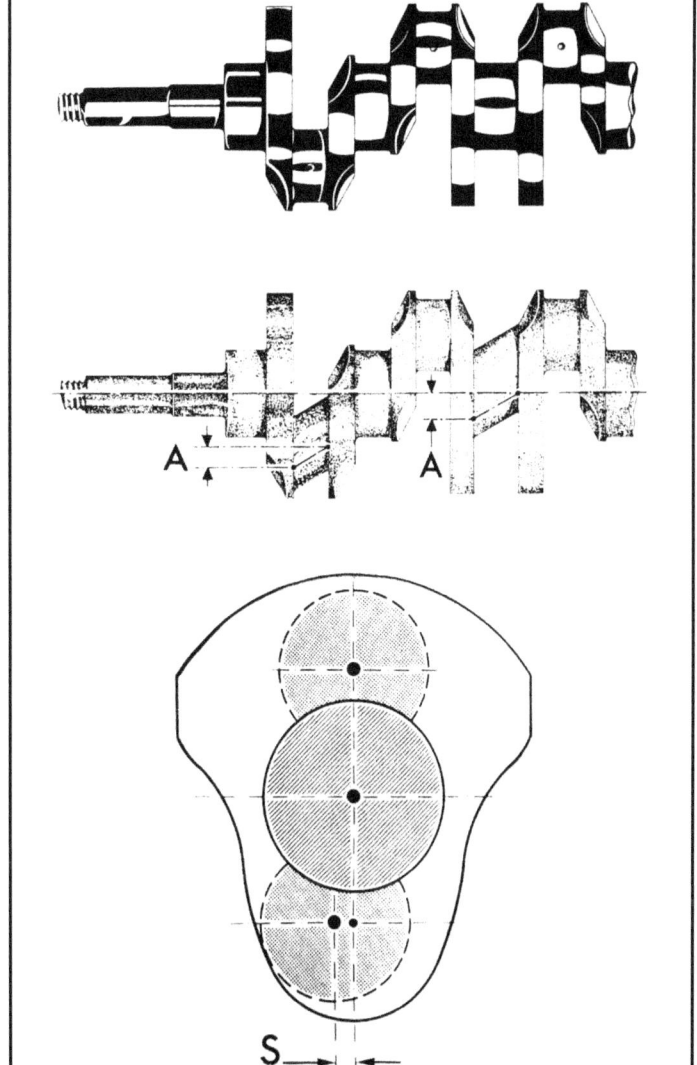

ENGINE OVERHAUL ON BENCH

INSPECTION AND CHECKING

- Drill out the aluminium pipe plugs which seal the oil passages.

  Clean the passages with a wire swab, then inject hot fuel oil and dry off with compressed air; at the same time wash the crankshaft thoroughly.

  Fit new pipe plugs and stake in place with tool **A.2.0103**.

- If the crankshaft has been reground or the ring gear replaced, check the static balance as follows:

  - set the crankshaft and flywheel assembly up on parallel stands on a perfectly level surface (check with a spirit level); if the shaft is balanced it should remain steady in any position; if it tends to rotate, apply mastic to the side opposite that showing a tendency to move downwards; the weight of mastic so applied indicates the balance weight required;

  - remove an equal weight of metal from the crank counterweights by grinding, or reduce weight by drilling holes in the rim of flywheel at a point diametrically opposite the position of the weight added:

  maximum permissible out-of-balance: 30 g. cm (.4 in. oz.).

  If the necessary equipment is available, the crankshaft should be balanced dynamically.
  After balancing remove the flywheel from the crankshaft.

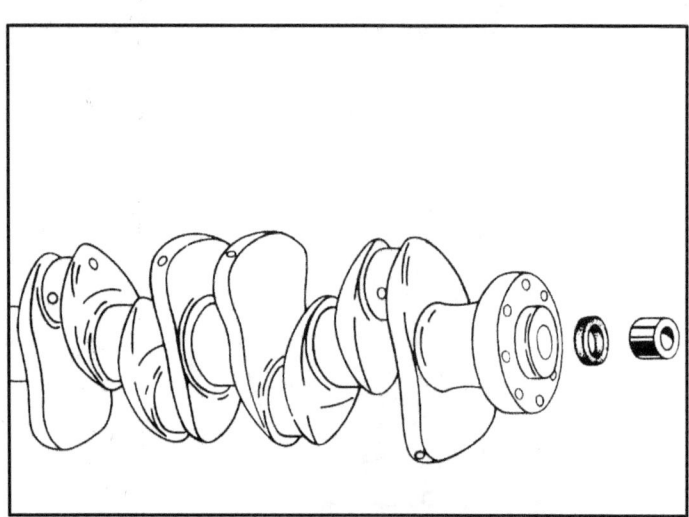

- Check that the felt washer and the bushing which centres the direct drive shaft onto the crankshaft are in good condition.

- To fit new felt washer and bushing proceed as follows:

  - soak the felt in engine oil at 45° C (113° F) for about an hour; let cool down, then install the washer in its seat;

  - soak the bushing in engine oil at 120° C (248° F) for about 4 hours; let cool down, then install the bushing into the crankshaft with the aid of a punch

  16.035 ± .002 mm (.6313 ± .0001 in.) in diameter.

ENGINE OVERHAUL ON BENCH

INSPECTION AND CHECKING

Cylinder block

- Complete the engine disassembly by removing:
  - the oil filter;
  - the rear cover;
  - the oil vent elbow and the pipe;
  - the plate for mounting of starting motor.

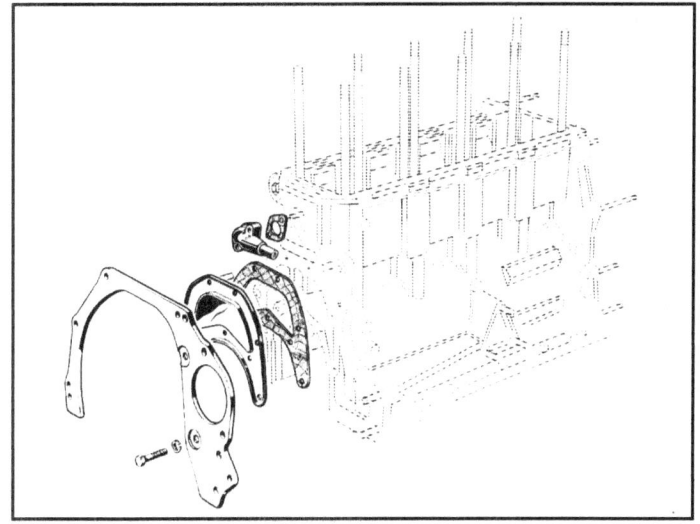

- Wash the cylinder block thoroughly with a solution of sodium bicarbonate in hot water. Rinse with running water, followed by hot fuel oil. Dry with compressed air and check that all water and oilways are completely clear.

- Test water and oil ducts under pressure, as follows:
  - seal off system with suitable flanges, one of which must have a union through which water can be forced under pressure;
  - raise water pressure to about **5 kg/cm²** (71 psi) and check that this pressure is maintained after the inlet cock is closed. If not, find the leak and decide whether the cylinder block can be repaired or must be replaced.

- Check that the cylinder head studs show no sign of warping, straining and that the threads are in good conditions.
  If the studs are damaged, withdraw them with a suitable puller and fit new ones.

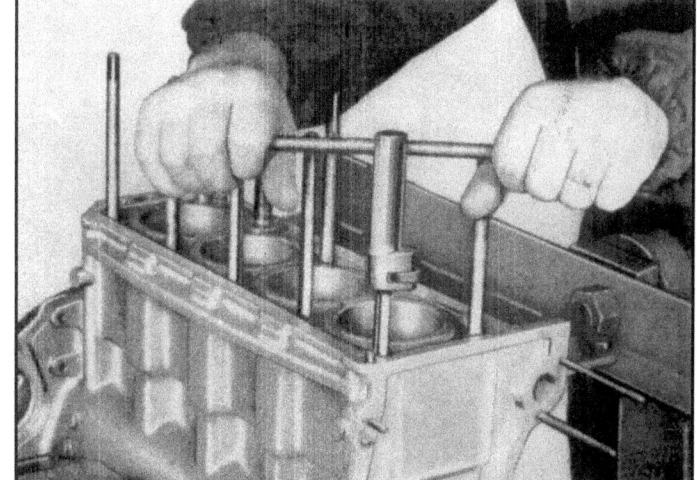

ENGINE OVERHAUL ON BENCH

REASSEMBLY

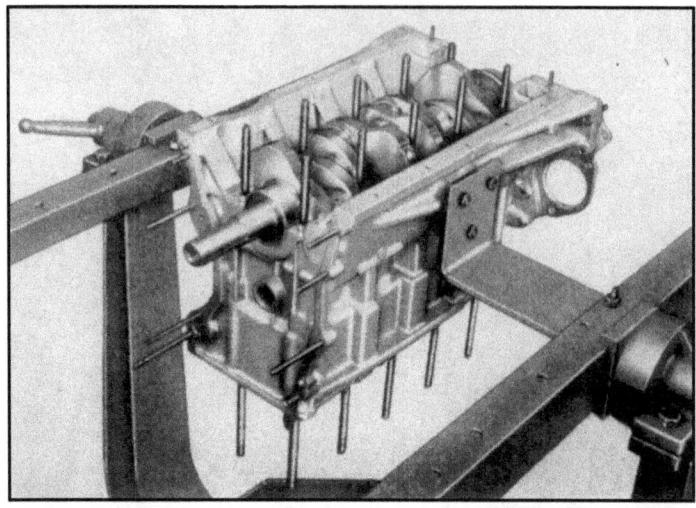

Reinstall the crankshaft

- Fit the main bearing half-shells into their housings in the crankcase and apply a film of engine oil.

- Fit the crankshaft into the crankcase along with the rear oil sealing half-rings.

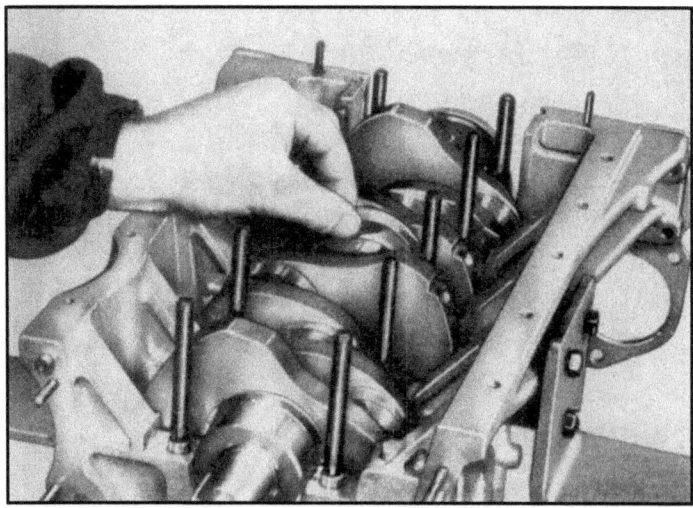

- Fit the upper thrust washers into their seatings by slipping them round the center main journal.

  The oil grooves on the thrust washers should be turned towards the working surfaces on the crankshaft.

- Fit the half-shells into the main bearing caps.

  Fit the center cap, complete with half-shells and thrust washers, on respective studs.

  Fit the remaining caps in accordance with the numbers marked on them.

ENGINE OVERHAUL ON BENCH

REASSEMBLY

- Insert the rubber plugs, sealing the oil passages, between rear main bearing cap and crankcase with the aid of the driver **A.3.0113** (Ref. Tool Bulletin no. 47/2).

- Lubetorque the main bearing cap nuts to **4.7 - 5 kgm** (34 - 36.2 ft. lbs) starting from the central bearing.
- Check pinch of main bearings caps as follows:
  - slacken one nut and check that pinch is **.08 - .10 mm** (.0030 - .0039 in.) with a feeler gauge.

  If pinch is below the correct figure or nil, rub the cap faces on very fine emery cloth laid on a surface plate until the prescribed clearance is obtained.

- Check that crankshaft end play is as prescribed:

  .07 - .26 mm (.003 - .010 in.)

  wear limit: .50 mm (.019 in.).

  If end play exceeds the prescribed wear limit, fit thicker thrust washers (see table on page 71).

ENGINE OVERHAUL ON BENCH

REASSEMBLY

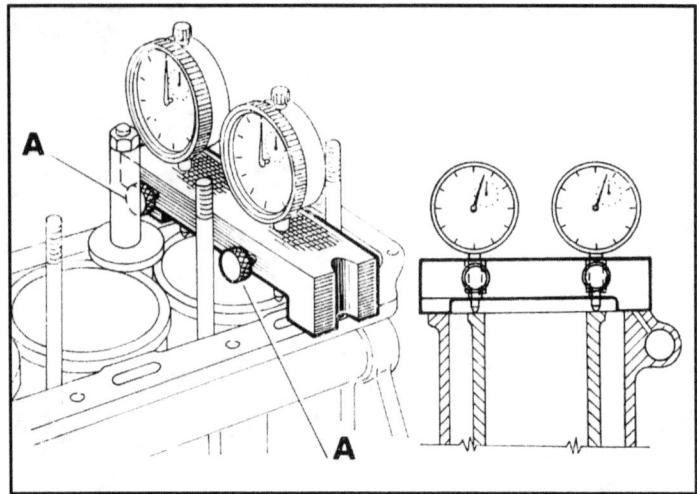

Reassemble the barrels, pistons and con. rods

- Insert the barrels with their seals into the cylinder block according to the reference numbers. Secure the dial gauges to the tool **C.6.0148** with setscrews « A » (Ref. Tool Bulletin no. 144) and check the projection of barrels from cylinder block:
  specified projection: F = .00 - .06 mm (.000 - .002 in.).

- Fit the parts of barrel retaining tool **A.2.0117** (Ref. Tool Bulletin no. 77/1) on cylinder head.

- Fit pistons, wrist pins and half-shells on con. rods making sure that con. rods and pistons are coupled according to reference numbers stamped on them.

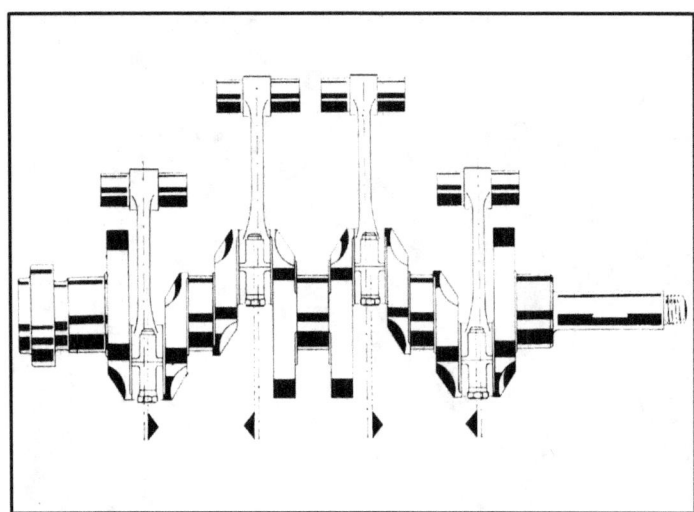

- Apply engine oil film to pistons and rings and insert con. rod and piston assemblies into the barrels with the aid of the suitable sleeve and in accordance with the reference numbers.
  The con. rods, being asymmetric, must be positioned as shown in the figure.

Note - Make sure the gaps of piston rings are staggered.

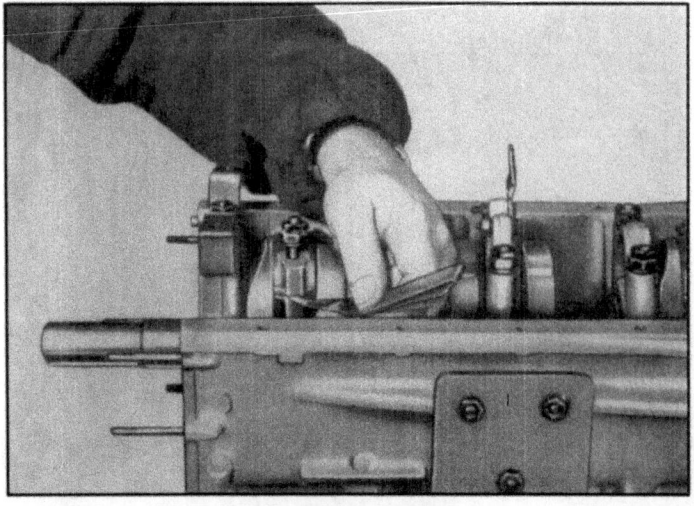

- Fit connecting rod caps complete with half bearings, in accordance with the numbers marked on them; lubetorque bolts with a torque wrench to:
  5 - 5.3 kgm (36.2 - 38.3 ft. lbs.)

- Check pinch of connecting rod caps as follows:
  - slacken one nut and check that pinch is **.08 - .10 mm** (.0030 - .0039 in.) with a feeler gauge.

  If pinch is below the correct figure or nil, rub the cap faces on very fine emery cloth laid on a surface plate until the prescribed clearance is obtained.

- Fit the stop nuts.

ENGINE OVERHAUL ON BENCH

REASSEMBLY

Reassemble the engine

- Insert the rear packing on the crankshaft with the tool **A.3.0178**.

- Rotate the crankshaft to bring no. 1 piston at TDC; then install the flywheel on crankshaft and align the mark cut in the flywheel with the centerline of crankpins 1 and 4 as shown in the figure.

- Fit new safety plates.

- Smear the bolts with oil and tighten to **4.2 - 4.5 kgm** (30.4 - 32.5 ft-lbs).
  To do this, hold the flywheel with tool no. **A.2.0145**. (Ref. Tool Bulletin no. 124.) Carefully bend the tabs of safety plates.

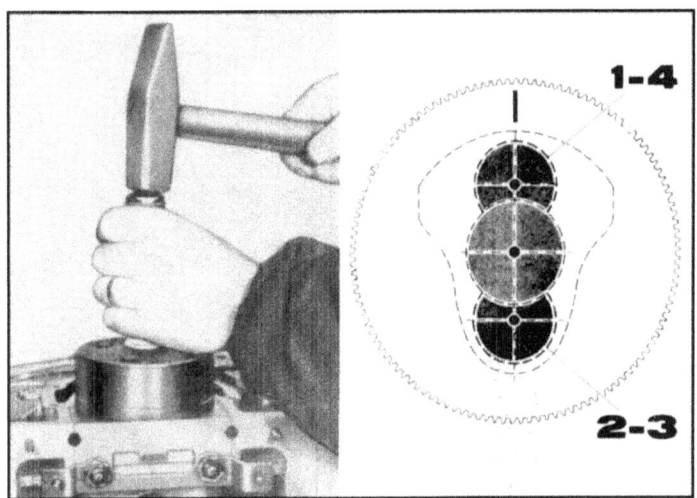

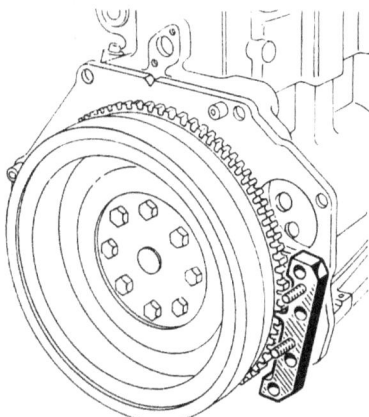

Complete the engine reassembly as follows:

- Refit:
  - the chain and the drive and idle sprockets making sure the timing reference marks are aligned (see page 31);
  - the timing chain;
  - the oil pump drive pinion;
  - the ignition distributor, the oil pump and the front cover as a unit; to do this, follow the instructions given on page 26 and 31.

Replace the front packing with a new one, if necessary; to install this packing use the special tool **A.3.0146**.
Fit the drive pulley on crankshaft with tool **A.5.0126**.

- Renew the gasket and place the cylinder head on cylinder block; tighten the nuts to the torque specified on page 13.

- Connect the timing chain and stretch it with the tensioner while cranking the engine slowly.

- Install the water pump and the fan on front cover.

On completion of reassembly, carry out the valve timing as described on page 16.

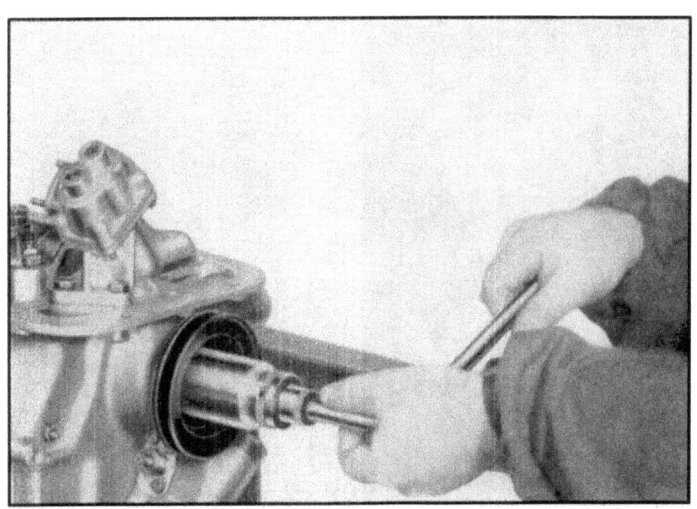

ENGINE OVERHAUL ON BENCH

CHECKING THE VALVE TIMING

Check the position of TDC

- Apply:
  - the protractor to crankcase (scale **C.6.0111**; spacer **A.2.0180**);
  - the pointer to flywheel **A.2.0179** (Ref. Tool Bulletin no. 140).
  - the brace **A.2.0122** to flywheel, for rotating the crankshaft.
- Rotate the crankshaft until the pointer and the zero on the scale are in line.

- Place the TDC checking tool **C.6.0122** (Ref. Tool Bulletin no. 117) in the seating of no. 1 cylinder spark plug and zero set the dial indicator:
  - move the flywheel 5° to the right and 5° to the left on the zero line and read the dial indicator in each position.

  If both readings are the same the protractor is in the correct position and the TDC of the piston corresponds to the zero of the graduated scale.

  If this is not the case, adjust the protractor on the crankcase until the two readings coincide and then lock the scale in position.

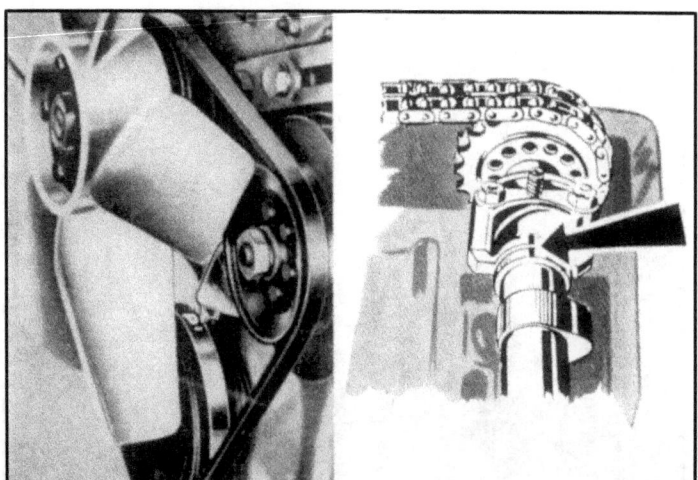

Check the reference marks

- Set the pointer on the flywheel so that it coincides with the zero on the scale.
- Check that the marks cut on the camshaft flanges and on the fan drive pulley **P** are in line.

ENGINE OVERHAUL ON BENCH

CHECKING THE VALVE TIMING

Check the valve opening and closing angles

- Using the feeler gauge **C.6.0123** (Ref. Tool Bulletin no. 122) check that, with the engine cold, clearance between the unlobed profile of each cam and the top of valve cup is:

  intake valves: .475 - .500 mm
  (.0187 - .0197 in.)

  exhaust valves: .525 - .550 mm
  (.0206 - .0216 in.).

- Place the tool **A.2.0120** on no. 1 cylinder and position the dial gauges so that sensing needles rest on the valve cups.

- Rotate the crankshaft and trace the dwell arc of each cam by observing where the index of the dial gauge of each cam remains stationary.

- Zero set the dial gauge.

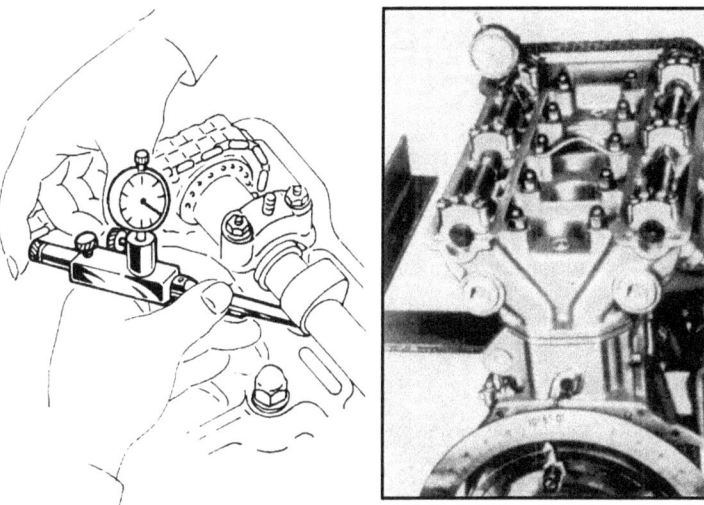

Intake valve

Opening

- Rotate the crankshaft counterclockwise (viewed from flywheel end) until a valve lift of **.20 mm** (.0078 in.) is indicated on the dial gauge.
  The reading on protractor scale should be:

  6° ± 1° 30′.

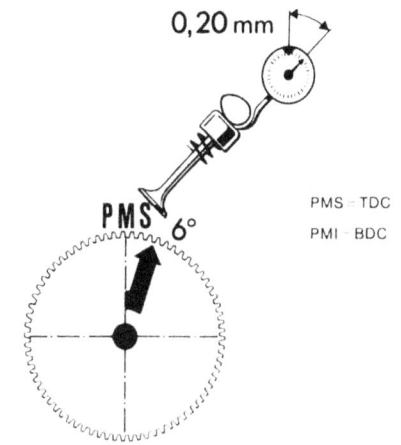

PMS = TDC
PMI = BDC

Closing

- Continue to turn the crankshaft counterclockwise (flywheel end) until the intake valve is completely closed and the dial gauge index remains stationary.
  Zero set the dial.
  Then rotate the crankshaft clockwise for about half a turn; again rotate it counterclockwise until a valve lift of **.20 mm** (.0078 in.) is indicated.
  The reading on protractor scale should be:

  54° ± 1° 30′.

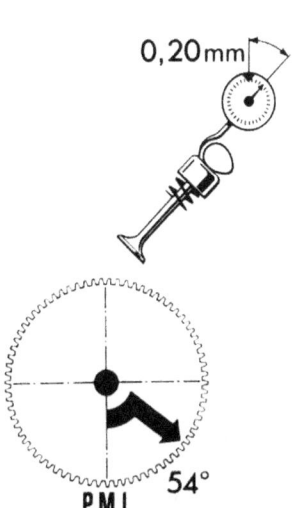

ENGINE OVERHAUL ON BENCH

CHECKING THE VALVE TIMING

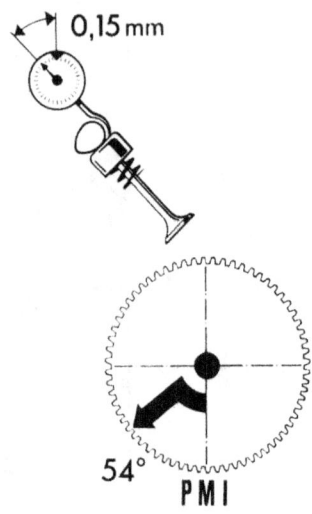

Exhaust valve

Opening

- Zero set the dial gauge as previously described.
- Rotate the crankshaft counterclockwise (flywheel end) until a valve lift of **.15 mm** (.006 in.) is indicated on the dial gauge. The reading on protractor scale should be:

  54° ± 1° 30′.

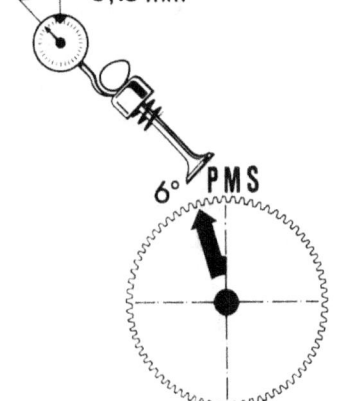

PMS = TDC
PMI = BDC
Scarico = exhaust
Aspirazione = intake

Closing

- Continue to turn the crankshaft counterclockwise (flywheel end) until the exhaust valve is completely closed and the dial gauge index remains stationary.

  Zero set the dial.

  Then rotate the crankshaft clockwise for about half a turn; again rotate it counterclockwise until a valve lift of **.15 mm** (.006 in.) is indicated.
  The reading on protractor scale should be:

  6° ± 1° 30′.

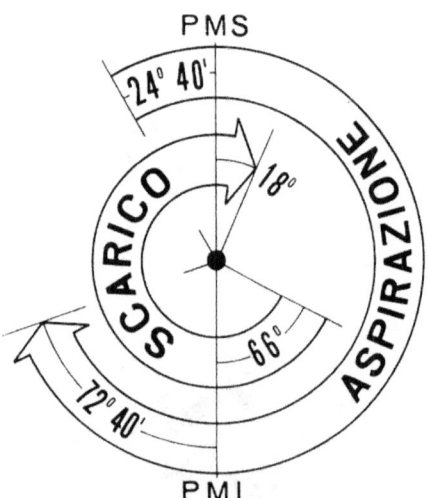

Actual diagram of valve timing

- if the results of timing check are as prescribed, the valve timing actual diagram with the engine cold is a shown.

Direction of rotation as viewed from engine front end.

ENGINE OVERHAUL ON BENCH

ENGINE RUNNING IN

Running in and testing on bench

- After overhaul, if piston & barrel assemblies, rings and/or main & con. rod bearings has been renewed, the engine must be carefully run in.
- Set the engine up on a suitable test bench provided with a hydraulic brake and connect the test equipments, the cooling and electric circuits.
- Follow the running in schedule shown in the table and record the power output at each speed.

Note - To calculate the power output use the following formula:

Power = weight × rpm × bench constant.

BERLINA			
Test duration minutes	RPM	Power output	
		Cv*	HP
5'	1000	—	—
5'	2000	4.4	4.3
5'	3000	14.7	14.5
10'	4000	34.8	34.3
15'	4500	49.5	48.8
10'	5000	68.0	67.1
5'	5500	90.75	89.5
5'	6000	**	**
10'	adjustments	—	—

* These figures do not represent maximum power at full throttle.

** At this engine speed full throttle power is recorded and a check is made of fuel consumption which should be: **220 ÷ 240 g/Cvh** (.49-.53 lb/HP/h).

Testing and checking

- During engine running in check the advance for correct values:

    Static advance: **3° ± 2°**.

    Maximum advance: **43° ± 3° at 5000 rpm**.

    Adjust as required by acting on distributor body, bearing in mind that it is better to have correct timing at high speeds.

- Check that oil pressure is maintained as follows:

    maximum pressure: **4.5 - 5 kg/cm²** (65 - 70 psi);

    minimum pressure at full speed: **3.5 kg/cm²** (50 psi);

    minimum pressure at idling speed: **.5 - 1 kg/cm²** (7 - 14 psi).

- During the tests check the following temperatures:

    water: 85° - 90° C (185° - 194° F)

    oil: 90° - 100° C (194° - 212° F).

ENGINE OVERHAUL ON BENCH

ENGINE RUNNING IN

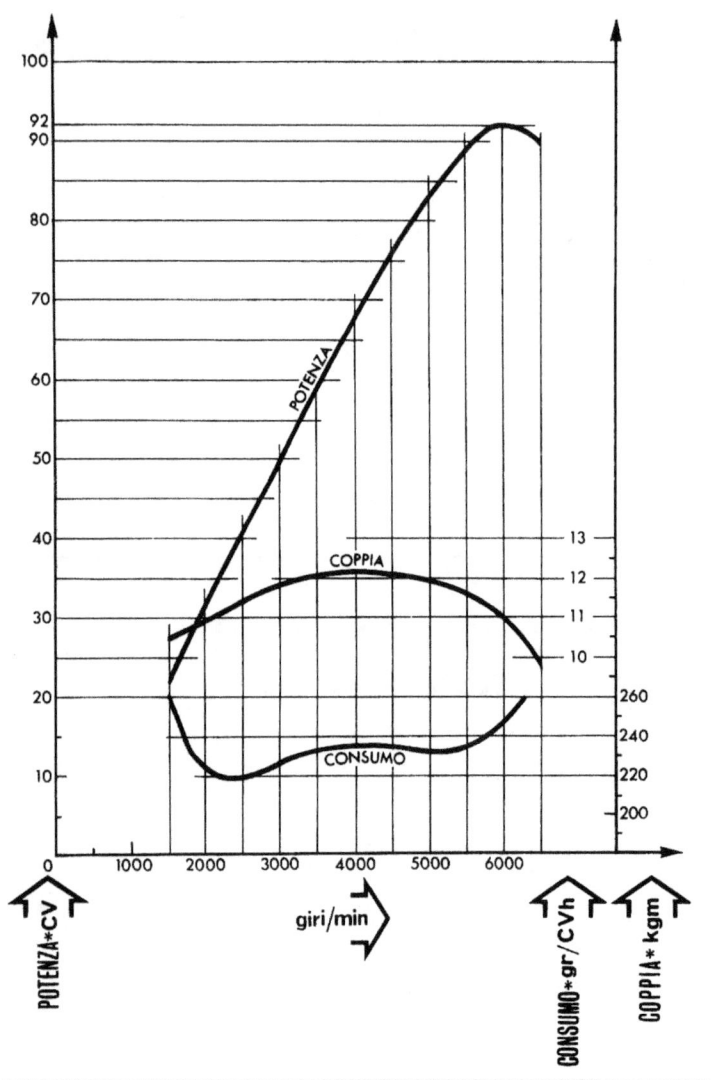

Engine performance graph

These graphs depict the average performance attained with a run in engine equipped with all accessories and the same induction and exhaust system as that installed on the car.

Potenza = Power output
Coppia = Torque
Consumo = Fuel consumption
giri/min = RPM

Distance	Maximum speeds					
	1st gear	2nd gear	3rd gear	4th gear	5th gear	
1st **1000 km** (600 miles)	26 (16)	44 (27)	64 (40)	87 (54)	110 (68)	km/h (mph)
1000 to 3000 km (600 to 1900 miles)	32 (20)	54 (33)	79 (50)	107 (66)	135 (84)	km/h (mph)

Road running in

After engine reconditioning, in order to allow the main units to bed down gradually a running in period must be observed during which the maximum performance must never be demanded of the car.

AUXILIARY EQUIPMENT

FUEL PUMP

Fuel pump

Removal from engine

Disconnect the inlet and delivery hose.

Loosen the screws securing pump to crankcase and remove the pump; withdraw the push rod from its housing in the crankcase.

Disassembly

Loosen the two screws **1** and remove the top cover, the gasket **2** and the funnel **13**.

Withdraw from the top of pump body:

3 the filter gauze;

4 the seat of inlet valve spring;

- the springs **5** and **14** of inlet and outlet valves;

- valve assembly **6** and **15**.

Loosen the screws which join together pump body and bottom cover.

Remove from the bottom cover:

8 the diaphragm assembly;

9 the rubber cup;

10 the diaphragm return spring.

Unscrew the spring seat **12** from bottom cover and remove the rocker arm return spring **11**.

Pull the pivot pin **17** out of bottom cover and remove the rocker arm **16**.

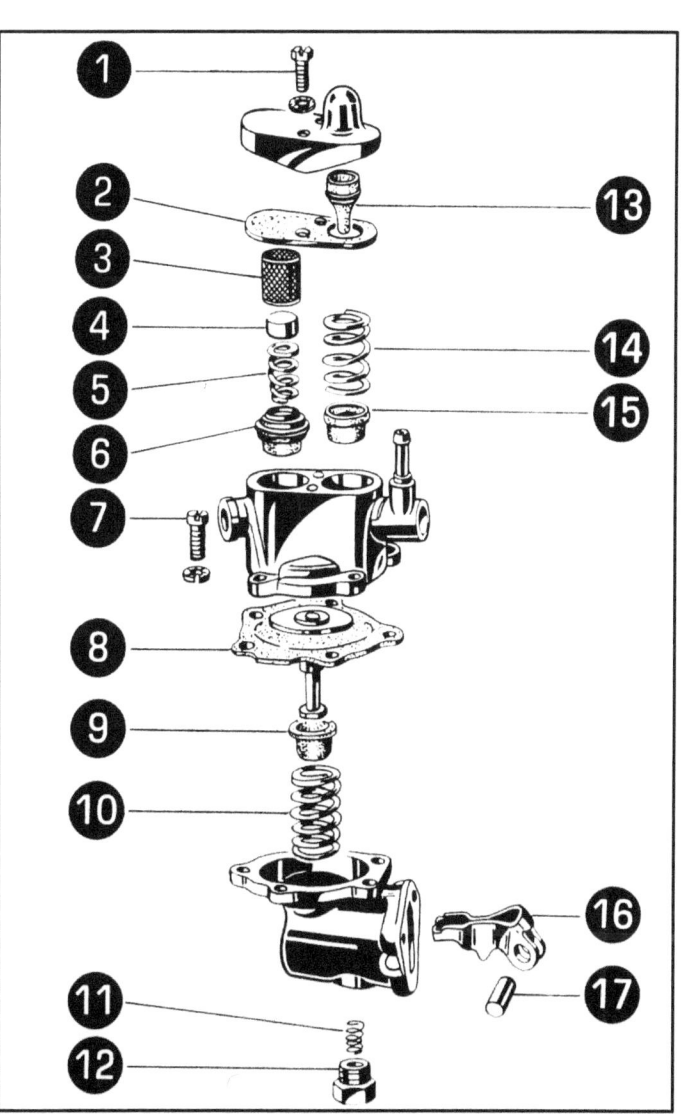

AUXILIARY EQUIPMENT

FUEL PUMP

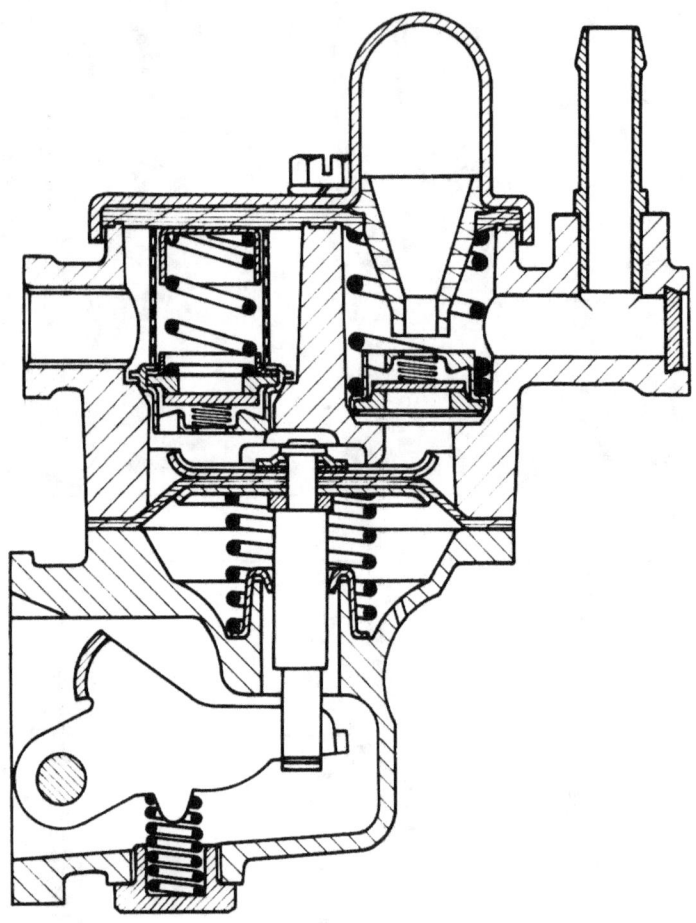

Inspection, reassembly and testing

- Clean the inlet and outlet valves with petrol; if worn, renew them.

- Check the diaphragm for good condition and make sure it is firmly gripped between the retaining discs. Renew the diaphragm assembly if worn or damaged.

- Check the rocker arm pivot pin for any sign of wear or seizing; renew it, if necessary.

- Check the operation of the following springs:
  - rocker arm return;
  - valve closing;
  - diaphragm return.

  Replace them with new ones, if necessary.

  Renew the filter gauze.

  On installation renew the gasket between pump mounting flange and crankcase.

  Reassemble the pump by reversing the order of disassembly.

- Set the pump on a suitable test bench and carry out the following performance tests;

  rate of operation corresponding to an engine speed of **2500 - 3000 rpm**;

  delivery with no outlet pressure: **110 lt/h** (24.2 gph GB) (29 gph US);

  outlet pressure with no flow: **3-4 m H_2O** (4.2 - 5.6 psi);

  delivery with an outlet pressure of **2 m H_2O** (2.8 psi): **60 lt/h** (13.2 gph GB) (15.8 gph US)

AUXILIARY EQUIPMENT

SOLEX C. 32 PAIA 7 CARBURETTOR

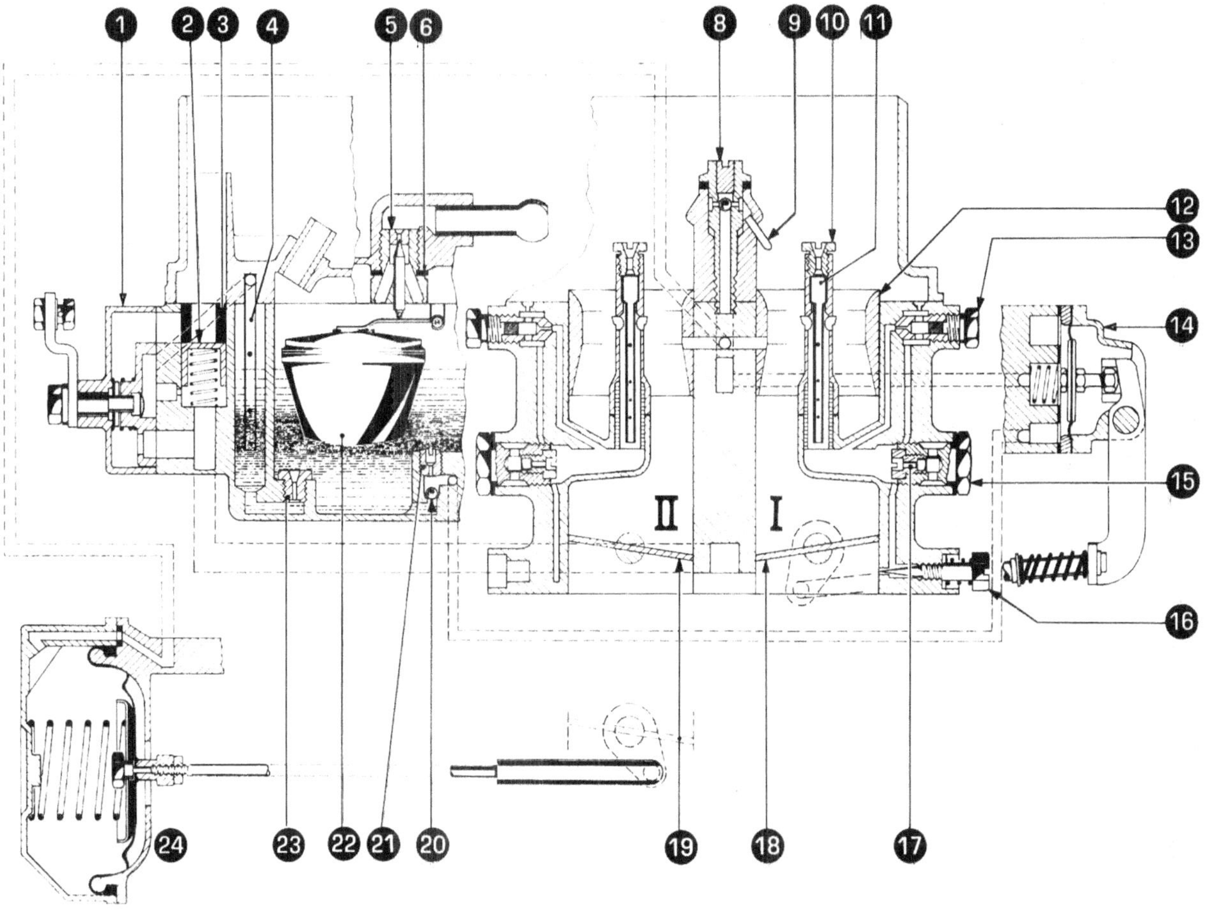

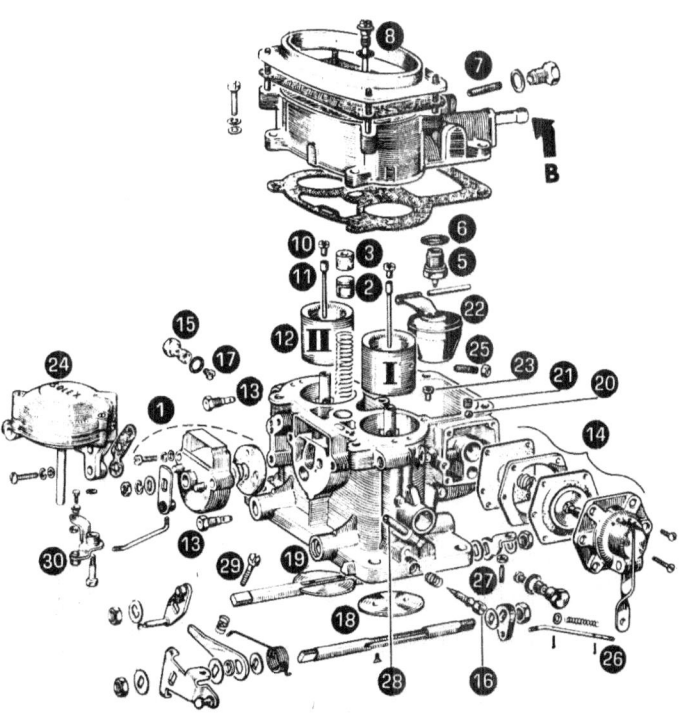

B. Fuel inlet

1. Choke assembly
2. Choke plunger
3. Choke plunger limit stop
4. Choke air metering
5. Needle valve seat
6. Copper gasket for needle valve seat
7. Filter gauze
8. Accelerating pump outlet valve
9. Accelerating pump nozzle
10. Main air metering
11. Mixture tube
12. Venturi
13. Idling jet
14. Accelerating pump
15. Main jet carrier
16. Idling mixture adjusting screw
17. Main jet
18. 1st barrel throttle
19. 2nd barrel throttle
20. Accelerating pump inlet valve
21. Accelerating pump bypass jet
22. Float
23. Choke jet
24. Vacuum capsule
25. Setscrew and locknut for securing venturi
26. Accelerating pump stroke adjuster
27. 2nd barrel throttle adjusting screw
28. Suction port for distributor vacuum advance regulator
29. 1st throttle idle adjusting screw
30. Choke control lever

AUXILIARY EQUIPMENT

SOLEX C. 32 PAIA 7 CARBURETTOR

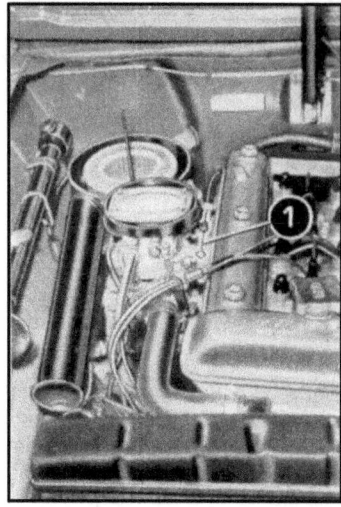 

Remove:

- the cover from air cleaner housing; to do this unscrew the wing nut and the clamp on carburettor;
- the choke control **1** from carburettor;
- the accelerator control **2** from carburettor;
- the suction pipe **3** for distributor vacuum advance regulator;
- the fuel feed pipe **4**;
- the nuts **5** from studs securing the carburettor body to intake manifold (special tool **A.5.0108**).

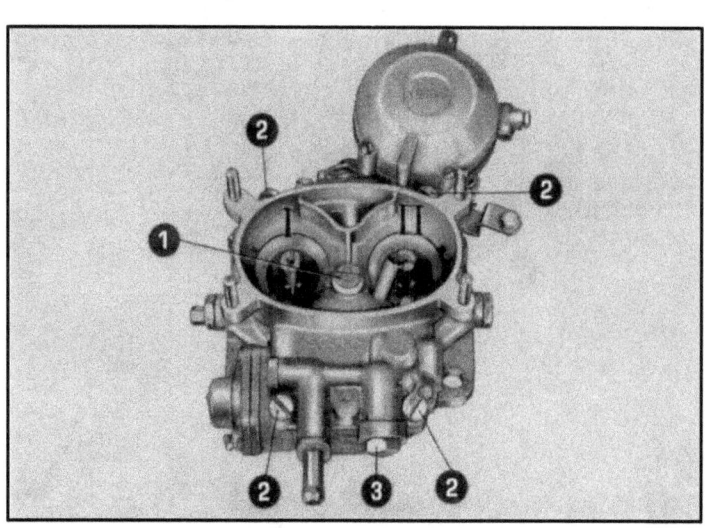

Disassembly

Remove:

1 the accelerating pump outlet valve;

2 the four screws securing the cover to the carburettor body;

- the float from its chamber.

Unscrew the gauze element seat **3** and clean the element from foreign matter that may have been collected on it.

Check the cover flange for warping and the joining surface for smoothness; if not, smooth it on emery cloth laid on a surface plate.

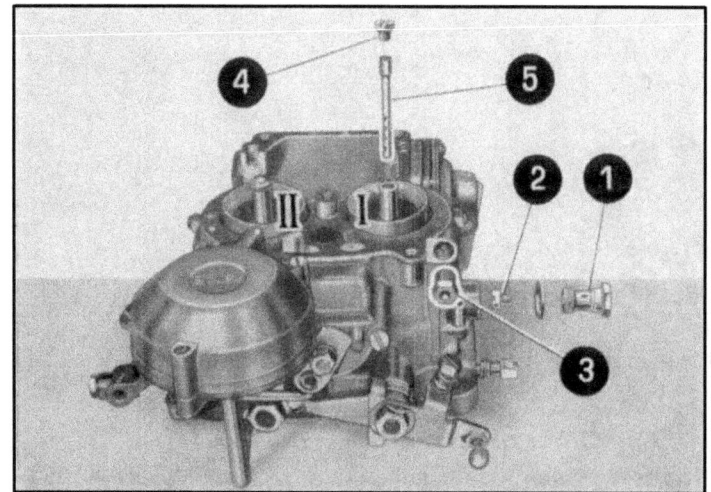

Take out from both barrels the jet carriers **1** with the main jets **2**, the idling jets **3**, the main air meterings **4** and the mixture tubes **5**.

Check that the figures stamped on the jets are as shown in the table below.

Do not alter the jet diameter with the use of sharp tools or metal probes.

	1st barrel	2nd barrel
Main jet	125	130
Main air metering	190	190
Idling jet	45	70
Mixture tube	17 T	17 T

AUXILIARY EQUIPMENT

SOLEX C. 32 PAIA 7 CARBURETTOR

Accelerating pump

- Unscrew the accelerating pump bypass jet **1** from the bottom of float chamber.
- Upset the carburettor with care in order to take the ball out of the valve seat.

  Pump bypass jet: 40.

- Loosen the six screws **2** securing the pump to carburettor body:
  - withdraw the split pin which locks the control lever **3** to the linkage;
  - check the diaphragm for good operating conditions.

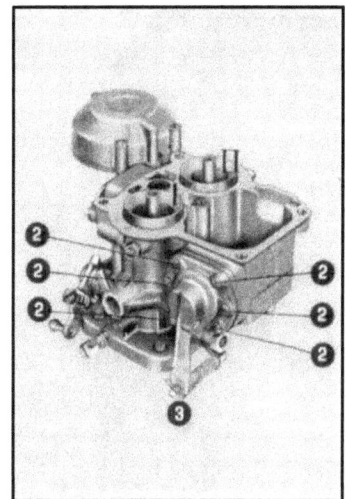

- Reassemble the pump and temporarily insert the split pin **1** in the first hole of stroke adjuster.
- Check pump delivery:
  the flow should be: **4-6 cc per 20 strokes.**

  If the flow is not within the specified limits correct it by adjusting the pump stroke. Small increments can be obtained by inserting shims between the split pin **1** and the control lever.
  Shifting the pin by one hole in the adjuster rod causes a 100 % increment in pump flow.

  Note - The pump nozzle **2**, a calibrated jet, is not turnable but fixed in the position giving the best result. **It is strictly prohibited to alter the nozzle calibrated hole.**

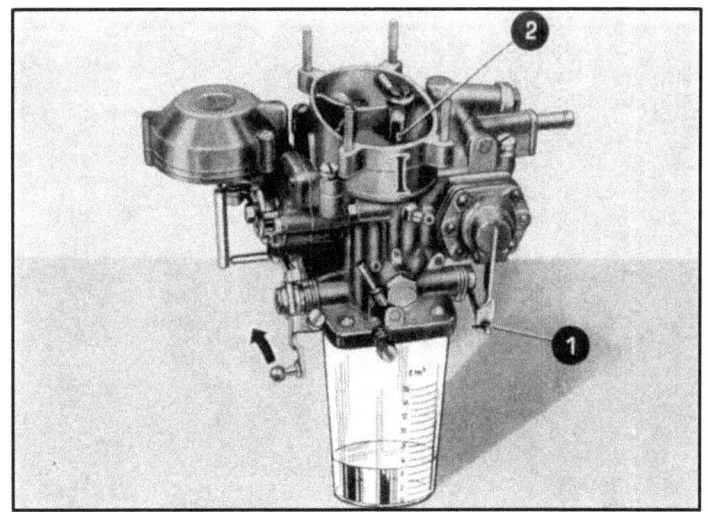

Choke

- Loosen the two screws **1** securing the choke assembly to carburettor body.
- Check that the surface of the valve disc and the mating surface on carburettor body are flat and smooth.
- Withdraw the limit stop **2** and check that the plunger **3** slides freely without binding.
- Check the spring **4** for proper operation.
- Take the choke jet **5** out of float chamber bottom.

  Choke jet: 120.

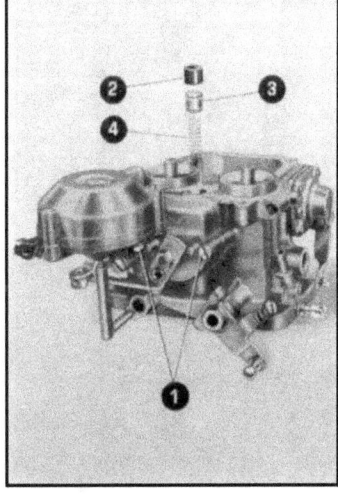

AUXILIARY EQUIPMENT

SOLEX C. 32 PAIA 7 CARBURETTOR

Throttle valves

It is not advisable to remove the throttles unless absolutely necessary.

To remove the throttles loosen the screws **1**. If the throttle spindles show signs of scoring or seizing, replace them (bore and rebush the seats in the carburettor body, if necessary).

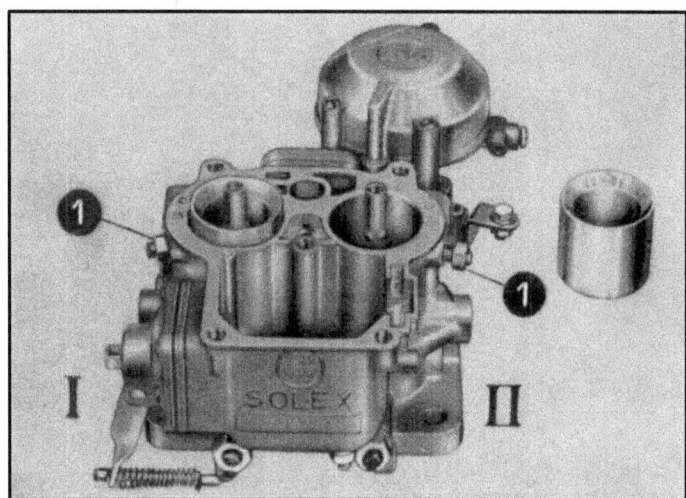

Venturi

- Loosen the setscrews **1**.
- Take the venturi tubes out of carburettor body.

Note - A built-in dowel properly position the venturi tubes with respect to carburettor body so that any misfit on reassembly is avoided.

2nd throttle actuating vacuum capsule

The second throttle actuating vacuum capsule starts to operate when more power is needed.

Usually, if the engine is accelerated with no load, the vacuum capsule should not operate.

If the car, during a road test, should not attain the maximum speed range, check the vacuum capsule for proper operation as follows:

a) check that the throttle is not seized in its barrel owing to wrong adjustment of throttle opening screws;

b) check that linkage connecting the throttle to the vacuum capsule works freely without any binding;

c) check that the vacuum pipe is not obstructed throughout its run from 1st venturi to vacuum chamber;

d) check that the rubber diaphragm is properly fitted but not squeezed between the capsule halves in such a way as to obstruct the suction port.

Unless strictly necessary, it is recommended not to disassemble the vacuum capsule to avoid damaging the rubber diaphragm on reassembly.

AUXILIARY EQUIPMENT

SOLEX C. 32 PAIA 7 CARBURETTOR

Level of fuel in float chamber

- To check the level of fuel in float chamber proceed as follows:
  - reinstall the carburettor onto car;
  - place the car on level ground;
  - run the engine at slow speed for about one minute then stop the engine;
  - detach the feed pipe from carburettor and discharge the fuel from pipe completely;
  - remove cover and float from chamber;

    take measurement with a gauge as shown;
  - the distance from fuel level to float chamber flange should be **18 - 19 mm** (.71 - .75 in.).

- The fuel level can also be measured with the more accurate and quicker method of communicating vessels as follows:
  - fit the indicator in place of main jet;
  - actuate the fuel pump and check that the level is **13 mm** (.51 in.) below the flange mating surface.

If the level is not as above specified, check the needle valve and the float:

needle valve seat = 175;

copper gasket under valve seat: 1 mm (.039 in.) **thick**

float weight: 7.2 grs (.25 oz.).

Do not touch at all the float arm; insert shims as required under the valve seat.
If the thouble persists check the feed pump delivery.

Note - After refitting the carburettor to engine adjust idle as outlined under « Engine tune up ».

AUXILIARY EQUIPMENT

LUBRICATION

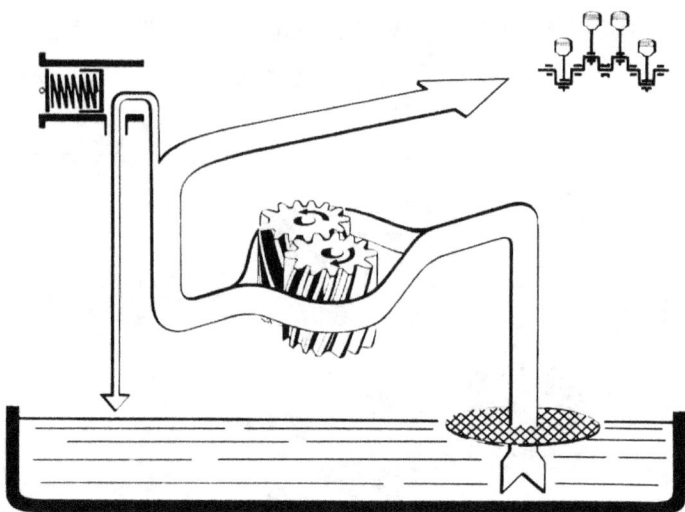

OIL PUMP

- For removal of pump from engine see page 25.

Disassembly

- Unscrew the nuts securing the gear housing to pump body and disassemble the pump as follows.
- Withdraw the pump driven gear from its spindle in gear housing.
- Pull out the pump drive gear from pump shaft with the aid of a press.
- Withdraw the pin keying the driven pinion to pump shaft and remove the pinion.
- Remove the split pin retaining the relief valve plunger.
- Then remove:
  - the spring seat:
  - the spring:
  - the plunger (with tool **A.3.0210**).

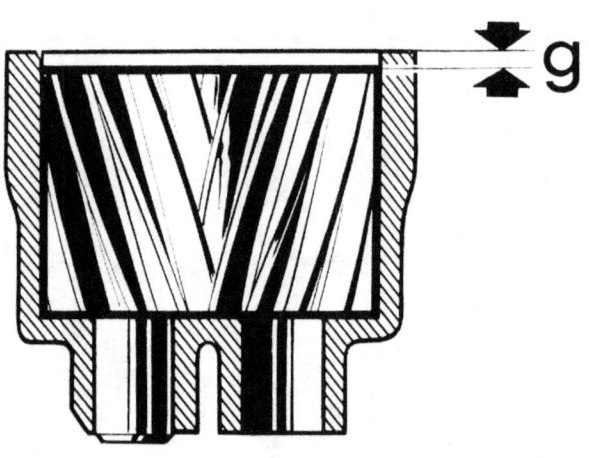

Inspection and checking

- Check the gear end play **g** with a feeler gauge

  permissible end play: .2 - .5 mm (.0078 - .0197 in.).

- Inspect the gear teeth for excessive wear. Check the abutment surfaces of gears for any sign of scoring or scratching.

- Check the radial clearance **r** between gears and housing:

  specified clearance: .020 - .062 mm (.0008 - .0024 in.).

- Check that the driven gear spindle is firmly fitted into its seat.

AUXILIARY EQUIPMENT
LUBRICATION

- Check:
  - the working surface of relief valve plunger **1**: if it shows sign of scratches, smooth them out;
  - the spring **2** against the following specifications:
    free length **48.25 mm** (1.9 in.)
    length under a load of
    15.71 kg (34.6 lbs) = **32.25 mm** (1.27 in.);
  - the condition of coupling slot **3** and that the play between slot and tooth on distributor drive shaft **7** is not excessive.

- Inspect the surface of mounting flange **4**. It must be perfectly flat and smooth to prevent oil leakage.

Reassembly

Reassemble the pump as follows:

- Insert the driven pinion **5** on shaft and secure it with the dowel pin **6**.

- Fit the shaft into pump body and shrink the drive gear, previously heated at **80° - 100° C** (176° - 212° F), on the shaft.

- Reassemble the pump in reverse order of disassembly.

- On completion of reassembly, check that the pump gears **8** and **9** run freely; tap lightly on gear housing with a lead mallet, if necessary.

- Reinstall the oil pump on the engine as outlined on page 26.

Oil pressure test

- Check oil pressure under the following conditions:

  a) **idle range**: min. **.5 - 1 kg/cm^2**
  (7 - 14 psi)

  b) **top speed range:** min. **3.5 kg/cm^2**
  (50 psi)

  max. **4.5 - 5 kg/cm^2**
  (65 - 70 psi)

- In the case a drop in pressure is indicated by the gauge and no external cause, such as the abnormal wear of crankshaft bearings, oil leakage from seals, etc. is ascertained, the trouble may be due to worn pump gears of gear housing.
  Other causes of pressure drop may be the yielding of spring **2**, oil leakage past the relief valve **1** or the sticking of valve plunger in its cylinder.

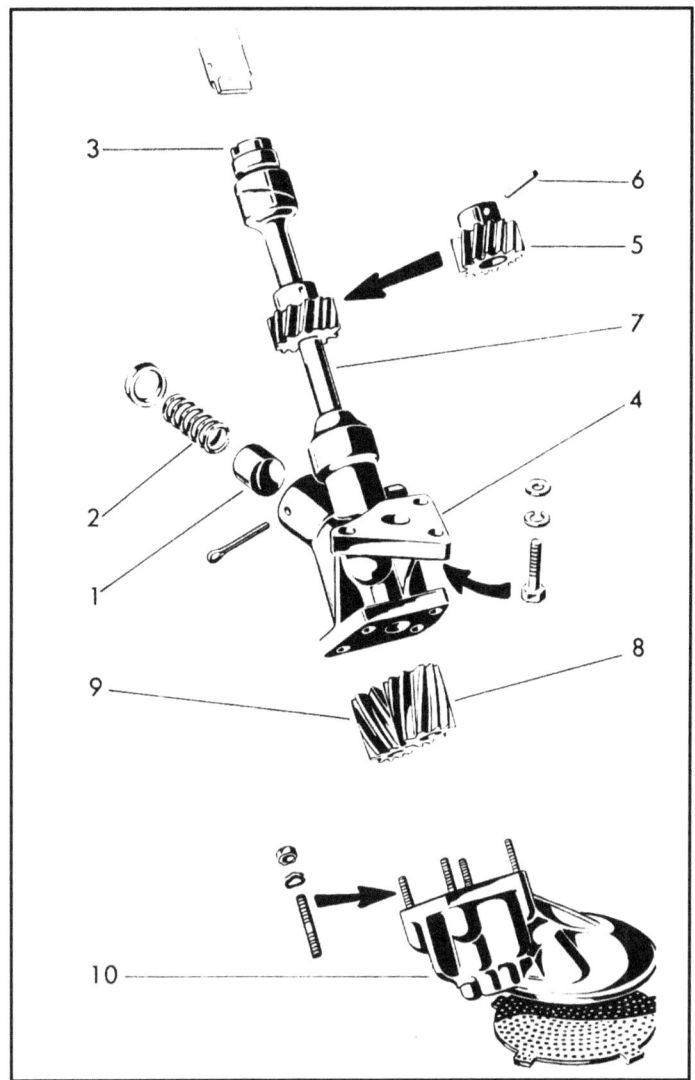

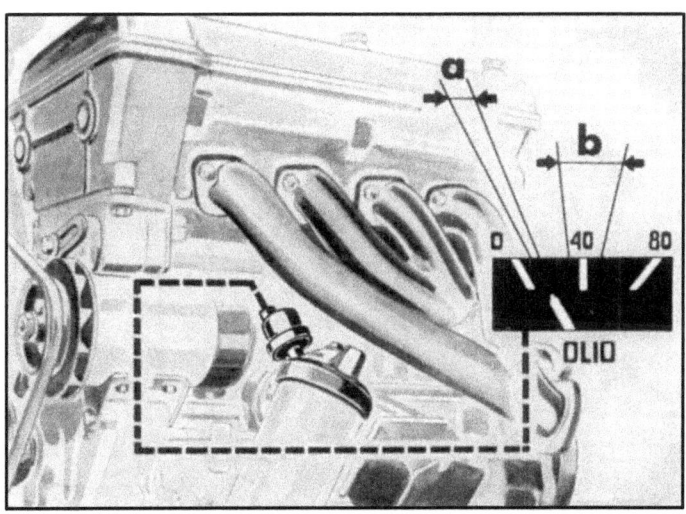

AUXILIARY EQUIPMENT

COOLING SYSTEM

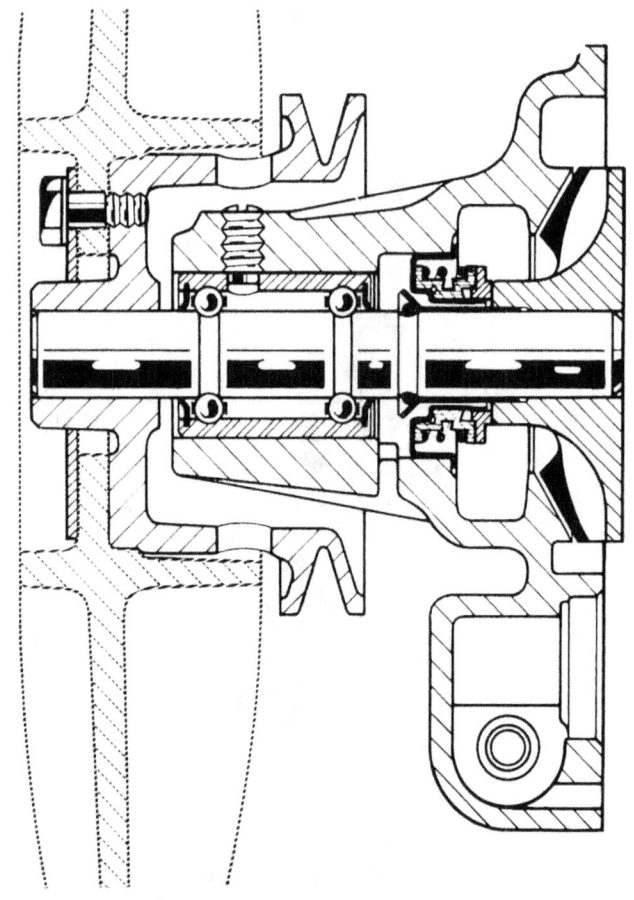

WATER PUMP

- Remove the water pump from engine as instructed under « Overhaul without removing engine » page 29.

Disassembly

- Loosen the screw fastening the fan to the pulley and remove the fan.

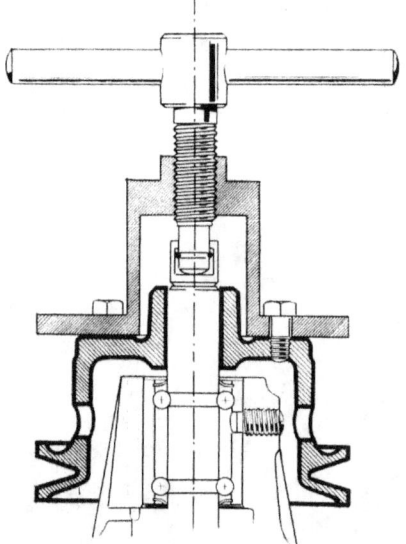

- Withdraw the pulley from the shaft with the puller **A.3.0147**.
- Loosen the grubscrew securing the bearing to pump body.
- With the aid of a press, remove the shaft, the impeller and the packing as a unit from pump body.

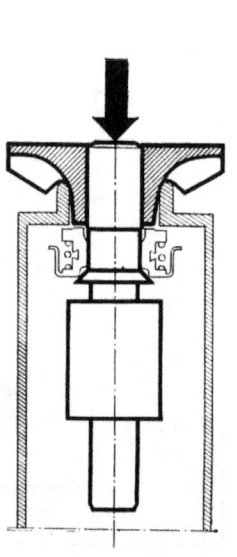

- Remove the following items only if repair or replacement is required:
  - the impeller from pump shaft (with tool **A.3.0136**);
  - the packing, the thrower and the retainer ring.

Inspection and checking

- Check the packing and the bearing for good conditions; if the bearing is damaged, replace the bearing and shaft assembly.
- Check that the impeller is not worn or corroded.

AUXILIARY EQUIPMENT

COOLING SYSTEM

- Descale the parts by rubbing and washing in a solution of sodium bicarbonate in water; then rinse thoroughly in fresh water.
- Make sure the water outlet port is not obstructed.
- On reassembly, replace non satisfactory parts with new ones.

Reassembly

- Refit the thrower retainer ring **1** to shaft with the tools **A.3.0155** and **A.3.0137**.
- Insert the thrower **2** onto shaft with the tool **A.3.0137**.
- Heat the pump body to **80° C** (176° F) and insert the shaft assembly into the pump body taking care to align the hole in the bearing with the threaded seat for the grubscrew.

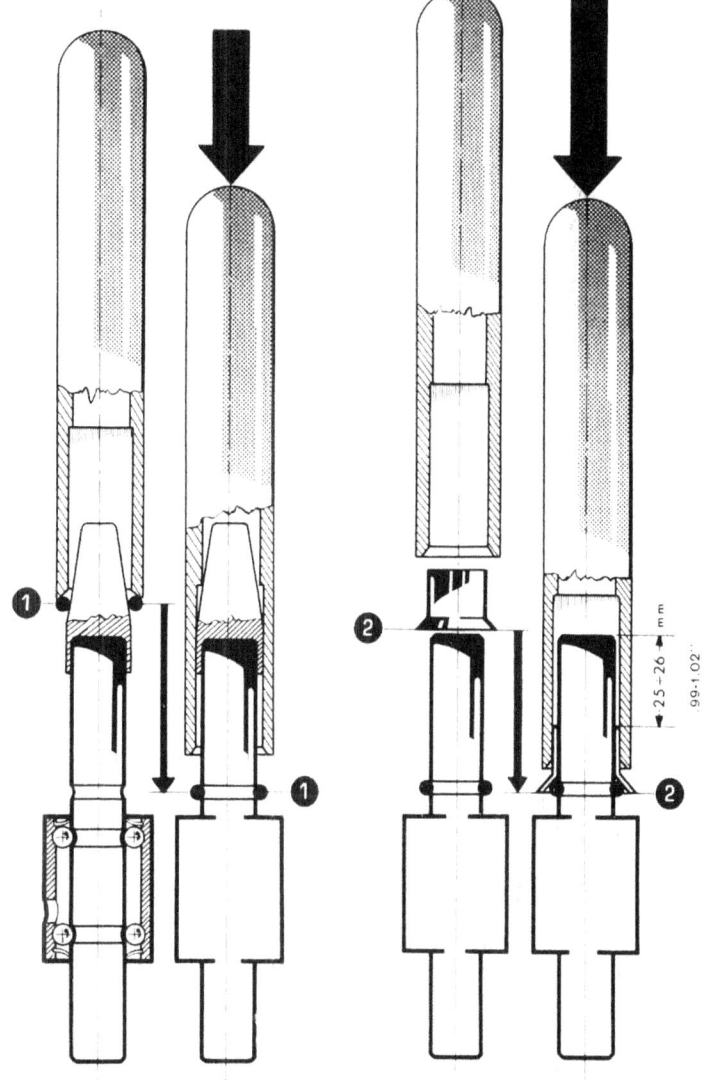

- Fit the packing **3** into the pump body with the tool **A.3.0177**.
  It is recommended to replace the packing at every reassembly.
- Heat the impeller to about **80° C** (176° F) and shrink it onto the shaft with the aid of a press.
  Stop pressing in when the clearance **S** between impeller vanes and pump body is: **.5 mm** (.02 in.).
  Heat the pulley at **80°-100° C** (176°-212° F) and install it on pump shaft.

Note - To mount the pump on engine follow the instructions given on page 29.

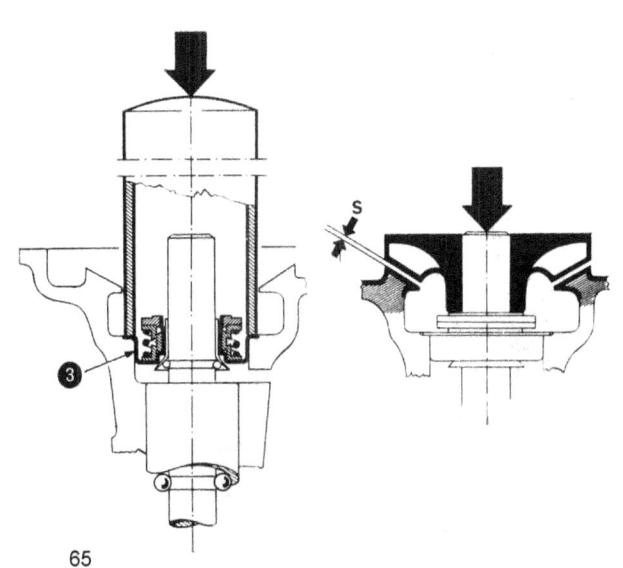

AUXILIARY EQUIPMENT

COOLING SYSTEM - EXHAUST SYSTEM

Thermostat

- The thermostat is installed in the water outlet duct from intake manifold jacket.
- For disassembly, remove the outlet duct elbow and take out the thermostat.

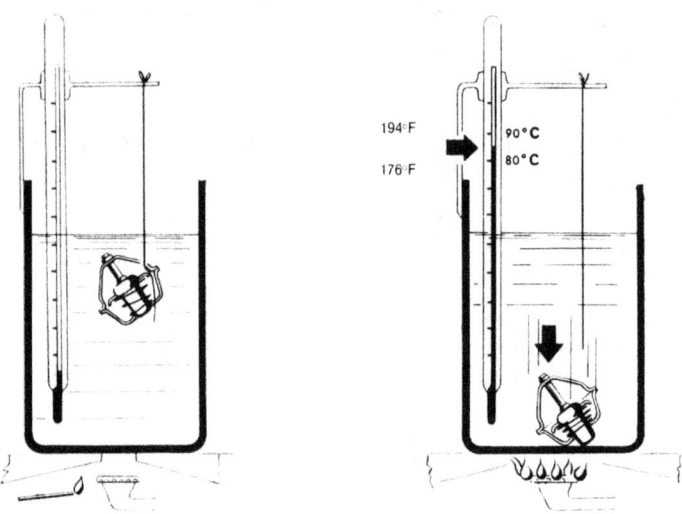

- Check the thermostat for proper operation as follows:
  - dip it in a water container;
  - heat the water so that the temperature gradient is **1° C** every 2 minutes;
  - check that the valve starts opening at the prescribed temperature of **82-87° C** (180 - 189° F).

The above check can also be performed by the following empirical method: hang the valve to a nylon string; at the prescribed temperature the thermostat sinking to the container bottom indicates the opening of valve.

Exhaust system

- Overhaul the exhaust manifold as follows:
  - free the exhaust pipe from supports at the points **S**;
  - detach the exhaust manifold from cylinder head and exhaust pipe;
  - thoroughly clean the inside of manifold with a wire swab.
- Check that the mounting flanges are not warped out of flat; true them, if necessary.
- Make sure the rubber pads and gaskets are in sound conditions.
- Check that the exhaust pipe is in good working conditions.

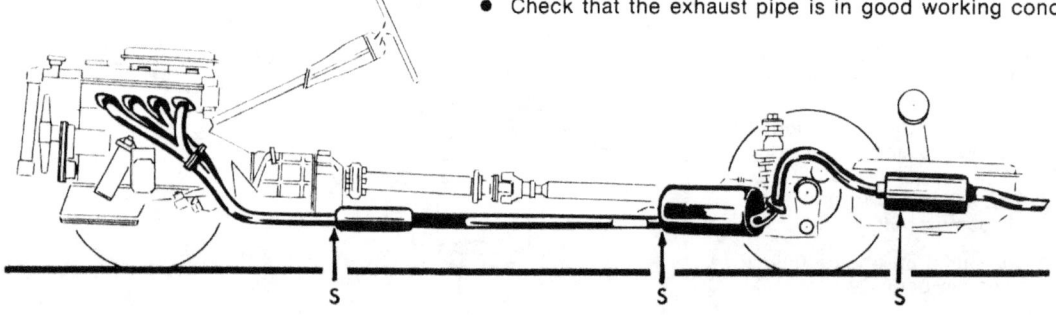

DIMENSIONS AND TOLERANCES
ENGINE

66
DIMENSIONS AND TOLERANCES
VALVES

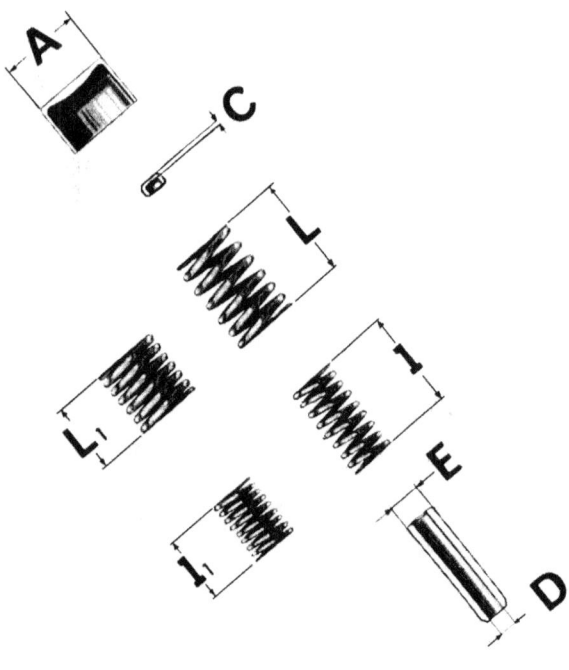
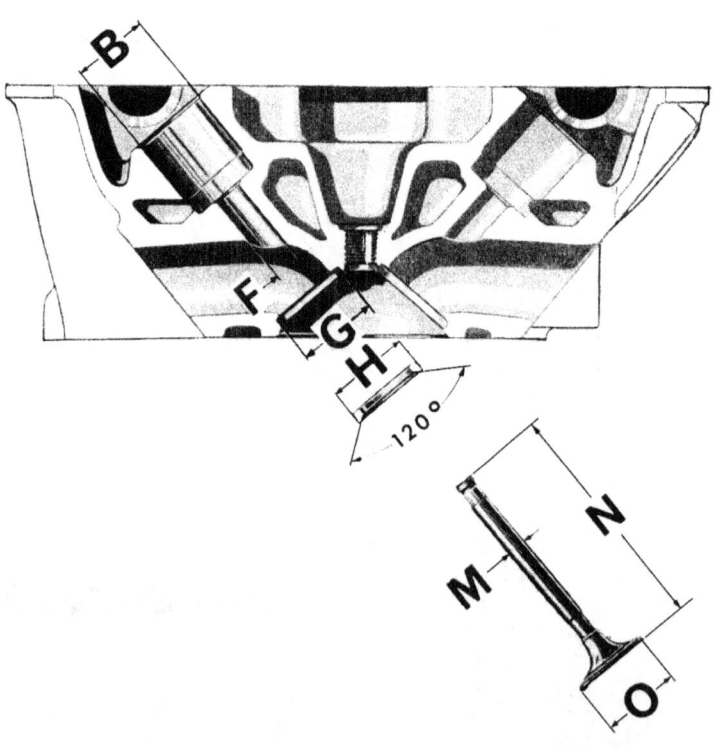

DIMENSIONS AND TOLERANCES

VALVES

		Standard	Oversized	CLEARANCES	
				New	Wear limit
VALVE CUP	A	34.973 - 34.989 mm (1.3773 - 1.3775")	35.173 - 35.189 mm (1.3848 - 1.3853")	.011 - .052 mm (.0005 - .0020")	.070 mm (.0027")
CUP SEAT	B	35.000 - 35.025 mm (1.3779 - 1.3789")	35.200 - 35.225 mm (1.3859 - 1.3068")		

ADJUSTING PAD	C	Thickness ranging from **1.3** to **3.5 mm** in increments of **.025 mm** (.051 to .138") (.001")

			Free length		Length under load	Test load
SPRING	large	L	51.3 mm (2.02")	L_1	27.5 mm (1.08")	35.6 - 37.1 kg (78.5 - 81.8 lbs)
	small	l	46.5 mm (1.83")	l_1	26.0 mm (1.02")	21.2 - 23.16 kg (46.7 - 51.1 lbs)

VALVE GUIDE	D	9.000 - 9.015 mm (.3544 - .3549") installed	
	E	14.033 - 14.044 mm (.5525 - .5529") removed	interference .015 - .044 mm (.0007 - .0017")
GUIDE SEAT	F	14.000 - 14.018 mm (.5512 - .5518")	

		INTAKE		EXHAUST			
		Standard	Oversized	Standard	Oversized		
SEAT INSERT HOUSING	H	42.472 - 42.497 mm (1.6722 - 1.6731")	42.772 - 42.797 mm (1.6840 - 1.6849")	38.472 - 38.497 mm (1.5147 - 1.5156")	38.772 - 38.797 mm (1.5265 - 1.5274")	Interference	.100 - .176 mm (.004 - .0017")
SEAT INSERT	G	42.597 - 42.648 mm (1.6771 - 1.6790")	42.897 - 42.948 mm (1.6889 - 1.6908")	38.597 - 38.648 mm (1.5196 - 1.5215")	38.897 - 38.948 mm (1.5314 - 1.5333")		

		SANTAMBROGIO		ATE				
		Intake	Exhaust	Exhaust only				
VALVE	M	8.960 - 8.987 mm (.3527 - .3538")	8.935 - 8.960 mm (.3518 - .3527")	8.935 - 8.960 mm (.3518 - .3527")	Clearance D minus M	Intake: .013 - .053 mm (.0006 - .0022")	Wear limit = .1 mm (.004")
	N	106.630-107.030 mm (4.1981 - 4.2137")	105.900-106.300 mm (4.1693 - 4.1850")	106.050-106.150 mm (4.1753 - 4.1791")		Exhaust: .040 - .080 mm (.0017 - .0031")	
	O	41.000 - 41.150 mm (1.614 - 1.620")	37.000 - 37.150 mm (1.4567 - 1.4625")	37.000 - 37.200 mm (1.4567 - 1.4645")			

DIMENSIONS AND TOLERANCES

CAMSHAFTS

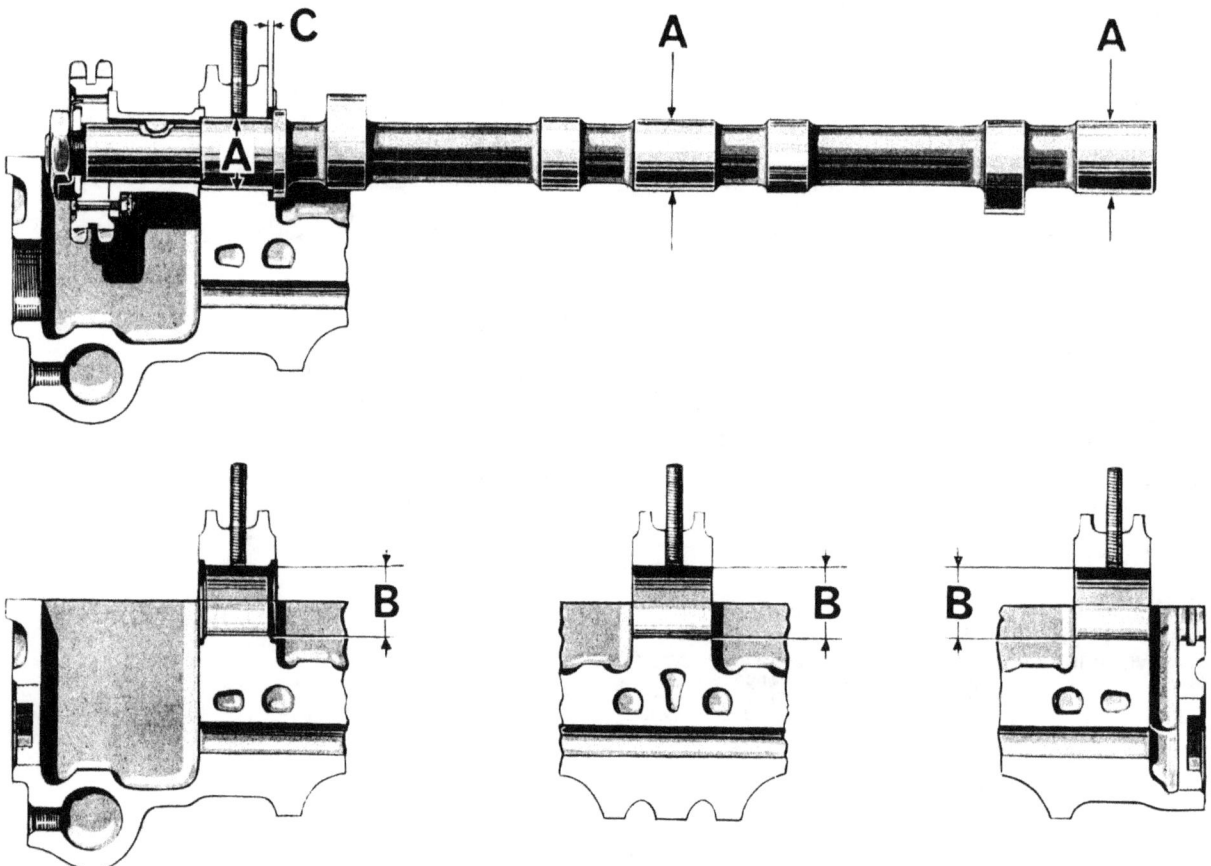

JOURNAL	A	26.959 - 26.980 mm (1.0614 - 1.0622")	Clearance	.020 - .074 mm (.0008 - .0028")
BEARING	B	27.000 - 27.033 mm (1.0630 - 1.0642")		

END PLAY	C	.065 - .182 mm (.0026 - .0071")

DIMENSIONS AND TOLERANCES

CYLINDER BARRELS - PISTONS

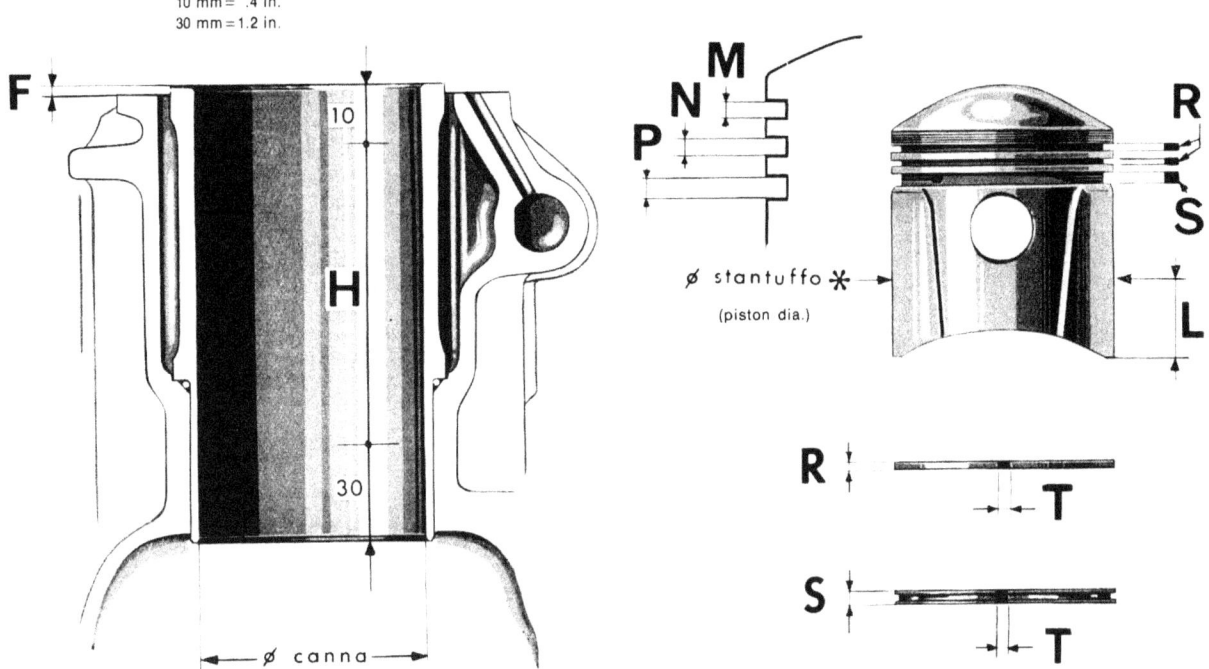

10 mm = .4 in.
30 mm = 1.2 in.

ø canna (barrel dia.)

ø stantuffo * (piston dia.)

* to be measured at right angle to wrist pin hole

PISTON MAKE	BARREL - TO - PISTON FIT					
	CLASS **A** BLUE		CLASS **B** PINK		CLASS **C** GREEN	
	PISTON O.D.	BARREL I.D.	PISTON O.D.	BARREL I.D.	PISTON O.D.	BARREL I.D.
BORGO	77.920 - 77.930 mm (3.0677 - 3.0681")	77.985 - 77.994 mm (3.0703 - 3.0706")	77.931 - 77.940 mm (3.0682 - 3.0685")	77.995 - 78.004 mm (3.0707 - 3.0710")	77.941 - 77.950 mm (3.0686 - 3.0688")	78.005 - 78.014 mm (3.0711 - 3.0714")
MAHLE	77.945 - 77.955 mm (3.0687 - 3.0690")		77.956 - 77.965 mm (3.0691 - 3.0694")		77.966 - 77.975 mm (3.0695 - 3.0698")	

BARREL-TO-PISTON CLEARANCE	BORGO	.055 - .074 mm (.0022 - .0029")	wear limit	.15 mm (.0059")
	MAHLE	.030 - .049 mm (.0012 - .0019")		

BARREL	Projection from cylinder block	F	.00 - .06 mm (.000 - .002")
	Reading points	H	Diameter (see table)
			Elongation .010 mm (.0004") new barrels
			.100 mm (.004") wear limit
			Surface roughness 20 - 40 microinches RMS

PISTON	Dia. reading point	L	11 mm (.43") (MAHLE)
			12 mm (.47") (BORGO)
	Ring grooves	Chromium-plated	M	1.785-1.800 mm (.0703-.0708")
		Oil scraper	N	1.775-1.790 mm (.0699-.0704")
		Oil control	P	4.015-4.030 mm (.1581-.1586")

Thickness of compression scraper rings	R	1.728-1.740 mm (.0681-.0685")
Thickness of oil control ring	S	3.978-3.990 mm (.1567-.1571")

End play M minus R =	.045-.072 mm (.0018-.0028")	Wear limit = .10 mm .004"
End play N minus R =	.035-.062 mm (.0014-.0024")	
End play P minus S =	.025-.052 mm (.0010-.0020")	

Gap of rings	T	.300-.450 mm (.012-.017") wear limit = 1 mm (.039")	to be inspected in ring gauge or in cylinder barrels

DIMENSIONS AND TOLERANCES

CONNECTING RODS

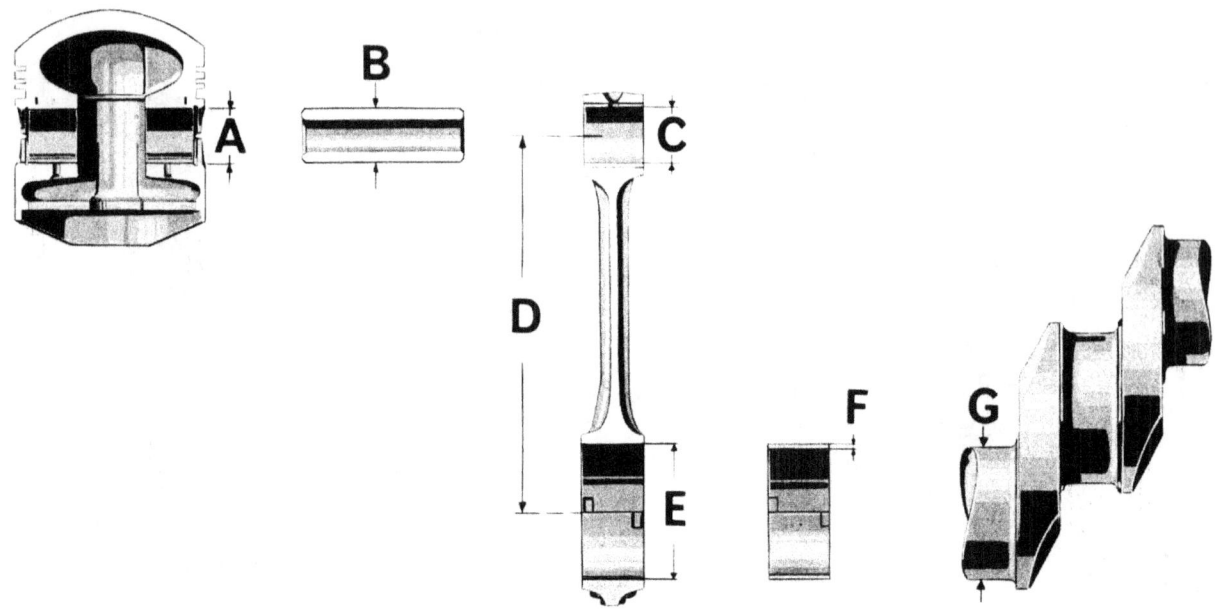

PISTON PIN HOLE I.D.	BORGO	A	BLACK	WHITE
			22.000 - 22.002 mm (.86614 - .86621")	22.003 - 22.005 mm (.86626 - .86633")
	MAHLE		21.996 - 21.999 mm (.86597 - .86608")	21.999 - 22.002 mm (.86608 - .86621")
PISTON PIN O.D.		B	21.994 - 21.997 mm (.86590 - .86602")	21.997 - 22.000 mm (.86602 - .86614")

		BLACK	WHITE
CLEARANCE A minus B	BORGO	.003 - .008 mm (.00012 - .0003")	.003 - .007 mm (.00012 - .0002")
	MAHLE	+.005 to -.001 mm (+.00019 to -.00004")	+.005 to -.001 mm (+.00019 to -.00004")
CLEARANCE C minus B		.008 - .021 mm (.0003 - .0008")	.005 - .017 mm (.0002 - .0006")

CONNECTING ROD	C	22.005 - 22.015 mm (.8664 - .8667")
	D	147.955 - 148.045 mm (5.8250 - 5.8285")
	E	53.695 - 53.708 mm (2.1140 - 2.1144")

CLEARANCE (E minus twice F) minus G	.025 - .063 mm (.0010 - .0025") wear limit = .15 mm (.006")

CONNECTING ROD BEARING THICKNESS	F	Standard	1.829 - 1.835 mm (.0720 - .0722")
		1st oversize	1.956 - 1.962 mm (.0770 - .0772")
		2nd oversize	2.083 - 2.089 mm (.0820 - .0822")

DIMENSIONS AND TOLERANCES

CRANKSHAFT

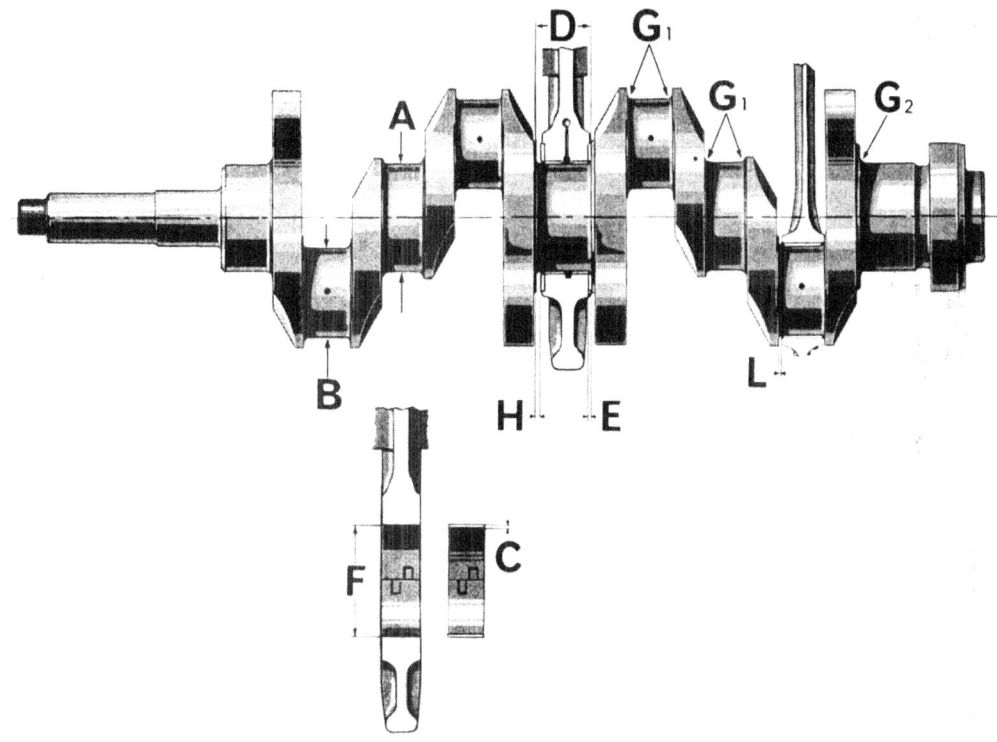

			STANDARD	UNDERSIZE	
				1st	2nd
JOURNALS	MAIN	A	59.960 - 59.973 mm (2.3606 - 2.3611")	59.706 - 59.719 mm (2.3506 - 2.3511")	59.452 - 59.465 mm (2.3407 - 2.3411")
	CON. ROD	B	49.987 - 50.000 mm (1.9680 - 1.9685")	49.733 - 49.746 mm (1.9581 - 1.9585")	49.479 - 49.492 mm (1.9480 - 1.9485")

MAX. TAPER = .01 mm (.0004") on journal full length

MAX. MISALIGMENT = .01 mm (.0004")

MAX. ELONGATION = .007 mm (.0003")

MAX. OUT OF PARALLELISM = .015 mm (.0006") on journal full length

MAX. SURFACE ROUGHNESS = 6 microinches RMS

		STANDARD	OVERSIZE	
			1st	2nd
MAIN BEARING THICKNESS	C	1.829 - 1.835 mm (.0720 - .0722")	1.956 - 1.962 mm (.0770 - .0772")	2.083 - 2.089 mm (.0820 - .0822")
MAIN JOURNAL LENGTH	D	30.000 - 30.035 mm (1.1811 - 1.1824")	30.127 - 30.162 mm (1.1861 - 1.1874")	30.254 - 30.289 mm (1.1911 - 1.1924")
THRUST RING THICKNESS	E	2.311 - 2.362 mm (.0911 - .0929")	2.374 - 2.425 mm (.0935 - .0954")	2.438 - 2.489 mm (.0960 - .0980")

MAIN BEARING SEAT		F	63.657 - 63.676 mm (2.5062 - 2.5069")
FILLET RADII	CRANKPINS AND MAIN JOURNALS	G_1	1.7 - 2.1 mm (.069 - .082")
	MAIN JOURNAL (flywheel side only)	G_2	3.7 - 4.1 mm (.146 - .161")

CLEARANCE (F minus twice C) minus A	.014 - .058 mm (.0006 - .0022")

END PLAY	CON. ROD	H	.076 - .263 mm (.003 - .010")
	CRANKSHAFT	L	.200 - .300 mm (.008 - .012")

NOTES

CLUTCH

CLUTCH

ADJUSTMENT DATA AND INSPECTION SPECIFICATIONS

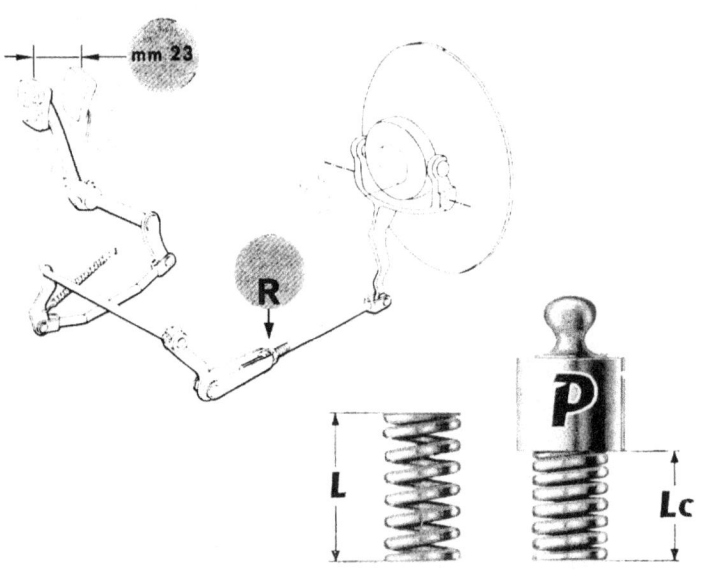

Pedal free travel: **23 mm** (about 1 in.).

When pedal free travel is reduced to **10 - 12 mm** (about 1/2 in.) owing to wear of driven plate facing, the free travel must be restored by adjusting the nut **R**.

After the adjustment firmly secure the adjusting nut with its locknut.

Length of engaging spring:
L = **43.5 to 45.5 mm** (1.71 to 1.79 in.);
Lc = **29 mm** (1.14 in.) under a load
P = **45 - 49 kg** (99 to 108 lbs).

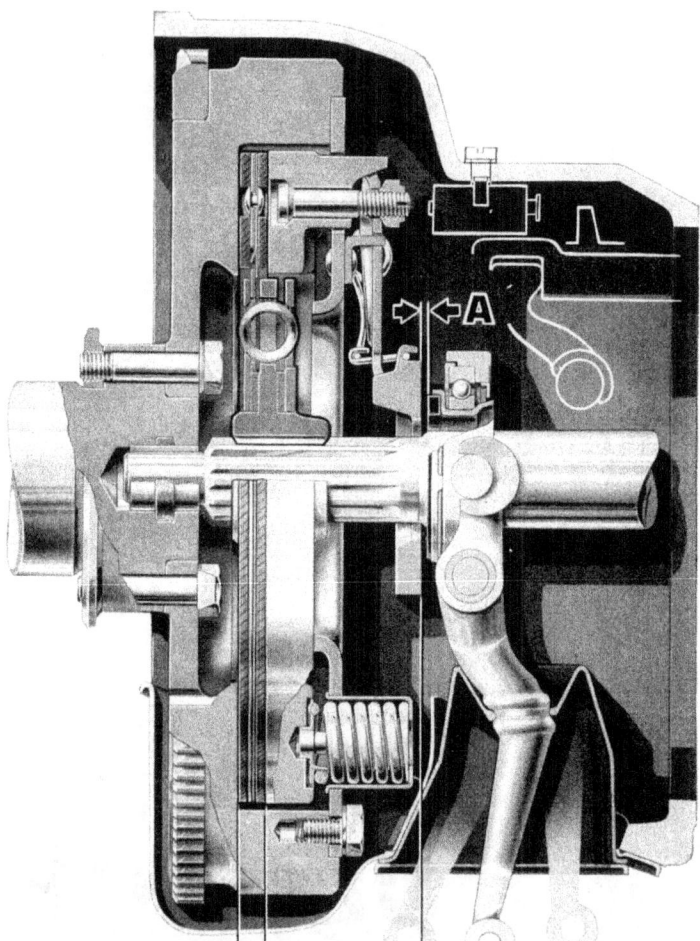

A = **2 mm** (0.79 in.).

Clearance between the thrust ring and throwout bearing.

With this amount of clearance the pedal free travel is **23 mm** (about 1 in.).

B = **9.1 to 9.4 mm** (.358 to .370 in.).

Thickness of driven plate when engaged (with new facings).

Wear limit: about **6 mm** (.236 in.).

C = **48.8 to 50.4 mm** (1.93 to 1.94 in.).

Distance between pressure plate face and thrust ring face.
This dimension is to be measured on a suitable fixture and indipendently of driven plate thickness.

CLUTCH

REMOVAL AND DISASSEMBLY

Removal from car

- Remove the gearbox as described on page 82.
- Unscrew the screws securing the clutch unit to the flywheel.
- Remove the clutch unit, driven plate included, taking care not to soil the facings with oil or grease.

Disassembling the clutch unit

- Set up the clutch unit on the jig **C.6.0104** (Ref. Tool Bulletin no. 50); screw all the way down the screws so as to compress the engaging springs.
- Clear the thrust ring from spring retainers and remove the ring.
- If necessary, remove the stakings which lock the nuts to the toggle lever bolts and without rotating the nuts unscrew the bolts with a screwdriver; then take out the toggle levers.
- Mark the position of thrust ring with respect to the flange; on reassembly, align these parts again according to the reference marks made so that balance of the system is not altered.
- Loosen the screws slowly and in diagonal order so as to relieve the springs gradually.
- Break down the unit in its parts.

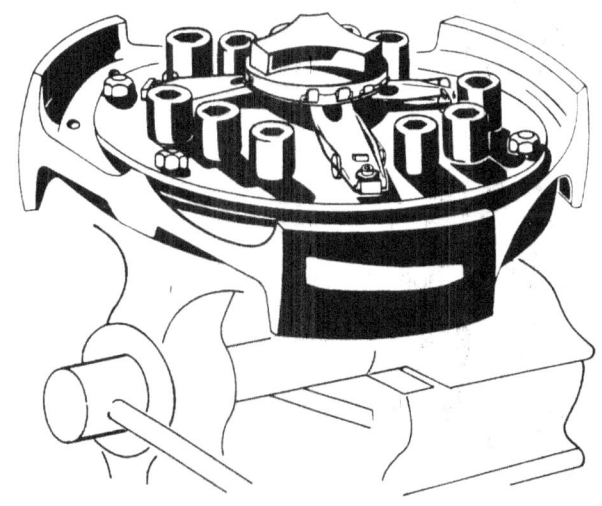

 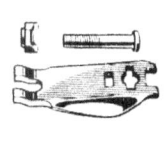 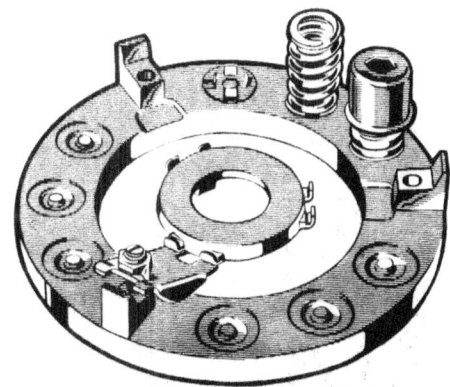

CLUTCH

INSPECTION AND CHECKING

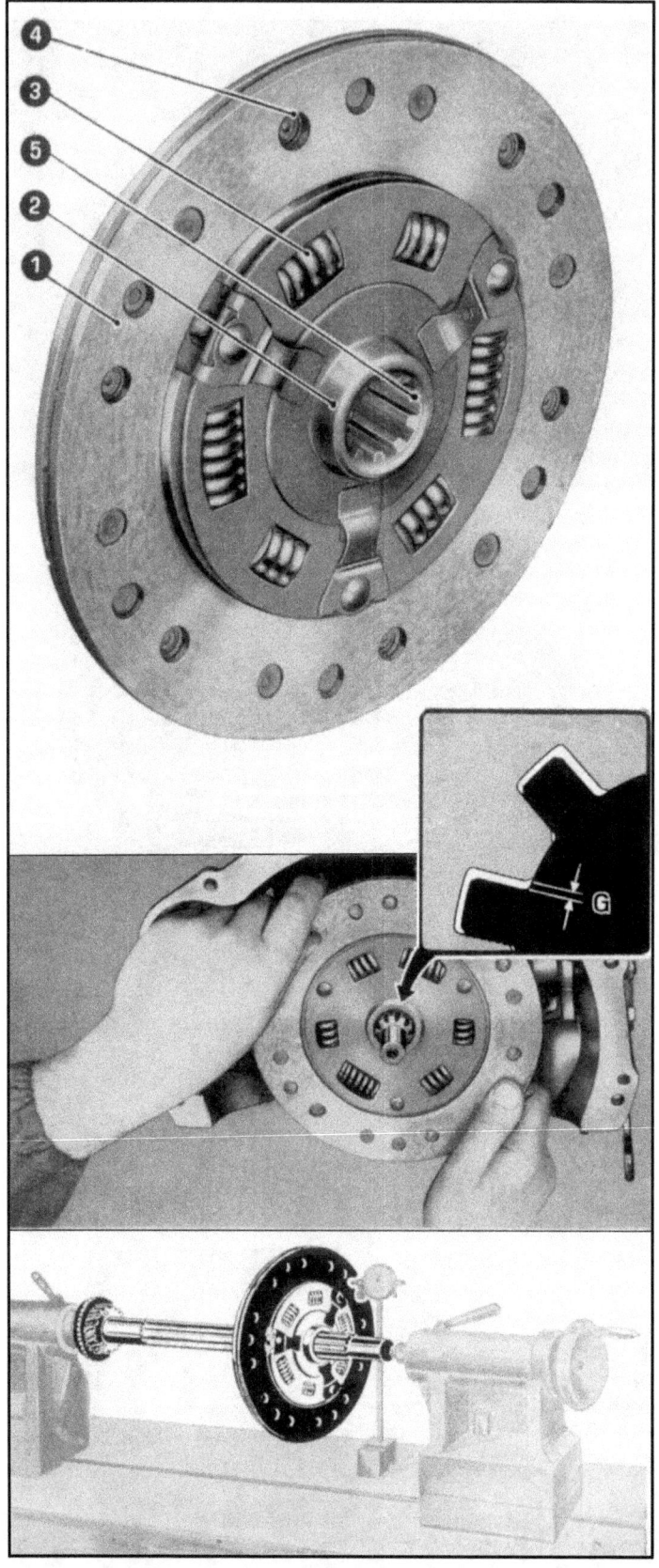

- Check that:

1. driven plate facings are dry; if they are stained with lubricants the affected area must be cleaned with petrol and dressed with a wire brush; however, reface the plate if facings are deeply soaked with oil;

2. driven plate is firmly secured to its hub;

3. springs in the coupling work properly;

4. facing rivets are well riveted into their holes;

5. with a suitable stone smooth off possible dents of burrs on the egdes of hub splines.

- Check the clearance between side faces of splines in the clutch driven plate and in the gearbox direct drive shaft.

  Factory assembly clearance:

  G = .03 to .11 mm (.0012 to .0043 in.).
  Wear limit: **.3 mm** (.0118 in.).

- Slide the driven plate onto the direct drive shaft and place the parts so assembled between centers as shown.
  Check flatness and run out of plate with a dial gauge:

  max. permissible run out = **.50 mm** (.02 in.)

  If necessary, true the plate by exerting pressure only on the side faces of plate.

CLUTCH

INSPECTION AND CHECKING

- Check that pressure plate and flywheel friction surfaces are smooth and flat. Re-grind the surfaces, if necessary.

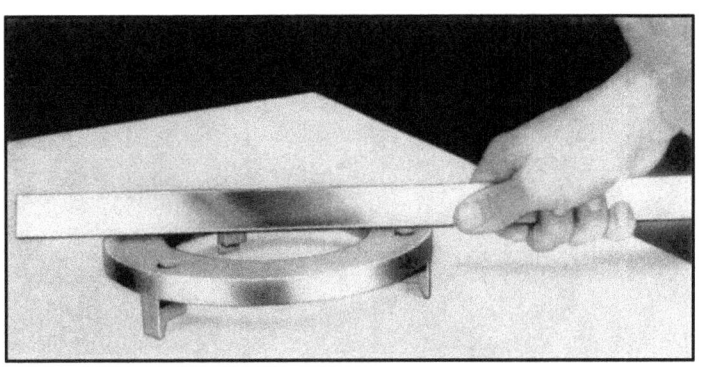

- Check the throwout bearing for any undue noise or excessive play; make sure the graphite ring projection **S** is not reduced to such a point as to leave uncovered the inner seat edge.

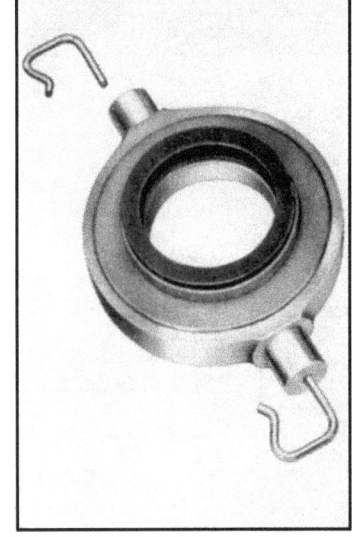

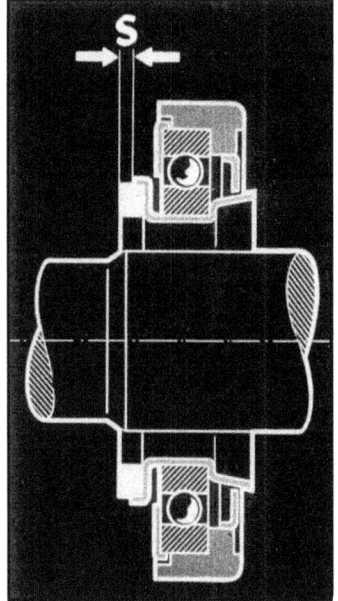

- Check that the bushing centering the direct drive shaft onto crankshaft shows no sign of seizing or excessive wear.

- If necessary, replace the bushing and the felt washer with new ones. On reassembling, lubricate the bushing and soak the felt with warm engine oil (see page 42).

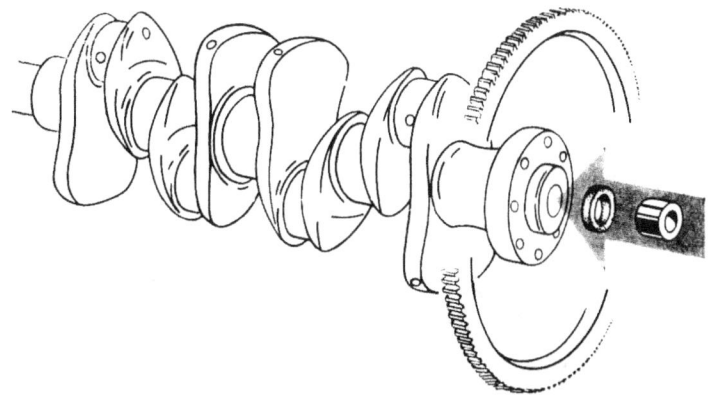

CLUTCH

REASSEMBLY, CHECKING AND REINSTALLATION

Reassembly

- Assemble the clutch on the jig **C.6.0104**. On reassembly, make sure to align the thrust ring and the flange according to the reference marks so as not to alter the balance of the system.

  Before assembling the thrust ring inspect it to make sure the surfaces which bear the toggle lever reaction, are not excessively indented. With an oil stone smooth out the gals and bring the surfaces flat in the same plane.

- Check that the levers are in the same plane with a dial gauge and remove possible damage from bearing surfaces with an oil stone.

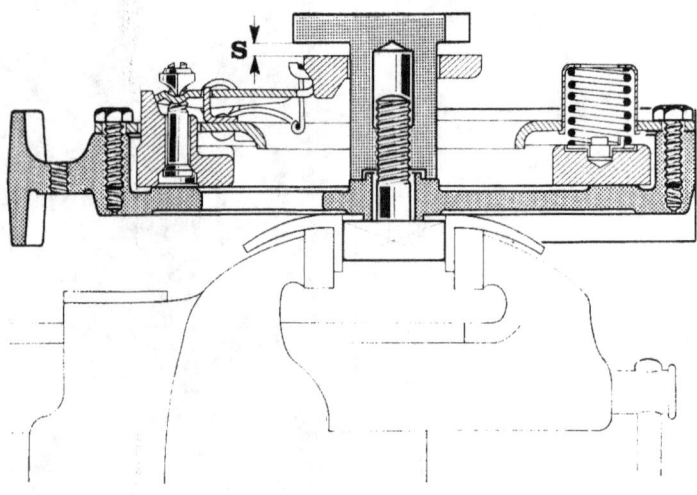

- Assemble the thrust ring and engage the spring retainers.

- With a feeler gauge check that the distance **S** between the reference plane of the jig and the thrust ring is **1 ± .8 mm** (.039 ± .031 in.).

  If the above distance is not as prescribed, adjust the position of toggle levers by acting on the respective bolts with the 14 mm wrench (special tool no. **A.5.0166**).

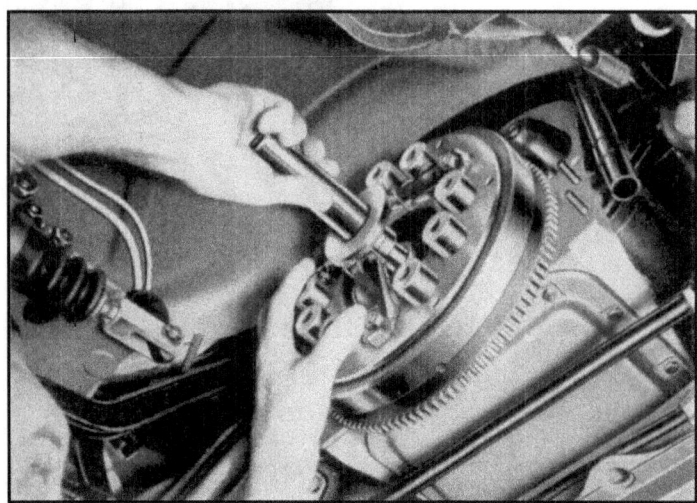

Reinstallation of clutch unit

- Assemble the clutch unit to flywheel centering the driven plate on flywheel with the tool **A.4.0103**; then gradually tighten the clutch mounting bolts.

GEARBOX

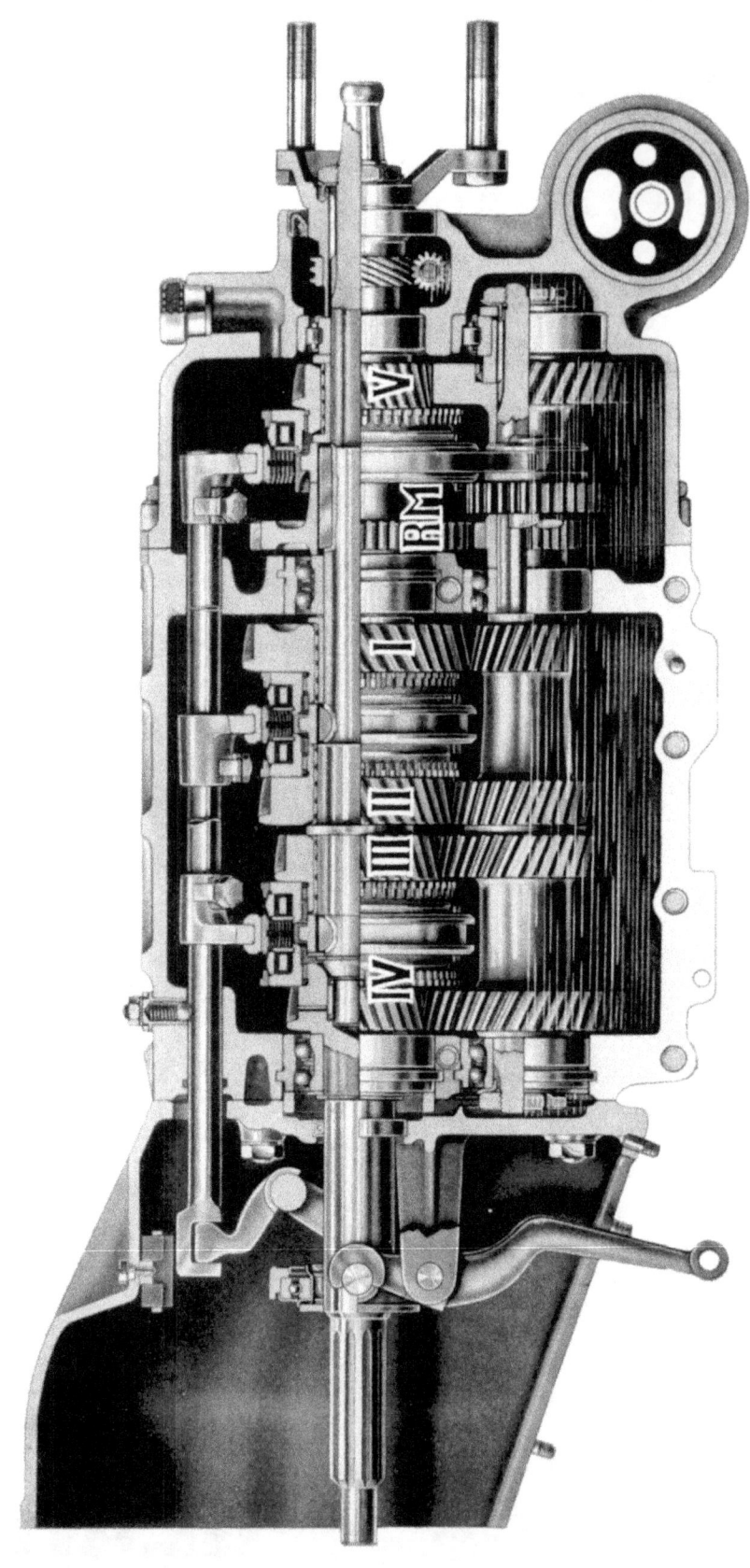

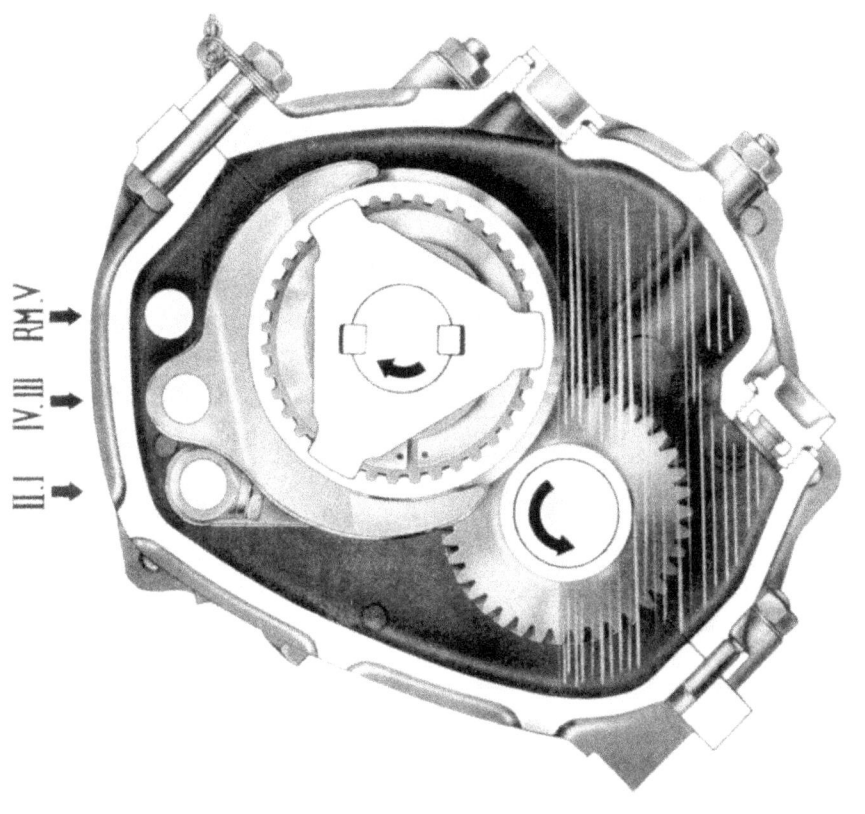

Transmission ratios

1st gear 3.304 : 1
2nd gear 1.988 : 1
3rd gear 1.355 : 1
4th gear 1.000 : 1
5th gear .791 : 1
REVERSE 3.010 : 1

GEARBOX

REMOVAL FROM CAR

Disconnect:

- the propeller shaft front section from rear section at the intermediate joint flange **1**;
- the support of propeller shaft central bearing **2**;
- the cross plate **3**;
- the odometer flexible shaft **4**;
- the exhaust pipe bracket **5** from gearbox.

Note - For floor-mounted gearshift remove:

- the carpet and the tunnel cover;
- the boot;
- the gearshift lever from gear engaging and selecting swivel;

- the clutch protection cover **6**;
- the gear selecting lever **7**;
- the leads **8** of back up light switch;
- the clutch disengaging lever **9**;
- the gear engaging lever **10**.

Unscrew:

- the bolts securing the crossmember to the floor;
- the bolt fastening the gearbox to the crossmember and remove the crossmember;
- the bolts securing gearbox to engine.

Remove the gearbox and the propeller shaft front section as a unit.
Drain oil from gearbox.
Disconnect the front section of propeller shaft from the flexible coupling with the tool **A.2.0124**.

Note - Reassemble the gearbox onto the car in reverse order of removal.

GEARBOX

DISASSEMBLY

- Place the gearbox assembly on a suitable stand.

- Unscrew the ring nut securing the flexible coupling yoke (keep the yoke from rotating by bringing a bolt at rest against the housing as shown) then remove the yoke.

- Unscrew the nuts securing the rear cover and remove the cover.

Note - For floor-mounted gearshift, engage the 3rd gear to remove the gearbox rear cover.

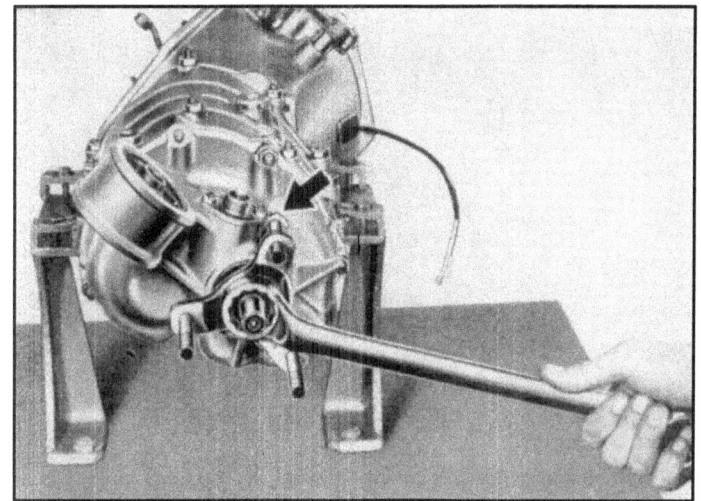

- Unscrew the bolt securing the 5th gear and reverse gear engaging fork so that the striking rod can be moved out thus freeing the gear engaging lever.

- Remove the back-up light switch.

- Remove the throwout bearing from the fork.

- Unscrew the nut securing the gear engaging lever to the shaft and remove the lever.

- Remove the small retainer ring from the groove in the shaft with suitable pliers.

- Remove the large retainer ring, which secure the seat for reverse gear return spring, from the groove in the boss with suitable pliers and remove the spring seat.

- Withdraw the shaft.

- Unscrew the nuts securing the clutch housing to the gearbox half-casings and remove the housing.

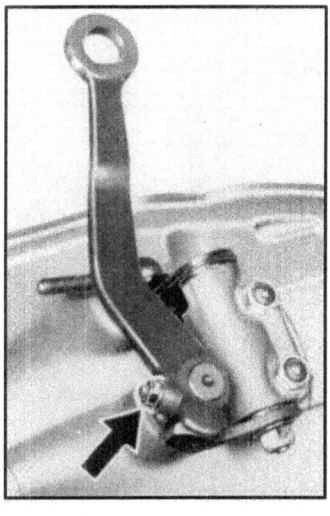 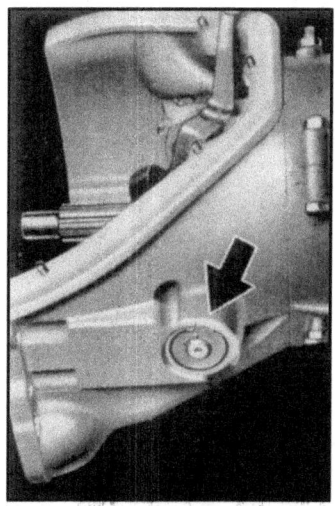

GEARBOX

DISASSEMBLY

- Unscrew the nuts fastening the half-casings; separate the casing by tapping lightly with a soft mallet and remove the shaft assemblies.

Warning: take care not to damage the half-casing joining surfaces as these must seal without a gasket.

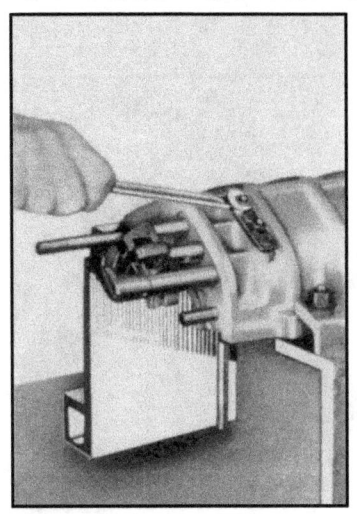

- Unscrew the nuts securing the plate which holds the striking rod ball plungers and withdraw plungers, springs and balls.
- Loosen the setscrews locking the forks to the striking rods, slide out the rods and remove the interlock rollers.

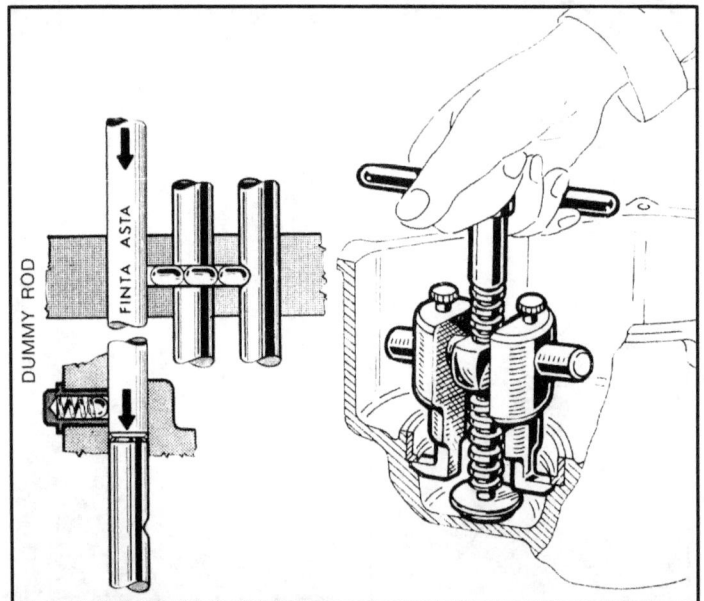

- If only one striking rod has to be taken out to repair a fault proceed as follows:
  - insert a dummy rod from the end opposite that of striking rod withdrawal, so as to hold in position the ball and the interlock rollers.

If necessary, remove the outer race of the countershaft rear bearing from the cover with the puller **A.3.0212** (Ref. Tool Bulletin no. 128).

This bearing race should be reinstalled with a suitable punch and the aid of a press.

GEARBOX

DIRECT DRIVE & MAINSHAFT

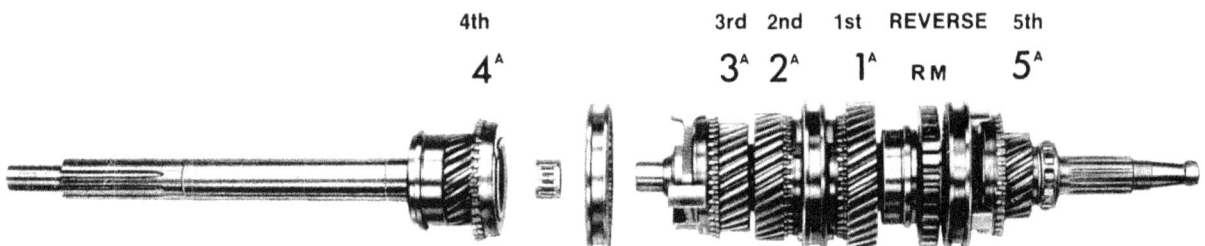

- Separate the mainshaft from the direct drive shaft and remove the roller bearing cage (the races are the shafts themselves).

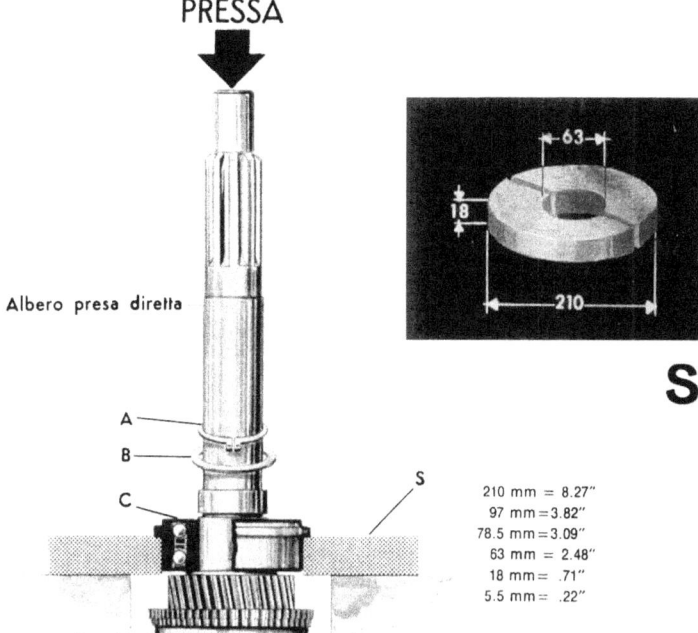

Disassemble the direct drive shaft

- Remove the retainer ring **A** and withdraw the shim **B**.
- Press off the bearing **C** using two half plates **S** as shown.

210 mm = 8.27"
97 mm = 3.82"
78.5 mm = 3.09"
63 mm = 2.48"
18 mm = .71"
5.5 mm = .22"

Pressa = Press
Albero presa diretta = Direct drive shaft
4° vel. = 4th gear

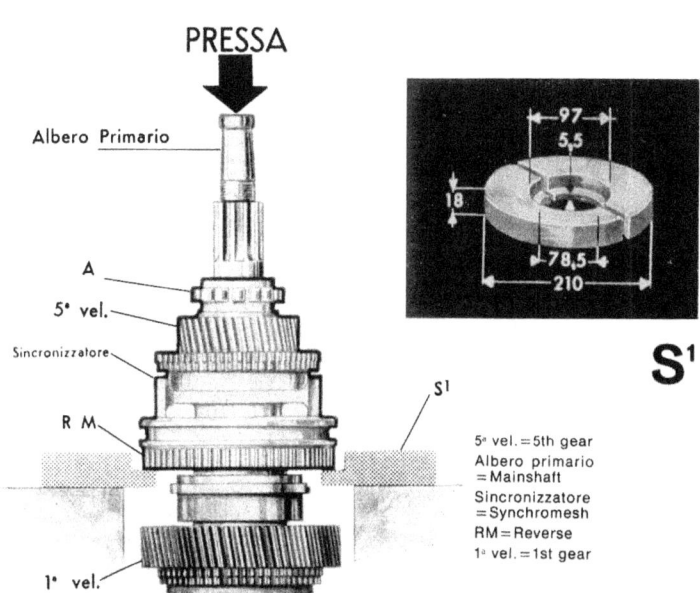

Disassemble the mainshaft

- Using the half-plates **S¹** press off the rear bearing **A** of the **5th** speed gear with its synchronizing hub and sleeve, the **reverse gear** and remove the key.

5° vel. = 5th gear
Albero primario = Mainshaft
Sincronizzatore = Synchromesh
RM = Reverse
1° vel. = 1st gear

GEARBOX

MAINSHAFT

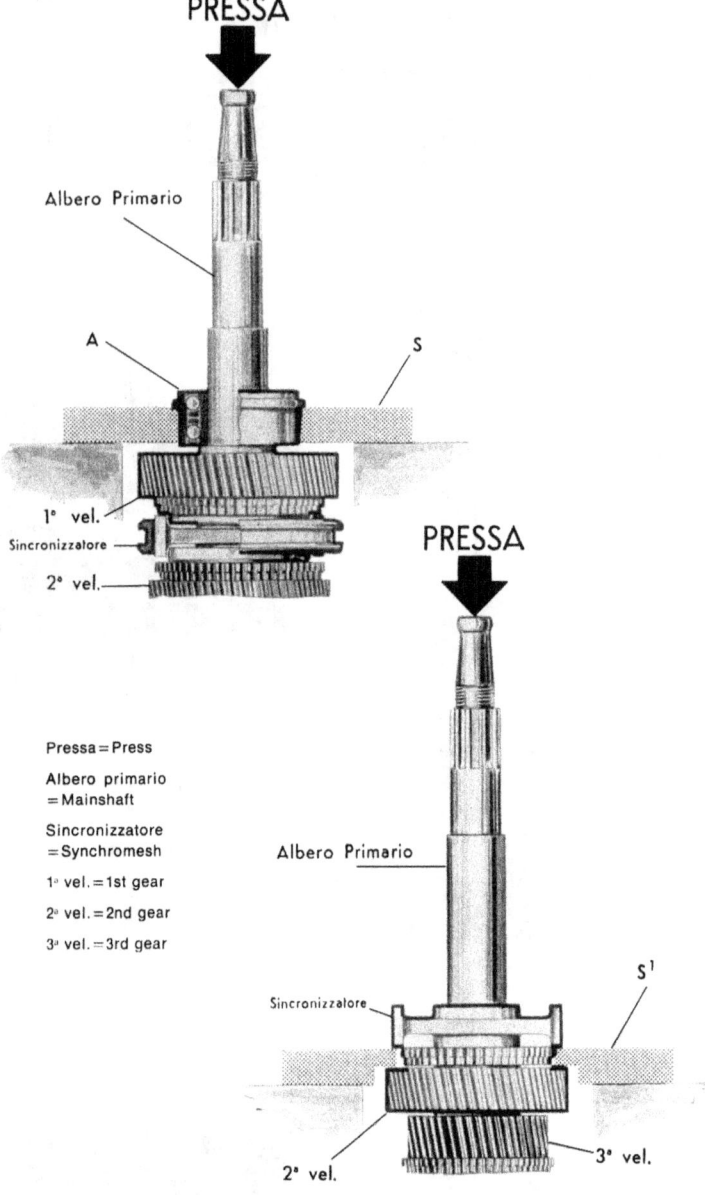

Pressa = Press
Albero primario = Mainshaft
Sincronizzatore = Synchromesh
1ª vel. = 1st gear
2ª vel. = 2nd gear
3ª vel. = 3rd gear

- Press off the intermediate bearing **A** using the half-plates **S**.
- Withdraw the shims, the **1st** speed gear with its bushing and the engaging sleeve of **1st** and **2nd** speed gears.

- Press off the synchronizing hub of **1st** and **2nd** speed gears using the half-plates **S¹**.
- Remove the keys and slide out the **2nd** speed gear.

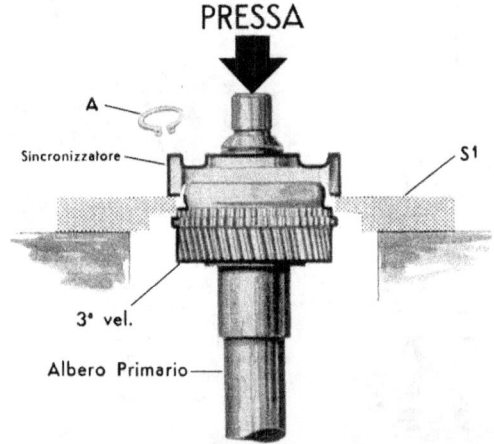

- Remove the retainer ring **A** of the **3rd & 4th** speed gear synchronizing hub.
- Press off the hub using the half-plates **S¹**.
- Slide out the **3rd** speed gear and remove the keys.

GEARBOX

COUNTERSHAFT

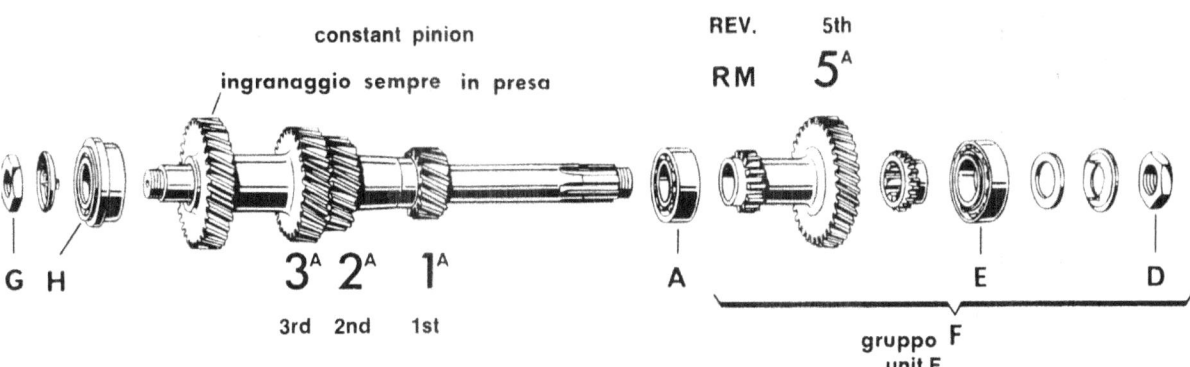

- Grip the shaft in a vice with lead jaws.
- Unscrew the nut **D**, remove the roller bearing **E** and the **reverse & 5th** speed gear assembly (unit **F**).

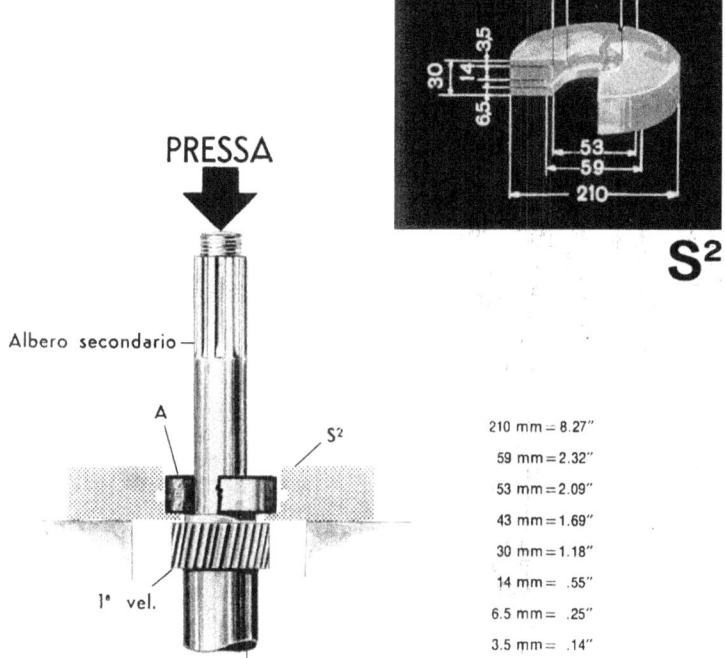

- Withdraw the intermediate bearing **A** using two half-plates **S²** as shown.

Pressa = Press
Albero secondario = Countershaft
1ª vel. = 1st gear
ingranaggio sempre in presa = Constant pinion

210 mm = 8.27"
59 mm = 2.32"
53 mm = 2.09"
43 mm = 1.69"
30 mm = 1.18"
14 mm = .55"
6.5 mm = .25"
3.5 mm = .14"

- Again grip the shaft between lead jaws and unscrew the nut **G** securing the front bearing.

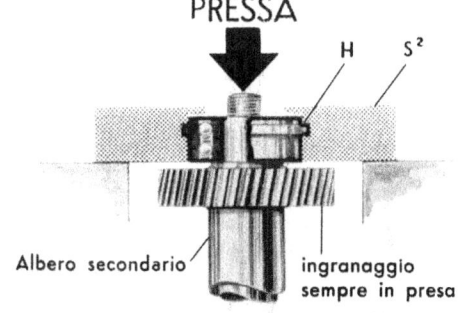

- Slip the half-plates **S²** over the rim **H** of front bearing and withdraw the bearing.

GEARBOX

SYNCHROMESH: OPERATING PRINCIPLE

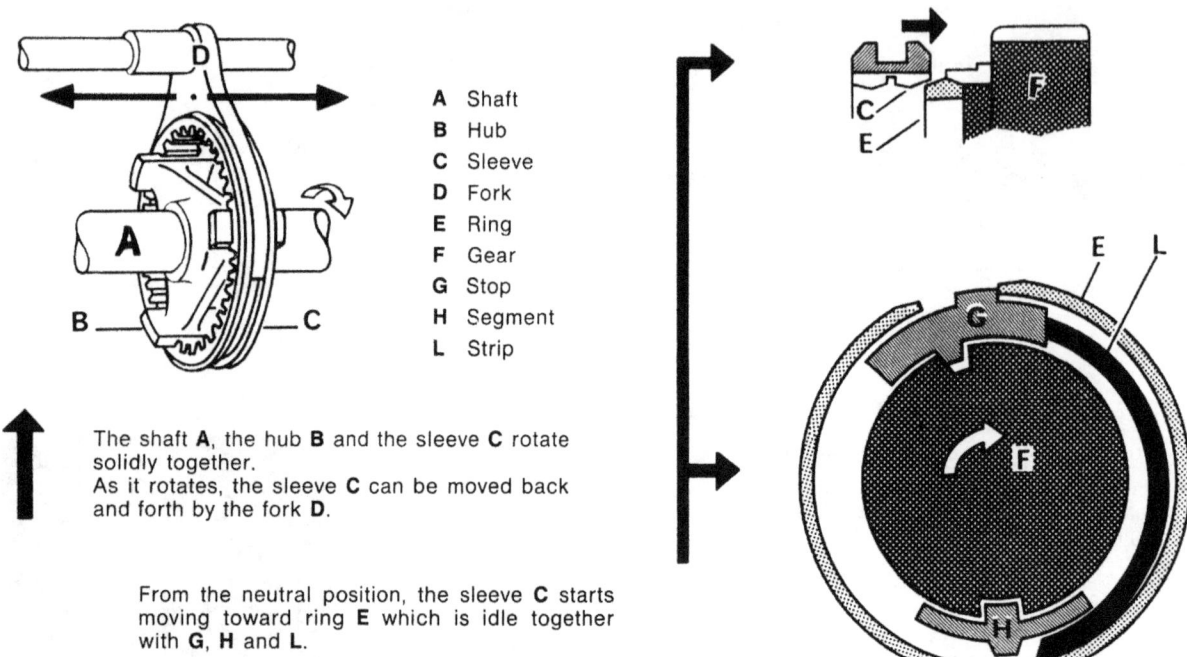

A Shaft
B Hub
C Sleeve
D Fork
E Ring
F Gear
G Stop
H Segment
L Strip

The shaft **A**, the hub **B** and the sleeve **C** rotate solidly together.
As it rotates, the sleeve **C** can be moved back and forth by the fork **D**.

From the neutral position, the sleeve **C** starts moving toward ring **E** which is idle together with **G**, **H** and **L**.

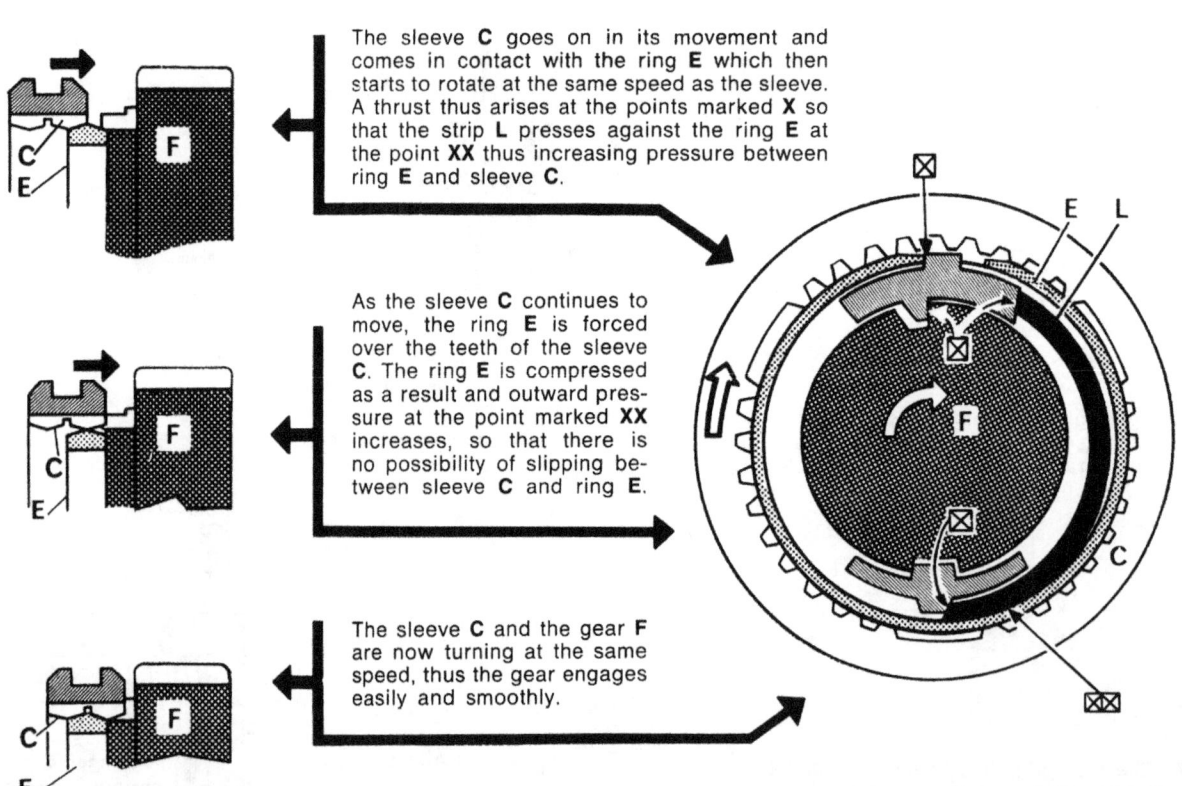

The sleeve **C** goes on in its movement and comes in contact with the ring **E** which then starts to rotate at the same speed as the sleeve. A thrust thus arises at the points marked **X** so that the strip **L** presses against the ring **E** at the point **XX** thus increasing pressure between ring **E** and sleeve **C**.

As the sleeve **C** continues to move, the ring **E** is forced over the teeth of the sleeve **C**. The ring **E** is compressed as a result and outward pressure at the point marked **XX** increases, so that there is no possibility of slipping between sleeve **C** and ring **E**.

The sleeve **C** and the gear **F** are now turning at the same speed, thus the gear engages easily and smoothly.

GEARBOX

SYNCHROMESH INSPECTION

- Disassemble the synchromesh unit by removing the retainer ring with suitable pliers as shown.

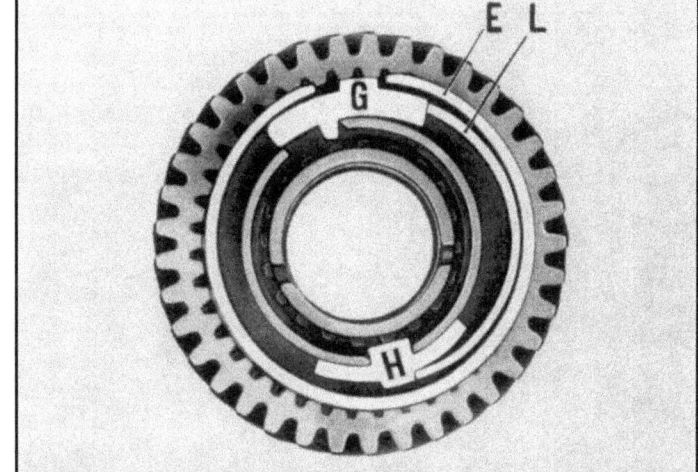

1st gear synchromesh unit

- Check that:
  - the engaging teeth shown no sign of seizing or excessive wear;
  - the synchronizing sleeves slide freely on their hubs.

- Check that all synchronizing elements are in good conditions:
  - the rings **E** must shown no sign of excessive wear;
  - the stop **G** and the segment **H** must show no sign of scoring at the contact points with the strips.

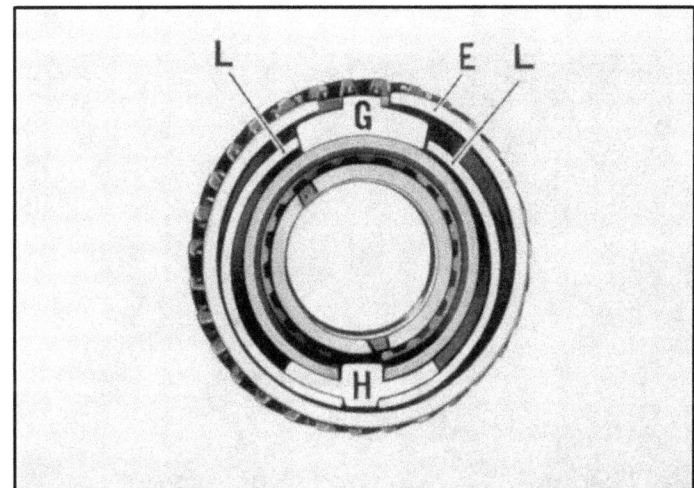

2nd, 3rd, 4th & 5th gear synchromesh units

- Reassemble the synchromesh units, taking care that the stop **G**, the segment **H**, the strips **L**, and the ring **E** are properly positioned.

GEARBOX

CHANGING SILENTBLOK MOUNTING PADS
INSPECTION AND CHECKING

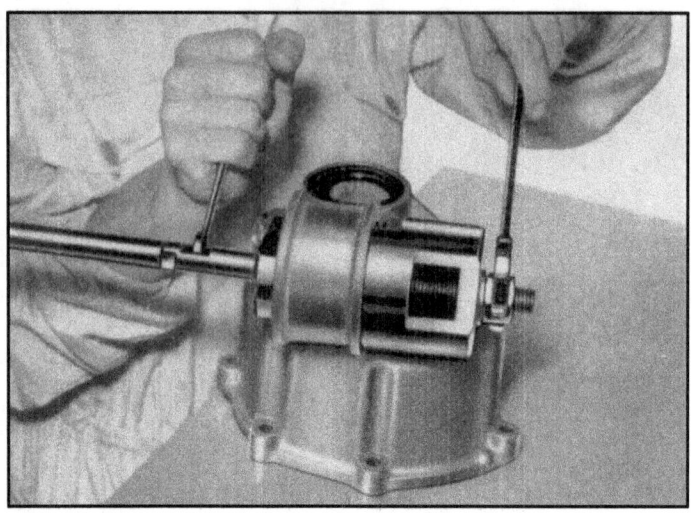

Changing silentblock mounting pads

- If necessary, remove the silentblock mounting pads supporting the engine/gearbox unit with the tool **A.3.0118** (Ref. Tool Bulletin no. 46/1. Use the same tool for refitting the silentblock mounting pad.

Note - Removal and refitting of silentblock can be performed without removing the gearbox from car.
However, it is necessary to carry out the preparatory steps for engine removal in order to enable the operator to tilt the engine gearbox unit and to use the proper special tool.

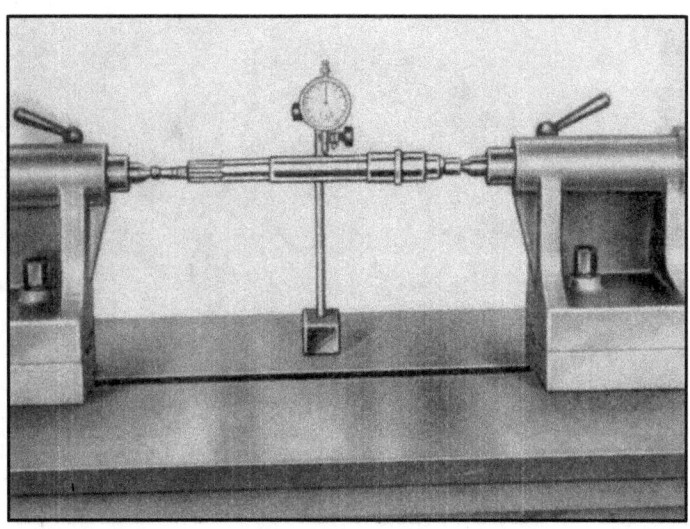

Inspection and checking

- Place the mainshaft between centers and check the run-out with a dial gauge. The run-out should not exceed: **.05 mm** (.002 in.).
  If this is exceeded, straighten the shaft with a press or replace it with a new one.
- Check that bearings show no sign of seizing or excessive wear.

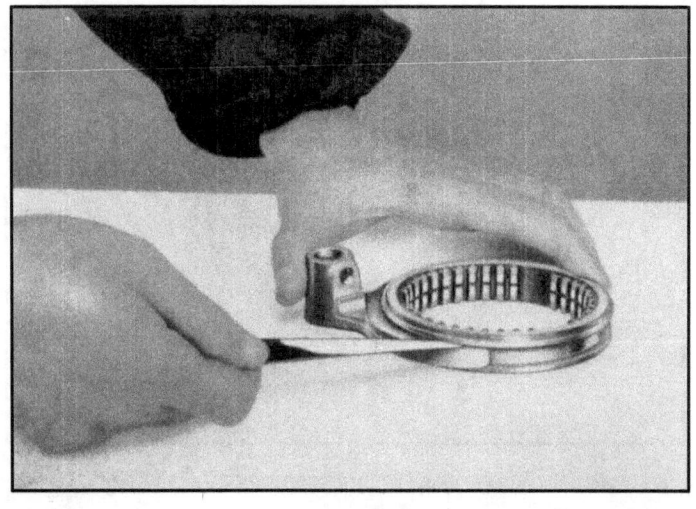

- Check that the working surfaces of the forks and sleeves show no sign of seizing or excessive wear.
- Check that the end play between forks and sleeves is:

  .25 - .50 mm (.0098 - .0197 in.)

  wear limit: .70 mm (.0275 in.).

GEARBOX

INSPECTION AND CHECKING

- Check that interlock rollers slide freely in their grooves and that working surfaces of rollers and striking rods are perfectly smooth.
  If a roller should stick, blend the fillet of the striking rod notch with a file.

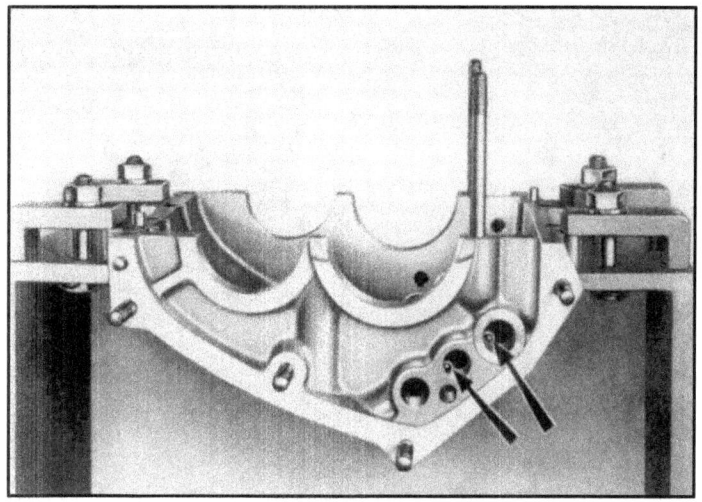

- Check the ball springs for good appearance, and that lengths and load are as prescribed:

  $L = 15.2$ mm (.598 in.)
  $Lc = 10$ mm (.394 in.) under a load
  $C = 4.67 \div 5.505$ kg (10.4 - 12.1 lbs).

- Check the balls and the notches in striking rods for good conditions.

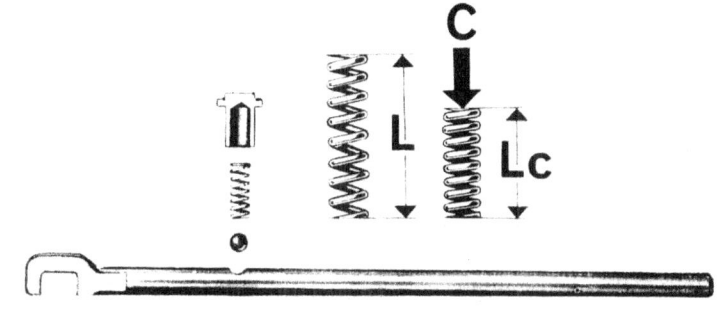

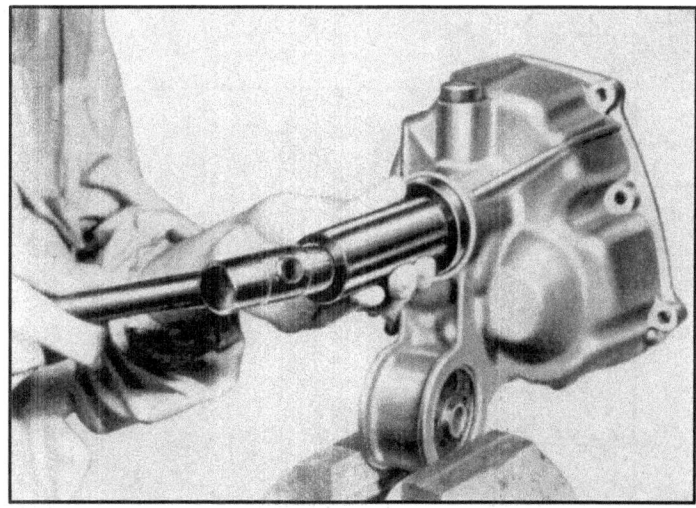

- Inspect the packings in front and rear covers for good appearance.
  However, it is always advisable to replace them. For installing the packings use the tool **A.3.0180**.

GEARBOX

REASSEMBLY

- Place the mainshaft on the tool **A.3.0185** and reverse the order of disassembly according to the following:
  - before assembling, heat the synchronizing hubs to **150° C** (302° F);
  - with the retainer rings fitted, there should be no end play on the direct drive shaft and on **3rd & 4th** speed gear hub; if end play exists, take it up by shiming as required;
  - the end play on mainshaft driven gears with all parts assembled and with the nut locked to a torque of **7.5 - 8 kgm** (54.3 - 57.8 ft-lbs) should not exceed:

    .24 mm (.0095 in.) **for 1st speed gear**

    .21 mm (.0083 in.) **for 2nd & 3rd speed gears**.

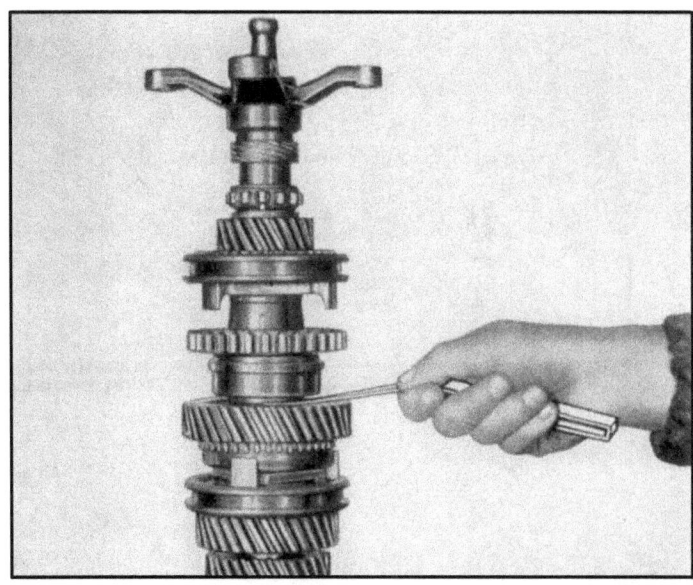

- Tighten the countershaft nuts to a torque of **8 kgm** (57.8 ft-lbs).

- After reassembling the direct drive and mainshaft, proceed as follows:
  - install the flexible coupling yoke on the mainshaft and lock the nut to **12 kgm** (86.8 ft-lbs) with a torque wrench and the tool **A. 5.0127**;
  - fit the group of two shafts into the half-casing and with a vernier caliper check that:

    A = 42 - 42.2 mm (1.654 - 1.661 in.).

If not so, replace the shim between 1st gear bushing and mainshaft bearing inner race accordingly.

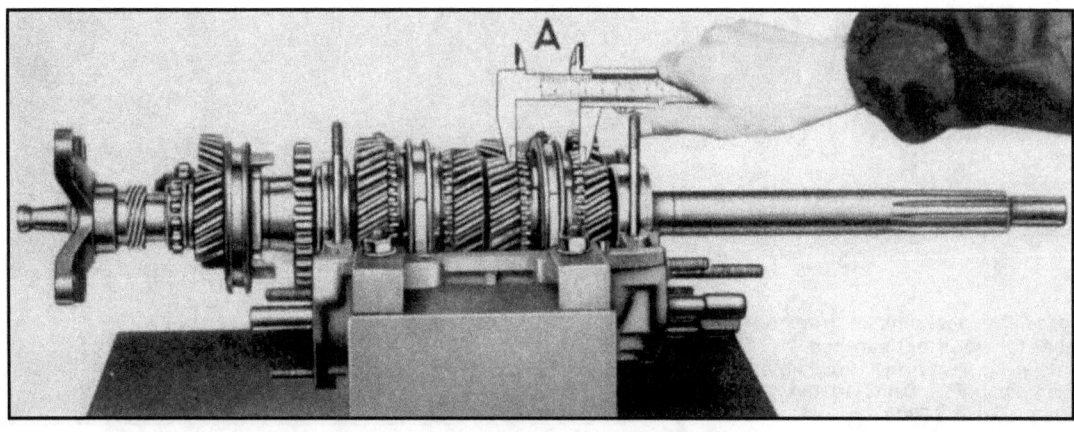

GEARBOX
REASSEMBLY

- Before setting the forks on the respective striking rods make certain that:
  - in neutral position, the sleeves of **3rd & 4th** speed and **1st & 2nd** speed gears are equally spaced between the abutments in the engaging teeth of driven gears; to do this use a vernier caliper;

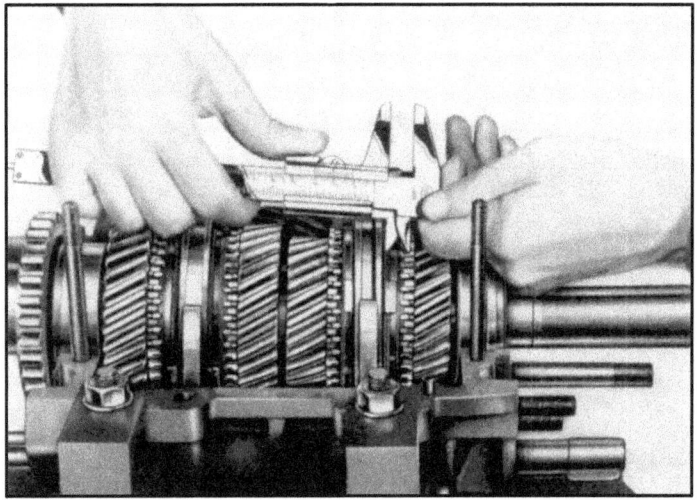

  - in neutral position, the **5th** speed sleeve rear edge is at **10 mm** (.394 in.) from the abutment in the gear engaging teeth.

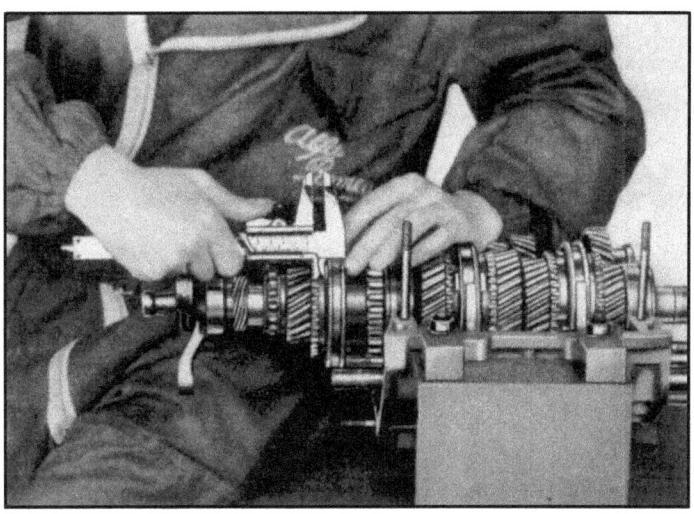

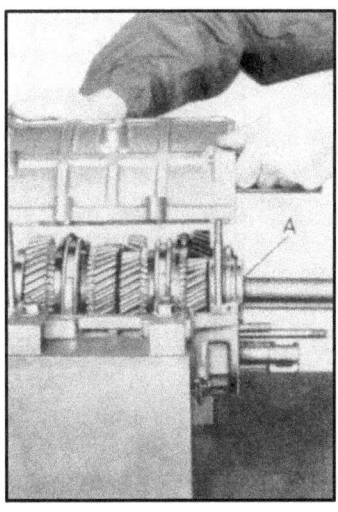

- Before joining the two half-casings together:
  - set the centering ring **A** in its seat;
  - insert the sliding pinion of reverse gear train onto its spindle.
- Install the clutch cover on gearbox. Use the tool **A.3.0114** (Ref. Tool Bulletin no. 24/1) to protect te packing during reassembly.

For floor-mounted gearshift check that, in neutral position, the finger of inner swivel is engaged with the **3rd & 4th** gear striking rod.

GEARBOX

ADJUSTMENT OF CONTROL LINKAGE

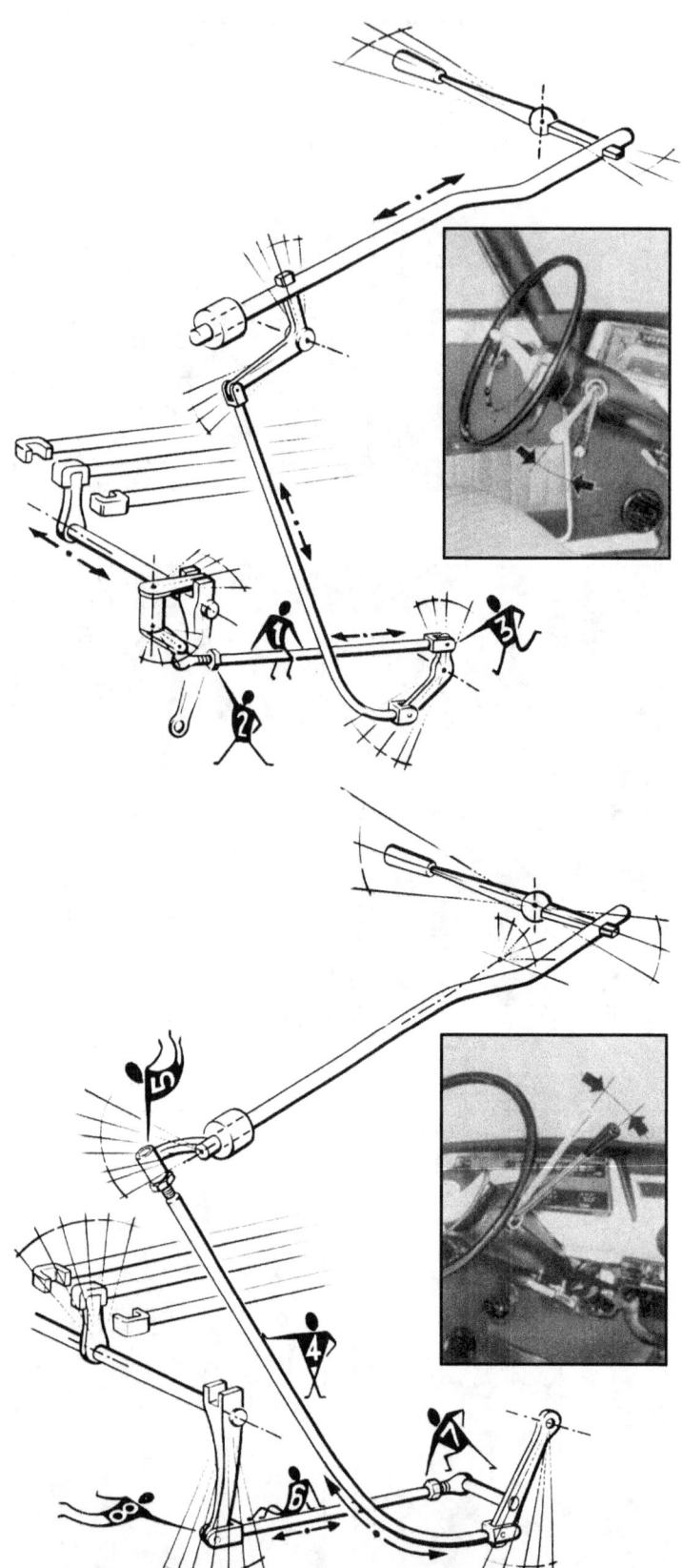

Checking gear selector control

- Engage the **1st** or **2nd** gear and check that the shift lever can be moved further toward the steering wheel.

- Engage **5th** or **reverse** gear and check that the shift lever can be moved further toward the dashboard.

- Check that both the above travels are approximately the same.

- If there is no travel toward the steering wheel or it is shorter than travel toward the dashboard **lengthen** the push-pull rod **1** by acting on the adjuster **2**.

- If on the other hand there is no travel toward the dashboard or it is shorter than travel toward the steering wheel, **shorten** the push-pull rod **1** by acting on the adjuster **2**.

To adjust the rod, free it from the lever **3** by removing the pivot pin.

Checking the gear engaging control

- Engage one of the odd gears (**1st**, **3rd** or **5th**) and check that the shift lever can be moved further after engagement.

- Engage one of the even gears (**2nd** or **4th**) or the **reverse** and check that shift lever can be moved further after engagement.

- Check that both the above travels are approximately the same.

- If there is no travel with odd gears or it is shorter than travel with even gears or reverse, **shorten** the push-pull rod **4** by acting on the adjuster **5**.

- If on the other hand there is no travel with even gears or the **reverse**, or it is shorter than travel with odd gears, **lengthen** the rod **4** by acting on the adjuster **5**.

If the correct travel cannot be obtained by the above adjustments, adjust the lower push-pul rod **6** by means of the adjuster **7**. To adjust this rod, detach it from the lever **8** by removing the pivot pin.

SPECIAL INSTRUCTIONS FOR
GIULIA T. I. SUPER
GIULIA SPRINT G. T.

The following pages deal with the special features regarding the GIULIA TI SUPER and GIULIA SPRINT GT models. For items not covered here refer to GIULIA TI model.

GIULIA T. I. SUPER

TECHNICAL FEATURES

Engine		
	Number and layout of cylinders	4 in line
	Bore and stroke	78 x 82 mm
	Total displacement	1570 cc
	Maximum power at 6,500 rpm HP	112 DIN / 129 SAE

Steering gear	Recirculating ball or worm-and-roller type	
Chassis		
	Wheel track front	1310 mm
	Wheel track rear	1270 mm
	Wheel base	2510 mm
	Minimum turning circle	10900 mm
	Overall length	4115 mm
	Overall width	1560 mm
	Overall height	1430 mm
	Dry weight	910 kg
	Number of seats	4
	Tyres (Pirelli Cinturato HS)	155-15

Inflation pressures with cold tyres			FRONT	REAR
	touring riding with only short burst of speed	with LOW load	1.7 kg/cm² (24.1 psi)	1.7 kg/cm² (24.1 psi)
		with FULL load	1.9 kg/cm² (27 psi)	1.9 kg/cm² (27 psi)
	continuous top speed on HIGHWAYS	with LOW load	2.0 kg/cm² (28.4 psi)	2.2 kg/cm² (31.3 psi)
		with FULL load	2.2 kg/cm² (31.3 psi)	2.2 kg/cm² (31.3 psi)

Performance after running-in (maximum speeds) with 41 : 8 final drive	km/h	mph		km/h	mph
1st	44	27	4th	146	91
2nd	73	45	5th	over 185	115
3rd	108	67	Reverse	48	30

The performances shown are intended for use in ambient conditions as found in center Europe.

GIULIA T. I. SUPER

IGNITION

Checking LODGE RL 47 plugs

- Earth the centre electrode of the plug by means of a screwdriver. If the plug sparked properly, now the engine will slow down.

- WARNING: do not disconnect the cables from the plugs with the engine running or the distributor capacitor may be damaged.

- Remove any defective plugs and clean them with a wire brush.

- Reset the electrode gaps:

  D = .38 - .46 mm (.015 - .018 in.).

- Tighten the plugs with a torque wrench and tool **A.5.0115**, at a torque of **2.5 - 3.5 kgm** (18.1 - 25.3 ft. lbs) when cold, after smearing the threads with graphite grease.

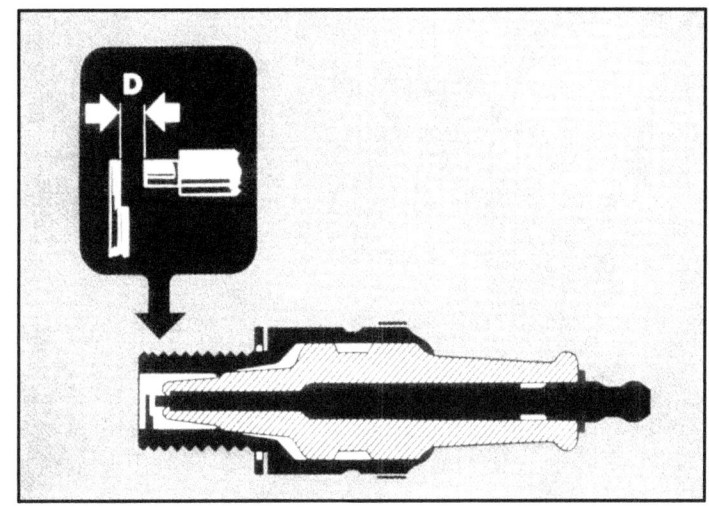

Distributor BOSCH JF 4

This distributor is fitted with the centrifugal advance governor.

- Check with a feeler gauge the gap between the points:

  S = .35 - .40 mm (.0138 - .0157 in.).

- If the points are corroded, smooth them out with a small file and then wash them in petrol.

- Adjust the gap to the correct value by means of the adjusting screw **2** (use a screwdriver and feeler gauge).

- Lubricate by introducing a few drops of oil into the oiler **3** and saturate the felt **1**.

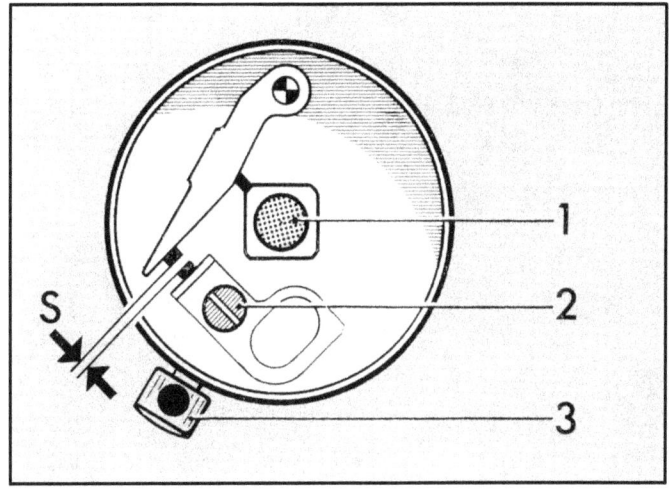

Timing check

- The timing check should be carried out as indicated on page 11.

  Check the values of ignition advance:

  Fixed advance = **5° ± 2° before TDC**

  Maximum advance = **46° ± 3° at 5000 rpm**.

  If the maximum advance is outside these limits, alter the fixed advance, as it is preferable to have the advance exactly right at the higher engine speeds.

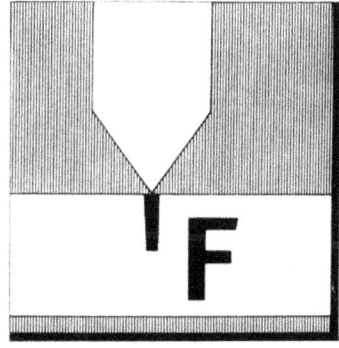

F = Fixed advance reference mark on the drive pulley.

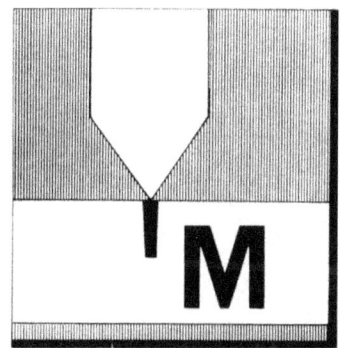

M = Maximum advance reference mark on the drive pulley.

GIULIA T.I. SUPER

ELECTRIC FUEL PUMP

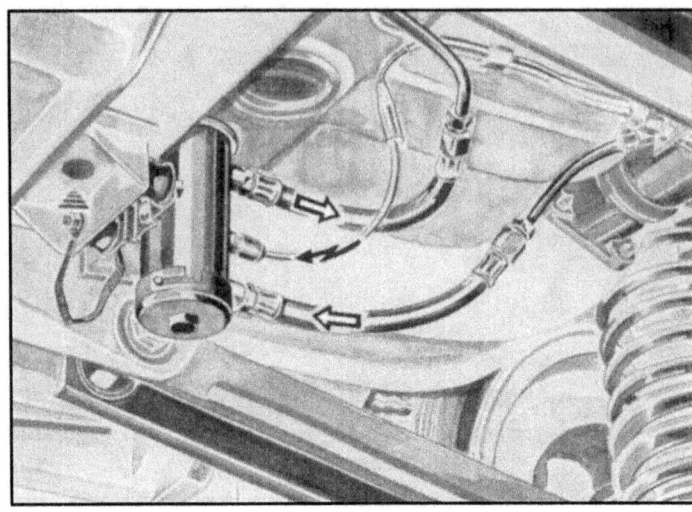

- The Bendix electric fuel pump is located under the floorboards.
- To remove the fuel pump from the car proceed as follows:
  - remove the connectors to the inlet and delivery pipes;
  - disconnect the electrical cable;
  - remove the pump by unscrewing the nuts securing it to the body.

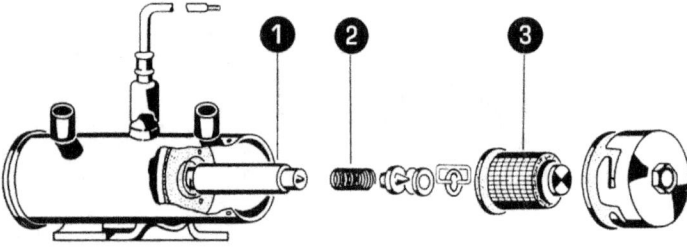

Inspection and checking

- Remove the pump cover and disassemble the pump into its component parts.
- Check:
  1 that the pump plunger is not worn or scored;
  2 that the plunger return spring is in good condition;
  • that the gaskets are in good condition;
  3 that the petrol filter is efficient.
- Carefully clean the parts with petrol and dry with compressed air.

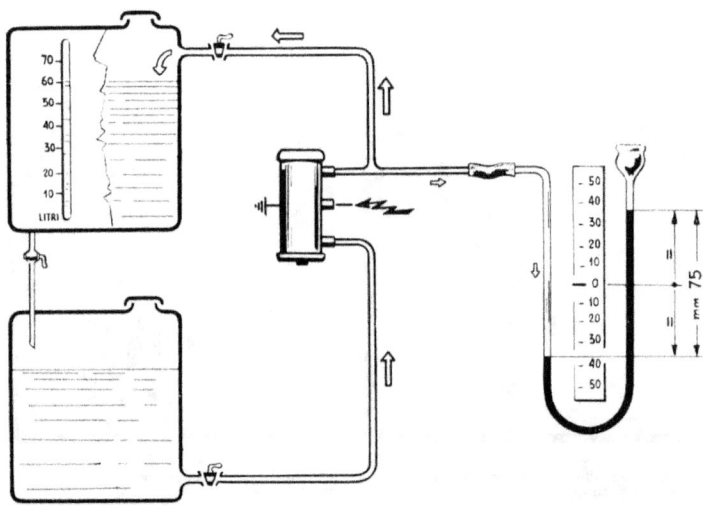

- Reassemble the pump.
- Set up the pump on a suitable test bench and check the following:

  Outlet pressure = **75 mm Hg** (1.5 psi)

  Delivery = **60 - 70 lt/h**
  (13.2 - 15.4 gph GB)
  (15.9 - 18.5 gph US).

- If these requirements are not met, replace the pump by a new one.

Refitting

- Refit the pump to the car, checking that:
  - the feed and ground connections to the pump are correct;
  - there are no air locks in the pipes or connectors;
  - the pipes are not buckled or obstructed.

GIULIA T. I. SUPER

WEBER 45 DCOE 14 CARBURETTOR

Removal from the engine

- Remove:
  - the air intake cover from the carburettor; first remove the air intake tube clamps;
  - the air intake box **5** from the carburettor;
  - the choke wire **2** from the carburettor body;
  - the throttle control **4** from the carburettor body;
  - the petrol feed pipe **3**;
  - the nuts **1** from the studs which fix the carburettor body to the intake manifold.

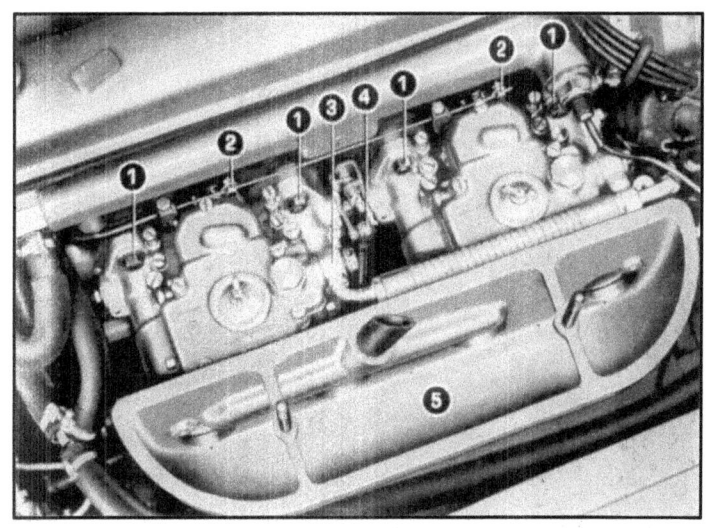

Dismantling

- Remove:
  - the cover from the carburettor and disassemble the petrol filter gauze, the float, the needle valve, the gasket.

Warning: lift off the cover very carefully so as not to distort the float.

- Remove:

  1 the idling jet holder and its jet;

  2 the main jet;

  3 the inlet valve from the acceleration pump (screw plugs, ball seats and balls);

  4 the acceleration pump delivery valve;

  5 the acceleration pump jet;

  6 the choke jet;

  7 the inspection screws from the steady acceleration port trap;

  8 the idling mixture adjusting screw;

  9 the choke assembly.

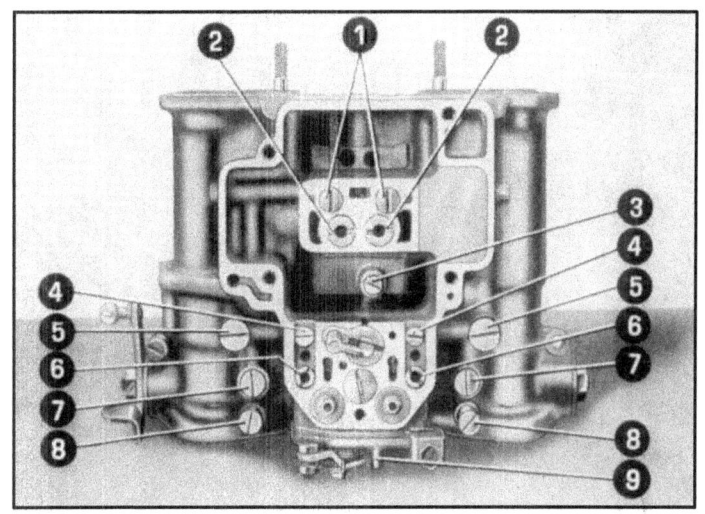

- Remove:
  - the acceleration pump **10**, after detaching the spring plate **11** from its seat on the body by means of a screwdriver;
  - the choke valves **12** with their springs and spring seats after releasing the circlips from the body.

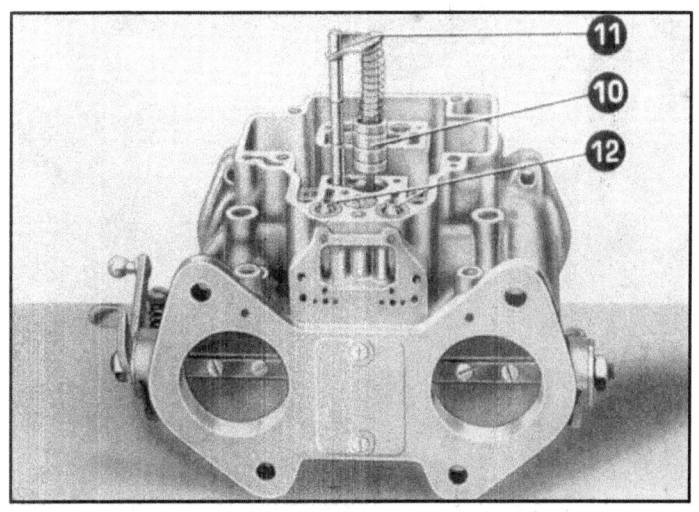

GIULIA T.I. SUPER
WEBER 45 DCOE 14 CARBURETTOR

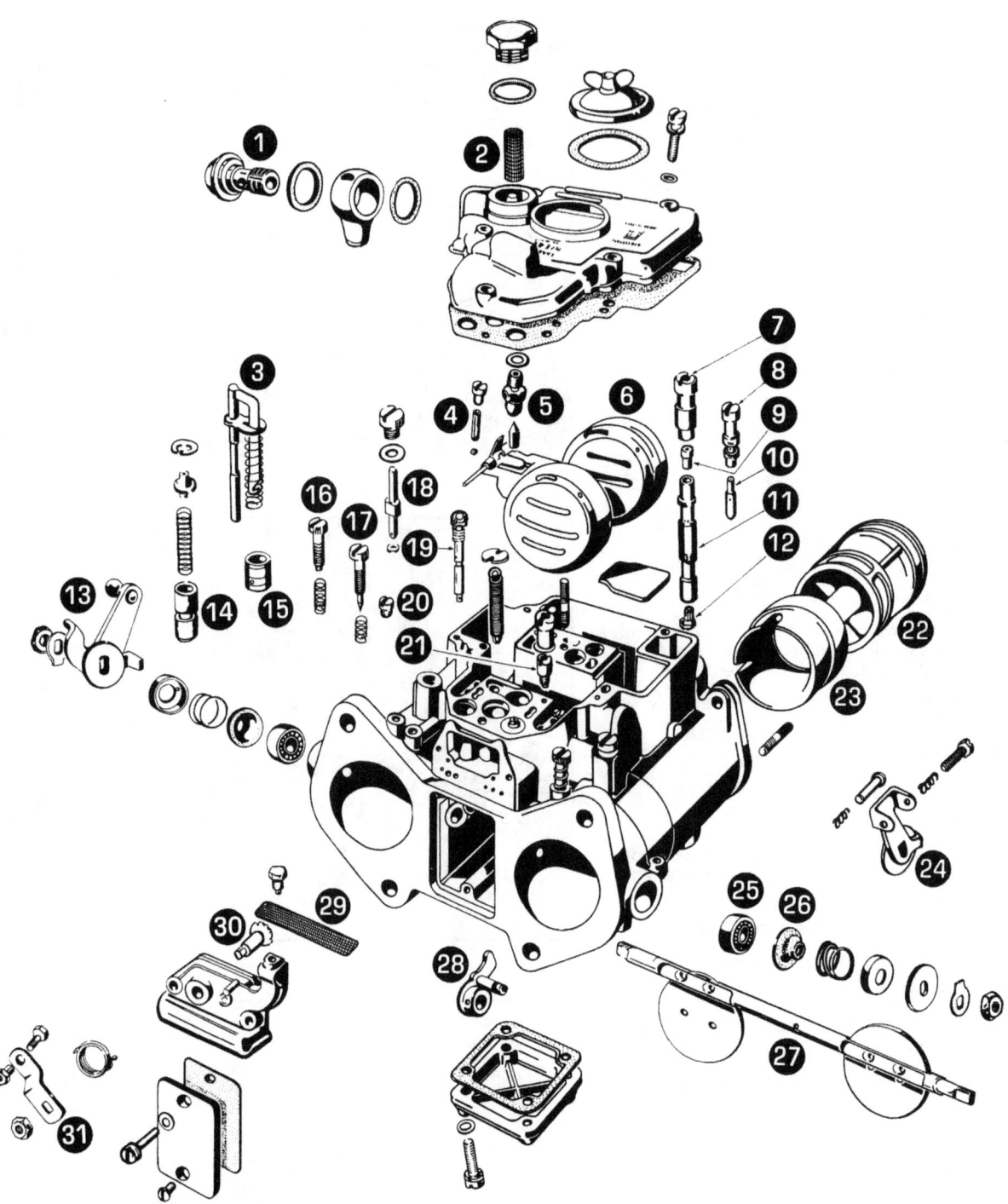

GIULIA T.I. SUPER

WEBER 45 DCOE 14 CARBURETTOR

1 Petrol inlet connector
2 Filter gauze
3 Acceleration pump control rod
4 Acceleration delivery valve
5 Needle valve
6 Float
7 Mixture tube holder
8 Idler jet holder
9 Air restrictor jet
10 Idler jet
11 Mixture tube
12 Main jet
13 Throttle control lever (rear carburettor)
14 Choke valve
15 Acceleration pump plunger
16 Throttle adjusting screw (rear carburettor)
17 Idling mixture adjusting screw
18 Acceleration pump jet
19 Choke jet
20 Steady acceleration port inspection screw
21 Inlet and outlet valve
22 Mixer
23 Venturi
24 Throttle control lever (front carburettor)
25 Ball bearing
26 Dust cover
27 Spindle with throttle valves
28 Acceleration pump control lever
29 Choke air filter gauze
30 Toothed quadrant for choke valve
31 Choke control lever

WEBER 45 DCOE 14 CARBURETTOR

GIULIA T.I. SUPER

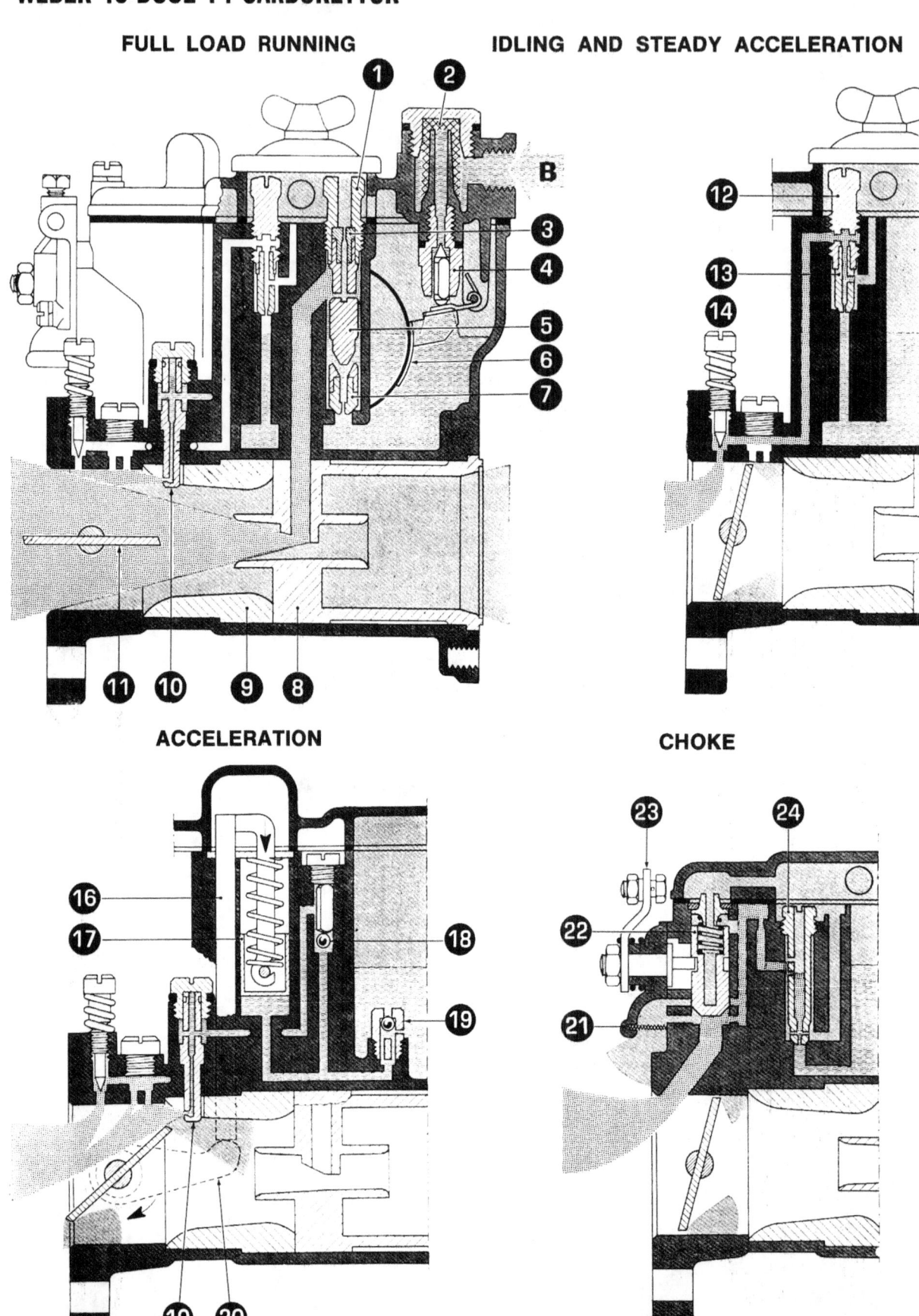

101A
GIULIA T.I. SUPER
WEBER 45 DCOE 14 CARBURETTOR

IDLING AND STEADY ACCELERATION

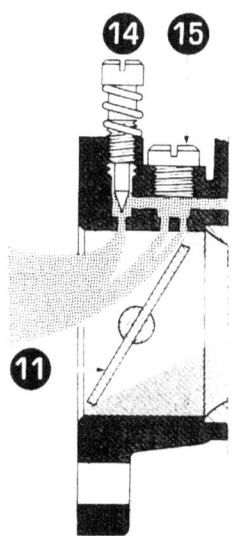

CHOKE

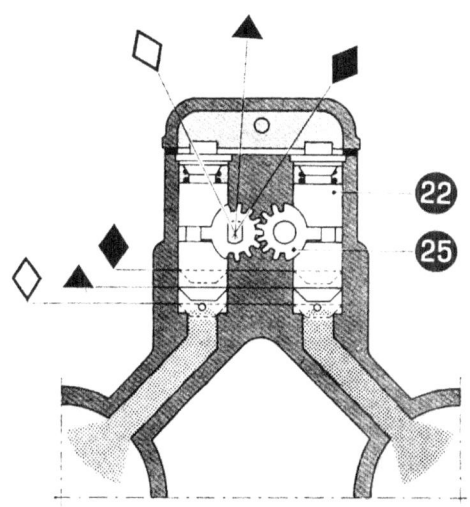

- **B** Petrol intake
- **1** Mixture tube holder
- **2** Filter gauze
- **3** Air restrictor
- **4** Needle valve
- **5** Mixture tube
- **6** Float
- **7** Main jet
- **8** Mixer
- **9** Venturi
- **10** Acceleration pump jet
- **11** Throttle valve
- **12** Idler jet holder
- **13** Idler jet
- **14** Idling mixture adjusting screw
- **15** Steady acceleration port inspection screw
- **16** Acceleration pump control rod
- **17** Acceleratiton pump plunger
- **18** Delivery ball valve
- **19** Inlet and outlet valve
- **20** Pump control lever
- **21** Choke air filter gauze
- **22** Choke valve
- **23** Choke control lever
- **24** Choke jet
- **25** Toothed quadrant for choke valve

Position of valve plunger **22** and choke control lever **23**:

 Choke in

 Choke partly in

 Choke out

GIULIA T. I. SUPER

WEBER 45 DCOE 14 CARBURETTOR

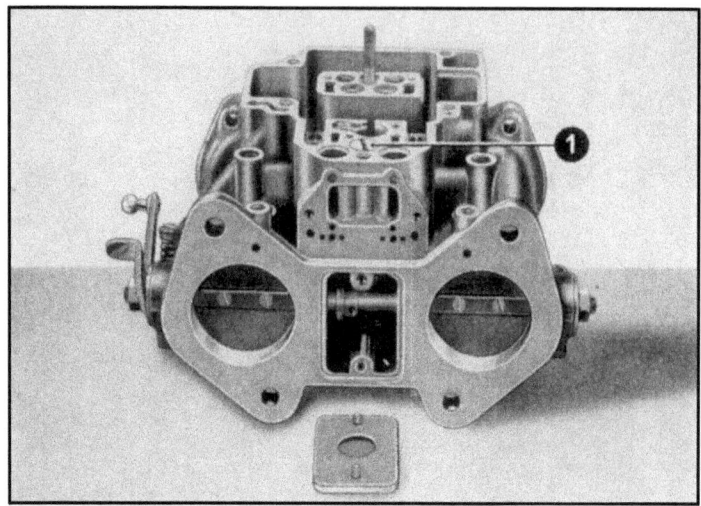

Unless absolutely necessary, it is inadvisable to remove the throttle valve spindle.

If this operation has to be performed:

- remove the small cover as shown;
- disengage the spindle return spring after removing the retaining plate **1**;

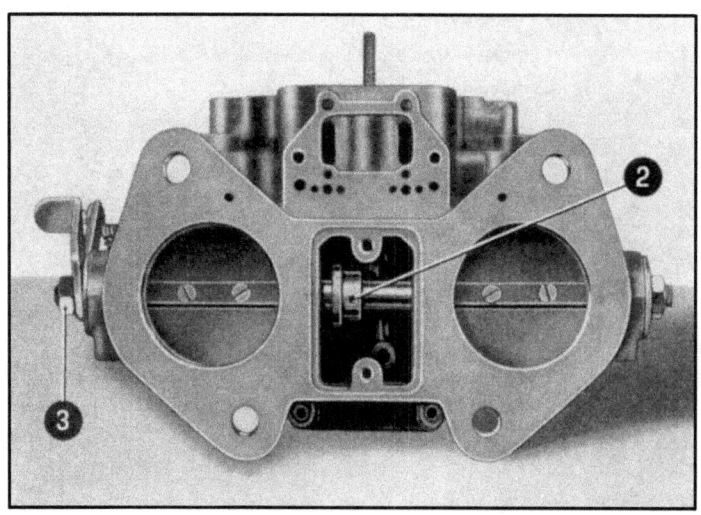

- mark the positions of the throttle valves with respect to the spindle and of the spindle to the body of the carburettor;
- detach the throttle valves from the spindle;
- remove the locking pin **2** from the pump control lever;
- unscrew the nut **3** and withdraw from the spindle the control lever with its shim, the spring retaining cover, the spring and the dust cover;
- withdraw the spindle from the opposite side, at the same time removing the acceleration pump control lever, the spring and the retaining cover.

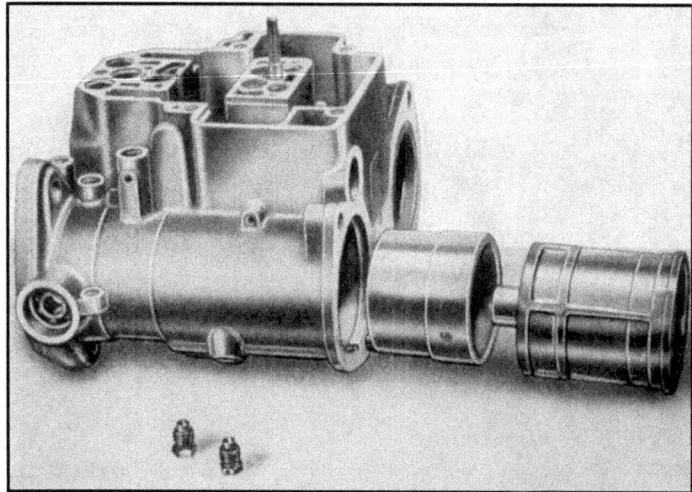

- Remove the end cover from the float chamber, situated in the lower part of the carburettor.
- Remove the mixers and the venturis after having loosened the setscrews.

GIULIA T.I. SUPER

WEBER 45 DCOE 14 CARBURETTOR

Cleaning

- Very carefully wash with petrol and clean with compressed air all the parts dismantled, being careful to remove all impurities which may have been deposited in the filter trap bottom, the float chamber bottom, in the passages or in the calibrated jet bores, the air restrictors (air calibrators), the mixture tubes, the idling mixture passages, steady acceleration ports, etc.

Warning: when cleaning jets and calibrated bores in general, **never use metal needles or other tools** which may change the diameters of the bores.

Inspection and checking

- Check that the numbers stamped on the jets are in agreement with those given in the table.

Choke

1 jet	65

Idling

2 jet holder	—
3 jet	55
• axial hole	220
• air calibrator hole	120

Acceleration

4 screw plug	—
5 pump jet	50

Running

6 main jet holder	—
7 air calibrator	180
8 mixture tube (8 radial holes)	100
9 main jet summer	115
winter	120
10 Venturi	30.00 mm

Note - The diffusing jets, air calibrator jets (or restrictors), etc. are marked in the positions shown in the figures.

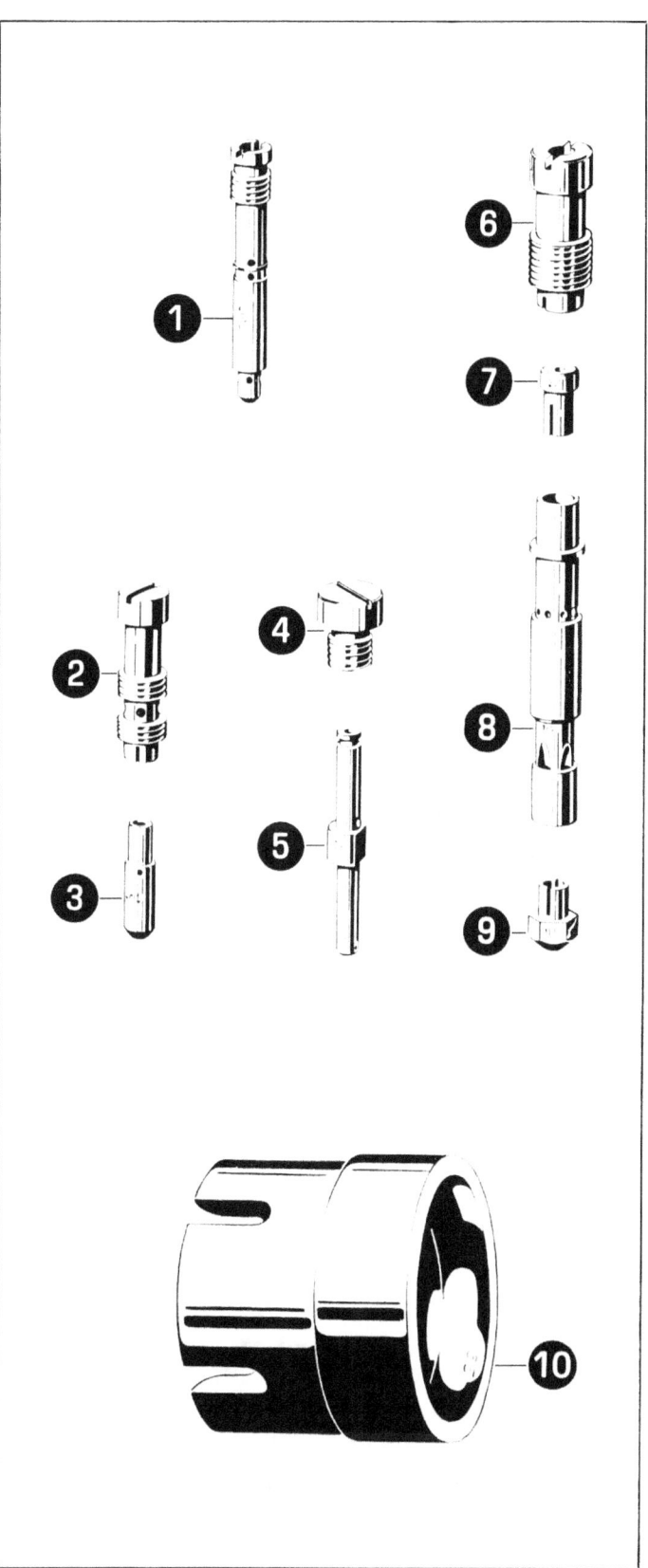

GIULIA T.I. SUPER

WEBER 45 DCOE 14 CARBURETTOR

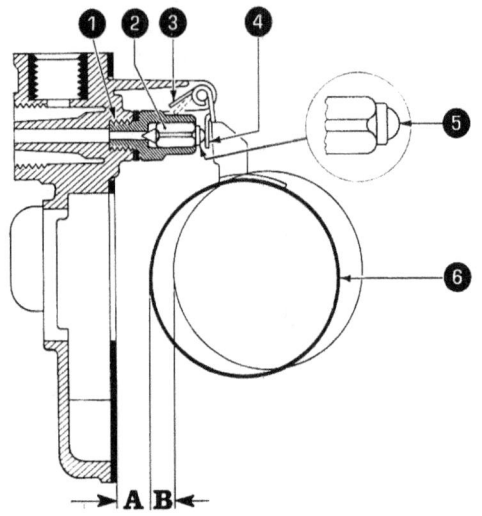

The float level should be set by following the instructions below:

- Make sure that the float is of the correct weight (**26 grs** - .9 oz.), that it is not leaking anywhere and is not dented, and that it can rotate freely about the pivot pin.

  The weight of the float cannot be altered; consequently, haphazard repairs (tinning, etc.) can impair the proper operation of the float itself.

- Check that the needle valve **1** is well screwed into the seating and that the spring loaded ball **5**, part of the needle **2**, is not jammed.

- Hold the carburettor cover in a vertical position as shown in the figure so that the float **6** does not depress the ball **5** mounted on the needle **2**.

  With the cover vertical and the float tongue **4** in light contact with the needle ball, the two floats should be at a distance from the cover joining surface of **A = 8.5 mm** (.33 in.) with the gasket fitted and well stuck to the cover.

- When the level has been set, check that the travel **B** of the float is **6.5 mm** (.26 in.) adjusting if necessary the position of the float pivot tail **3**.

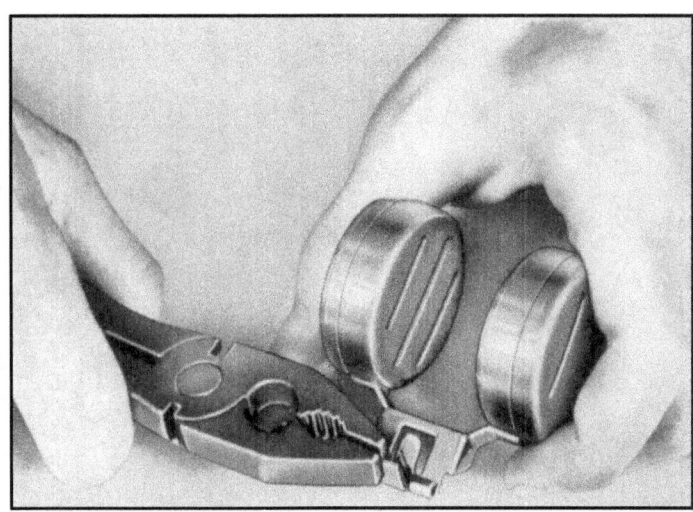

- If the float position is not correct, alter the position of the float tongue itself to achieve the correct level, making sure that the tongue remains at right angle to the needle centerline and that its contact surface has no notches which might impede the free movement of the needle.

- Then fit the carburettor cover and check that the float can move freely without friction on the walls of the float chamber.

GIULIA T. I. SUPER

WEBER 45 DCOE 14 CARBURETTOR

PRECAUTION

The float level should be checked whenever the float or the needle valve has been changed. In the latter case it is also advisable to change the gasket.

The adjustment described above will correspond to a fuel level, from the upper face of the float chamber, of **29 ± .5 mm** (1.14 ± .02 in.).

This level can be checked as shown on page 108.

- Check that the joining surfaces or the cover itself and on the carburettor body are in good condition. If necessary, where it is possible to grind without impairing the values which are the basis of the calibration of the carburettor, (petrol level with respect to the positions of the jets), remove the minimum necessary amount of material.

Note - When grinding is finished the whole of the carburettor must be carefully cleaned to remove all traces of dust which may have been deposited in the channels, traps, etc. during the work.

- Check the condition of all seals.

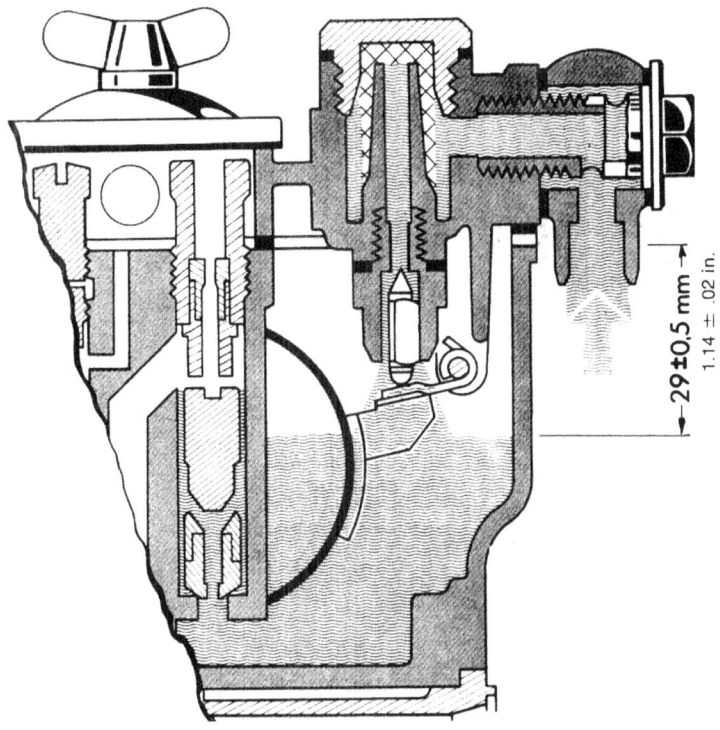

Reassembling the carburettor

The carburettor should be reassembled in reverse order of disassembly, bearing in mind the following points:

- Lubricate the ball bearings supporting the throttle valve spindle with bearing grease.

- Before the spindle is fitted to the body and to avoid distortion of the spindle while tightening the nut at the end opposite to the control lever, it is advisable to tighten this nut in a vice fitted with lead jaws, gripping the spindle itself close to the nut to avoid damaging the milled seatings for the throttle valves.

- The reference marks made on the throttle valves and on the spindle must coincide.

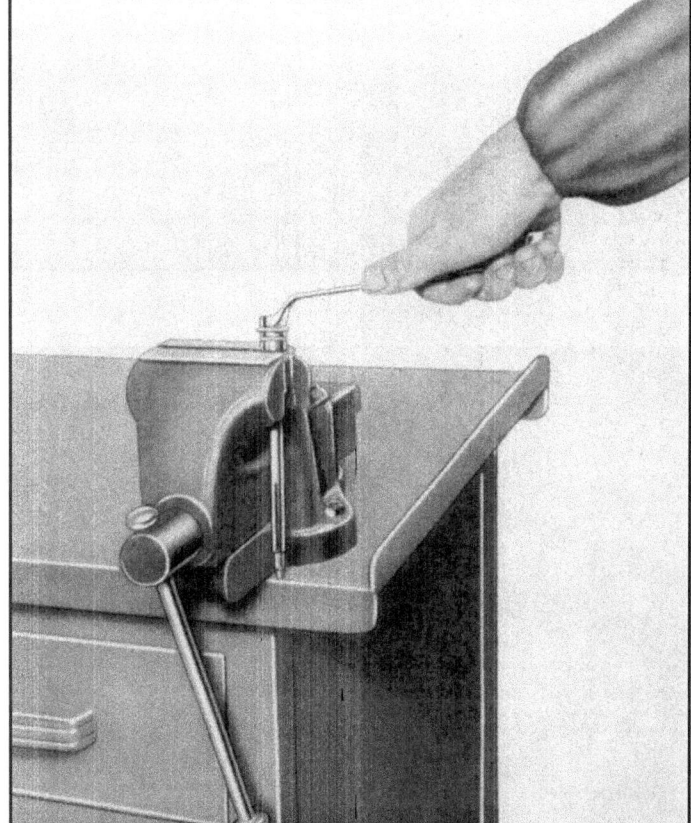

GIULIA T.I. SUPER

WEBER 45 DCOE 14 CARBURETTOR

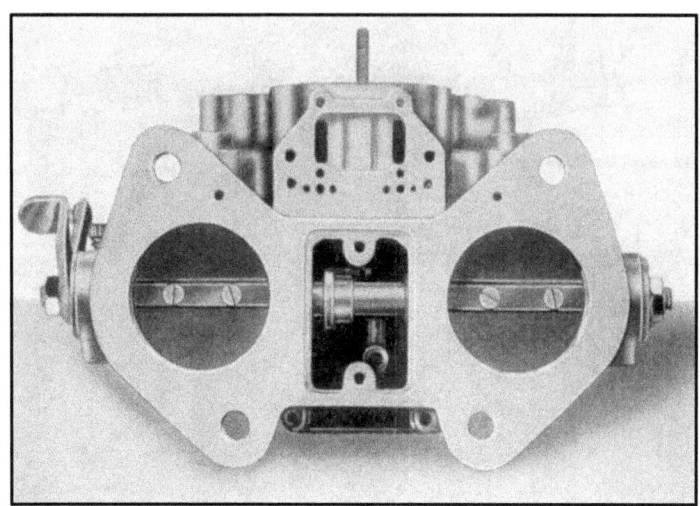

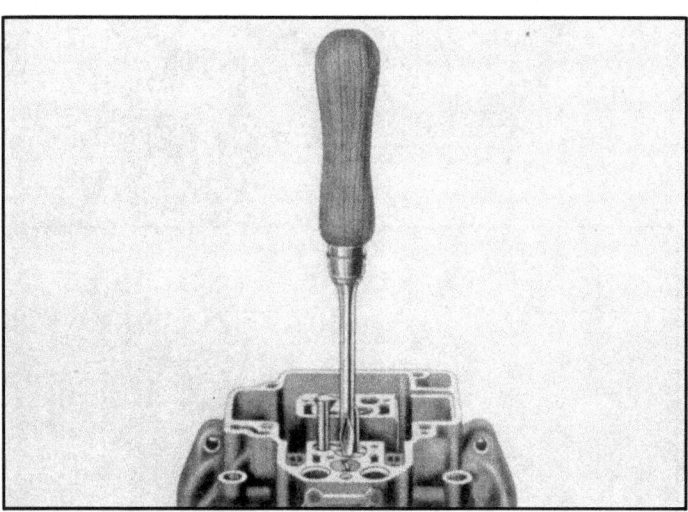

- Before fitting the throttle valves to the spindle, fully unscrew the opening adjustin screws.

- Fit, centre and secure one throttle at a time, taking particular care with the centring so as to obtain a proper fit with the throttles in contact with the bores of the barrels. With a correctly centred throttle, if it is looked at in back light, no light should be seen around the valve. Some light may be tolerated in the areas close to the spindle.

  When the first valve has been fitted, the second should be fitted in the same way.

  Before fitting the return spring, check that the spindle complete with valves rotates freely.

- To refit the acceleration pump on the body press on the spring plate with a screwdriver so as to insert the plate into its proper groove on the body.

- To refit the two plungers of the choke assembly, press with a screwdriver on the retainer rings so as to force them into their respective grooves on the body.

- The jet assemblies must be firmly secured into the carburettor.

- The idling mixture adjusting screws should never be screwed fully home to avoid breaking the needle seat.

- In refitting to the carburettor the cover complete with float, make sure that the float itself is well clear from the float chamber walls.

- When reassembly is complete, check the tightness of all seals to ensure that there will be no leakage.

Provisional idling adjustment

Before refitting the carburettor to the engine carry out a provisional adjustment of the adjusting screws in the following manner:

1 Idling mixture adjusting screw: two turns from the closed position.

2 Throttle opening adjusting screw: half a turn from the point of contact.

GIULIA T. I. SUPER

WEBER 45 DCOE 14 CARBURETTOR

Refitting the carburettors to the engine

When refitting the carburettors to the engine **make sure that there are no defects in the joints between the carburettor and the engine**, so as to prevent seepage of air downstream the carburettors.

Any such seepage would cause irregular carburetion and consequent malfunctioning of the engine.

Alignment of throttles, idling adjustment and adjustment of control linkage.

To obtain good matching of the two carburettors and correct adjustment of the control linkage, proceed as follows:

a) **Alignment of throttles:**

- disconnect the control linkage **T** from the carburettors;

- almost fully loosen the screws **F** and **S** until the throttle control lever stop is just making contact against the boss;

- then screw in the screw **S** until contact is made, so that the throttles in the two carburettors are aligned;

- screw in screw **F** until it makes contact, then screw it in a further half turn.

b) **Idling speed adjustment**

When the throttles have been aligned and still with the control linkage disconnected:

- check that the spark plugs and the ignition system are in good order;

- unscrew the screws **M about one turn** from the closed position;

- start the engine and warm it up;

- operate the throttles a few times, making sure that they function without sticking;

- screw in progressively the screws **M** until the engine runs smoothly;

- unscrew the screw **F** very slowly until the engine is idling at 600 to 700 rpm.

If the engine starts to race, tighten the screws **M** slightly. **On no account should these screws be screwed right down.**

GIULIA T.I. SUPER

WEBER 45 DCOE 14 CARBURETTOR

Adjustment of control linkage

When the throttles have been aligned and the idling adjusted, proceed with the adjustment of the carburettor control linkage.
For this purpose the adjustable rod should have been reconnected to the throttle control lever. Having slackened the locknut on the rod, adjust rod length so that there is a slight preload on the lever itself when the pedal is in the rest position.

Checking the fuel level in the float chambers with the carburettors on the car

If it is necessary to carry out this check, level the car and for each carburettor carry out the following operations:

- Remove the jet inspection cover and both main jets.

- By means of a syringe, draw off from the wells a quantity of petrol sufficient to cause a substantial lowering of the level.

- Refit the cover and run the engine at idling speed for some seconds.

- Again remove the cover and measure with a gauge the fuel level with respect to the upper face of the float chamber. The level should be **29 ± .5 mm** (1.14 ± .02 in.). If this is not so, adjust the float as directed on page 104 and check the tightness of the needle valve, renewing it if there is any leak.

GIULIA T. I. SUPER

VALVE CLEARANCES
TIMING CHECK

Checking valve clearances

- Check that the valve clearances measured with the engine cold and at the dwell arc of the cams, is within the limits given in the diagram.

Timing check

- With the valve clearances as specified. check the opening and closing angles of the valves as directed on pp. 48 et seq.

- This check is carried out by observing that for a lift of the intake and exhaust valves of **.05 mm** (.002 in.) the readings on the protractor correspond to the **actual values** given in the diagram.

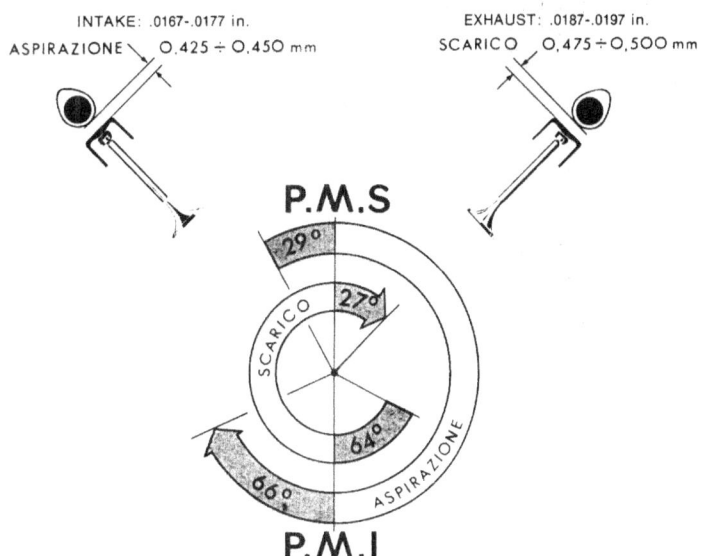

Scarico = Exhaust
Aspirazione = Intake
PMS = TDC
PMI = BDC

DIMENSIONS AND TOLERANCES

Variations with respect to the GIULIA TI:

		BARREL - TO - PISTON FIT				
		CLASS **A** BLUE		CLASS **B** PINK		CLASS **C** GREEN	
		PISTON O.D.	BARREL I.D.	PISTON O.D.	BARREL I.D.	PISTON O.D.	BARREL I.D.
PISTON MAKE	BORGO only	77.910 - 77.920 mm (3.0673 - 3.0677")	77.985 - 77.994 mm (3.0703 - 3.0706")	77.920 - 77.930 mm (3.0677 - 3.0681")	77.995 - 78.004 mm (3.0707 - 3.0710")	77.930 - 77.940 mm (3.0681 - 3.0685")	78.005 - 78.014 mm (3.0711 - 3.0714")

BARREL-TO-PISTON CLEARANCE .065 - .084 mm - wear limit = .15 mm
(.0026 - .0033") (.006")

GIULIA SPRINT G.T.

TECHNICAL FEATURES

Engine		
	Number and layout of cylinders	4 in line
	Bore and stroke	78 x 82 mm
	Total displacement	1570 cc
	Maximum power at 6,000 rpm . . . HP	106 DIN / 122 SAE

Chassis		
	Wheel track — rear	1310 mm
	Wheel track — front	1270 mm
	Wheel base	2350 mm
	Minimum turning circle	10700 mm
	Overall length	4080 mm
	Overal width	1580 mm
	Overall height	1315 mm
	Dry weight	950 kg
	Number of seats	4
	Tyres (Michelin XA - Pirelli cinturato S)	155 x 15

Inflation pressures with cold tyres

			FRONT	REAR
With reduced load and short bursts of maximum speed	MICHELIN		1.7 kg/cm² (24.1 psi)	1.7 kg/cm² (24.1 psi)
	PIRELLI		1.7 kg/cm² (24.1 psi)	1.8 kg/cm² (25.6 psi)
With full load and continuous maximum speed (HIGHWAYS)	MICHELIN		1.9 kg/cm² (27 psi)	1.9 kg/cm² (27 psi)
	PIRELLI		1.8 kg/cm² (25.6 psi)	2.1 kg/cm² (29.8 psi)

Performance after running in (max. speeds) with 41:9 final drive

	km/h	mph		km/h	mph
1st	43	27	4th	142	112
2nd	73	45	5th	over 180	89
3rd	106	66	Reverse	48	30

The maximum speeds indicated should not be exceeded or mechanical damage may result.

The performance given are applicable for use in normal Central European environmental conditions.

Fuel consumption

Per 100 km, (CUNA standard) with full load . . . . . . abt. 9.5 lts
(29.8 mpg GB)
(24.8 mpg US)

GIULIA SPRINT G.T.

IGNITION

Distributor

For inspection and checking the distributor see the GIULIA T.I. Super (page 97).

Timing check

The timing is checked in the manner described on page 11 of the Manual.

Check the ignition advance values:

Static advance: 3° ± 1° before **TDC**

Max. advance: 43° $^{+0°}_{-3°}$ at 5300 rpm.

If the max. advance is greater than or smaller than the specified value, adjust the static advance, as it is preferable to have the advance exact at the high speeds.

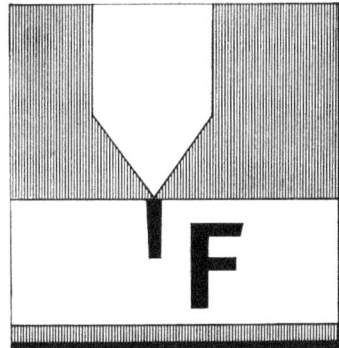

F = Fixed advance reference mark on the drive pulley.

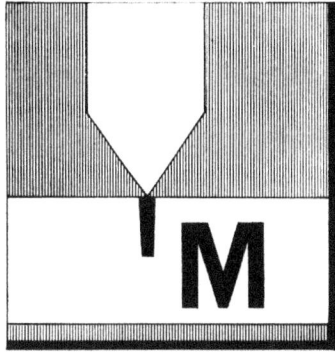

M = Maximum advance reference mark on the drive pulley.

WEBER 40 DCOE 4 CARBURETTOR

- For overhaul and adjustment of the carburettors, see **GIULIA T.I. Super** (page 99).

Adjustment data:

1 Main jets (with 1/8" dia. ball)	127
Main air restrictor jets	220
2 Idling jets	50
axial hole	150
air restrictor jet	120
3 Choke jets F 5	65
4 Acceleration pump jets	35
- Venturis	30.00 mm

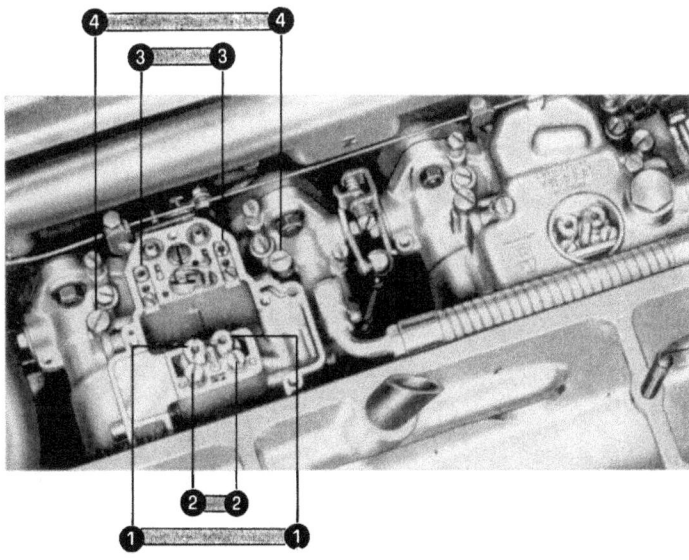

GIULIA SPRINT G.T.

VALVE CLEARANCES
TIMING CHECK

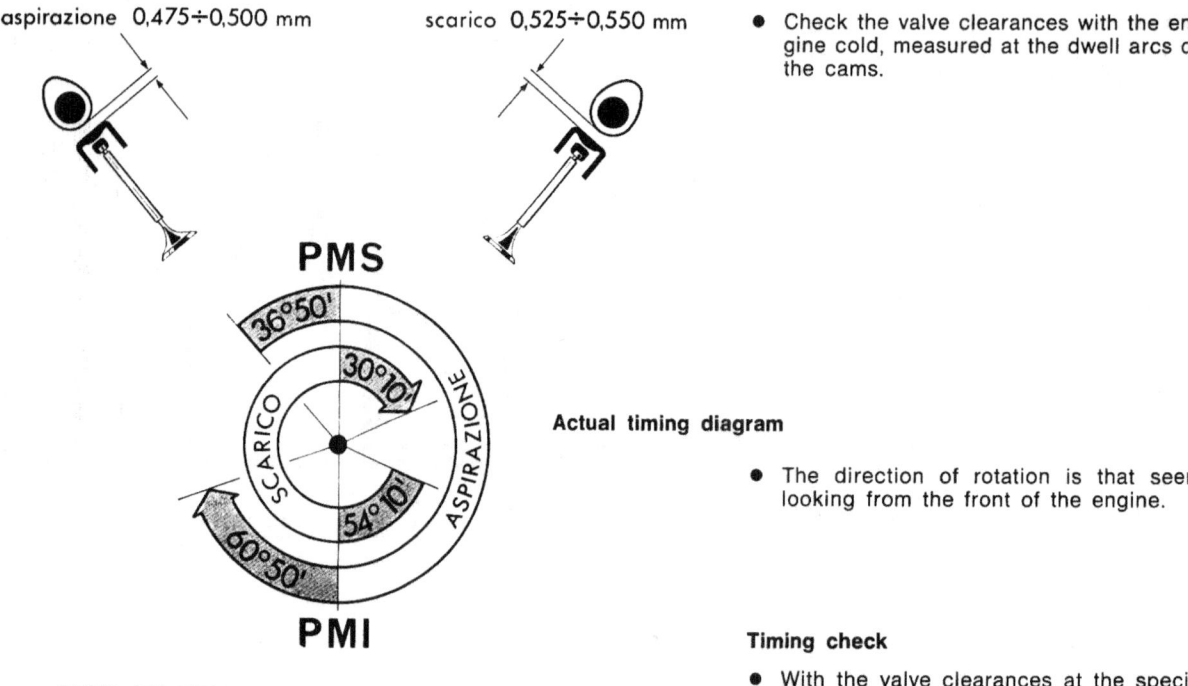

aspirazione 0,475÷0,500 mm
scarico 0,525÷0,550 mm

INTAKE: .0187-.0197 in.
EXHAUST: .0206-.0216 in.

PMS = TDC
PMI = BDC
Aspirazione = Intake
Scarico = Exhaust

- Check the valve clearances with the engine cold, measured at the dwell arcs of the cams.

Actual timing diagram

- The direction of rotation is that seen looking from the front of the engine.

Timing check

- With the valve clearances at the specified values, check the opening and closing angles of the valves in the manner described on pp. 48 etc. The nominal values are given in the following table.

	INTAKE		EXHAUST	
	OPENING	CLOSING	OPENING	CLOSING
VALVE LIFT	.20 mm (.0078 in.)		.15 mm (.0059 in.)	
Angular reading on the protractor fitted on the flywheel	18° 30' before **TDC**	42° 30' after **BDC**	42° 30' before **BDC**	18° 30' after **TDC**
	permissible angular tolerance ± **1° 30'**			

SHOP MANUAL No. 2

PROPELLER SHAFT
REAR AXLE
REAR SUSPENSION

(FACTORY MANUAL)

GIULIA 1300
GIULIA 1300 Ti
GIULIA Ti SUPER
GIULIA SPRINT GT
GIULIA GTC
GIULIA Ti
GIULIA SUPER
GIULIA SPRINT GT VELOCE
SPIDER 1600

CONTENTS

3 Servicing instructions

PROPELLER SHAFT

6 Cutaway view
7 Removal from car - Disassembly
8 Inspection and checking
9 Reassembly
10 Reassembly - Reinstallation

REAR AXLE AND SUSPENSION

Rear axle

12 General
13 Cutaway view
14 In-car repairs
17 Removal
18 Disassembly on bench
19 Inspection and checking
20 Reassembly on bench
27 Reinstallation

Rear suspension

28 Cutaway view
30 Pads & rebound straps - Shock absorbers
32 Reaction trunnion
33 Suspension springs
34 Radius rods

SERVICING INSTRUCTIONS

When disassembling and reassembling always use the correct wrenches, extractors and tools (standard and special) to avoid damage to parts.

To loosen close-fitting steel parts lightly tap with a copper or aluminum mallet; for light alloy parts (covers, housings, etc.) use a wooden or plastic mallet.

When disassembling check that specially coupled parts are stamped with the correct number or reference mark; any original parts (previously replaced) found unmarked should be so stamped.

Components of different assemblies should be kept separate and nuts should be loosely screwed onto their original studs or bolts.

Before washing parts, brush or wipe off the thickest grime (to avoid soiling the solvent in the washing tank), then wash with paraffin or hot water and soda and remove any remaining dirt with compressed air; dry all parts immediately after washing so that they do not rust.

Deformed parts must be trued with the use of a hydraulic press or some other suitable means of applying pressure; hammering reduces mechanical strength and should be strictly avoided.

After parts have been ground or honed, wash them thoroughly and blow the parts with compressed air in order to remove all traces of emery powder.

When reassembling, clean components (particularly after regrinding) with compressed air or a clean dry brush.

When reassembling lubricate all mechanical parts properly (except carbon bushings) to prevent seizing and scoring when the engine is first run.

Use a brush and absolutely clean oil to apply a film of oil to all parts which have to be lubricated on reassembly; the brush, the oil and its container, should be kept completely free from dust and should be used for the above purpose only.

With adhesive paper or clean rags mask out those parts of the engine remained uncovered after disassembling to prevent dust or foreign matter from entering them.

When reassembling, renew all gaskets, oil sealing rings, spring washers, tabwashers, safety plates, locknuts and any components not in perfect condition.

Use always genuine ALFA ROMEO spares.

4

GIULIA 1300
GIULIA 1300 ti

GIULIA TI
GIULIA TI SUPER
GIULIA SUPER

GIULIA SPRINT GT
GIULIA SPRINT GT VELOCE

GIULIA GTC

SPIDER 1600

PROPELLER SHAFT

6
PROPELLER SHAFT

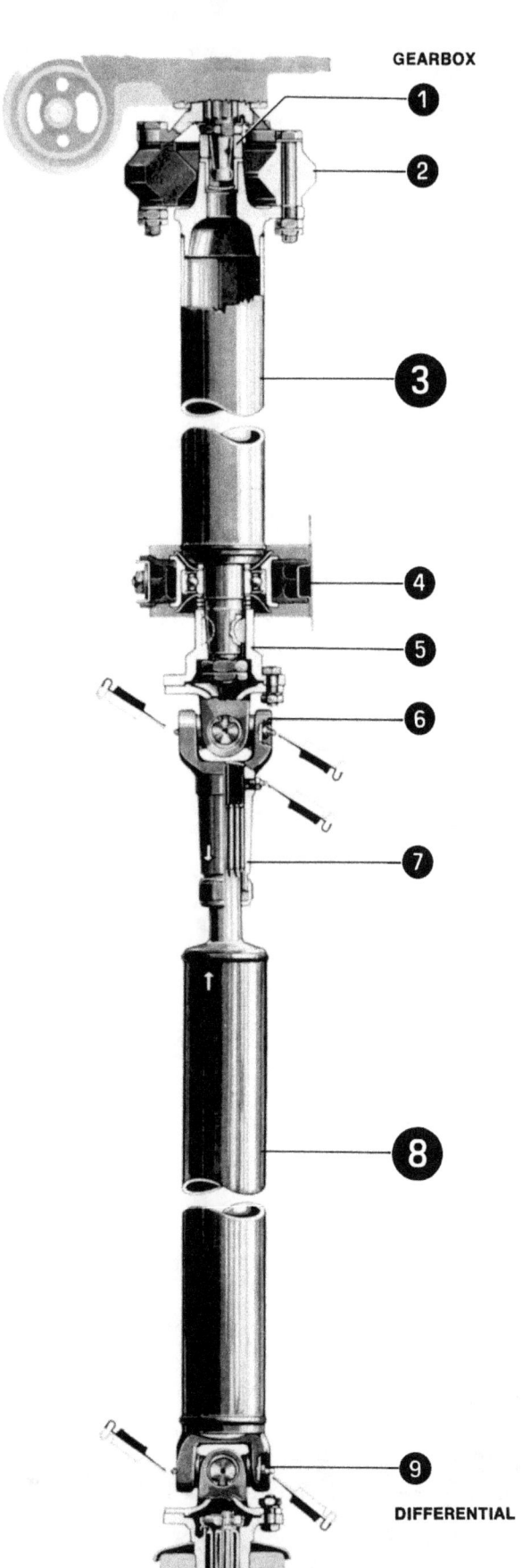

1. Grease seal
2. Flexible coupling
3. Shaft front section
4. Intermediate support, with ball bearing, elastically attached to body
5. Front shaft yoke
6. Universal joint, on needle bearings
7. Sliding yoke
8. Shaft rear section
9. Universal joint, on needle bearings

⌐╦┐ Grease fittings
⇒ ⇐ Alignment marks

PROPELLER SHAFT

REMOVAL FROM CAR - DISASSEMBLY

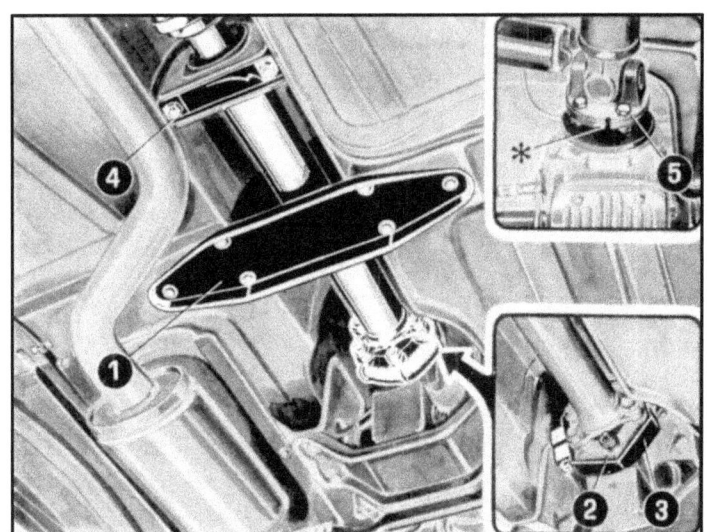

- Remove:
  - the center cross-member **1**;
  - hold the coupling securely with tool **3** (A.2.0124) and remove the bolts **2** fastening the flexible coupling to gearbox output shaft yoke;
  - loosen nuts **4** attaching intermediate support plate to body;
  - Remove bolts **5** fastening the propeller shaft yoke to differential input shaft yoke; before removing, countermark the parts for a proper reassembly as shown ✻.

- Take the propeller shaft away as a unit.

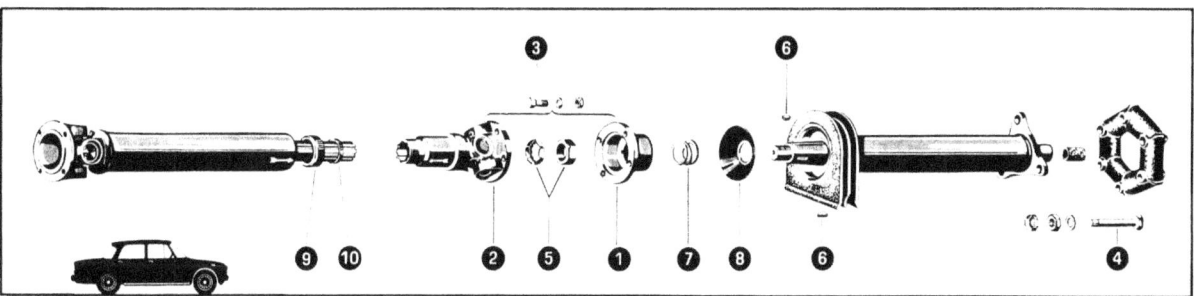

- Mark yokes **1** and **2** of front and rear section of propeller shaft for a correct reassembly; loosen bolts **3** and separate the two sections.

- If necessary, disassemble the shaft front section as follows:
  - loosen bolts **4** and remove flexible joint from yoke;
  - mark yoke **1** and front section of shaft for correct reassembly; then remove nut and palnut **5** and withdraw yoke from shaft.

- Remove keys **6**, spring **7** and slingers **8**.

- Unscrew the ring nut **9** and the seal **10** of yoke **2** and remove the yoke itself.

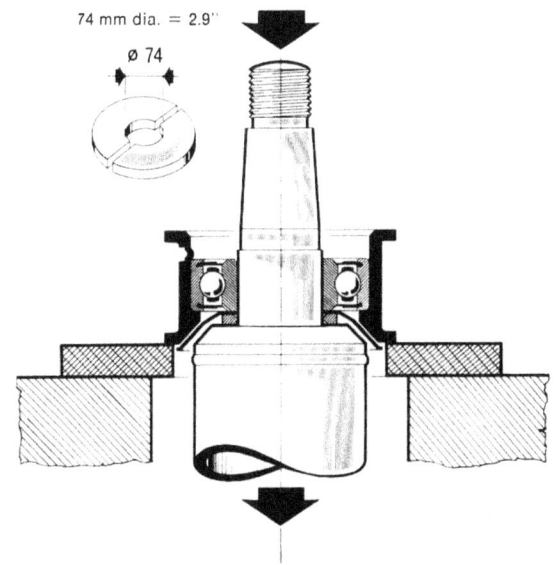

- If the bearing or support needs replacement, withdraw the support assembly by using suitable half-plates and proceeding as shown in figure.

- Take the bearing out of the support with a punch.

- Replace the support if distorted during disassembly.

PROPELLER SHAFT

INSPECTION AND CHECKING

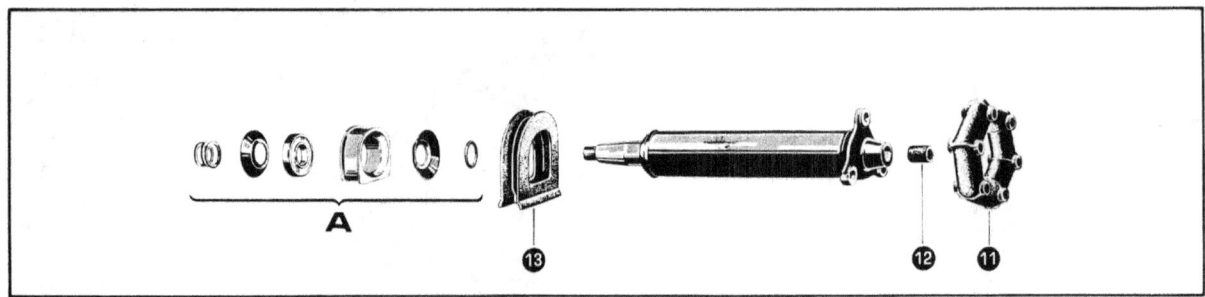

FRONT SECTION

- Check rubber collar **13** and components **A** of bearing assembly for sound conditions; replace damaged parts.
- Check felt **12**; replace it, if necessary.
- Check rubber coupling **11** for damage or distortion; replace it, if necessary.

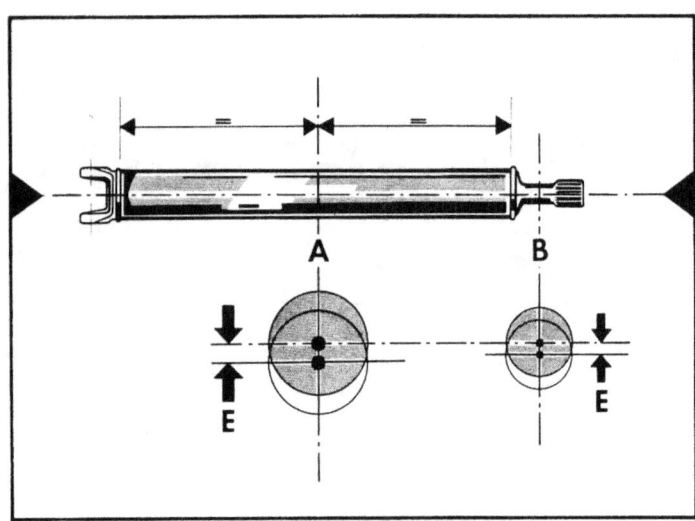

REAR SECTION

- Check the run-out **E** of shaft rear section at **A** and **B**:
  — max. run-out at **A** = .4 mm (.016")
  — max. run-out at **B** = .1 mm (.004")

  If run-out exceeds the above limits straighten the shaft in a hydraulic press. If truing is so difficult that vibrations could take place when shaft is reinstalled, replace the shaft.
  If so, the whole shaft must be rebalanced dynamically.

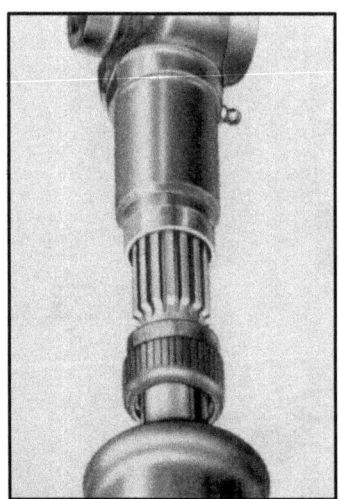

- Check the splines in the shaft and sliding yoke for good appearance; check that grease fittings on yoke and U-joints are not obstructed.
- Check yoke felt gasket: if damaged, replace it.
- Check that play **G** between splines is as follows:

  factory setting: .04 mm (.0016")
  wear limit: .2 mm (.0078")

PROPELLER SHAFT

REASSEMBLY

- Install the ball bearing in its seat and stake in place with a suitable punch to prevent any axial movement of the bearing.

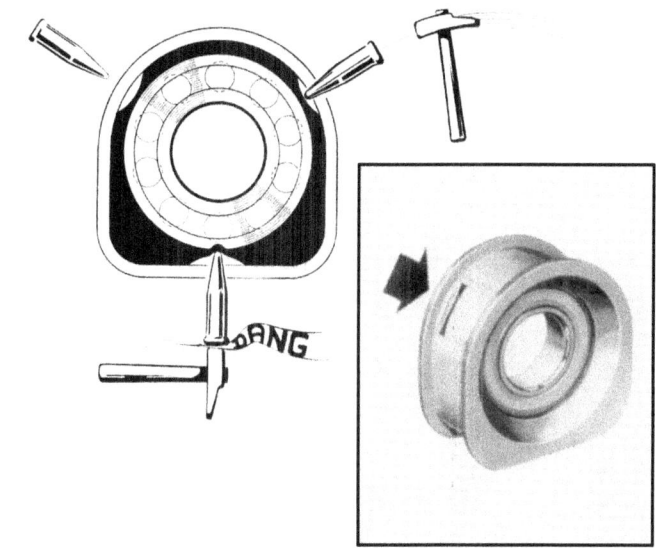

- Reassemble the front section of shaft in the following sequence:
  - the bearing spacer **14**;
  - the slinger **15**;
  - the bearing seat and rubber collar assemby **16**;
  - the slinger **8**;
  - the slinger spring **7**;
  - the keys **6**;
  - the yoke **1** according to the alignment marks.

  Tighten nut and palnut **5**.

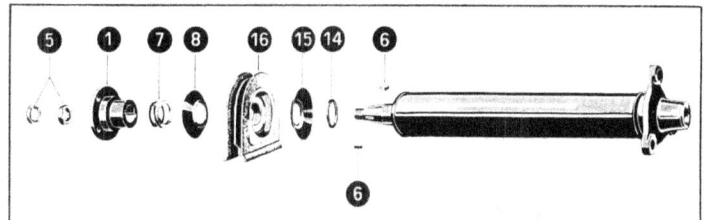

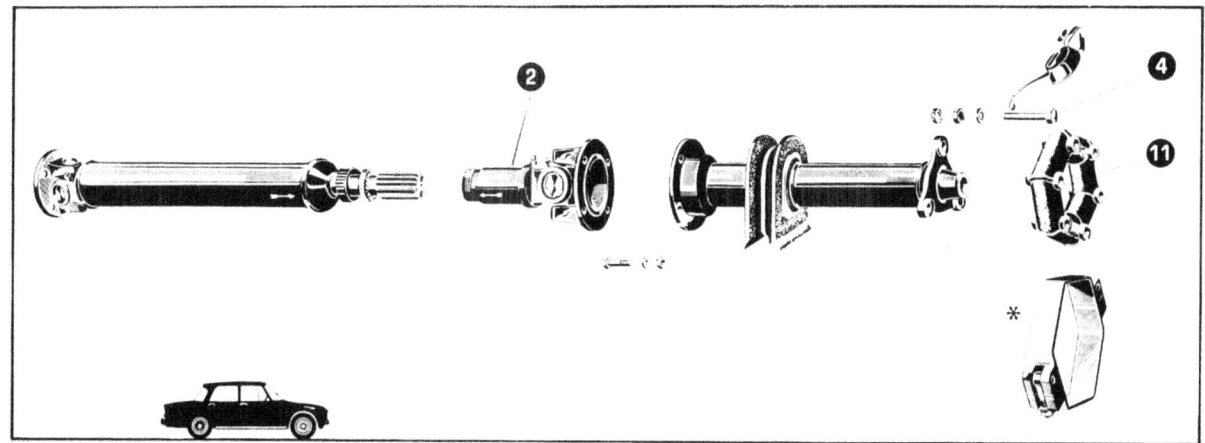

- Connect yoke **2** and rear shaft according to alignment marks.

- Join together front and rear sections of shaft according to alignment marks previously made.

- Place the rubber coupling **11** on front shaft yoke with the aid of the tool *****A.2.0124**; the mounting bolts should be oiled to prevent them from binding in the bushing when being locked.

- Torque the nuts on mounting bolts to **4 - 4.5 Kgm.** (32.6-39.7 lb. ft.) with tool **A.5.0162**.

10
PROPELLER SHAFT

REASSEMBLY - REINSTALLATION

Note - If a suitable balancing machine is available, dynamically balance the shaft assembly (Max. out of balance 12 gr. cm.² - test speed 5000 rpm).
The dynamic balancing is essential when any component of shaft has been replaced. If the propeller shaft is out of balance, apply balance weights in the proper positions.

- Reinstall the propeller shaft assembly as follows:

  - pack the bushing for centering prop. shaft and gearbox output shaft with grease (about 1/2 cc.) AGIP F.1 GREASE 15 - SHELL RETINAX G;

  - Connect shaft yoke to differential yoke according to alignment marks previously made;

  - torque the nuts of connecting bolts to **3.5-4 Kgm** (25.3 - 28.9 lb-ft) with tool **A.5.0162**.

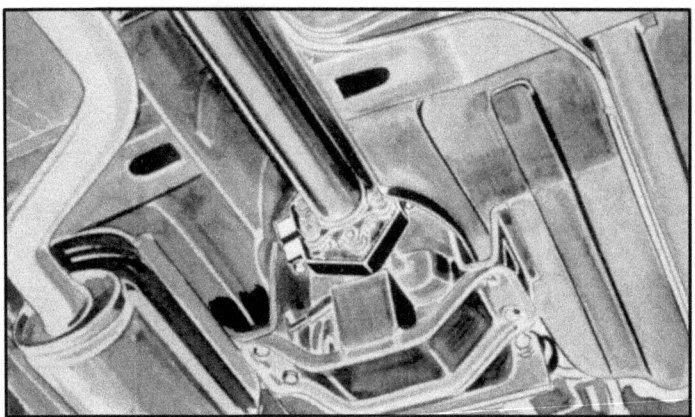

  - Mount the rubber coupling onto the gearbox yoke with the aid of the tool **A.2.0124**; the mounting bolts should be oiled to prevent them from binding in the bushing when being locked.

  - Torque the nuts to **4.5 - 5.5 Kgm** (32.6 - 39.7 lb-ft) with tool **A.5.0162**.

- Complete the reinstallation of the shaft in reverse order of removal.

REAR AXLE AND SUSPENSION

REAR AXLE

GENERAL

The live axle is attached to the body through:
- two rubber-bushed radius rods which counteract tractive and braking efforts longitudinally;
- a trunnion reacting to transversal efforts and mounted on rubber bushings;
- vertical coil springs secured to the radius rods and telescopic hydraulic shock absorbers coaxial with the springs.

Upward movement of rear axle in restricted by bumper pads and downward by rebound straps. The differential, with the hypoid final drive, is housed in the aluminum carrier to which the two axle tubes enclosing the semifloating axle shafts are connected.

A magnetic plug in the carrier retains metal particles suspended in the oil.

OVERALL GEARBOX/REAR AXLE RATIOS

	Final drive	**41 : 8**	**41 : 9**	**43 : 9**	**41 : 10**	**41 : 11**
	1st	16.933 : 1	15.049 : 1	15.783 : 1	13.546 : 1	12.314 : 1
	2nd	10.189 : 1	9.055 : 1	9.496 : 1	8.151 : 1	7.409 : 1
	3rd	6.944 : 1	6.172 : 1	6.472 : 1	5.555 : 1	5.050 : 1
Gear	4th	5.125 : 1	4.555 : 1	4.777 : 1	4.100 : 1	3.727 : 1
	5th	4.054 : 1	3.603 : 1	3.778 : 1	3.243 : 1	2.948 : 1
	Rev.	15.426 : 1	13.710 : 1	14.378 : 1	12.341 : 1	11.218 : 1
GIULIA 1300 (4 speed)			■			
GIULIA 1300 ti		■				
GIULIA TI		■	□		□	
GIULIA TI SUPER		■	□	□	□	□
GIULIA SUPER / **GIULIA SPRINT GT** / **GIULIA SPRINT GT Veloce** / **GIULIA GTC**			■			
SPIDER 1600			■			

■ standard
□ optional

REAR AXLE

14
REAR AXLE

IN-CAR REPAIRS

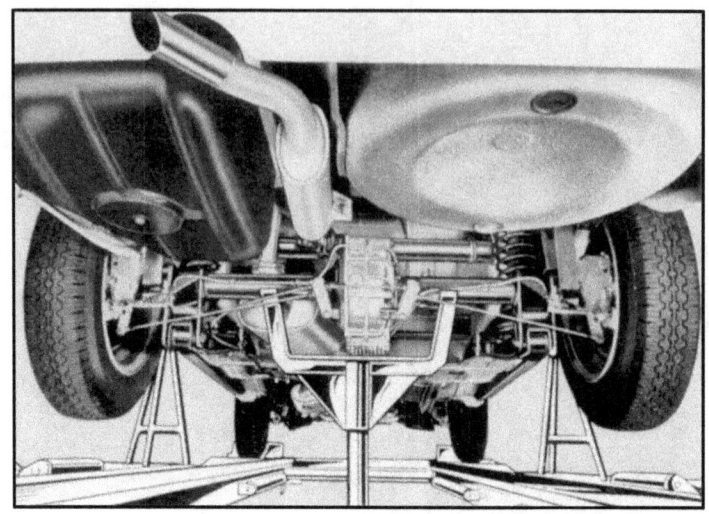

Axle shaft, wheel bearings and packing replacement

- Loosen the wheel nuts;
- Jack up the car as shown and put stands under the jack sockets;
- Remove the wheels and lower the lift.

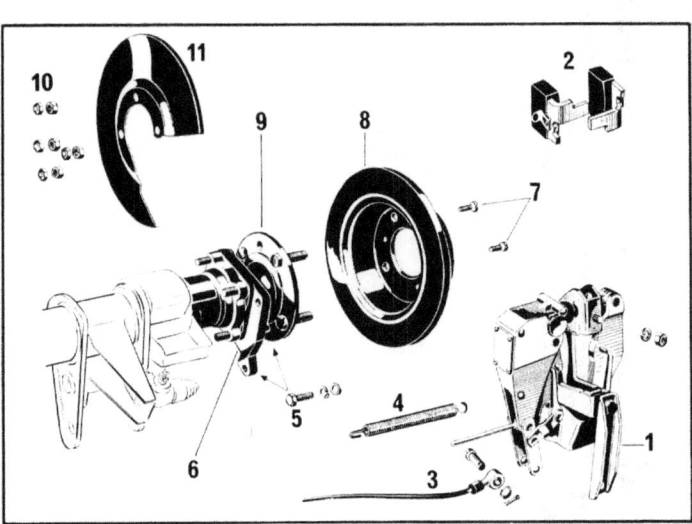

- Free the pad retaining plate **1** at one end only and take the pads out;
- Disconnect the hand brake cable **3**;
- Remove the return spring **4** from both attachment points;
- Loosen screws **5** fastening the brake caliper to its bracket **6**; remove the caliper by withdrawing the push rod from slave cylinder;
- Loosen screws **7** attaching the brake disc **8** to wheel hub **9** and remove the disc;
- Unscrew nuts **10** securing the bearing housing to axle tube and remove the splash shield **11**.

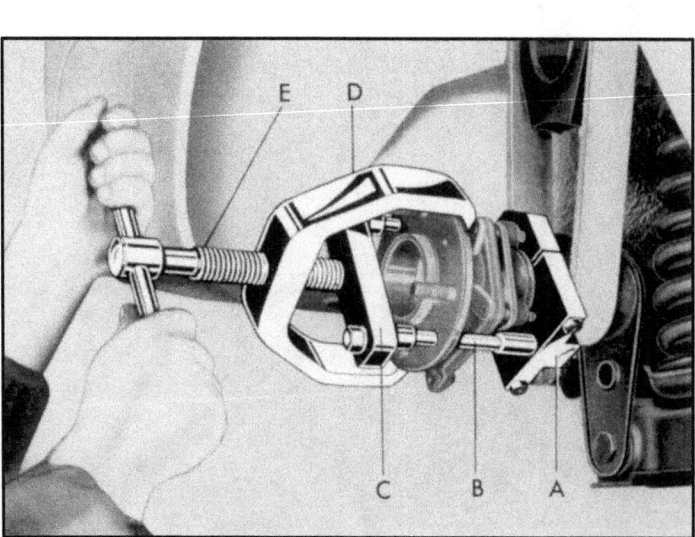

- Withdraw the axle shaft as follows (Ref. Tool Bulletin no. 33/2);
  - Install the abutment **A, tool A.3.0109/1**, on axle tube;
  - Pass offset pins **B** of the tool **A.3.0109** through the holes into the axle shaft flange and tighten by hand the nuts against the plate **C**;
  - Mount the puller **D** as shown and withdraw the axle shaft by turning the screw **E**.

REAR AXLE

IN-CAR REPAIRS

- If necessary, remove the axle shaft bearing as follows:
  - unscrew the bearing ring nut with the tool **A.5.0120**;

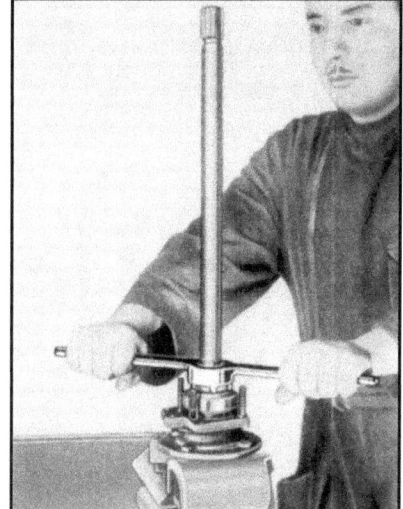

  - mount the plate **P** of tool **A.3.0109** (Tool Bulletin no. 33/2) on the bearing housing and tighten the nuts;
  - pass the offset pins **B** through the holes into the shaft flange so that they rest against the bearing housing;
  - mount the puller **D** onto the shaft flange making sure the screw **E** is perfectly centered and withdraw the shaft.

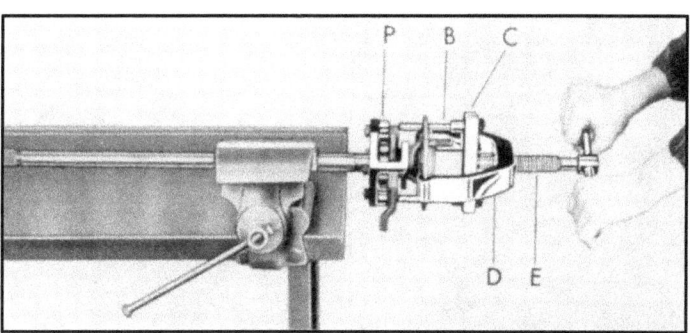

Withdrawing the axle shafts from cars with drum brakes
- loosen the attaching screws and remove the brake drums;
- loosen the nuts fastening the shoe back plates to axle tube;
- pass offset pins **B** of the tool **A.3.0109** (Tool Bulletin no. 33/2) through the holes into the axle shaft flange against the plate **T**;
- mount the puller **D** as shown and withdraw the shaft by turning the screw **E**.

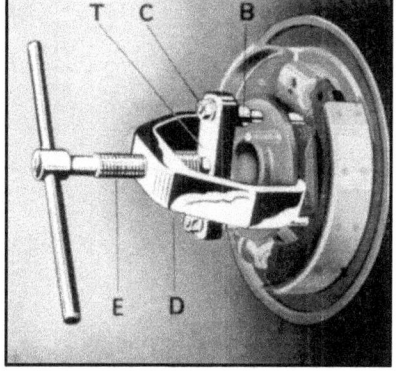

Inspection and check
- Check the conditions of oil seal packing; replace it, if necessary. To refit the packing use tool **A. 3.0160**.
- Check the run out of axle shaft with a dial indicator:
  maximum run out: .10 mm (.0039")
  Minor adjustment is possible by cold straightening the axle shaft with a suitable press. Replace the shaft, if necessary.

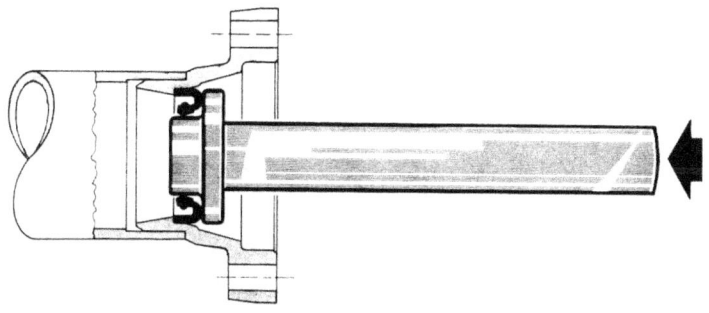

REAR AXLE

IN-CAR REPAIRS

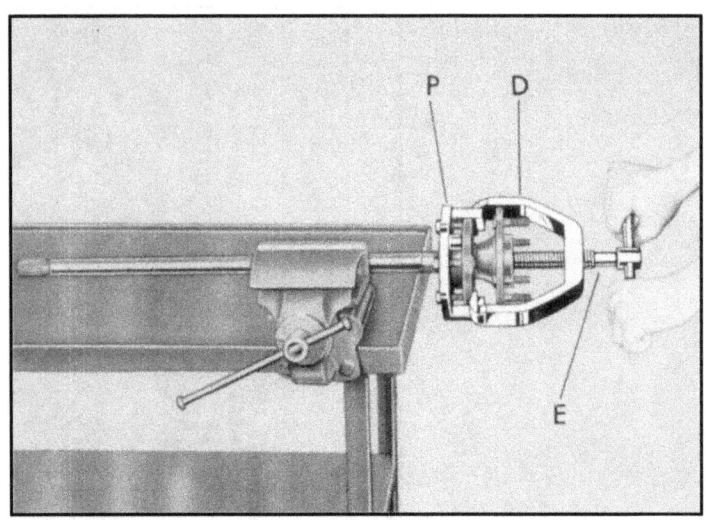

Reassembly

- Install bearing housing and bearing onto axle shaft; to insert bearing, proceed as follows (Tool Bulletin no. 33/2):
  - mount the plate **P** of tool **A.3.0109** on bearing housing and tighten the nuts;
  - engage the puller **D** with the brackets of plate **P**;
  - the bearing can now be driven in place by turning the screw **E** against the end of the shaft as shown;
  - screw in the bearing ring nut with tool **A.5.0120**;
  - Bend the tabs of tabwasher.

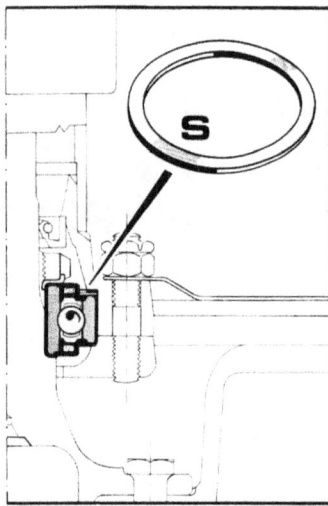

- Insert the axle shaft into axle tube and start axle splines into side gear, taking care not to damage the oil seal packing and the baffle in the axle tube.
- Push shaft in until it bottoms by tapping with a mallet on a punch placed in the shaft flange hollow.
- Install the splash shield on caliper bracket and torque the attaching nuts ✶ to **4.8 - 5.5 Kgm** (34.8 - 32.7 lb-ft.) with the tool **A.5.0146**; secure with the pal nuts.
- After installation, check that the axle shaft has no end play: if any play exists, take it up by inserting shims **S** as required between outer race of bearing and bearing housing.

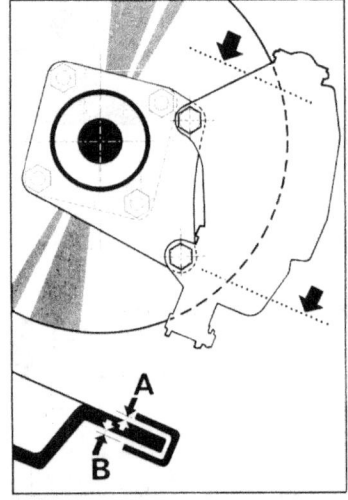
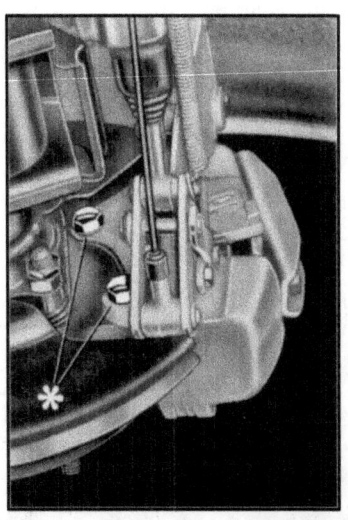

- Mount the caliper to its bracket keeping in mind that:
  - the difference in gap **A** and **B** between disc and caliper on each side should not exceed **.5 mm** (.02"); if necessary, insert shims between caliper and bracket;
  - torque the bolts ✶ attaching caliper to bracket to **2.3 - 2.8 Kgm** (16.7 - 20.2 lb-ft.).

REAR AXLE

REMOVAL

- Place the car on a lift and drain oil from differential;
  - loosen the wheel nuts;
  - jack up the rear end of car as shown and put stands under the jack sockets;
  - remove the wheels;

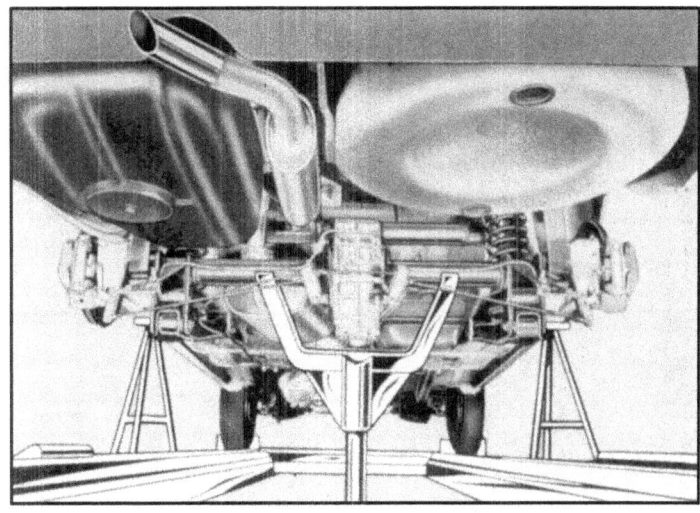

1 Disconnect the brake lines from three-way union;
2 loosen bolts attaching propeller shaft to differential;
3 remove cotter pin and nut attaching reaction trunnion to rear axle;
4 withdraw pins connecting hand brake cables to shackles at the differential carrier;
- disconnect hand brake cables from levers at the brake calipers;
5 Unscrew the nuts attaching shock absorbers to suspension radius rods, remove rubber pads and fully collapse the shock absorbers;
6 loosen the screws attaching the rebound straps and bumper pads; to do this easily, raise the rear axle so as to unload the straps.

 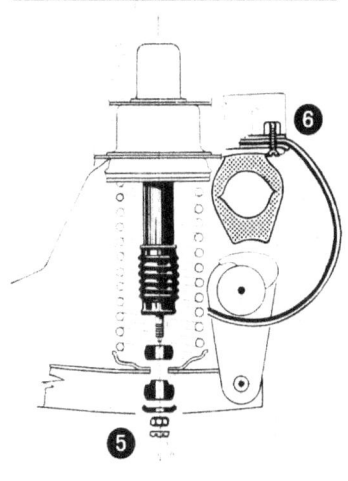

- Insert pin **B** of tool **A.2.0143** (Tool Bulletin no. 114) into the holes of radius rods attaching lugs;
- rotate handle **D** until the bracket **F** of tool rests firmly against the radius rod attachment;
- pass the wrench through the port in the tool and unscrew the nut on the bolt mounting the radius rod to rear axle;
- rotate handle **D** in such a way as to lower the bracket **F** and to relieve the spring;
- remove the special tool and get the rear axle free from the reaction trunnion by slightly shifting the axle toward the off side;
- put down the axle by lowering the jack.

Cars with drum brakes

- Hook the tool **A.2.0143** up to the axle tube with the beak **A** and rotate handle **D** until the bracket **E** rests firmly against the radius rod attachment;
- remove the rear axle the same way as directed for cars with disc brakes.

 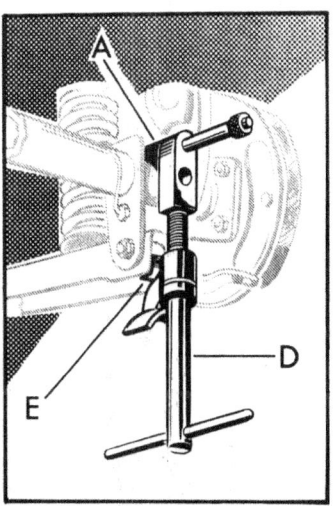

DISC BRAKES   DRUM BRAKES

REAR AXLE

DISASSEMBLY ON BENCH

- Place the rear axle on a suitable stand;
- Remove:
  - brake caliper assemblies;
  - brake discs and axle shafts (refer to page 14);
  - axle tubes;
  - and disassemble the differential carrier.

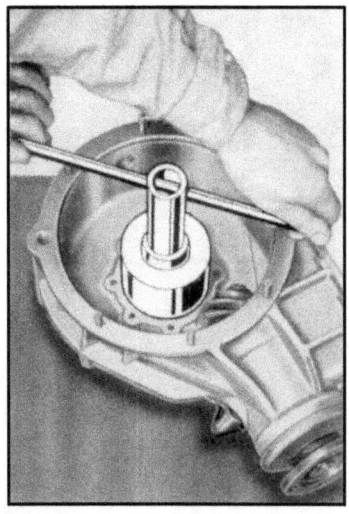
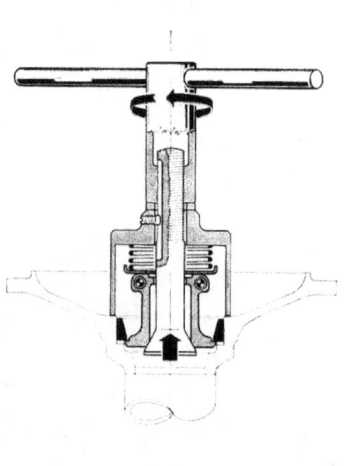

- If necessary, withdraw the bearing cups from differential carrier and left-hand axle tube with tool **A.3.0115**; take out and retain the shims.
  For withdrawal, set the parts upright and proceed as shown in the illustrations.

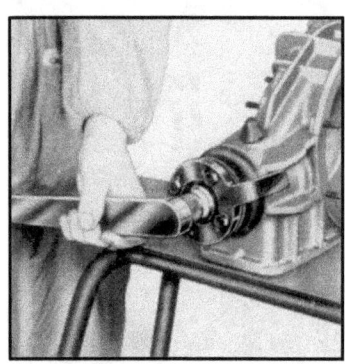
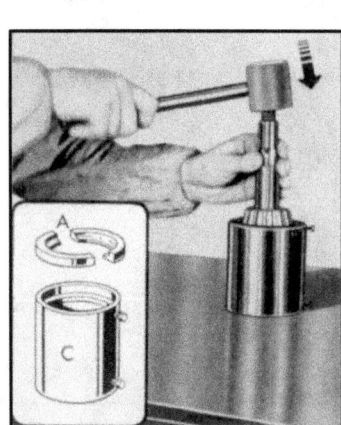
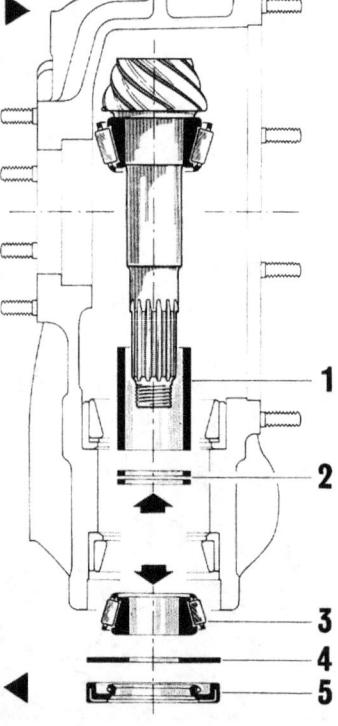

- Remove final drive pinion and shaft from differential carrier as follows;
  - free the flange securing ring nut from the tabwasher;
  - install tool **A.2.0144** (Tool Bulletin no. 116) onto the flange with the suitable bolts to prevent the pinion from rotating when unscrewing the ring nut;
  - insert the bushing **A.5.0104** (Tool Bulletin no. 74/1) and unscrew the ring nut;
  - withdraw the pinion & shaft assembly from carrier by tapping with a soft mallet;
  - slide out spacer **1** and retain shims **2**;
  - remove the oil seal packing **5**, the slinger **4** and the front bearing cone **3** from differential carrier.
- If necessary, withdraw the rear bearing cone with tool **A.3.0150** (Tool Bulletin no. 92); for withdrawal, fit the half rings **A** (of the proper type) onto the pinion and rest the parts so arranged against the base **C**; to slide out the bearing, tap lightly on pinion shaft end with a soft mallet.

REAR AXLE

DISASSEMBLY ON BENCH - INSPECTION AND CHECKING

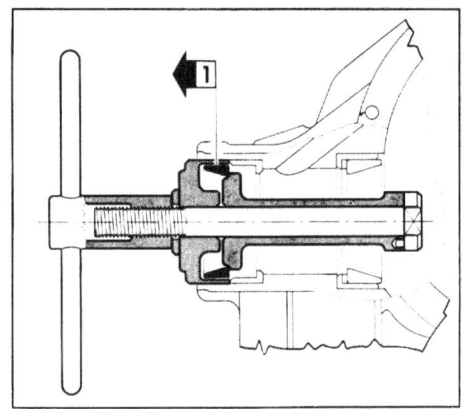

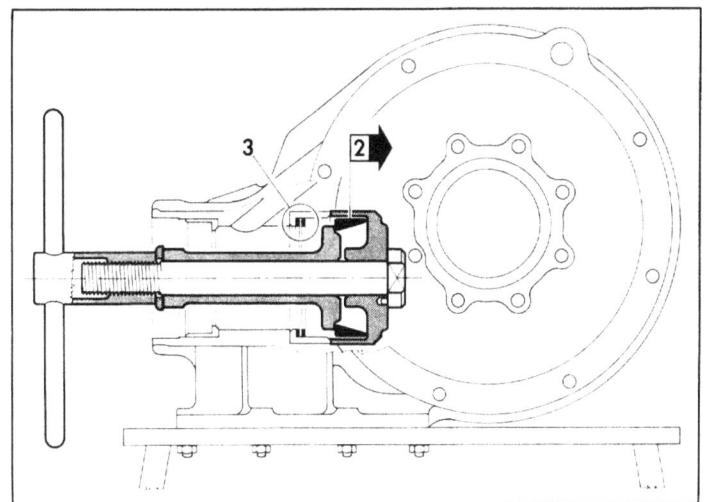

- With tool **A.3.0207** (Tool Bulletin no. 100/1) withdraw:
  1 front bearing cup;
  2 rear bearing cup.
  Remove and retain shims **3**.

Differential case

- If necessary, pull the bearing cones out of differential case with tool **A.3.0212** (Tool Bulletin no. 128).
- Loosen the screws attaching the ring gear to differential case after unlocking from tabwashers; then countermark and remove the ring gear from case.
- Drive out the shaft of differential pinions from the side opposite the key; take out pinions and side gears with their shims.

INSPECTION AND CHECKING

a) Final drive.
Check the pinion and ring gear teeth for any sign of binding or excessive wear. If teeth are badly worn, replace the pinion and ring gear assembly.

WARNING - Pinion and ring gear are supplied as a matched set only, therefore they are not available separately.

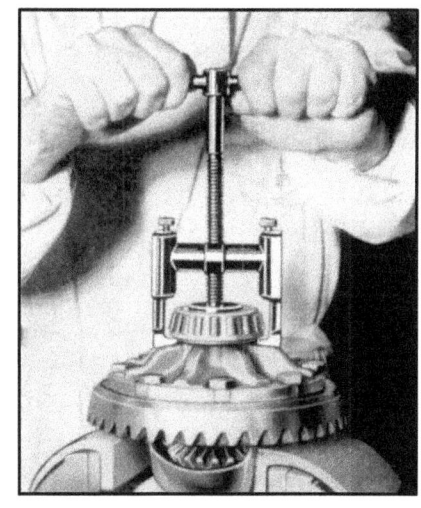

b) Roller bearings.
Check pinion bearings (**3** and **4**) and differential case bearing **5** for any sign of scoring, scratching, binding or excessive wear; replace them, if necessary.

c) Differential pinion and side gears.
Check teeth of gears **6** and **7** for scoring, dents or excessive wear.

- Check the differential pinion shaft **8** for sign of binding or excessive wear; replace damaged parts, if necessary. Clean all the components thoroughly.

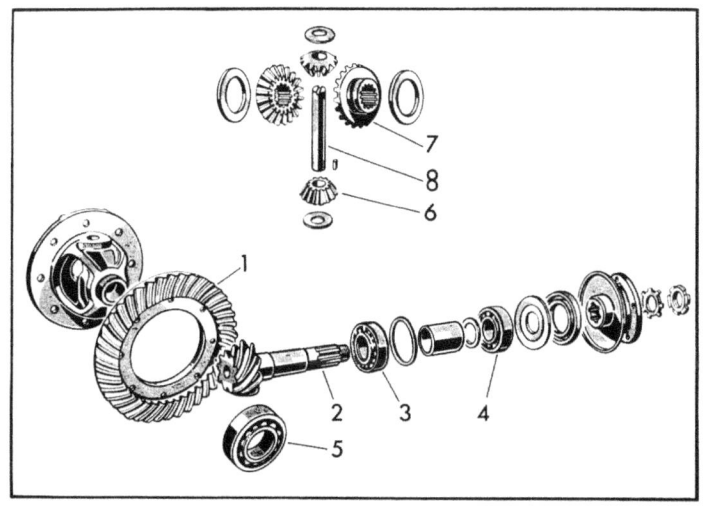

REAR AXLE

REASSEMBLY ON BENCH

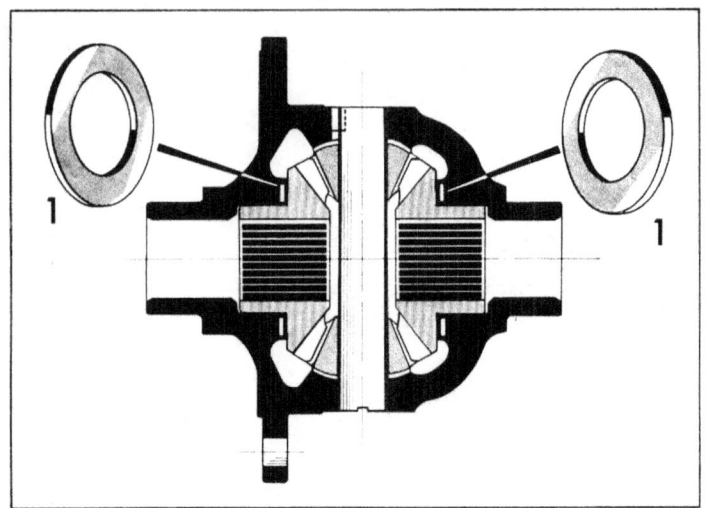

Reassembling the differential case

- Fit:
  - the side gears and the shims **1** previously retained;
  - the differential pinions and thrust washers;
  - the differential pinion shaft;
  - Check that backlash between pinion and side gears does not exceed **.05 mm** (.002''); if this condition is fulfilled, **the gears must rotate freely by hand.**
  To adjust the backlash, insert or remove shims **1** as required between the side gears and differential case.

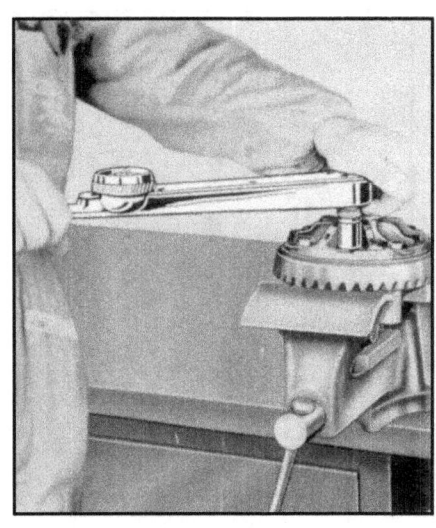 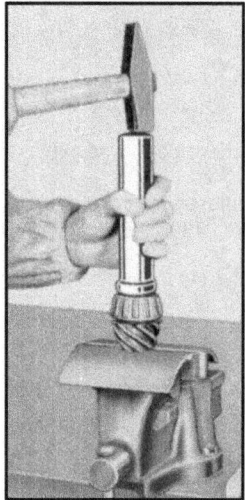

- Install the ring gear according to the markings previously made on differential case and dry torque the attaching screws to: **4.5-5.0 Kgm** (32.6-36.1 lb-ft).
- Safety lock the screws with the tabwashers.

Reassembling final drive pinion

- Drive rear bearing cone onto pinion shaft with the tool **A.3.0170**.

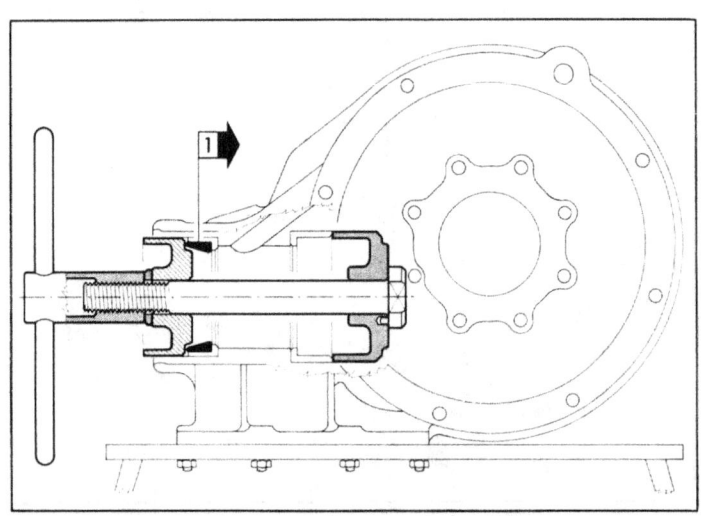

- With tool **A.3.0207** (Tool Bulletin 100/1) drive into their seats:
  1 pinion front bearing cup;

REAR AXLE

REASSEMBLY ON BENCH

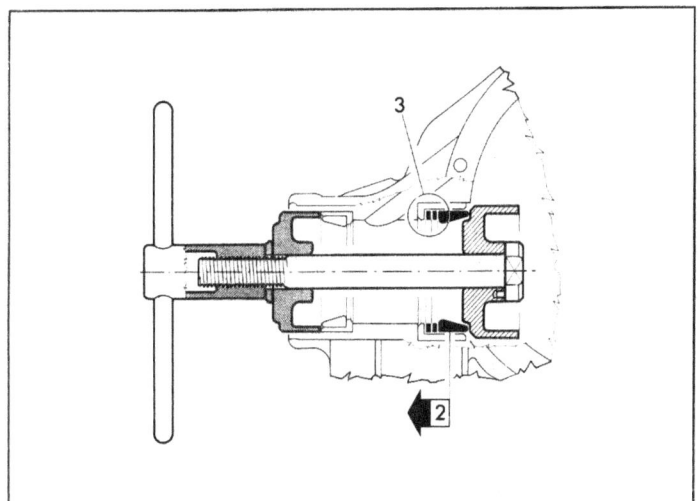

2 shims 3 and pinion rear bearing cup.

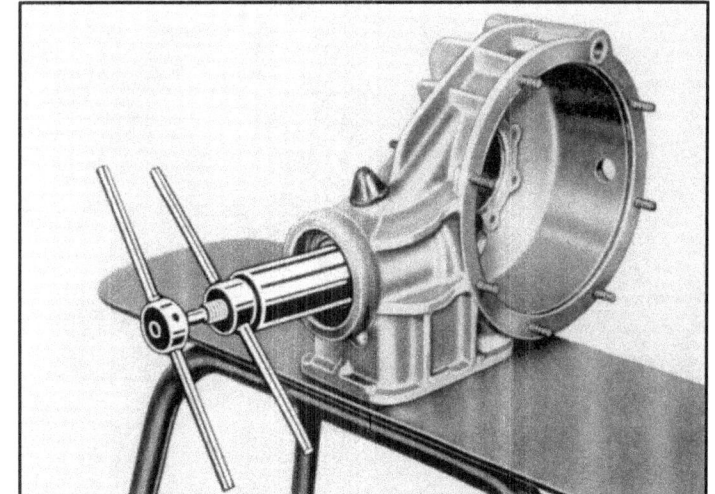

- Drive onto pinion shaft:
  1 the bearing spacer;
  2 the shims previously retained.
- At this stage of assembly insert the pinion into differential carrier.
- Then assemble:
  - the front bearing cone 3 with tool **A.3.0168**;
  - the slinger.

Warning: do not install the oil seal packing.

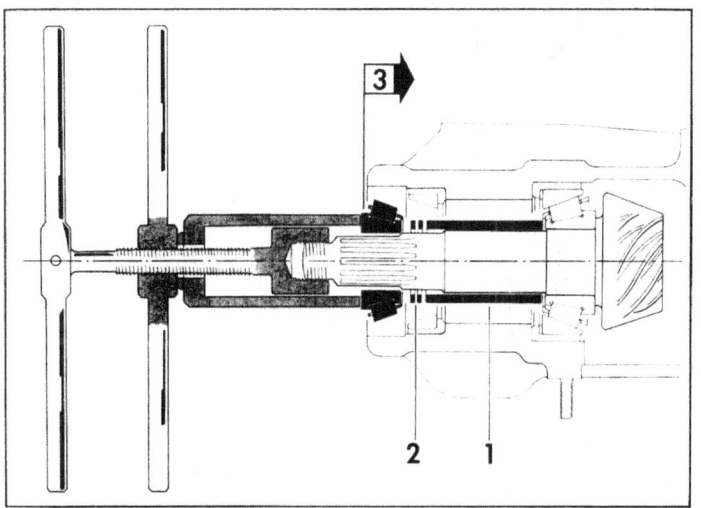

22
REAR AXLE

REASSEMBLY ON BENCH

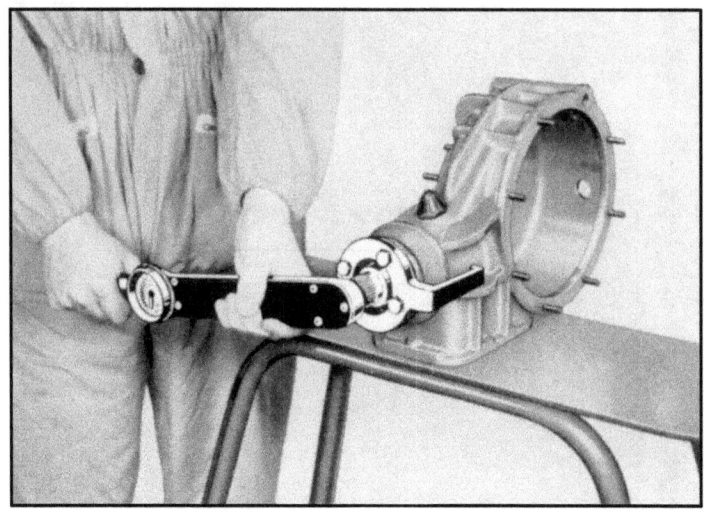

- Assemble the flange on pinion shaft and tighten the ring nut to **8-14 Kgm** (58 - 100 lb-ft); before tightening, insert bushing **A.5.0104** and prevent pinion from rotating with tool **A.2.0144**.

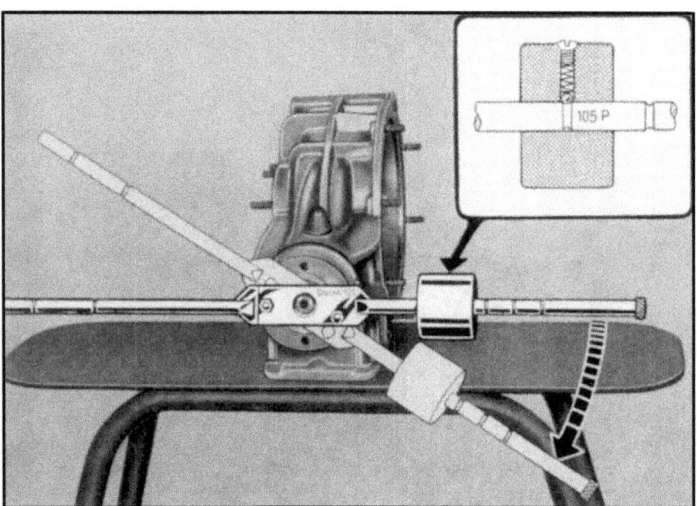

Checking the pre-load of pinion bearings

- Install the tool **C.5.0100** (Tool Bulletin no. 20/1) on the flange;
  - rotate the tool in both directions to settle the bearings;
  - position the weight in the slot marked 105 P;
  - check that, when leaving the tool arm free in horizontal position, the weight moves downward slowly through about 30 degrees.

  In such a condition the pre-load is correct and the revolving torque should be:
  11.5 - 15.5 Kgcm (10 - 13.5 lb-in.).

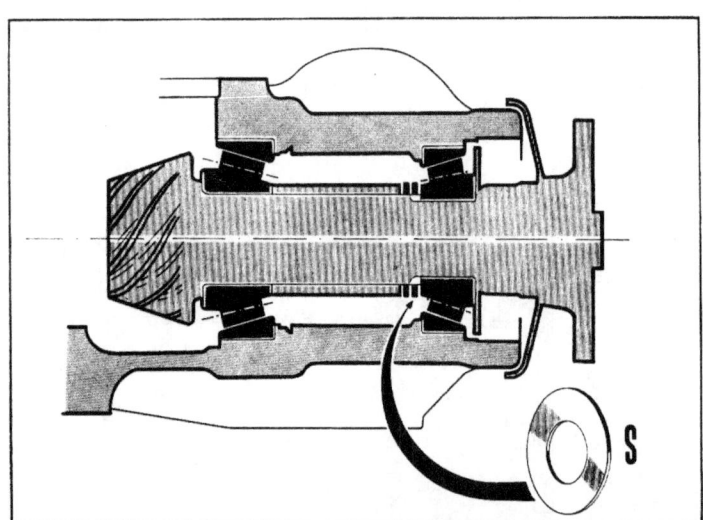

- If this is not the case, remove pinion from differential carrier and change thickness of shims between spacer and bearing cup taking in mind that:
  — **adding shims decreases the pre-load;**
  — **removing shims increases the pre-load.**
- Proceed by trial and errors until the correct pre-load is obtained.

REAR AXLE

REASSEMBLY ON BENCH

ADJUSTING THE DISTANCE OF FINAL DRIVE PINION FROM RING GEAR CENTER LINE

23A
REAR AXLE

REASSEMBLY ON BENCH

Checking and adjusting the distance of final drive pinion from ring gear center line

- The distance **B** from pinion top to ring gear center line should be 57 mm plus or minus the value (in hundredths of millimeter) metal stamped on pinion head.
  Specifically: if this value is preceded by the plus mark, the distance shall be 57 mm plus the figure stamped on pinion and viceversa.

- To check proceed as follows:
  - withdraw the R.H. bearing cup from differential carrier with tool **A.3.0115** (see page 18);
  - place the dummy shaft **U** (tool **C.6.0114** see Tool Bulletin no. 27/1) in the R.H. bearing seat and fasten in place by tightening nut **C** manually;
  - mount a dial indicator on to the support **V** (tool **C.5.0116**) and zero set the dial against the reference gauge **C.6.0101** to the nominal dimension **D = 70 mm**.
    The dimension **D** (70 mm) corresponds to the distance between the pinion top surface and the generating line of dummy shaft **U**.

$$70 \text{ mm} = 57 \text{ mm (B)} + \frac{\text{dummy shaft dia.}}{2}$$

- Rest the dial indicator support against the pinion top and check that the readings recorded (positive or negative with respect to **D**) are in accordance with the figure stamped on pinion both in sign and value.

- If this condition is not fulfilled, the pinion must be readjusted to correct assembly position by varying the thickness of shims S_1 in between the rear bearing cup and the seat in differential carrier:
  — **add shims to bring the pinion nearer to ring gear;**
  — **remove shims to bring the pinion farther off the ring gear.**

Warning: in order not to alter the pinion bearing pre-load, **it is necessary also to add or remove shims S_2** in between spacer and front bearing cone accordingly.

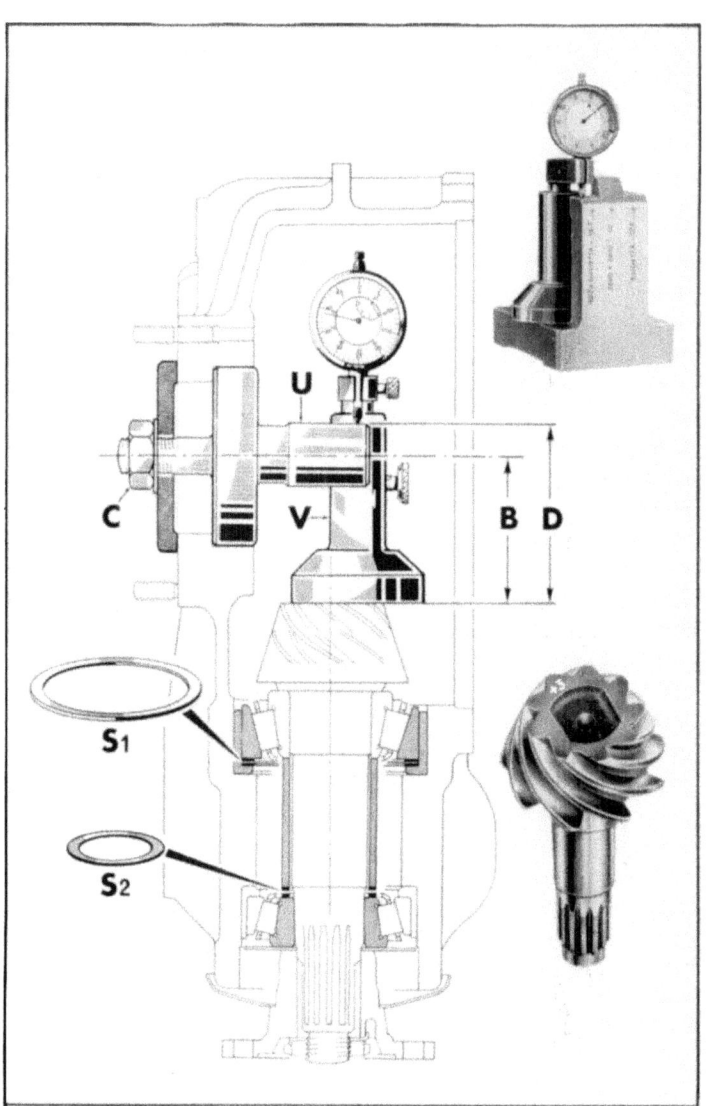

ACTUAL EXAMPLE

	D.I.R.	Mark on pinion	Adjustment
1st example	− 4	+ 2	− 6 (subtract)
2nd example	+ 4	− 2	+ 6 (add)
3rd example	− 2	+ 4	− 6 (subtract)
4th example	+ 2	− 4	+ 6 (add)
5th example	− 4	− 2	− 2 (subtract)
6th example	+ 4	+ 2	+ 2 (add)
7th example	− 2	− 4	+ 2 (add)
8th example	+ 2	+ 4	− 2 (subtract)

ADJUSTMENT S_1 = (algebraic subtraction) (± Dial indicator reading) **minus** (± Mark on pinion)

REAR AXLE

REASSEMBLY ON BENCH

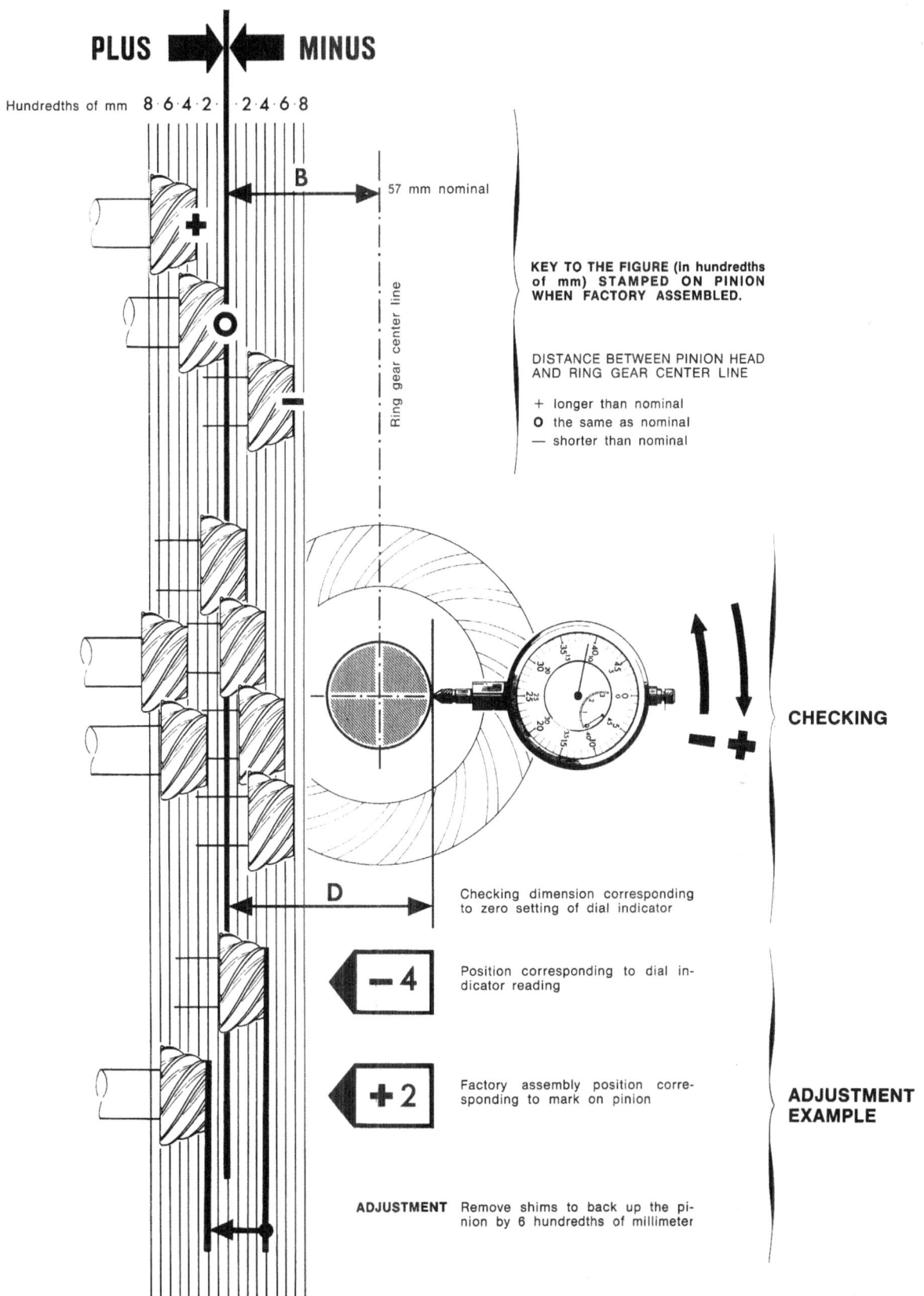

REAR AXLE

REASSEMBLY ON BENCH

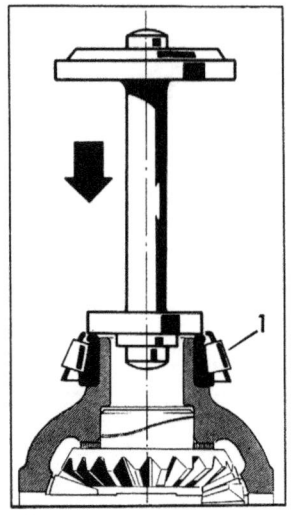
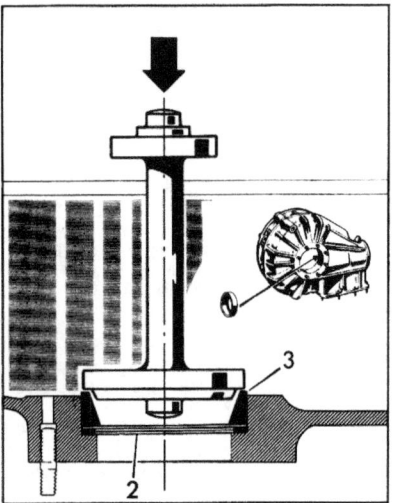

Checking the total pre-load of pinion & ring gear bearings

- Drive cones **1** of side bearings onto differential with tool **A.3.0208**.
- Into R.H. bearing seat in differential carrier insert:
  2 shims previously retained;
  3 bearing cup with tool **A.3.0208**.
- Assemble the differential case assembly to the differential carrier.

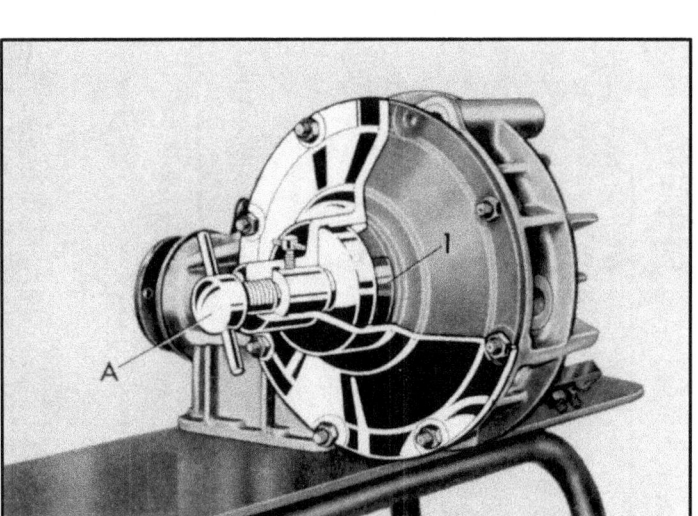

- Place the cup **1** of differential carrier L.H. bearing on tool **C. 6.0115** (Tool Bulletin no. 102/2);
  • mount the tool so arranged on L.H. flange of differential carrier and fasten with nuts;
  • rotate handle **A** until a provisional clearance is obtained between pinion and ring gear.

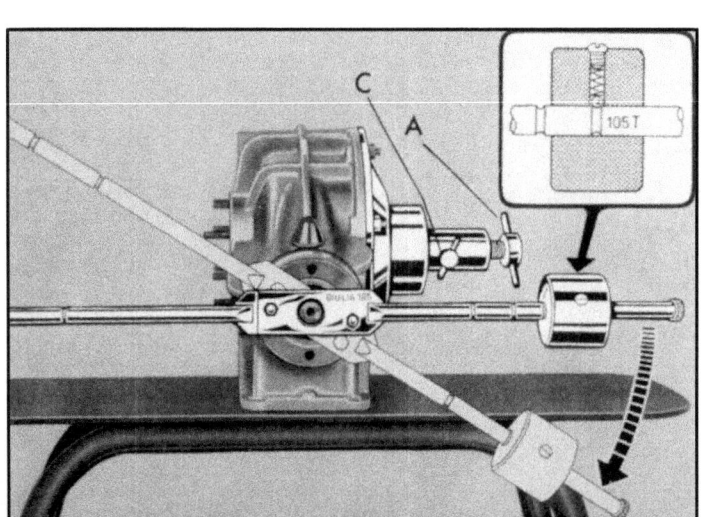

• Install the tool **C.5.0100** (Tool Bulletin no. 20/1) for checking the bearing pre-load on pinion shaft flange;
• rotate the tool in both directions to settle the bearings;
• position the weight in the slot marked 105 T and check that, when leaving the tool arm free in horizontal position, the weight moves downward slowly through about 30 degrees.
In such a condition the total revolving torque of pinion and ring gear should be:
16.5 - 24.5 Kgcm (14.5 - 21 lb-in.).
If this is not the case, rotate handle **A** of tool **C.6.0115** until the prescribed pre-load is obtained.
Then lock the setscrew **C**.

Note: the pre-load shall be checked in four different position of the ring gear; to do this, rotate the pinion of a complete turn after each check.

REAR AXLE

REASSEMBLY ON BENCH

Checking and adjusting the backlash of final drive

- Tighten the setscrew **B** (Tool Bulletin no. 102/2) into the drain plug boss so as to lock the ring gear;

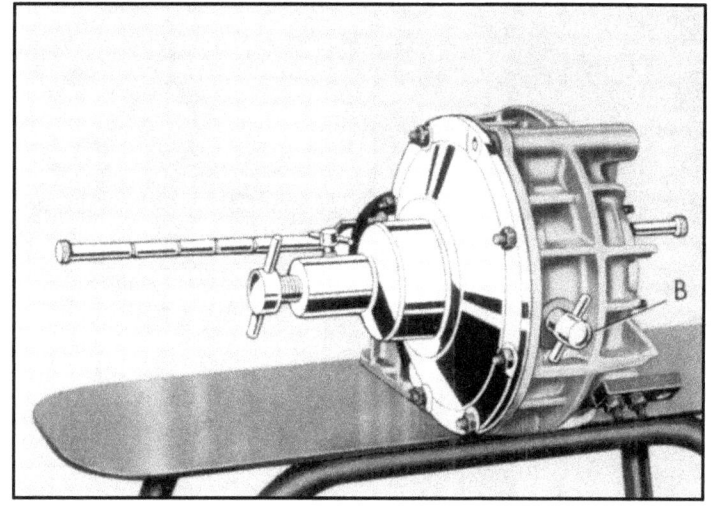

- have the sensing needle of a dial indicator resting against the centre plate of tool **C.5.0100** (Tool Bulletin no. 20/1) in correspondence of the reference mark 45 mm apart from pinion center line;
- swing the tool in both directions and take readings of backlash on dial indicator:
  specified value: .15-.25 mm (.006-.009'')
  This correponds to an actual backlash at the final drive teeth of **.05 - .10 mm (.002-.004'')**.

Note: the backlash shall be checked in four different positions of the ring gear; to do this, rotate the pinion of a complete turn after each check and lock the ring gear against rotation by setscrew **B**.

- If the backlash is not as prescribed, adjust as follows:
  - remove the tool **C.6.0115** from differential carrier and take out the differential case;
  - change shims as required between R.H. bearing cup and seat, bearing in mind that:
    — **removing shims decreases the backlash;**
    — **adding shims increases the backlash.**

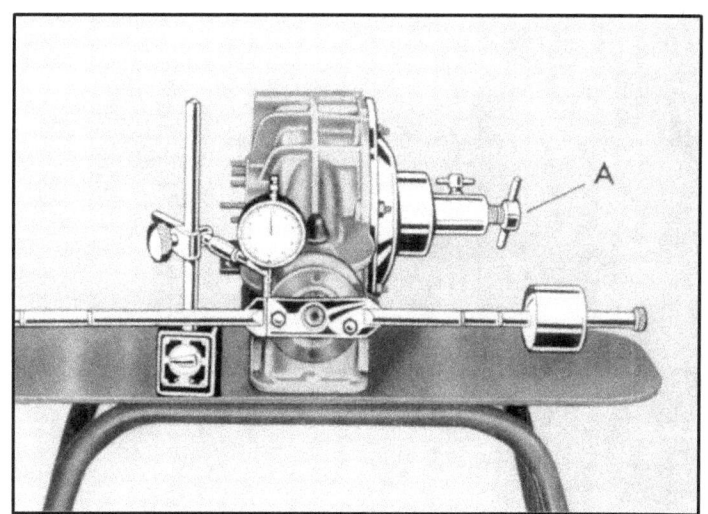

- Reassemble the R.H. bearing cup and shims **S** as per above procedure to the differential carrier with the tool **A.3.0208**.
- Reinstall the differential case and the tool **C.6.0115** in place of the L.H. axle tube.
- Adjust screw **A** of tool **C.6.0115** so as to obtain the specified bearing pre-load: check the total pinion & ring gear bearing pre-load and check for the correct backlash.
  Repeat the adjustment procedure, if necessary.

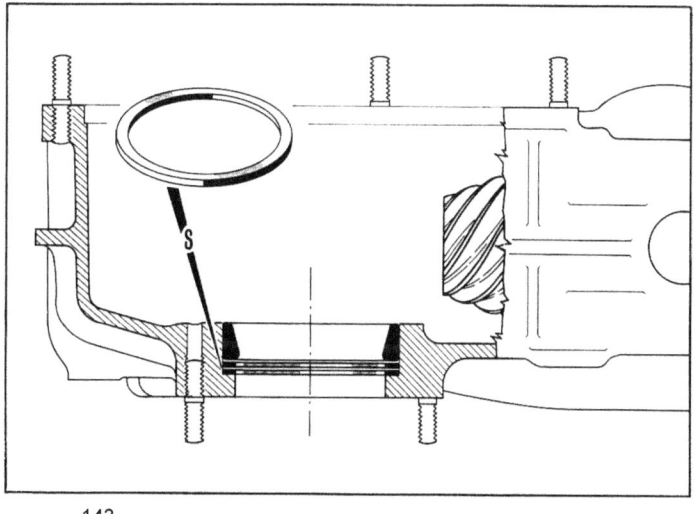

REAR AXLE

REASSEMBLY ON BENCH

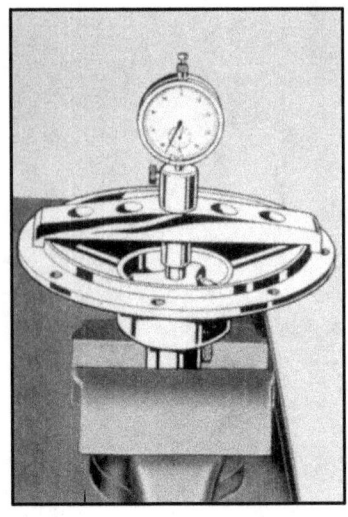
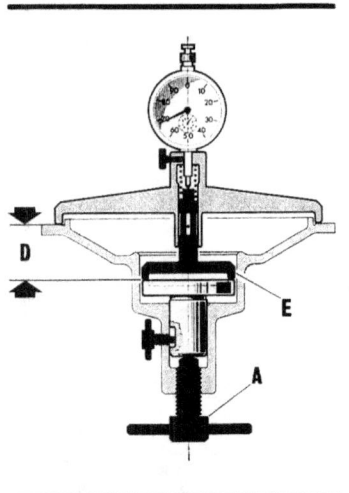
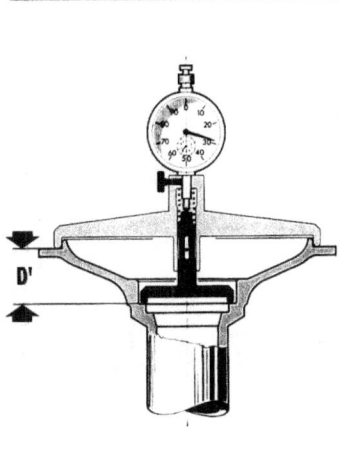
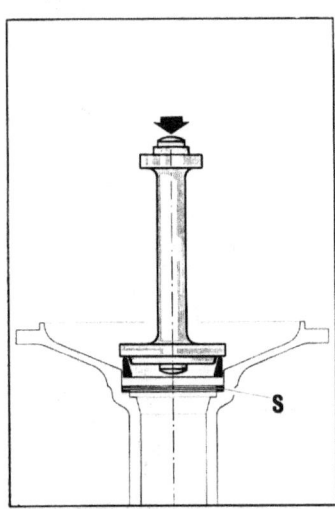

Reassembling the differential

- After the pre-load and backlash are set as specified, it is necessary to determine the thickness of shims between L.H. bearing cup and its seat. Proceed as follows:
  - remove tool **C.6.0115** from differential carrier;
  - withdraw the bearing cup previously fitted and, without disturbing the screw **A**, record the dimension **D** with a dial indicator and the tool **E (C.6.0102)** as shown;
  - take a reading of dimension **D'** in the L.H. axle tube.

  The difference **D - D'**, diminished by **.05 mm (.002")**, will give the thickness of shims to be inserted between bearing cup and the seat in the axle tube.

Note: the reason for decreasing the thickness of shims by .05 mm (.002") lies in the fact that, while the bearing cup makes a loose fit in tool during the measurement, in the axle tube the cup makes a press fit; as a consequence, the cup shrinks radially causing a reduction in pinion-to-ring gear clearance which eventually results in a greater bearing pre-load.

- Install shims **S** of thickness as previously determined within bearing seat in L.H. axle tube; then drive the bearing cup in place with tool **A.3.0208.**

- Assemble the R.H. & L.H. axle shaft and fasten with the attaching nuts; **do not bend the tabs of tabwashers.**

- Again check the backlash and the pre-load of differential case bearings:

  — **if the pre-load is as specified and the backlash lower than normal**, add shims at the R.H. bearing and remove **the same thickness** from the pack of shims at the L.H. bearing; vice-versa if the backlash is greater than normal;

  — **if the backlash is as specified and the pre-load is wrong**, add or remove the same quantity of shims from both bearings according to whether the pre-load must be increased or diminished respectively.

REAR AXLE

REASSEMBLY ON BENCH - REINSTALLATION

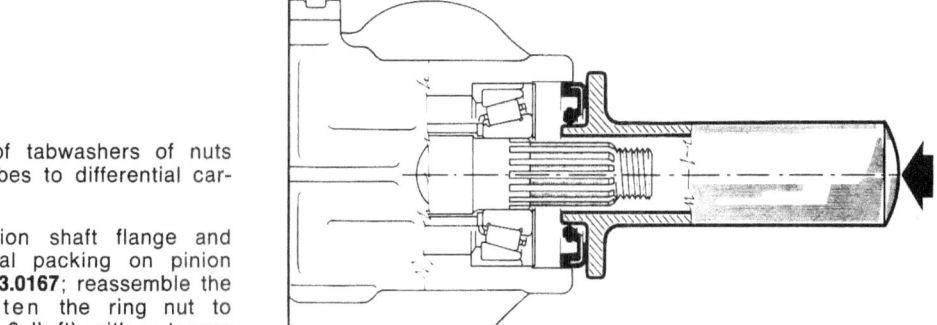

- Bend the tabs of tabwashers of nuts attaching axle tubes to differential carrier.

- Remove the pinion shaft flange and drive the oil seal packing on pinion shaft with tool **A.3.0167**; reassemble the flange and tighten the ring nut to **8-14 Kgm** (58-101.2 lb-ft) with a torque wrench and the bushing **A.5.0104**; counteract flange rotation with tool **A.2.0144**.

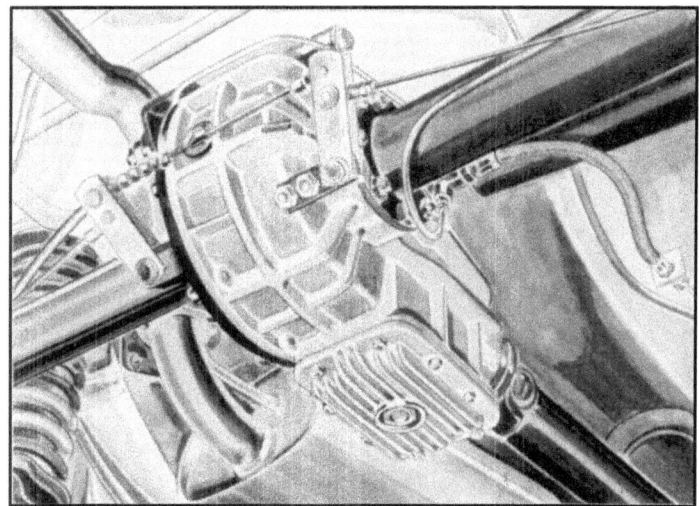

- If previously removed, drive the bearing on to axle shaft with tool **A.3.0109**; tighten the ring nut with the wrench **A.5.0120**.

- Insert the axle shaft into the tube and drive it into the differential side gear splines.

- Complete the reassembly as directed on page 16.

- Install the rear axle assembly to the body by reversing the removal procedure.

TIGHTENING TORQUE SPECIFICATION

	Kgm	lb - ft
Screws securing ring gear to differential case	4.5 - 5	32.6 - 36.1
Ring nut securing flange to final drive pinion	8 - 14	58 - 101.2
Nuts securing bearing housing to rear axle tubes	4.8 - 5.5	34.8 - 39.7
Nuts securing radius rods to body	10 - 11.5	72 - 94
Nuts securing radius rods to rear axle tubes	11.5 - 13	83 - 94
Nut securing reaction trunnion to body	4.8 - 5.5	34.8 - 39.7
Nut securing reaction trunnion to differential carrier	11 - 15	79.6 - 108.5
Screws securing brake cylinders to axle tubes (Dunlop brakes)	.4 - .5	2.9 - 3.6
Screws securing rear brake caliper to support Dunlop brakes	2.3 - 2.8	16.7 - 20.2
Screws securing rear brake caliper to support ATE brakes	5.5 - 6.5	39.8 - 47.0
Nuts securing wheels	6 - 8	43.4 - 57.8
Bolts joining differential flange to propeller shaft yoke	3.5 - 4	25.3 - 28.9

REAR SUSPENSION

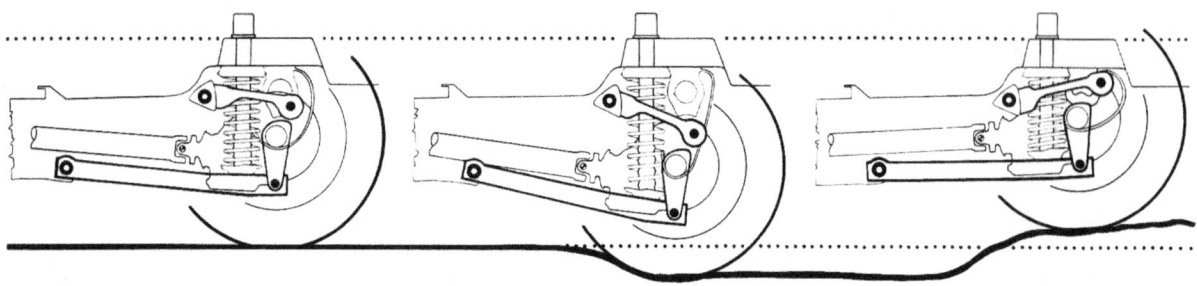

Suspension springing: suspension members move up and down while the car remains level.

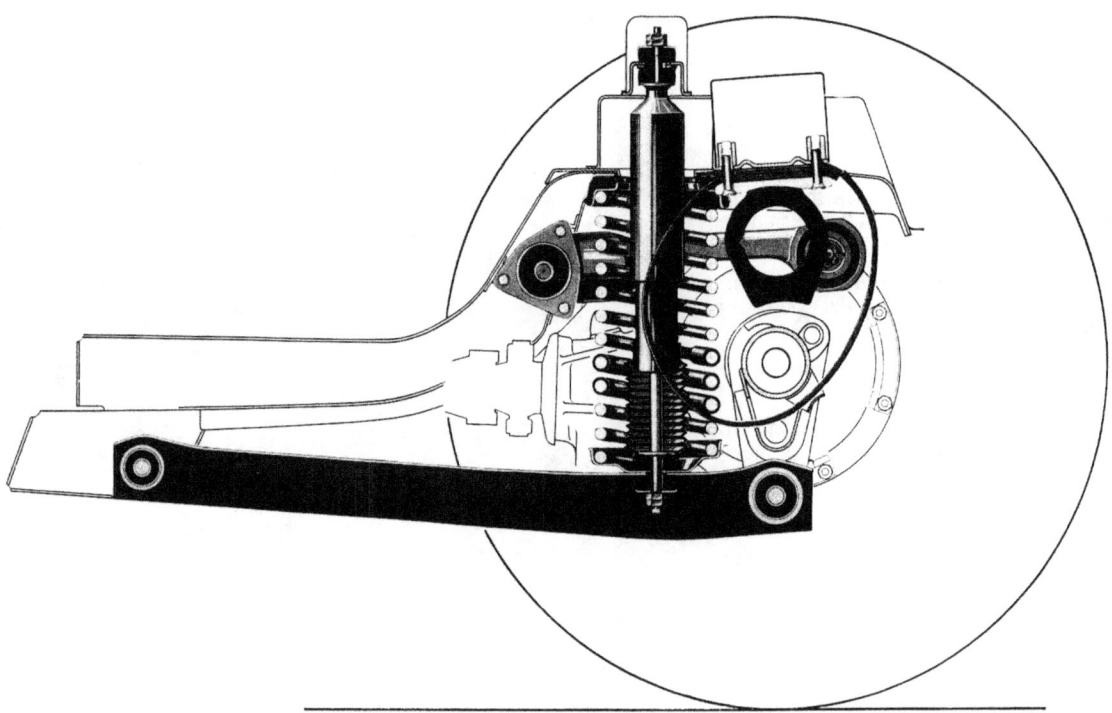

The rear suspension consists of coil springs and large diameter telescopic shock absorbers coaxial with the springs. The upward movement of the rear axle is limited by a rubber pad and the rebound by a fabric and rubber strap.

REAR SUSPENSION

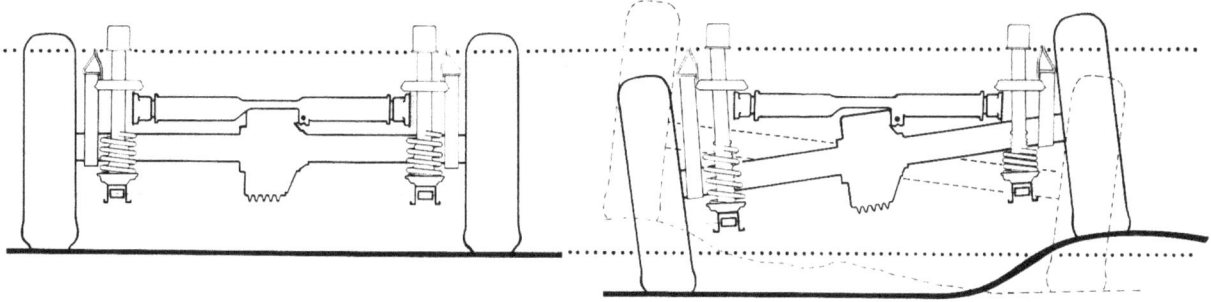

Suspension tilting: the rear axle pivots on the reaction trunnion fixed to the body while the car remains level.

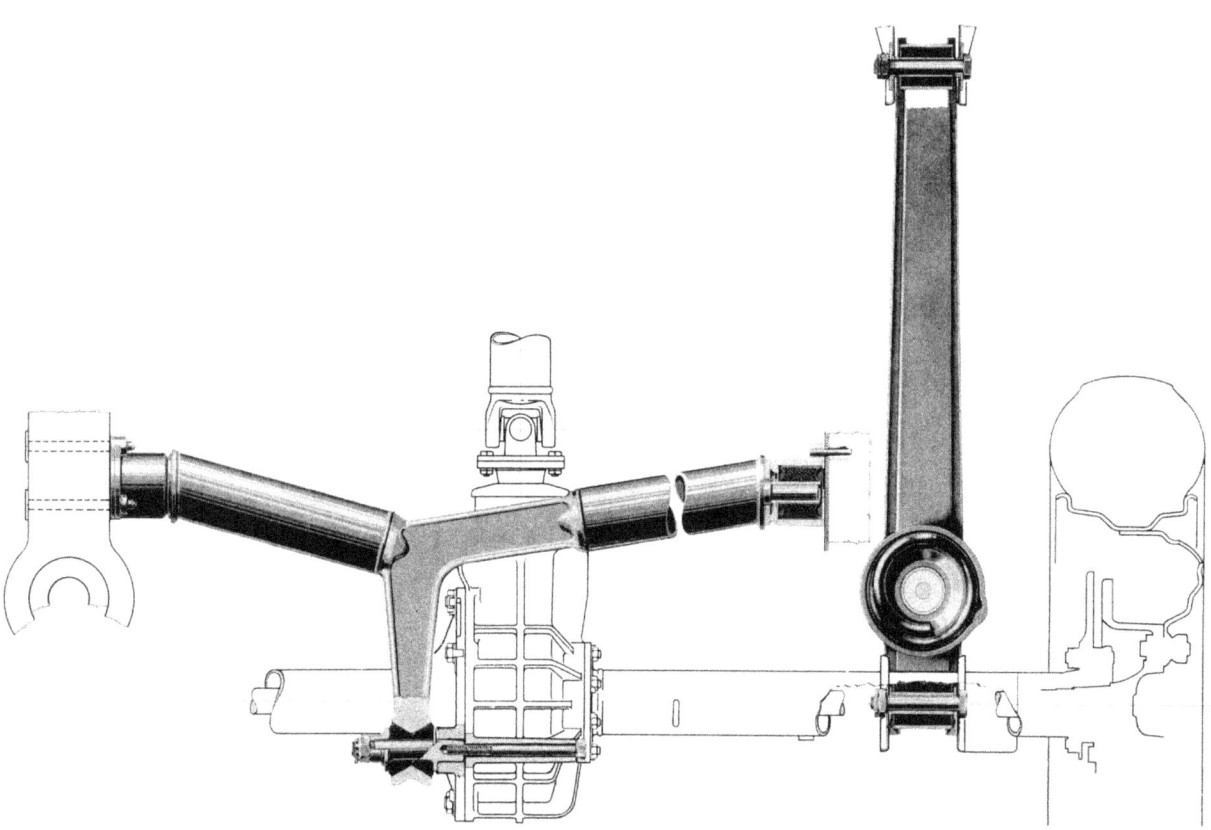

30
REAR SUSPENSION

PADS & REBOUND STRAPS - SHOCK ABSORBERS

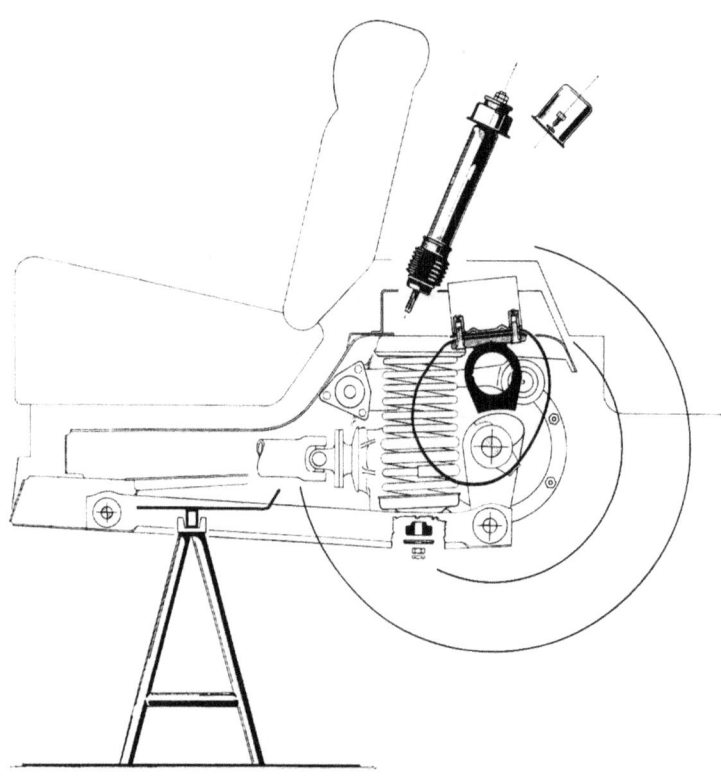

Removal of rebound straps and rubber pads

- Load the rear end of car so as to slacken the rebound straps slightly.
- Remove screws attaching rebound straps and pads.
- Replace defective parts.

Note: when reassembling pads and rebound straps make sure they are in the same position as before removal.

Removal of shock absorbers

- Disconnect the shock absorbers from radius rods.
- Fully collapse the shock absorbers.
- From the luggage compartment remove the shock upper attachments and withdraw the shocks upward; to do this easily take away the rear seat backrest.

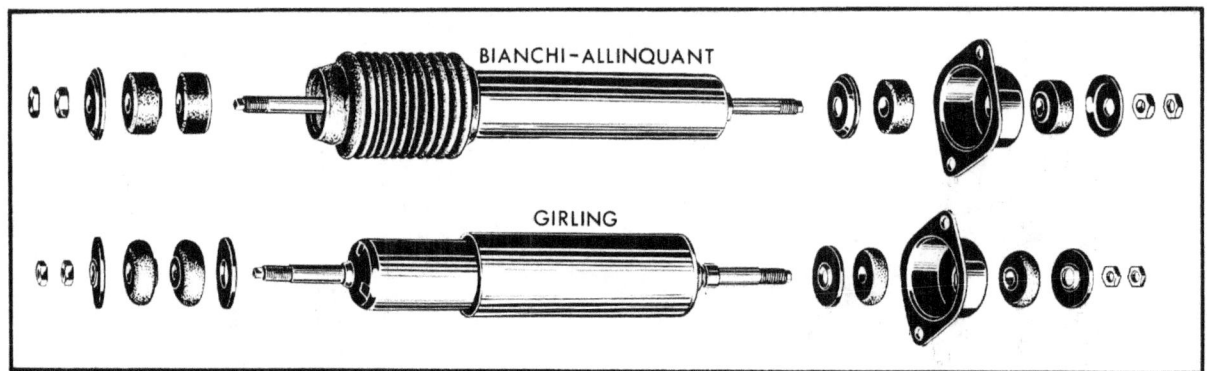

Shock absorber inspection and testing

- Inspect the shock absorber barrel and the cover for distortion.
- Check the cover for binding against the shock absorber barrel and for any sign of oil leaks.
- Check that shock absorber mounting pads are in good condition and replace if necessary.
- Check the shock absorbers on the test rig for correct damping action at high and low speed.

31
REAR SUSPENSION

SHOCK ABSORBERS

- Test as directed in Tool Bulletin no. 32/1 and specifically:
  - draw the zero reference line with the rig under no load;
  - install the shock absorber to be tested on the rig;
  - turn the control knob to slow speed and start the rig motor: the writing needle will record the corresponding curve;
  - then turn to high speed and record the curve.

The readings should fall within the limits given in the table below.

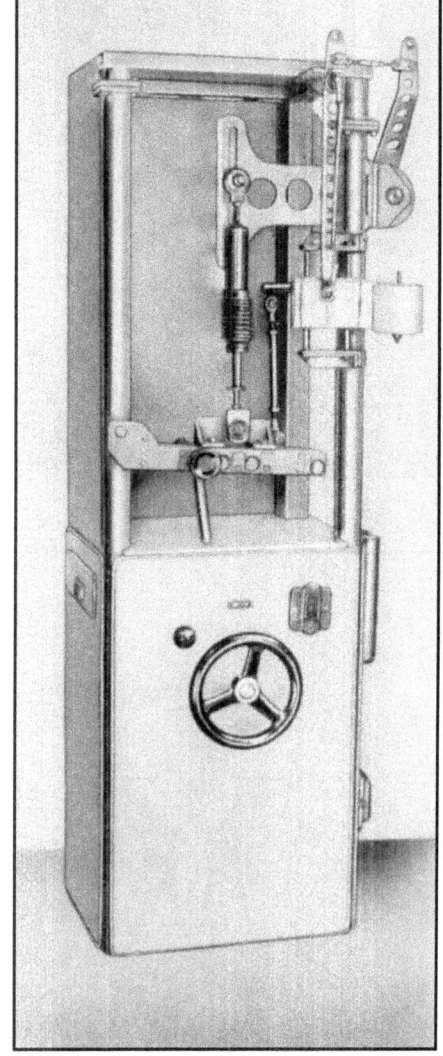

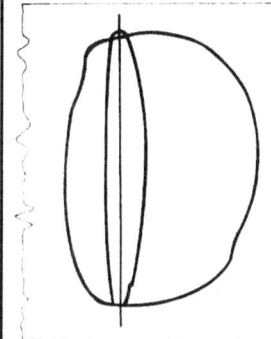

Rear shock absorber rating:

MAKE	EXTENSION		COMPRESSION	
	High speed	Low speed	High speed	Low speed
Bianchi Allinquant	135-190 Kg 300-418 lbs	19- 55 Kg 41-121 lbs	50- 80 Kg 110-176 lbs	9-22 Kg 20-48 lbs
Girling	121-190 Kg 270-418 lbs	13- 32 Kg 29- 70 lbs	27- 42 Kg 60- 92 lbs	9-18 Kg 20-39 lbs

Note: shock absorbers must be tested when cool. In the event the shock has been left inactive for a long time, cycle it through a few strokes before testing.

Replace shocks with new ones if test results do not fall within the above limits.

Take readings with the suitable transparent chart (the chart shown is rated in Kgs).

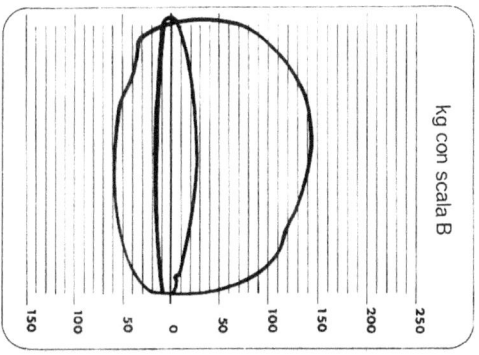

Reinstall the shock absorbers by reversing the order of removal. Inspect the mounting pads and replace, if necessary.

REAR SUSPENSION

REACTION TRUNNION

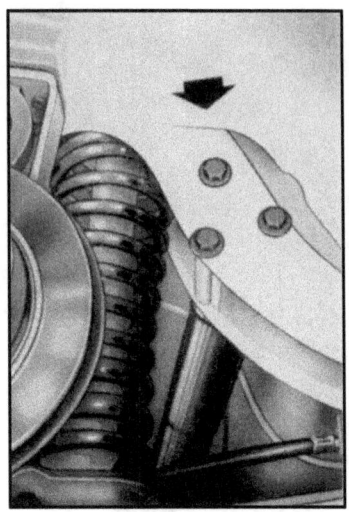
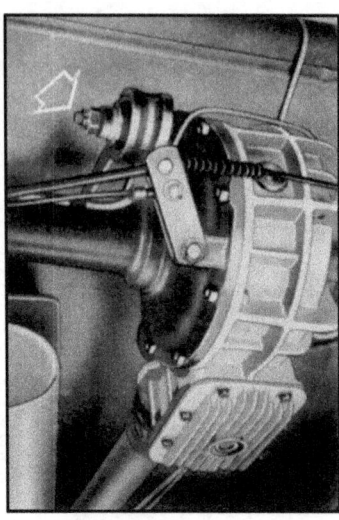

Removal of reaction trunnion from car

- Remove the rear section of the exhaust pipe;
  - loosen the screws attaching the trunnion rubber bushing seats to the body;
  - unscrew the nut attaching the trunnion to the pin on rear axle;
  - swing down the trunnion and take it away.

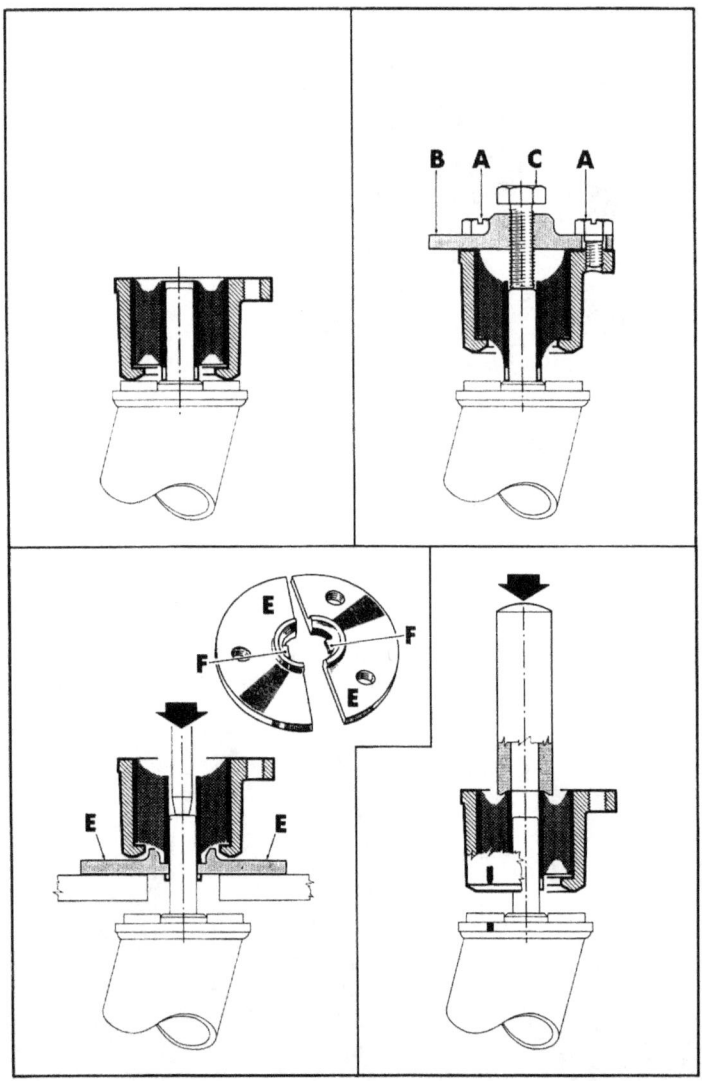

Inspection and replacement

- Check the pads for the attachment of trunnion to rear axle for any sign of deterioration; replace, if necessary.
- Check the rubber bushings and their seats for good condition. If necessary, replace them as follows:
  - secure the flange **B** of the tool **A.3.0163** (Tool Bulletin no. 101) to the rubber bushing seat with the three screws **A**; tighten screw **C** so as to stretch the rubber until enough gap is left to insert the half-plates **E**;
  - when inserting the half-plates take care to match the tabs **F** with slots in the inner sleeve of rubber bushing; then, slacken screw **C**;
  - remove the flange **B** and pull the bushing and the seat out as a unit by using a suitable punch.

To reinstall the rubber bushings on trunnion align the reference marks on bushing seat and trunnion and drive the bushing with tool **A.3.0164.**

REAR SUSPENSION

REACTION TRUNNION - SUSPENSION SPRINGS

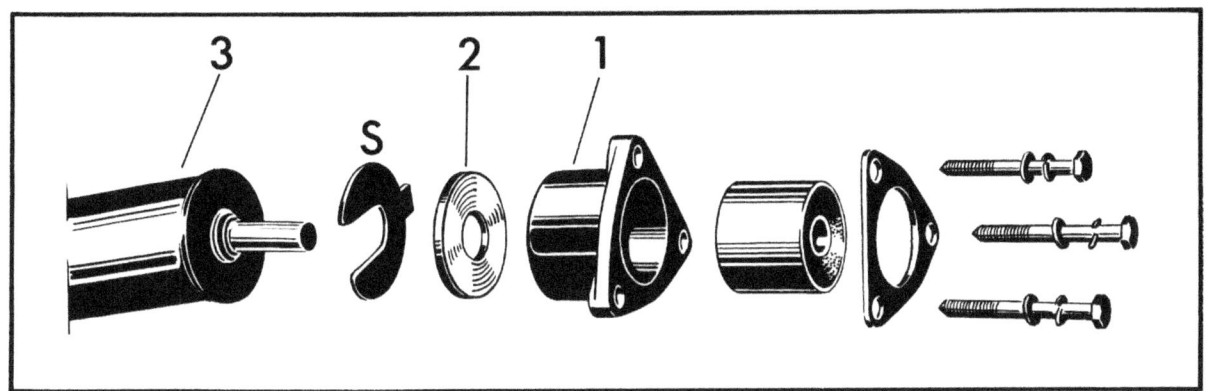

Reinstalling the reaction trunnion

- Proceed in reverse order of removal. On reinstallation check that total gap **L** (right side + left side) between rubber bushing seat **1** and the plastic washers **2** does not exceed **1 mm** (.04''); if necessary, add shims **S** between the trunnion beam **3** and the plastic washer; then electric weld such a shim to the trunnion. When selecting the thickness of shims to be added, keep in mind that a maximum interference fit of **1 mm** (.04'') is allowed between reaction trunnion and body.

- Tighten with a torque wrench:
  - the screws attaching reaction trunnion to body to **4.8 - 5.5 Kgm** (34.8 - 39.7 lb-ft);
  - the nut securing reaction trunnion to rear axle to **11 - 15 Kgm** (79.6 - 108.5 lb-ft).

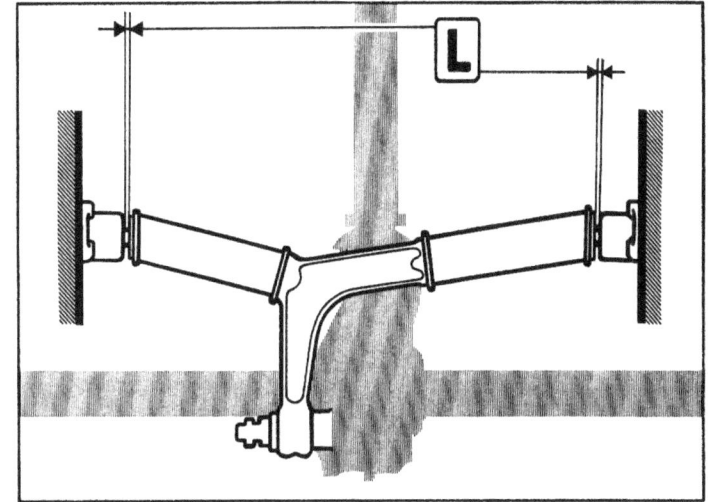

Suspension springs

- Remove the springs with tool **A.2.0143** as directed on page 17.
- Check the springs against the specifications given in the table and for any sign of distortion.

		LENGTH		STATIC TEST	
		Free	Under test load	Test load	Color mark
G I U L I A	1300 1300 ti Super	449 mm 17.7''		321 -341 Kg 706 -750 lbs	Blue Blue
	ti	461 mm 18.3''		341.5-362.5 Kg 752 -798 lbs	—
	ti Super	405 mm 15.9''	252 mm 9.9''	245.4-260.6 Kg 540 -574 lbs	Blue Blue
	Sprint GT GTC	429 mm 16.9''		265 Kg 584 lbs	White-White White-Blue
	Sprint GT Veloce	437 mm 17.2''		268.7-285.3 Kg 592 -627 lbs	Blue-Blue White-Blue
	Spider 1600	429 mm 16.9''		257 -273 Kg 566 -600 lbs	White-White White-Blue

34
REAR SUSPENSION

RADIUS RODS

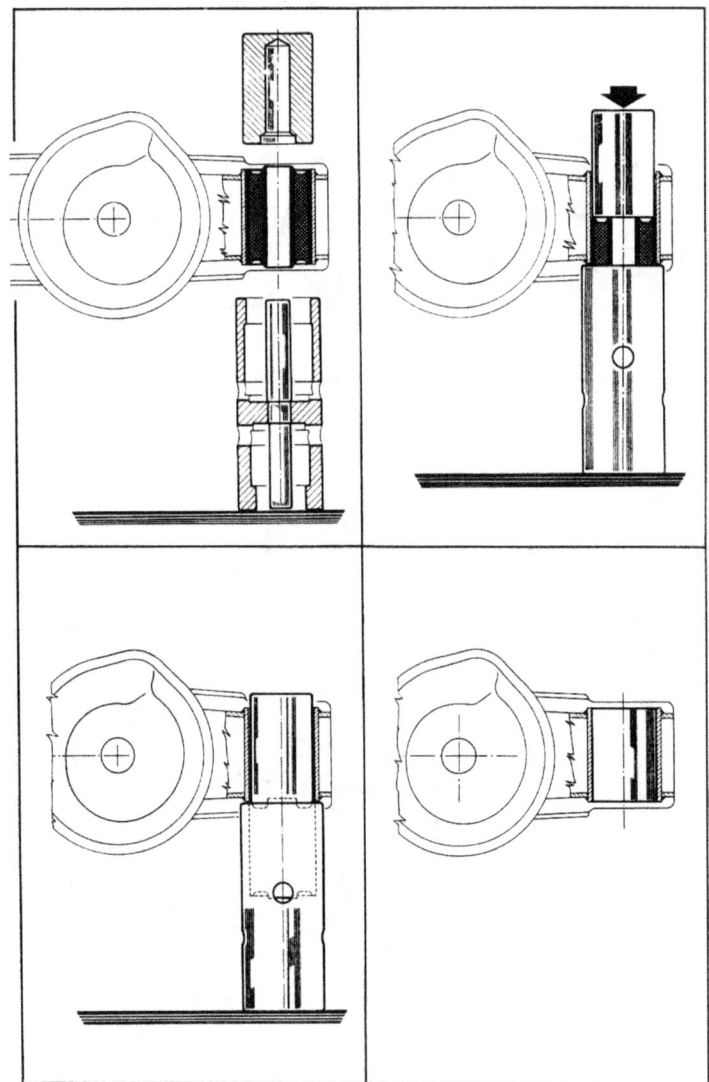

Removing the radius rods

- Take the spring away from the radius rod to be removed with the tool **A.2.0143** as directed on page 17.
- Withdraw the bolt connecting radius rod to body and remove the rod.

Inspection and replacement

- Check the front and rear rubber bushings of the radius rod for any sign of damage to the rubber.
- If damaged, remove the rubber bushing with the tool **A.3.0211** (see figure).

- Insert the new rubber bushing with tool **A.3.0211**.
- Reinstall the radius rod onto the car in reverse order of removal.
- Tighten with a torque wrench:
  - the nuts securing radius rods to rear axle to **11.5-13 Kgm** (83-94 lb-ft);
  - the nuts securing radius rods to body to **10-11.5 Kgm** (72-33 lb-ft).

WARNING

On completion of suspension assembly check the car for correct alignment.
To carry out this check disconnect the shock absorbers and stabilizer rod and put the car under static load.

The dimension **C** between axle tube and rubber buffer must be as specified in the table below. If necessary add shims in **2** as required and remove seat **3**.

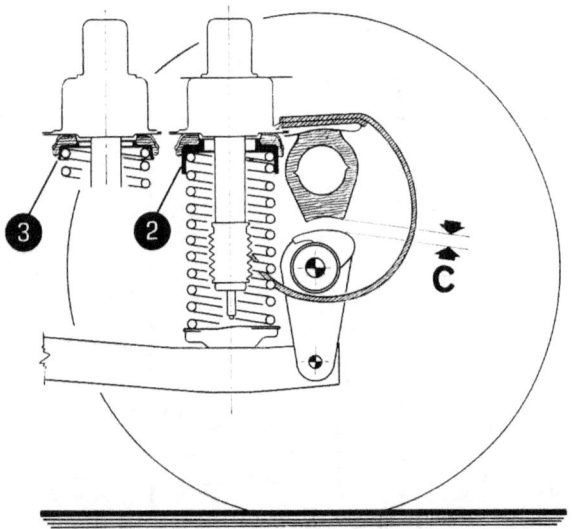

C	Model
10 ± 5 mm .2/.6''	Giulia 1300, Giulia 1300 ti, Giulia TI, Giulia Super
20 ± 5 mm .6/1.0''	Giulia TI Super
15 ± 5 mm .4/.8''	Giulia Sprint GT, Giulia Sprint GT Vel.
12 ± 5 mm .3/.7''	Giulia GTC
33 ± 5 mm 1.1/1.5''	Spider 1600

SHOP MANUAL No. 3

BRAKES

**DRUM BRAKES
HYDRAULIC SYSTEM
DUNLOP DISC BRAKES
ATE DISC BRAKES (FACTORY MANUAL)**

BRAKE SYSTEMS

Early Giulia 1600 models are fitted with drum brakes front and rear, disc front brakes being introduced at the end of 1964 and fitted to all models produced after that date. Giulia TI and Sprint GT models are equipped with four disc brake assemblies and a vacuum servo unit. The brakes on all four wheels are hydraulically operated by the brake pedal, the handbrake operating the rear brakes only through a mechanical linkage. The brake pedal is directly connected to the master cylinder where pressure on the fluid is generated and passed to the brakes by a system of metal and flexible pipes.

Front drum brakes are of the three leading shoe type arranged in a fully-floating configuration, each shoe being operated by a separate wheel cylinder. Rear wheel drum brakes each have one leading and one trailing shoe, both being operated by a single wheel cylinder.

Disc brakes have a fixed caliper with two self-adjusting friction pads between which the disc rotates. The friction pads are applied by two pistons operated by hydraulic pressure from the master cylinder, both pistons operating simultaneously to exert equal pressure on the pads. On Dunlop braking systems, the rear disc brakes are actuated through a pair of pressed steel levers by pushrods connected to remote operating cylinders mounted on the rear axle.

MAINTENANCE

Regularly check the level of the fluid in the master cylinder supply tank and replenish if necessary up to the MAX mark on the tank. Wipe dirt from around the filler cap before removing it and check that the vent hole in the cap is unobstructed. If frequent topping-up is required the system should be examined for leaks, but it should be noted that disc brake systems will need more frequent topping-up than all-drum systems, due to the wheel cylinder movement compensating for friction pad wear. The recommended fluid is Castrol Girling Amber. **Never use anything but the recommended fluid.**

On cars equipped with four disc brake assemblies no adjustment is necessary, wear being automatically taken up by the brake mechanisms. Drum brakes must be adjusted when brake pedal travel becomes excessive, at all four wheels on earlier cars or at the rear wheels only when disc front brakes are fitted.

FRONT DRUM BRAKE ADJUSTMENT

Three adjusters are provided on the drum front brake plate, one for each brake shoe. **As the shoes are fully-floating, any adjustments made to one shoe will also affect the others therefore shoe adjustments must be made carefully and accurately to ensure equal pressure on each shoe when the brakes are applied.** If the brakes are adjusted in an incorrect manner it is possible for a brake shoe to be cracked under the effects of heavy braking, apart from the obvious consequence of brake inefficiency.

Jack up the car so that the front wheels can be turned freely. Refer to the diagram and slacken each of the brake shoe adjusters to its fullest extent, this operation ensuring that each shoe is in the same position relative to the others. Now tighten the adjusters equally and alternately until the shoes just contact the brake drum. This condition can be felt by turning the wheel after each adjustment is made. When resistance to turning can be felt, slacken off the adjusters equally by one to three clicks, or until the wheel just rotates freely. Press the brake pedal several times then check again for free rotation, slackening the adjusters further if necessary.

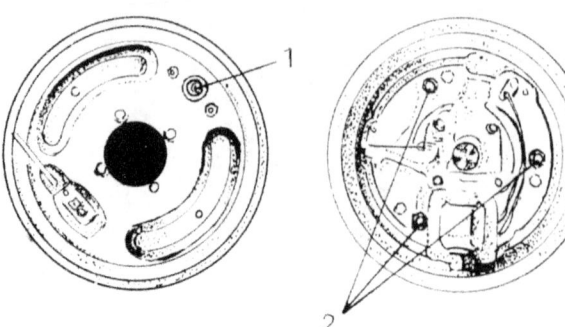

The rear and front drum brake adjusters

1 Rear brake shoe adjuster   2 Front brake shoe adjusters

REAR DRUM BRAKE ADJUSTMENT

Chock the front wheels, jack up the rear of the car and release the handbrake. See the diagram above, tighten the adjuster shown until the brake shoes can be felt touching the drum when the wheel is rotated, then slacken the adjuster until the wheel can just be rotated freely. If the adjuster needs to be slackened more than three-quarters of a turn to allow the wheel to rotate freely misalignment of the brake shoes could be indicated, in which case shoe alignment should be checked in the following manner. Remove the road wheel and the brake drum, then fit tool C.6.0106 to the brake assembly, see the diagram below. If the brake lining does not contact the gauge plate over the whole of its length, the brake shoe alignment screw at the rear of the brake plate should be turned until this condition is fulfilled. Repeat the operation on the second shoe. With the shoes set parallel to the drum in this manner, readjust the brake as previously described.

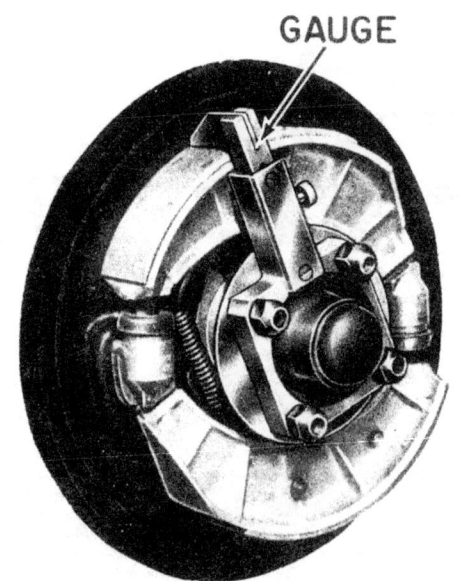

Check the brake shoes operate parallel to the drum

PREVENTATIVE MAINTENANCE

Regularly examine friction pads, brake linings and all pipes, unions and hoses. Change the brake fluid every year or 11,250 miles. Every 22,500 miles check all flexible hoses and fluid seals in the system and renew if necessary. Do not leave brake fluid in unsealed containers as it will absorb moisture which can be dangerous. It is best to discard fluid drained from the system or after bleeding.

Observe absolute cleanliness when working on all parts of the hydraulic system.

DRUM BRAKES

REMOVE AND REFIT FRONT BRAKE SHOES

Jack up the car and remove the road wheel and brake drum. Refer to the diagram, mark the brake shoes 5 for refitting in their original positions and remove the return spring 16. Carefully lift out the brake shoes, noting that each shoe guide is slotted into the adjacent shoe.

REFITTING

Clean the brake drum and backing plate thoroughly, using care to avoid dirt entering the wheel cylinder seals or wheel bearings. Make sure that the return spring is correctly fitted and that the brake shoe guides are correctly aligned. Slacken off all three brake shoe adjusters completely before refitting the drum and, when assembly is completed, adjust the brake as previously described.

REMOVE AND REFIT REAR BRAKE SHOES

Chock the front wheels, jack up the rear wheel and release the handbrake, then remove the brake drum. Refer to the diagram, remove the return springs 2 and 8 and lift out the brake shoes.

REFITTING

Clean the brake drum and backing plate thoroughly, using care to avoid dirt entering the wheel cylinder seals or bearings. Make sure that the return springs are correctly refitted, noting that the waisted spring is fitted to the wheel cylinder side of the assembly. Check that the shoes are slotted into the wheel cylinder and adjuster pistons and slacken the adjuster completely before refitting the drum. On completion, adjust the brakes as previously described.

HANDBRAKE ADJUSTMENT

Always check the adjustment of the rear shoes prior to adjusting the handbrake cable as adjustment of the rear brake shoes will automatically take up excessive handbrake free movement. If not, check the rear brake shoes and renew them if they are badly worn. If the handbrake is slack due to cable stretching or if it has been refitted after a servicing operation, act on the handbrake cable adjuster beneath the car. The cable is correctly adjusted when the rear wheels can be locked with the handbrake moved through half its total travel.

RELINING BRAKE SHOES

If the linings are worn down to the rivets, renewal is necessary. It is not recommended that owners attempt to reline brake shoes themselves. It is important that the linings should be properly bedded to the shoes, ground for concentricity and correctly chamfered at their leading and trailing edges. For this reason it is best to obtain sets of replacement shoes, or have the relining carried out by a service station. **Do not allow grease, oil or brake fluid to contact brake linings.** If the linings are contaminated in any way they must be renewed as they cannot be successfully cleaned.

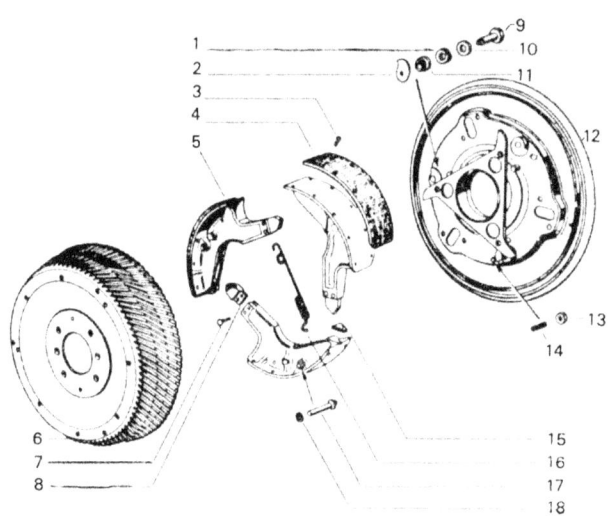

Components of the front drum brake assembly

1 Spring wsher
2 Adjuster cam
3 Lining rivet
4 Brake lining
5 Brake shoe
6 Brake drum
7 Rivet
8 Guide
9 Pivot pin
10 Washer
11 Bush
12 Backplate
13 Nut
14 Guide pin
15 Guide
16 Shoe return Spring
17 Adjusting pin
18 Washer

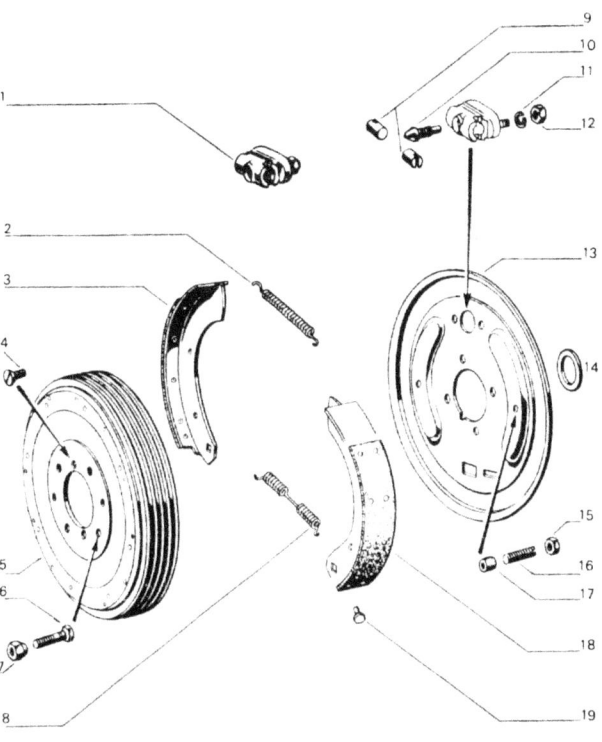

Components of a typical rear drum brake assembly

Key to Diagram
1 Brake adjuster assembly
2 Adjuster side shoe return spring
3 Brake shoe
4 Screw
5 Brake drum
6 Bolt
7 Nut
8 Cylinder side shoe return spring
9 Adjuster piston
10 Adjuster wedge
11 Lockwasher
12 Nut
13 Backplate
14 Shim
15 Nut
16 Shoe alignment adjuster
17 Piston
18 Brake lining
19 Rivet

HYDRAULIC SYSTEM

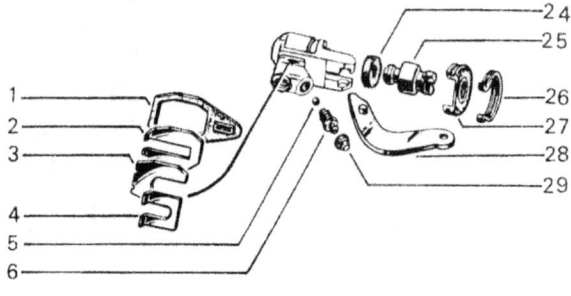
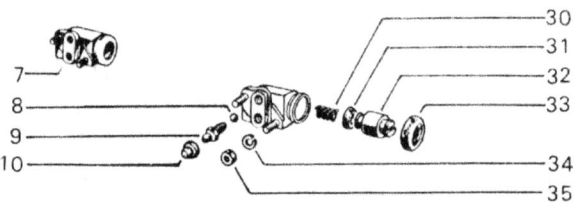
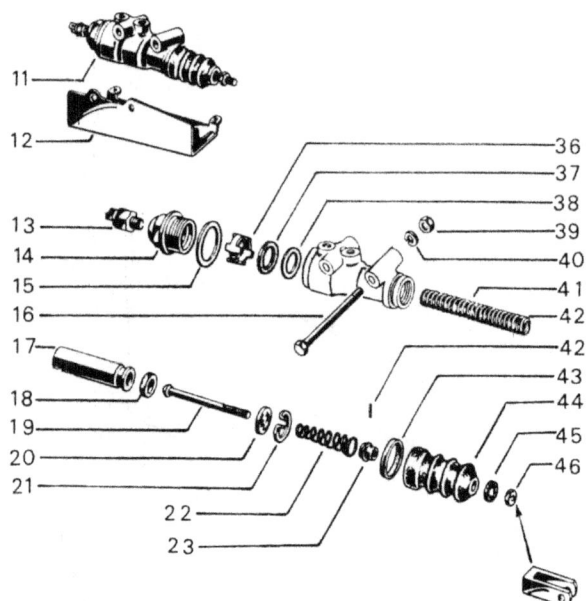

SERVICING HYDRAULIC WHEEL CYLINDERS

Remove the road wheel, drum and brake shoes. Disconnect the brake pipe or hose from the cylinder which is to be removed and use a plug to prevent fluid loss. Refer to the diagram which shows the components of both the front and rear wheel cylinders.

To remove a rear wheel cylinder, detach the handbrake operating lever 28 and the dust cover 1, retaining spring 2, securing plate 3 and spring clip 4, noting the arrangement of these components to ensure correct refitting.

To remove a front wheel cylinder, remove the attaching nuts 35 and lockwashers 34.

Remove the internal components from the cylinder housing and unscrew the bleeder screw, collecting the steel ball from behind the screw. Discard the rubber cups, seals and covers and thoroughly clean the remaining parts in the correct grade of brake fluid. Inspect the piston and cylinder bore for scoring or corrosion and renew any unserviceable component.

Dip the internal parts in brake fluid and reassemble the cylinder, using the fingers to insert the new rubber cups and to fit the new rubber seals to avoid damaging the edges. Install the wheel cylinder onto the brake backing plate and connect the brake pipe or hose. Fit a new dust cover 1 to rear brake assemblies if the original cover is worn or perished. Refit the shoes, drum and road wheel, then bleed the brakes.

SERVICING MASTER CYLINDER

Disconnect the brake line from the connection on the master cylinder and plug the pipe to prevent the entry of dirt. Tape the master cylinder connection to prevent fluid from draining from the supply tank. Remove the two securing bolts and the clevis pin connector and lift out the master cylinder.

Drain the brake fluid from the supply tank. Unscrew the clevis pin fork and its locknut and remove the retaining rings and rubber boot. Using a suitable tool, carefully remove the circlip 21 and withdraw and separate the internal parts.

Thoroughly clean the internal parts with brake fluid and inspect them for wear or damage, renewing any part found to be unserviceable. Check the surface of the piston and the bore of the cylinder and renew either component if there are signs of scoring or corrosion. Always fit new rubber cups and seals.

Reassemble the master cylinder in the reverse order of dismantling, coating all internal parts with brake fluid and assembling them wet with the fluid.

Fit the master cylinder assembly to the car in the reverse order of removal. **There must be a minimum clearance of .040 inch between the piston and pushrod to prevent the rubber cup from obstructing the brake supply tank feed port.** With the brake pedal in the rest position, adjust for a free play of .040 inch minimum by means of the clevis fork adjusting nut. On completion, refill the supply tank with the correct grade of brake fluid and bleed the system.

Components of the brake cylinders.

The rear wheel cylinder is at the top, followed by the front wheel cylinder and the master cylinder

1. Dust cap
2. Retaining spring
3. Securing plate
4. Spring clip
5. Ball
6. Bleeder screw
7. Wheel brake cylinder
8. Ball
9. Bleeder screw
10. Dust cap
11. Master cylinder assembly
12. Mounting bracket
13. Brake light switch
14. Closing plug
15. Seal ring
16. Mounting bolt
17. Piston
18. Piston cup
19. Pushrod
20. Stop washer
21. Circlip
22. Return spring
23. Spring seat
24. Piston cup
25. Piston
26. Retaining ring
27. Dust cover
28. Handbrake operating lever
29. Dust cap
30. Return spring
31. Piston cup
32. Piston
33. Dust cap
34. Spring washer
35. Nut
36. Spacer
37. Main piston seal
38. Washer
39. Nut
40. Spring washer
41. Return spring
42. Pin
43. Retaining ring
44. Rubber boot
45. Retaining ring
46. Locknut

HYDRAULIC SYSTEM

BLEEDING THE HYDRAULIC SYSTEM

This is not routine maintenance and is only necessary if air has entered the system due to parts being dismantled or because the fluid level in the master cylinder supply tank has dropped too low. The need for bleeding is indicated by a spongy feeling of the brake pedal accompanied by poor braking performance. Do not bleed the brakes with any drum or caliper removed. Always bleed the brake furthest from the master cylinder first, finishing with the brake nearest the master cylinder.

VACUUM ASSIST SERVO UNIT

The vacuum servo unit operates in conjunction with the master cylinder and assists the pressure on the fluid applied at the brake pedal. The vacuum cylinder in the servo is connected to the engine intake manifold by a hose which incorporates a vacuum control valve. The control valve and servo air filter can be renewed if either is defective, but a faulty vacuum servo unit must be renewed as an assembly. To test the operation of the vacuum servo mechanism, switch off the engine and depress the brake pedal several times to clear all the vacuum from the unit. Hold a steady light pressure on the brake pedal and start the engine. If the servo is working correctly, the brake pedal should move further downward without further foot pressure, due to the build up of vacuum in the unit. Failure of the servo unit does not impair the effeciency of the braking system, but greater pedal pressure will be needed to stop the car.

HYDRAULIC PRESSURE REGULATOR

This device is inserted in the hydraulic pressure line to the rear brake to regulate the pressure and provide a balanced braking action. It ensures that under heavy braking a greater proportion of the effort is applied to the front wheels and so prevents the rear brakes from locking the wheels under these conditions.

There is an adjusting nut on the valve, but this is sealed at the factory and should **not** be disturbed.

Layout of tandem brake system

1 Brake pedal
2 Fluid reservoirs (with min level senders)
3 Vacuum servo and master cylinder
4 Vacuum port
5 Brake pistons
6 Brake pads
7 Brake discs
8 Air bleed screws
9 Stop light switch
10 Pressure regulating valve
11 Warning light for min fluid level

DUAL BRAKING (TANDEM) SYSTEM

On later models of these cars, a dual braking system is fitted in which there are two separate hydraulic circuits as shown in the diagram.

A tandem master cylinder is used in which there are two pistons, each with its own hydraulic fluid reservoir, of which one serves the two front brakes and the other the two rear brakes. Servo assistance is available on both circuits.

This system ensures that even in the event of a complete failure in one braking circuit a balanced brake application is still available on two wheels.

A further safety device takes the form of a warning lamp, located on the instrument panel, which will alert the driver if the level of the fluid in either reservoir falls below a minimum. It should be noted that on the 1750 Berlina model this warning lamp also serves to give notice of low pressure in the engine lubrication system.

BLEEDING THE DUAL HYDRAULIC SYSTEM

This operation is performed in a different manner from previously described and is as follows:

Fill the two reservoirs and take care to ensure that the level is not allowed to fall below three-quarters full as the fluid is used during the operation.

Push rubber pipes over the bleed nipples of a front and rear wheel on the same side of the car and lead the free ends into clean glass jars containing a supply of fluid.

Loosen the two bleed screws together and slowly press the brake pedal down and allow it to return of its own accord. At first the fluid expelled from the rubber pipes will be accompanied by air bubbles. Continue to work the brake pedal until both pipes discharge fluid completely free of bubbles then hold the pedal down, tighten the bleed screws and remove the pipes.

Repeat the procedure for the two wheels on the other side of the car.

DUNLOP DISC BRAKES

This page and those following contain information that was extracted and translated from the Alfa Romeo factory publication on the Dunlop disc brake system (Publication No. 930 September 1963). It should be noted that the factory never issued an English language version of this publication. Please note that rudimentary procedures such as 'how to bleed the system' etc., have been omitted.

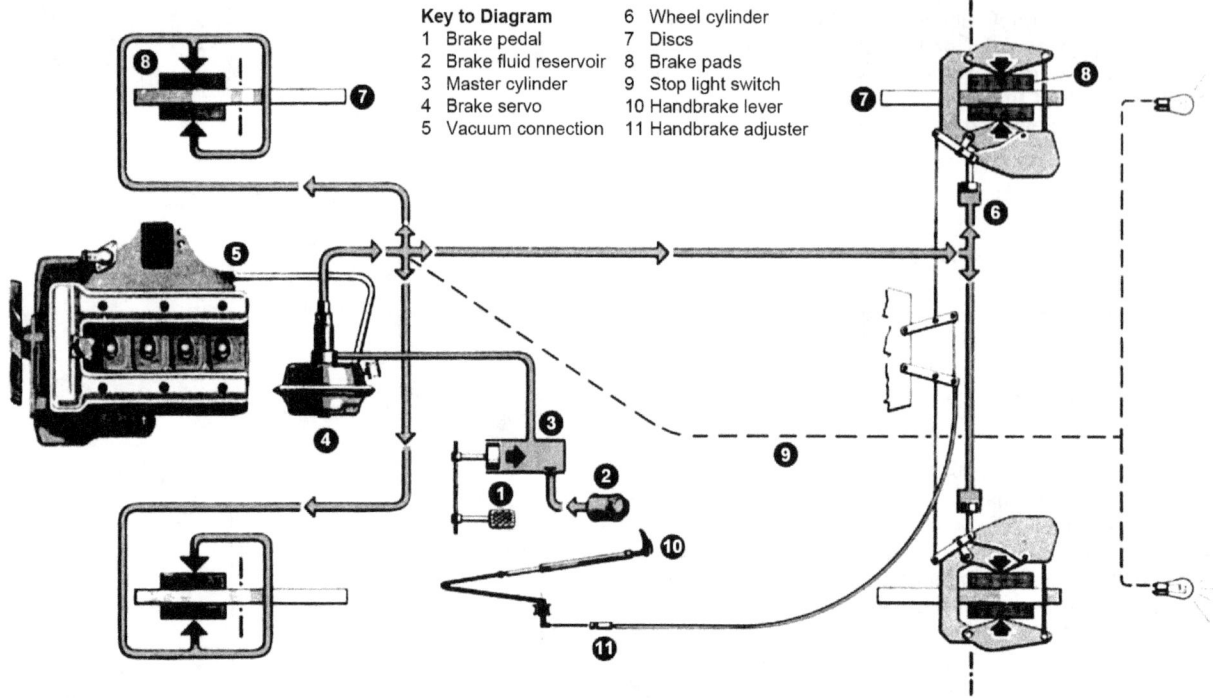

Key to Diagram
1. Brake pedal
2. Brake fluid reservoir
3. Master cylinder
4. Brake servo
5. Vacuum connection
6. Wheel cylinder
7. Discs
8. Brake pads
9. Stop light switch
10. Handbrake lever
11. Handbrake adjuster

GENERAL MAINTENANCE OF THE BRAKING SYSTEM

Every 4,000 km top, up the fluid in the brake reservoir using only CASTROL GIRLING BRAKE FLUID AMBER EXTRA HEAVY DUTY. Every 16,000 Km., or at least once a year, drain and replenish the brake fluid.

FRONT CALIPER MAINTENANCE

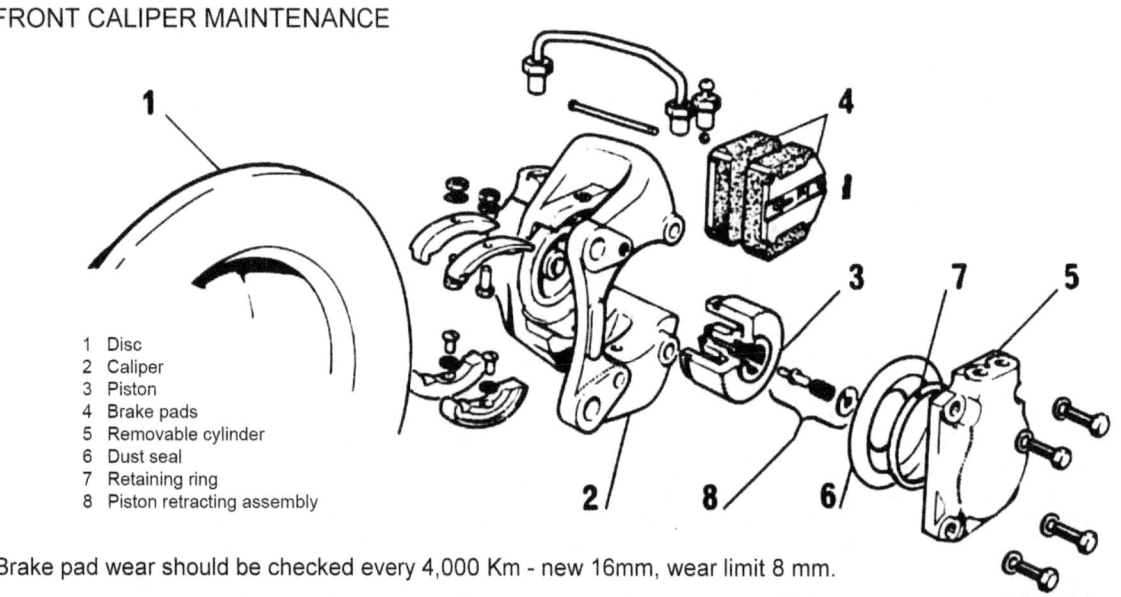

1. Disc
2. Caliper
3. Piston
4. Brake pads
5. Removable cylinder
6. Dust seal
7. Retaining ring
8. Piston retracting assembly

Brake pad wear should be checked every 4,000 Km - new 16mm, wear limit 8 mm.

The maximum eccentricity of the disk must not exceed 0.15 mm. If the eccentricity is greater, it is necessary to carefully check the mounting of the disc on the hub in order to eliminate any possible causes. If the problem persists, the disc must be replaced. The bolts securing the disc to the hub have a torque setting of 7.5 – 8.5 Kgm.

In the event of disassembly of the caliper or disc from its mounting, the position and number of previously installed shims must be observed. Upon reinstallation, it is necessary to check the lateral centering of the disc by comparing the distance between the caliper and the disc on each side, the difference between the two dimensions must not exceed 0.5 mm. Centering of the disc within the caliper can be achieved by the use of shim washers.

DIAGRAM SHOWING COMPONENT PARTS OF A REAR SELF-ADJUSTING DUNLOP CALIPER

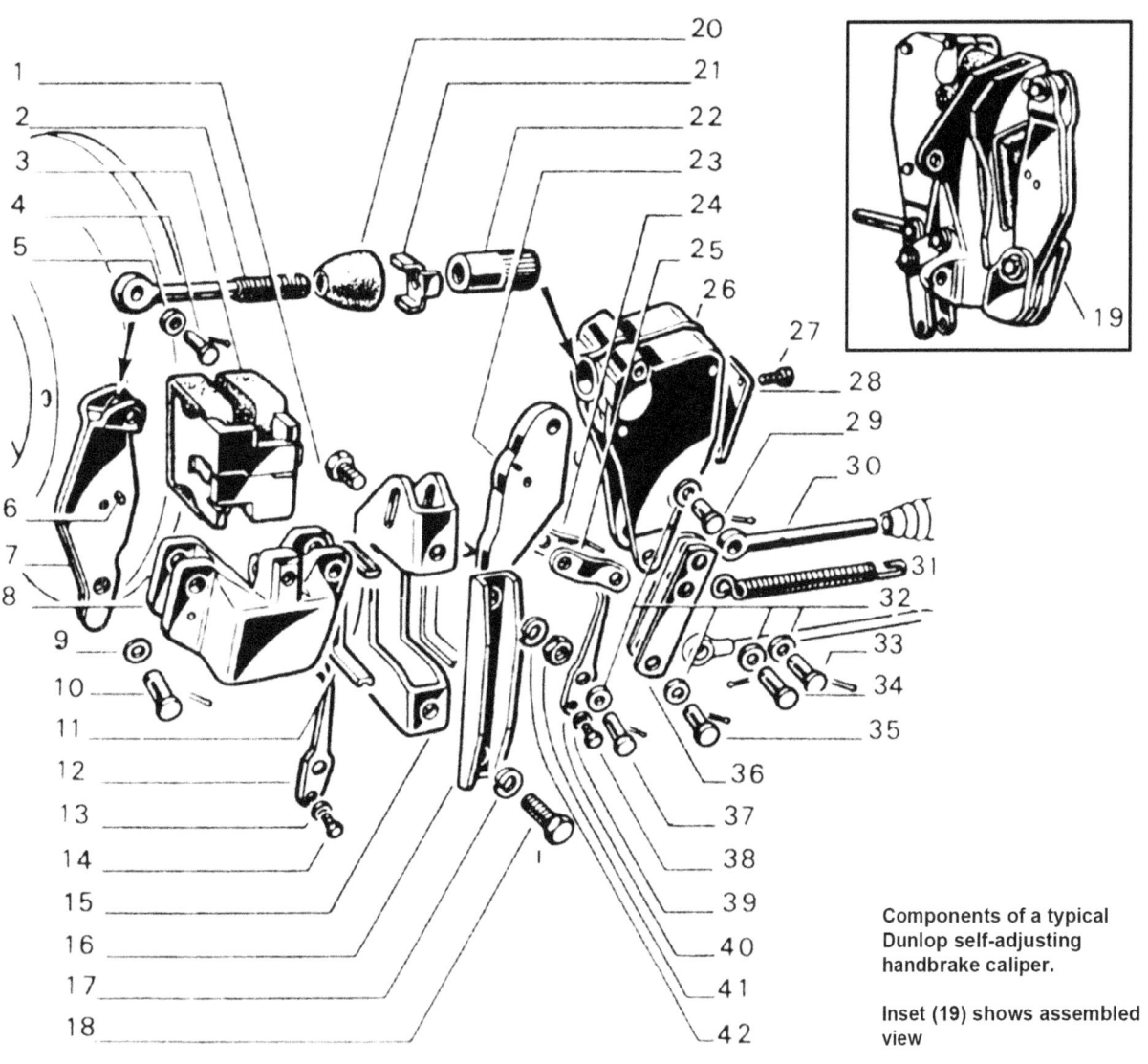

Components of a typical Dunlop self-adjusting handbrake caliper.

Inset (19) shows assembled view

1 Mounting bolt	15 Mounting frame	29 Clevis pin
2 Pullrod	16 Bracket	30 Pushrod
3 Brake pad	17 Spring washer	31 Return spring
4 Mounting bolt	18 Mounting bolt	32 Washer
5 Washer	19 Brake caliper	33 Mounting bolt
6 Pin	20 Dust cover	34 Clevis pin
7 Operating lever	21 Spring clip	35 Clevis pin
8 Brake pad carrier	22 Bush	36 H/brake operating lever
9 Washer	23 Operating lever	37 Clevis pin
10 Pivot pin	24 Operating link	38 Bolt
11 Guide	25 Operating link	39 Washer
12 Return lever	26 Operating lever	40 Return lever
13 Washer	27 Screw	41 Nut
14 Mounting bolt	28 Cover	42 Spring washer

This type of caliper does not normally require any servicing. However, the operation of the 'auto adjust' system can be seen by removing the cover (28) in the diagram and the mechanism can be checked by operating the handbrake.

REAR CALIPER MAINTENANCE

The brake is made up of a pair of pressed steel levers (1), hinged to the caliper (2) and connected together at their upper ends by a retaining pin that also secures a pullrod (3) which is connected to the automatic adjustment operating lever (4).

A push rod (5), connected to a hydraulic cylinder, acts on the lower end of operating lever (4) which by direct action and by means of the pullrod (3), applies a clamping action to the levers (1) which forces the brake pads in contact with the disc.

The brake pads are held in place by a removable bracket (6). The pads are supported by a housing that prevents them from being displaced, they are also kept centered by return levers (7), made of brass, bolted to the calipers. These return levers (7) have sufficient elasticity to retract the pads (after braking) and to accommodate pad wear while maintaining the specified disc to pad clearance (approximately 0.25 mm).

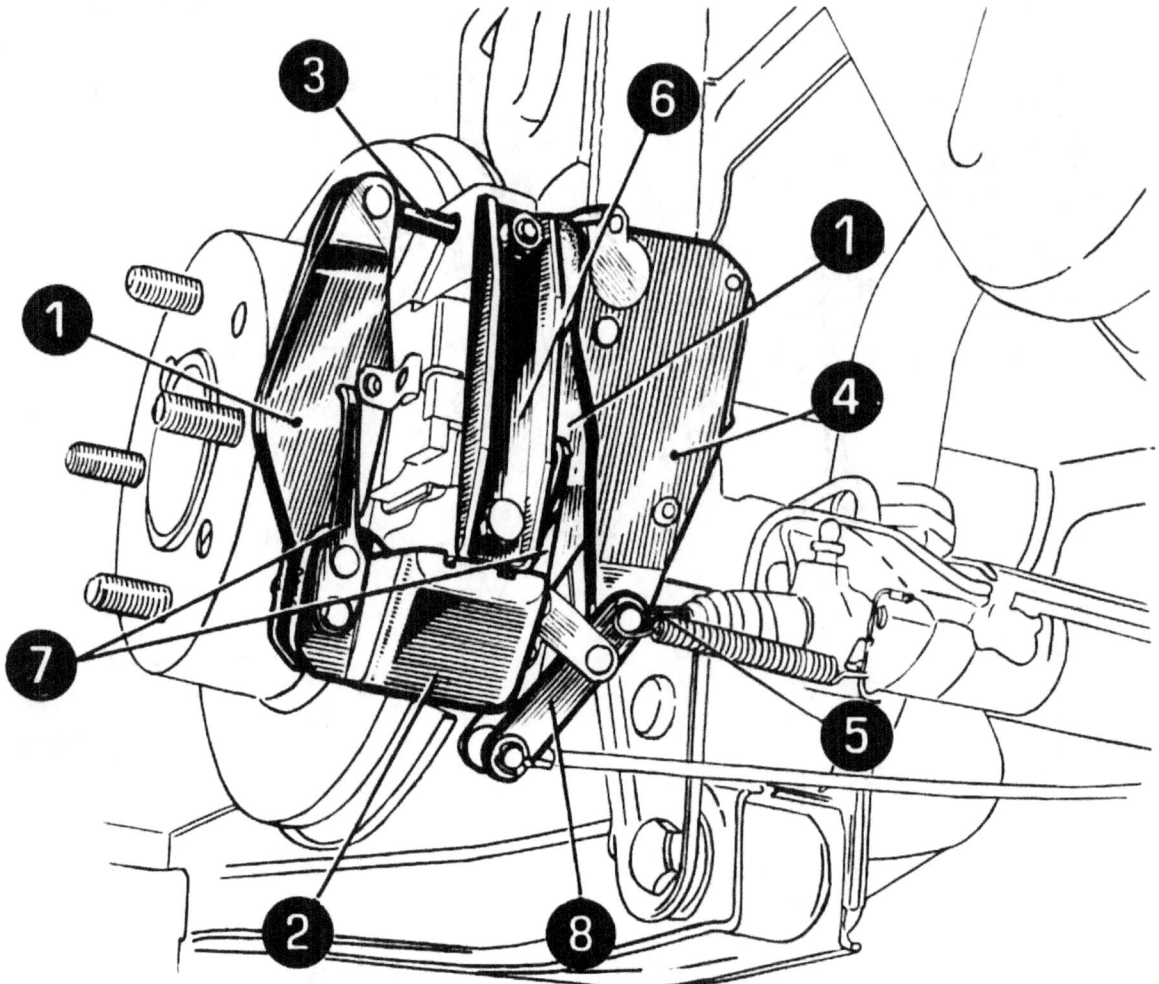

The self-adjusting mechanism is housed between the two halves of the caliper. The function of this mechanism is to take-up any excessive clearance between the brake pads and the disc. The adjustment device consists of a threaded, toothed bush positioned at the inner end of the pullrod (3). The teeth engage a pawl, connected by a spring, to the operating lever (4). Whenever the pad to disc clearance becomes excessive, the pawl engages the nearest tooth of the grooved bush and rotates it, thereby adjusting the length of the pullrod (3). The self-adjusting device cannot be overridden.

HANDBRAKE

The handbrake, which is mechanical in operation, also utilizes the hydraulically operated brake pads.

The handbrake is actuated by a cable attached between the levers (8) which act on the operating lever (4). The leverage exerted by the handbrake cable on the levers (8) forces the operating lever (4) towards the disc, thereby applying tension to the pullrod (3) which in turn pulls the levers (1) inwards and forces the brake pads against the disc.

REAR BRAKE PAD MAINTENANCE

The condition of the rear brake pads should be checked every 4,000 km. Remove the bracket (6) and remove the pads. Check the thickness of the pads, new 17.5 mm, wear limit 10 mm.

To replace the brake pads remove the retaining pin that attaches the pullrod (3) to the levers (1). Unscrew the pullrod counterclockwise until the threads begin to appear from the rubber dust cover.

Pull back the levers (1) and install the new brake pads, if necessary, fit new return levers (7).

Refit the pullrod to the levers (1), insert the retaining pin and secure it with a cotter pin, refit the bracket (6).

Take up any excess play by operating the levers (8) by hand, also checking that the return levers (7) and the automatic adjustment device are functioning correctly; complete the installation of the new pads by applying the brake pedal a number of times.

Finally, check and adjust the travel of the hand brake lever using the adjuster (11) - See diagram 1 - making sure that when the handbrake lever is in the fully off position there is no tension on the handbrake cable or preload on the handbrake caliper mechanism. The cable is correctly adjusted when the rear wheels can be locked with the handbrake lever moved through half of its total travel.

MOUNTING AND POSITIONING OF THE REAR CALIPER

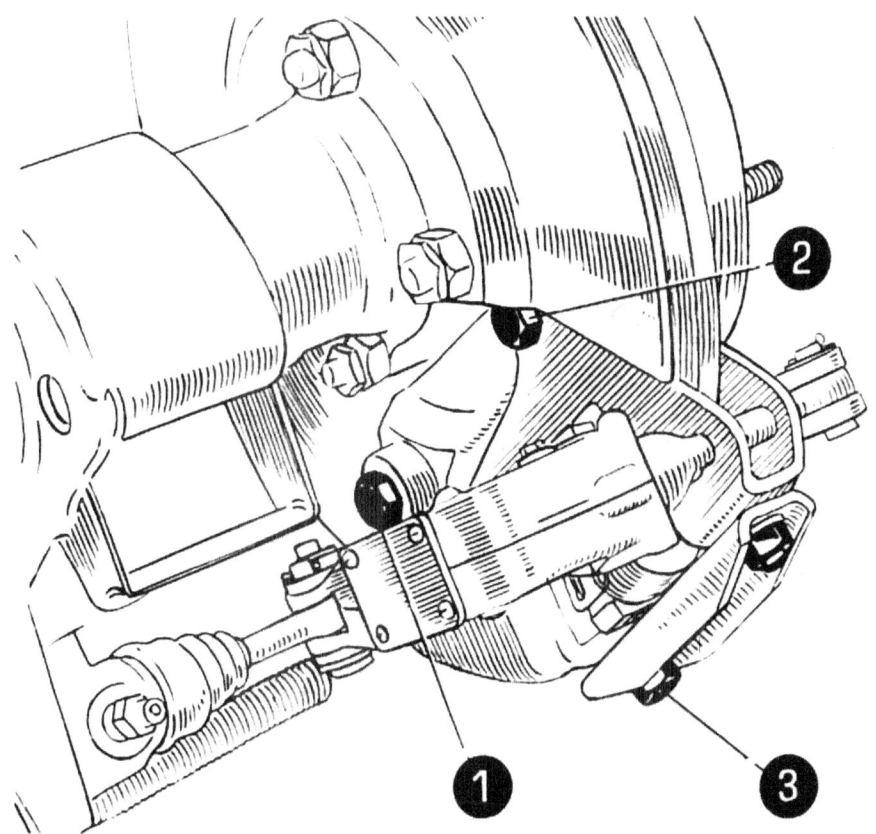

Position the brake caliper, complete with brake pads, install and hand tighten bolts (1) and (2) to temporarily hold the caliper in place.

Loosen the bolt (3) that holds the brake pad retaining bracket to the caliper.

Tighten bolts (1) and (2) to the prescribed torque, 2.3 - 2.8 Kgm then tighten bolt (3).

Check the clearance between the caliper and the disc on each side. The difference between the two dimensions must not exceed 0.5 mm. If the difference is greater than specified, remove the caliper and place appropriate shim washers on bolts (1) and (2).

ATE DISC BRAKES (SUPPLEMENTAL DATA)

BRAKE PAD WEAR LIMITS

The disc brake friction pads should be checked for wear every time the brakes are serviced. The brake pads should be renewed if they are less than .275 inch in thickness. The thickness of new brake pads together with backing plate is .59 inch. If only one brake pad is worn to the limit, all four brake pads must be renewed at the front or rear, whichever is the case. Never change the pads over in a caliper or interchange pads between calipers.

RENEWING BRAKE PADS

Refer to the factory publication that follows this page

ATE DRUM TYPE HANDBRAKE

This consists of a brake drum machined into the disc and includes a conventional type of expanding shoe mechanism for the handbrake, while the footbrake operates the calipers whose pads act on the disc which is in fact the rim of the drum/disc casting.

Servicing the ATE drum type handbrake is included in the factory publication that follows this page.

REMOVING AND DISMANTLING A CALIPER

1. Jack up the car and remove the road wheel. Remove the friction pads and disconnect the flexible hose from the caliper, using a plug to prevent fluid loss. With the caliper in a cool condition, remove the caliper attaching bolts and lift the caliper from the brake disc. If more than one caliper is removed at the same time, mark them for correct refitting.
2. Clamp the caliper assembly in a vice and remove the dust cover, using pliers (see the diagram below). Fit a piece of wood of approximately $\frac{3}{8}$ inch thickness into the caliper in the brake pad position to protect the pistons as they are ejected with compressed air. Remove the bleeder screw and apply a low-pressure compressed air nozzle at the bleeder screw opening to blow out the pistons.

Removing the dust shield from the caliper bore

3. Remove the retaining rings and rubber seals from the cylinder grooves, using a pointed instrument as shown (see below). Check all parts including the bores in the caliper halves for rust or score marks. Slight rust spots can be removed from the pistons with fine steel wool, but if the piston is scored or badly rusted it must be renewed. If the caliper bores are scored the complete caliper assembly should be renewed. Always fit new seals, dust covers, retaining rings, springs and retaining pins, these parts being obtainable in the form of a repair kit.

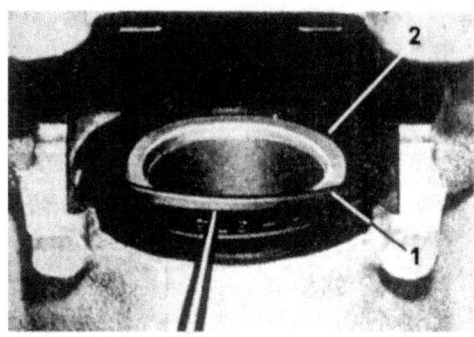

Removing rubber seal 1 and retaining ring 2 from the caliper bore

REASSEMBLING THE CALIPER

1. Thoroughly clean all internal parts with brake fluid and coat all parts with brake fluid during reassembly. Use the fingers to insert the rubber fluid seals into position to avoid damage to their edges. Slide the pistons into their bores.
2. Fit the rubber seals into the cylinder grooves and smear the inside of the dust cover with brake cylinder paste. Fit the dust cover and retainer and check that they are seated correctly. Check the positions of the pistons in the caliper bores, using the special tool as instructed in the factory publication that follows this page.
3. Refit the caliper assembly to the car, tightening the mounting bolts to a torque of 57.8 lb ft. (front) and 43.4 lb ft. (rear). Attach the brake hose and refit the friction pad assemblies, bleed the brakes and top-up the fluid supply tank.

BRAKE DISC MAINTENANCE

Remove the road wheel and the caliper attaching bolts. Remove the caliper and wire it to the suspension to avoid straining the brake hose, then remove the hub and disc assembly. Check the disc for runout, which should not exceed .008 inch. The brake disc can be reground in order to true it but, if it should be necessary to remove more than .02 inch from each side of the disc to achieve maximum runout measurement stated, the disc must be renewed.

Refit the disc, tighten the attaching bolts diagonally and evenly to a torque of 54.2 to 61.4 lb ft. Check the wheel bearings and repack them with grease. After refitting the hub, check the wheel bearing adjustment.

Ensure that the mounting faces of the caliper and the steering swivel are free from dirt and burrs then refit the caliper, tightening the attaching bolts to a torque of 57.8 lb ft. (front) 43.4 lb ft. (rear).

ATE DISC BRAKES (FACTORY MANUAL)

CONTENTS

A) <u>HYDRAULIC SYSTEM</u>

    1) <u>General</u> . . . . pag. 2

    2) <u>Operating principle</u> . . . . " 3

    3) <u>Maintenance directions</u> . . . . " 3

        a) general . . . . " 3

        b) check and replacement of brake fluid . . . . . " 3

        c) bleeding the system . . . . " 4

        d) check and replacement of pads . . . . " 5

    4) <u>Removal and reinstallation of caliper</u> . . . . . " 7

        a) removal from car . . . . " 7

        b) inspection and reinstallation . . . . " 7

    5) <u>Checking the disc for true rotation</u> . . . . " 7

B) <u>HAND BRAKE</u>

        a) running clearance adjustment with new linings . . " 9

        b) running clearance adjustment with worn linings . . " 10

"ATE" DISC BRAKES for GIULIA Models

Repair and Maintenance instructions

A) HYDRAULIC SYSTEM

1) General

The hydraulically-operated brake system consists of four disc-type brakes actuated through a master cylinder. The friction pads of front and rear brakes are directly actuated by the cylinders integral with the calipers.

The brakes automatically compensate for friction pad wear.

Each brake comprises a disc attached to the wheel hub and revolving between the jaws of a caliper installed on a suitable support.

Each caliper consists of two halves, joined together with four bolts, with cylinder cast integral with each half-caliper; in the cylinder bore a groove houses the piston seal.

Water and dust are prevented from entering the cylinder by proper excluders which are held in place by a retaining ring to the caliper and by their own elasticity on the piston.

The friction pads bonded to a backing plate are simultaneously forced toward the disc by pistons.

Two opposite retaining pins keep the pads in the calipers: the pad mounting slots are elongated to allow for slight movements of pads.

Furthermore two cross-shaped springs (mounted under the retaining pins) hold the pads pressed down in order to prevent vibrations and noise.

Each half-caliper has internal passages to transfer the fluid to the pistons. The inboard half-caliper has also the supply and the bleed fittings.

The components of front and rear calipers are not interchangeable.

2) Operating principle

When the brake pedal is depressed the fluid in the system (pipes, cylinders) is put under pressure by the displacement of plunger in master cylinder: such a pressure acts on the pistons which move inwards until the friction pads clamp the disc thus resulting in the braking action.

As the effort on the pedal increases, the pressure on pads also increases proportionately.

The movement of piston in the cylinder causes the seal (located in a groove in the cylinder bore) to deflect.

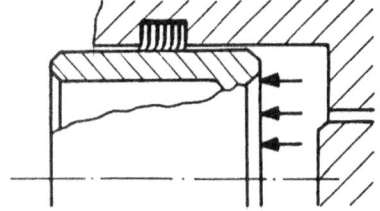

Piston in working position

When the brake pedal is released the plunger in the master cylinder comes back to starting position under the action of the return spring thus relieving pressure in the system.
At the same time the piston seal recovers and pushing back the piston restores the running clearance, .15 mm (.006") each side, between disc and friction pads.

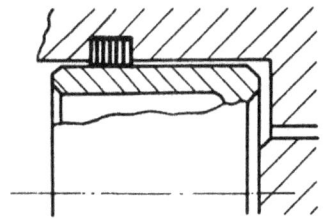

Piston in released position

Consequently, on brake release, the discs can again rotate freely. As the pads wear down the pistons travel a little further toward the disc because the pressure on piston overcomes the friction between piston and seal.

In this way the wear is automatically compensated for.

3) Maintenance directions

   a) General

   When servicing or greasing the car be careful not to let lubricants come in contact with discs and friction pads. Before cleaning the underside of car mask off the brake units.

   b) Check and replacement of brake fluid

   Every 3,750 mi. (6000 Km) check level of fluid in the reservoir; if necessary fill up with fluid freshly drawn from sealed containers.

When checking or filling up, take care not to contaminate the fluid with foreign matter, moisture or water.

<u>A remarkable drop in fluid level is undoubtedly caused by fluid leakage in the system: this should be traced and remedied immediately</u>.

- Every <u>11,250 mi.</u> (18,000 Km), or once a year whichever comes first, replace the brake fluid (specified fluid: ATE "Blau H").

For effective and reliable operation of brake system, the pipes must always be full of fluid and free from air bubbles. Excessive and resilient pedal travel is an indication of the presence of air in the system.

The use of compressed air guns for recharging the pipe lines is not permitted.

Should the flushing of brake circuit be required, use exclusively fluid of the specified type.

<u>Compressed air or alcohol must on no account be used to dry a flushed system.</u>

c) <u>Bleeding the system</u>

Bleeding is required when, due to the presence of air in the system a brake pedal spongy travel and sluggish response is felt. Proceed as follows:

- fill up the reservoir with the specified fluid (drawn from original containers opened just prior to use). Take care that during bleeding the fluid in the reservoir is maintained (not more than a quarter below full);

- start bleeding procedure with rear brakes:

  - fit a rubber pipe to the bleed screw and sink the other end into a small quantity of fluid in a glass container;
  - loosen the bleed screw;
  - slowly pump the brake pedal several times until the pipe discharges fluid free from air bubbles;
  - hold the pedal down and tighten the bleed screw.

If the bleeding has been carefully performed it will be found that when the brake pedal is pressed a firm and direct action on the fluid can be felt, immediately at the and of free travel.

If not repeat the procedure.

d) <u>Check and replacement of pads</u>

Friction pads should be checked for wear every 3750 mi. (6000 Km).

Proceed as follows:

- remove wheel from car;

- drive the upper retaining pin out of caliper by means of a punch;

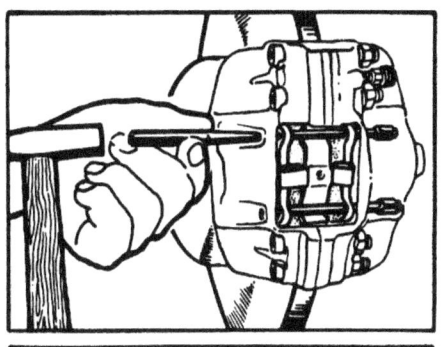

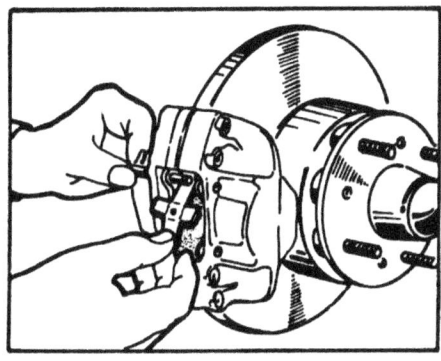

- remove the cross-shaped spring;
- drive out the lower retaining pin;

- withdraw the pads with the puller no. A.2.0150.

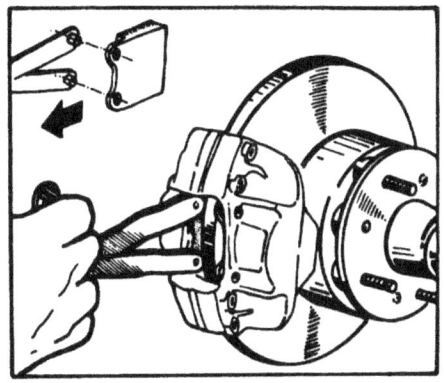

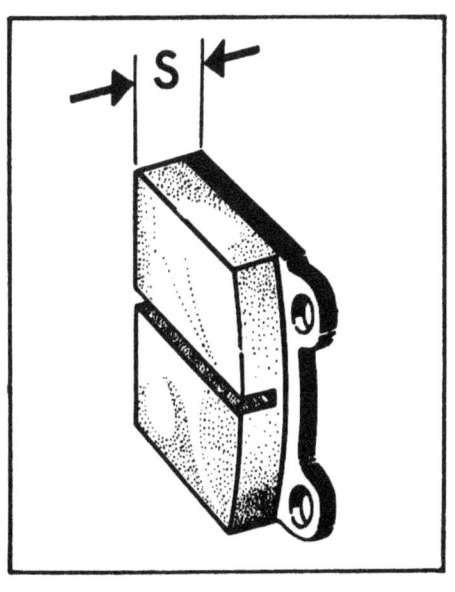

Check the pads for proper thickness:

$$S = \begin{cases} \text{New} & 15 \text{ mm } (.6") \\ \text{wear limit} & 7 \text{ mm } (.28") \end{cases}$$

Replace pads with new ones if necessary.

In case of uneven wear of a pad it is advisable to replace the whole set of front or rear brake pads.

Before reinstalling the pads:

- clean the pad housing: never use mineral base solvents or sharp edged tools;
- check the dust excluder and the retaining ring for sound conditions: if not so, replace them. Pack the inside of dust excluders with grease for ATE master cylinders.

- press the pistons to the bottom of cylinders with the aid of the resetting tool (no. A.2.0147) shown in the figure: do not use chance tools which might damage the pistons or the disc.

- check that the cross-shaped spring and the retaining pins are in good conditions: if not, replace them.

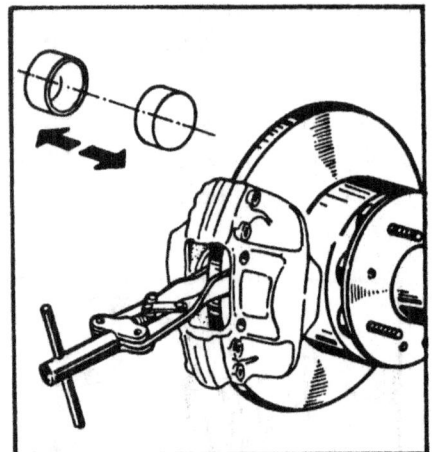

When resetting pistons, care should be taken to prevent fluid overflow from the reservoir.

- Make sure the pistons are correctly positioned in the caliper.
  To do so, rest the template 2 (no. A.2.0149/0160 for rear and front brakes respectively) against the reference surface of the caliper and make the check as shown below.

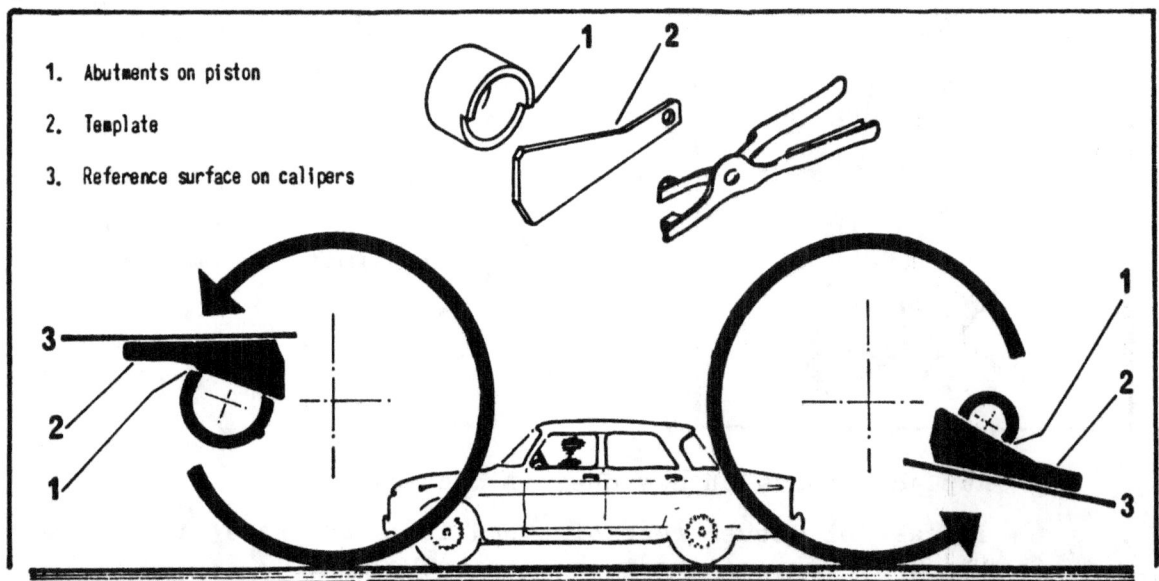

1. Abutments on piston
2. Template
3. Reference surface on calipers

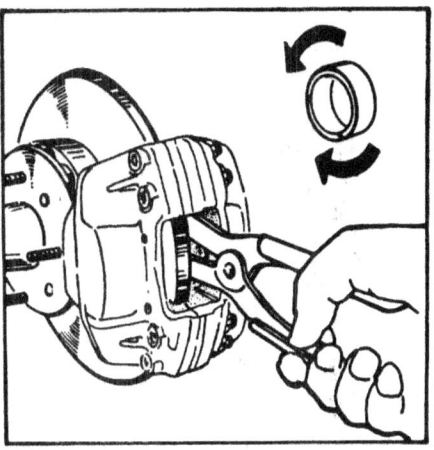

- If the pistons are not in the correct position true them as shown with the suitable pliers: no. A.2.0148/1 for rear brakes and A.2.0159 for front brakes.

- Insert the pads in the caliper; if new pads are installed make sure they slide freely in their housing and that upper edge of friction material does not protrude beyond disc outside diameter: if necessary remove the excess material until flush with the disc.

- Fit a retaining pin and then the cross-shaped spring; press down the free end of spring so as to permit the installation of the other retaining pin.

- With a suitable drift push the retaining pins fully home.

4) Removal and reinstallation of caliper

   a) Removal from car

- disconnect the fluid supply line;
- loosen the attaching screws and remove the caliper.

C a u t i o n :   avoid disassembling calipers when not at room temperature.

   b) Inspection and reinstallation:

- Check the attaching parts for good conditions and replace, if necessary;
- tighten the screws evenly to the following torque:

      Front caliper attaching screws 57.8 lb-ft (8 Kgm)
      Rear caliper attaching screws 43.4 lb-ft (6 Kgm)

5) Checking the disc for true rotation

When a brake disc is replaced it is necessary to check it for run-out after installation:

- use a dial indicator and the special tool A.2.0151 which is mounted to the caliper by means of the pad retaining pins.

Maximum permissible run out as measured at the swept surface should not exceed .22 mm (.0086").

N o t e : run-out readings can be misleading if bearing clearance is not as specified; therefore, check and adjust if necessary, according to factory instructions.

B) HAND BRAKE

It is mechanically operated and acts on the rear wheels through the shoes 2 which spread apart against a drum machined in the disc casting.

Pulling the hand brake handle causes the shoes, through the control linkage and the operating levers, to expand thus locking the wheels.

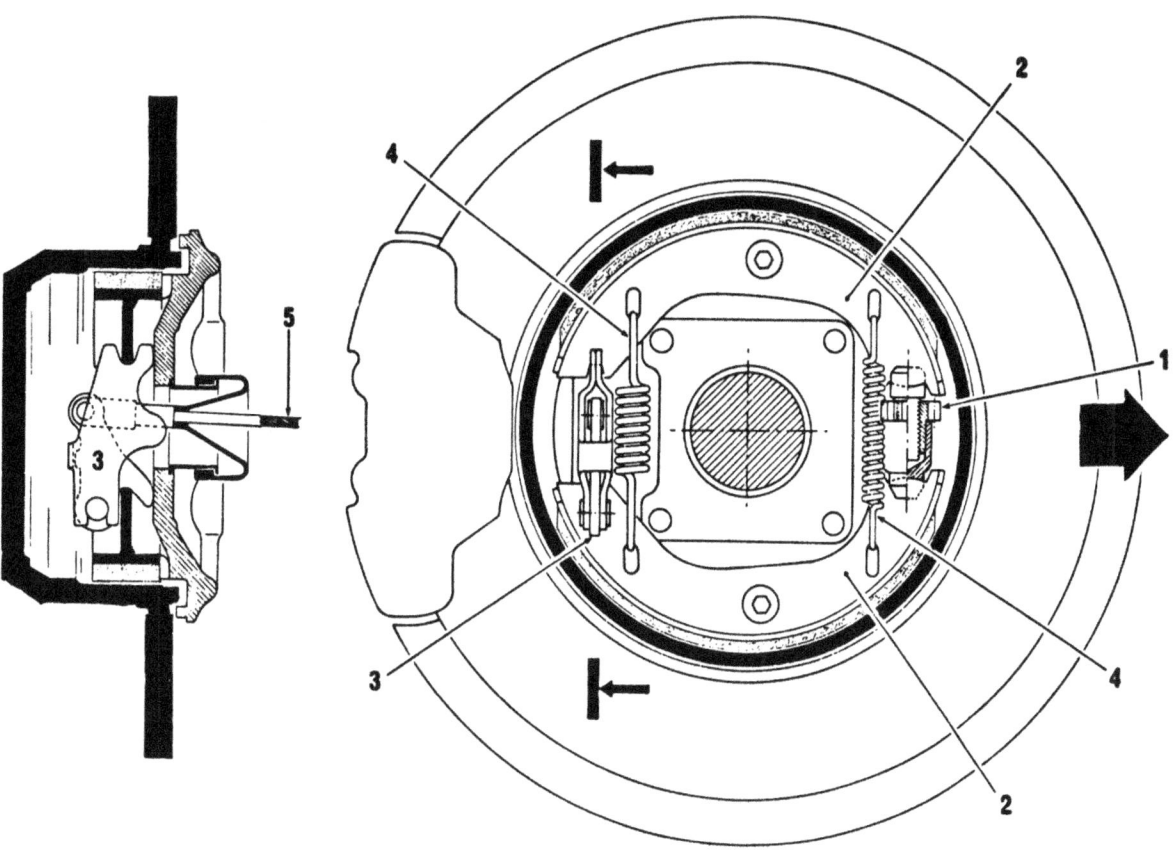

1 Adjuster - 2 Shoe - 3 Operating levers - 4 Return springs - 5 Control cable

a) Running clearance adjustment with new linings

When new shoes have been installed adjust the running clearance as follows:

- with the rear wheels removed, fully release the hand brake and make sure the control cables to the calipers are slackened;
- to adjust rotate the adjuster 1 with a screwdriver inserted through the hole in the disc brought into alignment with the adjuster;
- rotate the adjuster one notch at a time as shown in the illustration until hand brake shoes are just contacting the drum without locking: then back up the adjuster by two/four notches so that the disc rotates freely.

Proceed the same way for the other wheel.

- The hand brake is correctly adjusted when the wheels become locked as the handle is drawn through half its total travel. Make sure that, when the handle is released, the wheels rotate freely.

b) <u>Running clearance adjustment with worn linings</u>

To take up the excessive travel of hand brake handle, due to worn-down linings, proceed as follows a wheel at a time:

- jack up the wheel and with the hand brake in released position check that the wheel can rotate freely;

- act on the adjuster 1 as directed under a) above until shoes just contact the drum; then, back up the adjuster by two/four notches.

If necessary, adjust the control linkage too, by acting on the suitable slack adjusters.

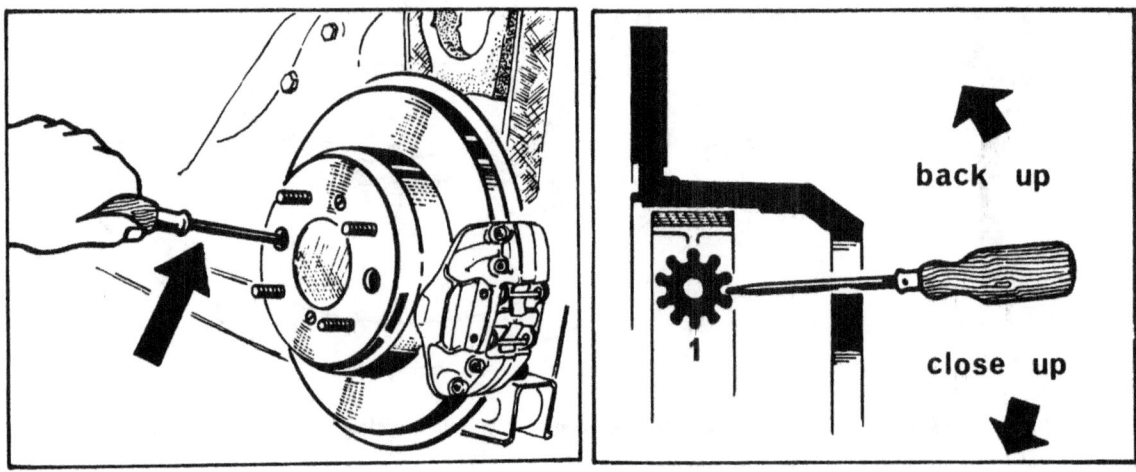

I M P O R T A N T   N O T E

Whenever a hand brake assembly is removed for replacement of parts or overhaul, on reassembly apply the sealing compound Minnesota EC 5305 in correspondence of the seats for the shoe mounting pins (as shown by arrows in the figure) in order to prevent dust or foreign matter from entering the brakes.

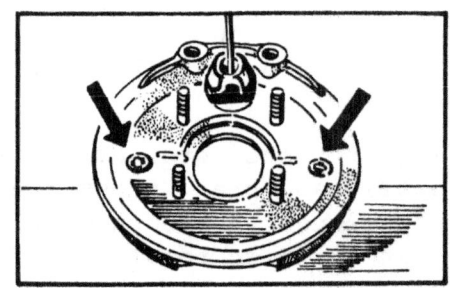

SHOP MANUAL No. 4

FRONT SUSPENSION

**GIULIA AND 1750 MODELS
(FACTORY MANUAL)**

**PLUS SUSPENSION SPECIFICATIONS FOR
GIULIA 1750 - GIULIA 2000 - MONTREAL
(FACTORY SUPPLEMENT - OCTOBER 1977)**

**WHEEL HUBS
SHOCK ABSORBERS AND STABILISER ROD
ZF STEERING BOX
BURMAN STEERING BOX
STEERING LINKAGE
STEERING ADJUSTMENTS**

TABLE OF CONTENTS

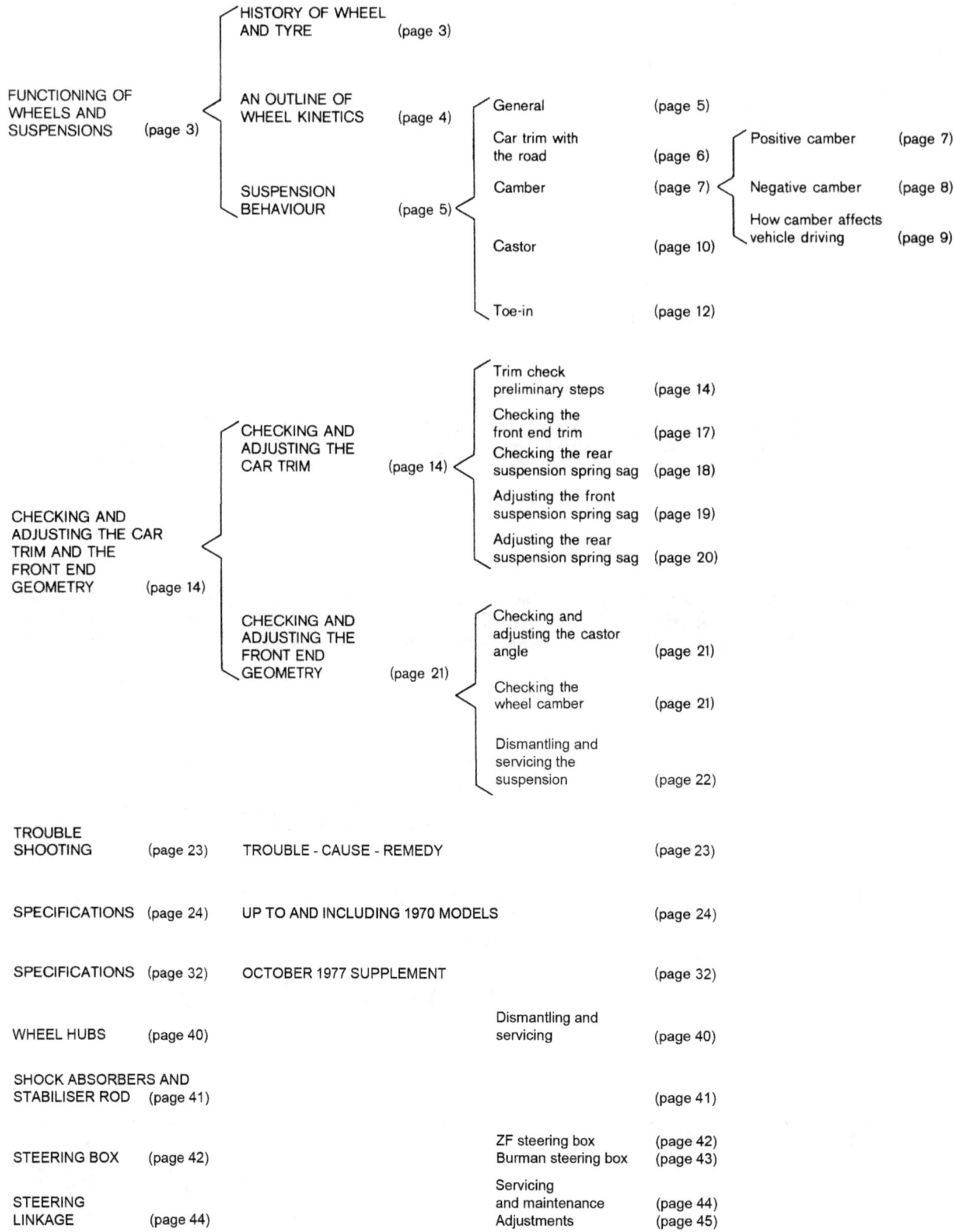

HISTORY OF WHEEL AND TYRE

It is believed that the wheel originated from the usage of a bole as a roll to overcome the sliding friction by converting it into rolling friction. Soon after, men realized that a lighter wheel would have been a better thing and this brought us to the spoke wheel. Then, a solid tire was used on the wheel rim and, in the nineteenth century, John Dunlop devised an air-filled high-pressure tyre. The vulcanizing process, introduced by Charles Goodyear in the 1920, gave the pneumatic tyre better characteristics; however the average life was just enough to cover about 4000 miles. In 1923 the low-pressure type of pneumatic tyre was developed, with a much longer life.

In the last decade, new types of tyres have been developed, especially in the U.S.A. Some of them, for example, have the inner surface coated with plastic material that, when the tyre is punctured, is forced by the internal air pressure to flow into and seal the hole left by puncture.

FUNCTIONING OF WHEELS AND SUSPENSIONS

AN OUTLINE OF WHEEL KINETICS

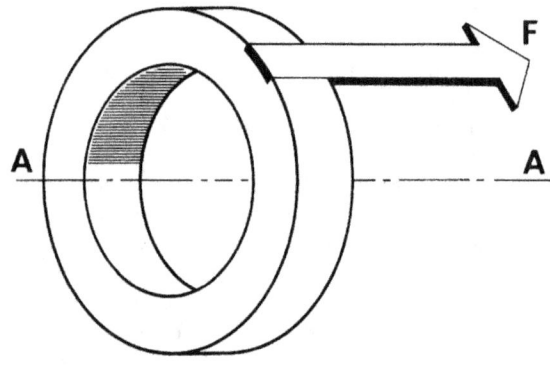

Suppose a force F is acting on a wheel: if the direction of the force F is parallel to the wheel axis, the force has no effect on wheel rotation; if the direction of the force is not parallel to the wheel axis, the force tends to produce or change the motion of the wheel in direct proportion to its magnitude.

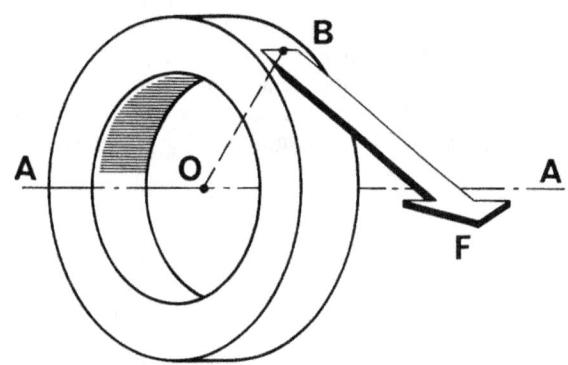

"Moment of a Force" is the product of the magnitude of the force F and the measure of its lever arm OB.
A moment applied to a wheel as outlined above tends to produce or change the wheel motion.

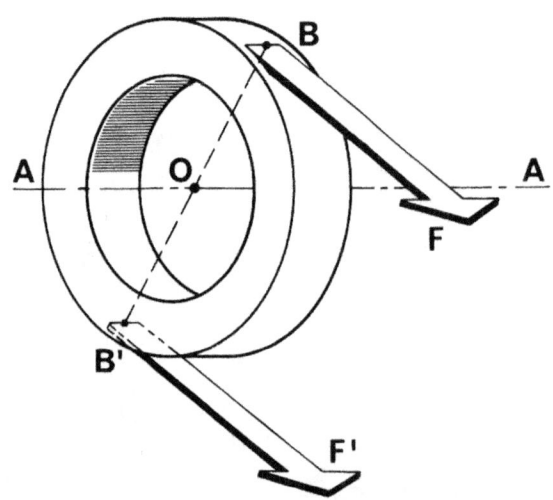

When a wheel is subjected to the action of two forces F and F1, whose moments about the axis are equal and opposite in direction, it remains in a state of balance. To distinguish between the directions of rotation the moments tend to produce, they are written with the sign "plus" when the direction is clockwise and "minus" when the direction is anti-clockwise.

FUNCTIONING OF WHEELS AND SUSPENSIONS AS FITTED

SUSPENSION BEHAVIOUR

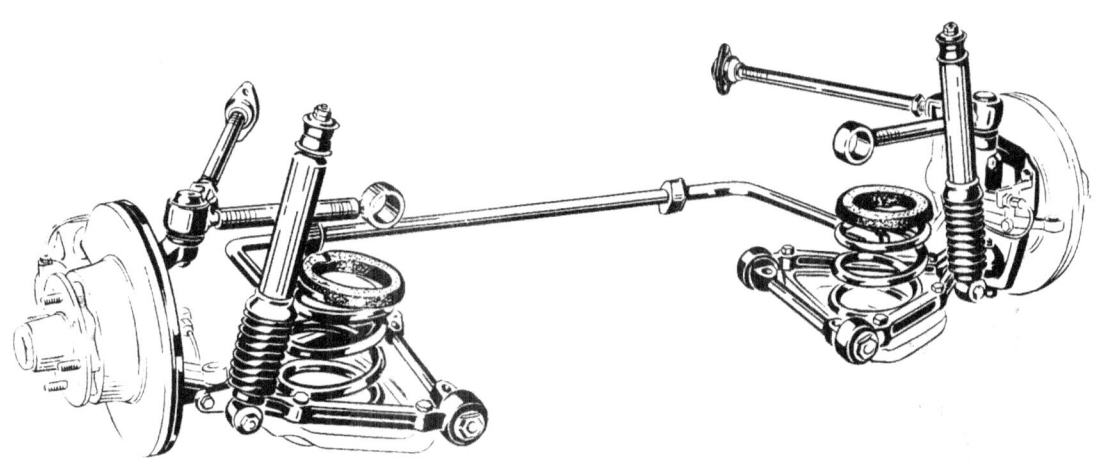

GENERAL

An essential feature of the suspensions dealt with in details in the following pages, is their direct attachments to the body.

Since the angular relationship between the suspension components and the frame varies as the car is moving, there is a number of position the suspension members can take. However, for the purpose of performing the necessary checks and adjustments a well definite position is chosen.

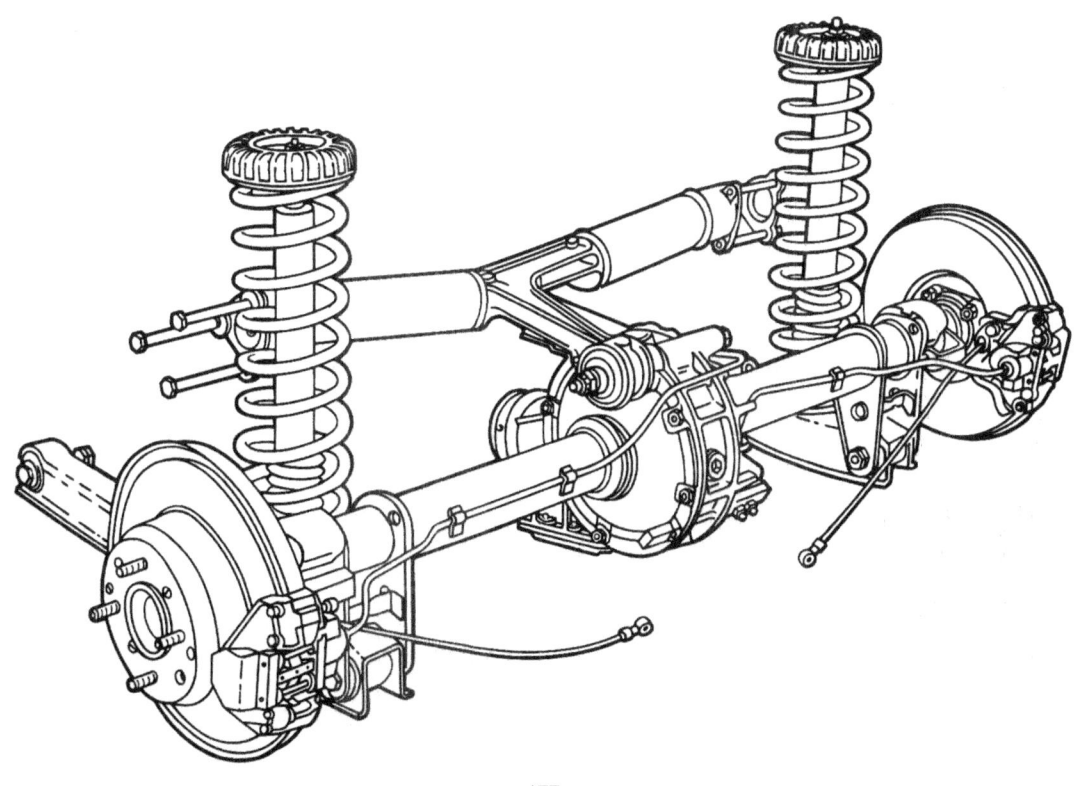

FUNCTIONING OF WHEELS AND SUSPENSIONS AS FITTED

SUSPENSION BEHAVIOUR

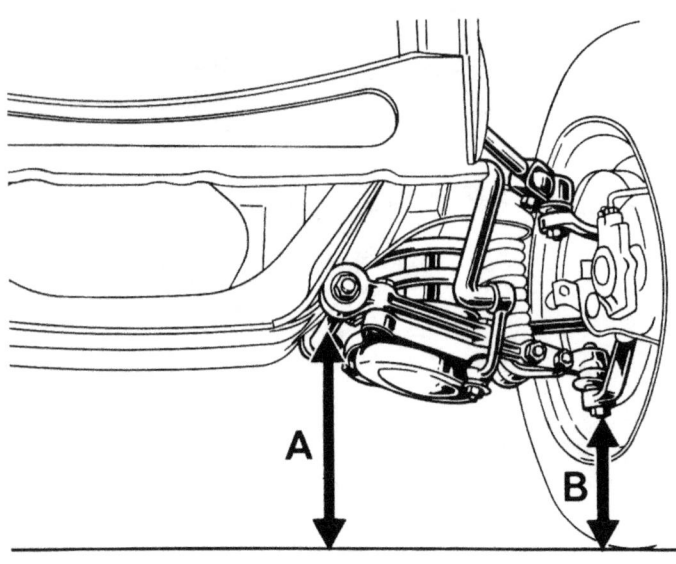

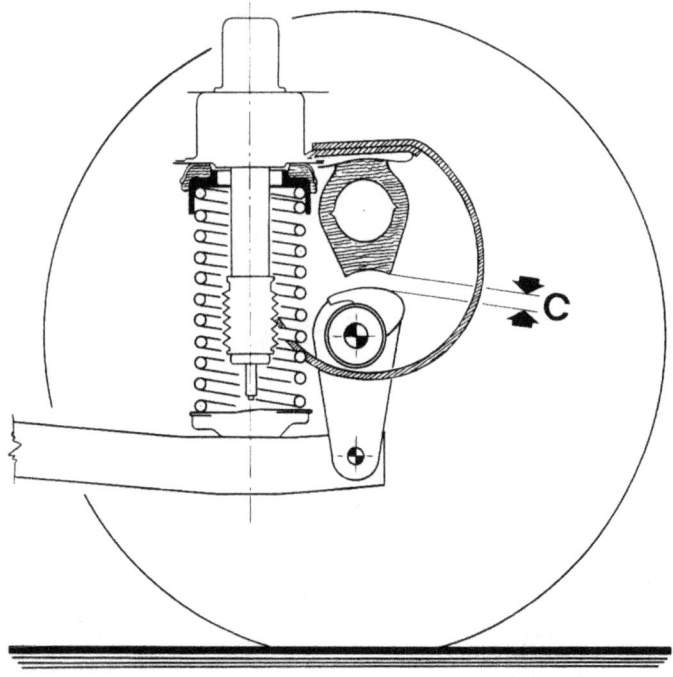

CAR TRIM WITH THE ROAD

The car trim is the height of front suspension (dimensions A and B) from the ground or the spring sag (dimension C) at the rear suspension.

These dimensions should fall within the preset limits as checked under suitable loading conditions and with shock absorbers and stabiliser rods disconnected.

The position of the suspensions in these conditions is hereinafter referred to as "trim" under static load.

There is a close relationship between the car trim and the front wheel alignment; so, if the trim varies the wheel angles also vary.

Therefore, the wheel alignment checks and adjustments should not be performed unless the car trim is as specified.

The regular inspection and maintenance of the front end geometry and car trim will ensure the perfect operation of suspensions both as far as the road holding and riding comfort are concerned.

FUNCTIONING OF WHEELS AND SUSPENSIONS AS FITTED

SUSPENSION BEHAVIOUR

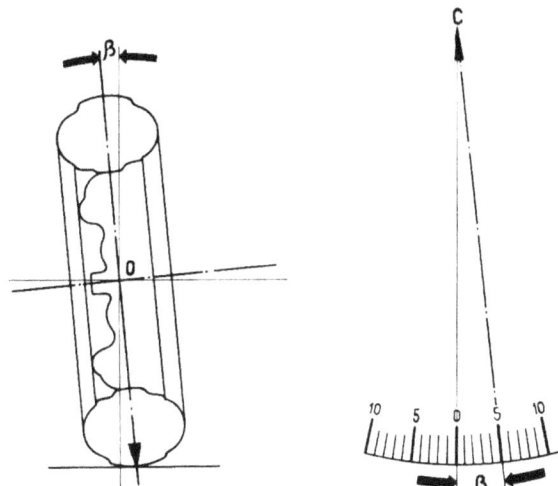

CAMBER

- Positive Camber (outward tilt of wheel top)

The camber angle is the angle β or the amount of wheel tilt measured in degrees from the vertical.

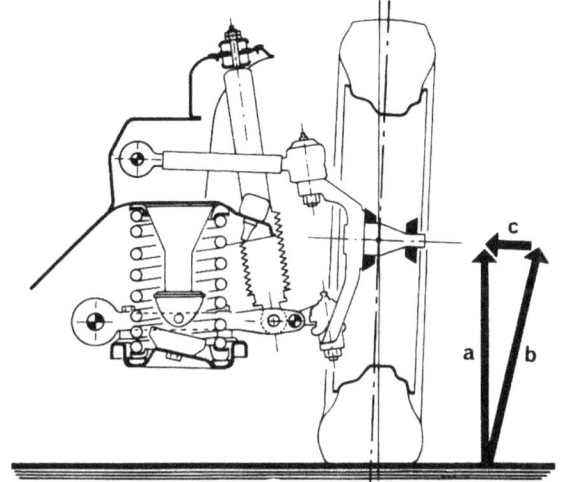

The wheel tilt does not remain constant but varies as the loading and springing conditions of front and rear suspension vary. One of the effects of camber is that of imposing the most of the wheel load on the hub bearing next to the steering axis.

- a = load reaction
- b = component force at right angle to wheel axis centreline
- c = component force along the wheel axis centreline

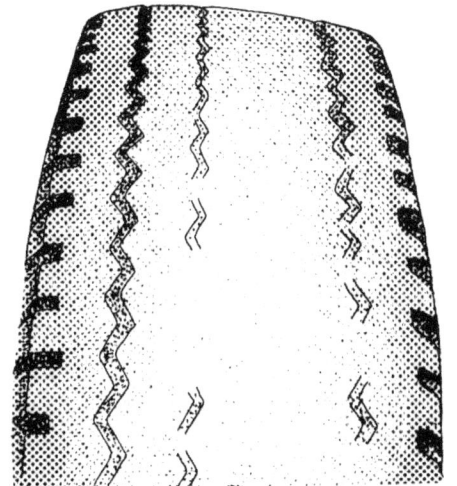

An excessive camber angle could cause the outside of the tread to wear down especially in conjunction with an incorrect toe-in.

179

FUNCTIONING OF WHEELS AND SUSPENSIONS AS FITTED

SUSPENSION BEHAVIOUR

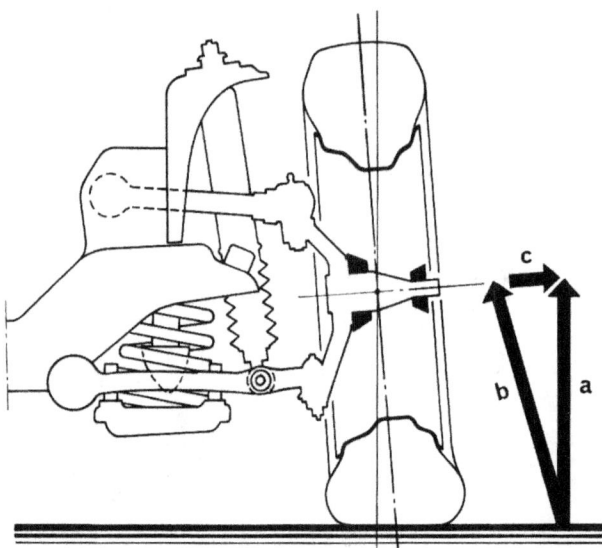

- Negative camber (inward tilt of wheel top)

If the camber is negative the wheels have an inward tilt at the top, the majority of the load is supported by the hub bearing farther from the steering axis and the inside of the tread wears excessively.

A wheel with a negative camber tends to slip out of its hub.

a = load reaction
b = component force at right angle to wheel axis centreline
c = component force along the wheel axis centreline.

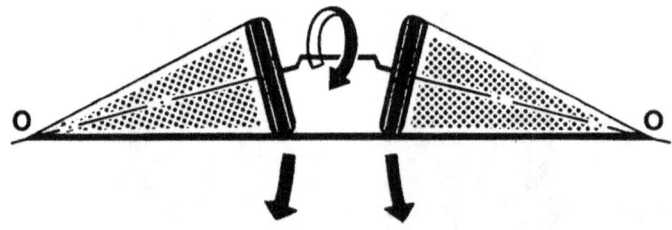

The front wheels when mounted with a camber angle behave like two cones tending to roll around their apex; thereby the wheels have a tendency toward moving apart.

This shows that too great a camber angle could cause the tyres to wear excessively. It is therefore essential that the camber angle be exactly that prescribed by design specifications.

FUNCTIONING OF WHEELS AND SUSPENSIONS AS FITTED

SUSPENSION BEHAVIOUR

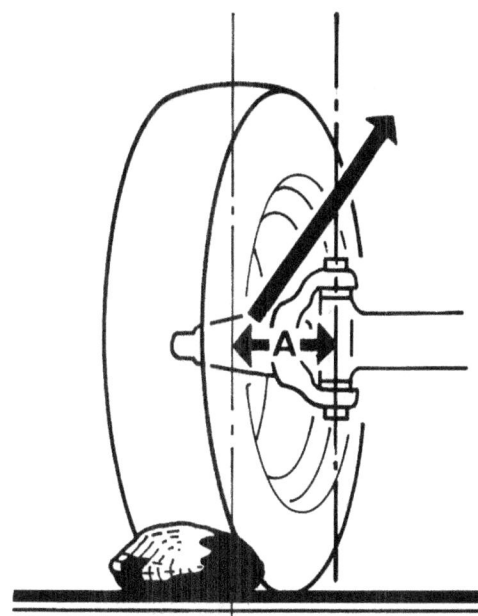

- How camber affects vehicle driving.

The figure shows a wheel with no camber angle.
As the wheel passes over a bump, the shock transfers to the steering gear greatly multiplied by the leverage A.

If the same wheel is so tilted that no more leverage A exists, it will transmit much less of the road shocks.
On Alfa Romeo cars the camber angle cannot be adjusted; however, it is a good rule to check whether the camber angle is as specified.
Actually, the point of intersection A is not at the road surface but slightly below; this means that in actual construction a certain amount of leverage A still exists.

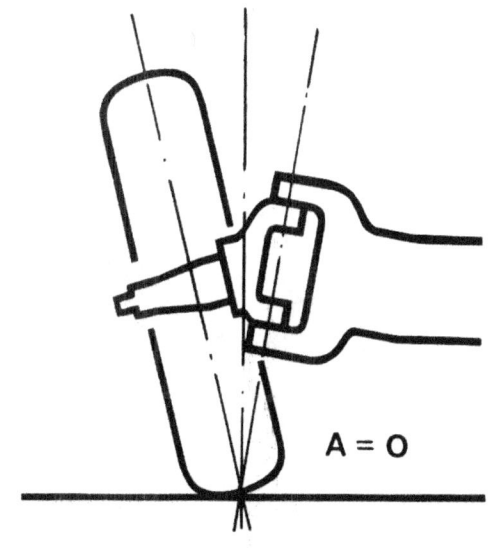

FUNCTIONING OF WHEELS AND SUSPENSIONS AS FITTED

SUSPENSION BEHAVIOUR

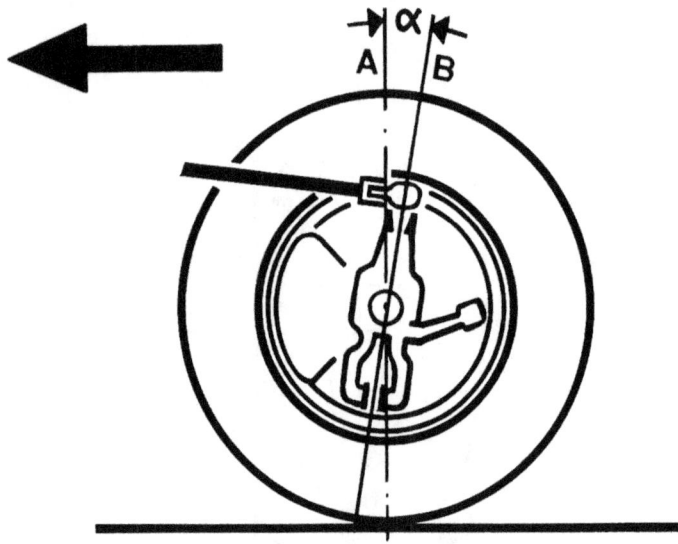

CASTOR

The castor angle α is the backward tilt of steering axis centreline B from the vertical A.

On Alfa Romeo cars the steering axis centreline is the centreline of stub axle ball joints passing through the road surface ahead of the wheel point of contact with the road.

Positive castor aids directional stability since it tries to keep the wheels straight ahead.

On Alfa Romeo cars the castor angle can be adjusted if checks performed with an optical aligner show such a need.

When castor angles are as specified, driving is easy and smooth. Any sideslip tendency can especially be prevented by making sure that the castor angle has the same value both at the near side and at the off side.

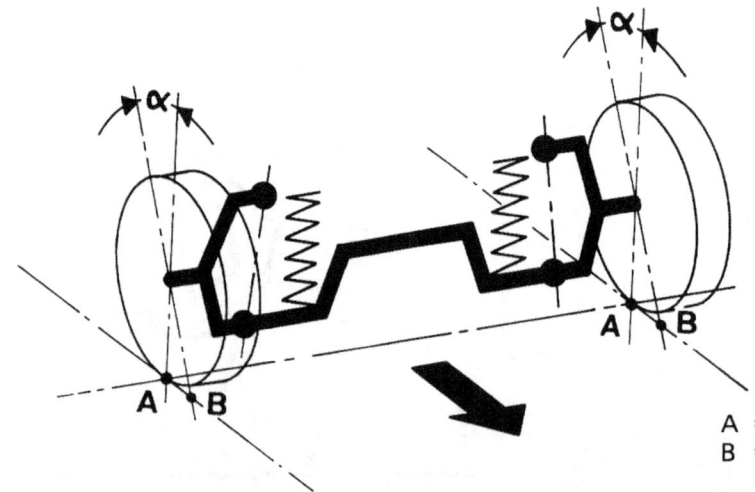

A = contact point with road surface
B = steering axis centreline intersection point

FUNCTIONING OF WHEELS AND SUSPENSIONS AS FITTED

SUSPENSION BEHAVIOUR

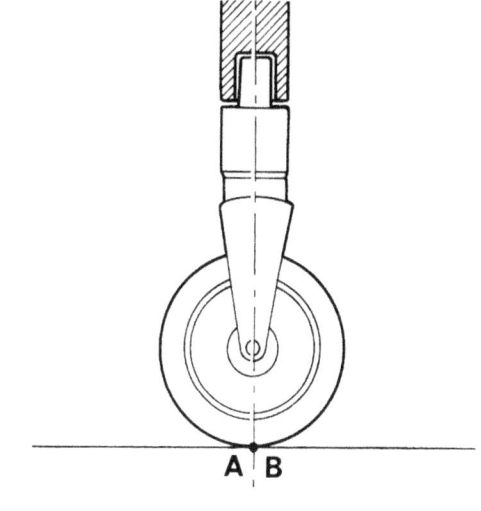

For a better understanding of the effects of caster angle, let us consider a table leg wheel and discuss the following three cases:

— No caster angle (A coinciding with B).

In this case there is no tendency toward recovery so that it is very difficult to keep the wheel straight ahead.

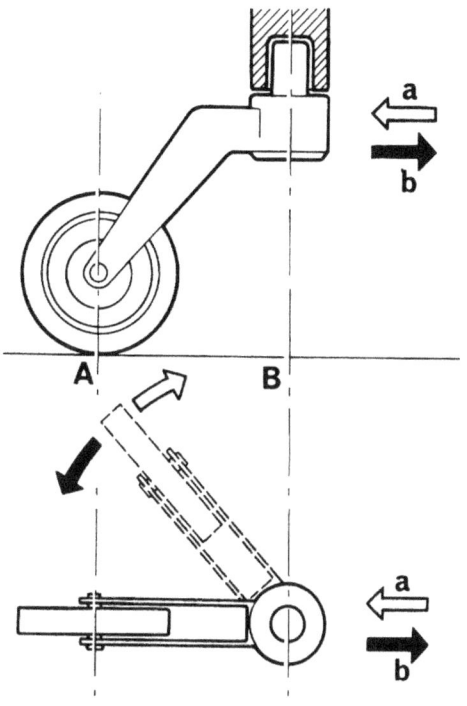

— Negative caster (A ahead of B in the direction "a").

In this case not only there is no recovery but a reversing couple takes place just from the start.

— Positive camber (A behind B in the direction "b").

In this case the wheel has the tendency toward recovery, that is, to "trail behind".

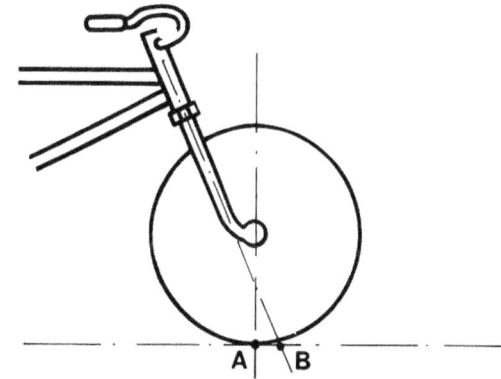

Such a behaviour is like that of the front wheel of a bicycle: the farther the intersection B of steering axis with road surface is ahead of wheel contact point A the more stable the wheel remains in straight forward direction.

The same considerations apply to a motor vehicle (see page 10).

FUNCTIONING OF WHEELS AND SUSPENSIONS AS FITTED

SUSPENSION BEHAVIOUR

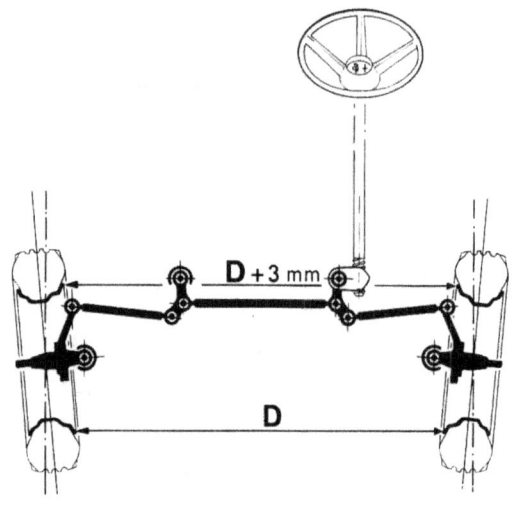

TOE–IN

Toe-in is the pointing in of the front wheels which attempt to roll inward instead of straight ahead (rear wheel drive).

Toe-in measurements are also obtained by difference between the tracks as read at the front and at the rear of the wheel rim on a plane passing by the centreline of hubs.

Rear wheel drive:
the front wheels tend to toe out.

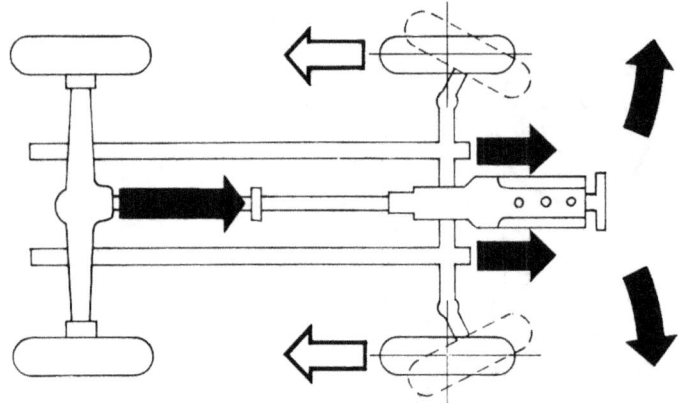

The purpose of toe-in is to ensure parallel rolling of front wheels, to stabilize steering as well as to prevent sideslipping and excessive wear of tyres. The toe in offsets the small deflections which come about when the car is moving forward. In fact, with rear wheel drive, due to the rolling resistance of the tyres on the road, the front wheels tend to roll parallel on the road, that is to toe-out.

Front wheel drive:
the front wheels tend to toe in.

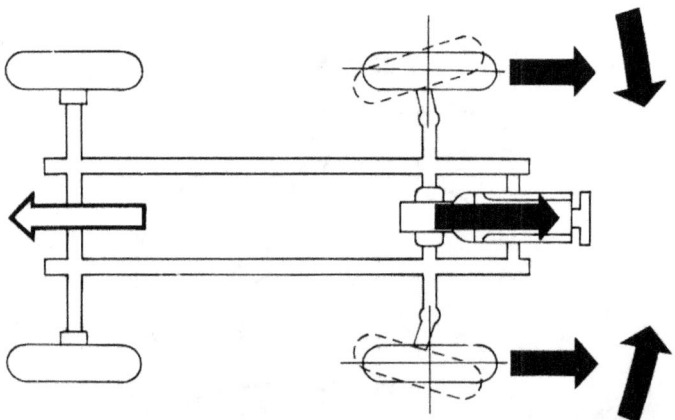

This is also the reason why the front wheels on a front drive vehicle are set to toe-out slightly when the car is standing still. On moving forward, the front wheels, being driving, tend to toe-in due to body resistance to motion.

FUNCTIONING OF WHEELS AND SUSPENSIONS AS FITTED

SUSPENSION BEHAVIOUR

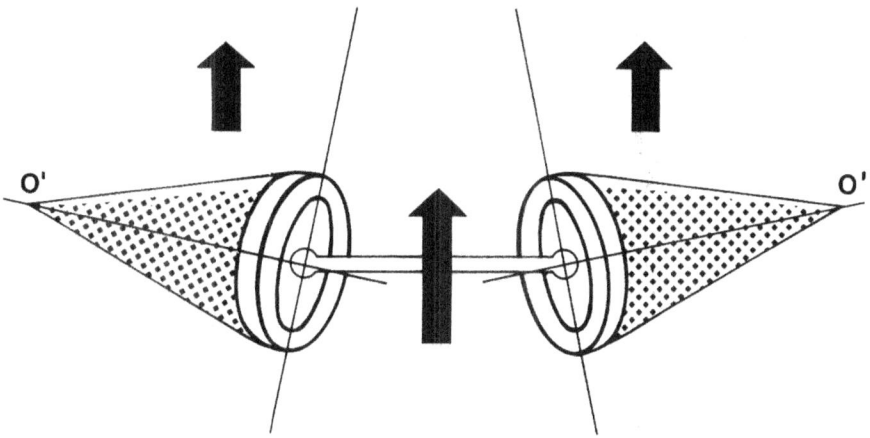

The toe-in allows to compensate for the sideslip tendency due to the camber angle (see page 8). Setting the wheels to toe-in, the two rolling centres O are shifted toward the front so that, in forward motion, the wheels roll parallel.

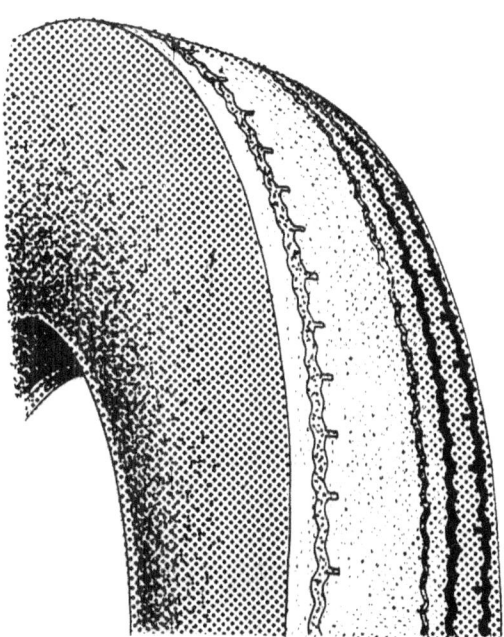

Improper toe-in greatly affects tyre wear. Feather-edge wear from excessive toe-in.

14
CHECKING AND ADJUSTING THE FRONT END GEOMETRY AND THE CAR TRIM WITH THE ROAD

CHECKING AND ADJUSTING THE CAR TRIM

TRIM CHECK PRELIMINARY STEPS.

Carrying out the preliminary steps before performing the "Trim" and "Front end geometry" checking procedure is essential for best accuracy.
Place the car to be tested over a pit (or a four-post lift).

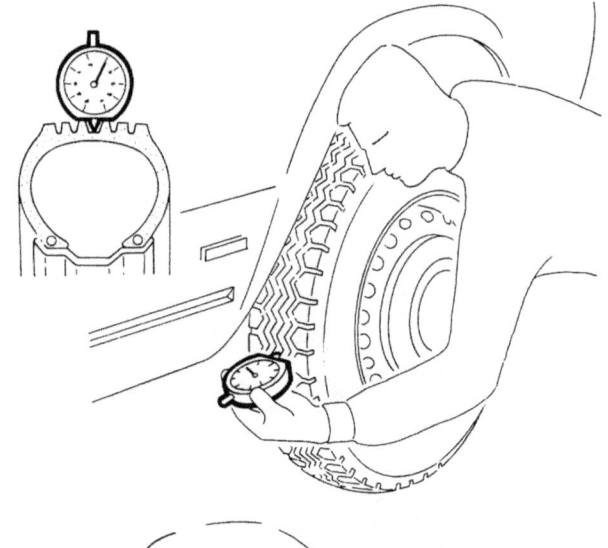

Check tyres for wear with a tread depth gauge. All four tyres should show the same amount of wear.

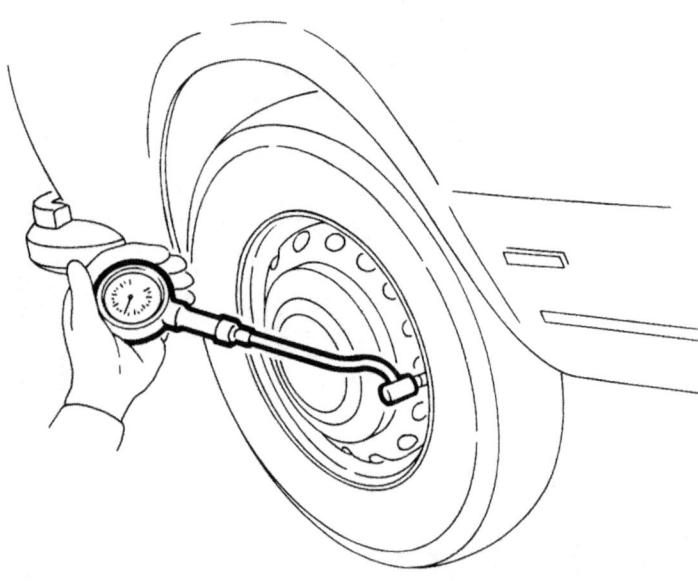

Check that tyre inflation pressure is as specified.

CHECKING AND ADJUSTING THE FRONT END GEOMETRY AND THE CAR TRIM WITH THE ROAD

CHECKING AND ADJUSTING THE CAR TRIM

Make sure the spare wheel, the jack and the tool kit are in the boot and that the fuel tank is full; otherwise put a weight in the luggage boot to compensate for the difference in load.

Put the car under static load by placing weights (sand bags or similar) as specified.

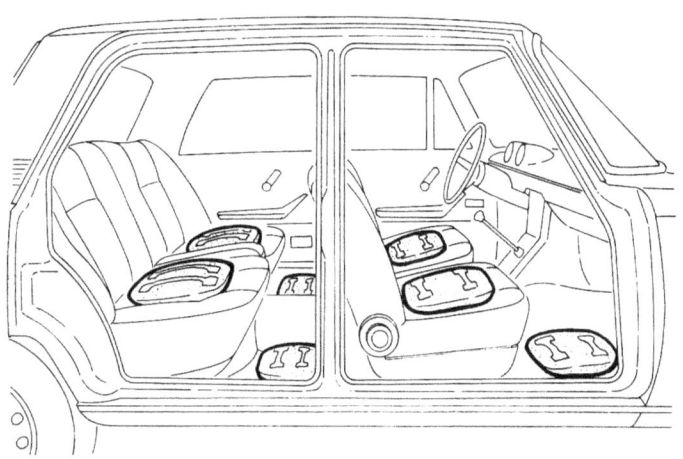

Disconnect the stabiliser rod of front and rear suspensions.

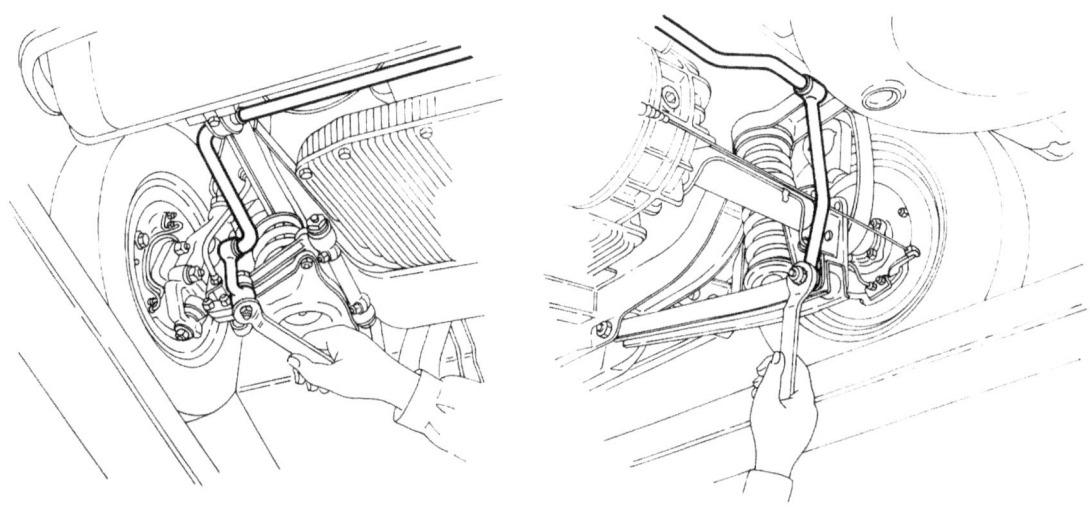

16
CHECKING AND ADJUSTING THE FRONT END GEOMETRY AND THE CAR TRIM WITH THE ROAD

CHECKING AND ADJUSTING THE CAR TRIM

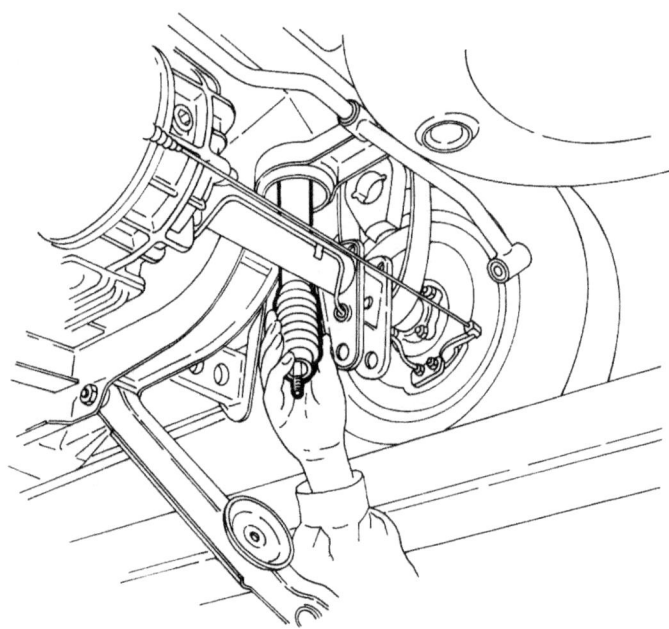

Disconnect the front and rear shock absorbers.

Rock the car up and down at the front first then at the rear to allow the suspensions to take up a static position.
This is a very important requirement if proper results have to be obtained.

CHECKING AND ADJUSTING THE FRONT END GEOMETRY AND THE CAR TRIM WITH THE ROAD

CHECKING AND ADJUSTING THE CAR TRIM

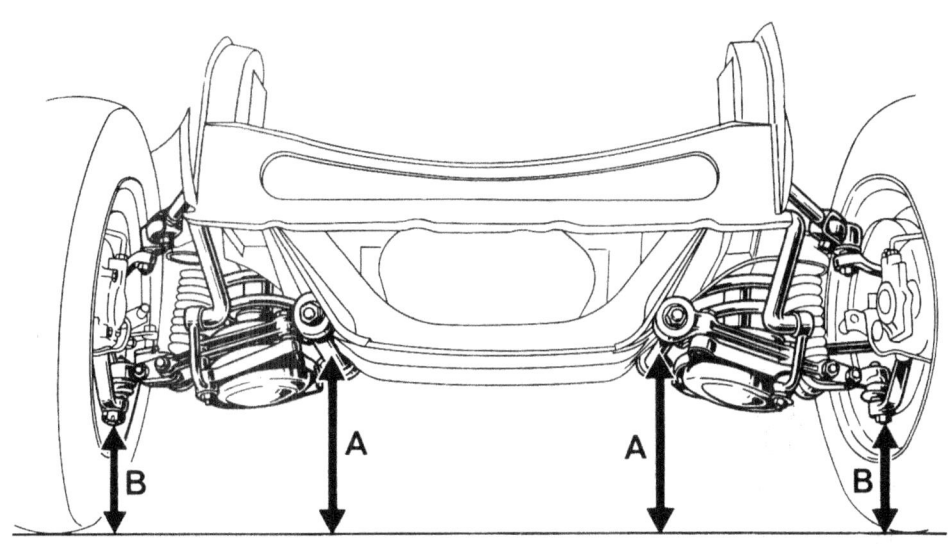

CHECKING THE FRONT END TRIM

The front suspension consists essentially of pivoted members which move up and down as the irregularities of the road are conveyed to them through the wheels.

With the car under static load, the suspension members settle to a well definite position and the suspension springs flex to a sag which can be checked by calculating the difference between the dimension A (distance from ground of lower wishbone shaft) and dimension B (distance from ground of bottom swivel pin).

Only if this requirement is met, the front wheel alignment can be checked and adjusted.

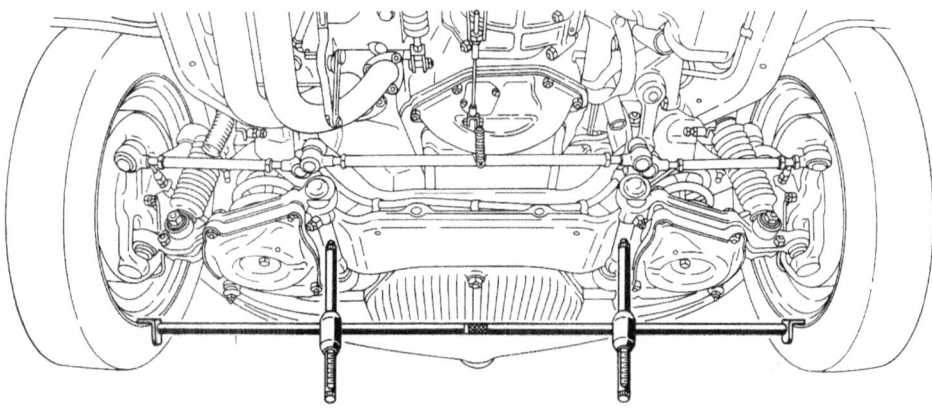

The front end trim can be easily checked with the special tool P.N. C.6.0125, which allows to take direct readings, by means of the suitable rules calibrated in millimetres, of the difference in value between A and B. The values of this difference should be as specified (according to the car model) in the table on page 46 et seq.

CHECKING AND ADJUSTING THE FRONT END GEOMETRY AND THE CAR TRIM WITH THE ROAD

CHECKING AND ADJUSTING THE CAR TRIM

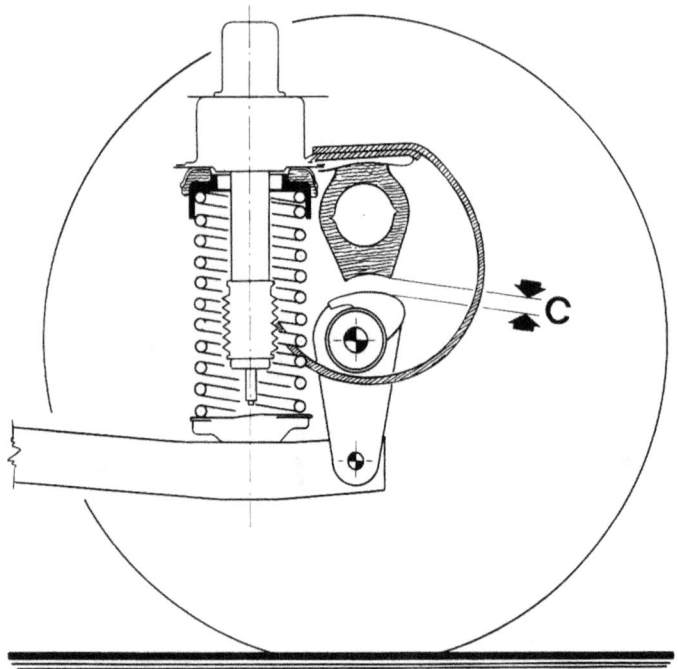

CHECKING THE REAR SUSPENSION SPRING SAG.

The rear suspension consists of a live axle controlled by two trailing arms and a T-arm.

The axle is elastically suspended by two coil springs, double acting telescopic shock absorbers and a stabiliser rod.

The rebound of rear axle is limited by straps and the upward movement by rubber pads.

The distance C between pad and axle housing serves as a reference for spring sag readings under static load condition.

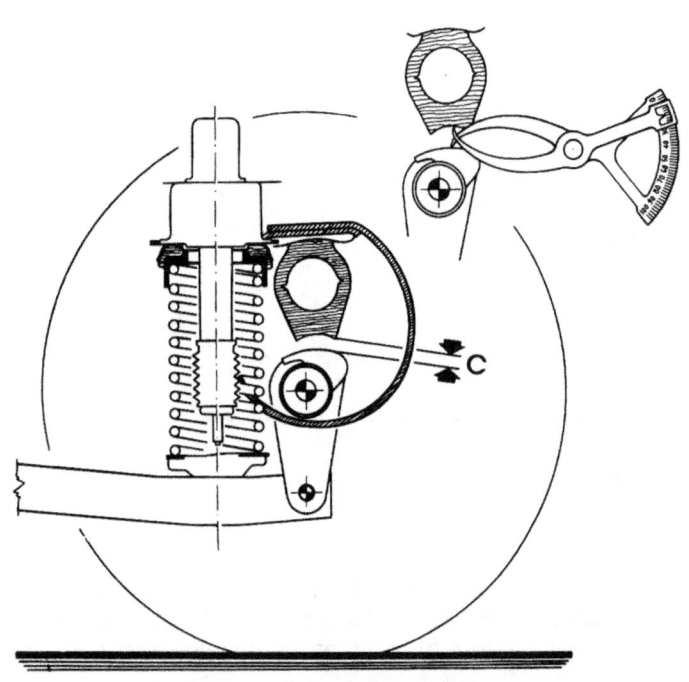

Check with a caliper that the dimension C between rubber pad and axle housing is as specified in the tables on page 46 et seq. according to the car model being tested.

CHECKING AND ADJUSTING THE FRONT END GEOMETRY AND THE CAR TRIM WITH THE ROAD

CHECKING AND ADJUSTING THE CAR TRIM

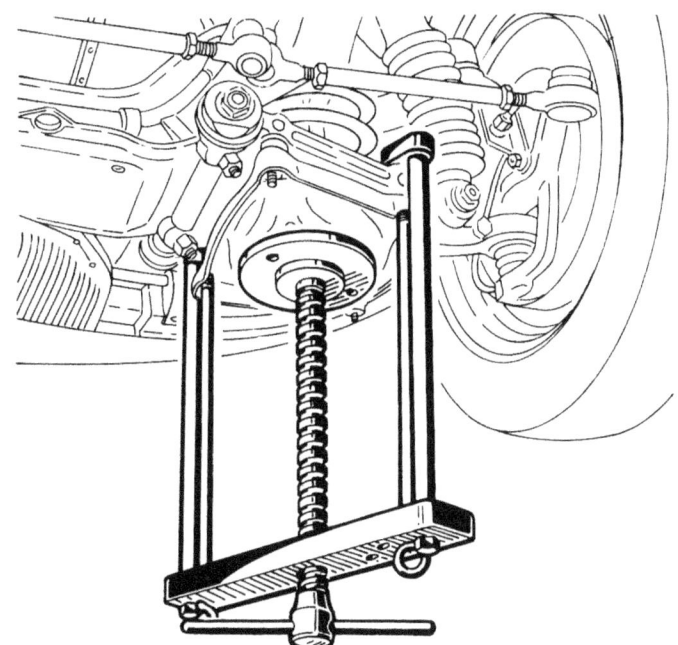

ADJUSTING THE FRONT SUSPENSION SPRING SAG.

In the event the dimensions A and B (see page 17) are not as specified, bring them within design limits as follows:

— remove the spring with the aid of special tool P.N. A.2.0169;

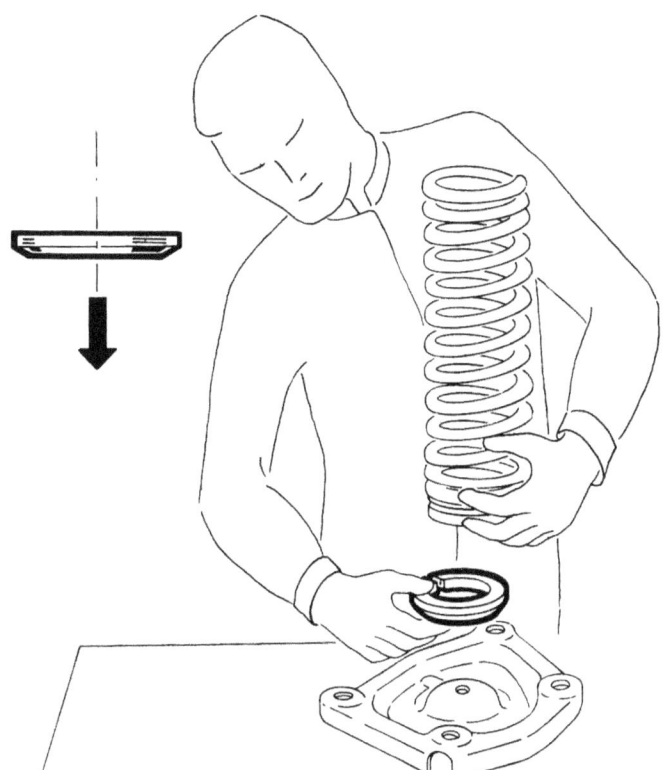

— add the suitable spacer with the chamfered edge downward;
— refit all parts properly.

CHECKING AND ADJUSTING THE FRONT END GEOMETRY AND THE CAR TRIM WITH THE ROAD

CHECKING AND ADJUSTING THE CAR TRIM

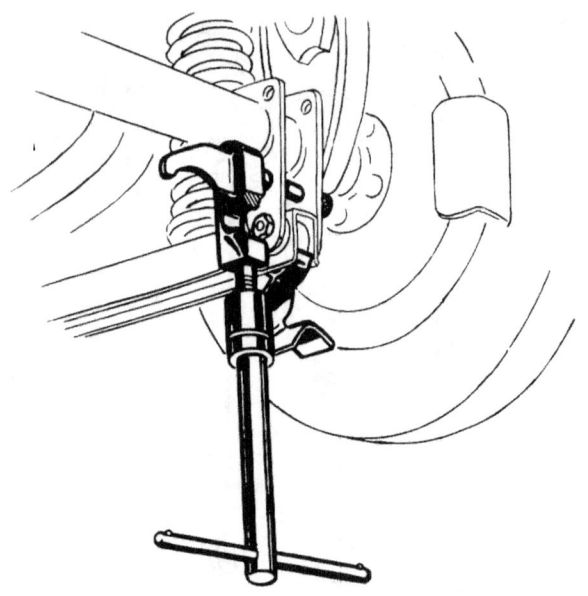

ADJUSTING THE REAR SUSPENSION SPRING SAG.

If the dimension C is not as specified, adjust it as follows:

– remove the spring with the aid of special tool P.N. A.2.0143;

– insert a spacer of suitable thickness between the spring and its seat.

The thickness of spacer should be so selected as to obtain the correct dimension C as specified (see tables on page 46 et seq.) for the affected model.

Then, refit all parts properly.

CHECKING AND ADJUSTING THE FRONT END GEOMETRY AND THE CAR TRIM WITH THE ROAD

CHECKING THE FRONT END GEOMETRY

ADJUSTMENTS

Before any checking and adjusting of the castor and camber angles is carried out the car must be standing on level ground, the tyre pressures must be correct and the car fully loaded. Make sure that the oil and water levels are correct and that the fuel tank is full. The front seats must be occupied by two passengers or weights must be put into the car as follows. 100 lbs on each of the front seats and 55 lbs in front of each front seat on the car floor. On Super 1.6, 110 lb on each seat, and 44 lb on each foot well, front and rear. Detach the anti-roll bar from the lower suspension arms and disconnect one end of each damper.

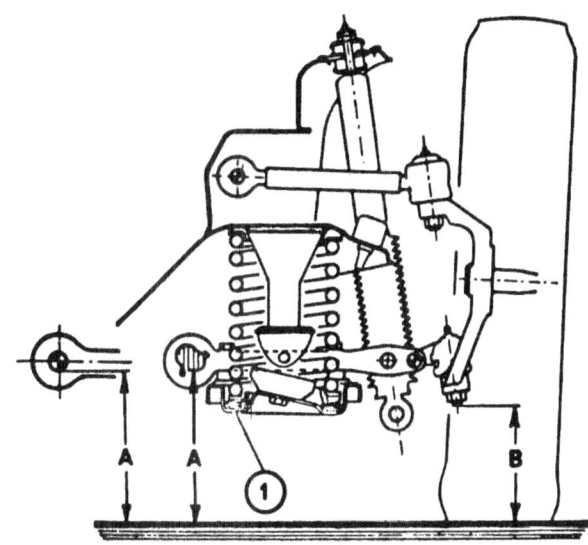

Checking the suspension adjustment

SUSPENSION ALIGNMENT

In order that this check may be carried out accurately, the car must be standing on a perfectly flat surface. Lift the front of the car 2 inches and allow it to drop to the rest position. Refer to diagram, measure the distance A from the lower suspension arm to the level surface and the distance B from the lower ball joint to the level surface. Deduct B from A and note the figure obtained. Push the front of the car down 2 inches and allow it to return. Now repeat the measuring procedure and again deduct B from A and note this second figure obtained. Add together both figures and divide the result by two in order to calculate an average figure. For suspensions equipped with an oval section lower pivot bolt the figure should be $1\frac{11}{32}$ inches plus or minus .118 inch. For suspensions equipped with round section lower pivot bolts the figure should be $1\frac{1}{2}$ inches plus or minus .118 inch. If the measurement is incorrect distance washers should be fitted below the spring in position 1. Washers are available in 3.5, 7.0 and 10.5 mm thicknesses. For 1750 models $A-B = 1.34 \pm .20$ inch.

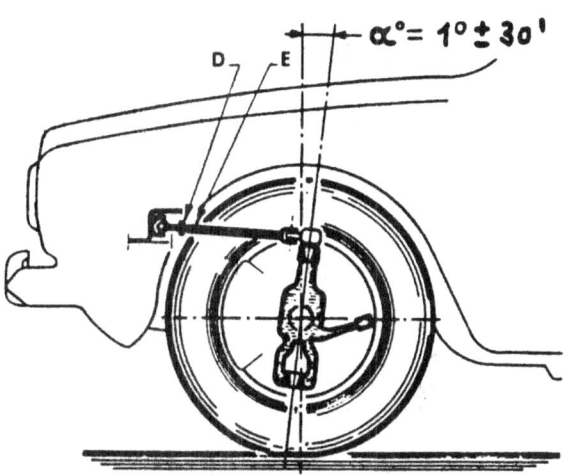

Checking and adjusting the castor angle

CASTOR ANGLE

This is the angle between the vertical line through the wheel centre and the line through the two ball joint centres as shown in the diagram. Using an approved gauge to measure the castor angle, which should be $1\frac{1}{2}$ deg. plus or minus $\frac{1}{2}$ deg. The difference in castor angle between the two wheels should not exceed 20'.

Adjustment is by slackening the locknut D and altering the length of the control rod E. Tighten the locknut when the correct setting is obtained.

CAMBER ANGLE

This is the angle of wheel inclination from the vertical when viewed from the front as shown in the diagram. Use an approved gauge to measure the camber angle, which should be 0 deg. 50' plus or minus 30'. The camber angle is preset and non-adjustable, so if camber angle is found to be incorrect a check should be made on the components of the front suspension and any worn or damaged parts which may be causing the condition renewed. On 1750 and 2000 models the camber angle is $20' \pm 30'$.

When the suspension geometry tests have been completed, reconnect the dampers and anti-roll bar and remove the loading weights.

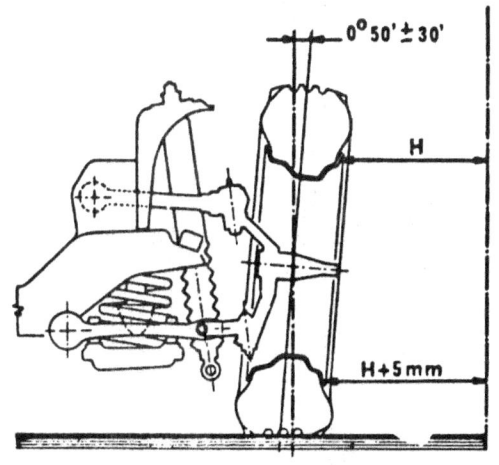

Checking the camber angle

DISMANTLING AND SERVICING SUSPENSION

Slacken the front wheel nuts, jack up the car under the front crossmember and support it on floor stands placed beneath the body sidemembers. Remove the wheels. Refer to the diagram to identify the components of the front suspension.

1. Remove the dampers, detach the brake hose and the caliper on cars fitted with disc brakes, or the brake hose and brake backing plate on cars fitted with drum brakes.
2. Detach the anti-roll bar connections from the lower wishbones and swing the arms of the anti-roll bar out of the way.
3. Remove the bolts from the spring retainer by first compressing the spring with tool A.2.0123. If no compressor is available, use a jack placed under the spring plate to compress the spring sufficiently for the bolts to be removed. Release the spring compressor or lower the jack and remove the spring from the suspension, together with the bearing washer and the top and bottom rubber mountings. Retain any shims which are fitted as they are necessary to set the suspension angle correctly.
4. Remove the ball joint from the upper suspension arm, using tool A.3.0156 or any suitable puller. Lift out the swivel joint complete. Unscrew the two attaching bolts and remove the lower wishbone from the front axle crossmember.
5. Disconnect the control rod from the upper suspension arm and remove the pivot bolt from the top of the crossmember. Lift out the upper suspension arm. Unscrew the two bolts attaching the control rod swivel joint to the car frame and remove the control rod.
6. Remove the lower ball joint from the lower wishbone assembly and remove the wishbone arms from the pivot bolt.

SERVICING

Examine the suspension arms for signs of damage or distortion. Check the condition of the suspension mounting bushes and renew them if they are worn, using tool A.3.0159 for this operation. The ball joints must swivel smoothly but have no free play. Check all parts for good condition and serviceability and renew parts where necessary. Coil springs should preferably be renewed in pairs. If one new spring only is to be fitted, make sure that the coloured paint marking on the new spring is the same as that on the old spring.

REFITTING

Refitting is a reversal of the removal procedure. The suspension should be assembled to the vehicle with the nuts and bolts installed finger-tight only. Final tightening should be carried out with the weight of the car resting on the wheels. Take care to ensure that every nut and bolt is fully tightened and bleed the brakes before road testing the car. It is always advisable to check and adjust the suspension geometry after assembling the suspension.

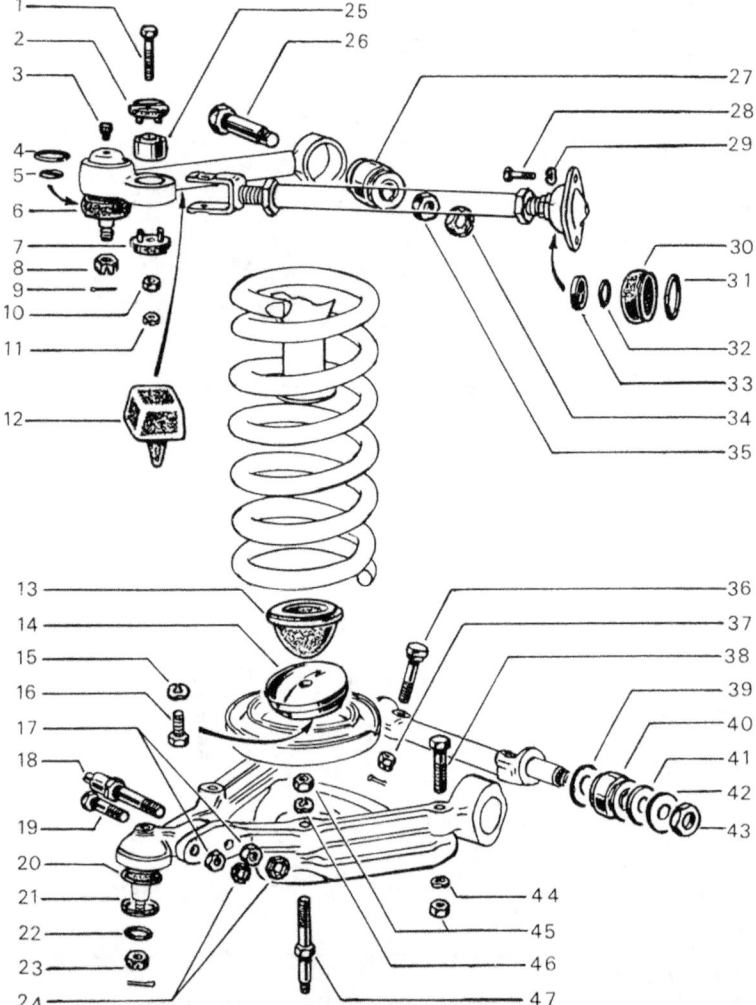

The components of the front suspension

Key to Diagram
1. Bolt
2. Locating washer
3. Screwed plug
4. Retaining ring
5. Retaining washer
6. Dust cover
7. Washer
8. Slotted nut
9. Splitpin
10. Nut
11. Locknut
12. Rebound buffer
13. Rebound buffer
14. Rubber seat
15. Spring washer
16. Bolt
17. Hexagonal nut
18. Suspension arm bolt
19. Mounting bolt
20. Dust cover
21. Retaining washer
22. Retaining washer
23. Slotted nut
24. Locknut
25. Bonded rubber bush
26. Mounting bolt
27. Bonded rubber bush
28. Securing screw
29. Washer
30. Rubber dust cover
31. Sealing ring
32. Retaining washer
33. Sealing ring
34. Locknut
35. Hexagonal nut
36. Mounting bolt
37. Slotted nut
38. Mounting bolt
39. Washer
40. Rubber bush
41. Washer
42. Washer
43. Hexagonal nut
44. Washer
45. Hexagonal nut
46. Washer
47. Mounting bolt

TROUBLE SHOOTING

TROUBLE	POSSIBLE CAUSE	REMEDY
Improper tyre wear	Camber incorrect	The camber (except on Giulietta, 2000, 2600 models) is not adjustable. If adjustment is needed, check the suspension attachments to body and the suspension arms.
	Toe in incorrect	Check and adjust as per specifications and directions given on page 34
	Tyre pressure uneven or incorrect	Inflate to correct pressure
	Wheel shimmy	Refer to the following item
Shimmy	Tyre pressure uneven or incorrect	Inflate to correct pressure
	Excessive wheel bearing play or wear	Carefully inspect and adjust the wheel hubs following strictly the specified pre-loads and directions
	Defective shock absorbers	Repair or replace, if necessary
	Wheels out of balance	Rebalance wheels as installed by means of the modern electronic wheel balancers
Car pulls to one side	Incorrect trim under static load	Check the sag of suspension springs as directed on page 14
	Tyre pressure uneven or incorrect	Inflate to correct pressure
	Front alignment off (wheel angles incorrect or uneven)	Check front wheel alignment and adjust as necessary
	Incorrect front wheel bearing play	Readjust the bearing play following strictly the directions given in the relevant Shop Manual
	Worn wheel bearings	Change bearings
	Defective shock absorbers	Repair or replace, if necessary
	Worn suspension joints	Renew suspension arm bushings
	Looseness at upper or lower ball joints	Renew worn ball joints
Wheel tramp	Tyre pressure uneven (possible air leakage)	Inflate to correct pressure and check the air valve for sound conditions
	Wheel ouf of balance	Rebalance wheels statically and dynamically
	Sagging springs	Change springs
	Defective shock absorbers	Change shock absorbers
	Bent wheel rim	Change wheel rim

SPECIFIC
dimensions in millimetres

LOADS FOR CAR TRIM

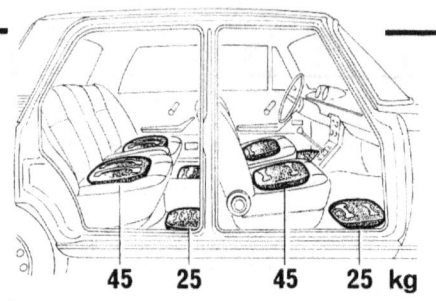

45 25 45 25 kg

- 4-door models:
  load as shown = 280 Kg total weight
- 2-door models:
  load the front only = 140 Kg total weight

		GIULIA 1300		GT 1300	
		former to chassis no. 645.000	from chassis no. 645.001	earlier than model year '68	model year '68
FRONT SPRING SAG	A minus B =	33 to 43 (1) 29 to 39 (2)	29 to 39	29 to 39 (2) 9 to 19 (3)	19 to 29
REAR SPRING SAG	C =	5 to 15	31 to 41	10 to 20	36 to 46
CAMBER	α = (4)	20' to 1°20'	− 10' to 50'	20' to 1°20'	− 10' to 50'
	F =	E + (2 to 9)	E + (−1 to 5)	E + (2 to 9)	E + (−1 to 5)

ATIONS
unless otherwise stated

(1) Wishbone shaft P.N. 105.00.21.301.02 (round cross-section)
(2) Wishbone shaft P.N. 105.14.21.301.00 (elongated cross-section)
(3) Wishbone shaft P.N. 105.41.21.301.00 (upper limiting buffer outside the spring)
(4) Maximum difference in castor angle between R.H. and L.H. wheel = 40′

JUNIOR	GIULIA 1300 TI			GTA 1300 JUNIOR	SPIDER 1300 JUNIOR		GIULIA SPRINT GT	SPIDER 1600
model year '69	earlier than model year '68	model year '68	model year '69		model year '68	model year '69		
19 to 29	29 to 39	29 to 39	29 to 39	29 to 39	19 to 29	19 to 29	33 to 43 (1) 29 to 39 (2)	23 to 33
36 to 46	5 to 15	31 to 41	31 to 41	36 to 46	28 to 38	28 to 38	10 to 20	28 to 38
− 10′ to 50′	20′ to 1°20′	− 10′ to 50′	− 10′ to 50′	− 10′ to 50′	− 10′ to 50′	− 10′ to 50′	20′ to 1°20′	20′ to 1°20′
—	—	—	—	—	—	—	—	—
E + (−1 to 5)	E + (2 to 9)	E + (−1 to 5)	E + (−1 to 5)	E + (−1 to 5)	E + (−1 to 5)	E + (−1 to 5)	E + (2 to 9)	E + (2 to 9)

SPECIFIC
dimensions in millimetres

			GIULIA 1300		GT 1300	
			former to chassis no. 645.000	from chassis no. 645.001	earlier than model year '68	model year '68
CASTOR		β = (5)	1° to 2°	1° to 2°	1° to 2°	1° to 2°
TOE-IN	L.H.D.	γ =	13'	13'	13'	13'
		G =	H + 3	H + 3	H + 3	H + 3
		M = (6)	N	N	N	N
	R.H.D.	γ =	13'	13'	13'	13'
		G =	H + 3	H + 3	H + 3	H + 3
		O = (7)	P	P	P	P

ATIONS
unless otherwise stated

(1) Wheel: 4 1/2j x 15 (390 mm dia.)
(2) Wheel: 5j or 5 1/2j x 14 (365 mm dia.)
(3) Steering arm P.N. 105.04.24.201.00
(4) Steering arm P.N. 105.49.24.201.00 marked with a white dot
(5) Max. difference in castor between R.H. and L.H. wheel = 20'
(6) Rod length: L = 530 to 550 mm; N = 264 to 280 mm.
(7) Rod length: L = 530 to 550 mm; P = 259 to 275 mm.

JUNIOR	GIULIA 1300 TI			GTA 1300 JUNIOR	SPIDER 1300 JUNIOR		GIULIA SPRINT GT	SPIDER 1600
model year '69	earlier than model year '68	model year '68	model year '69		model year '68	model year '69		
1° to 2°	1° to 2°	1° to 2°	1° to 2°	1° to 2°	1° to 2°	1° to 2°	1° to 2°	1° to 2°
13' (1) 14' (2)	13'	13'	13' (1) 14' (2)	14'	13'	13' (1) 14' (2)	13'	13'
H + 3	H + 3	H + 3	H + 3	H + 3	H + 3	H + 3	H + 3	H + 3
N − 5	N	N	N − 5	N	N	N − 5	N	N
13' (1) 14' (2)	13'	13'	13' (1) 14' (2)		13'	13' (1) 14' (2)	13'	13'
H + 3	H + 3	H + 3	H + 3		H + 3	H + 3	H + 3	H + 3
P (3) P + 5 (4)	P	P	P (3) P + 5 (4)		P	P (3) P + 5 (4)	P	P

LOADS FOR CAR TRIM

45   25   45   25 kg

- 4-door models:
  load as shown = 280 kg total weight
- 2-door models:
  load the front only = 140 Kg total weight
- * load the same as for 2-door models

SPECIFIC
dimensions in millimetres

		GIULIA TI	GIULIA TI SUPER *	GIULIA GTC	GIULIA SPRINT GTA
FRONT SPRING SAG	A minus B =	33 to 43 (1) 29 to 39 (2)	35 to 41	33 to 43 (1) 29 to 39 (2)	54 to 60
REAR SPRING SAG	C =	5 to 15	10 to 20	15 to 25	36 to 46
CAMBER	α = (4)	20' to 1°20'	20' to 1°20'	20' to 1°20'	20' to 1°20'
CAMBER	F =	E + (2 to 9)	E + (2 to 9)	E + (2 to 9)	E + (2 to 9)

ATIONS
unless otherwise stated

(1) Wishbone shaft P.N. 105.00.21.301.02 (round cross-section)
(2) Wishbone shaft P.N. 105.14.21.301.00 (elongated cross-section)
(3) Wishbone shaft P.N. 105.41.21.301.00 (upper limiting buffer outside the spring)
(4) Maximum difference in camber angle between R.H. and L.H. wheel = 40'

GIULIA SPRINT GT VELOCE	GIULIA SUPER			GIULIA 1600 S	1750 GT VELOCE		1750 BERLINA	1750 SPIDER VELOCE
	earlier than model year '68	model year '68	model year '69		L.H.D.	R.H.D.		
29 to 39 (2) / 9 to 19 (3)	33 to 43 (1) / 29 to 39 (2)	29 to 39	29 to 39	29 to 39	19 to 29	29 to 39	29 to 39	19 to 29
10 to 20	5 to 15	31 to 41	31 to 41	31 to 41	36 to 46	36 to 46	31 to 41	28 to 38
20' to 1°20'	20' to 1°20'	−10' to 50'	−10' to 50'	−10' to 50'	−10' to 50'	−10' to 50'	−10' to 50'	−10' to 50'
—	—	—	—	—	—	—	—	—
E + (2 to 9)	E + (2 to 9)	E + (−1 to 5)	E + (−1 to 5)	E + (−1 to 5)	E + (−1 to 5)	E + (−1 to 5)	E + (−1 to 5)	E + (−1 to 5)

SPECIFIC
dimensions in millimetres

		GIULIA TI	GIULIA TI SUPER	GIULIA GTC	GIULIA SPRINT GTA
CASTOR	$\beta =$ (5)	1° to 2°	30' to 1°30'	1° to 2°	30' to 1°30'
TOE-IN L.H.D.	$\gamma =$	13'	13'	13'	14'
	$G =$	H + 3	H + 3	H + 3	H + 3
	$M =$ (6)	N	N	N	N
TOE-IN R.H.D.	$\gamma =$	13'		13'	14'
	$G =$	H + 3		H + 3	H + 3
	$O =$ (7)	P		P	P

ATIONS
unless otherwise stated

(1) Wheel: 4 1/2j x 15 (390 mm dia.)
(2) Wheel: 5j or 5 1/2j x 14 (365 mm dia.)
(3) Steering arm P.N. 105.04.24.201.00
(4) Steering arm P.N. 105.49.24.201.00 marked with a white dot
(5) Maximum difference in castor between R.H. an L.H. wheel = 20'
(6) Rod length: L = 530 to 550 mm; N = 264 to 280 mm.
(7) Rod length: L = 530 to 550 mm; P = 259 to 275 mm.

GIULIA SPRINT GT VELOCE	GIULIA SUPER			GIULIA 1600 S	1750 GT VELOCE		1750 BERLINA	1750 SPIDER VELOCE
	earlier than model year '68	model year '68	model year '69		L.H.D.	R.H.D.		
1° to 2°	1° to 2°	1° to 2°	1° to 2°	1° to 2°	1° to 2°	1° to 2°	1° to 2°	1° to 2°
13'	13'	13'	13' (1) 14' (2)	13' (1) 14' (2)	14'		14'	14'
H + 3	H + 3	H + 3	H + 3	H + 3	H + 3		H + 3	H + 3
N	N	N	N − 5	N − 5	N − 5		N − 5	N − 5
13'	13'	13'	13' (1) 14' (2)	13' (1) 14' (2)		14'	14'	14'
H + 3	H + 3	H + 3	H + 3	H + 3		H + 3	H + 3	H + 3
P	P	P	P (3) P + 5 (4)	P + 5		P (3) P + 5 (4)	P (3) P + 5 (4)	P (3) P + 5 (4)

OCTOBER 1977 SUPPLEMENT

S P E C I F I C
dimensions in millimetres

LOADS FOR CAR TRIM

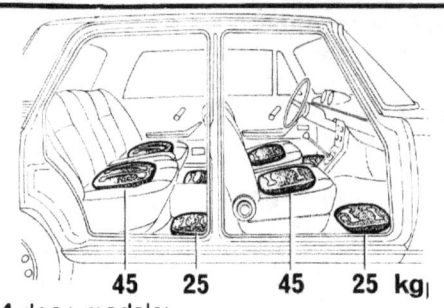

45 25 45 25 kg

- 4-door models:
  load as shown = 280 kg total weight
- 2-door models:
  load the front only = 140 kg total weight

	GIULIA 1300	GIULIA 1300 TI
	from chassis no. 1.029.001-L.H.D.	from chassis no. 1.029.001-L.H.D. / 765.001-R.H.D.
FRONT SPRING SAG — A minus B =	34 ± 5	34 ± 5
REAR SPRING SAG — C =	36 ± 5	36 ± 5
CAMBER — α = (1)	– 10' / + 50'	– 10' / + 50'
F =	E – 1 / + 5	E – 1 / + 5

A T I O N S
unless otherwise stated

(1) Maximum difference in camber angle between R.H. and L.H. wheel = 0° 40'
NOTE - Not adjustable. Check the chassis and suspension arms if necessary

1300 SUPER from chassis no. 2.220.001-L.H.D. 2.294.001-R.H.D.	1600 SUPER from chassis no. 1.875.001-L.H.D. 784.001-R.H.D.	1750 BERLINA from chassis no. 1.740.001-L.H.D. 1.464.001-R.H.D.	2000 BERLINA	2000 GT VELOCE	2000 SPIDER VELOCE
34 ± 5	34 ± 5	34 ± 5	34 ± 5	34 ± 5	24 ± 5
36 ± 5	36 ± 5	36 ± 5	36 ± 5	41 ± 5	33 ± 5
− 10' / + 50'	− 10' / + 50'	− 10' / + 50'	− 10' / + 50'	− 10' / + 50'	− 10' / + 50'
E − 1 / + 5	E − 1 / + 5	E − 1 / + 5	E − 1 / + 5	E − 1 / + 5	E − 1 / + 5

OCTOBER 1977 SUPPLEMENT

SPECIFIC dimensions in millimetres

		GIULIA 1300	GIULIA 1300 TI	
		from chassis no. 1.029.001-L.H.D.	from chassis no. 1.029.001-L.H.D.	from chassis no. 765.001-R.H.D.
CASTOR		$\beta =$ (4)	1° / 2°	1° / 2°	
TOE-IN	L.H.D.	$\gamma =$	13'	13' (1) 14' (2)	
		$G =$	H + 3	H + 3	
		$M =$	N (5)	N − 5 (5)	
	R.H.D.	$\gamma =$		13' (1) 14' (2)	
		$G =$		H + 3	
		$O =$			P + 5 (3) (6)

ATIONS
unless otherwise stated

(1) Wheel: 4 1/2 j x 15" – 390 mm dia.
(2) Wheel: 5 j or 5 1/2 j x 14" – 365 mm dia.
(3) Steering arm P.N. 105.49.24.201.00 marked with a white dot
(4) Maximum difference in castor between R.H. and L.H. wheel = 20'
(5) Side rod length N = 264/280 mm
(6) Side rod length P = 259/275 mm
L = Track rod length = 530/550 mm

1300 SUPER		1600 SUPER		1750 BERLINA		2000 BERLINA	2000 GT VELOCE	2000 SPIDER VELOCE
from chassis no.		from chassis no.		from chassis no.				
2.220.001	2.294.001	1.875.001	784.001	1.740.001	1.464.001			
L.H.D.	R.H.D.	L.H.D.	R.H.D.	L.H.D.	R.H.D.			
1°/2°		1°/2°		1°/2°		1°/2°	1°/2°	1°/2°
13' (1) 14' (2)		13' (1) 14' (2)		14'		14'	14'	14'
H + 3		H + 3		H + 3		H + 3	H + 3	H + 3
N – 5 (5)		N – 5 (5)		N – 5 (5)		N – 5 (5)	N – 5 (5)	N – 5 (5)
13' (1) 14' (2)		13' (1) 14' (2)		14'		14'	14'	14'
H + 3		H + 3		H + 3		H + 3	H + 3	H + 3
	P + 5 (3) (6)		P + 5 (3) (6)		P + 5 (3) (6)	P + 5 (6)	P + 5 (6)	P + 5 (6)

OCTOBER 1977 SUPPLEMENT

SPECIFIC dimensions in millimetres

LOADS FOR CAR TRIM
- 4-door models: load as shown = 280 kg total weight
- 2-door models: load the front only = 140 kg total weight

45 25 45 25 kg

	GT 1300 JUNIOR		JUNIOR 1300 ZAGATO
	from chassis no. 1.260.001-L.H.D.	from chassis no. 1.295.001-R.H.D.	from chassis no. 1.800.001-L.H.D.
FRONT SPRING SAG — A minus B =	24 ± 5	34 ± 5	24 ± 5
REAR SPRING SAG — C =	41 ± 5	41 ± 5	33 ± 5
CAMBER — α = (1)	−10' / +50'	−10' / +50'	−10' / +50'
F =	E − 1 / + 5	E − 1 / + 5	E − 1 / + 5

A T I O N S
unless otherwise stated

(1) Maximum difference in camber angle between R.H. and L.H. wheel = 0° 40'
NOTE - Not adjustable. Check the chassis and suspension arms if necessary

1750 GT VELOCE from chassis no. 1.375.001-L.H.D. / 1.454.001-R.H.D.	MONTREAL	SPIDER 1300 JUNIOR from chassis no. 1.841.001-L.H.D. / 1.855.001-R.H.D.	1750 SPIDER VELOCE from chassis no. 1.820.001-L.H.D. / 1.835.001-R.H.D.
34 ± 5	24 ± 5	24 ± 5	24 ± 5
41 ± 5	41 ± 5	33 ± 5	33 ± 5
− 10' / + 50'	− 10' / + 50'	− 10' / + 50'	− 10' / + 50'
E − 1 / + 5	E − 1 / + 5	E − 1 / + 5	E − 1 / + 5

OCTOBER 1977 SUPPLEMENT

SPECIFIC
dimensions in millimetres

	GT 1300 JUNIOR		JUNIOR 1300 ZAGATO
	from chassis no. 1.260.001-L.H.D.	from chassis no. 1.295.001-R.H.D.	from chassis no. 1.800.001-L.H.D.

CASTOR

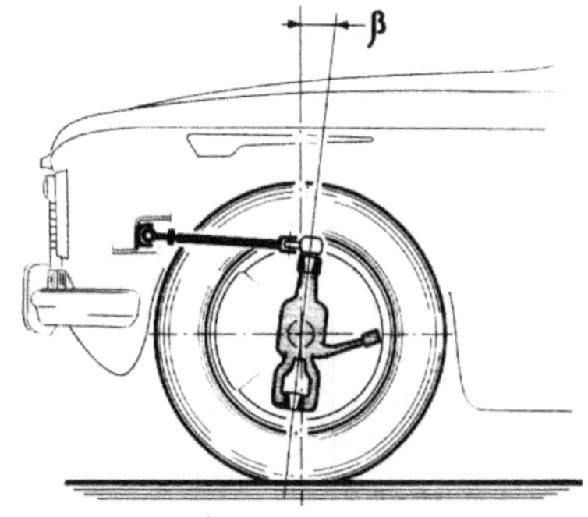

	GT 1300 JUNIOR	JUNIOR 1300 ZAGATO
$\beta =$ (4)	1° / 2°	1° / 2°

TOE-IN

L.H.D.

	GT 1300 JUNIOR	JUNIOR 1300 ZAGATO
$\gamma =$	13' (1) 14' (2)	14'
$G =$	H + 3	H + 3
$M =$	N − 5 (5)	N − 5 (5)

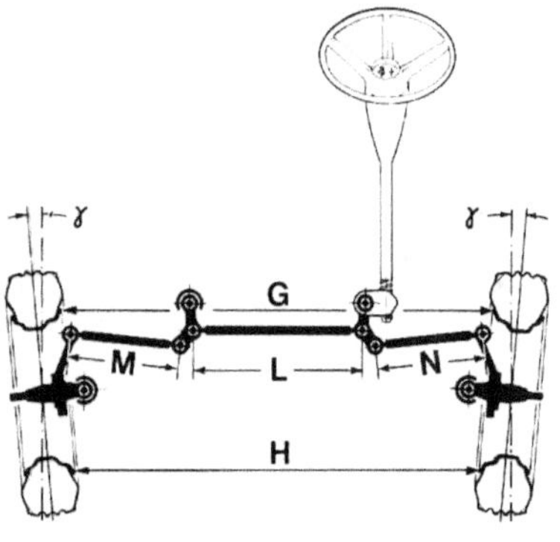

R.H.D.

	GT 1300 JUNIOR	JUNIOR 1300 ZAGATO
$\gamma =$	13' (1) 14' (2)	14'
$G =$	H + 3	H + 3
$O =$	P + 5 (3) (6)	

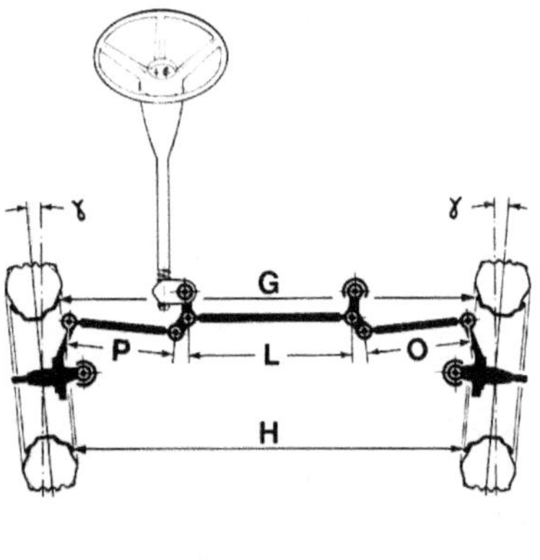

ATIONS
unless otherwise stated

(1) Wheel: 4 1/2 j x 15" — 390 mm dia.
(2) Wheel: 5 j or 5 1/2 j x 14" — 365 mm dia.
(3) Steering arm P.N. 105.49.24.201.00 marked with a white dot
(4) Maximum difference in castor between R.H. and L.H. wheel = 20'
(5) Side rod length N = 264/280 mm (for MONTREAL model = 256/272 mm)
(6) Side rod length P = 259/275 mm (for MONTREAL model = 256/272 mm)
L = Track rod length = 530/550 mm (for MONTREAL model = 643/663 mm)

1750 GT VELOCE		MONTREAL	SPIDER 1300 JUNIOR		1750 SPIDER VELOCE	
from chassis no. 1.375.001-L.H.D.	from chassis no. 1.454.001-R.H.D.		from chassis no. 1.841.001-L.H.D.	from chassis no. 1.855.001-R.H.D.	from chassis no. 1.820.001-L.H.D.	from chassis no. 1.835.001-R.H.D.
1° / 2°		1° / 2°	1° / 2°		1° / 2°	
14'		14'	13' (1) 14' (2)		14'	
H + 3		H + 3	H + 3		H + 3	
N − 5 (5)		N (5)	N − 5 (5)		N − 5 (5)	
14'		14'	13' (1) 14' (2)		14'	
H + 3		H + 3	H + 3		H + 3	
	P + 5 (3) (6)	P (6)	P + 5 (3) (6)		P + 5 (3) (6)	

WHEEL HUBS

REMOVAL

Remove the road wheel. On cars fitted with drum brakes, remove the drum attaching screws and pull off the drum. On cars fitted with disc brakes, dismount the caliper.

Refer to the diagram, remove the grease cap 3 and the splitpin and castellated nut 4 from the wheel spindle. Pull off the hub. If the bearings are to be renewed, prise out the oil seal 7 from the wheel hub and drive out the bearing outer races.

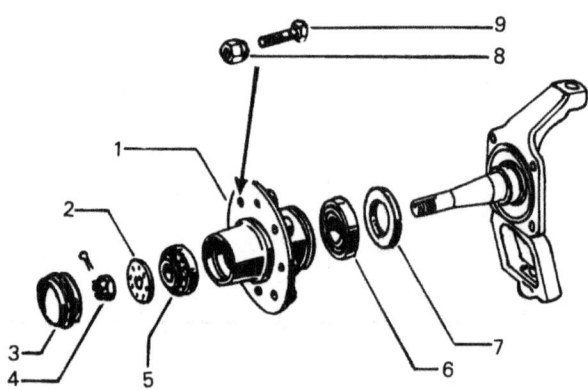

The components of the front wheel hub

Key to Diagram

1 Wheel hub
2 Locating Washer
3 Grease retaining cap
4 Hub securing nut
5 Outer wheel bearing
6 Inner wheel bearing
7 Oil seal
8 Wheel securing nut
9 Wheel securing stud

REFITTING

This is the reverse of the removal procedure. Use a suitable mandrel such as tool A.3.0120 to fit the outer bearing races into the hub. Lubricate the bearings with high melting point grease and fill the cavity in the wheel hub with two ounces of similar grease. Smear the outer lip of a new oil seal with grease and drive it into position, keeping it square. Refit the hub carefully to avoid distorting the swivel joint, the use of tool A.3.011 being recommended. On completion, adjust the bearing end float.

BEARING END FLOAT ADJUSTMENT

Jack up the car and remove the hub cap and the splitpin from the castellated nut 4. Leave the road wheel fitted. Turn the wheel and at the same time tighten the castellated nut to a torque of 18 lb ft to settle the bearings. Loosen the nut by half a turn then tap against the inside of the wheel swivel with a soft mallet to seat the outer bearing. Now tighten the nut to a torque of 10.8 lb ft. Loosen the nut by a quarter of a turn and insert a new splitpin, tightening the nut slightly if necessary to line up the hole in the wheel spindle with a slot in the nut. Check that it is possible to move the locating washer 2. If necessary, again tap against the rear of the swivel joint until the wheel can be rotated freely with no signs of binding. If a dial gauge is available to check the bearing end float, the figure obtained should be .002 to .005 inch. Lock the splitpin when the adjustment is satisfactory.

SHOCK ABSORBERS AND STABILISER ROD

SHOCK ABSORBERS

DAMPERS

The telescopic hydraulic dampers which are shown in the diagram are of the sealed type and require no maintenance. Should a damper become unserviceable a replacement must be fitted. Renew both dampers even if one of them appears to be satisfactory.

REMOVAL

Unscrew the nuts from the upper damper mounting and remove the cup washers and rubber bushes. Remove the nut, spring washer and plain washer from the damper lower mounting on the suspension arm and remove the damper, together with the cup washer and rubber mounting.

REFITTING

This is a reversal of the removal procedure, refer to the diagram for details of the correct fitting of the upper and lower rubber mountings.

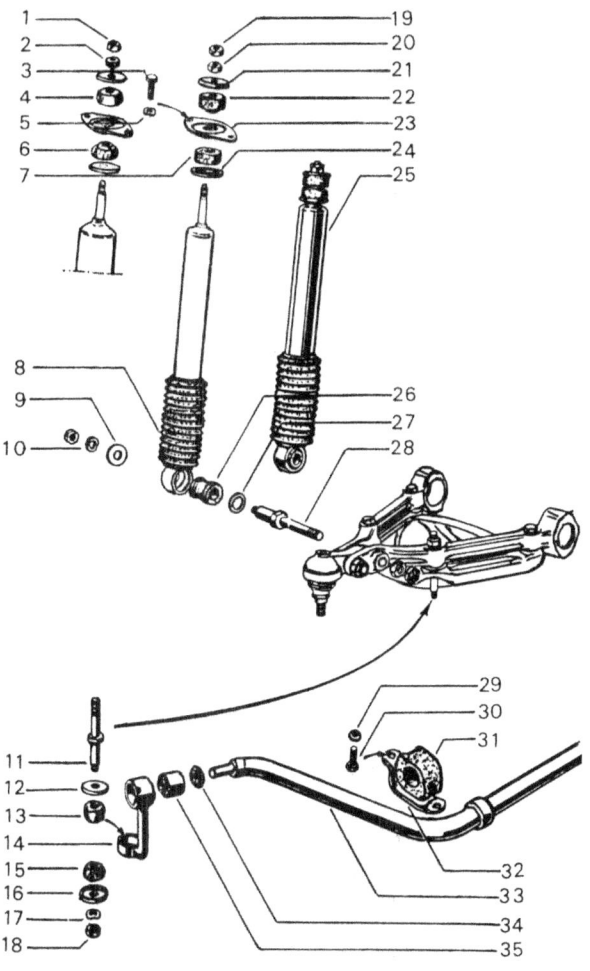

Damper and anti-roll bar components

Key to Diagram	
1 Locknut	18 Nut
2 Locknut	19 Locknut
3 Bolt	20 Securing nut
4 Rubber ring	21 Cup washer
5 Washer	22 Rubber bush
6 Rubber ring	23 Mounting flange
7 Rubber bush	24 Cup washer
8 Protection gaiter	25 Damper
9 Plain washer	26 Rubber bush
10 Spring washer	27 Plain washer
11 Mounting stud	28 Mounting stud
12 Washer	29 Spring washer
13 Rubber Bush	30 Bolt
14 Anti-roll bar link	31 Rubber bearing
15 Rubber bush	32 Clamp bracket
16 Cup washer	33 Anti-roll bar
17 Spring washer	34 Washer
	35 Bonded rubber bush

STABILISER ROD

REMOVAL

Refer to the diagram, disconnect the anti-roll bar from the attachment points on the lower suspension arms. Remove the two rubber bush clamps from the car body attachment points and remove the anti-roll bar. If the anti-roll bar is bent it is possible to straighten it in a cold condition under a press. Check that the arms are parallel to each other when viewed from the side. Check the rubber bushes at the body and suspension arm mounting points and renew them if they are worn or damaged.

REFITTING

Refitting is a reversal of the removal instructions.

42
ZF STEERING BOX

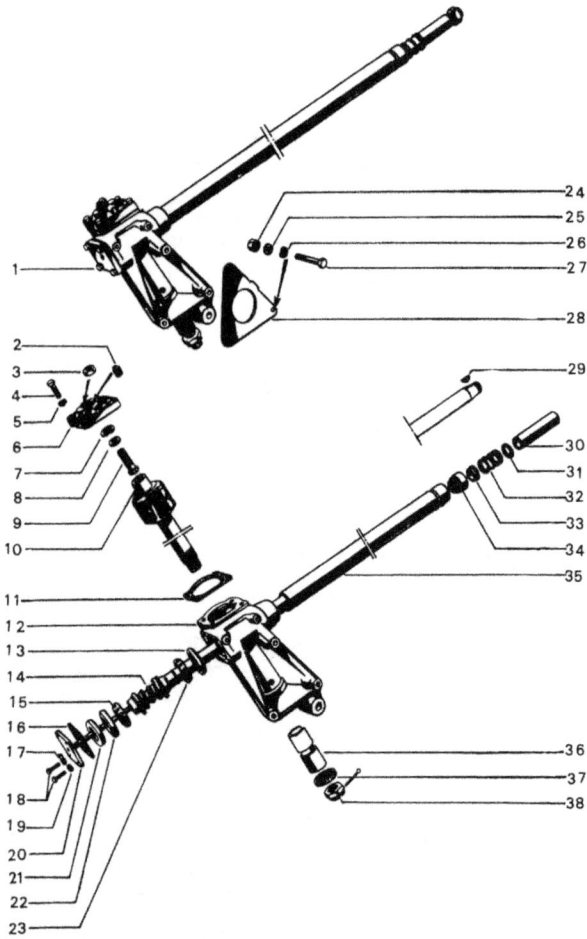

Components of the ZF steering box

1 Steering box assembly	14 Worm	27 Bolt
2 Oil filler plug	15 Lower bearing	28 Mounting plate
3 Nut	16 End cover shim	29 Key
4 Top cover screw	17 Lock washer	30 Sleeve
5 Spring washer	18 End cover screws	31 Ring
6 Top cover	19 Washer	32 Column spring
7 Retaining ring	20 End cover	33 Inner tube bush
8 Guide washer	21 Spacer	34 Spring seat
9 Adjusting screw	22 Lower bearing outer race	35 Outer tube
10 Rocker shaft		36 Bush
11 Gasket	23 Upper bearing	37 Oil seal
12 Housing	24 Nut	38 Castellated nut
13 Upper bearing outer race	25 Washer	
	26 Spring washer	

REMOVAL

1 Remove the padding from the steering wheel followed by the horn button, horn contact and cable sleeve guides. Remove the steering wheel attaching nut and retaining washer and pull the steering wheel from the tapered shaft by means of a suitable puller. Remove the key from the steering inner shaft.

2 Set the steering column lock to the 'Garage' position and detach the outer tube by removing the attaching bolts from the engine compartment and the car interior. Disconnect the cable terminals from the switch connectors.

3 Remove the ball joint from the steering drop arm and remove the steering box attaching bolts. Remove the air cleaner assembly then lift the steering box from the car.

DISMANTLING

1 Remove the splitpin and castellated nut from the rocker arm shaft. Mark the position of the steering drop arm to the shaft then remove the drop arm, using a suitable puller. Unscrew the plug from the top cover and drain the oil.

2 Slacken the locknut on the adjusting screw 9 then remove the top cover 6. Before removing the retaining ring 7 for the adjusting screw guide washer, check the clearance between the adjusting screw and the end of the steering rocker shaft. The correct clearance is .002 inch and, if necessary, a washer of different thickness should be fitted to obtain the specified clearance. Washers are available in six different thicknesses from 2.20 mm to 2.45 mm.

3 Remove the steering rocker shaft, taking care to avoid damaging the lower oil seal with the splines on the shaft. Remove the end cover 20 and withdraw the steering shaft from the housing, together with the shim 16, spacer 21 and the upper and lower shaft bearing assemblies.

SERVICING

Clean all parts in petrol or paraffin and dry them off. Check the components for wear or damage, particularly the steering worm and the teeth on the rocker shaft, and renew any component found unserviceable. The normal clearance between the rocker shaft and the bush 36 is .0005 inch. If this clearance is exceeded, a new bush should be fitted and reamed to give a shaft clearance of .0003 inch. Check the condition of the oil seal 37 and renew it if necessary.

REASSEMBLY

Reassembly is a reversal of the dismantling procedure, noting the following points. Refit the steering shaft and worm assembly and fit the end cover with the original shim. Now check the torque required to turn the steering shaft, which should be between .10 and .5 lb ft. If necessary, alter the thickness of the shim beneath the end cover to obtain a torque reading within the limits stated. Shims are available in five different thicknesses from .10 mm to .30 mm.

Fit the steering rocker shaft and place the drop arm over the shaft splines in accordance with the alignment marks made during dismantling. Set the drop arm in the central position and tighten the adjusting screw until all perceptible clearance between the worm and the steering rocker shaft is eliminated. Now turn the drop arm through an angle of 30 deg. in each direction and check the clearance in each position, again using the adjusting screw to eliminate any free play. When this is done correctly the steering should have a clearance-free movement without any sign of binding. Fit the guide washer retaining ring and lock the adjusting screw. Tighten the drop arm securing nut to a torque of 90 to 100 lb ft and lock with a new splitpin. On completion, refill the steering housing with SAE.90 oil.

REFITTING

Refitting the steering assembly to the car is a reversal of the removal procedure.

BURMAN STEERING BOX

REMOVAL

The removal of the Burman steering box is carried out in the same manner as that previously described for the removal of the ZF assembly.

DISMANTLING

Refer to the diagram for details of the components of the Burman steering box assembly.

1 Remove the splitpin and castellated nut from the rocker arm shaft. Mark the position of the steering drop arm to the shaft then remove the drop arm, using a suitable puller. Unscrew the plug from the top cover and drain the oil.

2 Unscrew the four bolts attaching the top cover to the housing and remove the cover, paper shim 11 and the roller 12. Remove the bolts securing the end cover 17 and remove the cover, together with the shim 18 and the bearing spacer 19. Remove the key 32, sleeve 33 and spring 34 from the end of the steering shaft. Push on the end of the shaft to remove the bearing outer race from the housing and collect the ten steel balls. Remove the remaining thirteen steel balls which will have fallen into the housing. Remove the steering column tube.

3 Turn the steering column clockwise and remove the second bearing outer race from the housing. Remove the rocker shaft 26 and the steering main nut 13 from the housing, then withdraw the lower shaft bearing and oil seal.

SERVICING

Clean all parts in petrol or paraffin and dry them off. Check the components for wear or damage and renew any component found unserviceable. Renew any worn bushes, noting that the steering shaft bush must be fitted with the oil groove toward the shaft. New bushes must be reamed until the shaft is a smooth sliding fit in the bush. If the steering shaft worm is worn or damaged, a new shaft must be fitted. The steering main nut and roller should be examined for signs of scoring or wear and parts renewed as required.

REASSEMBLY

Reassembly is a reversal of the dismantling procedure, noting the following points. Mount the steering column tube horizontally in a vice. Fit the upper bearing outer race over the steering shaft and insert the shaft a short distance into the tube. Retain the steel recirculatory balls in the steering main nut by the use of heavy grease. Insert the steering shaft into the housing and screw the worm carefully into the main nut until the nut is centrally positioned on the worm. Fit the bearing outer race on the steering shaft into the housing and refit the steering column flange to the housing, making sure that the gasket is correctly positioned. Retain the ten steel balls in the upper bearing with heavy grease, then push the bearing into the housing until it abuts against the steering column. Apply heavy grease and refit the thirteen balls in the same manner. Fit the end cover and shim and tighten the end cover attaching bolts.

There should be no perceptible end play on the steering worm with the end cover fitted. Alternative metal shims are available in .003 and .004 inch thicknesses, paper shims in .002 and .010 thicknesses. Select and fit an appropriate shim to remove end play, making sure that the steering is in the central position when making tests and adjustments.

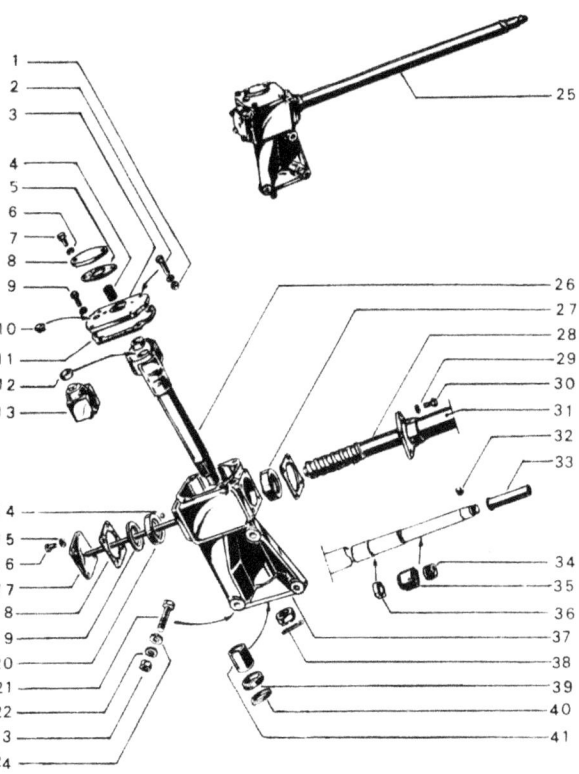

Components of the Burman steering box

Key to Diagram		
1 Nut	14 Ball	28 Wormshaft
2 Bolt	15 Lockwasher	29 Lockwasher
3 Top cover	16 Screw	30 Screw
4 Shaft spring	17 End cover	31 Outer tube
5 Shim	18 Shim	32 Key
6 Lockwasher	19 Spacer	33 Sleeve
7 Screw	20 Lower bearing	34 Inner tube spring
8 Small cover	21 Bolt	35 Ballbearing
9 Screw	22 Spring washer	36 Bush
10 Oil plug	23 Nut	37 Housing
11 Paper shim	24 Washer	38 Castellated nut
12 Main nut roller	25 Complete assy.	39 Oil seal
13 Main nut	26 Rocker shaft	40 Retainer
	27 Upper bearing	41 Bush

Fit the top cover and gasket and tighten the cover attaching bolts to a torque of 16.5 to 18 lb ft and check the steering column end float in the following manner. Fit a dial gauge assembly to the top of the steering column and read off the end float measurement while applying a load of 22 lbs to the lower end of the shaft. The end play should be between .002 and .010 inch. A shim of appropriate thickness must be fitted between the small cover and the top cover to obtain the figure quoted, making sure that the steering is in the central position when making tests and adjustments. Do not fit the spring 3 when making the adjustments.

When the adjustments have been completed, check that the steering can be turned freely from one lock to the other. Refit the steering drop arm to the rocker shaft in accordance with the marks made during dismantling, tighten the castellated nut and lock with a new splitpin.

REFITTING

Refitting the steering assembly to the car is a reversal of the removal procedure.

44
STEERING LINKAGE

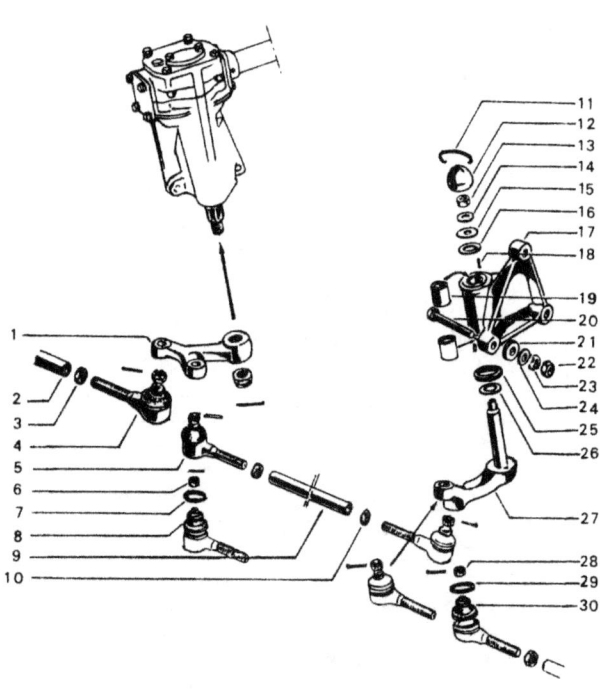

Components of the steering linkage

Key to Diagram

1. Steering drop arm
2. Track rod
3. Locknut
4. Track rod end
5. Tie rod end
6. Castellated nut
7. Retaining ring
8. Rubber cover
9. Tie rod
10. Locknut
11. Securing clip
12. Protective cover
13. Nut
14. Locking plate
15. Washer
16. Thrust washer
17. Idler arm bracket
18. Pin
19. Bush
20. Mounting bolt
21. Washer
22. Nut
23. Spring washer
24. Washer
25. Oil seal
26. Thrust washer
27. Idler arm
28. Castellated nut
29. Retaining ring
30. Rubber cover

The components of the steering linkage are shown in the diagram.

IDLER UNIT (REMOVAL AND REPLACEMENT)

Detach the tie rod and track rod ball joints from the idler arm then remove the mounting bolts from the idler arm bracket and lift the idler unit from the car. Remove the securing clip, protective cover and the pivot bolt nut and withdraw the idler arm from the bracket, collecting the washers, thrust washers and locking plate. Check the pivot bolt and bearing bushes for wear and renew parts as necessary. New bushes must be reamed out until the pivot bolt is a smooth sliding fit without side play. The pivot bolt must have no end play when it is refitted to the bracket and the nut tightened to a torque of 35 to 40 lb ft. Eliminate any end play by fitting thicker thrust washers. Tighten the mounting bolts to a torque of 35 to 40 lb ft when refitting the idler arm bracket to the car.

TIE ROD

If the tie rod ball joints are worn they should be renewed. Remove the splitpins and castellated nuts from both joints and remove the tie rod. Use a puller such as A.3.0157 to remove the ball joints. When refitting the unit to the car, tighten the ball joint castellated nuts to a torque of 32.6 to 41.9 lb ft and lock with a new splitpin.

TRACK RODS

Renew the track rod ball joints if they are worn, in the manner previously described for the tie rod joints. If the track rod ends are removed, count the number of turns taken to unscrew them so that they can be screwed in an equal number of turns when they are refitted. Tighten the ball joint castellated nuts to a torque of 32.6 to 41.9 lb ft and lock with a new splitpin. On completion, check the front wheel alignment.

STEERING UNIT MAINTENANCE

Every 3750 miles, remove the steering box oil filler plug and top up with the recommended lubricant until no more oil will enter.

BALL JOINTS

The steering ball joints are lubricated and sealed for life, so no routine maintenance is necessary. If the joints are worn or the oil seals are damaged the complete ball joint should be renewed.

STEERING ADJUSTMENTS

STEERING BOX

If there is any play in the steering, the steering box internal clearances should be checked and adjusted.

Before carrying out any adjustments to the steering box, a check should be made to ensure that worn ball joints or loose wheel bearings are not the cause of the trouble.

LOCKSTOPS

The lockstops limit the travel of the steering drop arm in one direction and the idler arm in the other direction. Lockstops are factory set to give the correct turning circle If adjustment should be necessary, slacken the locknuts and adjust the screws to obtain the desired left and right turning circles. Tighten the locknuts and recheck.

FRONT WHEEL ALIGNMENT

The car should be in a loaded condition on level ground before any checks and adjustments are made. With the wheels in the straight-ahead position, check the wheel alignment using an approved track setting gauge. Each wheel should be toed-in .06 inch (1.5 mm). Push the car forward until the wheels have turned through 180 deg. and recheck.

If adjustment is required, lock the steering wheel in the straight-ahead position by suitable means, then slacken the locknuts at each end of the track rods and at each end of the tie rod. Refer to the diagram, rotate the track rod 1 until the wheel on the steering box side is in the straight-ahead position. Measure accurately the length of the track rods thus obtained and adjust the track rod 2 on the other side to the same length. Now adjust the tie rod 3 to bring the wheel on the side away from the steering box into the straight-ahead position and tighten the tie rod locknuts. Finally, rotate the track rods 1 and 2 by equal amounts until the specified toe-in setting is obtained and tighten the locknuts.

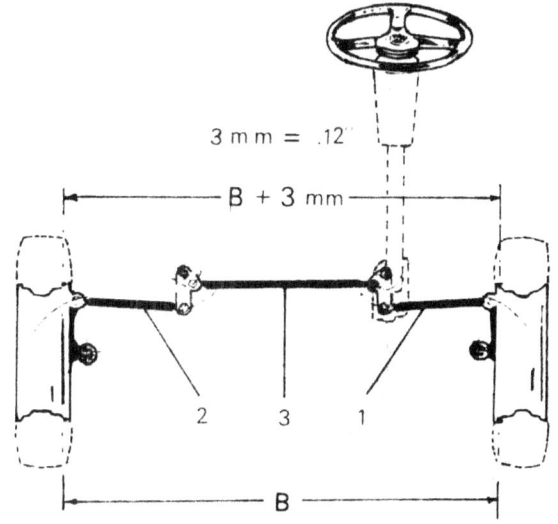

Checking and adjusting the front wheel alignment

Key to Diagram

1 Track rod
2 Track rod
3 Tie rod

NOTES

SHOP MANUAL No. 5
ELECTRICAL

BOSCH ALTERNATOR (FACTORY MANUAL)

GIULIA SUPER
1750 BERLINA
1750 GT VELOCE
1750 SPIDER VELOCE

REGULATOR (CONTROL BOX) ADJUSTMENTS
GENERATOR
STARTER MOTOR
WIPER MOTOR (BOSCH & MARELLI)
LAMPS
WIRING DIAGRAMS

INDEX TO MANUAL

Factory Manual - Bosch alternator

Control box and regulator	27
Generator	28
Starter motor	30
Windscreen wiper motor	32
Lamps and lighting	34

INDEX TO WIRING DIAGRAMS

1300 Spider Junior	35
1300 Giulia Ti	36
1300 GT Junior	37
1600 Spider Duetto	38
1600 Giulia Spider & Spider Veloce	39
1600 Giulia Sprint GT (Version 1)	40
1600 Giulia Sprint GT & Veloce (Version 2)	41
1600 Giulia Ti	42
1600 Giulia Super	43
1750 GT Veloce	44
1750 Berlina (Pre 1970)	45
1750 Berlina (1970 Onwards)	46
1750 Coupe	47
2000 Saloon	48
2000 Veloce	49

■ GIULIA SUPER ■ 1750 BERLINA ■ 1750 GT VELOCE ■ 1750 SPIDER VELOCE ■

ELECTRICAL UNITS: CHARGING SYSTEM ■
BOSCH K1 (RL) 14V 35A 20 ALTERNATOR ■

SHOP MANUAL

CONTENTS

1 Technical specification

CHARGING CIRCUIT

2 Wiring diagram
3 Regulator operating principles
4 In-car test

ALTERNATOR

5 Description
6 Preparatory steps for testing diodes
9 Testing diodes with a test lamp
10 Testing diodes with an ohmmeter

DISASSEMBLY & OVERHAUL

12 Special tools for replacing diodes
14 Pulley — Brush holder — End frame
15 Rotor - Ball bearing
16 Replacing diodes
18 Inspection and testing
20 Replacing one positive or negative diode

REASSEMBLY

21 Drive end frame
22 Brush — Negative diode heat sink
23 Positive diode heat sink
24 Connections
25 Rotor — Brush holder
26 Press-fit field diodes

SPECIFICATION

Slip ring out-of-round	max 0.03 mm.
Rotor out-of-round	max 0.05 mm.
Minimum length of carbon brushes	14 mm.
Brush spring pressure	300-400 gr.
Minimum O.D. of slip rings	31.5 mm.
Stator winding resistance	0.26 Ohm + 10%
Field winding resistance	4.0 Ohm + 10%
Tightening torque of drive pulley securing nut	3.5 – 4.0 Kgm
Tightening torque of field diodes	.135 – .175 Kgm
Ball bearing grease (1.5 gr per bearing)	Bosch Ft 1v 33 / Bosch Ft 70v 1
Diode lube	Bosch Ol 63v 2
Insulating compound for positive diode heat sink	Bosch Fl 87v 1

This Manual, supplied to all authorised ALFA ROMEO Repair Shops, contains instructions for the overhaul and reconditioning of the BOSCH K1 (RL) 14V 35A20 alternator.

The operations are amply illustrated so that the detail and unit concerned can be quickly identified and the tools to be used and the correct method of operation can be seen.

Only genuine spares should be used if any assemblies or parts have to be replaced; only in this way can complete interchangeability and fully satisfactory performance be guaranteed.

This Manual should be kept continuously up-to-date by the addition of new information and instructions issued at intervals by the Technical Service Division in the regular Information Sheets.

ALFA ROMEO
Direzione Assistenza

2
CHARGING CIRCUIT

WIRING DIAGRAM

The charging circuit consists of:
- Alternator   BOSCH   K1 (RL) 14V 35A 20
- Voltage regulator BOSCH   AD 1/14 V
- Warning Light

The wiring diagram of the charging circuit is as shown below.

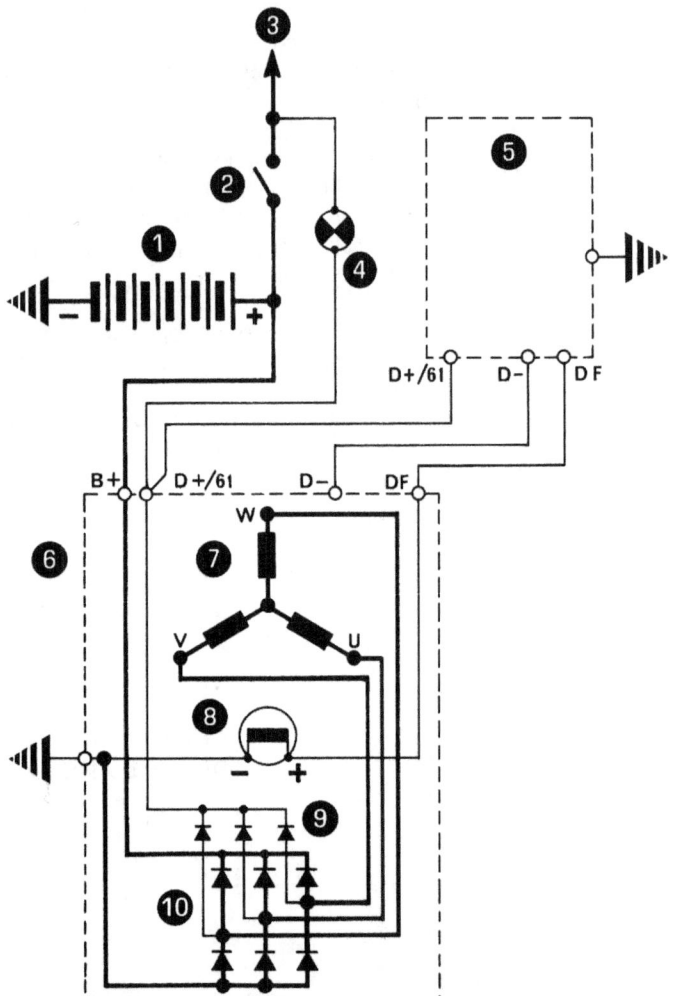

1 Battery
2 Switch
3 To accessory circuits
4 Warning light
5 Regulator
6 Alternator
7 Stator winding
8 Field winding
9 Field current diode rectifier
10 Output current diode rectifier.

D+/61 field rectifier terminal: connected to regulator terminal D+/61 and to warning light.

DF   field input terminal: connected to regulator terminal DF.

B+   battery terminal.

D−   ground terminal: connected to regulator terminal D−.

224

CHARGING CIRCUIT

REGULATOR OPERATING PRINCIPLES

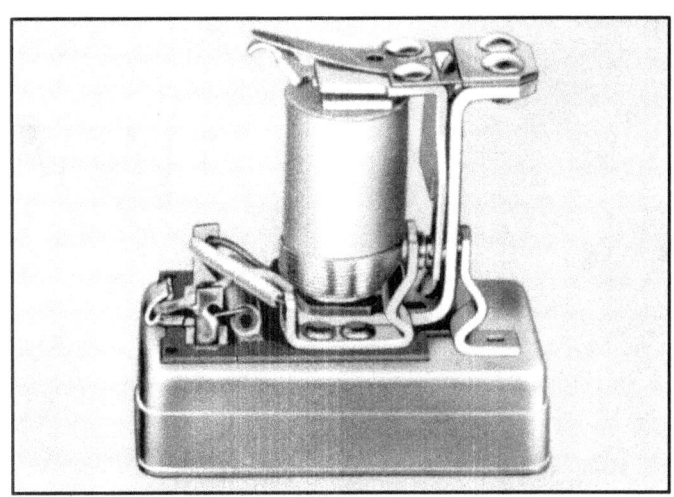

CONSTRUCTION

The alternator output is regulated by a resistance inserted in the alternator field circuit by the regulator.

Such a resistance is connected across the regulator terminals D+ and DF. The armature is under the tension of a spring which holds the points together for contact with the terminal D+ until it is overcome by the magnetism of the regulator winding parallel connected to the alternator terminals D+ and D−.

OPERATION

When the alternator starts, the output voltage is lower or barely attains 12 volts. Thus, full current flows from terminal D+ through armature points to the alternator field winding (DF).

As the alternator output increases the magnetism in the regulator winding also increases. When the voltage for which the regulator is set (about 13.8 volts) has been reached, the armature is pulled toward the core and the D+ points separate.

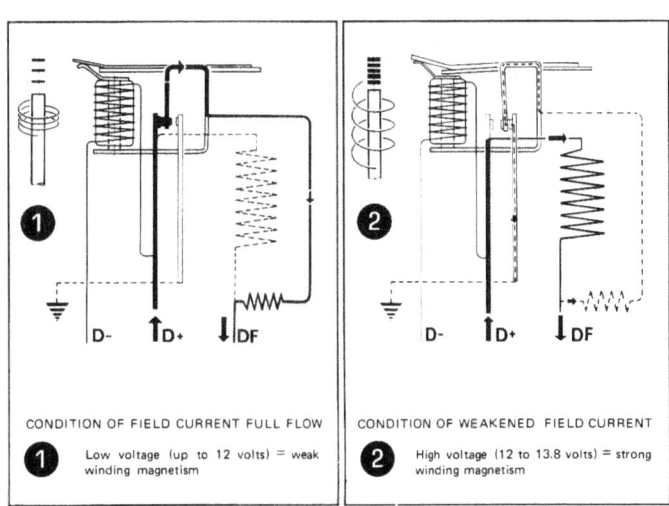

① CONDITION OF FIELD CURRENT FULL FLOW
  Low voltage (up to 12 volts) = weak winding magnetism

② CONDITION OF WEAKENED FIELD CURRENT
  High voltage (12 to 13.8 volts) = strong winding magnetism

The current bypasses the air gap between points and, flowing through the resistance in the alternator field circuit (a small part also flows back through the armature which is grounded via the other sets of points now closed) causes the alternator output to drop. As a consequence, the magnetic strength in the winding core also drops thus permitting the armature spring to pull the armature away from the core and the D+ points to close again. The entire sequence is repeated more or less rapidly according to the alternator RPM.

The regulator is factory set; therefore, if any trouble is experienced, do not attempt to repair the regulator but replace it with a new one.

4
CHARGING CIRCUIT

IN-CAR TEST

When the warning light or whatever else indicates that the charging system is developing troubles, a test should be made.
An in-car inspection can be performed after the engine has been stopped and left cool down to gain a safe access to the alternator. Cautiously disconnect the terminal B+ and connect an ammeter and a voltmeter as shown.

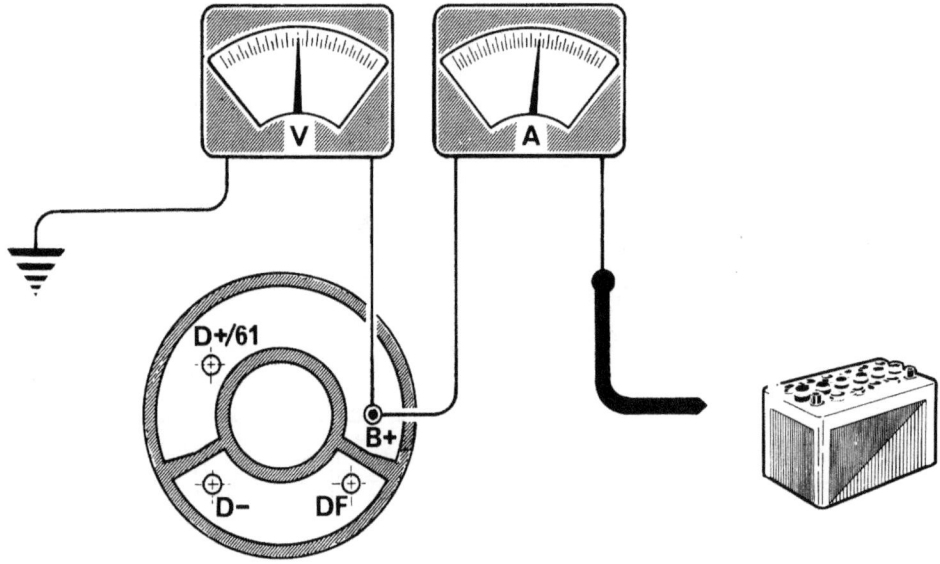

Start the engine.
Switch on some of the lines, e.g. the headlamp, then check charging current and voltage.
If the readings are 20 to 30 amps and 12 to 13 volts the alternator is operating properly and the trouble is somewhere else.
Check the connections carefully; inspect with special care the warning light circuit and the leads to the regulator.
Should the trouble persists even after faulty connections have been remedied, the alternator must be disassembled and thoroughly tested on a suitable tester.

ALTERNATOR

DESCRIPTION

The alternator is of the three phase, twelve pole type, with fan ventilation and a six diode rectifier.

Each phase winding of the stator is connected to one field diode whose output is in turn connected to the terminal D+/61 (refer to the diagram on page 2).

The six diode rectifier hook up is such that three diodes have positive polarity and the other three have negative polarity.

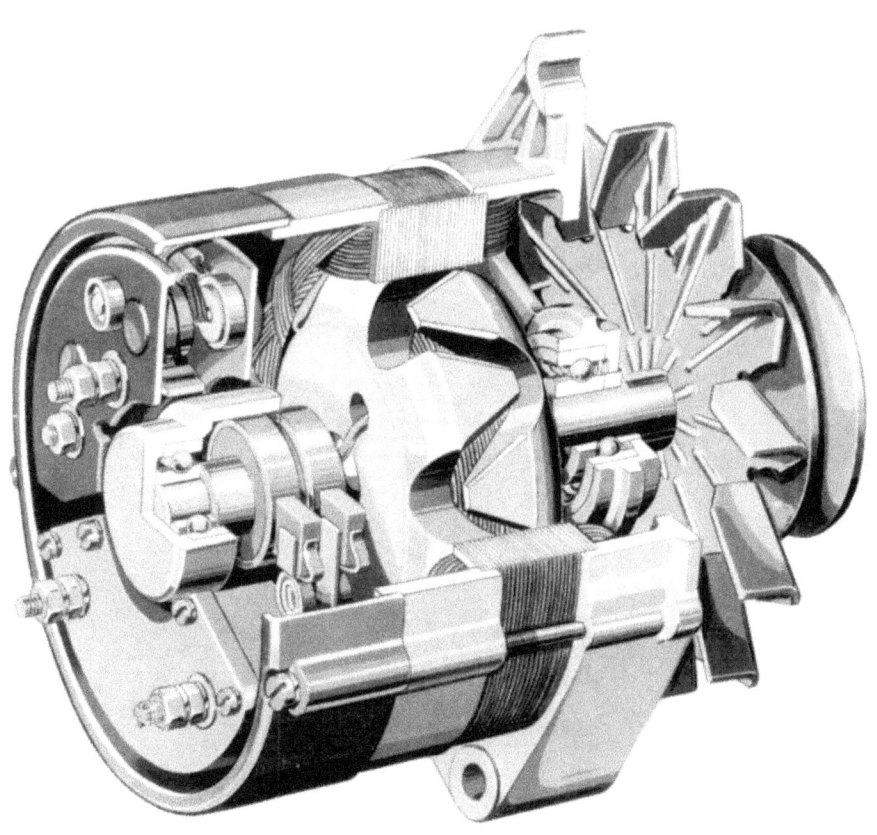

The positive diode heat sink is insulated from ground while the negative heat sink is grounded.

Between the two heat sinks there is the bracket of the three field diodes properly insulated from the alternator frame.

The stator windings are "Y" connected.

The field winding is wound on the mounting core between the rotor segments with twelve magnetic poles.

The field winding is excited through the slip rings.

ALTERNATOR

PREPARATORY STEPS FOR TESTING DIODES

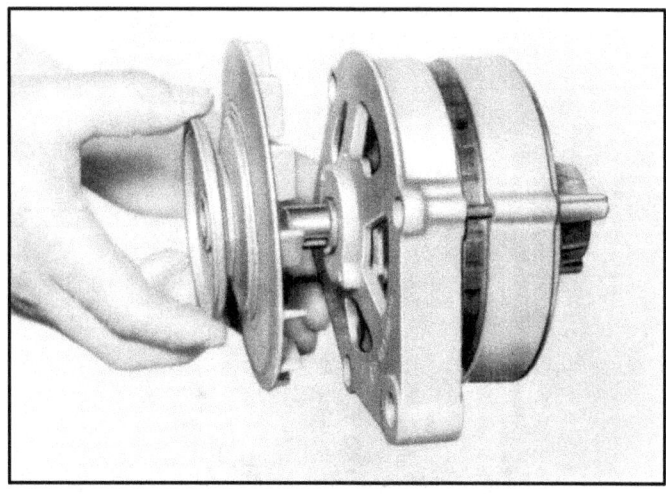

REMOVAL FROM CAR

- Disconnect the battery by detaching the negative terminal first to prevent possible shorts which may damage the diodes.
- Take the drive belt away and remove the alternator.
- Place the alternator on a clean bench.

DISASSEMBLY FOR TESTING DIODES

- Remove the drive pulley.
  For more details refer to page 14.

- Loosen the three attaching screws and remove the plastic ring.

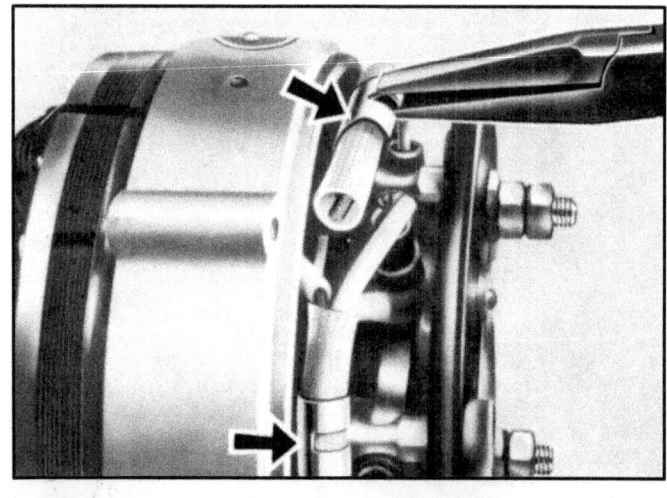

- Free the leads from clips with pliers. Spread apart the leads so that they can then be easily disconnected.

ALTERNATOR

PREPARATORY STEPS FOR TESTING DIODES

- Disconnect the three clusters of four leads by unsoldering or cutting them as shown.
- Withdraw and retain the insulating sheaths.

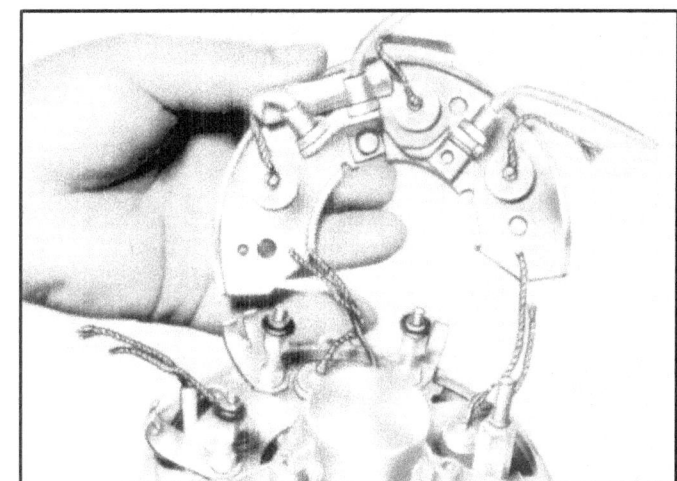

- Remove the positive diode heat sink complete with the field diode bracket.

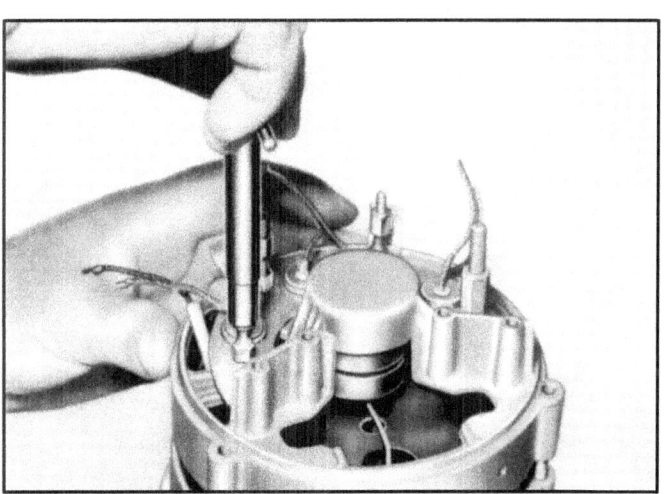

- Unscrew the spacers between the heat sinks and loosen the through bolts.

ALTERNATOR

PREPARATORY STEPS FOR TESTING DIODES

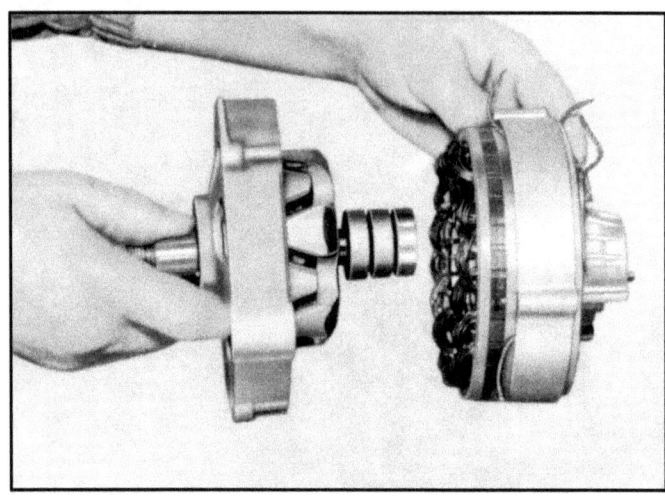

- Ease the rotor out of the stator frame.

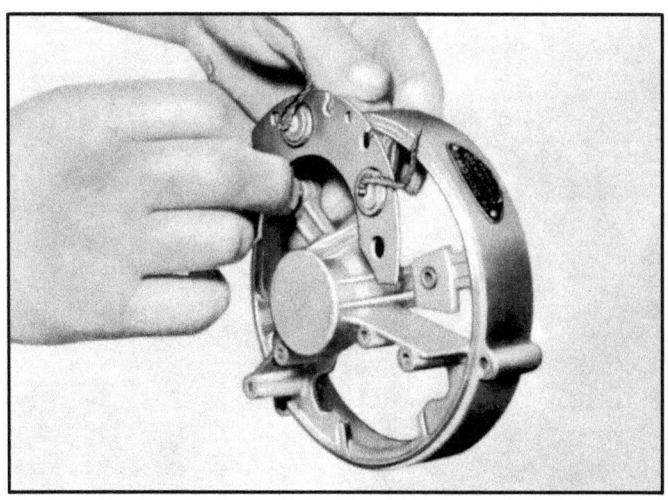

- Remove the negative diode heat sink.

At this stage each diode can be tested separately.

> CAUTION — Throughout testing do not keep diodes, especially when out of their heat sink, under current load for too long a time or they will suffer from overheating.

ALTERNATOR

TESTING DIODES WITH A TEST LAMP

TESTING A POSITIVE DIODE
Connect a 2 watt/12 volt test lamp across battery and positive diodes as shown. If diodes test good the lamp should light up in one direction and not in the other.
If the lamp fails to go on in both directions the diode is open circuited.
If the lamp goes on in both directions the diode is short circuited.

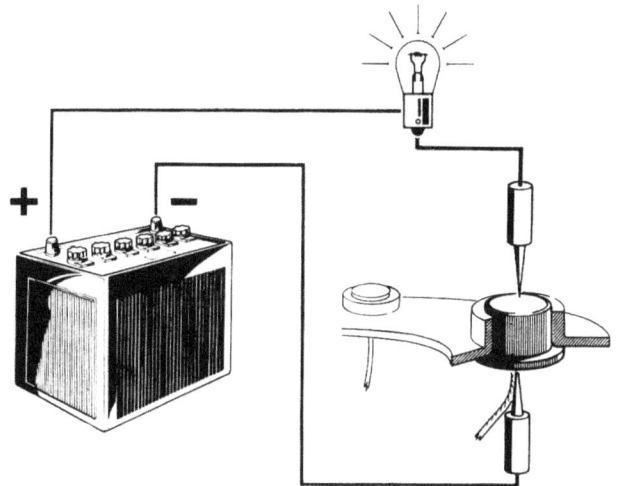

TESTING A NEGATIVE DIODE
Make the connections as shown and perform the test as outlined above.

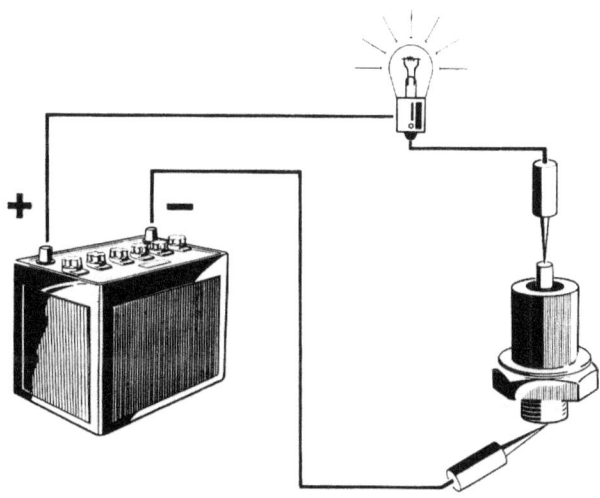

TESTING A FIELD DIODE
Make the connections as shown and perform the test the same way as for positive diodes.

10
ALTERNATOR

TESTING DIODES WITH AN OHMMETER

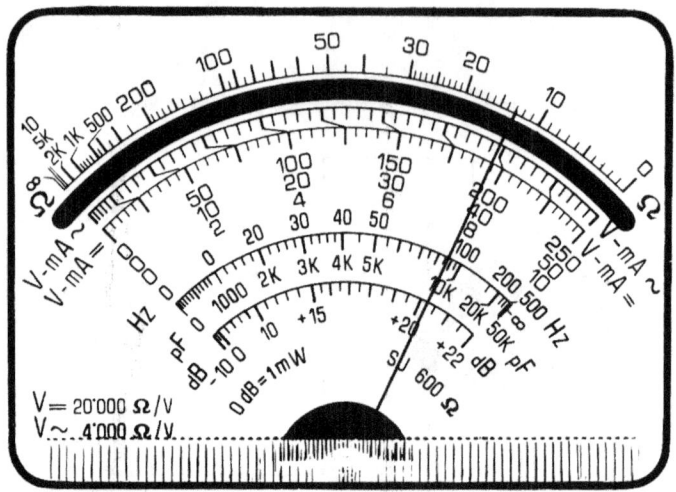

NOTE. For diode testing no exact reading is specified depending it upon the scale and the calibration of the ohmmeter.
Usually, an efficient diode will show a reading of some ohms in the flow-through direction and some kilo-ohms in the no-flow direction.
The purpose of the instrument is essentially to indicate whether the diode allows the current to flow in the proper direction and prevents it from flowing in the opposite direction.
Therefore, in the flow-through direction, the ohmmeter needle should swing quickly to the first one-third of the scale but not to zero which would mean that the diode is shorted.
As to the reading, it is enough that the value remains constant for diodes of the same polarity and function.

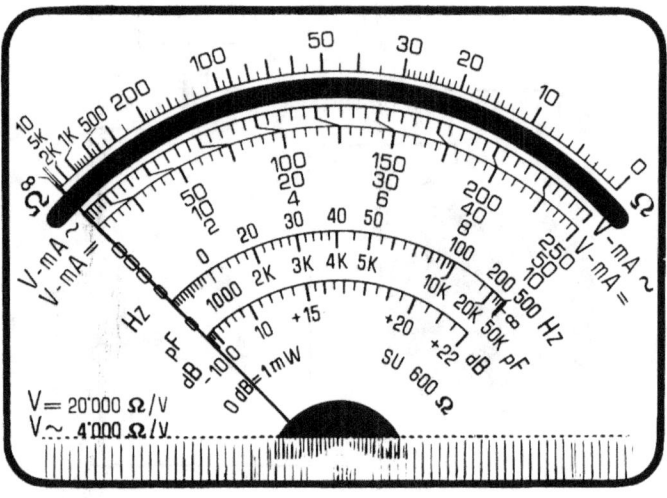

In the no-flow direction the ohmmeter needle should remain stationary at the high (Kilo-Ohm) range of the scale.

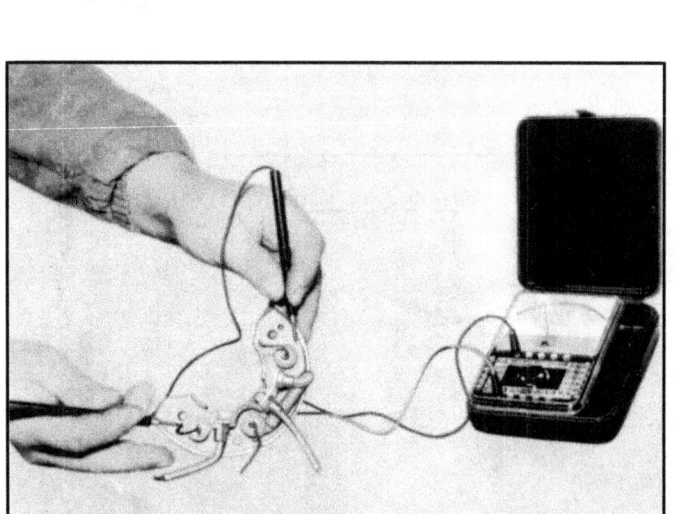

TESTING A POSITIVE DIODE WITH AN OHMMETER.
Placing the prods as shown the diode allows the current to pass through; therefore the needle will swing down the scale. Reversing the prods the current flow is blocked and the needle will remain stationary.
As to the ohm reading, refer to the note above.

ALTERNATOR

TESTING DIODES WITH AN OHMMETER

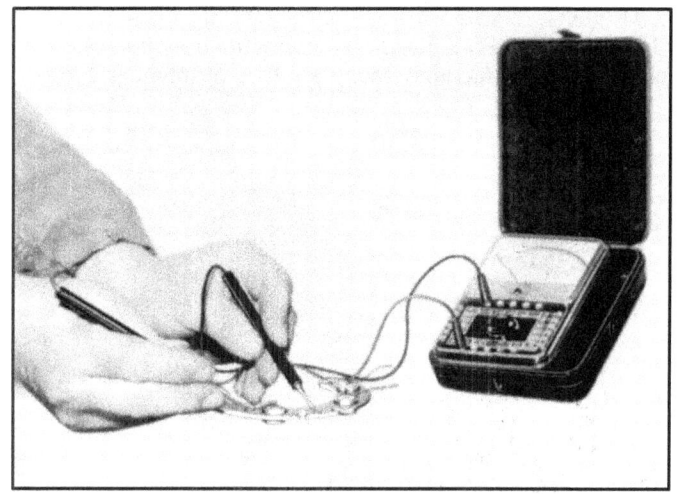

TESTING A NEGATIVE DIODE WITH AN OHMMETER
Proceed the same way as for positive diodes keeping in mind that the polarity is reversed.

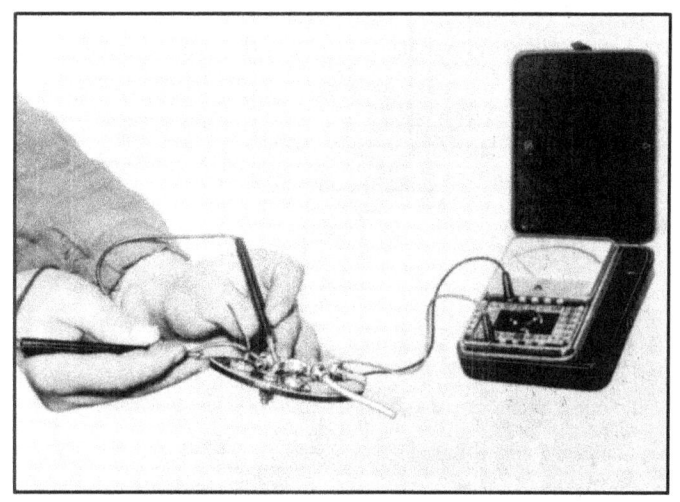

TESTING A FIELD DIODE WITH AN OHMMETER
Proceed the same way as for a positive diode.

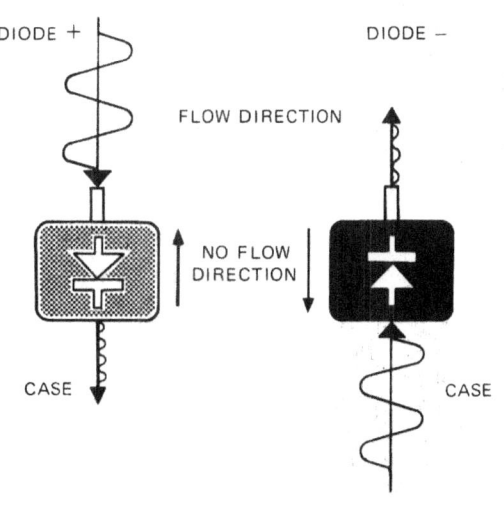

DISASSEMBLY

SPECIAL TOOLS FOR REPLACING DIODES

WARNING. The replacement of single diodes is not recommended unless strictly necessary. However, if a diode needs replacement, use the following special tools to be ordered to ALFA ROMEO or locally manufactured according to the drawings shown.

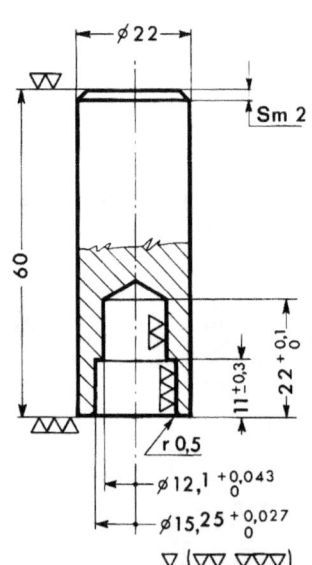

Material: C20 UNI 5332−64

Brinell Hd: $30D^2 \simeq 150$ kg/mm^2

DIMENSIONS IN MILLIMETRES

Surface Roughness:
∇ = 500 microinches AA−CLA
$\nabla\nabla$ = 125 microinches AA−CLA
$\nabla\nabla\nabla$ = 32 microinches AA−CLA

Tool for pulling diodes: A.3.0248

Tool for trueing the mounting boss of diodes: A.4.0122

DISASSEMBLY

SPECIAL TOOLS FOR REPLACING DIODES

Tool for driving diodes: A.3.0249

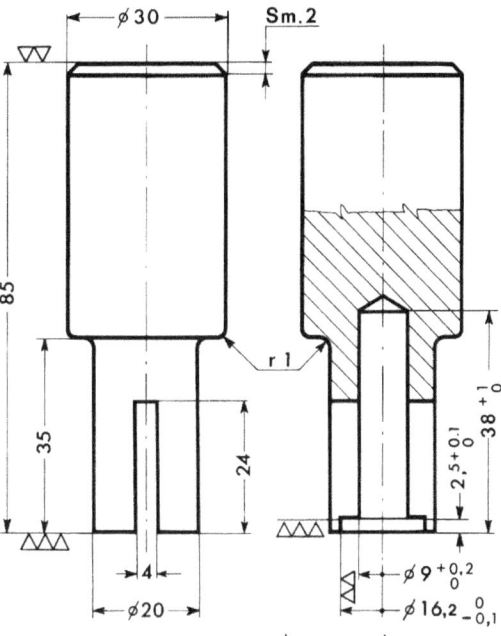

Tool for trueing diode mounting boss hole: A.4.0123

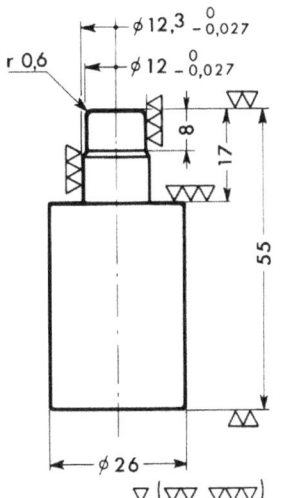

Support tool for pulling and driving diodes: A.3.0250.

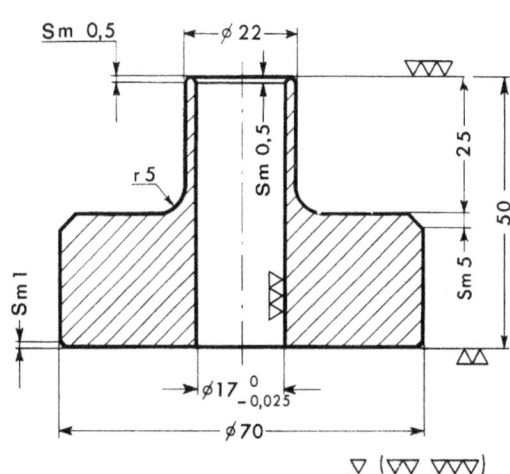

DISASSEMBLY

PULLEY - BRUSH HOLDER - END FRAME

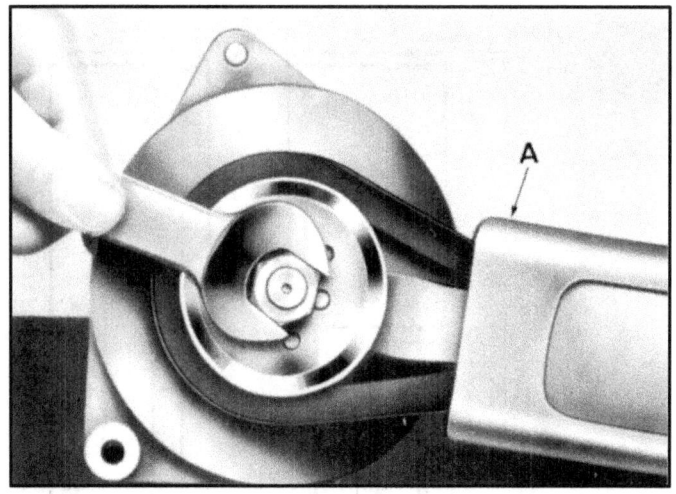

If no definite trouble is detected during the preceding tests, the alternator should be disassembled and thoroughly inspected as outlined on the following pages.

DISASSEMBLING THE ALTERNATOR
Hold the drive belt with a suitable tool (A) and unscrew the nut with a 22 mm wrench. Remove the drive pulley.

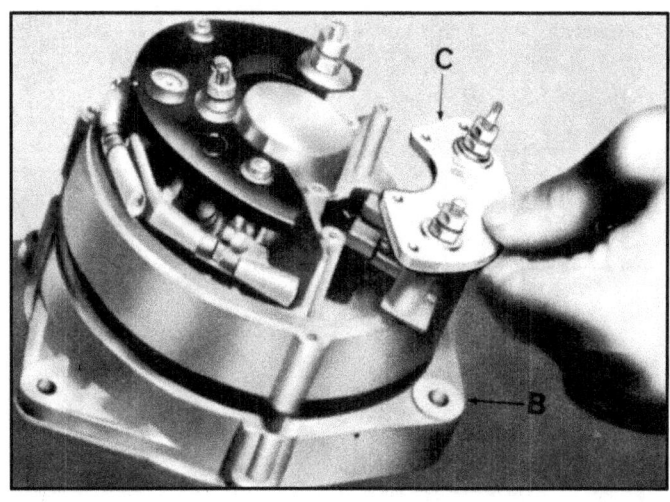

Mark the position of drive end frame (B) with respect to the other components. Loosen the screws attaching the brush holder (C), take away the screws and remove brush holder and brushes as a unit.

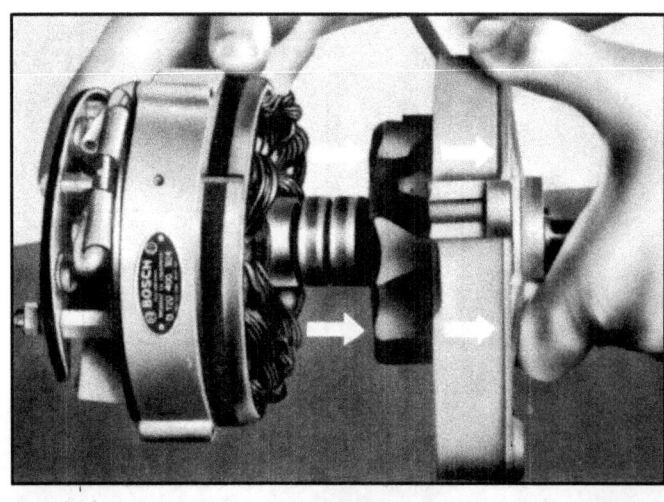

Loosen the drive end frame attaching screws and carefully withdraw the rotor and end frame as a unit from the stator.

DISASSEMBLY

ROTOR - BALL BEARING

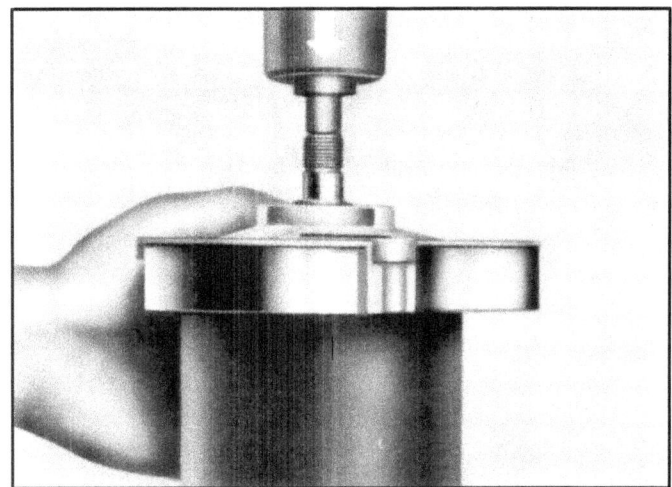

Pull the rotor apart from end cover with a suitable press and a support as shown. While doing this, keep the rotor stationary.

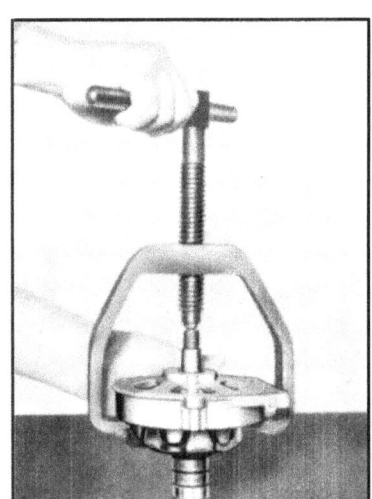

The rotor can also be withdrawn from the end frame by using a puller or the special tool A.3.0109. In case the special tool is used, screw the pulley attaching nut on the shaft threaded shank by about two threads to provide a wider thrust surface.

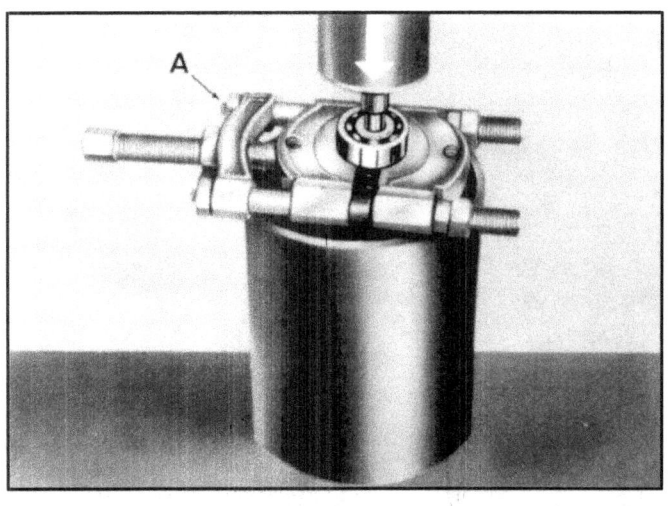

Remove the bearing from the slip ring side by means of a suitable clamp (A) and a press, or with a puller. Pressure should be applied to the inner race. If damaged on removal, replace the bearing with a new one.

OVERHAUL

REPLACING DIODES

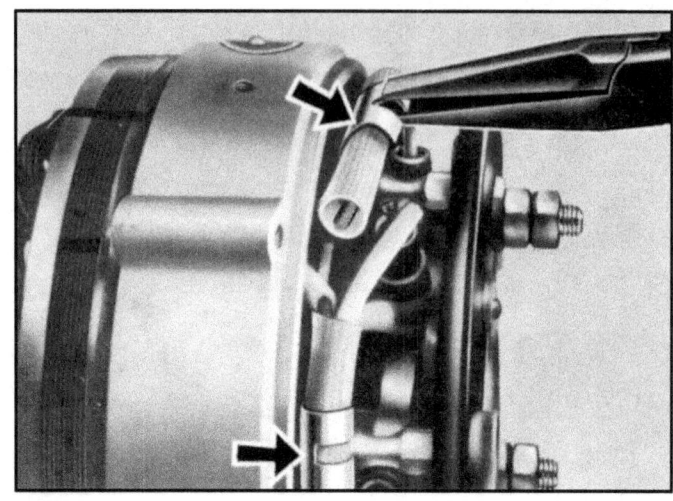

With suitable pliers free the leads to diodes and stator from the clips.
Spread apart the leads so that they can then be easily disconnected.

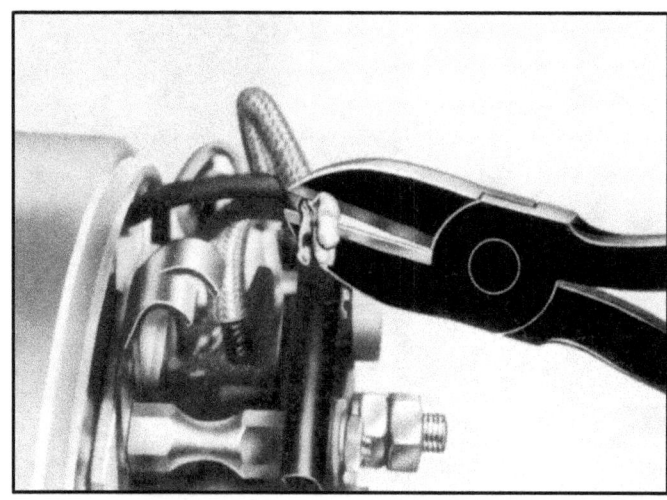

Disconnect the leads by unsoldering or cutting them as shown. Slip out and retain the insulating sheaths.

Before further disassembly, test diodes according to one of test procedure as applicable (refer to pages 9 - 11).

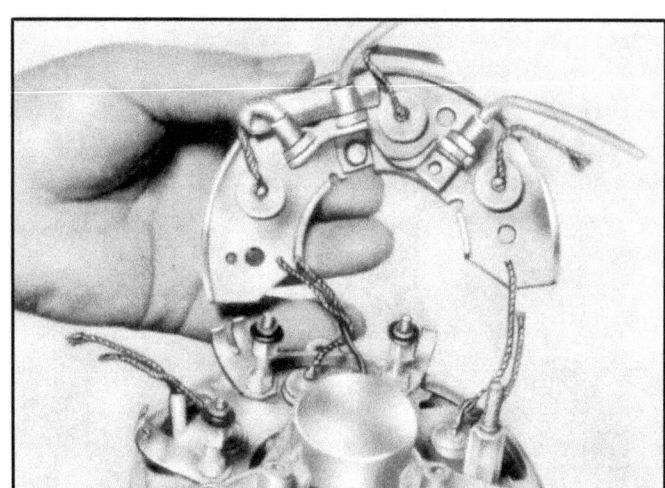

As recommended, replace the complete set of:
- three positive diodes
- three negative diodes
- three field diodes

Positive Diodes:
remove the positive diode heat sink.
When disassembling, special care should be given to the insulating washers.

OVERHAUL

REPLACING DIODES

Negative diodes:
take the negative diode heat sink away with a box spanner.

Field diodes:
In the event of screw-mount diodes: unscrew them with a suitable wrench. Handle the wrench so that it works flat in the plane of diode hex head.

In case of field diodes in unit with their bracket: Replace the set of three diodes complete with bracket.

CLEANING
For a thorough cleaning of the alternator component parts, petrol or trichloroethylene is recommended; however, use them sparingly.

OVERHAUL

INSPECTION AND TESTING

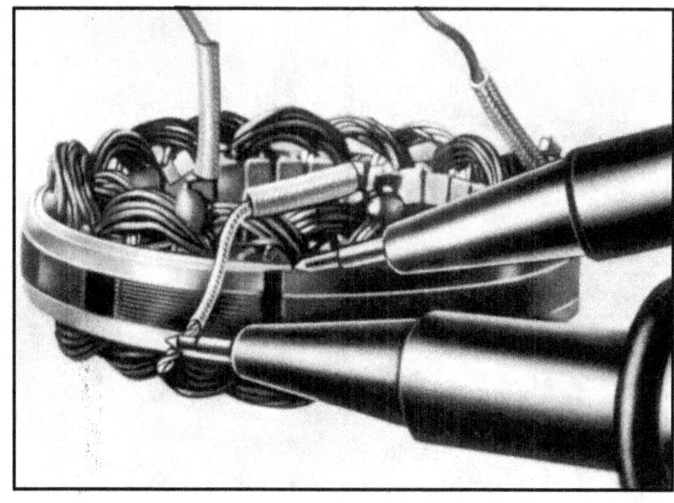

Check the stator windings for grounds with points.
Test voltage:
                        40 volts A.C.

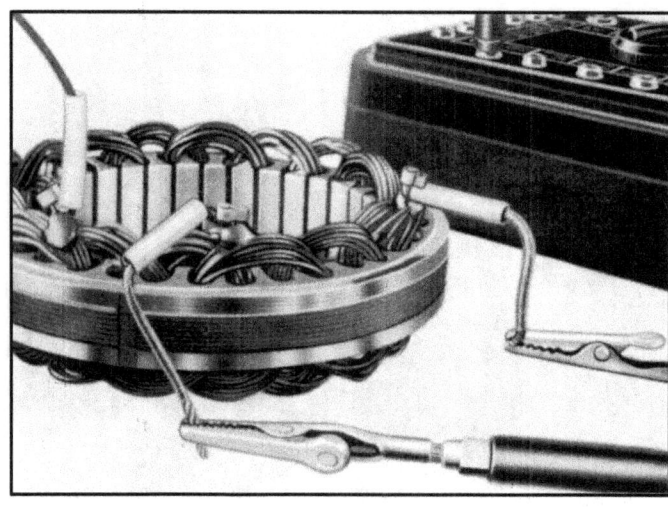

The resistance of each phase winding across output wires should be:
                      0.26 Ohm + 10%
Check windings for shorts and opens.

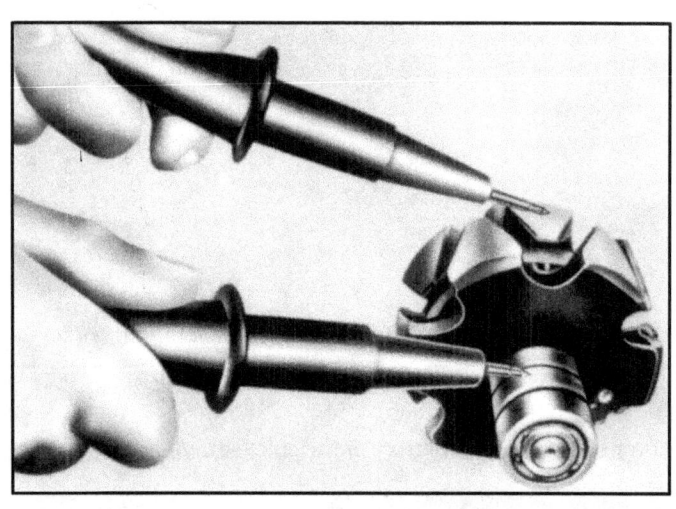

Check rotor poles for grounds with points.
Test voltage:
                        40 volts A.C.

OVERHAUL

INSPECTION AND TESTING

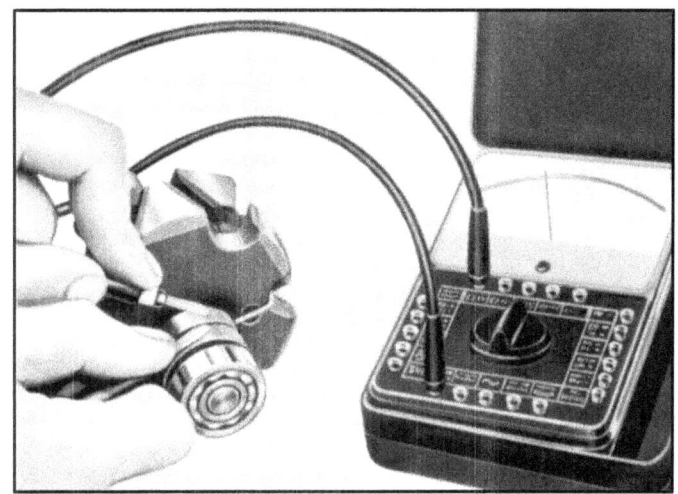

Check the field winding for shorts and opens.
The resistance should be:
4.0 Ohm + 10%

Turn the slip rings in a lathe.

After the slip rings have been turned in a lathe, check them for run out.
Maximum permissible out-of-round: 0.03 mm.
Minimum slip ring O.D.: 31.5 mm.
Rotor maximum out-of-round: 0.05 mm.

OVERHAUL

REPLACING ONE POSITIVE OR NEGATIVE DIODE

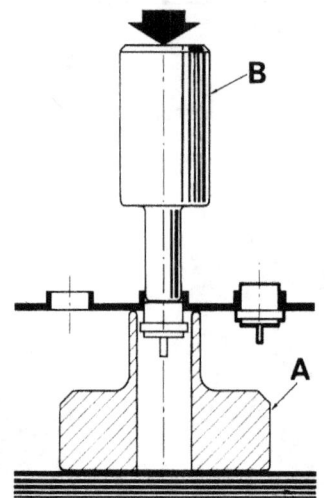

WARNING. Changing single diodes is not recommended.
However, if such a need arises, follow the directions given below.

PULLING
- Place the heat sink on the special tool A (A.3.0250) and press out the diode with tool B (A.3.0248).

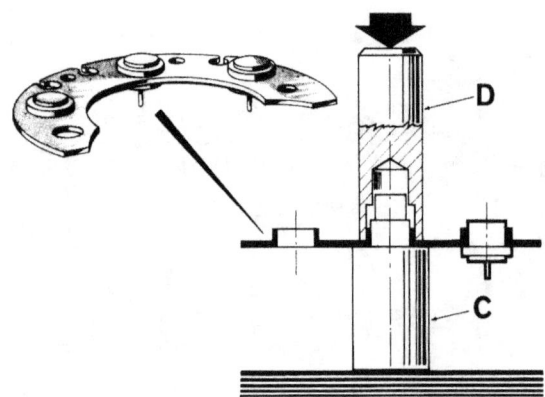

TRUEING THE MOUNTING BOSS
Before pressing in a new diode true the hole in the mounting boss as follows:
- Place the heat sink on special tool C (A.4.0123);
- True the boss with special tool D (A.4.0122).

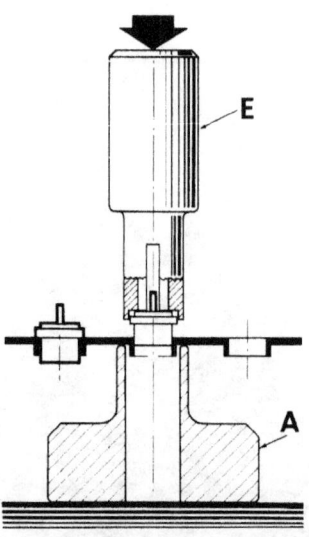

DRIVING
- Lubricate the hole in mounting boss with Bosch Ol 63 v2 oil.
- Place the heat sink on special tool A (A.3.0250).
- Press fully in the diode with tool E (A.3.0249)

NOTE — It is recommended to use an arbor press to perform all the above work.

On completion of the procedure, test diodes for proper operation.
(refer to pages 9 - 11).

REASSEMBLY

DRIVE END FRAME

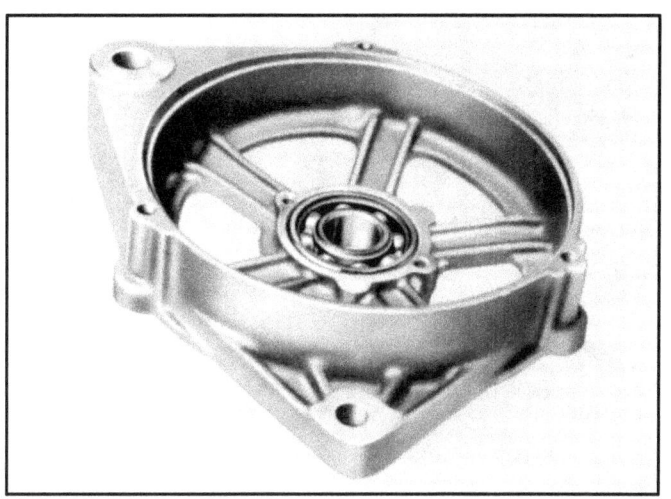

DRIVE END FRAME

Check the bearing for wear and change it, if necessary.
Usually, this bearing has an operating life of about 60,000 mi. and after that period it should be replaced with a new one.
Pack the bearing with Bosch Ft 1 v 33 grease; fit it in the frame with the close side down as shown. Secure the retainer with the screws.

Press the bearing (slip ring side) on rotor shaft. To do so, rest the rotor on a suitable support.

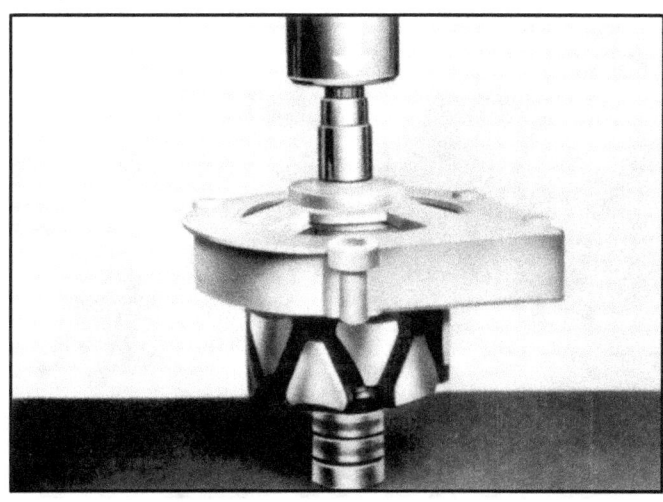

Press the drive end frame on rotor shaft. Make sure the resting surface is clean to prevent foreign matter from entering the bearing.

22
REASSEMBLY

BRUSH - NEGATIVE DIODE HEAT SINK

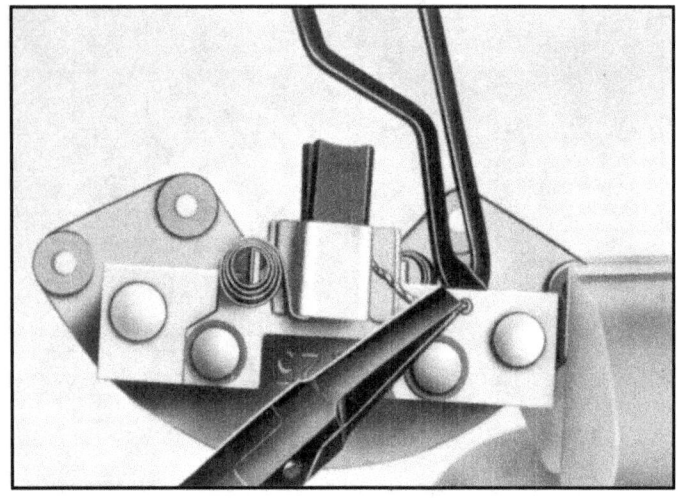

CAUTION:
While replacing the carbon brushes care should be taken to prevent the solder (tin with rosin flux only) from creeping along the copper wire.
Minimum length of carbon brushes: 14 mm.
After fitting, check brushes for binding.

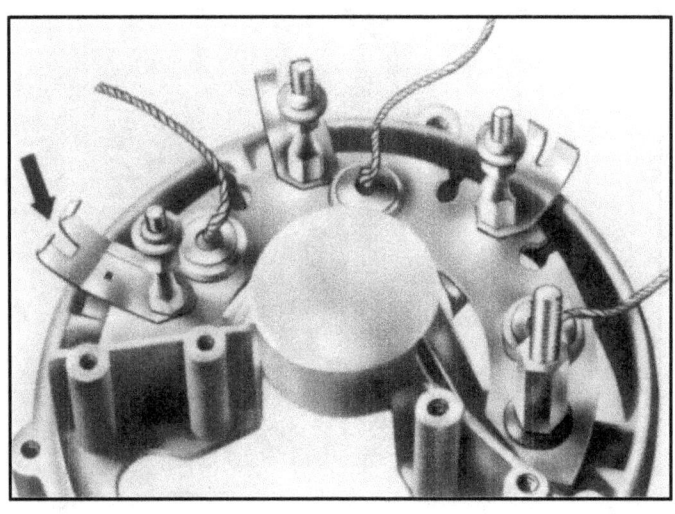

Fit the negative diode heat sink and the wire clips. Screw in the spacers so that the shorter threaded shank is outward. The longest clip must be fitted at the left side as shown. Properly fit the insulating washers.

Check terminal B+ for grounds.
Test voltage:
40 volts A.C.

REASSEMBLY

POSITIVE DIODE HEAT SINK

Install the positive diode heat sink, the insulating washers and the lockwashers. On the spacer next to the terminal D+/61, the special dished insulator instead of flat insulating washers must be fitted. Tighten the nuts with a box wrench.

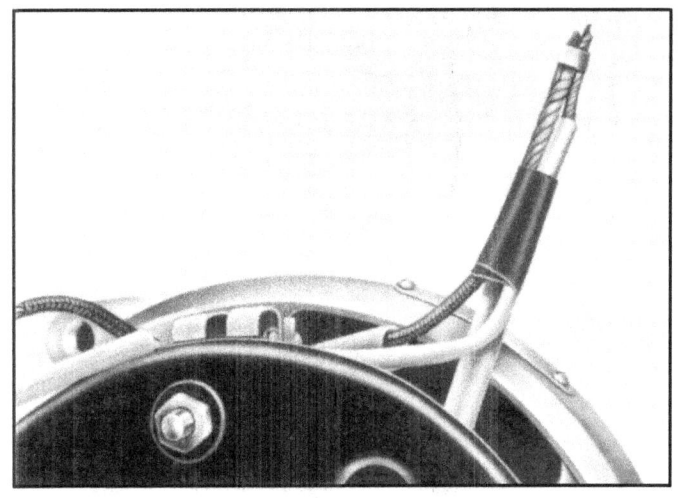

Fit the stator to the slip ring end frame. Bring together the positive and negative diode wires and slip on them the sheath. Also put sheaths over the field diode wires and stator winding leads. Tape provisionally together the four leads.
Mount and solder in place the metal ring. Take care that solder does not run down the wires for more than 4 mm.

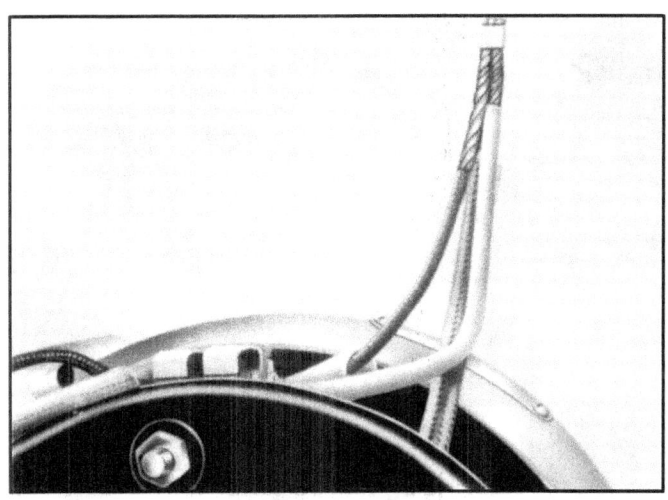

After soldering cut the ends of wires projecting beyond the metal ring.
Remove the tape.
Install the outer sheath.

REASSEMBLY

CONNECTIONS

Bend the clip tabs properly with pliers.

Position the sheath so that the field diode lead is fully protected as shown.

The stator winding output leads should be so positioned as to stand astride of negative diode heat sink as shown.

REASSEMBLY

ROTOR - BRUSH HOLDER

Make sure the leads are firmly secured with the clips. It is essential that the leads are fastened in the clips in such a way that an air gap of at least 1/8'' (3mm) exists between the leads and the frame; the insulating sheaths should project of at least 1/8'' over the solderings.

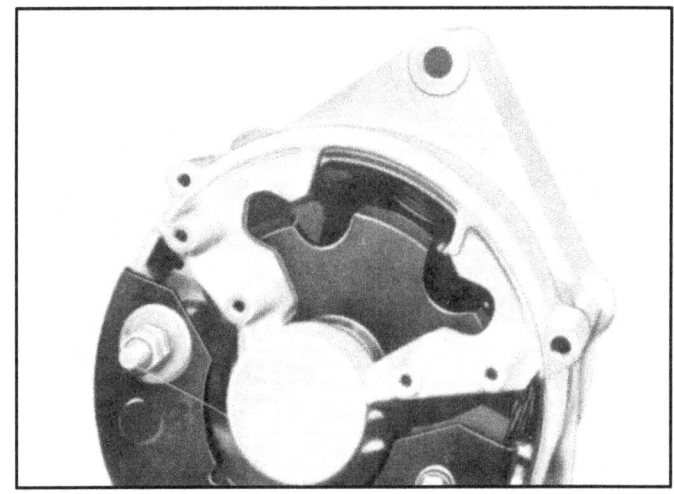

Install the rotor frame assembly according to the reference marks made on disassembly. Fit the brush holder, install the pulley and the fan and tighten the securing nut to: 25.3-28.9 lb. ft. (3.5-4 kgm). After reassembling, protect the positive diodes previously replaced with Bosch FI 87 v 1 compound.

REASSEMBLY PROCEDURE FOR ALTERNATORS WITH PRESS-FIT INSTEAD OF SCREW-MOUNT FIELD DIODES

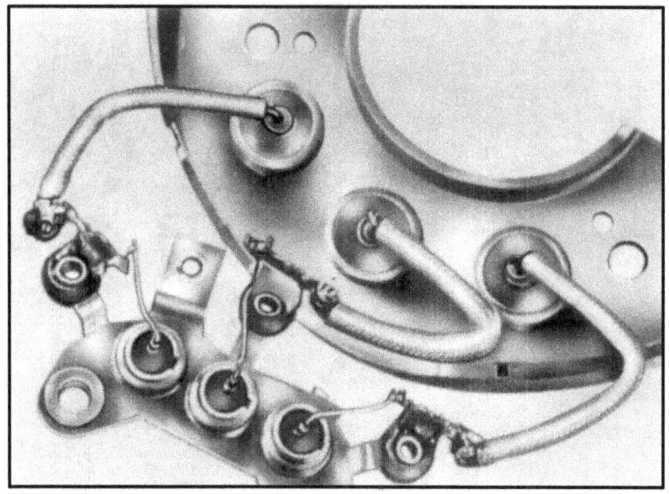

Before fitting the field diode bracket, solder the three positive diode wires to the field diode bracket itself.

After the field diode bracket has been fitted, connect by soldering the stator, negative diode and field diode leads.
When soldering, great care should be taken to avoid overheating the diodes.

Fit the brush holder. Raise the brushes and keep them up out of way for reassembly. Connect the D+ lead to the field diode bracket.
Place the wave washer into bearing seat.
Smear the ball bearing seat with Bosch Ft 70 v1 grease. Install the rotor onto the drive end frame by reversing the procedure outlined on page 14. Carefully insert the rotor and end frame assembly in the stator and secure with the three screws.
Fit the positive diode heat sink and lock it in place.
Fit the brush springs with the aid of a screwdriver or similar tool.

CONTROL BOX AND REGULATOR

The control box on cars equipped with alternators contains only a voltage regulator, the use of diodes in the alternator making a cut-out relay unnecessary. The alternator charging circuit is shown below.

On cars equipped with generators the control box contains a voltage regulator and a cut-out relay, this type of circuit being shown in the diagram to the right.

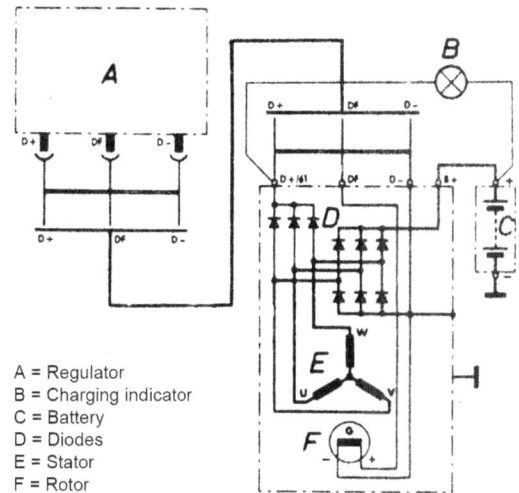

A = Regulator
B = Charging indicator
C = Battery
D = Diodes
E = Stator
F = Rotor

The alternator charging circuit

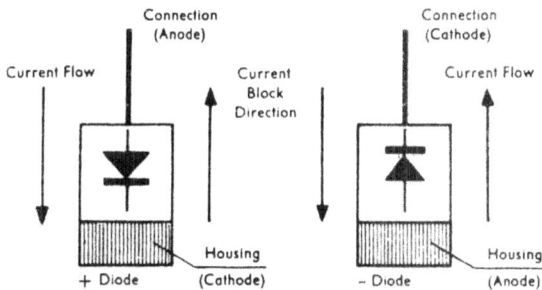

Current flow through positive and negative diodes

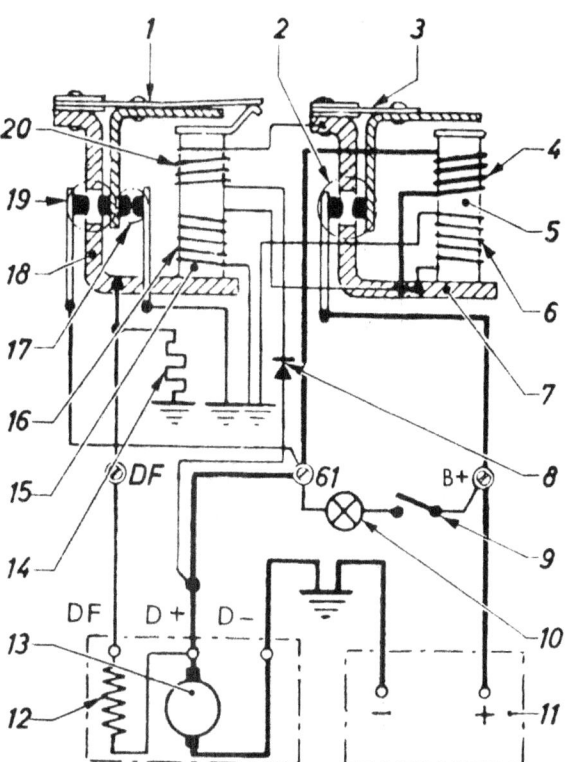

The generator charging circuit

Key to Diagram

1 Voltage regulator spring
2 Cut-out relay points
3 Cut-out relat spring
4 Cut-out relay current coil
5 Cut-out relay iron core
6 Cut-out relay voltage coil
7 Cut-out relay armature support
8 Varioge
9 Ignition switch
10 Charging indicator lamp
11 Battery
12 Field coils
13 Generator armature
14 Resistor
15 Regulator iron core
16 Regulator voltage coil
17 Regulator lower points
18 Regulator armature support
19 Regulator upper points
20 Regulator control coil

CHECKING THE CHARGING CIRCUIT

Do not disturb the control box settings until the generator or alternator has been checked as described in the following pages.

It must be stressed that the use of first grade electrical meters is essential to check and make any necessary adjustments to the control box. All checks and adjustments must be made as quickly as possible to avoid errors due to heating up of the control box operating coils. If the control box fails to respond correctly to any adjustment it should be examined at a service station.

ADJUSTING THE VOLTAGE REGULATOR

1 Remove the red battery lead from the control box B+ terminal. Connect the voltmeter positive lead to the B+ terminal and the negative lead to earth on the base of the control box.
2 Start the engine and slowly increase its speed while observing the voltmeter. The reading should be between 13.5 and 14.5 volts. If the reading is not within the specified range, remove the control box cover and adjust the voltage regulator armature spring to obtain a reading between the figures quoted. If the reading fluctuates, the contacts are dirty and must be cleaned as described later.
3 Replace the control box cover and recheck the setting.

ADJUSTING THE GENERATOR CUT-OUT

1 Connect the voltmeter positive lead to the control box terminal 61 and the negative lead to earth. Connect an ammeter in series with the B+ terminal and disconnect the red wire.
2 Start the engine and increase the speed while observing the voltmeter. The voltage will increase until the cut-out relay points close, then drop slightly as the circuit is completed to the battery. The highest voltage reading just before it drops off is the closing voltage. This voltage should be between 12.3 and 13.4 volts. If the voltage as tested is not between these limits, remove the control box cover and adjust the closing voltage by bending the cut-out relay spring support. Increase the tension on the spring to increase the closing voltage, decrease tension to decrease the voltage.
3 Replace the control box cover and recheck the setting.

CLEANING CONTACT POINTS

Clean the contact points in the voltage regulator and cut-out relay with fine glasspaper. Clean off all dust with methylated spirits.

28
GENERATOR

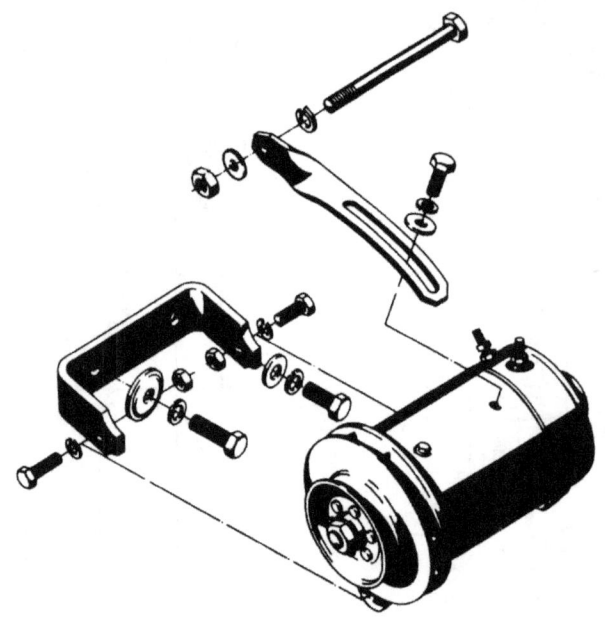

Generator mounting details

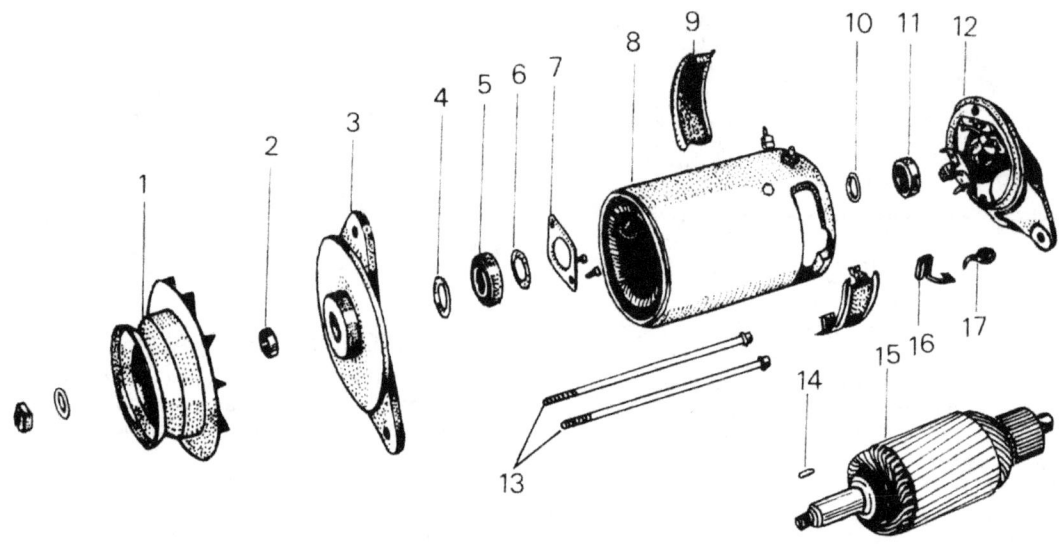

The generator components

Key to Diagram
1 Pulley
2 Spacer
3 Drive end bracket
4 Oil deflector
5 Bearing
6 Coverplate
7 Retaining plate
8 Generator housing
9 Coverband
10 Sealing washer
11 Bearing
12 Commutator end bracket
13 Through-bolts
14 Key
15 Armature
16 Brush
17 Brush spring

GENERATOR

TESTING THE GENERATOR OUTPUT

1 Check that a loose drive belt is not the cause of the trouble.
2 Switch off all the lights and accessories. Start the engine and connect an ammeter in series with the battery and control box by disconnecting the red lead from the B+ control box terminal, then connecting the ammeter between the terminal and the red wire. Raise the engine speed and check the ammeter reading. The output should be 20 amps minimum at 2500 rev/min.
3 If the generator is in order, check the continuity of the cables to the control box. If they are in order, remove the ammeter and reconnect the cable, then test the control box as previously described.

REMOVING THE GENERATOR

Refer to the diagram, remove the fan belt and then disconnect the battery. Disconnect the wires from the generator. Remove the adjuster bolt and washers, the two pivot bolts, nuts and washers then lift out the generator.

DISMANTLING THE GENERATOR

Refer to the diagram, remove the brush cover bands 9. Loosen the screw securing the connecting lead to the commutator end bracket and remove the through-bolts and end bracket from the housing. Remove the pulley securing nut and withdraw the pulley from the shaft, using a suitable puller. Remove the key 14 from the shaft and pull off the drive end bracket. Remove the bearing retainer plate and press the bearing from the drive end bracket.

SERVICING THE BRUSHGEAR

Lift the brushes up in their holders and secure them by positioning each spring at the side of its brush. Fit the commutator end bracket over the commutator and release the brushes. Hold back each spring in turn and move the brushes by pulling gently on their flexible connectors. If a brush moves sluggishly or sticks in its holder, remove it and ease the sides against a smooth file. Refit in its original position. Renew and bed to the commutator any brush which is less than the permissible minimum of .47 inch in length. Renew any brush spring which gives a spring balance reading of less than 16 oz.

SERVICING THE COMMUTATOR

A commutator in good condition will be smooth and free from pitting and burned segments. Clean with a cloth and petrol and, if necessary, polish with fine glasspaper. **Do not use emerycloth.** Skim a badly worn commutator in a lathe, using a high speed and taking a light cut with a sharp tool. Remove the minimum amount necessary to clean up, then polish with fine glasspaper. Undercut the insulation between the segments to a depth of .002 inch using a special saw or a hacksaw blade ground to the thickness of the insulation.

THE ARMATURE

In the absence of armature testing facilities, the only check for faults which an owner can make is to substitute one which is known to be serviceable. Alternatively, have the armature tested for open circuits or internal earthing at a service station, fitting a new component if faults are indicated.

FIELD COILS

When testing with an ohmmeter, the reading should be between 3.5 and 3.85 ohms. If the reading is less than 3.5 ohms the field coils must be renewed by a service station.

RENEWING BEARINGS

It is most unlikely that noticeable bearing wear will occur during the life of the generator. However, if bearing wear is encountered, the bearings in the commutator end bracket and drive end bracket should be renewed.

GENERATOR REASSEMBLY AND REFITTING

This is the reverse of the dismantling procedure. If new brushes have been fitted, place a strip of fine glasspaper round the commutator and grind them in until they make good contact on their bearing faces. Reconnect the lead to the commutator end bracket and refit the brush cover bands. Adjust the fan belt tension.

30
STARTER MOTOR

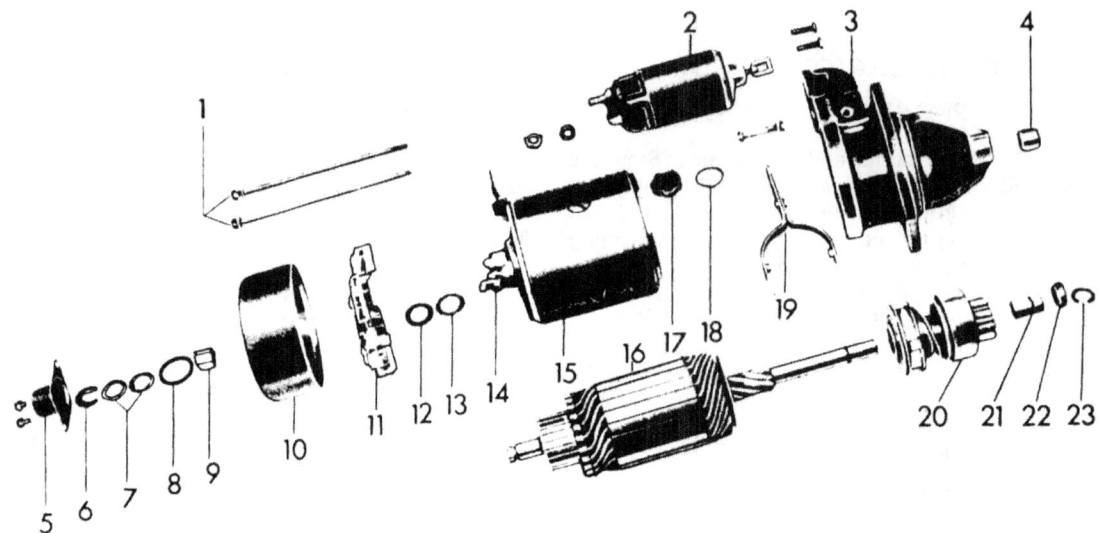

The starter components

Key to Diagram
1. Through-bolts
2. Solenoid
3. Drive end bracket
4. Bush
5. End cap
6. Retainer
7. Shims
8. Rubber seal
9. Bush
10. Commutator end bracket
11. Negative brush plate
12. Fibre washer
13. Washer
14. Positive brushes on field coils
15. Starter motor housing
16. Armature
17. Rubber washer
18. Washer
19. Engagement lever
20. Pinion and clutch
21. Bush
22. Thrust washer
23. Retainer

THE STARTER MOTOR

The Bosch starter is a brush type series wound motor equipped with an overrunning clutch and operated by a solenoid. The armature shaft is supported in sintered bronze bushes which are factory packed with lubricant and require no servicing between overhauls. The diagram above shows the starter components. When the starter is operated from the switch, the engagement lever moves the pinion into mesh with the flywheel ring gear. When the pinion meshes with the ring gear teeth, the solenoid contact disc closes the circuit and the starter motor operates to turn the engine over. When the engine starts, the speed of the flywheel causes the pinion to overrun the starter clutch and armature. The pinion continues to be engaged in the ring gear teeth until the engagement lever is released, when it returns under spring action.

TESTING THE STARTER MOTOR

Check that the battery is in good condition and fully charged and that its connections are clean and tight. Switch on the headlights and operate the starter switch. Current is reaching the starter if the lights go dim, in which case it will be necessary to remove the starter for servicing. If the lights do not go dim, check the switch and the starter cables. Check the brushes by the method described later, it not being necessary to remove the starter to do this. If the switch, cables and brushes are in order, the starter must be removed and serviced.

REMOVING THE STARTER MOTOR

Disconnect the battery, the main starter lead and the control wire. Remove the starter mounting bolts and lift out the starter.

SERVICING THE BRUSHGEAR

Remove the brush cover from the starter and detach the brushgear, marking the position of the brushes for correct reassembly. Renew any brush which is worn to less than $\frac{1}{2}$ inch in length. If a brush binds or sticks in its holder, remove it and ease the sides against a smooth file. When fitting new brushes, hold the connecting wire close to the work with a pair of flat-nosed pliers to prevent solder from flowing down the wire strands, otherwise the wire will become rigid and the brush unserviceable.

DISMANTLING THE STARTER MOTOR

Remove the brushgear as previously described. Remove the screws attaching the small cover at the end of the shaft and detach the cover. Remove the lockwasher and shim from the shaft and remove the two through-bolts. Detach the commutator end bracket then remove the brush holder plate, collecting the shims between the plate and the commutator.

STARTER MOTOR

Detach the starter solenoid by removing the two screws (see upper diagram). Remove the rubber and metal plate from the drive end bracket as shown (lower diagram). Remove the engagement lever pivot pin, engagement lever and the armature from the drive end bracket. Drive back the retaining ring on the armature shaft and remove the circlip, then pull off the retaining ring, overrunning clutch and pinion assembly.

THE COMMUTATOR

Clean the commutator with a cloth and petrol and, if necessary, polish with fine glasspaper. **Do not use emerycloth.** Skim a badly worn commutator in a lathe, using a high speed and taking a light cut with a sharp tool, noting that the minimum diameter for starter motor commutators is 1.25 inches. If cleaning up would remove enough metal to reduce the diameter below this figure the armature must be renewed. Undercut the insulation between the segments to a depth of .002 inch using a special saw or a hacksaw blade ground to the thickness of the insulation.

THE ARMATURE

A damaged armature should always be renewed. No attempt should be made to straighten a bent shaft or to machine the core.

TESTING THE FIELD COILS

Test the continuity with a 12-volt test lamp and current supply between the terminal post and each field brush in turn. Test for breakdown of the insulation by connecting a test lamp between the terminal post and the starter body. If the lamp lights, defective insulation is indicated. The renewal of field coils should be entrusted to a service station.

REPLACING BEARING BUSHES

Press out the old bearing bushes if they are worn and renew them as follows. Allow the new bushes to stand fully immersed in engine oil for at least 30 minutes before pressing them into the starter brackets. Press them into position with a shouldered mandrel having a polished pilot of the same diameter as the armature shaft and slightly longer than the bushes.

STARTER PINION AND CLUTCH

Do not clean the overrunning clutch with solvents as this would wash the grease from inside the clutch. Check the components for wear or damage and renew any found unserviceable. Coat the armature shaft splines and the contact areas for the engagement lever with high melting point grease.

REASSEMBLY AND REFITTING

These operations are the reverse of the dismantling and removal instructions.

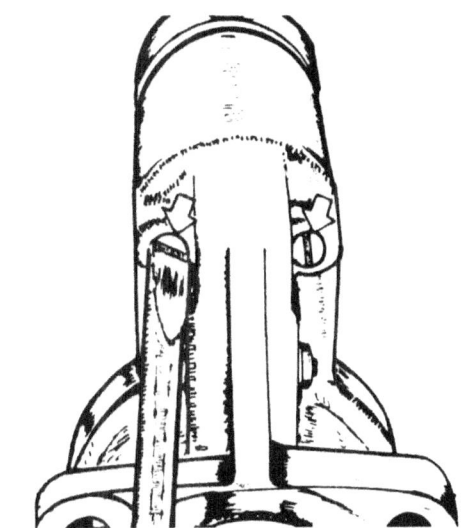

Removing the starter solenoid

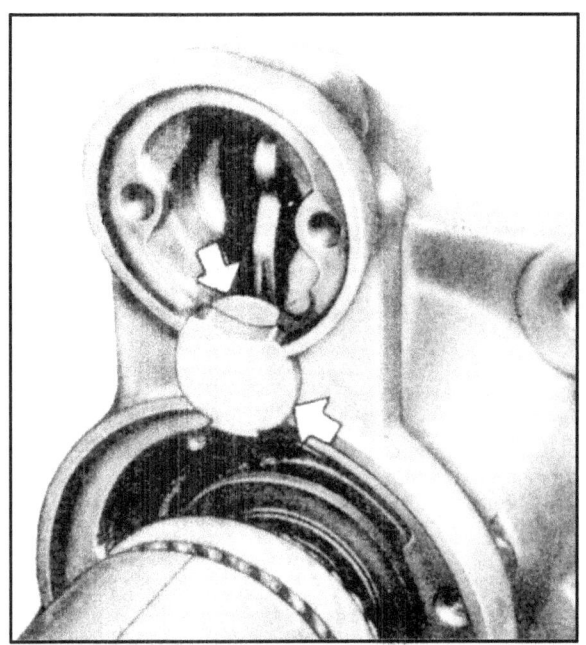

Remove the rubber and metal plate from the drive end bracket

WINDSCREEN WIPER MOTOR

The wiper assembly consists of a permanent magnet type motor with a reduction gearbox driving the wiper arms through a connecting linkage. Apart from renewal of worn wiperblades the wiper assembly needs no routine maintenance.

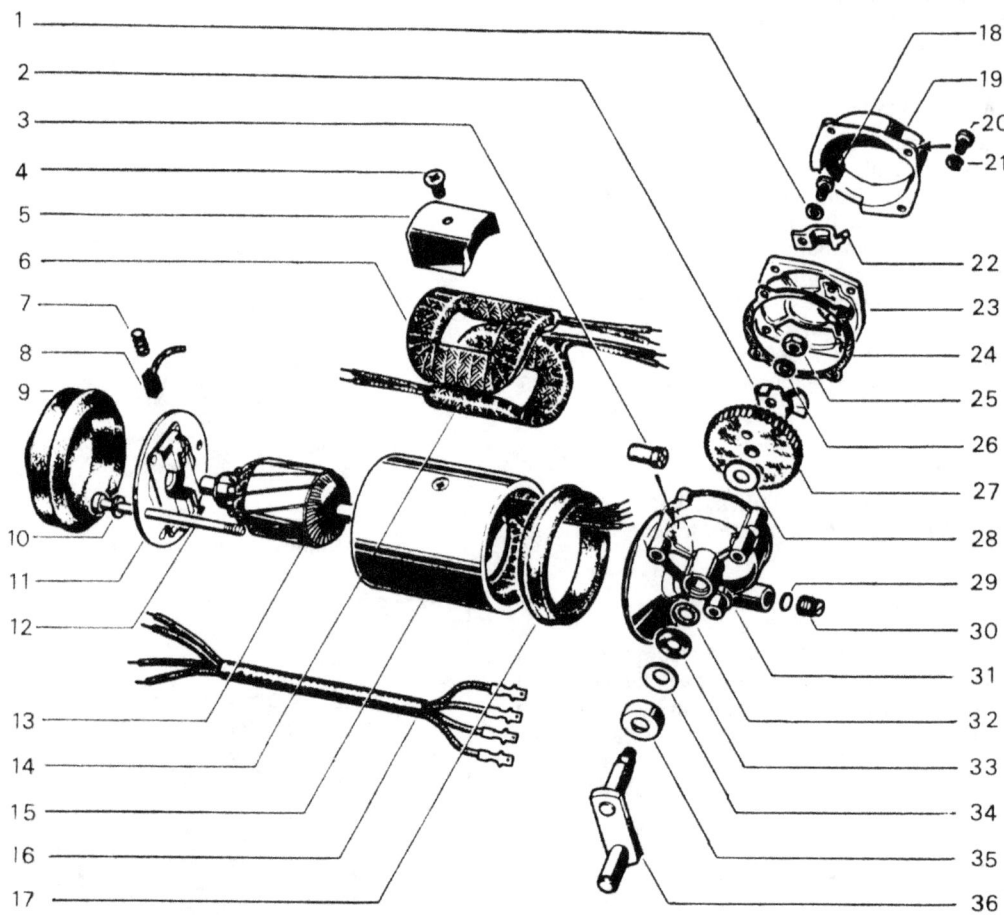

WIPER MOTOR OPERATIONAL CHECK

If the motor is completely inoperative, check the fuse and the connections at the fuse block and wiper switch. Disconnect the positive lead from the wiper motor terminal, turn on the ignition and wiper switches and use a voltmeter to check the voltage available to the motor, which should be 12-volts if the battery is fully charged. A further check can be made by connecting a temporary lead between the battery and the positive terminal of the wiper motor. If the motor then runs the fault is in the wiring circuit or switch. If not, the motor must be removed for service.

If the wiper operation is sluggish, detach the linkage crank arm from the motor and operate the wipers by hand to check for binds in the linkage.

REMOVING THE WIPER MOTOR

Detach the crank arm from the motor drive shaft, then disconnect the electrical connections and the wiper motor attaching nuts. Refit in the reverse order, making sure that the wiring is reconnected correctly.

Components of a Marelli wiper motor

1 Lockwasher
2 Limit stop control plate
3 Grommet
4 Screw
5 Field coil shoe
6 Field coil
7 Brush spring
8 Brush
9 Seal ring
10 Lockwasher
11 Brush holder
12 Through-bolt
13 Armature
14 Field coil
15 Housing
16 Wiring assembly
17 Seal ring
18 Screw
19 Protection cover
20 Screw
21 Lockwasher
22 Connection fastener
23 Cover
24 Gasket
25 Nut
26 Lockwasher
27 Gear
28 Shim
29 Thrust bearing
30 Adjusting screw
31 Drive end cover
32 O-ring seal
33 Plastic washer
34 Spring washer
35 Protection cover
36 Crank arm

WINDSCREEN WIPER MOTOR

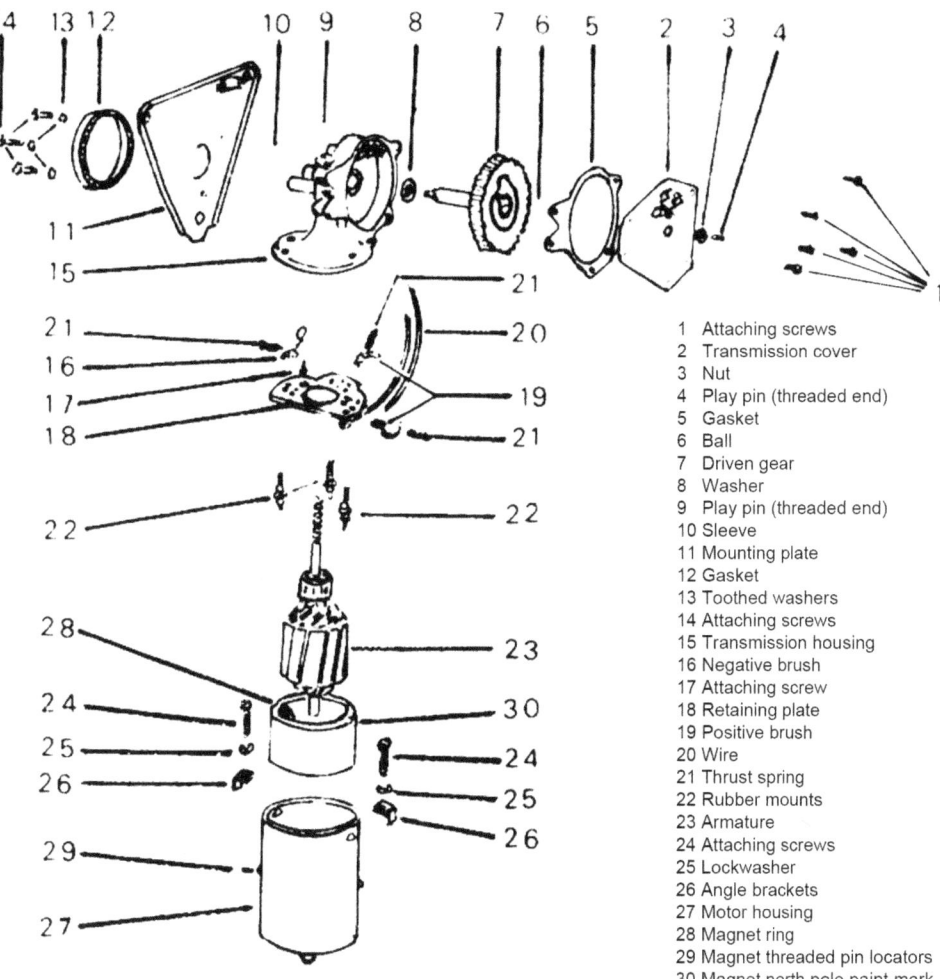

Components of a Bosch wiper motor

1. Attaching screws
2. Transmission cover
3. Nut
4. Play pin (threaded end)
5. Gasket
6. Ball
7. Driven gear
8. Washer
9. Play pin (threaded end)
10. Sleeve
11. Mounting plate
12. Gasket
13. Toothed washers
14. Attaching screws
15. Transmission housing
16. Negative brush
17. Attaching screw
18. Retaining plate
19. Positive brush
20. Wire
21. Thrust spring
22. Rubber mounts
23. Armature
24. Attaching screws
25. Lockwasher
26. Angle brackets
27. Motor housing
28. Magnet ring
29. Magnet threaded pin locators
30. Magnet north pole paint mark

CHECK AND REPLACE BRUSHES - BOSCH

Disassemble the transmission housing together with the armature from the motor housing and check that the brushes are free and that the brush springs function adequately. Renew the brushes if they are less than .24 inch in length. To remove a negative brush, remove the retaining screw from the commutator end frame. To remove a positive brush, the lead must be cut off at the brush holder. New positive brushes must be soldered into position, making sure that the solder does not run down the flexible lead as this would stiffen the lead and make the brush unserviceable. Clean the commutator with a cloth and petrol and polish with fine glasspaper. Lightly oil the armature shaft and lubricate the transmission with the correct grade of grease.

LAMPS AND LIGHTING

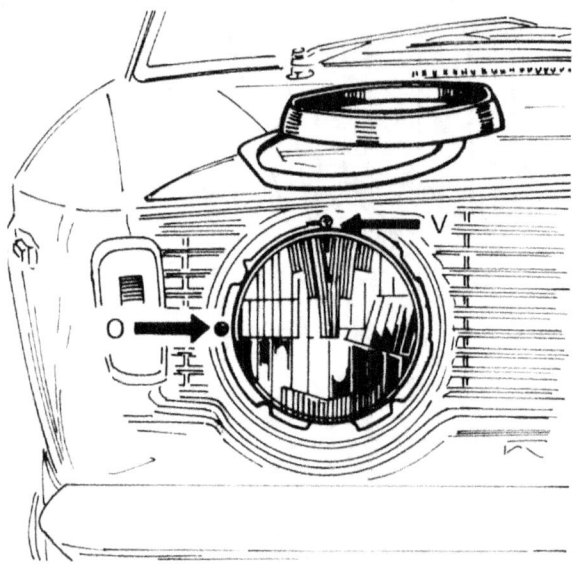

The headlamp beam setting screws

HEADLAMPS

Headlamps, of which there may be two or four according to model, should be set so that, when the car is in an unloaded condition, the main beams are parallel to each other and to the road. The diagram shows the headlamp adjustment screws which are accessible when the headlamp rim has been removed. Screw V is used to adjust the vertical alignment, screw O to adjust the horizontal alignment. Accurate beam setting is best carried out by a service station having special beam setting equipment.

PANEL AND WARNING LAMPS

The removal of the instrument panel will give access for the replacement of instrument and warning lights. When working on electrical units in this manner, the battery should be disconnected to avoid the occurence of accidental shortcircuits.

FLASHER UNIT

The flasher unit, in which a switch is operated by alternate heating and cooling of an actuating wire, is housed in a small cylindrical container behind the dashboard. A small relay to flash the pilot light is incorporated.

In case of trouble check the bulbs and main fuses. If one bulb is defective, the other bulb and the pilot light will flash at twice the normal speed, which will indicate this fault. If the flasher unit is defective it must be renewed. Mark the connections before removing the old unit to ensure that the new unit is correctly wired.

HAZARD WARNING SYSTEM

This system, when fitted, operates in conjunction with flashing direction indicator lights. When the hazard warning light switch on the instrument panel is turned on, all four flasher lights operate simultaneously through the flasher unit. The system will operate with the ignition switched off so that, if necessary, the car can be locked up and the lights left flashing in the event of a breakdown. As the system is meant as a warning to other traffic of a stationary vehicle, the hazard warning should not be switched on when the car is moving.

BULBS BURN FREQUENTLY

Check the control box settings.

NOTES

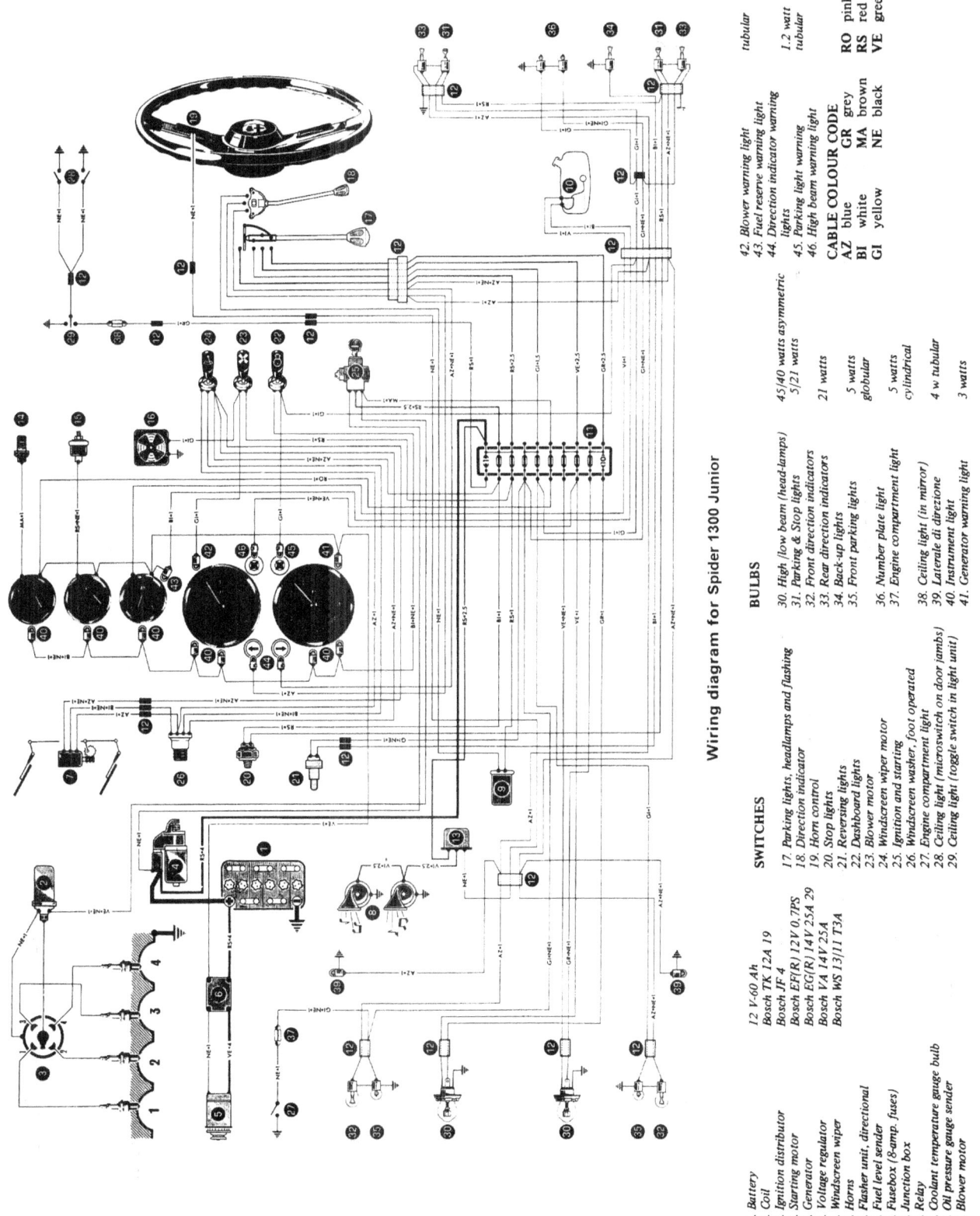

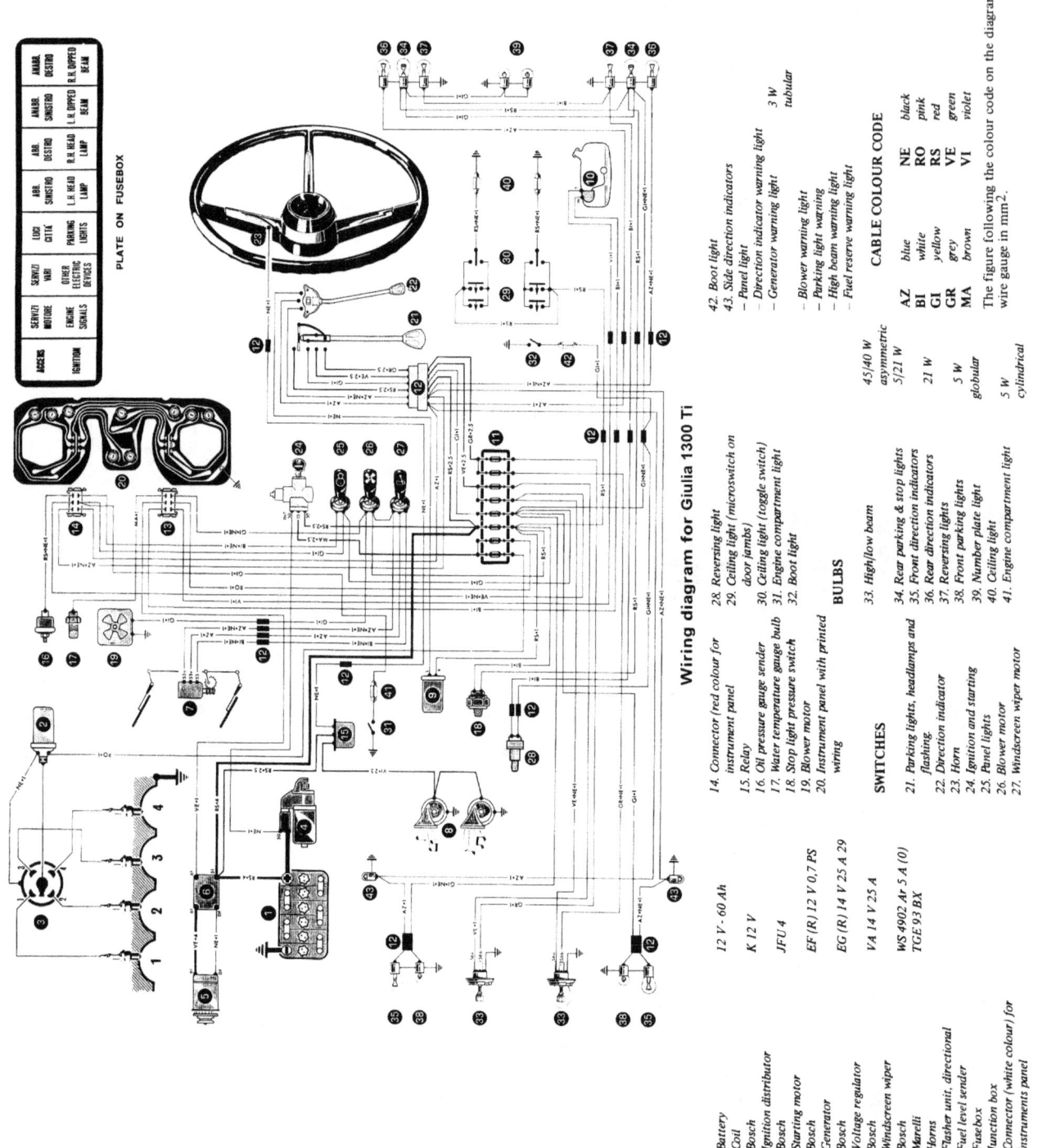

Wiring diagram for Giulia 1300 Ti

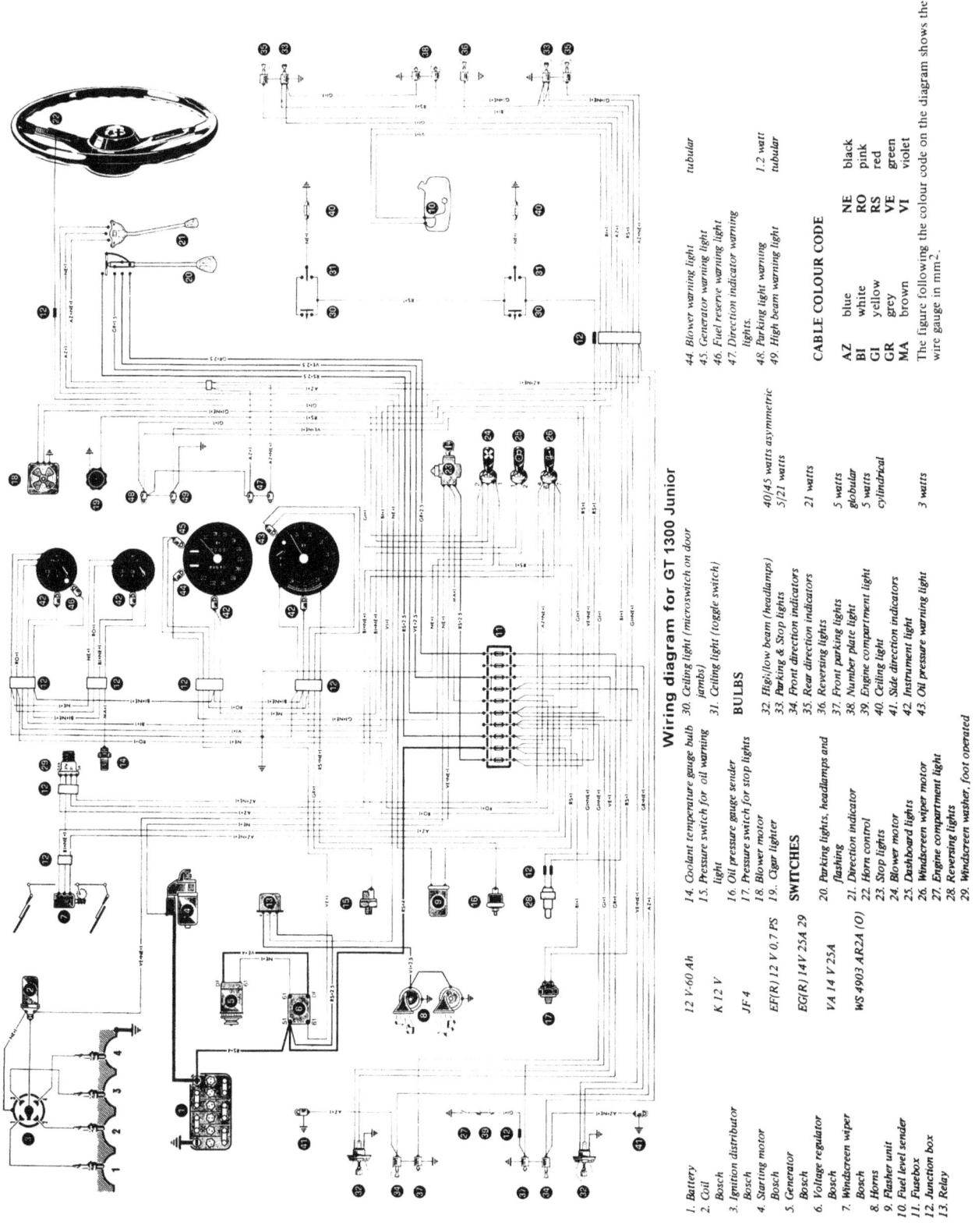

Wiring diagram for GT 1300 Junior

1. Battery — 12 V-60 Ah
2. Coil — Bosch
3. Ignition distributor — Bosch
4. Starting motor — Bosch
5. Generator — Bosch
6. Voltage regulator — Bosch
7. Windscreen wiper — Bosch
8. Horns — Bosch
9. Flasher unit
10. Fuel level sender
11. Fusebox
12. Junction box
13. Relay
14. Coolant temperature gauge bulb
15. Pressure switch for oil warning light
16. Oil pressure gauge sender
17. Pressure switch for stop lights
18. Blower motor
19. Cigar lighter

SWITCHES

20. Parking lights, headlamps and flashing
21. Direction indicator
22. Horn control
23. Stop lights
24. Blower motor
25. Dashboard lights
26. Windscreen wiper motor
27. Engine compartment light
28. Reversing lights
29. Windscreen washer, foot operated
30. Ceiling light (microswitch on door jambs)
31. Ceiling light (toggle switch)

BULBS

32. High-/low beam (headlamps) — 40/45 watts asymmetric
33. Parking & Stop lights — 5/21 watts
34. Front direction indicators
35. Rear direction indicators — 21 watts
36. Reversing lights
37. Front parking lights — 5 watts globular
38. Number plate light
39. Engine compartment light — 5 watts cylindrical
40. Ceiling light
41. Side direction indicators
42. Instrument light — 3 watts
43. Oil pressure warning light
44. Blower warning light
45. Generator warning light
46. Fuel reserve warning light
47. Direction indicator warning lights
48. Parking light warning — 1,2 watt tubular
49. High beam warning light — tubular

— 12 V-60 Ah
K 12 V
JF 4
EF(R) 12 V 0,7 PS
EG(R) 14V 25A 29
VA 14 V 25A
WS 4903 AR2A (O)

CABLE COLOUR CODE

AZ	blue	NE	black
BI	white	RO	pink
GI	yellow	RS	red
GR	grey	VE	green
MA	brown	VI	violet

The figure following the colour code on the diagram shows the wire gauge in mm².

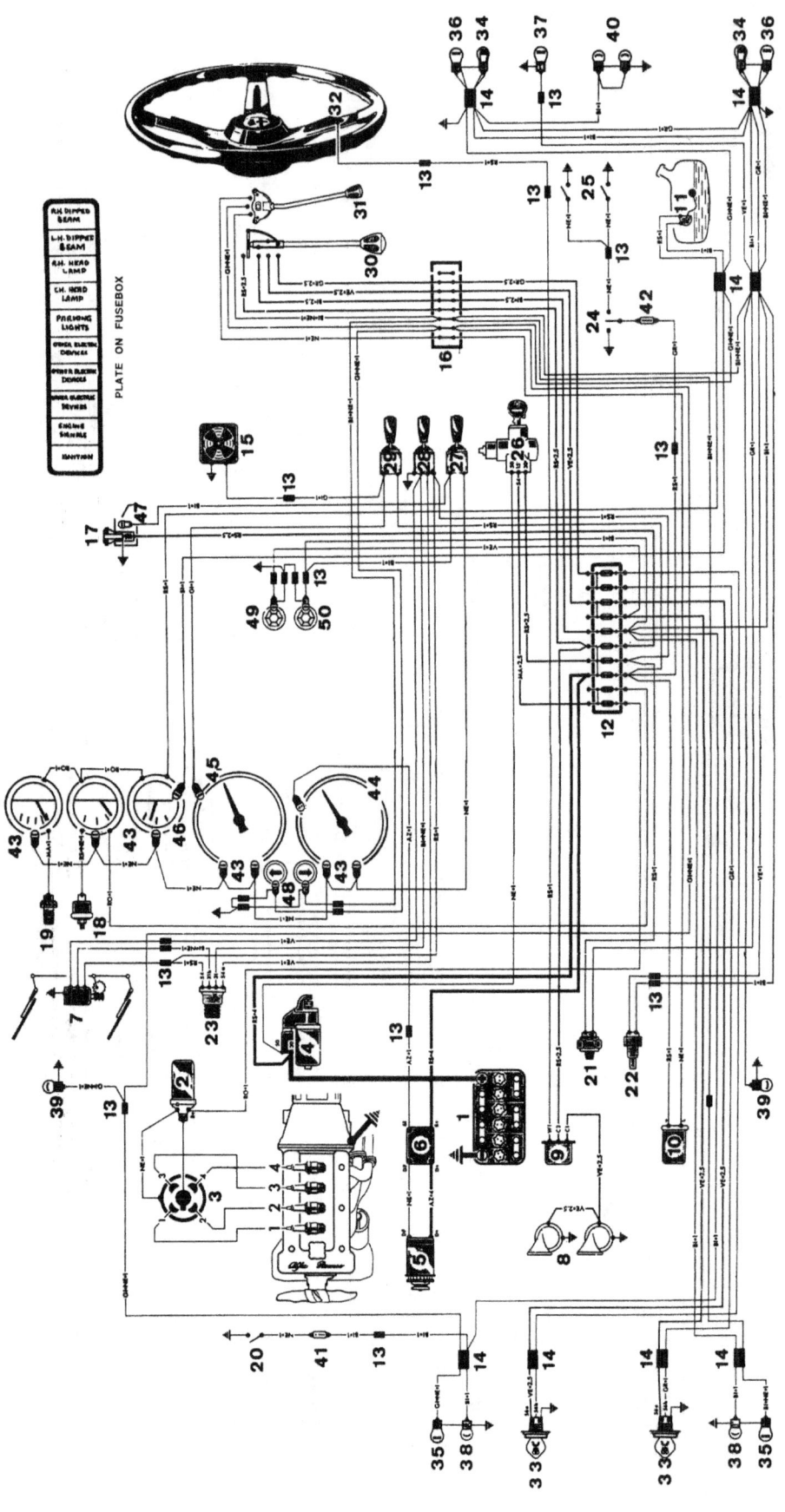

Wiring diagram for Spider Duetto 1600

Key to Diagram 1 Battery 2 Coil 3 Distributor 4 Starter 5 Generator 6 Regulator 7 Windscreen wiper 8 Horn 9 Electromagnetic relay 10 Flasher unit 11 Petrol gauge tank unit 12 Fuse box 13 Connectors (1-pole) 14 Connector block 15 Fan motor 16 Connector plate 17 Cigar lighter 18 Oil pressure switch 19 Temperature (water) switch

Switches 20 Bonnet light 21 Stop switch 22 Reverse light 23 Windscreen washer foot switch 24 Interior light switch (on rear view mirror) 25 Interior lights (on door posts) 26 Ignition/starter switches 27 Instruments light 28 Windscreen wiper motor 29 Fan motor 30 Side, headlights and flashers 31 Direction indicators 32 Horns

Bulbs 33 Headlights 45/40 watts asymmetric 34 Direction indicators, front 20 watts 37 Reverse light 20 watts 38 Side light, front 5 watts spherical 39 Flasher repeater 5 watts spherical 40 Number plate 5 watts spherical 41 Bonnet light 5 watts cylindrical 42 Interior light 5 watts cylindrical 43 Instrument combinations 3 watts tubular 44 Generator control lamp 3 watts tubular 45 Fan control lamp 3 watts tubular 46 Petrol reserve light 3 watts tubular 47 Cigar lighter 3 watts tubular 48 Direction indicator control lamp 1.2 watts tubular 49 High beam control lamp 1.2 watts tubular 50 Side light control lamp 1.2 watts tubular

Key to cable colour code AZ Pale blue GR Grey RO Pink BI White MA Brown RS Red GI Yellow NE Black VE Green
The figure after the colour code letters indicates the wire section in mm².

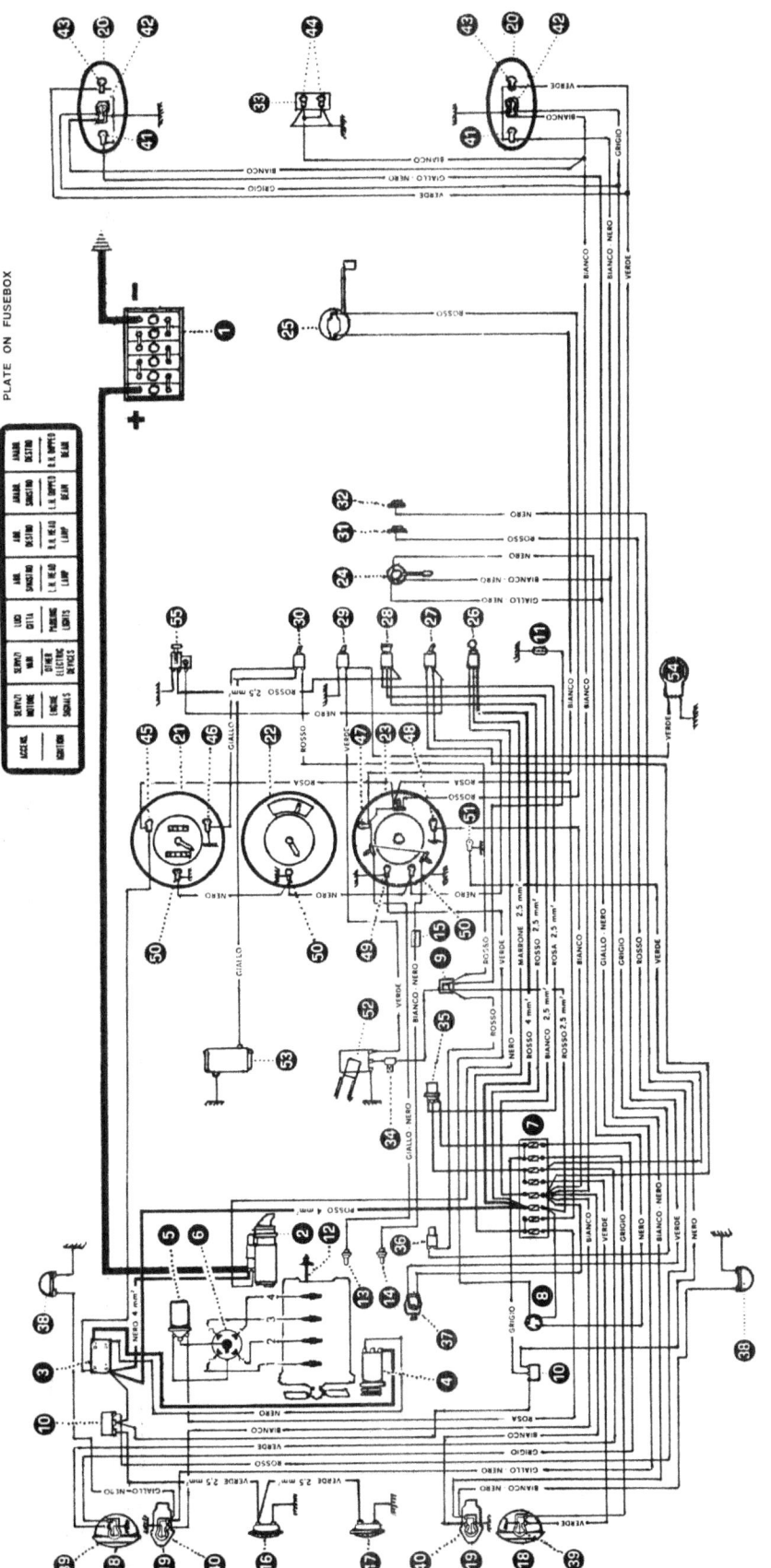

Wiring diagram for Giulia Spider and Giulia Spider Veloce

Key to Diagram 1 Battery 2 Starter motor 3 Control box 4 Generator 5 Ignition distributor 6 Ignition coil 7 Fuse boxes 8 Flasher relay 9 Connection 10 Electromagnetic relay 11 Map reading light 12 Earth connection 13 Water temperature sender unit 14 Oil temperature sender unit 15 Resistor for oil circuit 16 Horn 17 Horn 18 Headlamps 19 Front pilot lamps 20 Rear lamps 21 Speedometer 22 Revolution counter and oil pressure gauge 23 Oil and water temperature gauge with fuel contents gauge 24 Direction indicator switch 25 Fuel gauge tank unit 26 Ignition and starter switch 27 Instrument light switch 28 Light switch 29 Windscreen wiper switch 30 Heater blower switch 31 Horn push switch 32 Headlamp flasher switch 33 Number plate lights 34 Thermo switch 35 Dipswitch 36 Brake light switch 37 Reversing light switch 38 Side flasher lamps 52 Windscreen wiper motor 53 Heater blower motor 54 Foot switch for screen washer 55 Cigar lighter

Bulbs 39 Headlamp driving and dipped beam 45/40 watts 40 Front pilot lamps and flasher lamps 5/20 watts 41 Rear flasher lamps 20 watts 42 Tail/brake lights 5/20 watts 43 Reversing light 20 watts 44 Number plate lights 5 watts 45 Ignition warning light 3 watts 46 Heater blower warning light 3 watts 47 Fuel contents warning light 3 watts 48 Pilot warning light 3 watts 49 Direction indicator warning light 3 watts 50 Instrument lights 3 watts 51 Driving beam warning light 3 watts

Key to cable colour code Verde=Green Bianco=White Rosso=Red Grigio=Grey Nero=Black Rosa=Pink Marrone=Brown Giallo=Yellow Giallo-nero=Yellow-black Bianco-nero=White-black

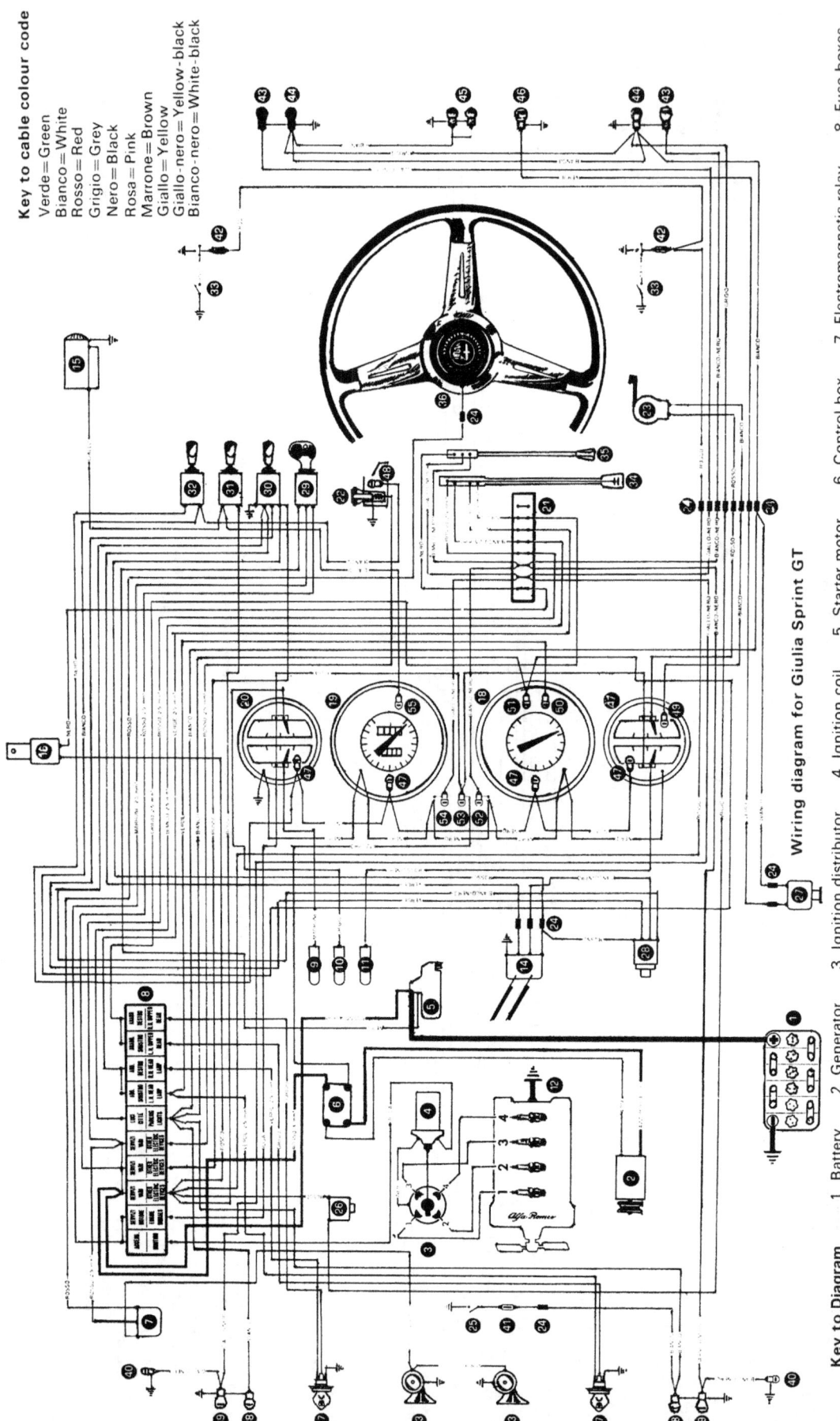

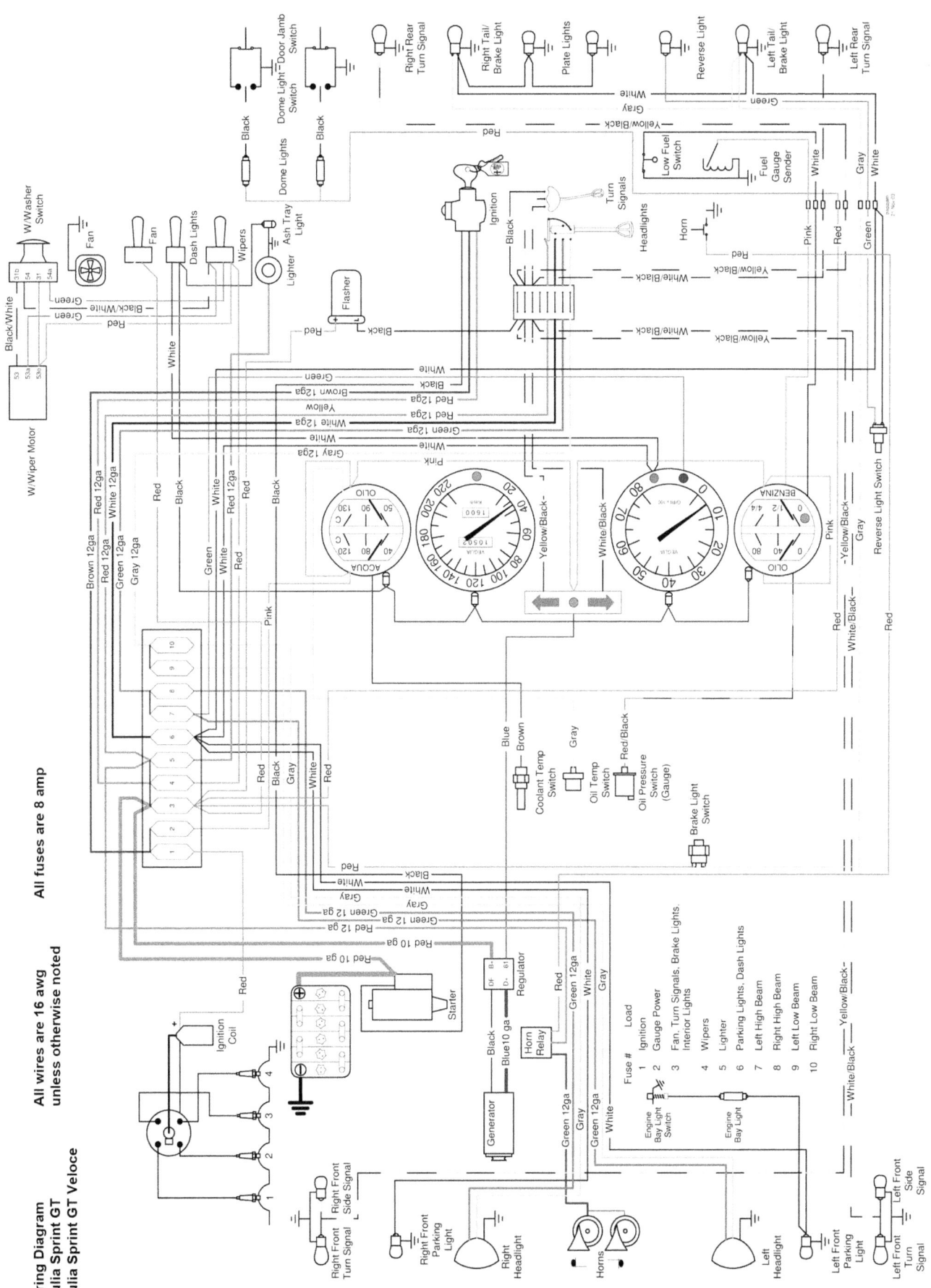

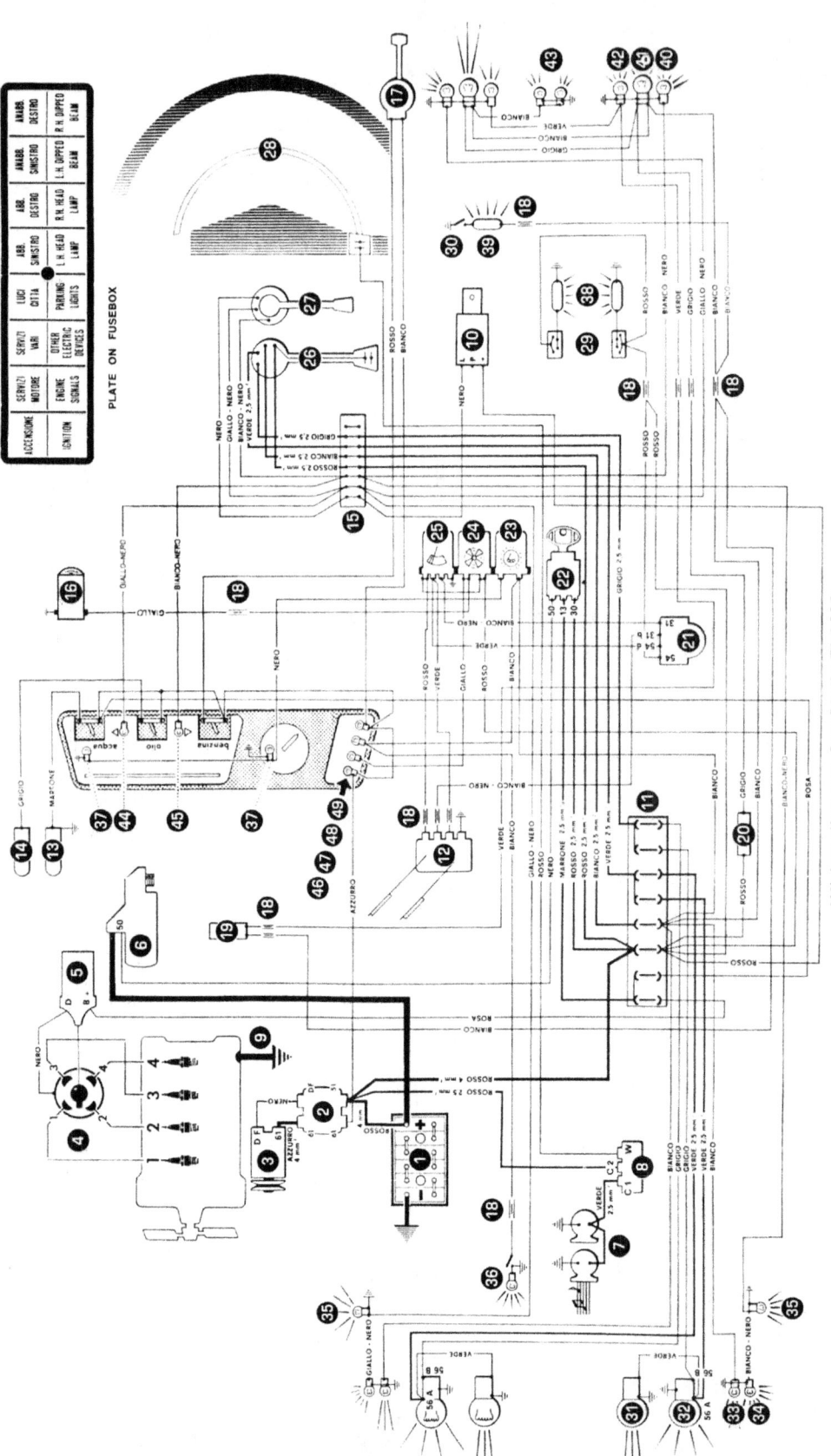

Wiring diagram for Giulia TI 1600

Key to Diagram 1 Battery 2 Control box 3 Generator 4 Ignition distributor 5 Ignition coil 6 Starter motor 7 Horns 8 Electromagnetic relay 9 Socket for inspection lamp 10 Flasher relay 11 Fuse boxes 12 Windscreen wiper 13 Temperature sender unit 14 Oil pressure gauge 15 Junction box 16 Heater blower 17 Fuel gauge tank unit 18 Cable connectors 19 Reversing light switch 20 Brake light switch 21 Foot switch for screen washer 22 Ignition and starter switch 23 Instrument light switch 24 Heater blower switch 25 Windscreen wiper switch 26 Light switch 27 Flasher lamp switch 28 Horn push switch 29 Three-way switch for inerior light 30 Luggage compartment switch

Bulbs 31 Headlamp driving beam 45/40 watts 32 Headlamp driving and dipped beam 45/40 watts 33 Front flasher lamp 5 watts 34 Front flasher lamp 20 watts 35 Side flasher lamps 5 watts 36 Engine compartment lamp 5 watts 37 Instrument lights 3 watts 38 Roof light 5 watts 39 Luggage compartment light 5 watts 40 Rear flasher lamps 20 watts 41 Tail light 5/20 watts 42 Reversing lamp 20 watts 43 Number plate lamp 5 watts 44 Direction indicator warning light 3 watts 45 Direction indicator warning light 3 watts 46 Ignition warning light 3 watts 47 Blower warning light 3 watts 48 Pilot warning light 3 watts 49 Fuel content warning light 3 watts

Key to cable colour code Verde = Green Bianco = White Rosso = Red Nero = Black Rosa = Pink Marrone = Brown Giallo = Yellow Giallo-nero = Yellow-black Bianco-nero = White-black Grigio = Grey

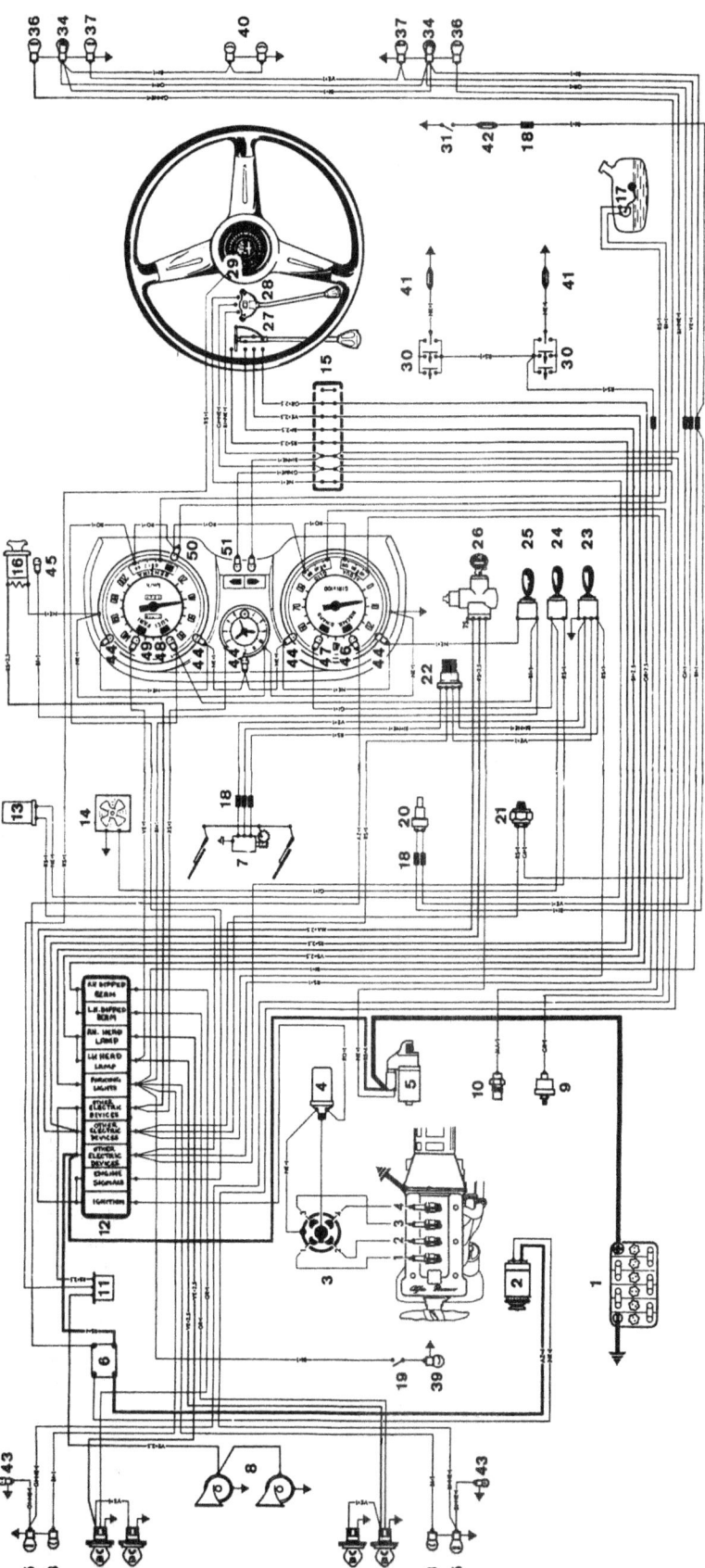

Wiring diagram for Giulia Super 1600

Key to Diagram 1 Battery 2 Generator 3 Distributor 4 Coil 5 Starter 6 Regulator 7 Windscreen wiper 8 Horn 9 Oil pressure switch 10 Temperature switch 11 Electromagnetic relay 12 Fuse box 13 Flasher unit 14 Fan motor 15 Connector plate 16 Cigar lighter 17 Petrol gauge tank unit 18 Connectors
Switches 19 Bonnet light 20 Reverse light 21 Stop switch 22 Windscreen washer, foot controlled 23 Windscreen wiper motor 24 Fan motor 25 Facia light (rheostat) 26 Ignition/starter switch 27 Side light, headlight and flashers 28 Direction indicators 29 Horns 30 Interior light (on door post) 31 Boot light
Bulbs 32 Headlight beam small model 45/40 watts asymmetric 33 Headlight beam large model 45/40 watts asymmetric 34 Side and stoplight, rear, 5/20 watts spherical bulb 5 watts 36 Direction indicator, rear 20 watts 37 Reverse light 20 watts 38 Side light, front, spherical bulb 5 watts 39 Bonnet light, 35 Direction indicator, front 20 watts 40 Number plate, spherical 5 watts 41 Interior light, cylindrical 5 watts 42 Boot light, cylindrical 5 watts 43 Flasher repeater, tubular 3 watts 44 Speedometer/petrol gauge light, tubular 3 watts 45 Cigar lighter light, tubular 3 watts 46 Generator control lamp, tubular 3 watts 47 Fan control lamp, tubular 3 watts 48 Dipped headlight control lamp, tubular 3 watts 49 High beam control lamp, tubular 3 watts 50 Petrol reserve control lamp, tubular 3 watts 51 Flasher control lamp, tubular 3 watts

Key to cable colour code AZ Pale blue GR Grey RO Pink BI White MA Brown RS Red GI Yellow NE Black VE Green
The figure after the colour code letters indicates the section of the wire in mm²

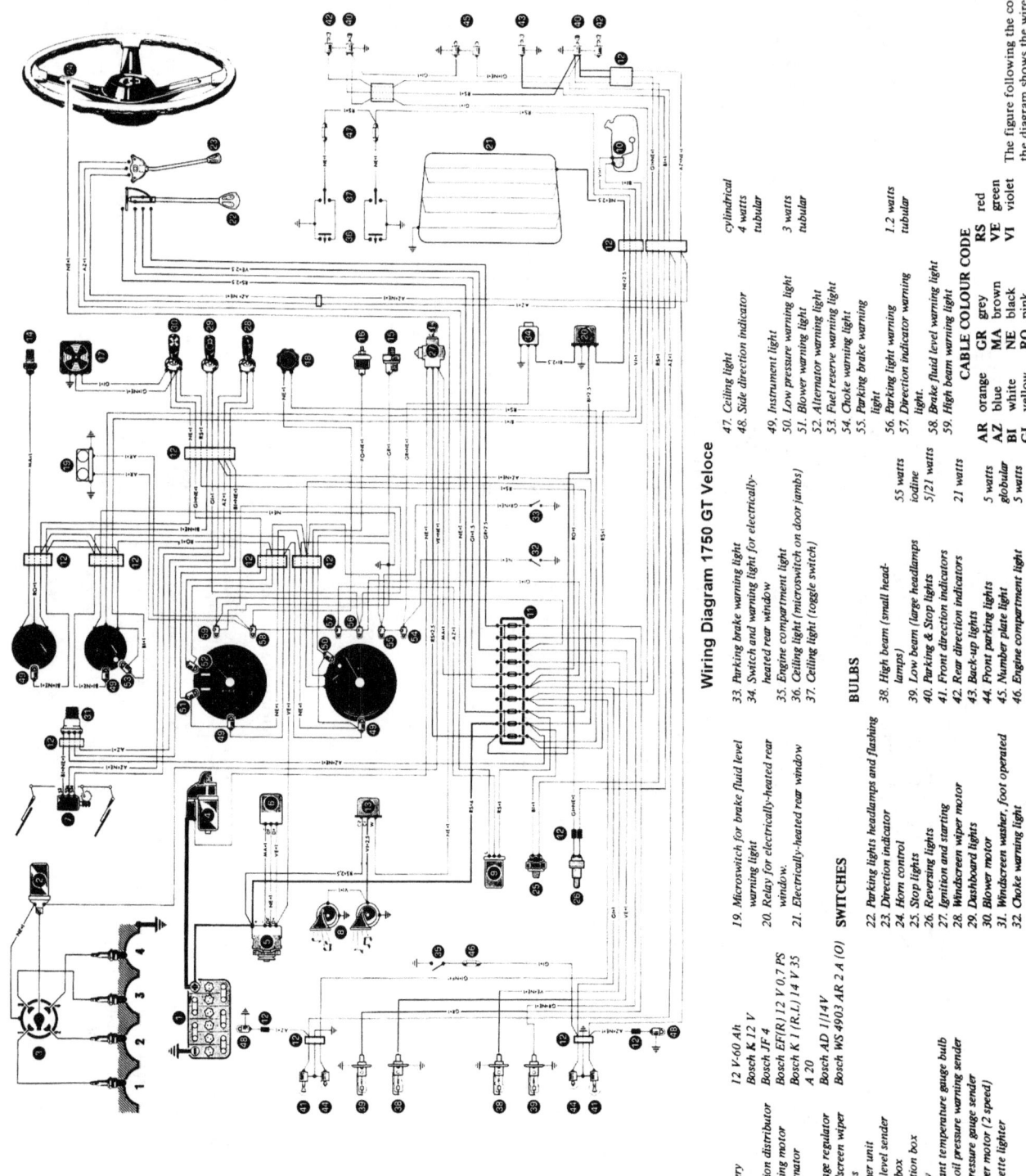

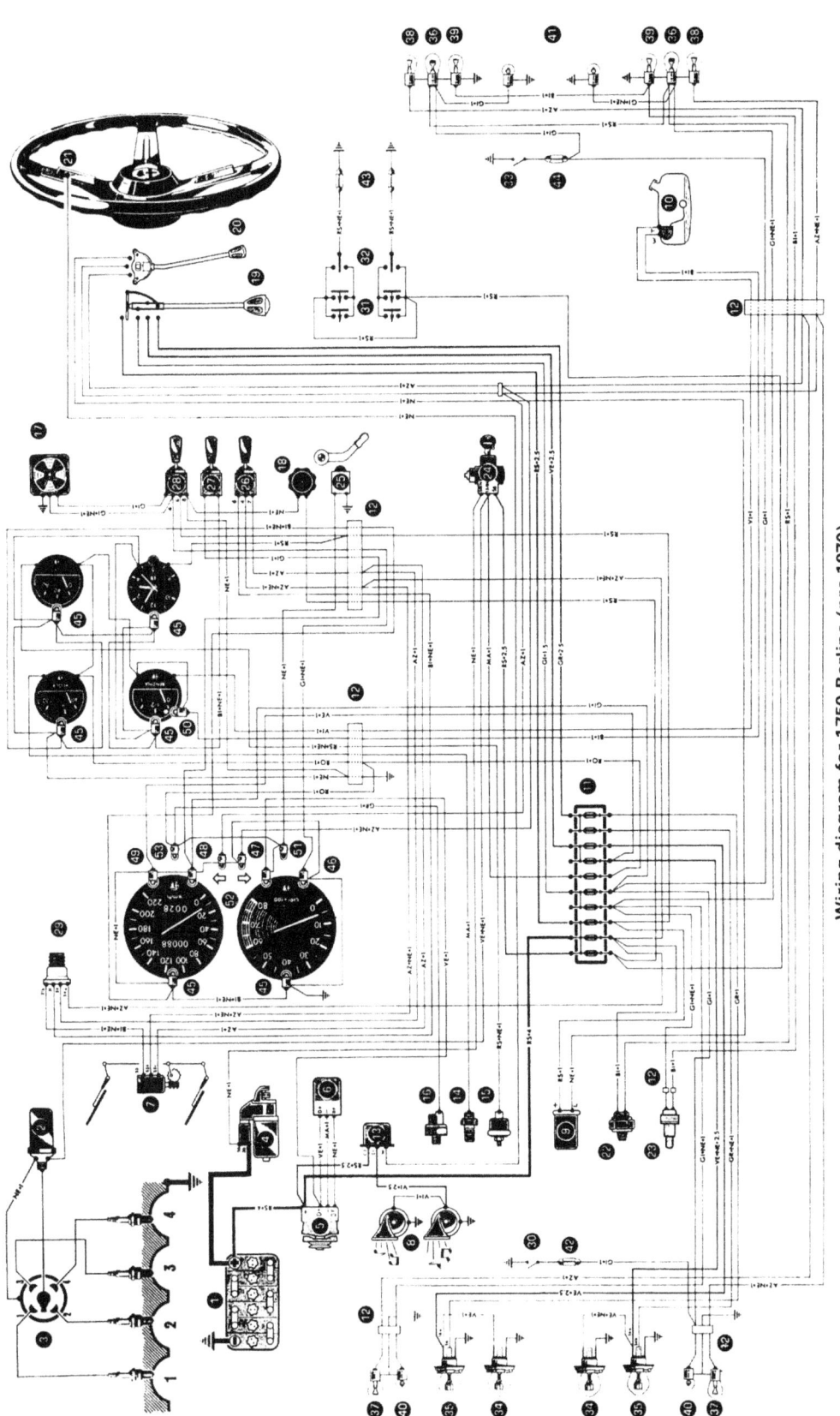

Wiring diagram for 1750 Berline (pre 1970)

Key to Diagram 1 Battery 2 Coil 3 Distributor 4 Starter 5 Alternator 6 Voltage regulator 7 Windscreen wiper motor 8 Horns 9 Flasher control 10 Fuel gauge transmitter 11 Fuse box 12 Connectors 13 Horn relay 14 Water temperature transmitter 15 Oil pressure transmitter 16 Minimum oil pressure 17 Two-speed heater/ventilator motor 18 Cigar lighter 19 Side, head and head flash switch 20 Direction indicator switch 21 Horn switch 22 Stop light switch 23 Reverse light switch 24 Ignition and starter switch 25 Choke warning 26 Wiper motor switch 27 Panel lights switch 28 Heater/ventilator motor switch 29 Windscreen washer plunger switch 30 Engine compartment light switch 31 Door pillar light switch 32 Independent interior light switch 33 Boot compartment switch 34 Inner headlamps 35 Outer headlamps 36 Rear parking and stop lights 37 Front direction indicator lamps 38 Rear direction indicator lamps 39 Reverse lights 40 Front parking lights 41 Index plate lights 42 Engine compartment lamp 43 Interior lamps 44 Boot compartment lamp 45 Instrument panel lamps 46 Heater fan warning lamp 47 Alternator charge warning lamp 48 Parking light warning 49 Main head beam warning light 50 Low fuel warning light 51 Choke warning light 52 Flasher repeater lamps 53 Oil pressure warning lamp
Key to colour code AZ Blue B1 White G1 Yellow GR Grey MA Maroon NE Black RO Pink RS Red VE Green V1 Violet
The number after the colour code letters indicates the thickness of the cable in sq mm

46

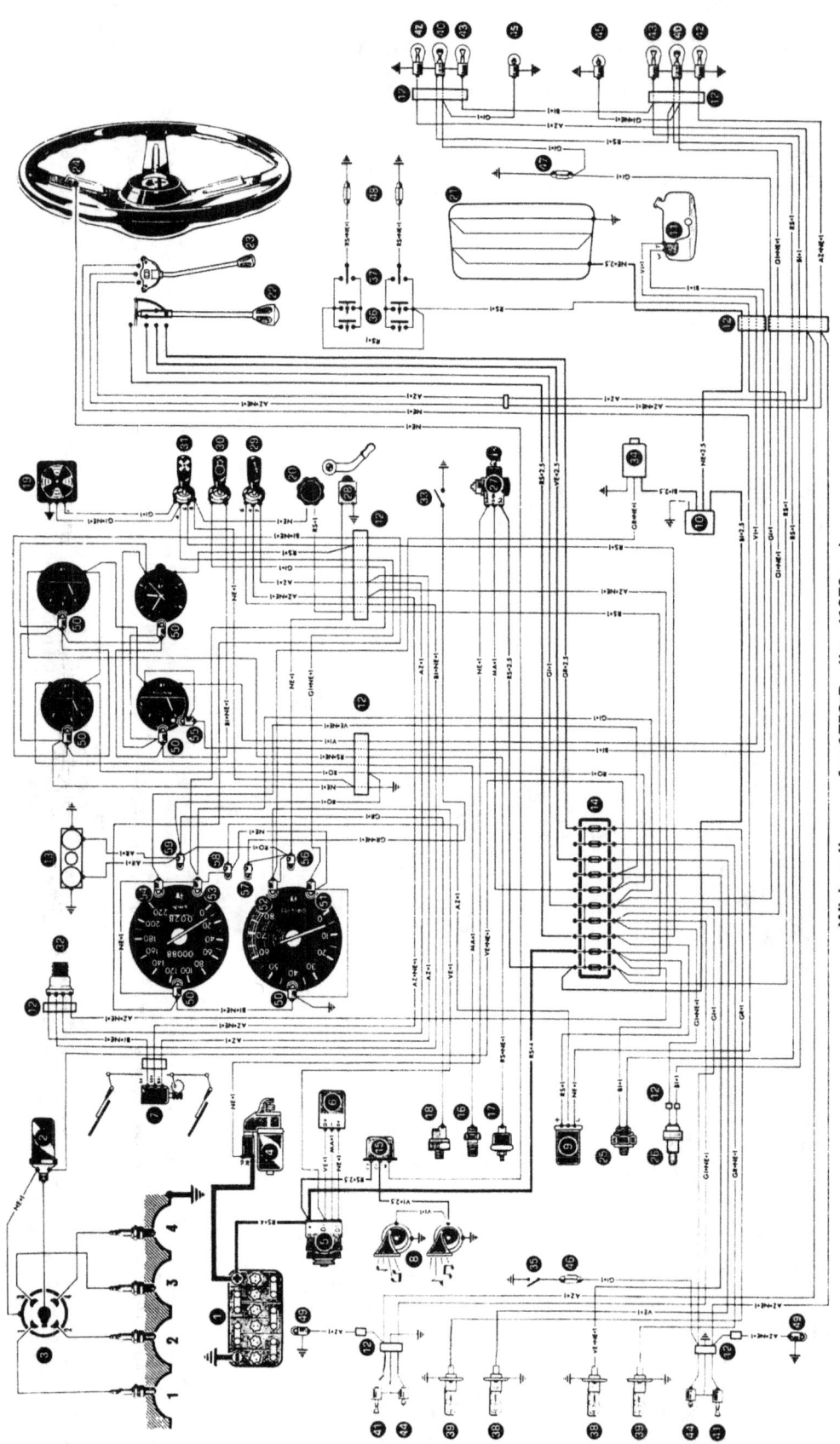

Wiring diagram for 1750 Berline (1970 on)

Key to Diagram — 1 Battery   2 Coil   3 Distributor   4 Starter   5 Alternator   6 Voltage regulator   7 Windscreen wiper motor   8 Horns   9 Flasher unit   10 Electro-magnetic relay for heated rear window (optional)   11 Fuel gauge transmitter   12 Connectors   13 Brake fluid (minimum) transmitter   14 Fuse box   15 Horn relay   16 Water temperature transmitter   17 Oil pressure transmitter   18 Oil pressure (minimum) transmitter   19 Two-speed heater ventilator motor   20 Cigar lighter   21 Heated rear window (option)   22 Side, head and head flash switch   23 Direction indicator switch   24 Horn switch   25 Stop light switch   26 Reverse light switch   27 Ignition and starter switch   28 Choke warning switch   29 Wiper motor switch   30 Instrument panel light switch   31 Heater/ventilator motor switch   32 Windscreen washer plunger switch   33 Handbrake warning light switch   34 Rear window heater switch   35 Engine compartment light switch   36 Door pillar light switch   37 Interior light switch   38 Inner headlamp   39 Outer headlamp   40 Stop and tail light   41 Front direction indicators   42 Rear direction indicators   43 Reverse lights   44 Front parking lights   45 Index plate lights   46 Engine compartment light   47 Boot compartment light   48 Interior lamps   49 Side repeater lamps   50 Instrument panel lights   51 Heater motor warning lamp   52 Alternator charge warning   53 Parking light warning   54 Headlamp warning   55 Low fuel warning light   56 Choke warning light   57 Heater warning light   58 Direction indicator warning repeater lamp   59 Minimum brake fluid warning light

Colour code and cable thickness — see pre 1970 Berline wiring diagram

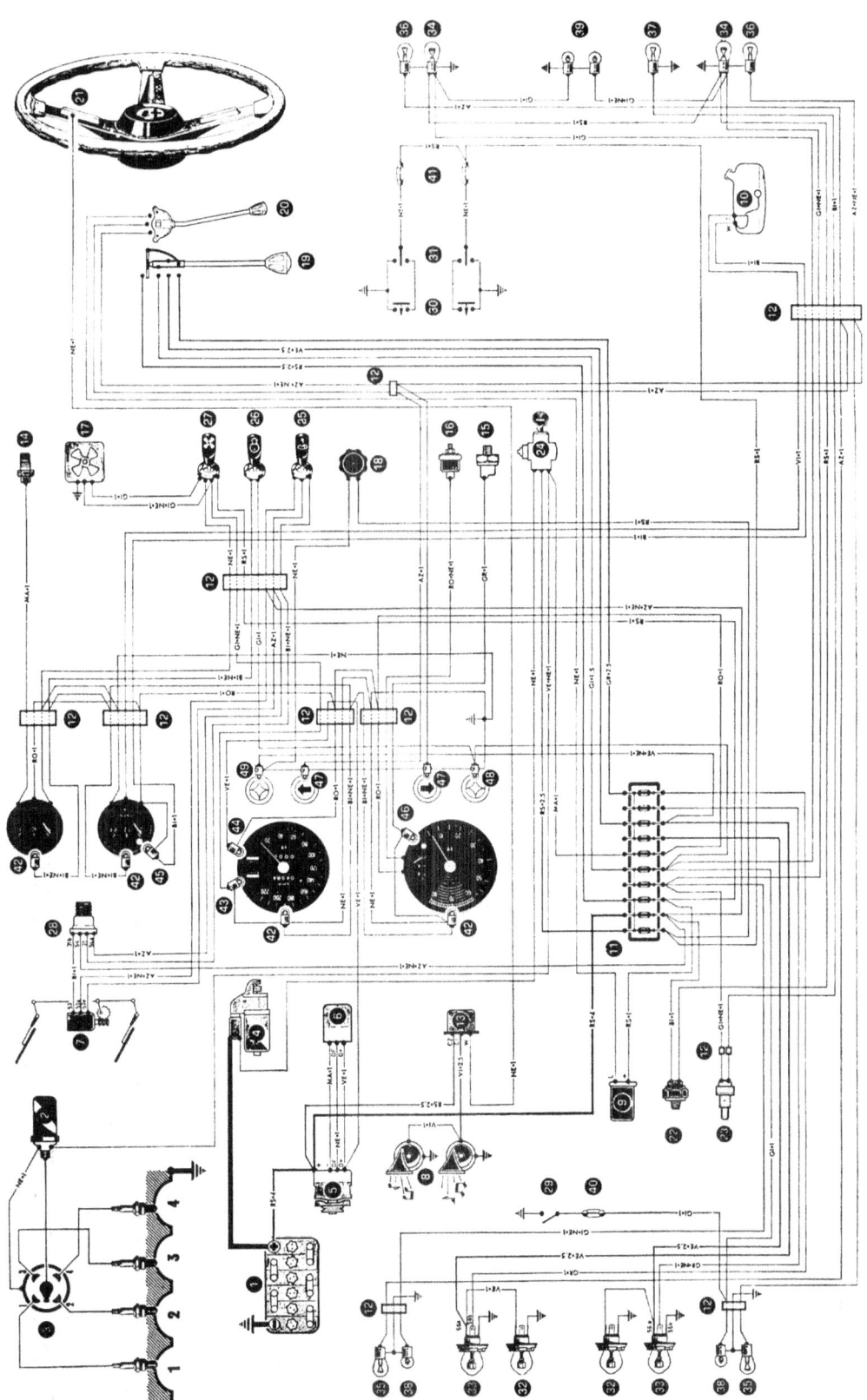

Wiring diagram 1750 Coupe

Key to Fig 13:8 Numbers 1 to 24, refer to **FIG 13:6** 25 Windscreen wiper motor switch 26 Instrument panel switch 27 Heater:ventilator motor switch
28 Windscreen washer plunger switch 29 Engine compartment light switch 30 Door pillar light switch 31 Independent interior light switch 32 Inner headlamps
33 Outer headlamps 34 Tail and stop lamp 35 Front direction indicators 36 Rear direction indicators 37 Reverse lamp 38 Front parking lights 39 Index plate
light 40 Engine compartment light 41 Interior lights 42 Instrument panel lights 43 Heater:ventilator fan warning light 44 Alternator charge warning
light 45 Low fuel warning light 46 Oil pressure warning lamp 47 Direction indicator warning repeater lights 48 Parking light indicator 49 Main head beam indicator
Colour code and cable thickness—see pre 1970 Berline wiring diagram

48

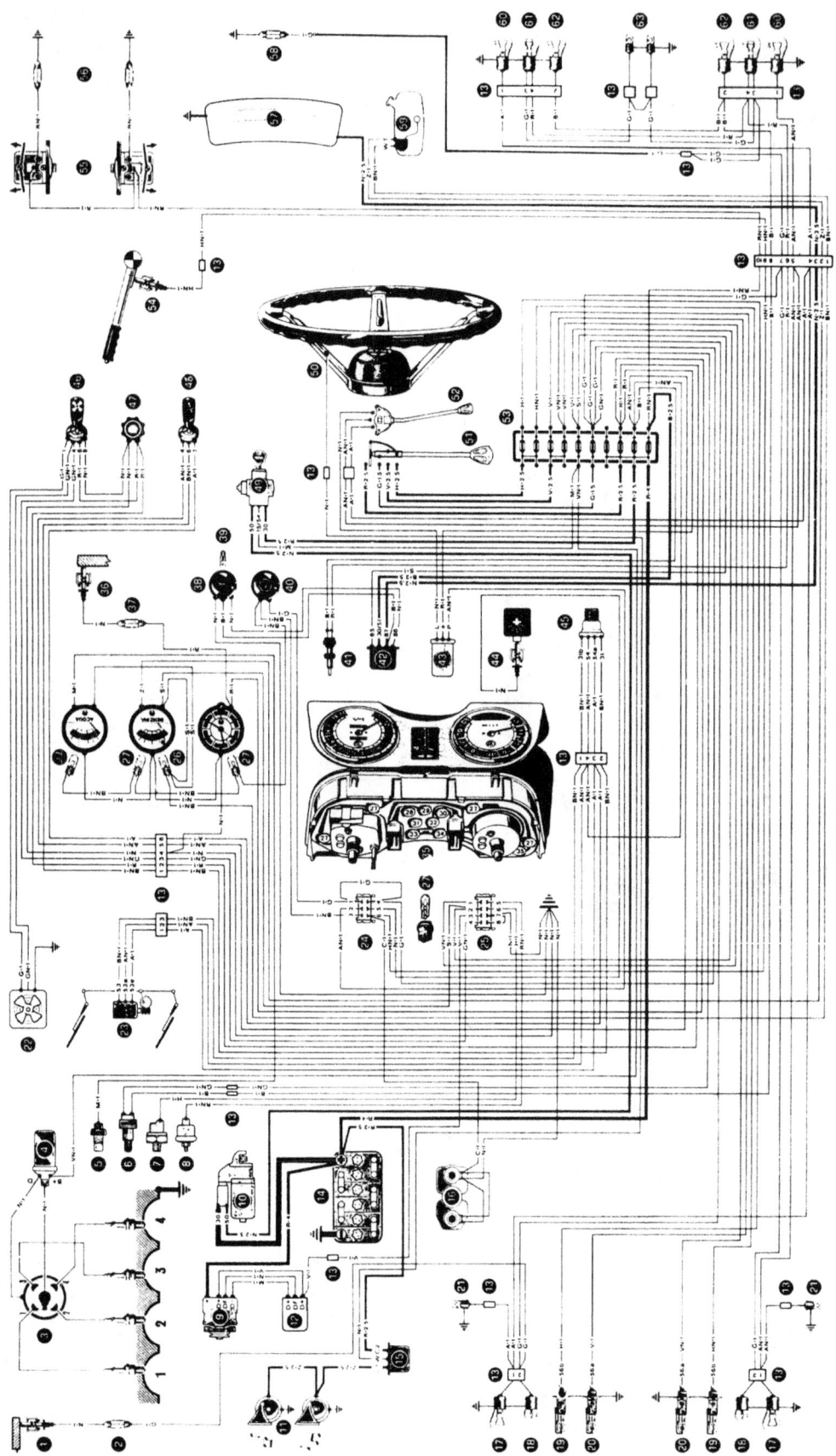

2000 Saloon wiring diagram

Key to Diagram 3 Distributor 4 Coil 5 Water temperature sender 7 Oil pressure warning sender 8 Oil pressure sender 9 Alternator 10 Starter 11 Horns 12 Voltage regulator 13 Connectors 14 Battery 15 Horn relay 16 Brake fluid warning sender 22 Two-speed heater fan 23 Wiper motor 24 Fuel tank unit 25 Connector (6-way) 26 Connector (8-way) 42 Heated window relay 43 Flasher control 47 Cigar lighter 53 Fuse box 57 Heated rear window 59 Choke warning lamp **Switches** 1 Engine compartment light 6 Reverse lamp 36 Glove box 38 Rear window 40 Instrument panel lamps 41 Stop lamp 44 Choke warning 54 Handbrake warning 45 Foot, windscreen wash 46 Heater fan 48 Wiper motor 49 Ignition and starter 50 Horn 51 Side, head and flasher 52 Direction indicators **Lamps** 2 Engine compartment 17 Front flashers 18 Side lamps 19 Dipped beam 20 Headlamp main beam 21 Side indicators 26 Reserve petrol warning 27 Instrument panel 28 Handbrake and fluid level warning 29 Flasher repeaters 30 Fan warning 31 Choke warning 32 Charge warning 33 Side lamp warning 34 Headlamp warning 35 Low oil pressure warning 37 Glove box 39 Heated window warning 56 Interior lights 58 Boot 60 Rear flashers 61 Rear and stop lamps 62 Reversing lamp 63 Number plate **Key to colour code** A Blue B White C Orange G Yellow H Grey M Maroon N Black R Red S Rose V Green Z Violet
The number after the colour letter indicates the section of the wire in sq mm

Wiring diagram for 2000 Veloce

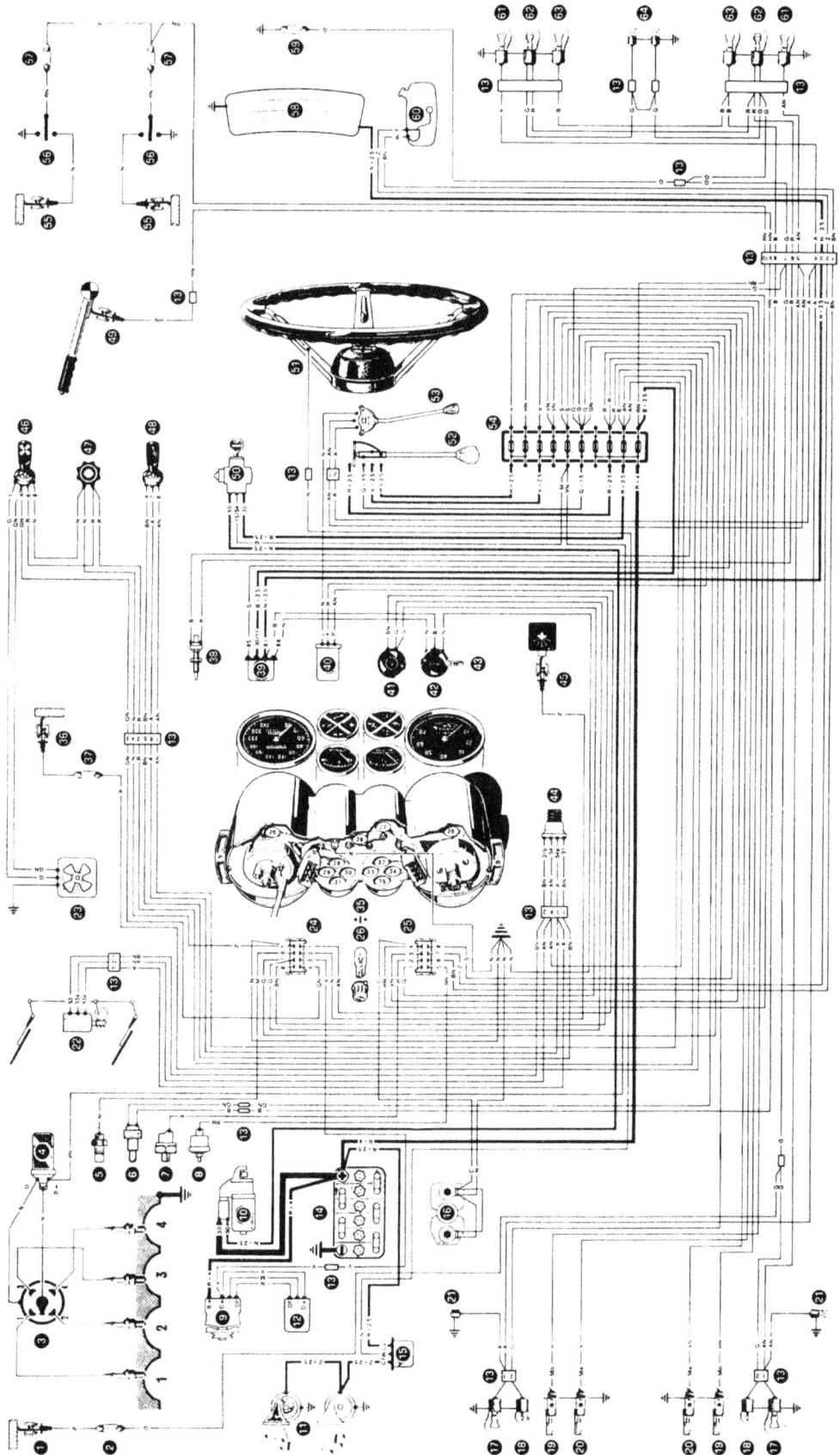

Equipment 3 Distributor 4 Coil 5 Water temperature sender 7 Oil pressure warning sender 8 Oil pressure sender 9 Alternator 10 Starter 11 Horns 12 Voltage regulator 13 Cable connectors 14 Battery 15 Horn relay 16 Brake fluid warning sender 22 Windscreen wiper 23 Two-speed heater fan 24 and 25 Connectors **Switches** 1 Engine compartment light 6 Reverse lamp 39 Heated window relay 40 Flasher control 47 Cigar lighter 54 Fuse block 58 Heated rear window 60 Fuel tank unit 44 Windscreen washer 45 Choke warning 46 Heater/ventilator motor 48 Wiper motor 49 Handbrake warning 41 Instrument panel light 42 Rear window heater 51 Horns 52 Side, head and head flash 53 Direction indicator 55 Door pillar 56 Interior light 50 Ignition and starter 26 Instrument panel **Lamps** 2 Engine compartment 17 Direction indicator (front) 18 Front parking 19 Dipped beam 20 Main beam 21 Side repeater 32 Headlamp warning 27 Reserve petrol warning 28 Flasher repeater 29 Battery charge warning 30 Choke engaged warning 31 Heater fan operating 43 Rear window heater warning 57 Interior 33 Handbrake and fluid level warning 34 Low oil pressure warning 35 Reversing 63 Parking light warning 37 Glove box 59 Boot 61 Rear direction indicator 62 Rear and stop 64 Index plate **Colour codes and cable thickness**—see **2000 Saloon wiring diagram**

NOTES

SHOP MANUAL No. 6
AIR CONDITIONING

**DIRECTIONS FOR CHECKING
AND RECHARGING
(FACTORY MANUAL)**

CONTENTS

FIRST SECTION

Operation of air conditioning system	Page	1
Compressor	"	3
Condenser	"	4
Expansion valve	"	5
Evaporator	"	5
Suction throttling valve	"	5
Service valve	"	7
Safety precautions	"	8

SECOND SECTION

Evacuating the system	"	9
Charging the system	"	11
Leak detector	"	12
Servicing the air conditioning system	"	12
Diagnosing troubles	"	14

FIRST SECTION

OPERATION OF AIR CONDITIONING SYSTEM

A car air conditioner operates in the same way as any standard refrigerator, that is it removes heat from a relatively less warm ambient and transfers it to a warmer ambient, exactly opposite to what happens by physical law: heat transfers from hot to cold things.

A car air conditioning system consists basically of the following components:

- compressor with magnetic clutch
- condenser
- receiver-dehydrator unit
- expansion
- evaporator

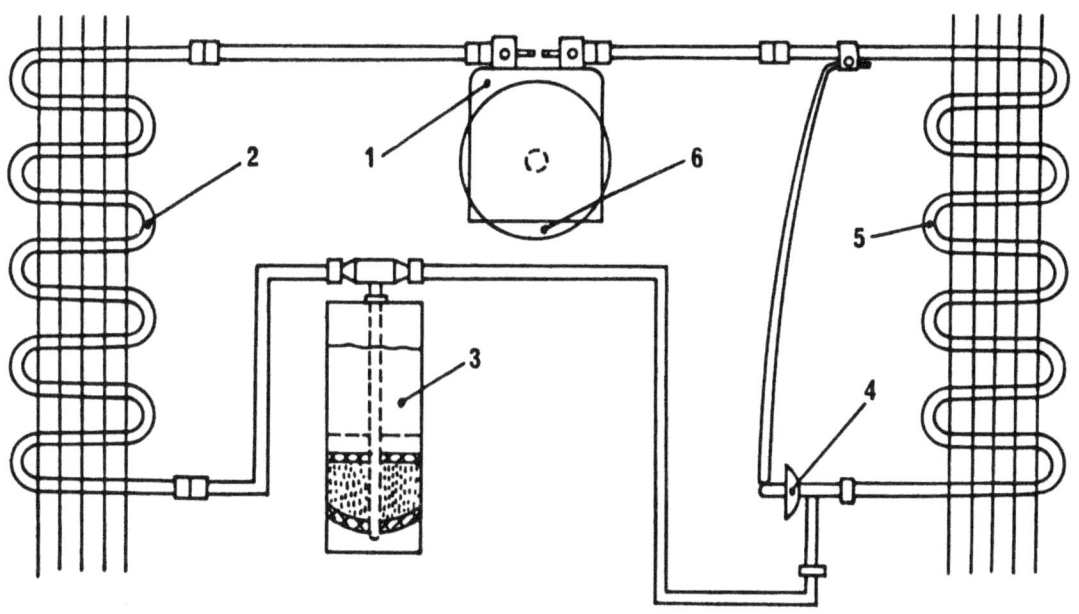

Fig. 1 - OPERATING DIAGRAM OF A CAR AIR CONDITIONER

1 - Compressor   4 - Expansion valve
2 - Condenser   5 - Evaporator
3 - Dehydrator   6 - Magnetic clutch

The refrigerant fluid is dichlorodifluoromethane (C Cl2 F2) known by the trade name of FREON 12. It is odourless, nonpoisonous, nonflammable and non corrosive: possible leaks of FREON are not dangerous for the parts involved and the persons.

The FREON has a boiling point of -22°F at atmospheric pressure; in the car air conditioning system it is used to produce the cooling effect through a cycle of evaporation and condensation.

The operating principles of an air conditioning system are the following:

The vaporized FREON is sucked by the compressor from the low pressure side of the circuit, it is compressed to about 10-18 Kg/cm^2 and delivered to the high pressure side of the circuit; as a consequence of the rise in pressure the temperature of the refrigerant increases to about 180-210°F.

The hot vapourised refrigerant enters the condenser through which air is circulated by electric blowers, engine cooling system fan or ram intake.

In the condenser the heat of refrigerant vapour is dissipated by the air, therefore the FREON temperature decreases until it condenses back from a vapour to a liquid at a temperature of about 100-120°F and the cycle starts over again.

The FREON in liquid form then passes through the dehydrator that absorbs any moisture that may have gotten into the system. The receiver dehydrator has also the purpose of assuring the supply of liquid refrigerant to the expansion valve; a sight glass on top of dehydrator allows to check the refrigerant fluid level; the sight glass should show clear fluid when FREON is:

- Totally in liquid state
- Totally in vapour state
- There is no FREON at all.

If there are instead bubbles or foam it means that vaporised and liquid FREON are mixed together.

From the dehydrator the FREON, still in liquid form, flows to the expansion valve which, by means of an automatically controlled restrictor, vaporises the liquid FREON causing a drop in pressure to take place.

This is where we get the cooling effect: the FREON changing back to a vapor state absorbs a great deal of heat, via the evaporator radiating fins, from the air circulated through them.

Thus, the air temperature drops suddenly, a dehumidifying process also takes place since a high percentage of moisture condensates on the cold surfaces of the evaporator; such a condensate is then disposed of.

The FREON at the evaporator outlet is in vapour state and rather cool despite of the high amount of heat removed from the air through the radiating core.

The cold vapourized FREON is sucked by the compressor and the cycle starts over again.

The evaporator is equipped with a three-speed blower system that forces the air of the passenger compartment of the car to pass through the evaporator radiating core; thus the air is cooled and returned to the car's interior.

Moreover on the evaporator there is a thermostatic switch which, depending on the temperature of the air passing through the radiating core, automatically declutches the compressor when the temperature drops below a certain level and re-engages the compressor magnetic clutch when the temperature again rises.

This is obtained by the thermostatic switch which open or closes the electric circuit actuating the compressor magnetic clutch: in this way the compressor pulley runs idle when the circuit is open while drives the compressor shaft when the circuit is closed.

The amount of heat absorbed by the evaporator and the temperature of the air flowing through the evaporator coils are regulated by the simultaneous action of the blower control and the thermostatic switch.

Finally, the expansion valve is automatically adjusted by means of a thermostat which increases or decreases the restrictor opening according to whether the temperature of the refrigerant vapour at the outlet of the evaporator coils is more or less high; in other words the expansion valve adjust itself in accord to the heat exchanging rate in the evaporator.

COMPRESSOR

The compressor is selected on the basis of its capacity and rpm rating so that it can provide enough refrigerant fluid delivery to obtain an efficient heat exchanging through the evaporator coils and the condenser cores.

The compressor capacity and the expansion valve calibration must be in such a relation in the system as to keep the pressures equalized within a certain interval; i.e. there should never be too high a pressure in the circuit downstream of the compressor and upstream of the expansion valve as well as too low a pressure downstream of the expansion valve and upstream of the compressor.

4

The compressor is driven by means of belts from a pulley on the crank shaft to a pulley keyed to the compressor shaft and electrically actuated by a magnetic clutch.

The compressor is of the single stage type and basically consists of the crankcase containing the crankshaft on ball bearings, the con rods, the pistons with rings and pins and the head containing inlet and outlet valve plates.

The compressor is equipped with service valve and a suction throttling valve; these components are described in detail on the following pages.

The compressor is lubricated with 280 grs of an oil specifically developed for air conditioners since it must be chemically compatible with FREON.

No regular oil change is required; nevertheless oil level must be topped up whenever the system has been discharged.

CONDENSER

The condenser is essentially a fin-and-tube radiator whose capacity varies according to the conditioner installation.

The condenser installed on cars are air cooled through ram air circulation or by means of a suitable blower.

In the condenser the refrigerant fluid temperature is dropped to condense the liquid back from a vapor to a liquid.

The proper functioning of the condenser depends on refrigerant fluid pressure and the flow of air circulated through the condenser core.

An inadequate heat exchanging in the condenser causes the fluid pressure to rise since condensation still occurs but at a higher pressure.

Too high a condensation pressure would force the overheated refrigerant vapours to mix with the liquid fluid and, so mixed, to enter the expansion valve thus impairing the efficiency of the system.

At the top of the condenser coils the heat of the refrigerant fluid is dissipated until condensation takes place; in the remaining part of the coils there is fluid in liquid state.

EXPANSION VALVE

In the expansion valve, placed at the inlet of the evaporator coils, the liquid refrigerant fluid passing through the valve restrictor changes back to a vapor state because of the sudden expansion to a much lower pressure.

Since the operation of the air conditioning system is related to the engine rpm which varies widely, the expansion valve requires a self-adjusting type of operation; such an adjustment is controlled by a thermostat which restricts more or less the flow of refrigerant fluid through the valve according to the temperature of the fluid at the evaporator outlet.

EVAPORATOR

The evaporator serves the purpose of absorbing heat from the air to be cooled as well as of drying the air.

The heat taken by the refrigerant from the air is a function of the difference in temperature between the air circulated through the radiating fins and the temperature of the fins as well as of the air flow rate.

The greater the air flow rate the more heat is picked up from the air by the radiating fins; therefore their temperature tends to increase.

Viceversa, with a low air flow rate, less heat is picked up and the temperature of the fins is lower.

To sum it up, the faster the air flow rate the higher the temperature at the evaporator outlet and viceversa; however, the majority of these temperature variations are corrected by the thermostat.

On the evaporator there are the doors for the controlled supply of air to the passenger's compartment as well as the switches for controlling the conditioner: the switch for the three-speed blower and the relay for cutting in and off the compressor; the latter is controlled in turn by the thermostatic switch in the evaporator unit.

SUCTION THROTTLING VALVE

Purpose of the suction throttling valve is to prevent the outlet pres sure of the compressor from exceeding a given value thus keeping constant the compressor power requirements and avoiding variations consistent with engine rpm.

In fact, when the car is running slowly and with a high ambient temperature, as the compressor outlet pressure augments, the power required by the compressor to operate also increases and if the engine runs at idle a considerable reduction of rpm could occur.

As the compressor outlet pressure rises up to its maximum rating (about 20 Kg/cm^2) the throttling valve gradually and evenly reduces the passage of refrigerant at the compressor suction side; the refrigerant, however, keeps flowing, via a by-pass, from the evaporator to the compressor, even if in small quantity so that cooling is still produced.

A pressure switch on the suction throttling valve cuts out the compressor should the standard operating pressure drop because of leaks of refrigerant. In such an event the pressure switch de-energizes the magnetic clutch, thus stopping the compressor.

On the suction throttling valve there also is an automatically-operated needle valve which allows to discharge and recharge the system without opening any drain plug; in fact, it is enough to screw the charging pipe to the valve connection, after having removed the knurled cap, to open automatically the valve and to close it as the pipe is disconnected.

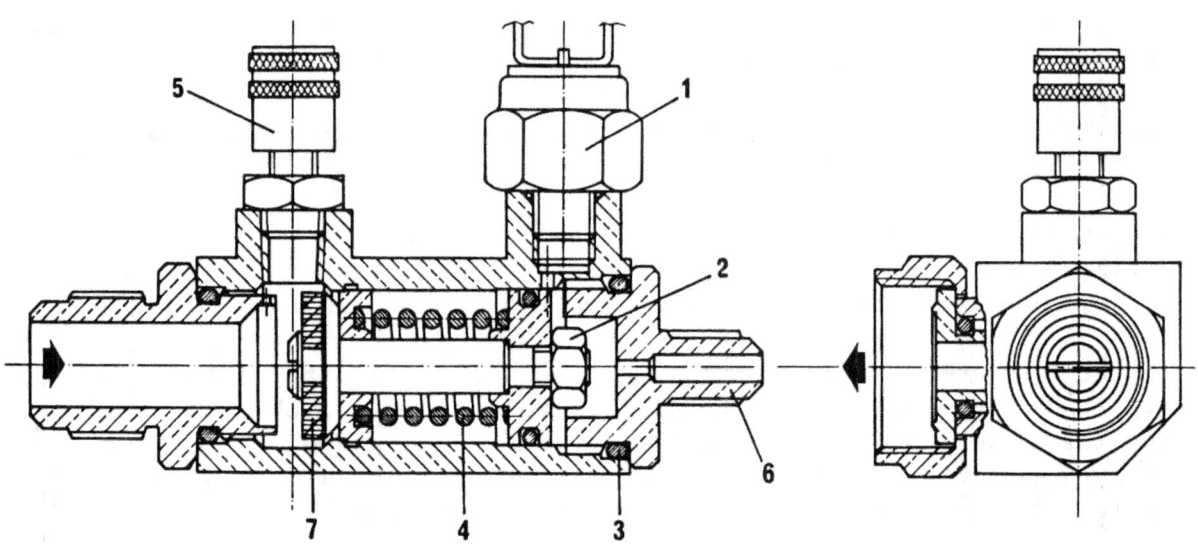

Fig. 2 - CUT-AWAY VIEW OF SUCTION THROTTLING VALVE

1 - Pressure switch
2 - Plunger
3 - Seal
4 - Return spring
5 - Needle valve for discharging and recharging the system
6 - Connection to the service valve
7 - Seal

SERVICE VALVE

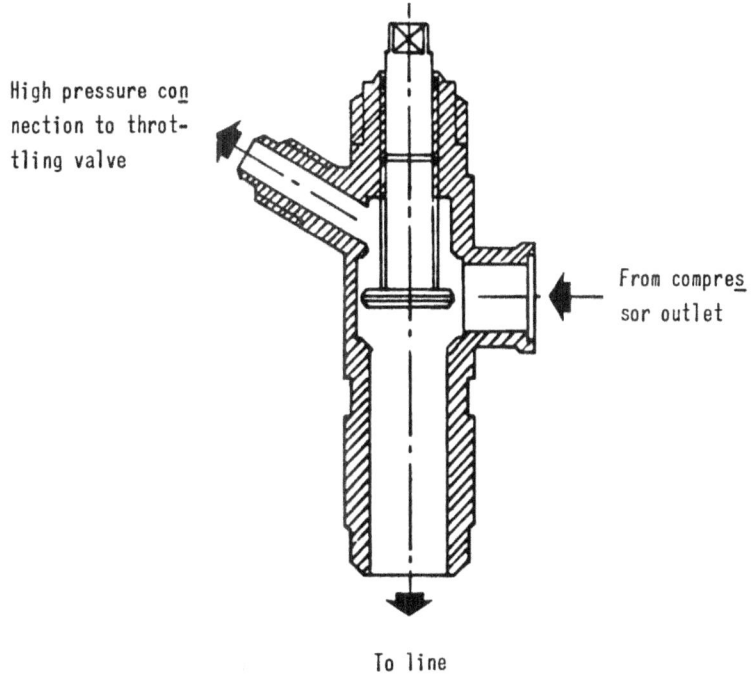

Fig. 3 - SERVICE VALVE IN OPERATING POSITION

The service valve at the compressor outlet in addition to connecting the compressor to the outlet pipe also provides a pressure connection for the throttling valve. The service valve could be used to shut off either the compressor-to-condenser connection or the high pressure bypass connection; however, since a recent modification to the system (use of a suction throttling valve) does away with shutting off the service valve, this valve is set constantly at its mid position as shown in the illustration.

Should the need for using the service valve arise, it can be operated by rotating its stem with a spanner.

Rotating the valve stem all the way clockwise stops the refrigerant flow to the condenser.

Conversely, rotating the valve stem all the way anticlockwise cuts off the refrigerant connection to the throttling valve through the by-pass.

SAFETY PRECAUTIONS

Although the FREON is classified as a safe refrigerant, it is usually used under pressure, therefore, the following precautions must be strictly observed in handling the refrigerant.

FREON is supplied in high pressure metal containers. Do not overheat the containers by leaving them in the sun for prolonged periods; the heat so applied would cause this pressure to build up excessively.

In winter months, charging or adding refrigerant may be difficult due to the low pressure in the container; in such a case, before charging, place the containers for about twenty minutes in a room at a temperature not exceeding 95°F; <u>never use</u> an open flame to heat the container.

Never leave the container in the charging station for prolonged periods.

While discharging the system, if FREON 12 comes into contact with an open flame (gas welding torch, stove, etc.) it is converted into a poisonous gas; therefore, it is advisable to discharge the system in a well ventilated room with no open flame nearby.

Extreme care must be taken to prevent any liquid refrigerant from coming in contact with the skin, it evaporates so quickly that it tends to freeze anything it contacts.

Always protect your eyes when handling refrigerant; you could damage your eyes seriously by getting refrigerant in them.

SECOND SECTION

EVACUATING THE SYSTEM

For an efficient operation of the air conditioner air and moisture must be kept out of the system. In fact, air is pumped by the compressor, power is absorbed, but no cooling effect is produced; moisture tends to freeze in the cold lines with consequent obstructions and malfunctions.

For the above said reasons, before refilling with FREON the system must be evacuated thoroughly.

PROCEED AS FOLLOWS:

1 - Evacuate the system by connecting the low pressure hose to the suction throttling valve and wait until all FREON has been discharged.

2 - Check oil level and add oil as necessary;

3 - Connect the high pressure hose to the conditioner service valve.

4 - Make the connections with the filling rig: low pressure to connection 1, high pressure to connection 8 and make sure that all valves of the filling rig are closed.

5 - Start the vacuum pump then open valves 6 and 7.

6 - Operate the vacuum pump for about 10 minutes then close valves 6 and 7 to shut off the pump and check for no leaks.

   Wait a few minutes and check whether vacuum registered on gauges remains constant, if not, retighten the connections; if leaks still persist, partially charge the circuit with about 300 grs of FREON and check for leaks with a leak detector.

7 - After the leaks have been corrected, discharge possible FREON remained in the circuit and again operate the vacuum pump, the vacuum should go as low as 0.8 - 0.6 mm Hg.

EDWARDS FILLING RIG

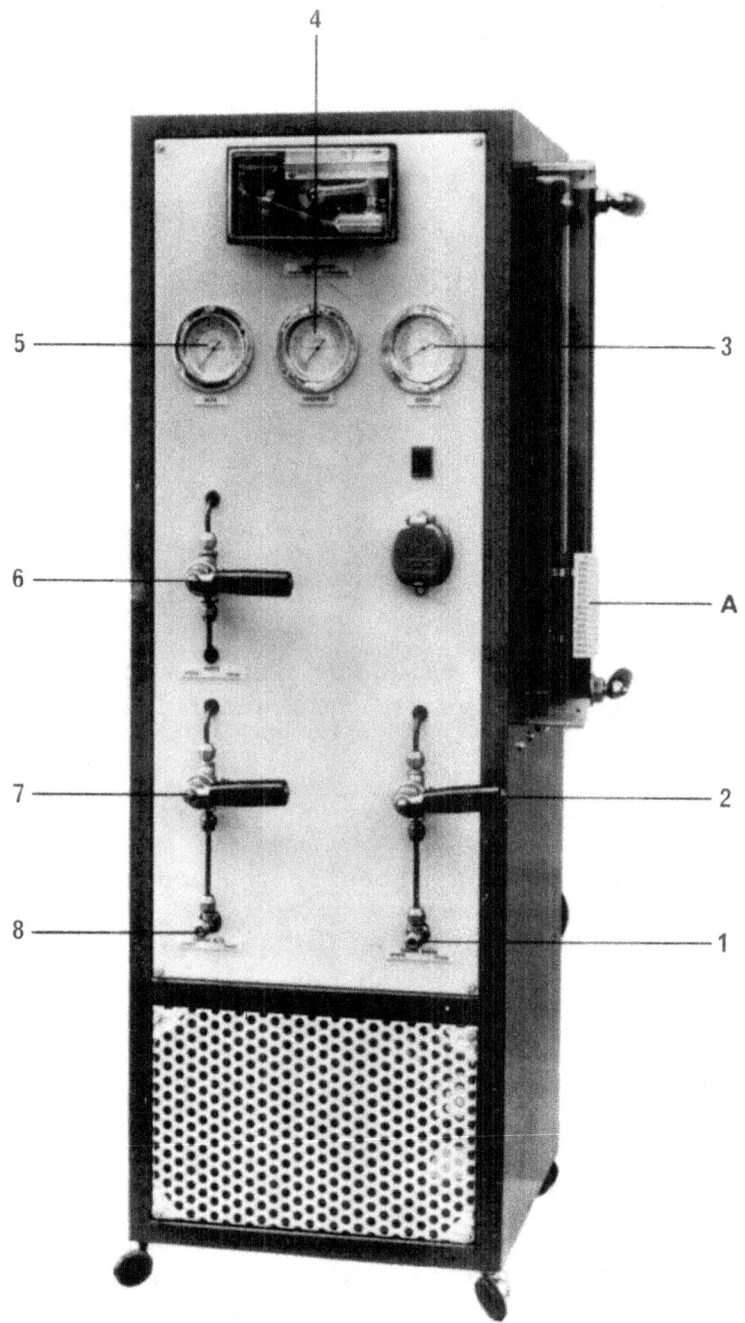

Important notes

Even if the specified vacuum is reached in a few minutes, continue vacuum pump operation for at least 30 minutes.

Before turning off the vacuum pump, always close the valve 6.

When making connections in the circuit or to the filling rig, lubricate the threads with the same type of oil as used in the compressor.

CHARGING THE SYSTEM

After the system has been evacuated as outlined above, it is ready for charging.

Proceed as follows:

1 - Check that all valves of filling rig are closed.

2 - Preset the indicator "A" for checking the quantity of FREON being charged.

3 - Slowly open the valve 2 first then the valve 7 and make sure that the FREON flows into the system until the specified charge (1 Kg) of refrigerant has been made.

4 - Should the FREON stop flowing into the system under its own pressure, run the engine at 1500 rpm and turn on the air conditioner.

5 - After the proper charge has been made, close the valves 2 and 7.

6 - Turn the service valve stem all the way anticlockwise and remove the hoses by disconnecting them from the suction throttling valve and the service valve first.

7 - Put the cap on the suction throttling valve connection, rotate the service valve stem by two complete turns clockwise and put the cap on service valve stem.

8 - Make a thorough test for leaks with a leak detector.

   After charging the system, test it for proper operation according to the directions given. Operate the system for some minutes, then observe the sight glass for foam; foam indicates an undercharge of refrigerant or the presence of moisture in the system.

LEAK DETECTOR

As already explained, the air conditioning system is a circuit along which FREON is pushed under pressure; for a reliable and long lasting operation of the system there must be no leakage of refrigerant from the system.

However, even though unlikely, FREON leaks might occur owing to a fault in the circuit, or a pipe improperly connected; since refrigerant leaks cannot be detected and traced visually, it is necessary to use a leak detector.

Several types of leak detectors are commercially available, one among those less expensive is the propane gas torch. In the presence of the FREON vapour its blue flame changes colour turning yellowish first, then violet/blue.

Alfa Romeo, for the service network, has selected an electronic type of leak detector, the best on the market for its high sensitivity. It must be handled with care but gives excellent results.

For its use, strictly follow the manufacturer's instructions.

SERVICING THE AIR CONDITIONING SYSTEM

The air conditioning system should be thoroughly tested when preparing it for summer operation, whenever repair works have been carried out on its components and whenever it is faulty.

Check as follows:

1 - Drive belts: the belt tension is correct when on pressing the belts down the amount of play is about 8-10 mm.

   If the tension is excessive the bearings of the compressor bracket and shaft will be overloaded.

   If the tension is insufficient the belts will slip especially at high rpm. If the pulleys are not perfectly aligned the bolts will wear prematurely.

2 - Attaching parts: while checking generally, the compressor attaching parts must be checked for tightness; being subject to vibrations these parts might become loose.

Whenever the compressor service valves are removed for whatever reasons, the seals must be renewed.

3 - <u>Condenser</u>: inspect the condenser fins for obstructions or foreign matter that might decrease the free flow of air and in turn the efficiency of the condenser.

If cleaning is performed with jets of air or water, make sure to direct the jet so as not to strike too hard the fins.

Should the magnetic clutch show such troubles as slipping, excessive play or noise due to an improper spring rating, the clutch must be replaced as a unit with a new one since presently its components cannot be repaired individually.

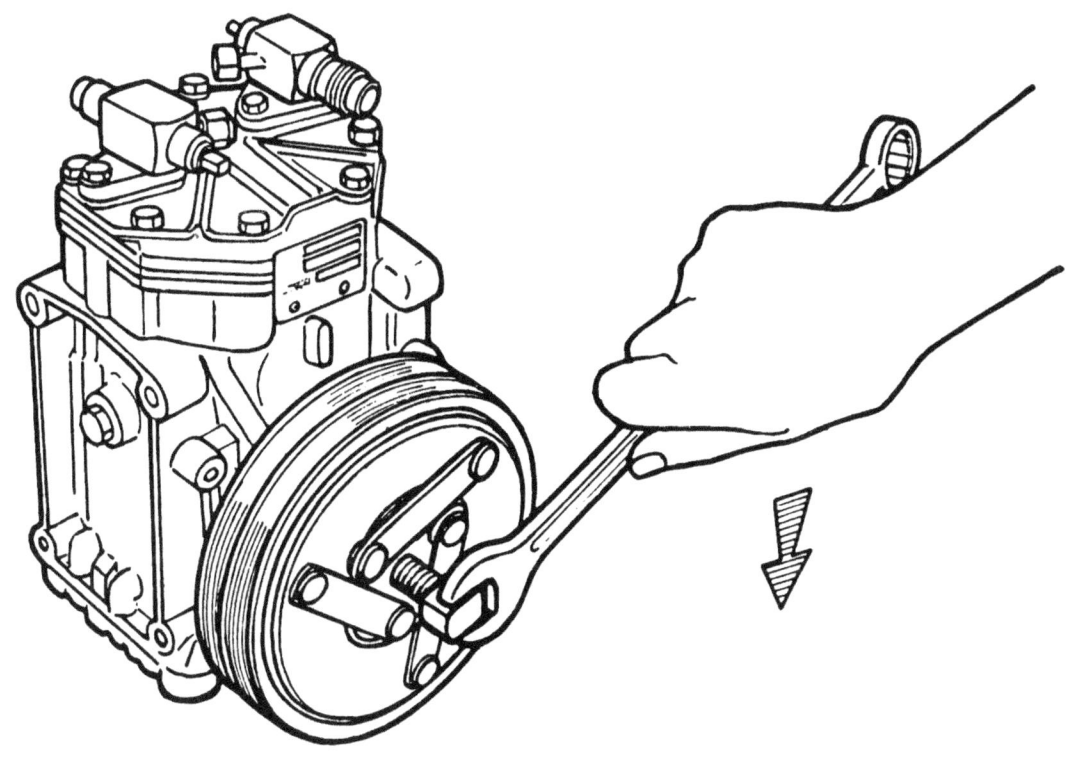

Fig. 4 - TIGHTEN THE SCREW TO REMOVE THE CLUTCH FROM SHAFT

To renew the magnetic clutch proceed as follows:

- Loosen the belt.
- Remove the clutch mounting bolt from compressor crankshaft.
- Install the puller (tool no. A.3.0403) onto the clutch and withdraw the clutch.
- Install the new clutch with its key on compressor crankshaft.
- Tighten the clutch mounting bolt to 2.4 - 2.8 kgm.

- Fit the drive belts.

Testing the system.

Operate the system for about ten minutes to allow all parts to warm up to the operating temperature and to cool sufficiently the passenger's compartment.

At this test stage, only the temperature of the air discharged by the evaporator outlets can be determined.

The system performance is good when the discharge air temperature is approximately half the ambient temperature.

The temperature of the car's interior cannot be taken as a reference because it depends on several factors out of control such as the passenger's compartment volume, tightness of door weatherstrips, number of persons being accomodated, condition of body insulating material.

To read the discharge air temperature use a suitable thermometer kept hanging on the outlet by means of an insulating support and not with bare hands whose heat could alter the reading.

If the system so tested shows poor performance, more complete diagnostic checks must be performed.

Diagnosing troubles

For a more complete test procedure readings must be taken of the suction pressure S.P. and delivery pressure D.P.

The pressure readings are then compared to standard, or normal, system pressures so as to locate the troubles and remedy them with the aid of the attached trouble shooting chart.

To connect the pressure gauge set of the filling rig to the system proceed as follows:

1 - Rotate the conditioner service valve stem anticlockwise until it goes.

2 - Remove the high pressure by-pass between the service valve and the suction throttling valve.

3 - Connect the service valve to the high pressure gauge of filling

rig with the suitable connector.

4 - Connect the needle valve of the suction throttling valve unit to the low pressure gauge with the suitable connector.

5 - Disconnect the two leads from the pressure switch and connect together the leads so as to get continuity to feed the magnetic clutch.

6 - Rotate clockwise the service valve stem by two complete turns.

With connections so made, operate the conditioner for about ten minutes, then read the pressures registered on high and low pressure gauges. For interpreting correctly the trouble shooting chart, the standard values of pressures are given below as a reference.

Suction pressure S.P.

Too high when exceeding	2.5 Kg/cm^2
Normal	0.8 - 2.5 Kg/cm^2
Too low when below	0.8 Kg/cm^2

Delivery pressure D.P.

Too high when exceeding	20 Kg/cm^2
Normal	10 - 20 Kg/cm^2
Too low when below	10 Kg/cm^2

To disconnect the pressure gauges and put again the system in working conditions, proceed as follows:

1 - Rotate the conditioner service valve stem anticlockwise until it goes.

2 - Disconnect the high pressure gauge from the service valve.

3 - Disconnect the low pressure gauge from the needle valve.

4 - Connect the high pressure by-pass across service valve and suction throttling valve.

5 - Rotate the service valve stem by two complete turns.

6 - Reconnect the leads to the pressure switch.

After the trouble has been diagnosed with the aid of the shooting chart again test the system performance.

TROUBLE SHOOTING CHART

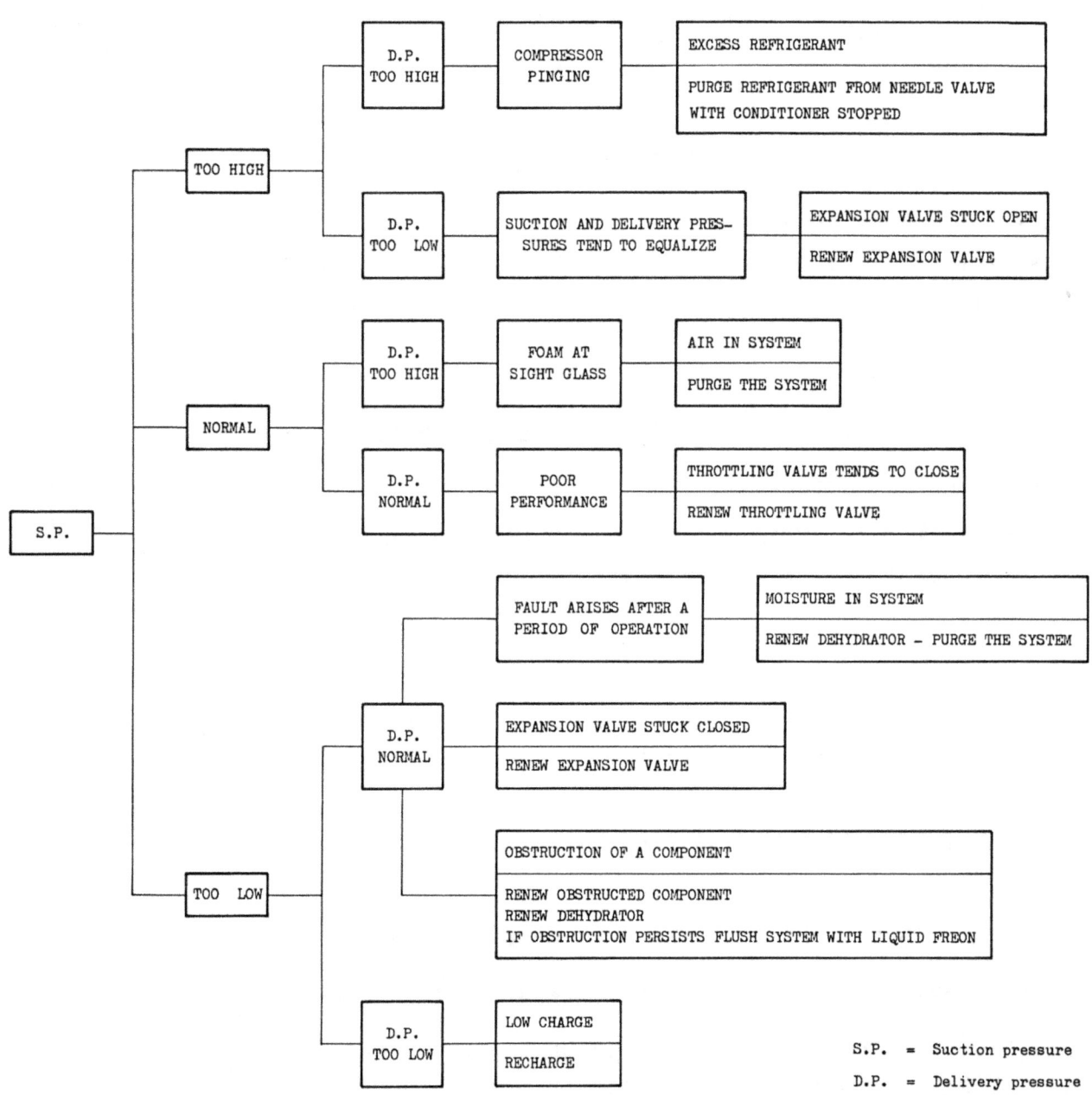

SHOP MANUAL No. 7

BODY

(FACTORY MANUAL)

GIULIA AND 1750 MODELS

INDEX TO MANUAL

REMOVAL AND INSTALLATION

Windscreen and rear window glass	1
Doors, door glass and door components	6
Front seats	19
Instrument panel – facia	20
Console	24
Headliner	27
Body insulation and sound deadening	35

CHECKING AND ADJUSTING

Door locks	36
Hood – bonnet	39
Trunk lid – boot lid	42
Door weather strip	43
Sealing the trunk – boot area	44

REMOVAL AND INSTALLATION

WINDSCREEN AND REAR WINDOW GLASS

The same procedure applies to all Saloon and Coupe models. Giulia and 1750 Saloon are shown for example purpose.

Proceed the same way both for the windscreen and the rear window.

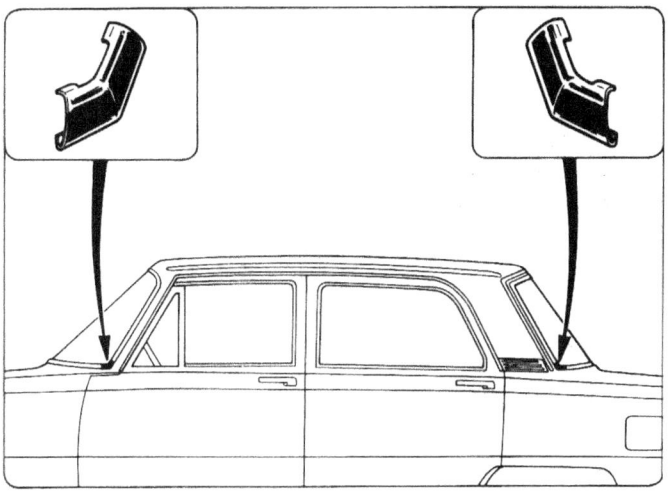

REMOVAL

- Take the corner finishers away of the mouldings.

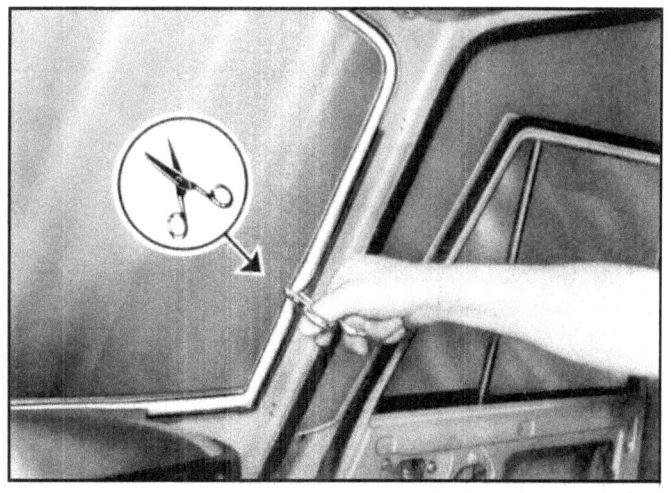

- From inside out, apply pressure evenly distributed on the glass; from the outside, have an assistant holding the glass when it pops out of weatherstrip.
To make the windscreen removal easier, cut the inner lip of weatherstrip with scissors; in this case the weatherstrip must then be renewed.

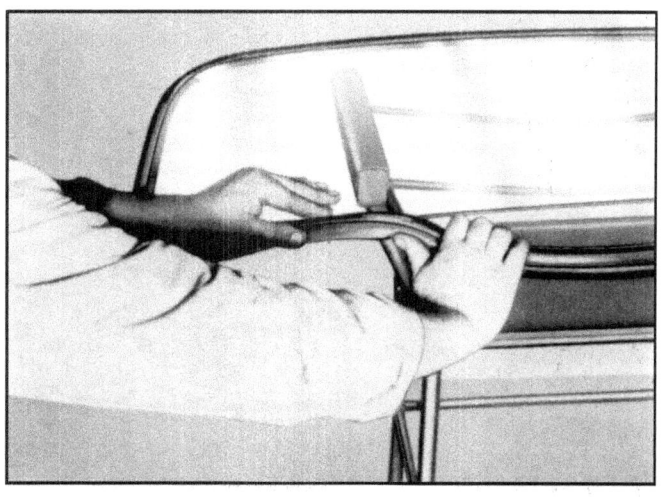

INSTALLATION

- 1 – Carefully clean the edges of the glass and install the weatherstrip on it.

REMOVAL AND INSTALLATION

WINDSCREEN AND REAR WINDOW GLASS

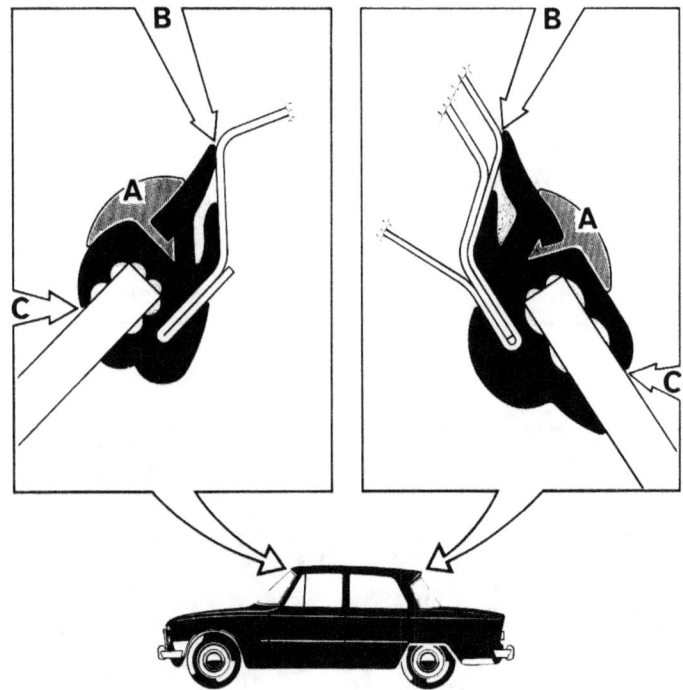

- 2 – In order to facilitate the installation of the metal moulding A, spray liquid soap to lubricate the weatherstrip.

- 3 – Install the metal moulding.

NOTE – The operations 1-2-3 are to be carried out when the weatherstrip needs replacement.
To perform these operations it is advisable to rest the glass on the suitable stand P.N. A.9.0104.

REMOVAL AND INSTALLATION

WINDSCREEN AND REAR WINDOW GLASS

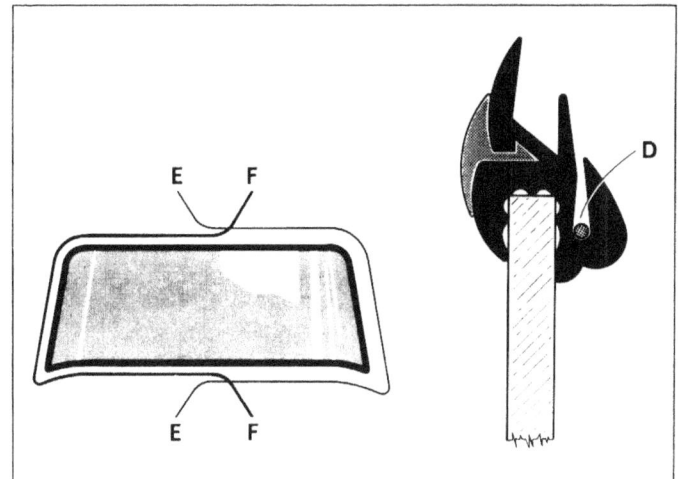

- Wrap two cords EE–FF around the outer groove D of weatherstrip as shown.

- Lay a bead of petroleum jelly around the glass opening for ease of installation.

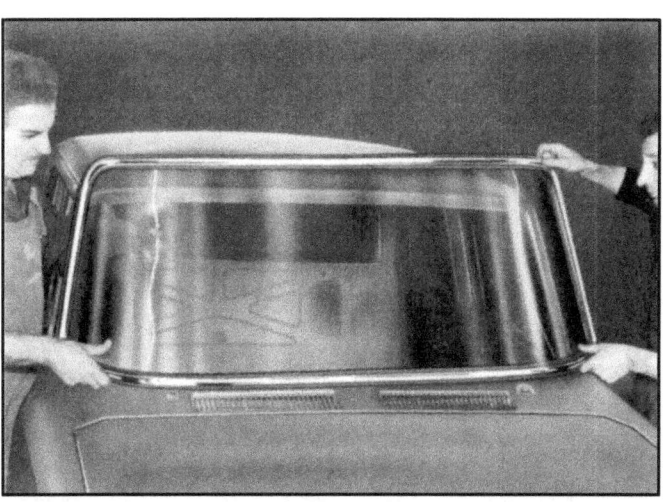

- Place the glass in the opening.

REMOVAL AND INSTALLATION

WINDSCREEN AND REAR WINDOW GLASS

- From the outside apply pressure over the glass.

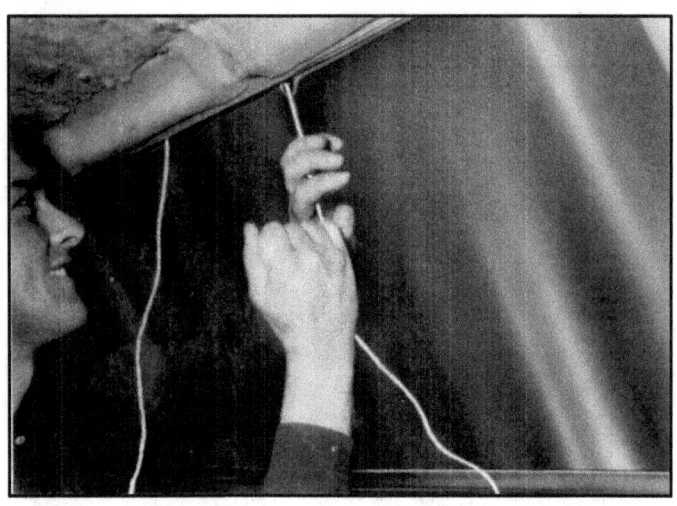

- At the same time, an assistant, pulling from the inside the ends of the cords one at a time, will facilitate the seating of weatherstrip into the glass opening.

- Tap lightly with the hand on the glass especially in the corners.

REMOVAL AND INSTALLATION

WINDSCREEN AND REAR WINDOW GLASS

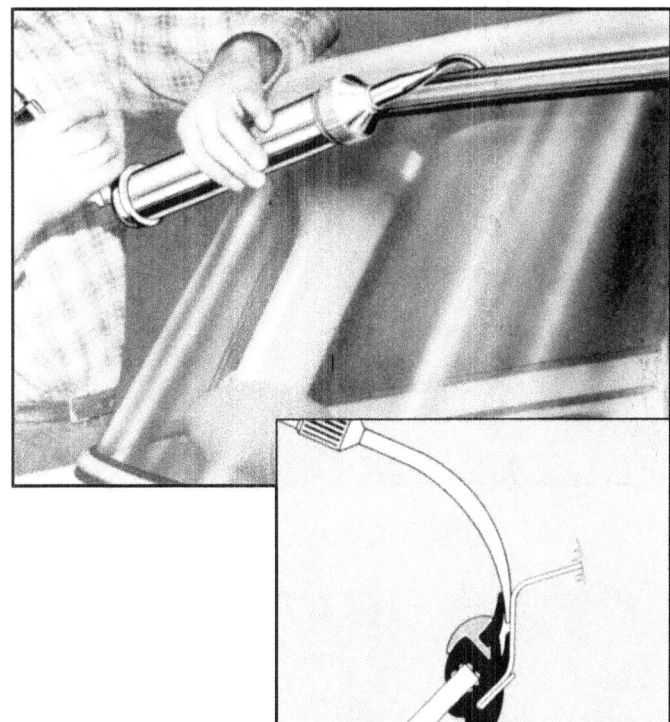

- Insert the spout of the gun under the weatherstrip lips B and C and apply the specified sealing compound.
(See page 2, upper diagram).

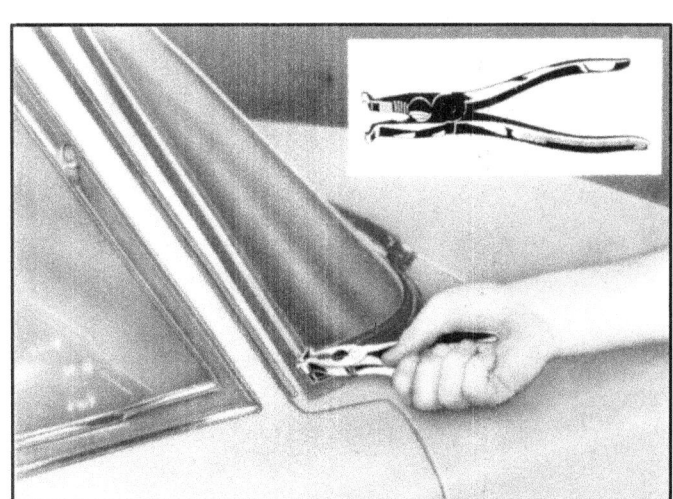

- Refit the corner finishers and secure them in place with the pliers, special tool P.N. A.9.0035

NOTE — Should the weatherstrip show sign of defect which might impair the waterproofing of the windscreen, it must be changed with a new one.
The perfect sealing against water leaks depends upon the way the above mentioned procedure is performed especially as far as care in applying the sealing compound is concerned.

REMOVAL AND INSTALLATION

DOORS

> The same procedure applies to all Saloon models.
> 1750 Saloon is shown for example purpose.

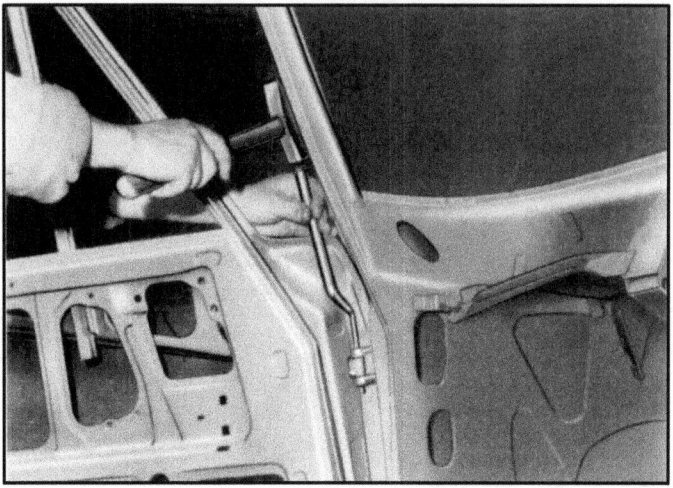

REMOVAL

- Remove the spreader plug and withdraw the hinge pins by tapping lightly with a hammer on a suitable punch which can be easily manufactured or purchased locally.
  Start from the lower hinge.
  Hold the door when the hinge pin slips out of the upper hinge.

NOTE – To gain access to the hinge pins of rear doors, open up the front doors.

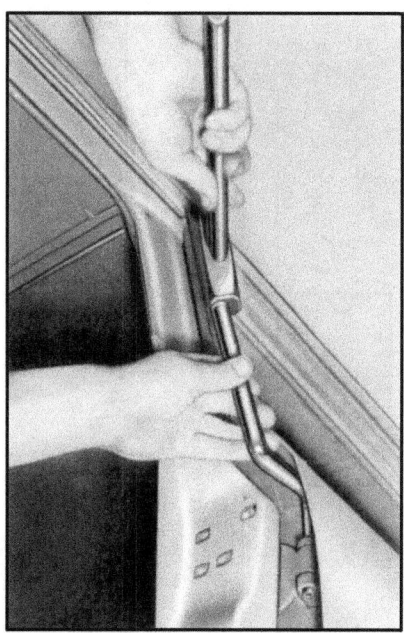

INSTALLATION

Reverse the removal procedure.

NOTE – If the doors are out of alignment, any adjustment should be made by acting only on the adjustable hinges. To prevent shortening the life of the hinge pins never put the doors under undue strains even by hand.

REMOVAL AND INSTALLATION

DOOR TRIM PANELS

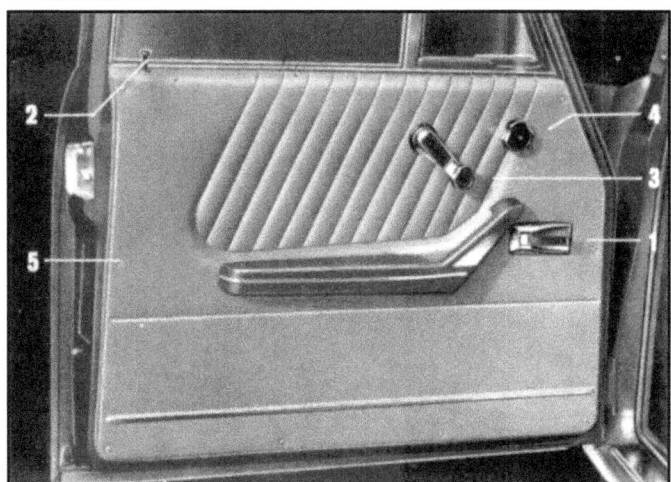

1750 Saloon is shown for example purpose.

REMOVAL

- Take the safety lock button 2 out by unscrewing it.

- Remove the remote control handle support 1, the window regulator handle 3, the vent window knob 4 (front doors) by unscrewing the attaching screws.

- Take the trim panel away by loosening the attaching screws 5.

- Detach the plastic sheet as shown.

INSTALLATION

Proceed in reverse order of removal.

REMOVAL AND INSTALLATION

DOOR GLASS FRAMES

> The same procedure applies to all Saloon models.
> 1750 Saloon is shown for example purpose.

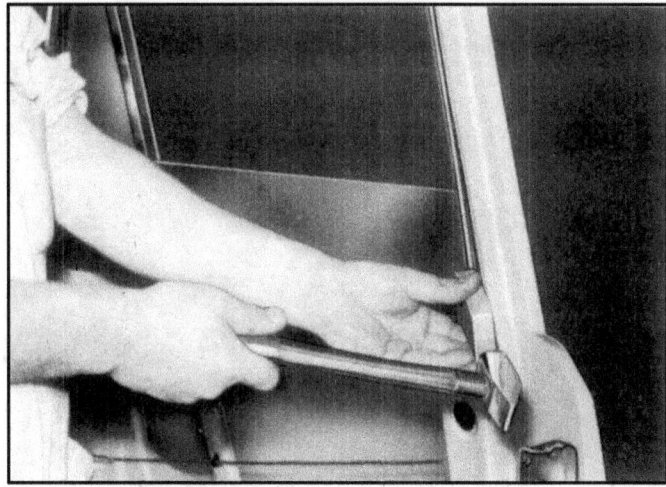

REMOVAL

- Start removing the upper frame of door glass by tapping lightly with a mallet and a wooden block at the sides as shown.

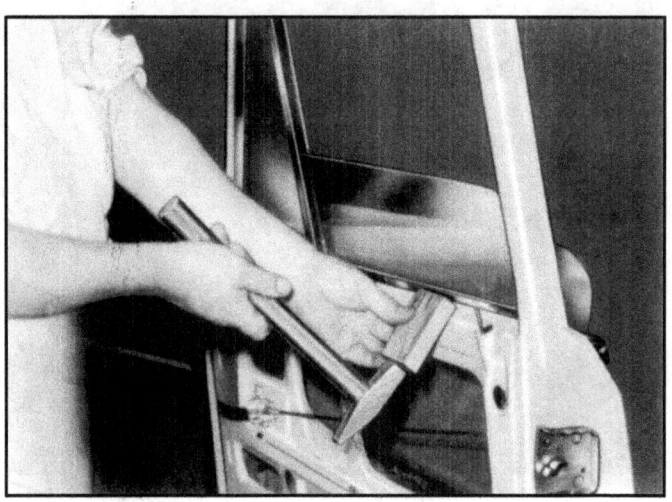

- Remove the lower frame in the same way as outlined above.

INSTALLATION

Slide into position the lower frame first, then the upper frame and push them in place by applying even pressure.

REMOVAL AND INSTALLATION

DOOR LOCKS

1750 Saloon is shown for example purpose.

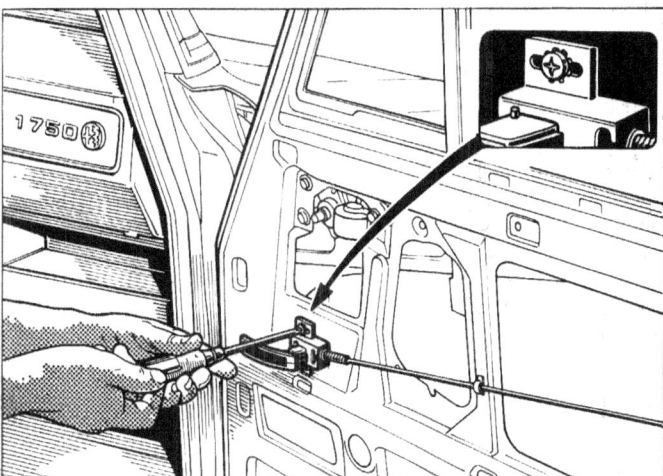

FRONT DOOR LOCKS

REMOVAL

- Remove the door trim panel and detach the plastic sheet. (see page 7).

- Loosen the two screws securing the support of remote control handle.

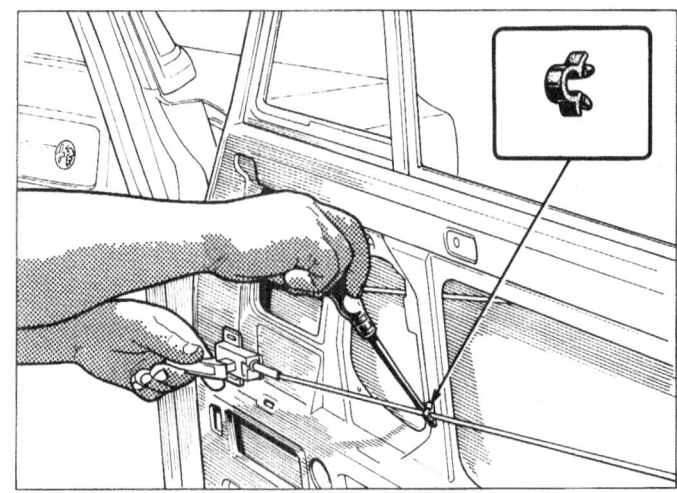

- Pry out of its seat the remote control rod guide.

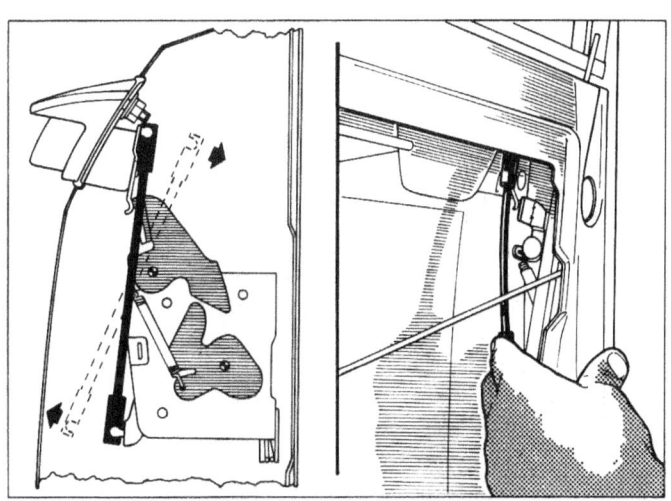

- Disconnect the outside handle-to-lock link.

REMOVAL AND INSTALLATION

DOOR LOCKS

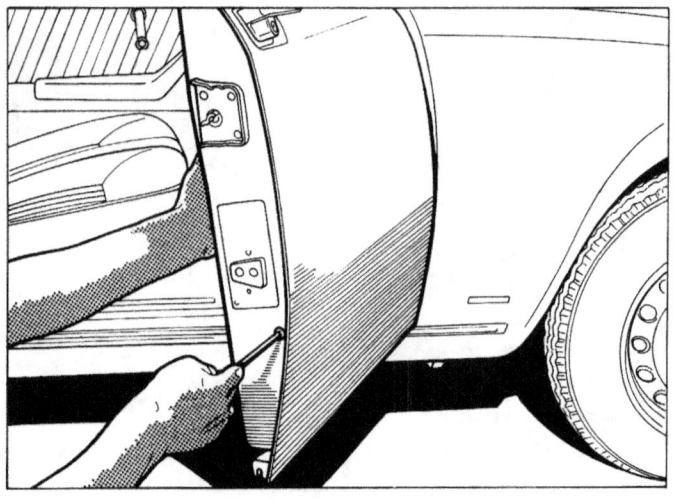

- Unscrew the attaching screws and remove the glass run channel.

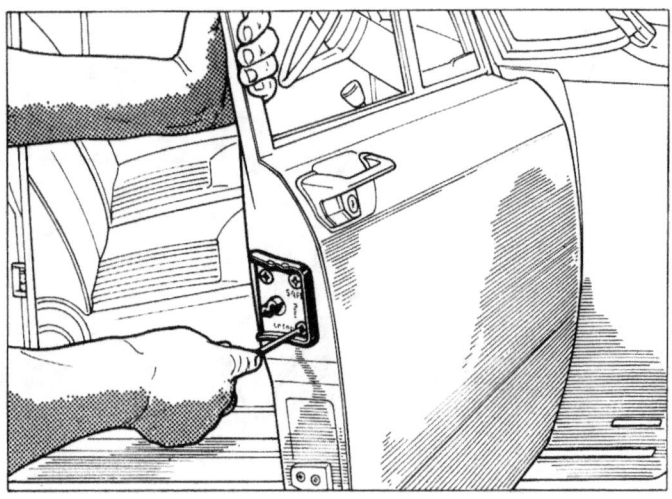

- Remove the screws securing the dovetail and take the dovetail away.

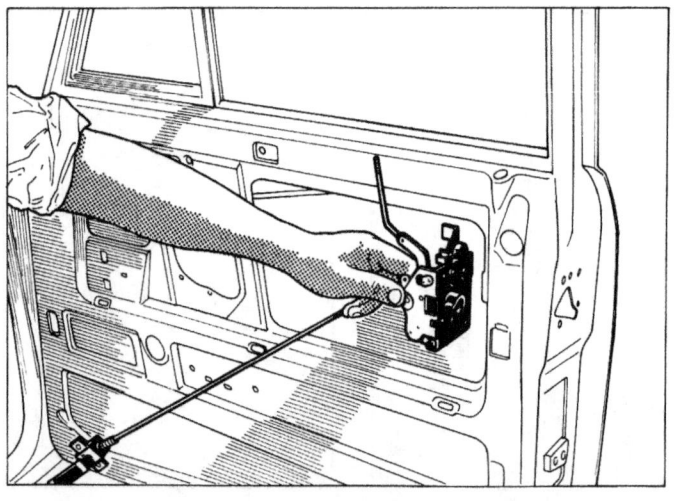

- Remove the remote control rod and the lock as a unit.

INSTALLATION

Reverse the removal procedure.

REMOVAL AND INSTALLATION

DOOR LOCKS

REAR DOOR LOCKS

REMOVAL

- Remove the door trim panel and detach the plastic sheet. (See page 7).
- Remove nut and washer securing the support of remote control rod and safety button.

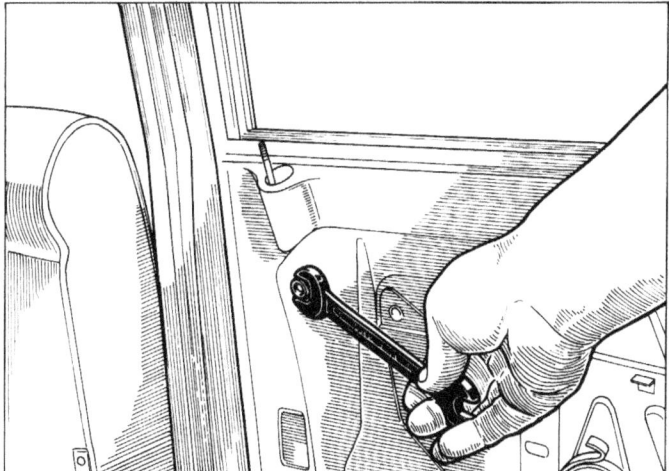

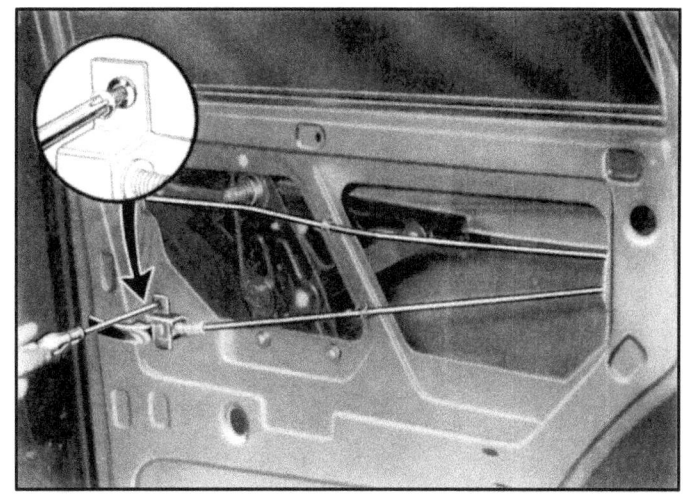

- Remove the screws securing the support of remote control handle.

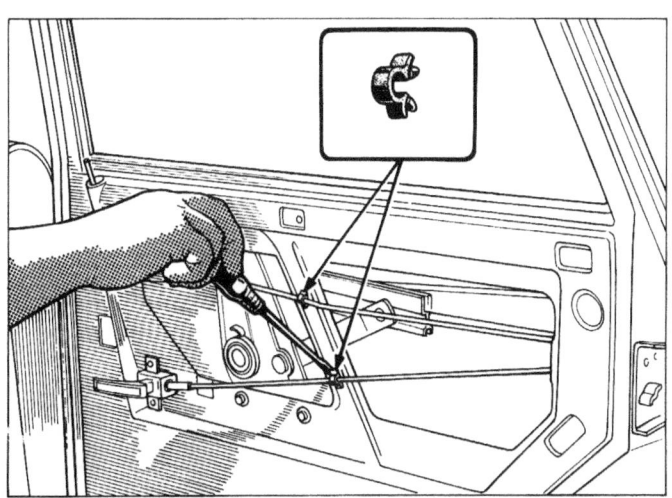

- Pry out of their seats the guides of remote control rods of door locks and safety catch.

REMOVAL AND INSTALLATION

DOOR LOCKS

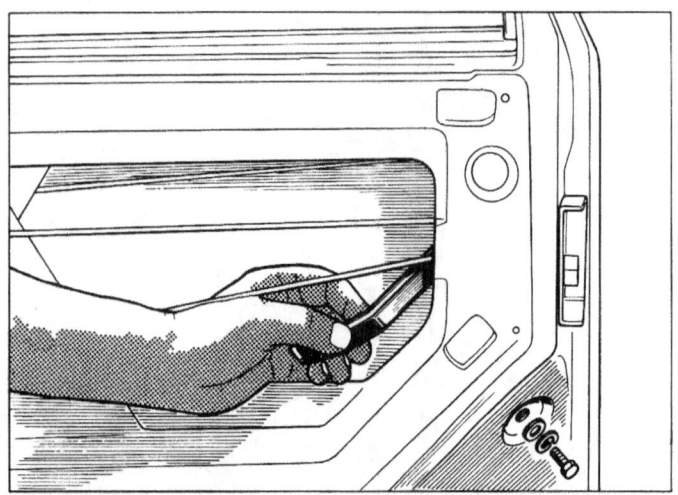

- Remove the securing screw and withdraw the rear glass channel.

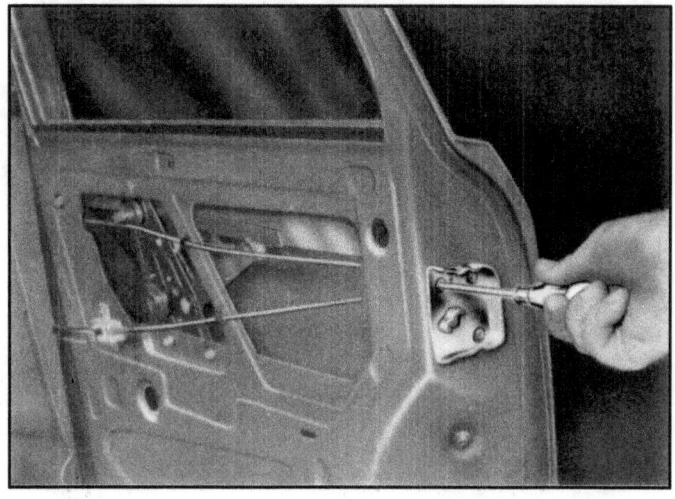

- Remove the screws securing the dovetail and take the dovetail away.

- Remove the lock, the remote control rod and the safety catch rod as a unit.

INSTALLATION

Reverse the order of removal.

NOTE — On Giulia Saloon and all Coupe models the safety catch is controlled by the inside door handle; therefore, it is necessary to disconnect the related control link.

REMOVAL AND INSTALLATION

WINDOW REGULATORS

> The same procedure applies to all models in this range.
> 1750 Saloon is shown for example purpose.

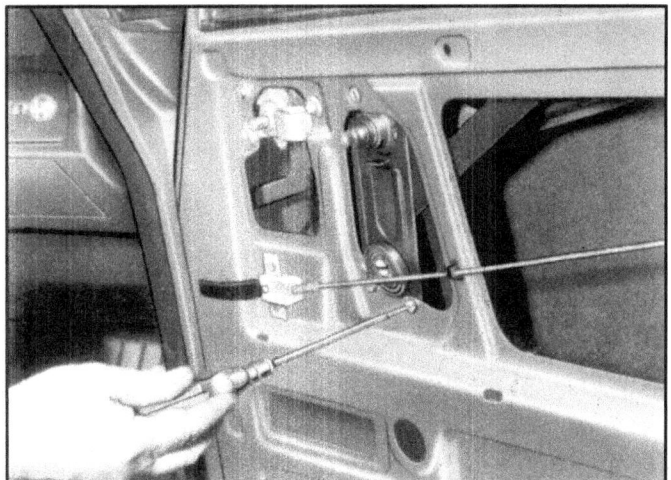

REMOVAL

- Remove the door trim panel and detach the plastic sheet. (See page 7).

- Remove the screws securing the window regulator.

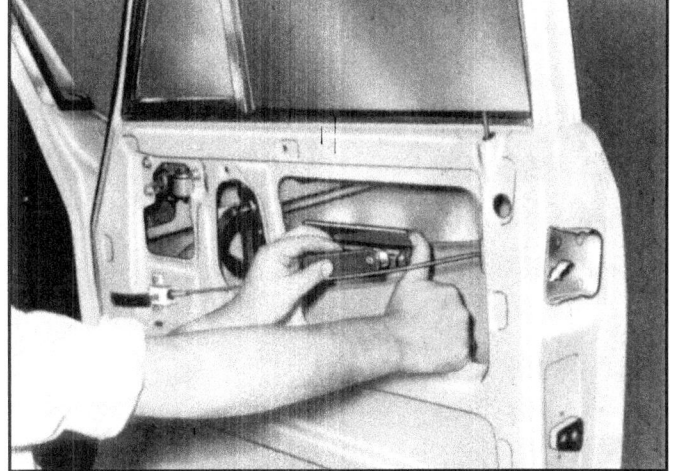

- With the handle, wind the regulator so that the end of the lever is positioned as shown in the glass support slot (the regulators at the rear have two levers).

- Disconnect the end of the lever from the glass support as shown (at the rear both levers should be disconnected).

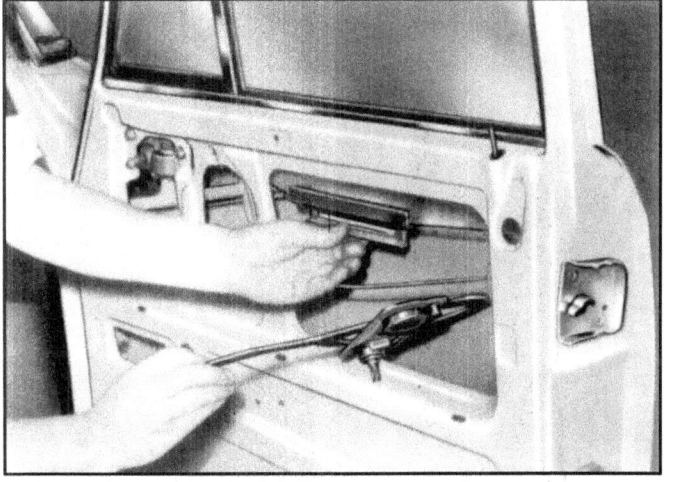

- Push the glass upward.
- Take the window regulator out of the door frame.

INSTALLATION

Reverse the order of removal.

REMOVAL AND INSTALLATION

DOOR GLASSES

> The same procedure applies to all models in this range.
> Giulia and 1750 Saloon are shown for example purpose.

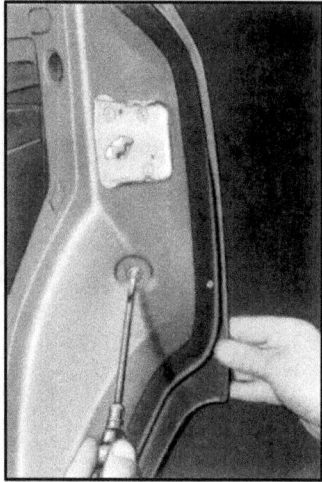

The operations are the same for the glasses of front and rear doors.

REMOVAL

- Remove the door glass frames. (See page 8).
- Remove the door trim panel and detach the plastic sheet. (See page 7).
- Remove the window regulator. (See page 13).
- Remove the screws securing:
  - the front glass channel on front doors;
  - the rear glass channel on rear doors.

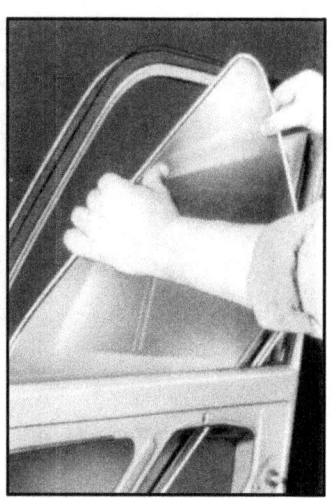

- Tilt the glass by 90 degrees so that the bottom edge is brought parallel with the rear post of door frame (front door glass) and with the front of door frame (rear door glass).

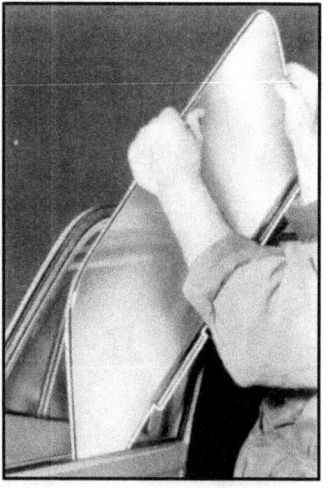

- Tip the glass inward and lift it out carefully.

INSTALLATION

Proceed in reverse order of removal.

REMOVAL AND INSTALLATION

FRONT VENT WINDOWS

1750 Saloon is shown for example purpose.

REMOVAL

- Remove the door trim panel and detach the plastic sheet. (See page 7).

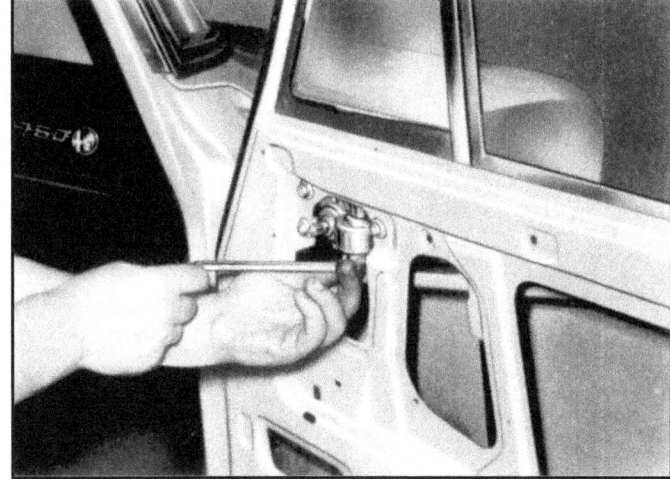

- With a Phillips screwdriver remove the vent window securing screw.

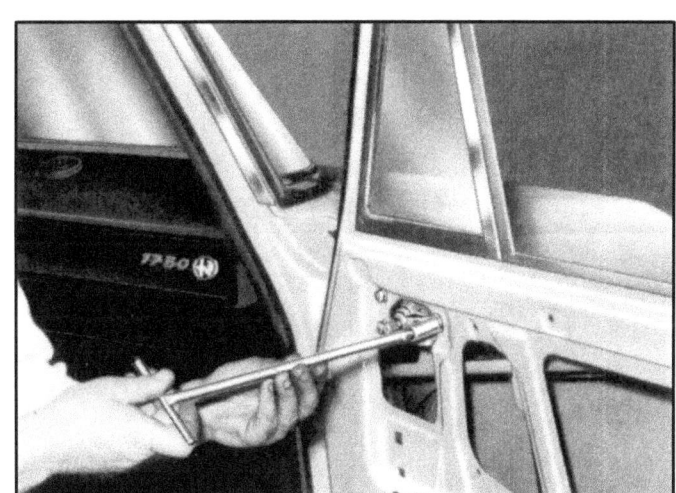

- With a socket wrench remove the screws securing the vent window control mechanism.

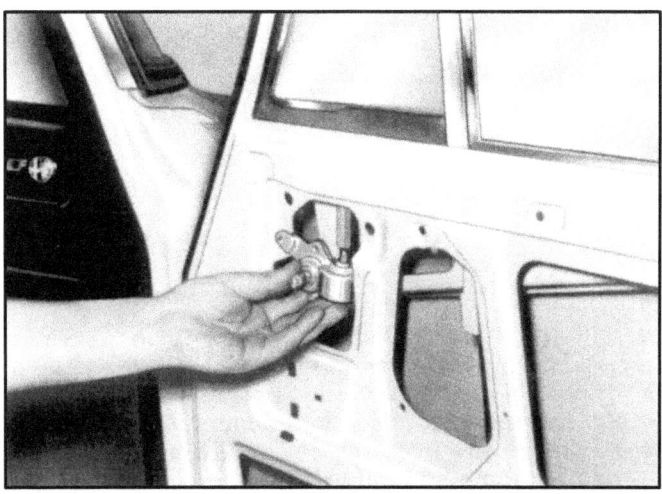

- Remove the vent window control mechanism.

REMOVAL AND INSTALLATION

FRONT VENT WINDOWS

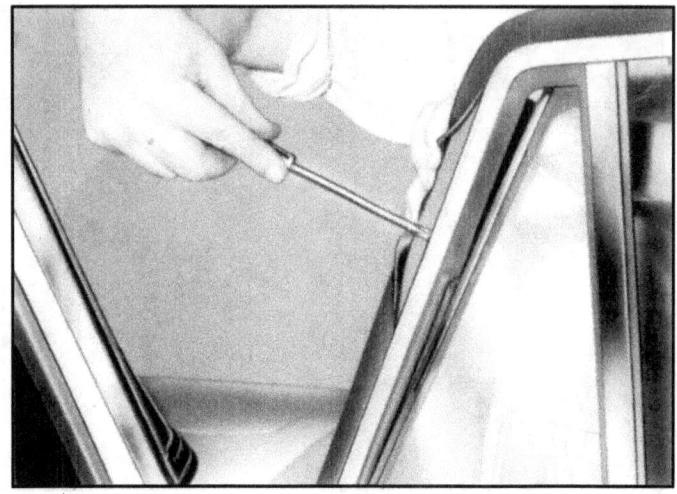

- Separate the weatherstrip from the frame and remove the screws securing the vent window pivot bracket.

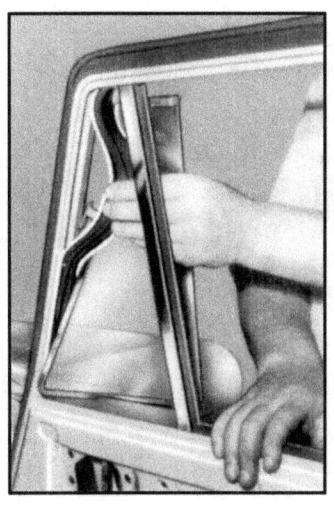
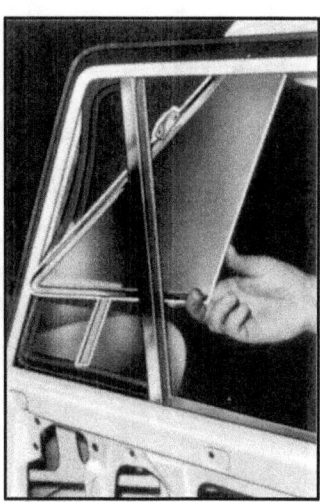

- Tilt the vent window so that it can be lifted out of the opening.

INSTALLATION

Reverse the removal procedure.

NOTE — On Giulia 1300-1300TI-1600S Saloon models and GTA Coupe models, in the event the vent window catch peg has come off the glass, stick it again in place as follows:
- Thoroughly clean the affected surfaces with alcohol.
- Apply a thin coat of cement to both surfaces.
- Secure the peg to the glass with a clamp and keep it so clamped until the cement is dried (about 24 hours at room temperature).

REMOVAL AND INSTALLATION

DOOR WEATHERSTRIPS

> The same procedure applies to all Saloon models.
> Giulia Saloon is shown for example purpose.

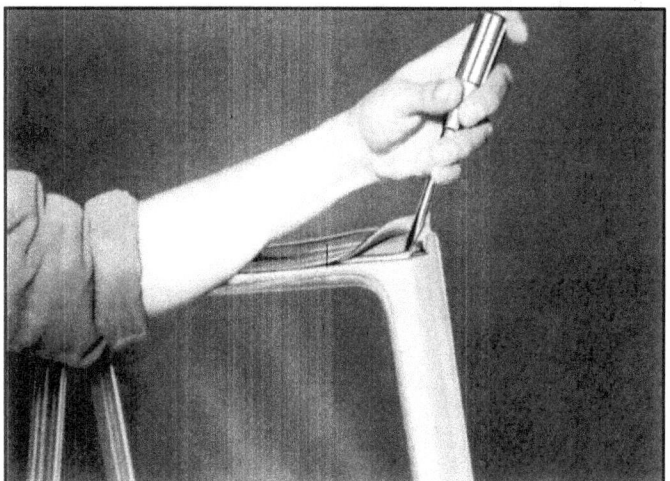

REMOVAL

- At the door top, lift off the edge of metal strip retaining the weatherstrip.

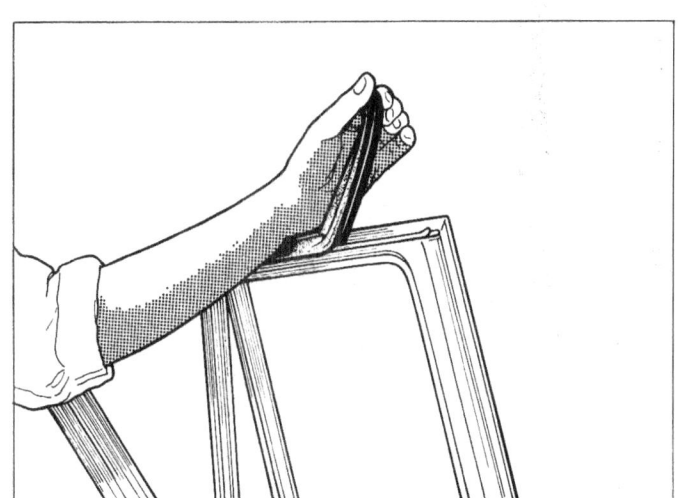

- Pull the weatherstrip away from the metal strip.

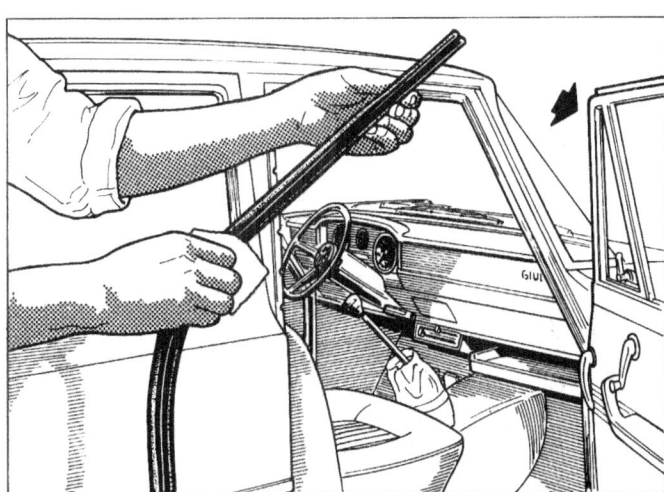

INSTALLATION

- Cover the weatherstrip with petroleum jelly or similar.

REMOVAL AND INSTALLATION

DOOR WEATHERSTRIPS

- Place the weatherstrip onto the metal strip:
  — on front doors start from the front post;
  — on rear doors start from the rear post.

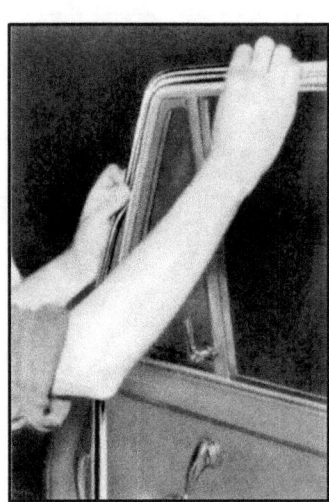
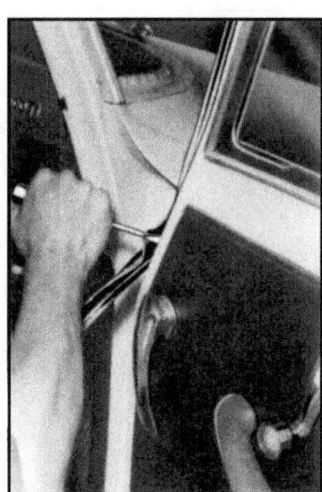

- Slide the weatherstrip along the metal strip.
- Use a screwdriver or a similar tool as an aid.
- Bend down the edge of weatherstrip retainer previously lifted.

REMOVAL AND INSTALLATION

FRONT SEATS

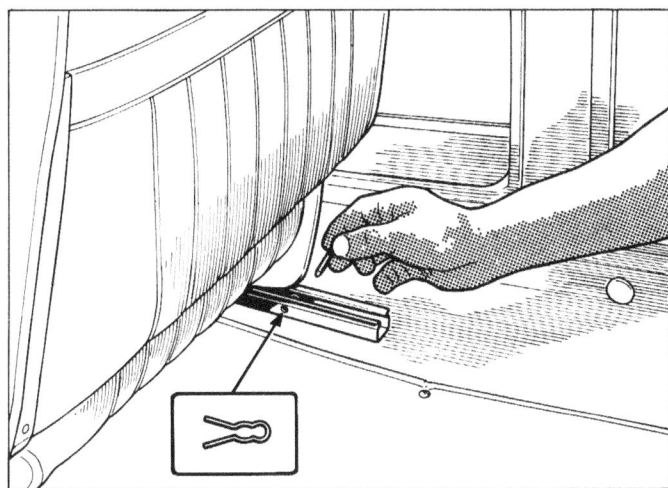

1750 Saloon is shown for example purpose.

REMOVAL

- Remove the clip and withdraw the limit stop from the slide.

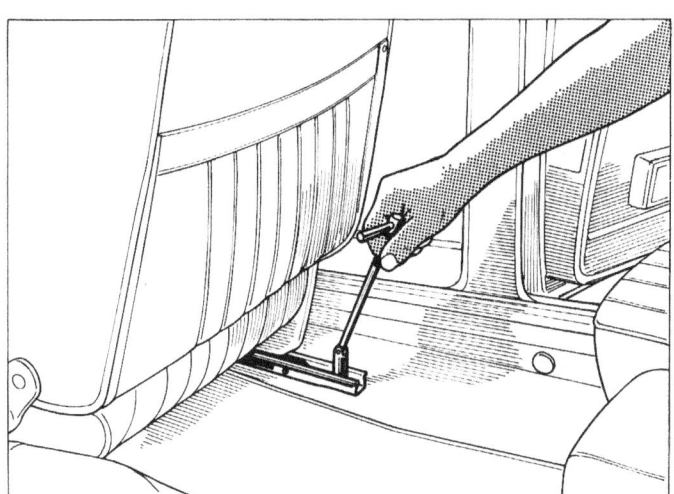

- Remove the front and rear slide attaching screws.

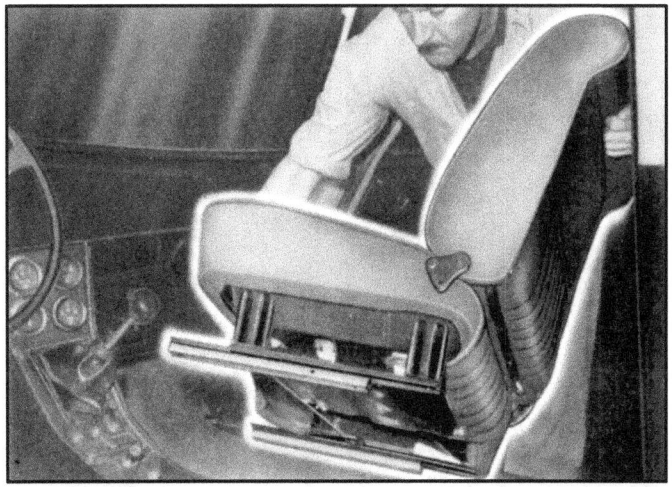

- Remove the seat.

INSTALLATION

Reverse the order of removal.

REMOVAL AND INSTALLATION

FACIA BOARD

1750 Saloon is shown for example purpose.

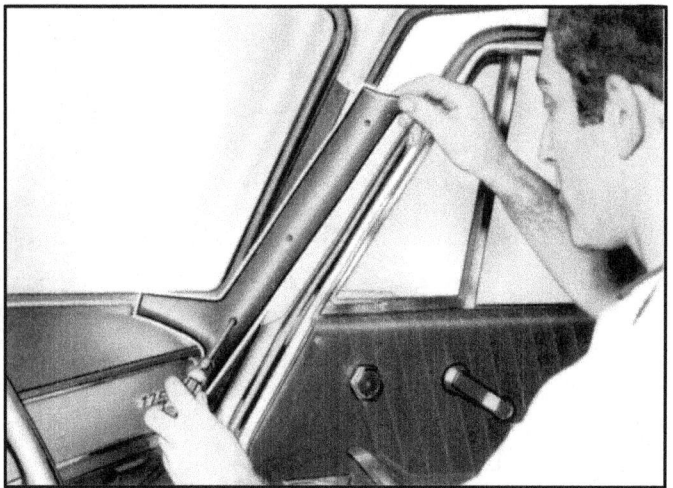

REMOVAL

CAUTION — Before commencing removal, disconnect battery terminals.

- Remove the trim panels from windscreen pillars.

- Remove the air outlets by lifting them off so as to separate them from the rubber ducts underneath.

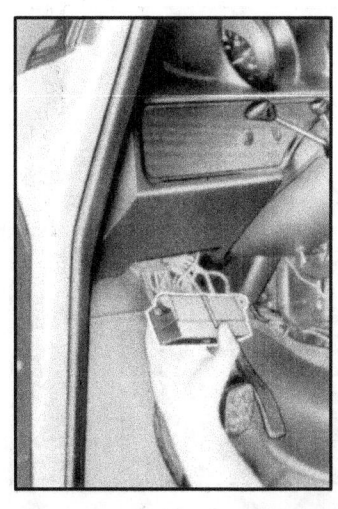

- Unscrew the attaching nuts:
  — at the right side gain access from the glove box;
  — at the left side gain access by detaching the fusebox.

REMOVAL AND INSTALLATION

FACIA BOARD

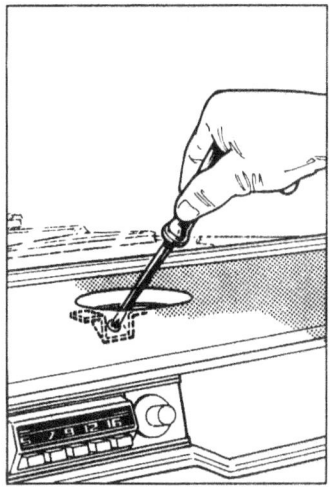 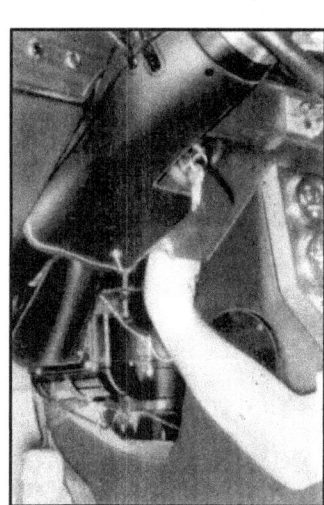

- Remove the centre attaching screws.
- From the underside, unscrew the two wingnuts securing the panel to the console.

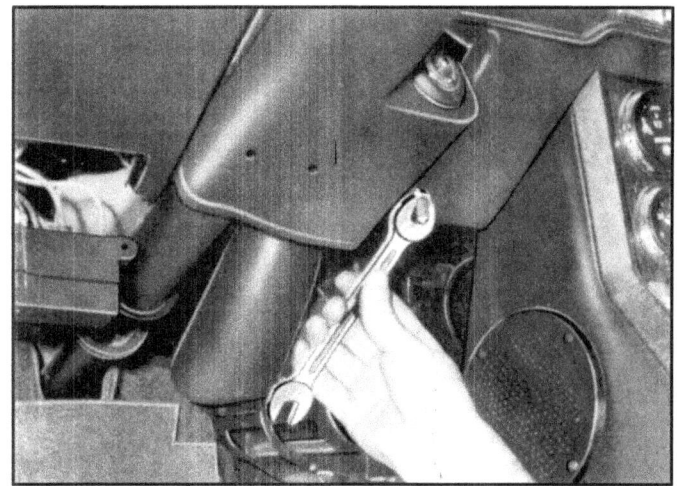

- Unscrew the ringnut securing the tripometer reset.

- Take out the instruments, disconnect wires and lamp holders.

REMOVAL AND INSTALLATION

FACIA BOARD

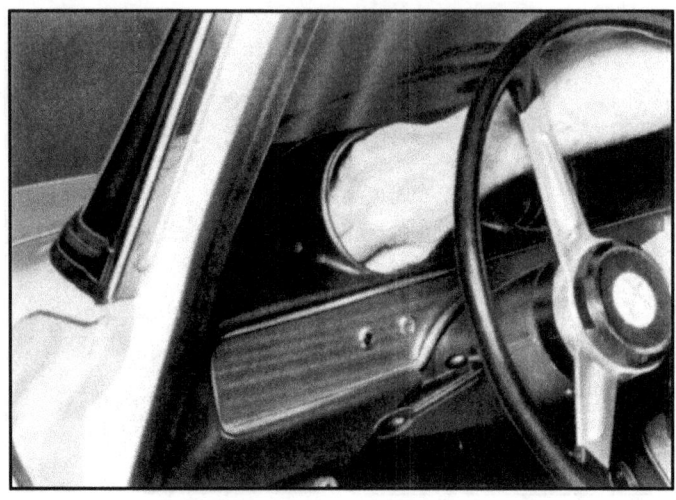

- From the inside, disconnect wires of warning lights and direction indicators.

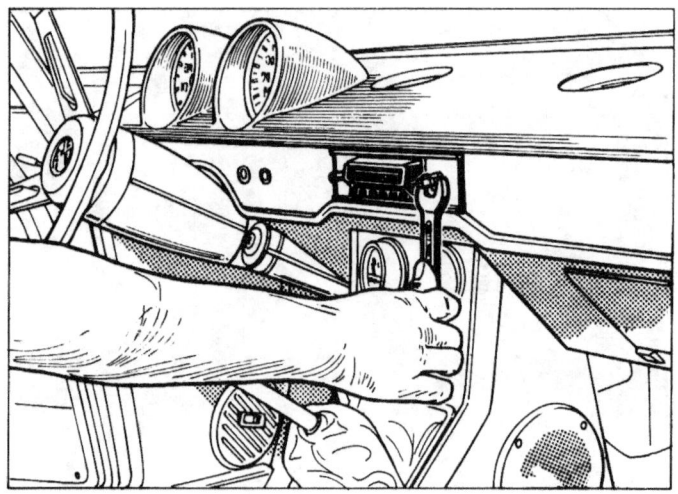

- Free the radio (if so equipped) from the facia board.

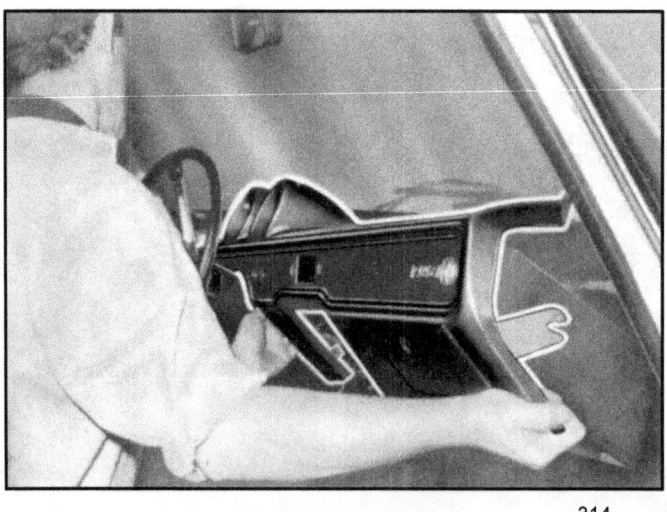

- Remove board.

REMOVAL AND INSTALLATION

FACIA BOARD

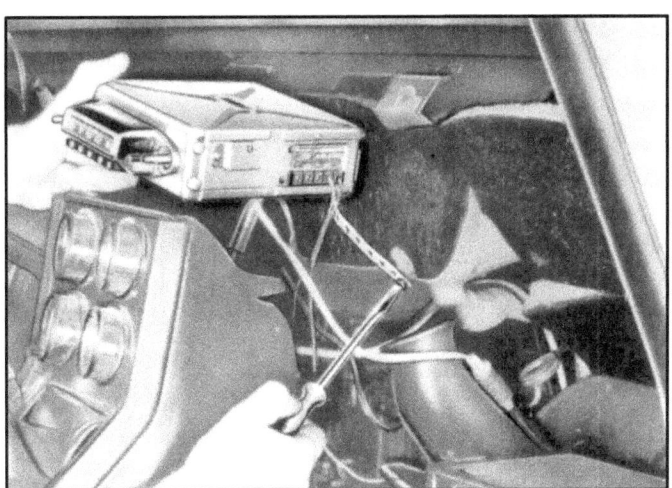

- Disconnect wires and remove the radio.

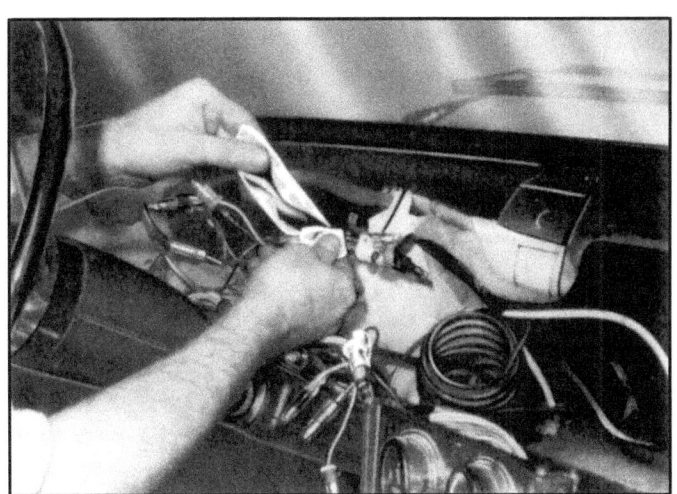

- In order to perform the subsequent operations easily, it is advisable to tie the wires together in a bundle.

INSTALLATION

Reverse the removal procedure.

REMOVAL AND INSTALLATION

CONSOLE

> 1750 Saloon is shown for example purpose.

NOTE — When removing the console, it is unnecessary to remove the facia board too; only carry out the following:

— unscrew the wingnuts securing console to facia board (see upper right-hand image page 21).

— slacken the facia board attaching nuts at the sides (see lower images page 20).

— raise the facia board just enough to allow to remove the console.

REMOVAL

- Remove front seats (see page 19).
- Disconnect the wiring junction gaining access from behind the console (unless the facia board has not been previously removed).

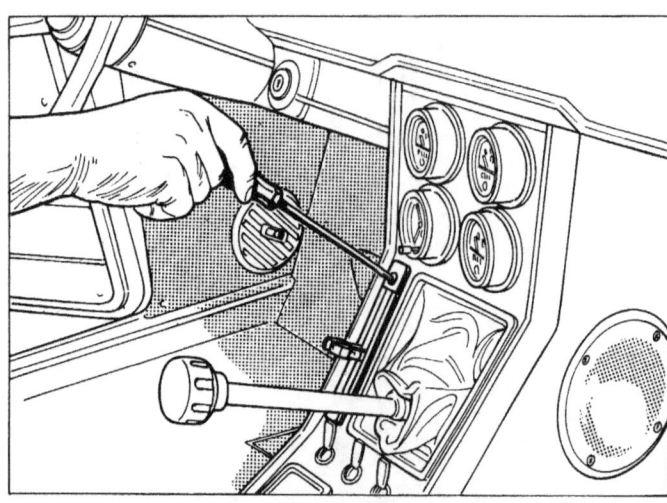

- Remove the escutcheon from heater control panel.

REMOVAL AND INSTALLATION

CONSOLE

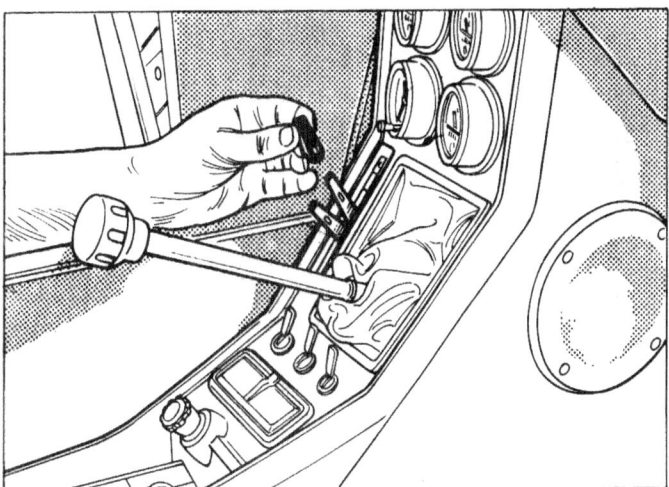

- Remove knobs from heater control levers.

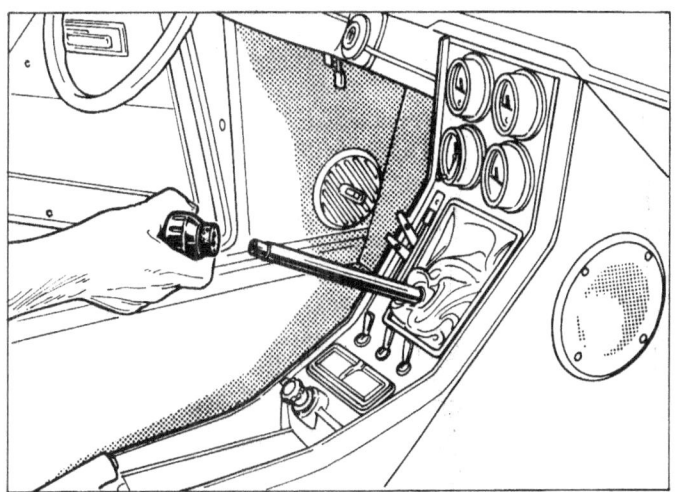

- Remove gear lever knob.

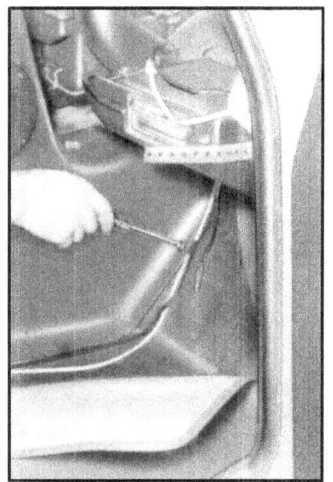
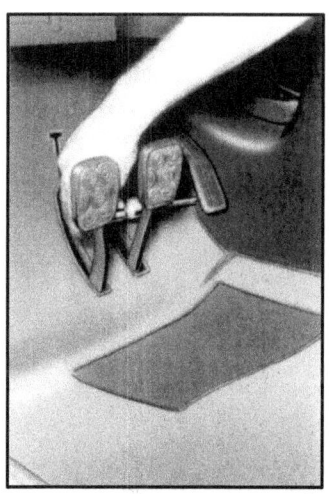

- Remove carpets and slacken off console side attaching screws.

REMOVAL AND INSTALLATION

CONSOLE

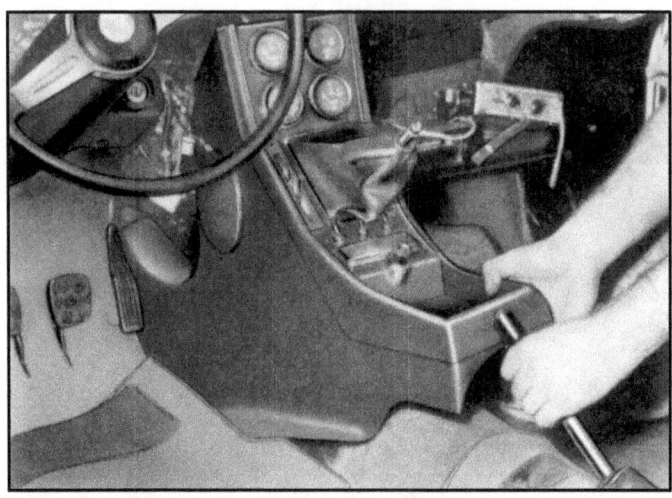

- Pull up handbrake lever and raise the console as shown.

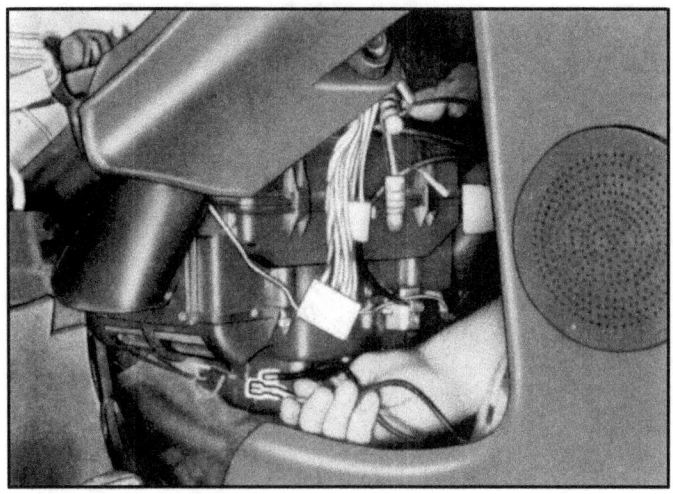

- Disconnect heater junction to allow the console to be removed.

INSTALLATION

Reverse the removal procedure.

REMOVAL AND INSTALLATION

ROOF TRIMMING

> The same procedure applies to all Saloon and Coupe models.
> Giulia and 1750 Saloon are shown for example purpose.

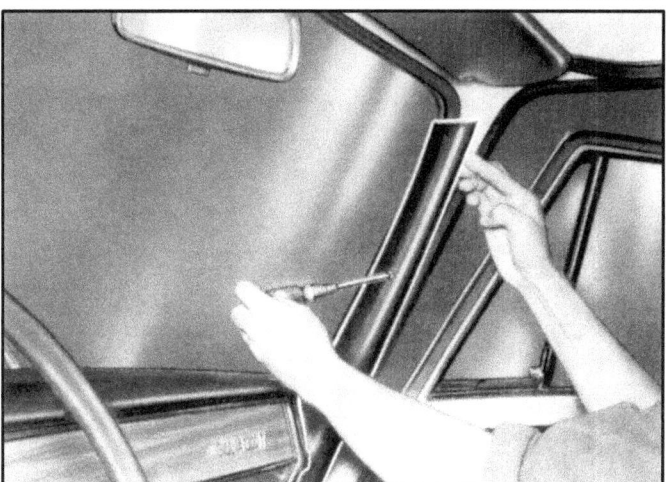

REMOVAL

- Remove trim panels from windscreen pillars.

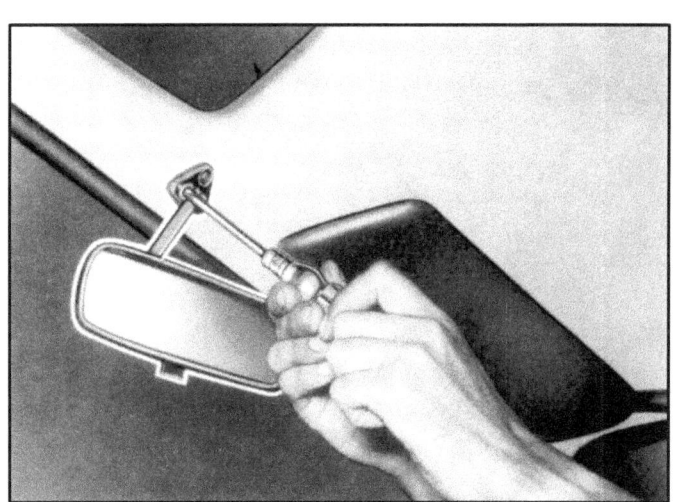

- Remove mirror and sun visors.

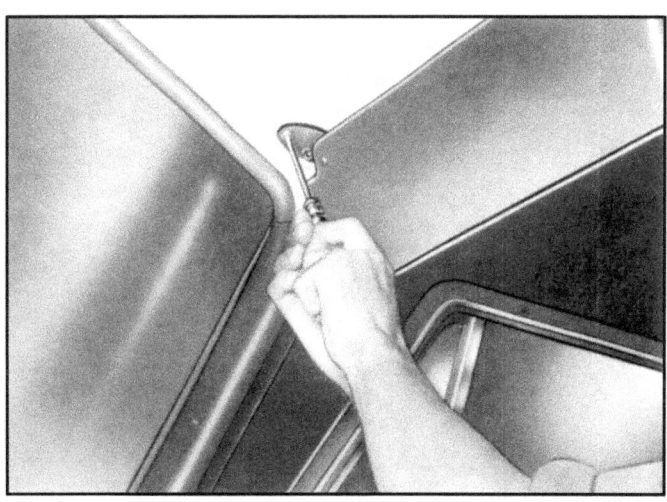

REMOVAL AND INSTALLATION

ROOF TRIMMING

- Remove windscreen and rear window. (see page 1).
- Carefully remove the sealing compound with a suitable spatula (wooden or plastic) in order not to damage the paint layers; then, clean thoroughly with a suitable solvent.

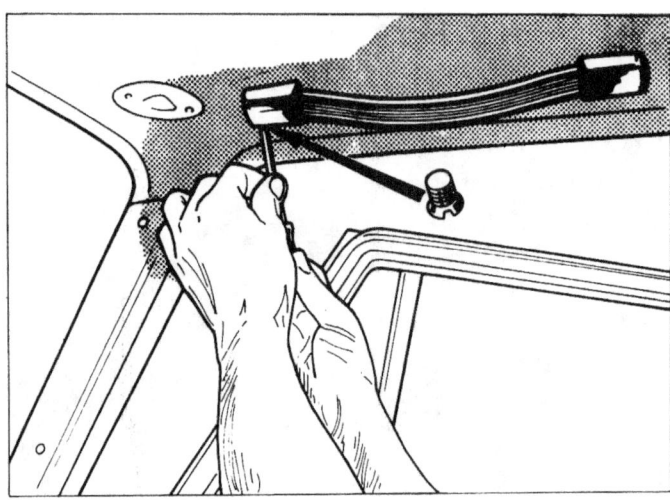

- Loosen the setscrews and remove the finishers over the ends of grab handle at passenger's side, then remove the grab handle.

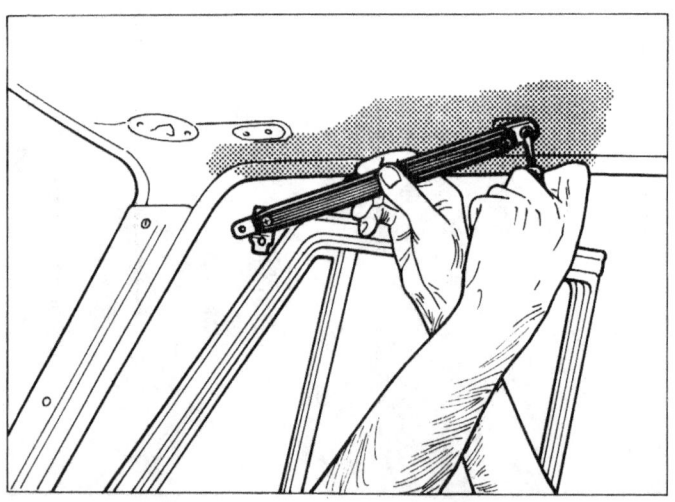

REMOVAL AND INSTALLATION

ROOF TRIMMING

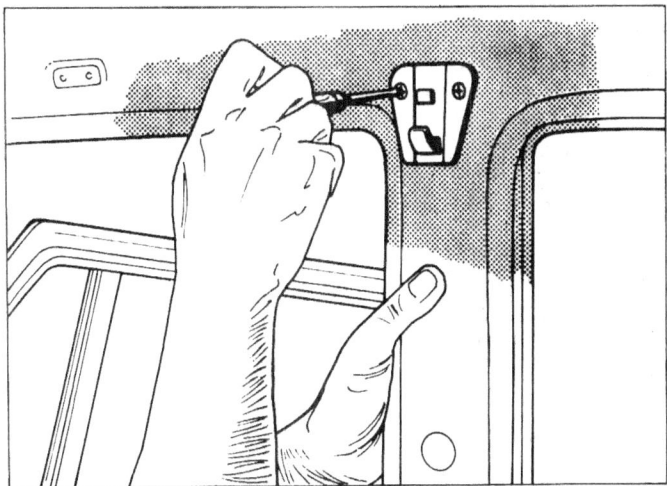

- Remove clothes-pegs.

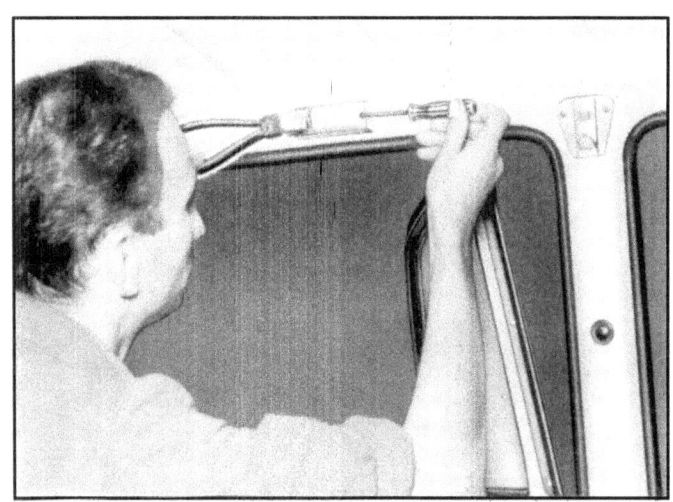

- Remove the rear handle and light units.

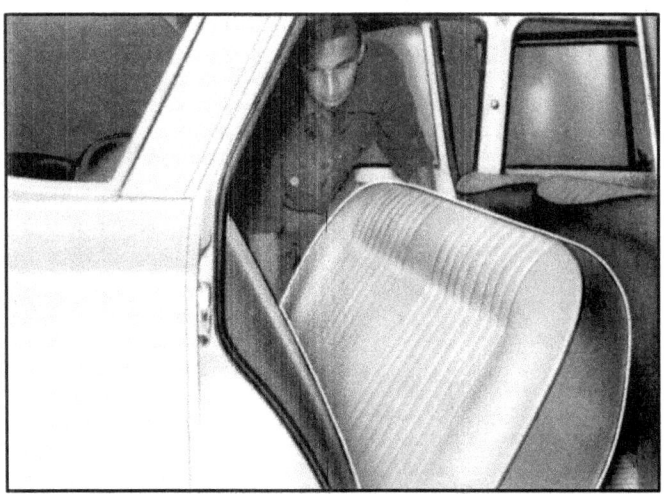

- Remove the rear seat cushion.

REMOVAL AND INSTALLATION

ROOF TRIMMING

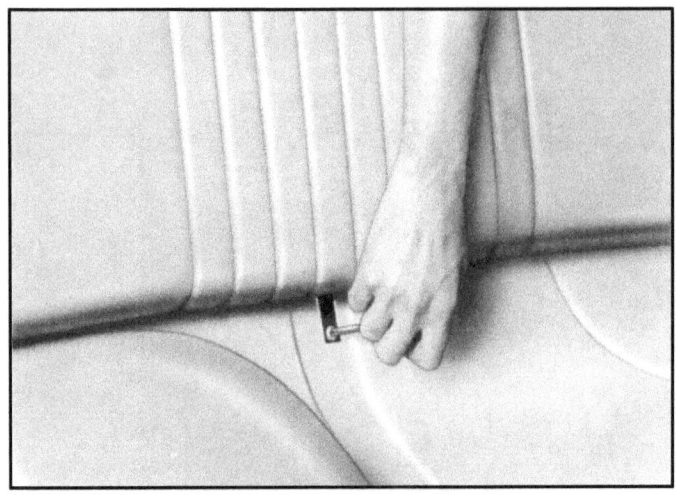

- Remove the attaching screws at the bottom and take away the squab.

- Detach the front edge of parcel shelf trim.

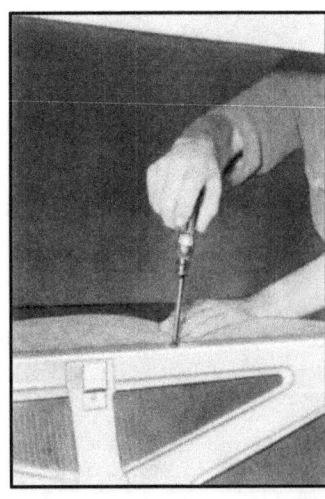

- Slacken off the attaching screws and remove rear parcel shelf.

REMOVAL AND INSTALLATION

ROOF TRIMMING

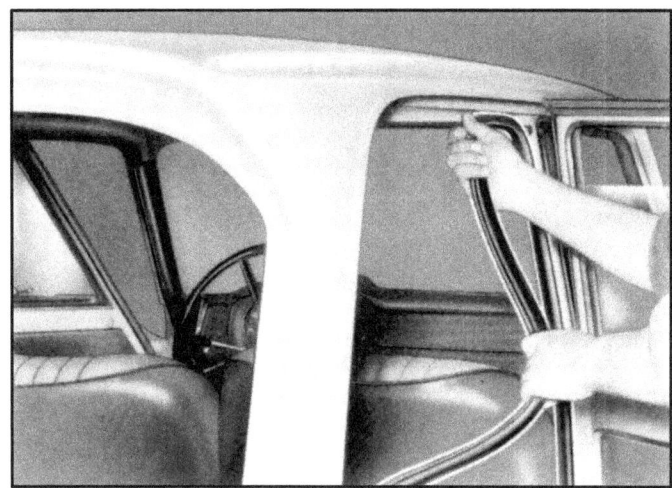

- Disengage door opening weatherstrips from the clips.

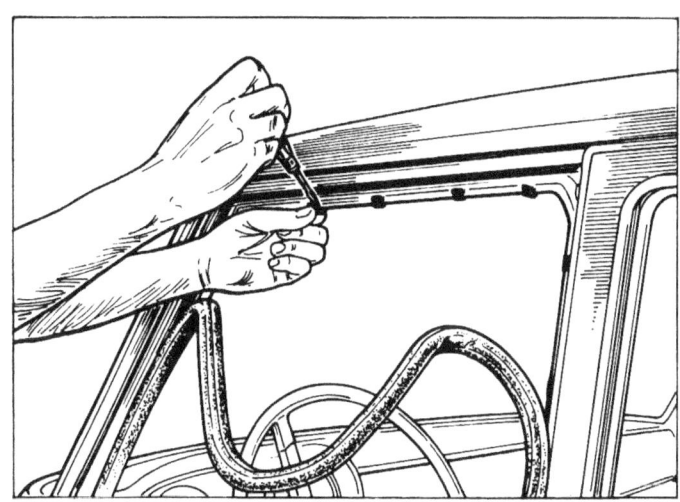

- Remove the clips along the edge affecting roof trim.

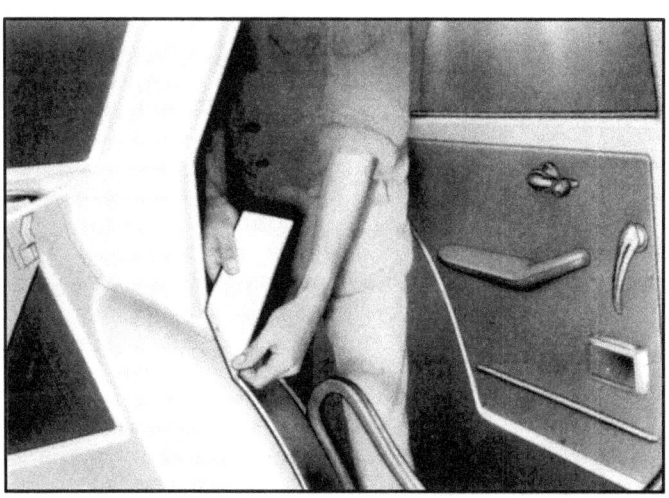

- Detach wheelarch edge trim.

REMOVAL AND INSTALLATION

ROOF TRIMMING

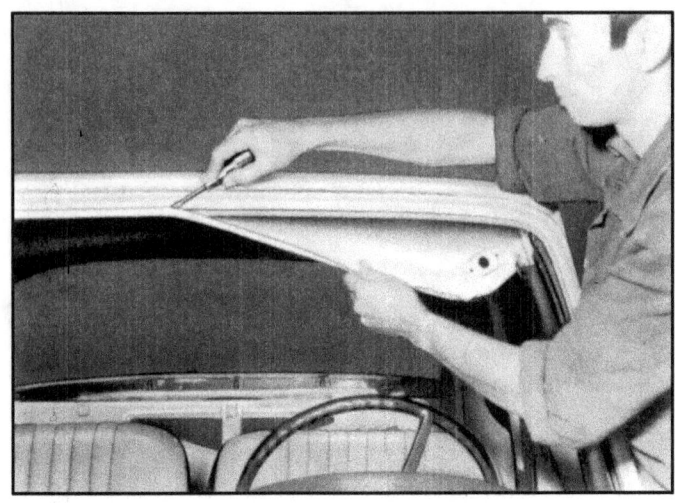

- Detach roof trim starting from the front header and proceeding toward the rear window.

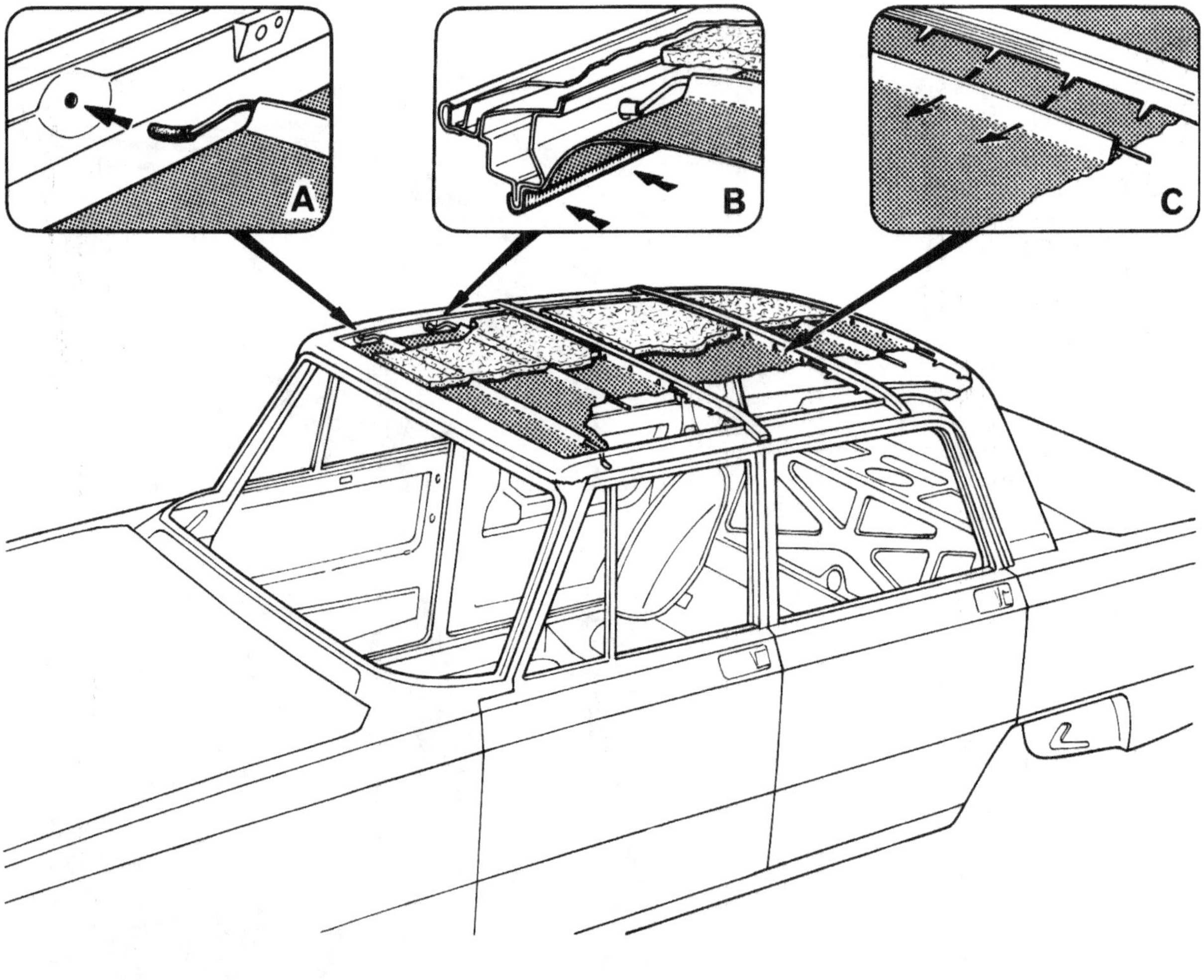

A – Mounting holes for roof trim stiffening bows.
B – Areas in which roof trim is stuck to roof panel.
C – Hooks for fastening trim bows to roof ribs.

REMOVAL AND INSTALLATION

ROOF TRIMMING

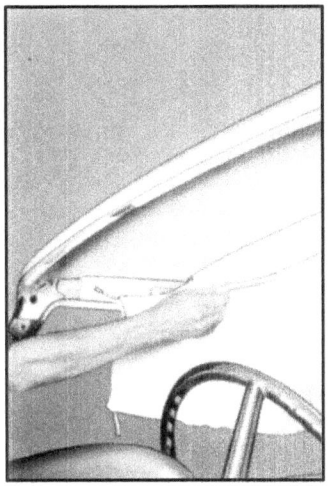 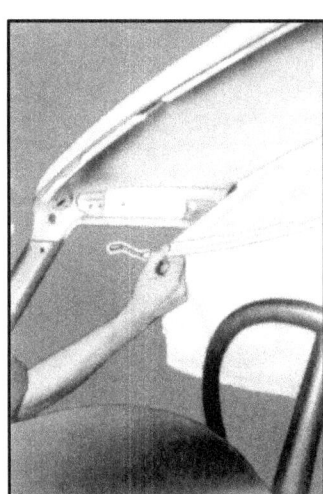

- Take front stiffening bow out of its mounting holes (see detailed image 'A' on page 32), then remove next bow, too.

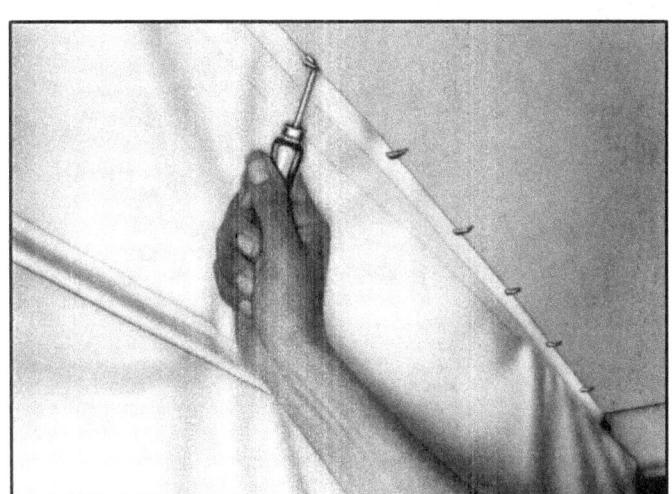

- Use special tool P.N. A.9.0103 to straighten the bow fastening hooks on first roof rib so that the bow can be removed (see detailed image 'C' page 32), then, repeat the procedure for the second rib.

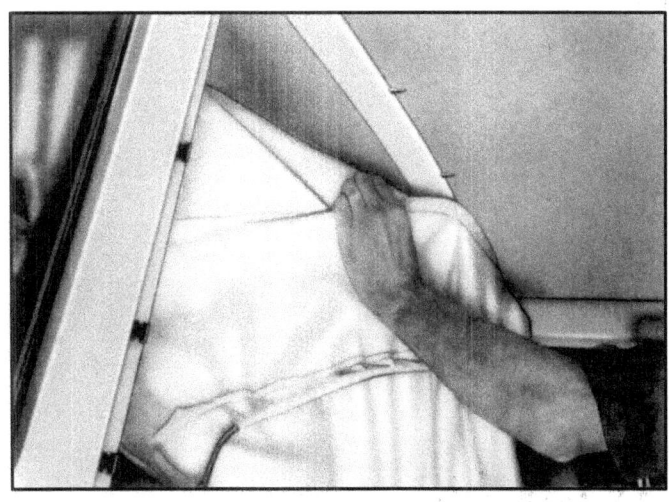

34
REMOVAL AND INSTALLATION

ROOF TRIMMING

- Take out of mounting holes the rim bow located just after the second rib.
- Straighten hooks and remove the rear bow from the rib.

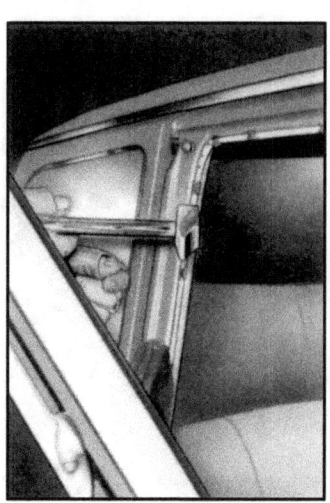
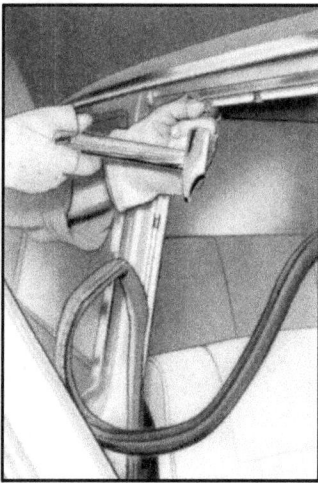

INSTALLATION

Reverse removal procedure.

WARNING — To ensure proper weatherstrip fitting, carefully reset the clips, replacing those damaged or missing with new ones.

REMOVAL AND INSTALLATION

INSULATION PADDING

Soundproofing is obtained by lining the body as shown below with insulation pads of the following types:

— "Sound deadening" panels
Consisting of bituminized material applied at 120 degrees centigrade to the sheet metal so as to ensure perfect adhesion.

— "Sound obsorbing" panels
Made up with layers of natural and artificial fibers, they are bonded with suitable resins and have high porosity and light weight characteristics; together with bituminized panels they are glued to the body inside with neoprene cements of standard type commonly available on the market.

On repairing, renew all soundproofing pads not in good conditions so that the insulation properties of car are not impaired.

The illustration below shows how insulation pads are applied to the 1750 Saloon.

 Sound absorbing panels

 Sound deadening panels

CHECKING AND ADJUSTING

DOOR LOCKS

> The same procedure applies to all Saloon and Coupe models.
> 1750 Saloon is shown for example purpose.

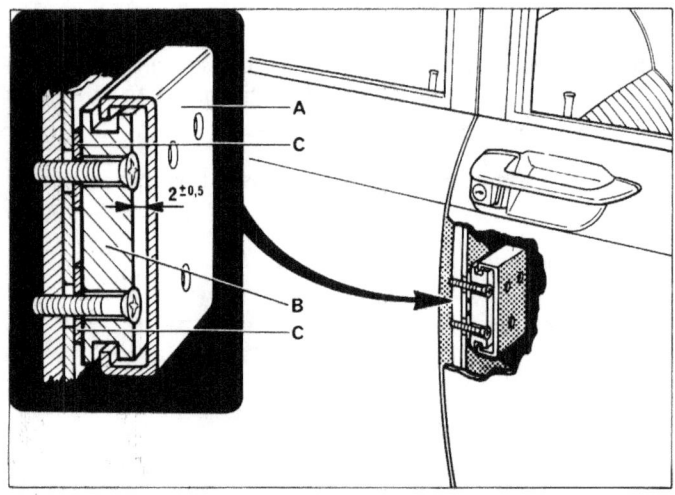

To remedy possible noise from door locks, it is necessary:

- To check that there is a clearance of 1.5 mm minimum and 2.5 mm maximum between the dovetail and striker by inserting a plastigage or similar between them.
If clearance is not as specified, slacken the striker screws and add or remove shims (0.5, 1, 2 mm), taking care to keep the striker parallel with the dovetail.

A — Dovetail
B — Striker
C — Spacer

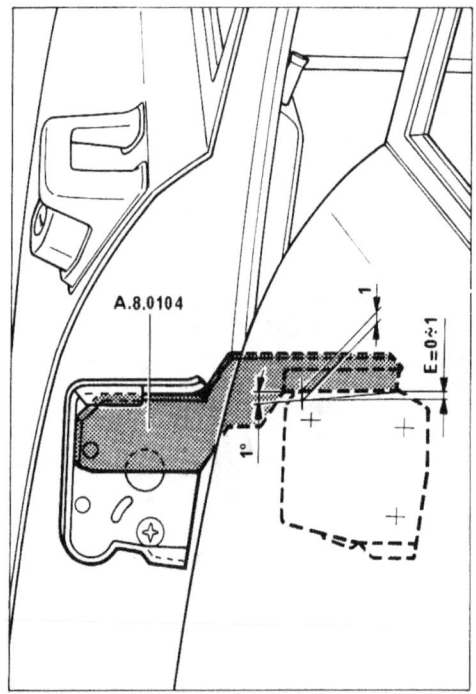

- To check for proper alignment of striker, proceed as follows:

KEIPER MAKE LOCKS

— Place the template, special tool P.N. A.8.0104, into the dovetail and make sure it fits properly against the dovetail top edge. The proper ajustment of striker is when engagement E with dovetail falls within 0 and a maximum interference fit of 1 mm and downward tilt does not exceed 1 degree. Such a condition is fulfilled when 1 mm gap exists between the template and the leading edge of striker top.

CHECKING AND ADJUSTING

DOOR LOCKS

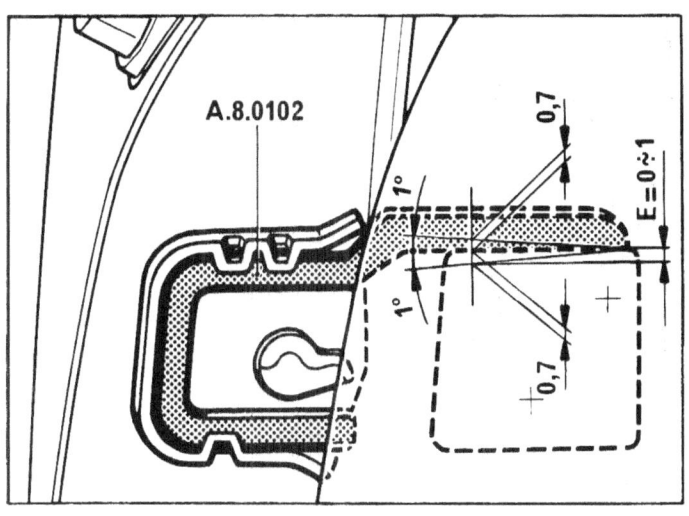

SAFE MAKE LOCKS

- Place the template, special tool P.N. A.8.0102, into the dovetail. The striker engagement E with dovetail should fall within O and a maximum interference fit of 1 mm; and should have a tilt of no more that 1 degree corresponding to a 0.7 mm gap.

NOTE: – on models with guide block, the lock striker should fit perfectly the dovetail or with an interference E from 0.5 to 1.5 mm maximum.

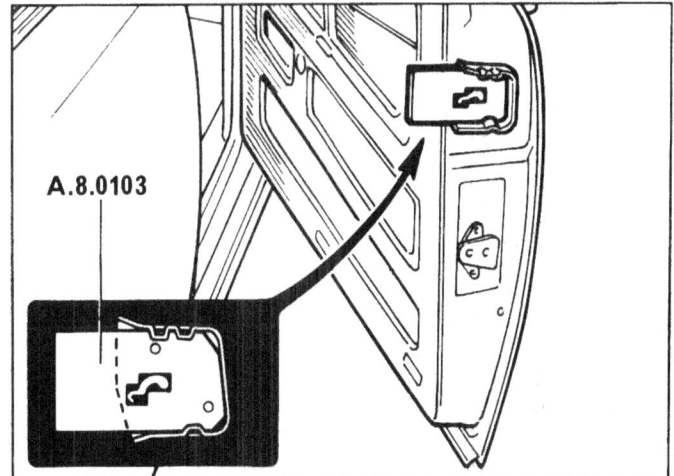

- Check the location of the catch with the aid of the template, special tool P.N. A.8.0103 and, in the event the catch has an interference fit, make the required adjustment as follows:

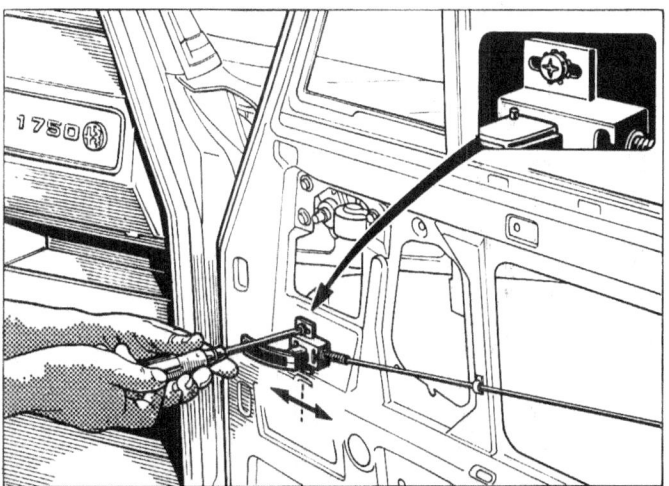

- Slacken the screws securing the bracket of inside door handle.
- Adjust the position of the bracket until no more interference exists in the fit as mentioned above.

38
CHECKING AND ADJUSTING

DOOR LOCKS

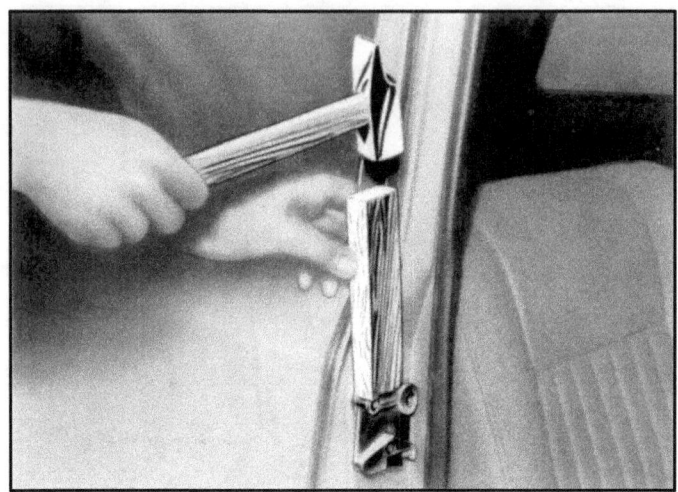

- For adjusting the position of the striker use a wooden block as shown.

- On completion of the above outlined procedure, lock striker screws to 130 Kgcm ± 5% with a torque wrench whose rating should be 80 to 320 Kgcm.

CAUTION — If the locks are to be securely fixed into alignment, their attaching screws must be tightened with a torque wrench, never with a screwdriver.

CHECKING AND ADJUSTING

ENGINE HOOD

1750 Saloon is shown for example purpose.

Should any interference exist between the leading edge of engine hood and the front panel top, proceed as follows:

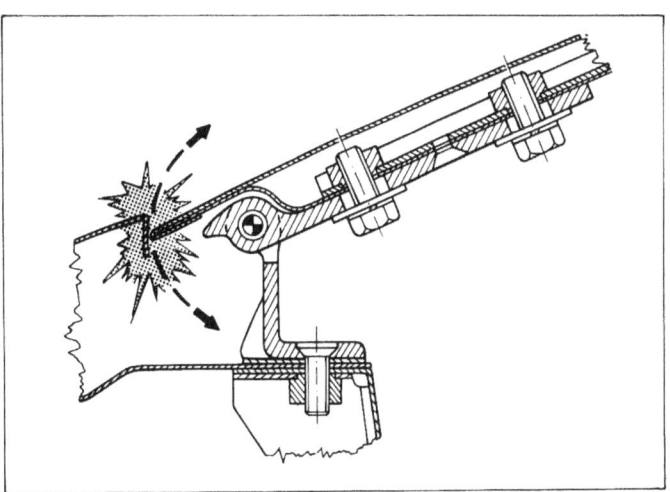

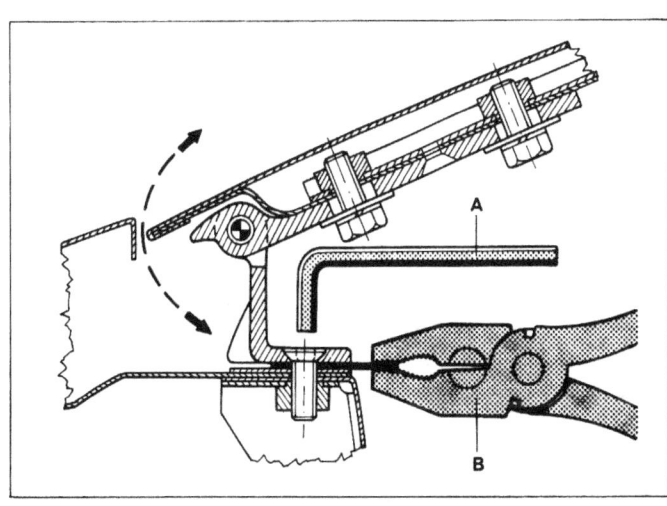

- With an Allen wrench A, loosen the screws attaching hinge to body (at the side affected by interference troubles).
- With pliers B, insert shims between hinge and body until hood rotates freely, then retighten the hinge attaching screws.

CHECKING AND ADJUSTING

ENGINE HOOD

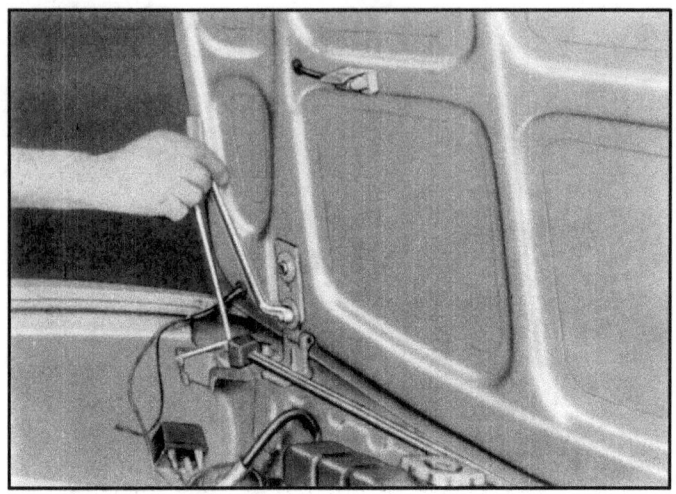

In the event engine hood is misaligned laterally or longitudinally:

- Slacken the two screws attaching hinge to hood panel.

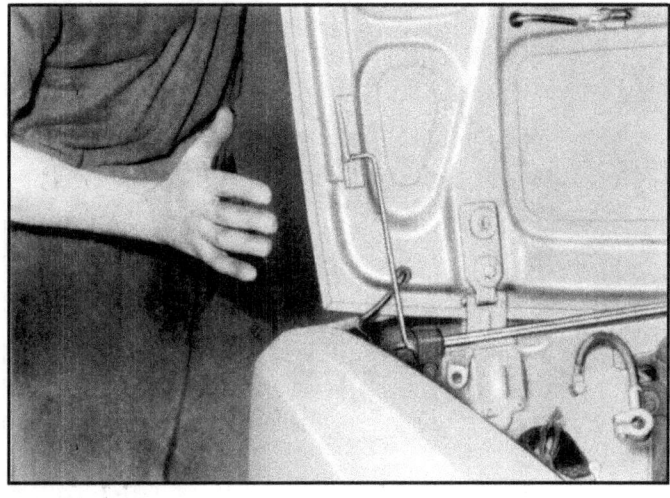

- Tapping by hand, move the hood as required.
- Check for proper alignment then retighten the screws.

If a misalignment of the hood rear edge is experienced as a consequence of the above operations:

- Remove windscreen wiper arms.
- Slacken one or both the ringnuts securing the scuttle top panel.

CHECKING AND ADJUSTING

ENGINE HOOD

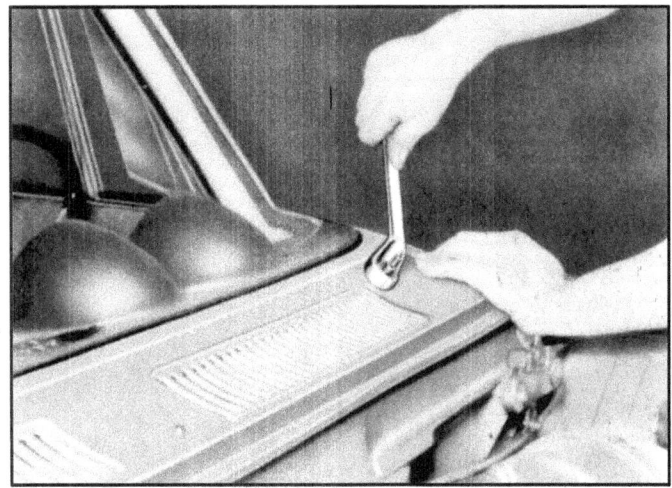

- Position the scuttle top as required and, holding the panel firmly in place, retighten the ringnuts.

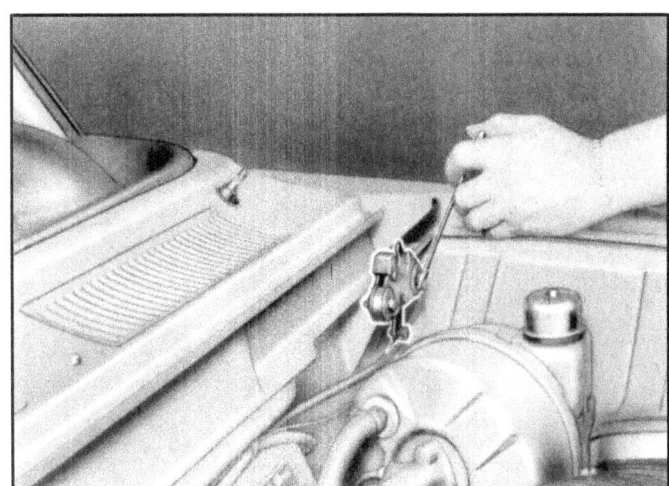

To adjust the hood locks:

- Slacken lock attaching screws.

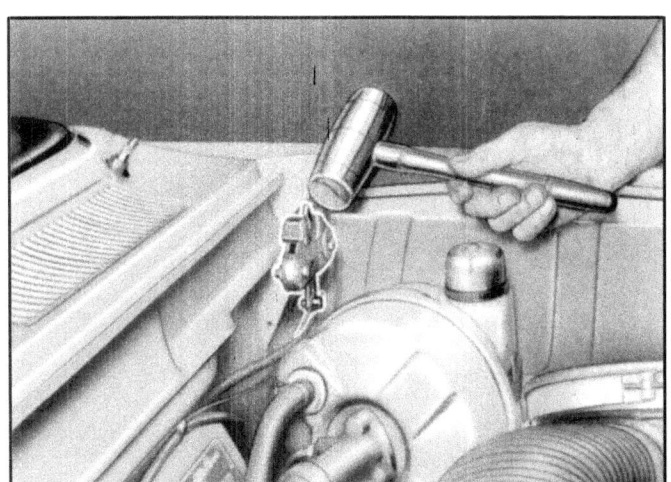

- Adjust the position of locks in such a way that both locks close at the same time when the hood is in proper alignment with the adjoining parts.
- Retighten lock attaching screws.

CHECKING AND ADJUSTING

LUGGAGE COMPARTMENT LID

1750 Saloon is shown for example purpose.

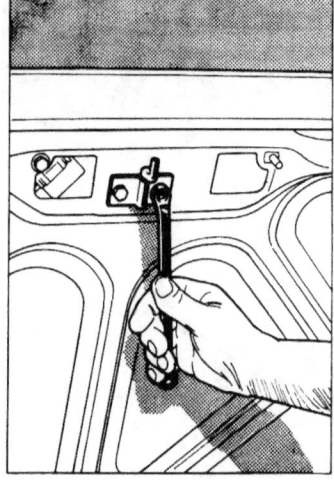
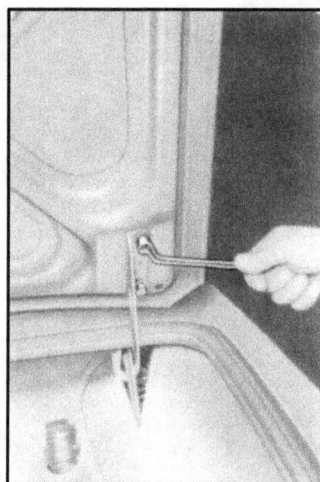

- Slacken the lock attaching screws.
- Slacken the lid hinge attaching screws.

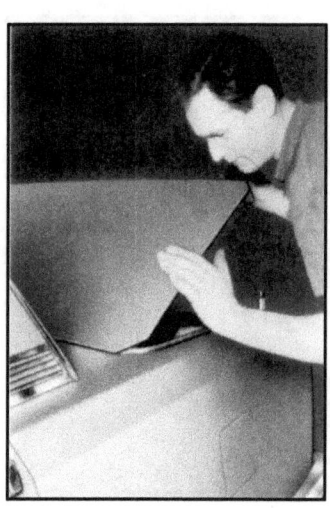
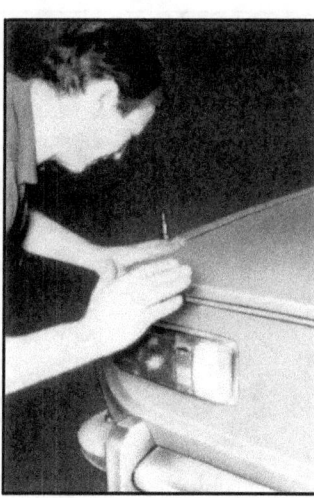

- Tapping by hand, move the lid as required.
- Check for proper alignment, then retighten the hinge screws.
- Adjust the position of the lock and tighten in place the attaching screws.

CHECKING AND ADJUSTING

DOOR WEATHERSTRIP LEAKAGE

The same procedure applies to all Saloon and Coupe models. 1750 Saloon is shown for example purpose.

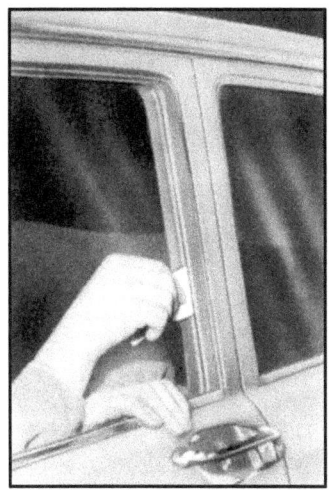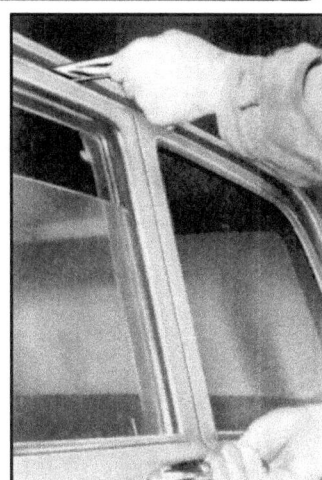

Should air or water leakage be experienced:

- Check weatherstrips for sound conditions and renew them, if necessary.
- Check for tightness by inserting a piece of paper between pillar and door. There should be some drag when trying to pull out the paper.

- Where needed, improve the tightness by bending outward the edge of sheet metal in the door opening. To do so, use a wooden block.

44
CHECKING AND ADJUSTING

LUGGAGE COMPARTMENT SEALING

> The same procedure applies to all models in this range.
> 1750 Saloon is shown for example purpose.

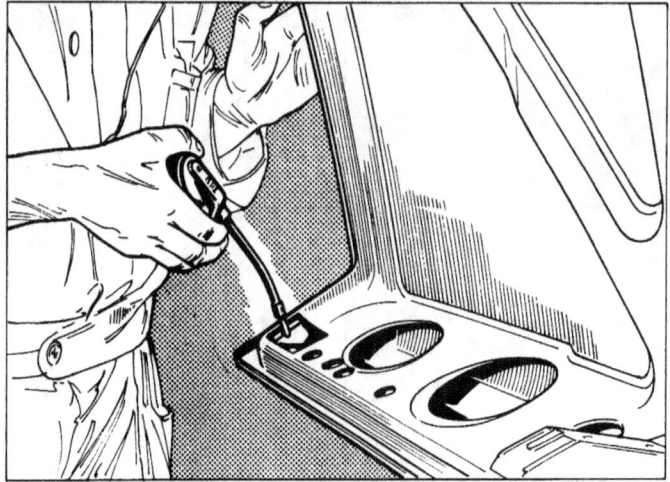

If water leakage is found, proceed as follows:

- Renew the rubber weatherstrips, if damaged.
- Check for proper sealing of lid weatherstrip by ensuring that the contacting surfaces are actually in contact.
- Check for proper sealing of screws attaching mouldings, lights, etc; if not so, apply sealing compound as required to the affected areas.

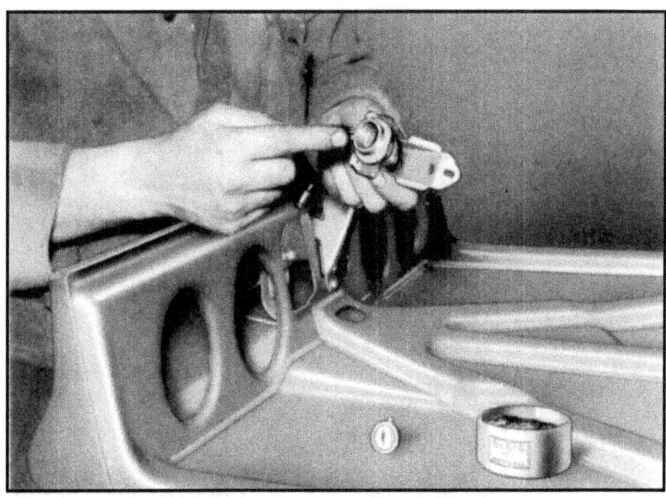

- Check the lock for proper sealing and remove it for greasing, if necessary.

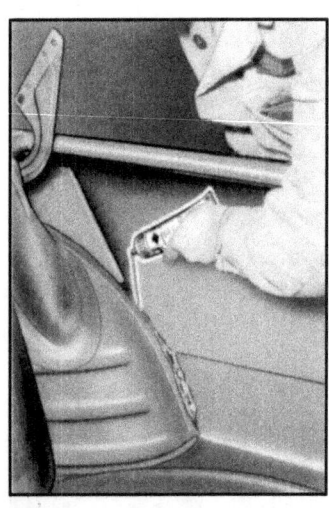 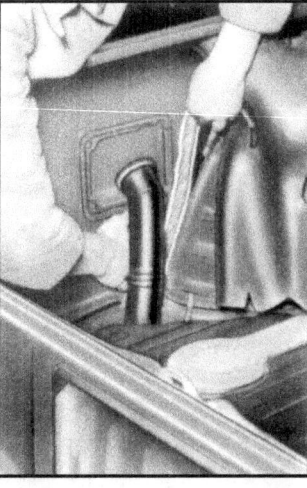

- Ensure that the joining lines of sheet metal seal properly together; if necessary, apply sealing compound in the interstices; then coat the wheelarch fillets with a suitable sealer.

Alfa Romeo Factory 'Technical Characteristics' publications.

As mentioned in the introduction to this manual, Alfa Romeo also issued individual 'Technical Characteristics' publications for each specific Giulia model (or series of models). The manuals listed below are a compilation of a number of the more significant of those technical publications, appropriately selected for either the carbureted or SPICA fuel injected models. While copies of the original 'Technical' publications can be sourced on the secondary market, they are scarce and relatively expensive. Consequently, we are pleased to be able to offer these reasonably priced alternatives to Alfa Rome Giulia owners worldwide.

Alfa Romeo Giulia Technical Manual (ISBN 9781588502261) for 1962 and onwards 1300cc, 1600cc and 1750cc Carbureted Models

This manual is a compilation of the factory 'Technical' publications listed below and, while the list is not inclusive, the publications were selected as being representative for the 1300cc, 1600cc and 1750cc series of carbureted Alfa Romeo Giulia models.

Factory 'Technical Characteristics' Publications for the Carbureted Giulia Series include:

(1) 1300cc GT 1300 Junior (1967 Publication)

(2) 1300cc Spider 1300 Junior (1968 Publication - plus 1969 Supplement)

(3) 1300cc Giulia TI (1969 Publication)

(4) 1600cc Giulia Ti, Spider & Sprint (1963 Publication)

(5) 1600cc Spider (1966 Publication)

(6) 1600cc Sprint GT Veloce (1966 Publication)

(7) 1600cc Giulia Super (1970 Publication)

(8) 1750cc Berlina, GT Veloce & Spider Veloce (1968 publication)

Alfa Romeo Giulia Technical Manual (ISBN 9781588502278) for 1969 and onwards 1750cc and 2000cc SPICA Fuel Injected Models

This manual is a compilation of the factory 'Technical' publications listed below and, while the list is not inclusive, the publications were selected as being representative for the 1750cc and 2000cc series of SPICA fuel injected Alfa Romeo Giulia models. It should be noted that the technical publications included in this manual are the only documents that were ever issued by the factory that contain the appropriate maintenance, repair, service, adjustment and trouble shooting information for the SPICA Fuel Injection system.

Technical Characteristics and Principal Inspection Specifications Manual for:

(1) 1750 Berlina, 1750 GT Veloce & 1750 Spider Veloce (1969 publication)

Instruction and Maintenance Manuals for Fuel Injection Models USA:

(2) 1750 All Models USA (1969 publication)

(3) 1750 All Models USA (1971 publication)

(4) 2000 All Models USA (1972 publication)

Technical Characteristics and Principal Inspection Specifications Manual for:

(5) 2000 Berlina, 2000 GT Veloce & 2000 Spider Veloce (1973 publication)

Instruction and Maintenance Manual for Fuel Injection Models USA:

(6) 2000 All models USA including Alfetta (1975 publication)

VELOCEPRESS MANUALS - MOTORCYCLE

1930'S BRITISH MOTORCYCLE CARBS & ELEC COMPONENTS (BOOK OF)
1930'S BRITISH MOTORCYCLE ENGINES (OVERHAUL & MAINTENANCE)
1930'S BRITISH MOTORCYCLE GEARBOXES & CLUTCHES (BOOK OF)
AJS 1932-1948 SINGLES & TWINS 250cc THRU 1000cc (BOOK OF)
AJS 1945-1960 SINGLES 350cc & 500cc MODELS 16 & 18 (BOOK OF)
AJS 1955-1965 SINGLES 350cc & 500cc (BOOK OF)
ARIEL 1932-1939 PREWAR MODELS (BOOK OF)
ARIEL 1933-1951 (WORKSHOP MANUAL)
ARIEL 1939-1960 4 STROKE SINGLES (BOOK OF)
ARIEL 1958-1964 LEADER & ARROW (BOOK OF)
BMW R26 R27 (1956-1967) FACTORY WORKSHOP MANUAL
BMW R50 R50S R60 R69S (1955-1969) FACTORY WORKSHOP MANUAL
BRIDGESTONE 90 SERIES FACTORY WSM & PARTS CATALOGUE
BRIDGESTONE 175 SERIES FACTORY WSM & PARTS CATALOGUE
BSA BANTAM ALL MODELS FROM 1948 ONWARDS (BOOK OF)
BSA SINGLES & V-TWINS UP TO 1927 (BOOK OF)
BSA SINGLES & V-TWINS UP TO 1935 (BOOK OF)
BSA SINGLES & V-TWINS 1936-1939 (BOOK OF)
BSA SINGLES & V-TWINS 1936-1952 (BOOK OF)
BSA OHV & SV SINGLES 250-600cc 1945-1954 (BOOK OF)
BSA OHV & SV SINGLES 250cc 1954-1970 (BOOK OF)
BSA OHV SINGLES 350 & 500cc 1955-1967 (BOOK OF)
BSA TWINS 1948-1962 (BOOK OF)
BSA TWINS 1962-1969 (SECOND BOOK OF)
CYCLEMOTOR (BOOK OF)
DOUGLAS 1929-1939 PREWAR ALL MODELS (BOOK OF)
DOUGLAS 1948-1957 POSTWAR ALL MODELS FACTORY SHOP MANUAL
DUCATI 160cc, 250cc & 350cc OHC MODELS FACTORY SHOP MANUAL
HONDA 50 ALL MODELS UP TO 1970 INC MONKEY & TRAIL (BOOK OF)
HONDA 90 ALL MODELS UP TO 1966 (BOOK OF)
HONDA 125-150cc TWINS C/CS/CB/CA FACTORY WORKSHOP MANUAL
HONDA 250-305 TWINS C/CS/CB FACTORY WORKSHOP MANUAL
HONDA C100 SUPER CUB FACTORY WORKSHOP MANUAL
HONDA C110 SPORT CUB 1962-1969 FACTORY WORKSHOP MANUAL
HONDA TWINS & SINGLES 50cc THRU 305cc 1960-1966 (BOOK OF)
HONDA TWINS ALL MODELS 125cc THRU 450cc UP TO 1968 (BOOK OF)
J.A.P. ENGINES 1927-1952 & MOTORCYCLES 1934-1952 (BOOK OF)
LAMBRETTA 1947-1957 ALL 125 & 150cc MODELS (BOOK OF)
LAMBRETTA 1957-1970 LI & TV MODELS (SECOND BOOK OF)
MATCHLESS 1931-1939 ALL MODELS 250cc THRU 990cc (BOOK OF)
MATCHLESS 1945-1956 350 & 500cc SINGLES (BOOK OF)
MATCHLESS 1955-1966 350 & 500cc SINGLES (BOOK OF)
NEW IMPERIAL ALL SV & OHV FROM 1935 ONWARDS (BOOK OF)
NORTON 1932-1939 PREWAR MODELS (BOOK OF)
NORTON 1932-1947 (BOOK OF)
NORTON 1938-1956 (BOOK OF)
NORTON 1955-1963 MODELS 19, 50 & ES2 (BOOK OF)
NORTON 1955-1965 DOMINATOR TWINS (BOOK OF)
NORTON 1957-1970 TWINS FACTORY WORKSHOP MANUAL
NSU PRIMA 1956-1964 (BOOK OF)
NSU QUICKLY 1953-1963 ALL MODELS (BOOK OF)
PANTHER 1932-1958 LIGHTWEIGHT MODELS 250 & 350cc (BOOK OF)
PANTHER 1938-1966 HEAVYWEIGHT MODELS 600 & 650cc (BOOK OF)
RALEIGH MOPEDS 1960-1969 (BOOK OF)
RALEIGH MOTORCYCLES 1919-1933 (BOOK OF)
ROYAL ENFIELD 1934-1946 SINGLES & V TWINS (BOOK OF)
ROYAL ENFIELD 1937-1953 SINGLES & V TWINS (BOOK OF)
ROYAL ENFIELD 1946-1962 SINGLES (BOOK OF)
ROYAL ENFIELD 1958-1966 250cc & 350cc SINGLES (SECOND BOOK OF)
ROYAL ENFIELD 736cc INTERCEPTOR FACTORY WORKSHOP MANUAL
RUDGE 1933-1939 (BOOK OF)
SUNBEAM 1928-1939 (BOOK OF)
SUNBEAM 1946-1957 S7 & S8 (BOOK OF)
SUZUKI 50cc & 80cc UP TO 1966 (BOOK OF)
SUZUKI T10 1963-1967 FACTORY WORKSHOP MANUAL
SUZUKI T20 & T200 1965-1969 FACTORY WORKSHOP MANUAL
TRIUMPH 1935-1939 PREWAR MODELS (BOOK OF)
TRIUMPH 1935-1949 (BOOK OF)
TRIUMPH 1937-1951 (WORKSHOP MANUAL)
TRIUMPH 1945-1955 FACTORY WORKSHOP MANUAL
TRIUMPH 1945-1958 TWINS (BOOK OF)
TRIUMPH 1956-1969 TWINS (BOOK OF)
VELOCETTE 1925-1970 ALL SINGLES & TWINS (BOOK OF)
VESPA 1951-1961 (BOOK OF)
VESPA 1955-1963 125 & 150cc & GS MODELS (SECOND BOOK OF)
VESPA 1955-1968 GS & SS (BOOK OF)
VESPA 1963-1972 90, 125 & 150cc (THIRD BOOK OF)
VILLIERS ENGINE UP TO 1959 INC. 3 WHEELERS (BOOK OF)
VILLIERS ENGINE UP TO 1969 (BOOK OF)
VINCENT 1935-1955 (WORKSHOP MANUAL)

VELOCEPRESS TECHNICAL BOOKS – MOTORCYCLE

CATALOG OF BRITISH MOTORCYCLES (1951 MODELS)
INDIAN PONYBIKE, BOY RACER & PAPOOSE ILL PARTS LIST & SALES LIT
MOTORCYCLE ENGINEERING (P.E. Irving)
SPEED AND HOW TO OBTAIN IT (Motor Cycle Magazine UK)
TUNING FOR SPEED (P.E. Irving)

VELOCEPRESS MANUALS - THREE WHEELER'S

BSA THREE WHEELER (BOOK OF)
VINTAGE MORGAN THREE WHEELER (BOOK OF)

VELOCEPRESS MANUALS - AUTOMOBILE

ALFA ROMEO GIULIA WORKSHOP MANUAL 1300 TO 2000cc 1962-1975
ALFA ROMEO GIULIA TECH MANUAL CARBURETED CARS FROM 1962
ALFA ROMEO GIULIA TECH MANUAL FUEL INJECTED CARS FROM 1969
AUSTIN-HEALEY 6-CYLINDER WORKSHOP MANUAL
AUSTIN-HEALEY SPRITE & MG MIDGET WORKSHOP MANUAL 1958-1971
BMW 600 LIMOUSINE FACTORY WORKSHOP MANUAL
BMW 600 LIMOUSINE OWNERS HAND BOOK & SERVICE MANUAL
BMW 2000 & 2002 1966-1976 WORKSHOP MANUAL
BMW ISETTA FACTORY WORKSHOP MANUAL
CORVAIR 1960-1969 WORKSHOP MANUAL
CORVETTE V8 1955-1962 WORKSHOP MANUAL
FIAT 500 FACTORY WORKSHOP MANUAL 1957-1973
FIAT 600, 600D & MULTIPLA FACTORY WORKSHOP MANUAL 1955-1969
JAGUAR E-TYPE 3.8 & 4.2 SERIES 1 & 2 WORKSHOP MANUAL
JAGUAR MK 7, 8, 9 & XK120, 140, 150 MANUAL 1948-1961
METROPOLITAN FACTORY WORKSHOP MANUAL
MGA & MGB OWNERS HANDBOOK & WORKSHOP MANUAL
MG MIDGET TC, TD, TF & TF1500 WORKSHOP MANUAL
PORSCHE 356 1948-1965 WORKSHOP MANUAL
PORSCHE 911 2.0, 2.2, 2.4 LITRE 1964-1973
PORSCHE 912 WORKSHOP MANUAL
TRIUMPH TR2, TR3, TR4 1953-1965 WORKSHOP MANUAL
VOLKSWAGEN TRANSPORTER, TRUCKS & WAGONS 1950-1979 WSM
VOLVO 1944-1968 ALL MODELS WORKSHOP MANUAL

VELOCEPRESS TECHNICAL BOOKS - AUTOMOBILE

FERRARI 250/GT SERVICE AND MAINTENANCE
FERRARI GUIDE TO PERFORMANCE
FERRARI OWNER'S HANDBOOK
FERRARI TUNING TIPS & MAINTENANCE TECHNIQUES
HOW TO BUILD A FIBERGLASS CAR
HOW TO BUILD A RACING CAR
HOW TO RESTORE THE MODEL 'A' FORD
MASERATI OWNER'S HANDBOOK
OBERT'S FIAT GUIDE
PERFORMANCE TUNING THE SUNBEAM TIGER
SOUPING THE VOLKSWAGEN
SOLEX CARBURETORS (EMPHASIS ON UK & EU AUTOMOBILES)
SU CARBURETORS (EMPHASIS ON UK AUTOMOBILES)
WEBER CARBURETORS (EMPHASIS ON ALFA & FIAT)

VELOCEPRESS BOOKS & GUIDES - AUTOMOBILE

ABARTH BUYERS GUIDE
COMPLETE CATALOG OF JAPANESE MOTOR VEHICLES
FERRARI 308 SERIES BUYER'S AND OWNER'S GUIDE
FERRARI BERLINETTA LUSSO
FERRARI BROCHURES AND SALES LITERATURE 1946-1967
FERRARI BROCHURES AND SALES LITERATURE 1968-1989
FERRARI OPP, MAINTENANCE & SERVICE H/BOOKS 1948-1963
FERRARI SERIAL NUMBERS PART I - ODD NUMBERS TO 21399
FERRARI SERIAL NUMBERS PART II - EVEN NUMBERS TO 1050
FERRARI SPYDER CALIFORNIA
HENRY'S FABULOUS MODEL "A" FORD
MASERATI BROCHURES AND SALES LITERATURE

VELOCEPRESS BOOKS – RACING

CARRERA PANAMERICANA - MEXICAN ROAD RACE (BOOK OF)
DIALED IN - THE JAN OPPERMAN STORY
IF HEMINGWAY HAD WRITTEN A RACING NOVEL
LE MANS 24 (THE BOOK THAT THE FILM WAS BASED ON)
VEDA ORR'S NEW REVISED HOT ROD PICTORIAL

AUTOBOOKS WORKSHOP MANUALS & BROOKLANDS ROAD TEST PORTFOLIOS

FOR A COMPLETE LISTING OF THE AUTOBOOKS & BROOKLANDS TITLES THAT WE CURRENTLY HAVE AVAILABLE, PLEASE VISIT OUR WEBSITE.

For a detailed description of any of the above titles please visit www.VelocePress.com

www.ingramcontent.com/pod-product-compliance
Lightning Source LLC
Chambersburg PA
CBHW060244240426
43673CB00047B/1877